Comic Books and Comic Strips in the United States

Recent Titles in
Bibliographies and Indexes in Popular Culture

Humor Scholarship: A Research Bibliography
Don L. F. Nilsen

The Comic Art Collection Catalog: An Author, Artist, Title, and Subject Catalog of the Comic Art Collection, Special Collections Divison, Michigan State University Libraries
Randall W. Scott, compiler

Animation, Caricature, and Gag and Political Cartoons in the United States and Canada: An International Bibliography
John A. Lent, compiler

Comic Art of Europe: An International, Comprehensive Bibliography
John A. Lent, compiler

Comic Books and Comic Strips in the United States

An International Bibliography

Compiled by John A. Lent

Foreword by Mort Walker

Introduction by Jerry Robinson

Bibliographies and Indexes in Popular Culture,
Number 4

Greenwood Press
Westport, Connecticut • London

Library of Congress Cataloging-in-Publication Data

Lent, John A.
Comic books and comic strips in the United States : an international bibliography / compiled by John A. Lent ; foreword by Mort Walker ; introduction by Jerry Robinson.
p. cm.—(Bibliographies and indexes in popular culture, ISSN 1066–0658 ; no. 4)
Includes bibliographical references and indexes.
ISBN 0–313–28211–0
1. Comic books, strips, etc.—United States—Bibliography.
I. Title. II. Series.
Z5956.C6L46 1994
[PN6725]
016.7415'973—dc20 94–10852

British Library Cataloguing in Publication Data is available.

Library of Congress Catalog Card Number: 94–10852
ISBN: 0–313–28211–0
ISSN: 1066–0658

First published in 1994

Greenwood Press, 88 Post Road West, Westport, CT 06881
An imprint of Greenwood Publishing Group, Inc.

Printed in the United States of America

The paper used in this book complies with the Permanent Paper Standard issued by the National Information Standards Organization (Z39.48–1984).

10 9 8 7 6 5 4 3 2

Contents

Our Changing Comics
A Foreword by Mort Walker

I have been in the comics business 70 years...all my life. My earliest recollection is of my father reading Moon Mullins and laughing till he couldn't breathe. This fascinated me so much that I learned to read the comics before I went to school and was drawing comics at the age of three. I sold my first cartoon to a national magazine when I was 11 and sold over 300 before I was 15. I had a regular weekly strip in the newspaper while I was in high school. As a professional I have had nine syndicated strips, four of them still running in over 3,000 newspapers.

So I have been involved and observed many changes in the comic strip business. In the beginning, the comics were mostly ethnic. "Down in Hogan's Alley" (The Yellow Kid) made fun of the Irish immigrants. The "Katzenjammer Kids" were German, "Alphonse and Gaston" were French, "Abie the Agent" was Jewish, etc. The dialogue was written in dialect. It was what you heard on the streets at the turn of the century, and nobody objected.

As sensitivities rose, most of those strips were phased out or changed. Blacks, for instance, were depicted as lazy and stupid and were supporting characters in almost every strip. When the mood changed, they were dropped completely, and blacks were not represented at all. Lately, they have gingerly returned to the mainline strips with the help of some ben-day shading, and are usually only featured in strips drawn by blacks themselves.

There was a period when con men like "Barney Google" had a big play, and boarding houses were the subject of many features. They reflected society as it was then in the 1920s and 1930s, but would be an anachronism today.

New inventions spawned their share of comics. The auto inspired "Gasoline Alley," and the airplane gave us "Barney Baxter," "Smilin'Jack," and "Tailspin Tommy." There were several about the movies like "Betty Boop" and "Minute Movies." As the novelty of these inventions faded, so did the strips.

Many strips attempted to capitalize on famous personalities such as Charlie Chaplin, Charlie Chan, Bob Hope, Lucille Ball, Hennie Youngman, Woody Allen, and others. No syndicate would touch a strip like that today.

Then there were the World War II years. Most of the comic characters donned uniforms, and many new features were launched with a military theme, none of which exist today.

Office strips proliferated, especially with a knockout secretary... "Winnie Winkle," "Tillie the Toiler," etc.,...their nerdy boyfriends and pompous bosses. Also there were the office boys, "Smitty," "Jerry on the Job," and others. Didn't kids go to school in those days?

There were strips about orphans, "Little Orphan Annie," "Little Annie Rooney," strips about cops, "Dick Tracy," "Clarence," "Potsy," explorers in Africa, "Tim Tyler," explorers in space, "Buck Rogers," "Flash Gordon," explorers in the Orient, "Terry and the Pirates," teenagers, "Archie," "Harold Teen," "Teena," "Emmy Lou," talking animals, "Pogo," "Bugs Bunny," "Mickey Mouse," and a host of others. All of these genres have virtually disappeared.

Story strips were introduced in the 1930s and grew to dominate the comics page. When TV hit the scene, it literally wiped them out. It took 12 weeks to tell a story in the strip that could be told on TV in a half hour. Strips couldn't compete. Readers were busier and didn't have the patience to keep up with the cartoon stories. Only a few are left.

Throughout the years, there has been a colorful eclectic variety of subjects that have burst on the scene, illuminated us for awhile, then fizzled and burned out. What we have left are predominately politically correct family strips. Of the top eight strips, six are family strips; "Blondie," "Calvin and Hobbes," "Hagar the Horrible," "Family Circus," "For Better or for Worse," and "Hi and Lois." The other two can even be construed as family strips, "Garfield" and "Beetle Bailey," if you construe enough.

Strips today tend to be more autobiographical than inventive. Artists are drawing themselves, their families and friends. "Hagar" and his wife were caricatures of Dik and Joan Browne. Bil Keane's characters are not only caricatures, they all have their real names. So does "Cathy." My characters were *all* taken from real people. Lynn Johnston and her husband, Rod, star in their own strip. I guess it helps to give the characters life, and it seems to be what the readers prefer because they keep voting for them in readership polls.

A lot of things have affected the changes in comic strips over the years, but probably the most powerful were the pressure groups. Ethnic groups, of course, felt they were the objects of ridicule and demanded that editors drop offensive strips. I get pressure from feminists, fat people, reformed alcoholics, bald people, religious groups, anti-violence groups, gays, secretaries, the military. No one wants to be the butt of the joke. It is threatening joke-telling because it has its effect on editors who are trying to please their readers, even though one angry reader can wipe out a million readers who want to have fun.

We have progressed from an era when we offended everyone to an age of fear of offending *anyone*. Neither is right. A healthy person should be able to laugh at himself. A gentle joke, well-taken, is good for the soul. Laughter heals and sheds light on the human condition, and it should be protected as vigorously as all those other rights.

It is interesting and informative to go back over the years and see how the comics reflected society at the moment. It probably tells our history better than most books. You can easily see from a cartoon at one glance how people dressed and talked and what affected their lives. Times change and the comics tag along. They are a part of our lives and that's what makes them so wonderful.

I just hope that our age today will not be recorded by a bunch of simpy, safe, and politically correct "comic" strips.

Mort Walker is best known for his "Beetle Bailey" comic strip, which he has drawn since 1950. But, he has also excelled in comic books, animation, and magazine cartooning; in 1948-1949, he was the top selling gag cartoonist in the United States. Other Walker strips have been "Hi and Lois," "Mrs. Fitz's Flats," "Boner's Ark," and "Sam and Silo." Since 1974, Walker has devoted much time to his cartoon art museum, which in recent years has become known as the International Museum of Cartoon Art. He has won numerous awards, including the Reuben, and has held many offices, including president of the National Cartoonists Society.

Preface

Whether attributable to a more visually-oriented world, or to a public with more leisure time and money to spend on them, the genres of comic art (animation, caricature, comic strips, comic books, gag and political cartoons) have had a phenomenal growth in recent years. There are many manifestations of this rapid maturation, including a burgeoning fandom (or should we say, "collectordom"?), the creation of comics icons, and the discovery of many uses for the medium.

The increasing number of fans and collectors has bloated circulations of some Japanese comics magazines to millions weekly, made *komiks* the "national book" of the Philippines, inflated original artwork prices to astonishingly-high levels in Europe and the United States, and supported more than 4,000 comic book stores and dozens of very well-attended comic fests in the United States.

In Cuba, a town has been nicknamed the "town of humor" to honor its cartoon tradition. In Japan, a temple is devoted to cartooning. In other countries, especially the Philippines, the majority of movie scripts are lifted from comics. Throughout the world, cartoon characters adorn all types of products—from letterheads and cereal in the West to trishaws and jeepneys in Asia.

Comic art has been used to build morale during wartime, to teach the Japanese people about their country's complex economy, to promote developmental programs in health and family planning in India and elsewhere, to promote peace and to denounce war, to teach religious stories of Buddha and Jesus Christ, to make people literate, and to relieve hunger in Africa and other parts of the world.

However, the medium has not lacked detractors who, for decades, have blamed comic strips and comic books for corrupting the youth, bastardizing grammar, stereotyping minorities, glamorizing war and crime, promoting ethnocentrism, and more recently, for not being politically correct.

Serious efforts to preserve and study comic art have correspondingly increased. In the United States, Belgium, Cuba, France, Switzerland, Sweden, Germany, Japan, Canada, Macedonia, and England, private and public museums and universities have established comic art collections. In a number of other countries, including India, United States, Korea, Brazil, colleges and universities have developed courses and programs in cartooning, both in techniques and theory. In various places, conferences of such far-flung disciplines as philosophy, history, mass communications, psychology, psychiatry, and popular culture have included comic art papers in their programs.

The literature on comic art has grown with these developments. Older periodicals, such as *Bédésup*, *Cartoonist PROfiles*, *Comic Art*, and *Comics Journal*, have been joined by *Inks*, *WittyWorld*, *Inkspot*, *El Wendigo*, *Seriejournalen* and others on every continent of the globe. Hundreds of book titles on comic art have appeared annually, including encyclopedias, especially those of Maurice Horn, catalogues, notably Randall Scott's mammoth works, anthologies of artists' works, histories of strips and characters, and biographies and profiles of cartoonists. Scholarly treatments such as David Kunzle's *History of the Comic Strip in the Nineteenth Century* and Thomas Inge's *Comics as Culture* are also included.

The European scholarly approach to comic art, pioneered by Horn, Couperie, Traini, Trinchero, Fuchs, and others, has now found a place in academia in a number of places. Getting there was often an arduous task as those who pioneered had to fight back the myopic, jealous, and snobbish nature of academic communities.

My own scholarly interest in comic art goes back more than 30 years. In 1963, I designed and conducted experimental studies in Syracuse, New York, elementary schools on possible effects of violent comic books on fourth graders. Although the experiments did not yield irrefutable proof one way or the other (fourth graders are a cunning lot), the project was nevertheless useful for, among other things, it alerted me to the abundance of literature available on comic art.

This bibliography on comic books and comic strips, one of four dealing with various regions of the world and all published by Greenwood, is an attempt to rectify this shortcoming in comic art scholarship. The other three books cover animation, caricature, gag, magazine, illustrative, and political cartoons of the United States, comic art of Europe, and comic art of Africa, Asia, Australia and Oceania, and Latin America and the Caribbean.

Organization, Objectives, Emphases

Comic art in this volume includes comic books and comic strips in the United States.

The first chapter treats these two genres together, starting with a resources section, consisting of entries on bibliographies, dictionaries, encyclopedias, catalogues, collections, checklists, guides, fanzines, indices, and a periodical directory. The latter provides names, addresses, typical contents, and inaugural dates of at least 128 comic art-related journals, magazines, and fanzines. A general studies section consists of items that either are too general or too vague to fit elsewhere or that are cross category in nature.

Also discussed is the collecting of comics, their portrayal in movies, television, and radio, and their relationship with other topics: *art*; *children*, including comics for children, child cartoonists, comics and juvenile delinquency; *education and culture*, with subcategories of culture, literacy, reading, and religion; *eroticism, pornography, sex*; *ethnicity*, *minorities*, *racism*, including also ethnic groups, stereotyping, the elderly, homosexuals; *humanism*, *social consciousness*, *relevancy*, including cartoons used to help humanity, cartoonists' deeds in support of various causes, social relevancy of comics; *professions*, meaning how they are portrayed in comics; *violence controversy*, including controversies over violent content, codes and "clean up," legislative action, ratings, and Dr. Frederic Wertham's campaign; *war*; and *women*, with subsections on female cartoonists, singling out 16, portrayals, sexism, sex role, and superheroines. The criterion used in giving a cartoonist, company, or character/title a separate listing in this and subsequent chapters is that they are the subject of at least two citations.

In chapter two, comic books are treated under general studies, historical, business, legal, and technical aspects, genres, comic book makers and their works, and anthologies. The general section subdivides into graphic novels and paraphernalia of comic book fandom, such as cards, games, and toys, while the history is broken down by periods of pre-golden, golden, and silver, and by publishers. Business aspects include production, singling out 15 individual companies, and distribution/sales, listing four companies separately.

Thirteen genres of comic books are listed, with 48 specific titles given separate subcategories. There may be cause for quibbling about placement of titles, especially some of those in the superhero category, but frankly, it has become an onerous chore determining genre—even deciding who is a hero/heroine.

The section on comic book makers and their works consists of autobiographies, biographies, memoirs, profiles, interviews, obituaries, and sketchbooks of individuals associated with comic books. One hundred and seventy-nine are singled out, having two or more citations. In this, as well as in the comic strip section, it was often difficult categorizing cartoonists by genre and even by country. Many cartoonists did both strips and comic books; others, comic books and animation. Some cartoonists are split by countries—their places of origin and those where they make their living or have gained their fame. Famous "American" comics people, such as Hal Foster, Alan Grant, Moebius, Alan Moore, or Arn Saba, were born elsewhere. Such multi-genre or multi-country cartoonists were usually placed where they were the more prominent; admittedly, some placements were made arbitrarily.

The anthologies category consists of multi-author collections of comics, reprints, and reviews. Under legal aspects, subcategories include censorship, control, copyright, licensing, plagiarism, creator's rights, guidelines, ratings, libel, obscenity, pornography, and violence. The user of this bibliography should also refer to the violence category in chapter one. Drawing, publishing, and writing are covered in the technical aspects part.

The third chapter is on comic strips, with much the same categorization used for comic books. One-hundred and forty-three individual strips are singled out in the characters and titles subcategory. Also, ninety-six cartoonists are given separate listings.

A serious effort was put forth to compile a comprehensive and usable bibliography. No item was too small or insignificant to be listed; if it dealt with comic art, it could become a citation. The compiler works on the premise that both systematically-researched and ephemeral materials are useful during the course of developing a field of study.

Having said that, I must point out some limitations on comprehensiveness. The accelerated interest in comic art (unfortunately, too often as a commercial investment, rather than reading experience) in recent years has seen a proliferation of literature, usually in quickly-slapped-together anthologies and collections. Not all of these books are included. The necessity to drop some was based on expediency, rather than evaluative, decisions. They were not readily available physically or accessible in library and other research depositories. In some other cases where materials were obtainable, a selective process had to be used because of the volume. For example, not all the collections of Disney character stories are here, nor are all the references to famous cartoonists who also excelled in painting or other arts. The German artist/caricaturist George Grosz comes to mind here. I saw hundreds of citations about him, but for the most part, chose those that dealt with him as a caricaturist.

The bibliography is representative in covering various publications, writing formats and styles, time periods, and languages. Most of the citations are current, ranging from the 1960s to present, although some date back to the eighteenth and nineteenth centuries.

Many problems surfaced in the course of doing this work. Dealing with such a voluminous amount of information presented (sometimes inaccurately) in different bibliographic styles can lead to much duplication. Although I have attempted to eliminate, or at least, to minimize duplication, some is bound to exist, for which I apologize.

As indicated already, categorization gave me a few headaches. In a number of periodicals, cartoonist profiles are intermingled with accounts of their characters or the titled works for which they are known. Thus, the user of this bibliography will find in the sections on characters and titles much biographical information about the creators of those works, and conversely, much on characters and titles in cartoonists' profiles and interviews.

At times it has been difficult to determine dates of periodicals. Some magazines, especially fanzines, are not dated. Others change series or alternate, without any seeming logic, between using dates and volume numbers or months and seasons of the year.

The citations are arranged alphabetically by author, or by article title when an author is not listed, and are numbered consecutively.

Search Process

The search for literature was mostly manual, since that is the way the compiler works, and because much of the literature, being journalistic, anecdotal, or brief, is not in computerized databases. Many bibliographies, indices, and bibliographic periodicals, too numerous to list here, were used. It is worth noting, however, that all volumes of *Reader's Guide to Periodical Literature*, 1890 to 1992, were searched.

On a regular basis and rather systematically, the compiler has attempted to keep abreast of the literature on mass communications and popular culture for at least 30 years. For the most part, works on comic art are expected to be found in those fields, as well as in art. Hundreds of journal titles in these three fields and others, published on all continents, are scanned regularly by the compiler.

No effort will be made to list all of these periodicals, only those that would be expected to yield some articles. Among these, all numbers of the following were searched: *Animag, Apropos, Art? Alternatives, Artsy, Breaking In, Canadian Cartoonist, The Cartoonist (Nigeria), Cartoonist PROfiles, Cine Cubano, Citizens Publishing, Comic Art Studies, Comicist, Comics Collector, Comics Interview, Comics Journal, Comics News Service from Poland, Comics Scene, Communication Abstracts, Communication Booknotes, Communication Monographs, Communication Quarterly, Critical Studies in Mass Communication, European Journal of Communication, Fat Comic, FCA S.O.B., FECO News, Fort Mudge Most, The Funnie's Paper, Gannett Center Journal, Gauntlet, Gazette, Hollywood Eclectern, Humerus, Humor, Index on Censorship, Journal of Communication, Journal of Popular Culture, Journal of Popular Film, Journalism History, Journalism Monographs, Journalism Quarterly, Kayhan Caricature, L'Ecran, Mass Comm Review, Media Development, Media History Digest, Minnesota Cartoonist, Nemo, Nordic Comics Revue, Public Culture, Puck Papers, The Quill, Seriejournalen, Studies in Latin American Popular Culture, Talking Turkey, Target, Trix, Watcher,* and *WittyWorld.*

Additionally, the compiler looked at the following periodicals with varying degrees of exhaustiveness, depending upon availability and relevance: *AAEC Notebook, Akrep, Albany Cartoon Journal, Amazing Heroes, Amazing World of DC Comics, Animation, Animato, Anime-zine, Archie, Association of Comics Enthusiasts Newsletter, Comic Cuts, (A Suivre), Baby Sue, B & W, Barks Collector, Bédésup, Big O, La Borsa del Fumetto, Bulls' Eye, Caniffites, CAPS, Caricature, Cartoon Art Museum Newsletter, Cartoon Quarterly, Cartoons, Cartoon Times, Chapters, Collector's Club Newsletter, Collectors Dream, Comic Art, Comic Book Marketplace, Comic Book Newsletter, Comic Book Price Guide, Comic Cellar, Comicguia, Comic Informer, Comic Reader, Comic Relief, Comics Business, Comics Buyer's Guide, Comics Feature, Comic Shop News, Comics International, Comics Release, Comics Retailer, Comics Review, Comics Score Board, Comic Strip News, Comics Values Monthly, The Comics World, Comix, Corto*

Maltese, *Daredevil Chronicles*, *Dreamline*, *The Duckburg Times*, *East Coast Animation*, *El Wendigo*, *FA*, *Fandom Annual*, *Fanfare*, *The Fans of Central Jersey*, *The Fan's Zine*, *FCA and Me, Too! Newsletter*, *Fenix*, *Foom*, *Four-Color Magazine*, *Fred Greenberg's Omnibus*, *Funny Times*, *Funnyworld*, *The Gag Recap*, *Get Animated!*, *Graphixus*, *Granma Weekly Review*, *Heroic Fantasy*, *Humour and Caricature*, *ICOM/INFO*, *Il Fumetto*, *Infinity*, *Inkspot*, *Inside Comics*, *Inspirational Comics*, *In Toon*, *IPI Report*, *Itchy Planet*, *Japanimation*, *The Jester*, *Kever*, *Keverinfo*, *Kitchen Sink Pipeline*, *The Licensing Book*, *Linus*, *LOC*, *Locus*, *Mangajin*, *Manhattan Comic News*, *Menomonee Falls Gazette*, *Menomonee Falls Guardian*, *Mieux Vaut en Rire*, *Monokel*, *National Cartoonists Society Newsletter*, *Near Mint*, *The New Comic News*, *Newsletter of Northern California Cartoon and Humour Association*, *Newtype*, *Okefenokee Star*, *Orion*, *Outworld's Bi-Monthly*, *Overstreet's Price Update*, *Panels*, *Penstuff*, *Pogo Is Back*, *Qua Brot*, *RBCC*, *Retail Express*, *Robin Snyder's History of the Comics*, *SAF Reporter*, *Serieskaberen*, *Sick*, *Small Press Comics Explosion*, *Society of Strip Illustration Newsletter*, *Speakeasy*, *Squa Tront*, *Story Board*, *TEGN*, *Transformation*, *Tratto*, *Triangle Comic Review*, *TV Guide*, *Twinkles*, *UCLA*, *Uncle Jam Quarterly*, *Vot der Dumboozle?*, *Wizzard*, *Witzend*, *World Cartoon Gallery (Skopje) Catalogue*, *The World of Comic Art*, *Worldwide Classics Newsletter*, and *Yellow Press*.

"Fugitive" materials, such as dissertations not indexed through the University of Michigan system, theses, catalogues, conference papers, and pamphlets also make up part of the bibliographies.

Besides using scores of libraries in the United States and beyond, as well as the interlibrary loan services, the compiler found other ways to gather sources on comic art. Some key writers in the field were asked to submit bibliographies of their works, and advertisements were placed in *WittyWorld International Cartoon Magazine* soliciting citations. The compiler became familiar with much literature as he prepared his regular bibliographic column for *WittyWorld* during the past seven years. Additional sources became available during my interviews with hundreds of cartoonists and comic art specialists around the world.

Acknowledgments

Bibliographic work, tedious and time-consuming as it is, can have its moments of pleasure and fulfillment. In the course of finishing this bibliography, there were a number of such times—while scavenging through stacks of books and periodicals at comics festivals and stores, while finding a cache of fanzines or a list of references in library and commercial catalogues, or while interviewing cartoonists and comics authorities worldwide.

The latter deserve my first words of gratitude. The hundreds of cartoonists I have interviewed in Asia, Canada, Caribbean, Europe, South America, and the United States are the most interesting, flexible, and generous professionals I have known. They have shared with me their experiences, cartoons, and scrapbooks and clippings, the latter useful for bibliographic purposes. They have showered me with hospitality, motored me around crowded cities, provided me translations, and, in some cases, given me the benefits of their own comic art research.

They should all be mentioned, but space does not permit. Especially helpful, and to whom I am very thankful, are: Norman Isaac and Deng Coy Miel in the Philippines; Ramli Badrudin and Gerardus Sudarta in Indonesia; Suresh Sawant, Abu Abraham, Sudhir Tailang, Anant Pai, and Pran in India; K.M.K. Madagama and W.R. Wijesoma in Sri Lanka; Harunoor Rasheed Harun, Nazrul Islam, and the staffs of *Cartoon* and *Immad* magazines in Bangladesh; the entire cartoonists club of Myanmar, and particularly U Ngwe Kyi and Maung Maung Aung; Chai Rachawat in Thailand; Lat and Zunar in Malaysia; Zhan Tong and his talented cartooning family in China; Zunzi, Chan Ya, Larry Feign, and Jimmy Pang in Hong Kong; Johnny Lau and Heng Kim Song in Singapore; Yukio Sugiura, Sampei Sato, and Yoshiro Kato in Japan; Tom Hoong and Shan Li in Taiwan; Polito, Ares, Boligán, and Lillo in Cuba; Bohuslav Pernecký, Viliam Živický, Koloman Leššo in Slovakia; Ane Vasilevski and other personnel at the Osten Gallery and *Osten* magazine in Macedonia; Chris Browne, Jerry Robinson, and Mort

Walker in the United States; Robert LaPalme in Canada, and Flavio Mario De Alcantava Calazans in Brazil.

Other individuals were also very kind during my travels in search of cartooning information: Milan Šoltés, Rev. Samuel Meshack, Dr. Josephine Joseph, Dr. B.P. Sanjay, Lim Cheng Tju, Fong Pick-Huei, Sankaran Ramanathan, Mohd. Hamdan Adnan, Marcel and Viviane Sadarnac, Hane Latt, U. Thiha (a) Thiha Saw, Kyaw Lin, Klára Kubičková, Keiko Tonegawa, Yutaka Kaneko, Toshiko Nakano, and Katsuhisa and Midori Ichitsuka.

Former and current students, whose graduate work I proudly supervised during the past 20 years, lent much appreciated support: Professor Oranuj Lertchanyarak (and husband, Kanongdej) and Dr. Charles Elliott, in Thailand and Hong Kong, respectively; Dr. Hongying Liu-Lengyel (and husband, Dr. Alfonz Lengyel) in China; Dr. John V. Vilanilam in India; Dr. Myung Jun Kim, Dr. Hoon Soon Kim, and Sang Kil Lee in Korea, and Dr. Hsiao Hsiang-wen and Chu-feng Tang in Taiwan. Others, such as Rei Okamoto and Aruna Rao, provided sources and insights concerning Japanese and Indian cartoons, respectively, and Dr. Fei Zhengxing, Kohava Simhi, Jim Dever, Dr. Maria Santana, Chyun-Fung Shi, and Betsi Grabe helped in recording and translating sources.

Cartoonists and comic art specialists who kindly sent information, especially lists of their own works, were John J. Appel, Jean-Claude Faur, Axel Frohn, Denis Gifford, Harold Hinds, Maurice Horn, Nat Karmichael, Les Lilley, Richard Langlois, Leonard Rifas, and Jerry Robinson. Horn donated a part of his library to me. Also providing sources were Gary Groth, Pete Coogan, Randall Scott, German Caceres, Robert Roberts, Joseph G. Szabo, and Tim Ernst. Mort Walker, Jerry Robinson, David Kunzle, and Maurice Horn gave these bibliographies much respectability by writing forewords that are informative and interesting.

Roseanne Lent typed the 1986 bibliography on comic art which I self published, and Michael Taney readied this one for publication.

The reader of any scholarly work has a right to know who paid the research bill, for here lies the potential for influence peddling. As with my previous works, this bibliography was completed without grants and with very minimal (and that given begrudgingly) help from my workplace. Instead, it was financed by my summer earnings, meager savings, and income tax refunds, as well as a loan from what I good naturedly, but gratefully, call the Bovalino's Ristorante "Foundation," my brother Russ's restaurant in Westlake, Ohio.

To all the people mentioned above, and hundreds of others, I express my sincerest appreciation.

John A. Lent

Introduction

by Jerry Robinson

Once considered a rather lowbrow and immature form of entertainment, albeit a popular one with newspaper readers and therefore a circulation builder, the comic strip during its 100-year history has gradually and grudgingly been recognized by the art and literary establishment as a unique and indigenous American art form. During its fifty-five year history, the modern comic book, has been banned, degraded, and held accountable for many of society's ills. However, "the seductress of the innocent," has also become respectable as art and literary expression, and both genres have been awarded such mainstream recognition as the Pulitzer Prize.

America has been habitually slow to recognize its own fertile inventions as "culture." Significant artistic achievement has been detected in such American phenomena as jazz, country and folk music, the movies, and even television. It may be set down as a law of cultural history that the vulgar amusements of today become the highbrow art of tomorrow. Italian opera, Elizabethan drama, and the comics were conceived for the entertainment of the masses. Gilbert Seldes, who included the comics among his "seven lively arts," effectively rebutted the cherished notion that if something is enjoyed by the masses and makes you laugh, it isn't art.

The combination of the picture and word endows the sequential narrative, as it is defined, with a unique power for storytelling and creative expression. It is at once a literary art in the tradition of the written word and a visual art with the ability to compress and expand time, develop character, and create a sense of immediacy through crosscutting and nonlinear plot development—techniques of the film, theater, and television. But unlike film, theater, and television, it is an intensely personal art more akin to the traditional children's illustrated book in that the reader literally holds the story in his hands. In Marshall McLuhan's terms, the comics are a "hot" medium.

Interestingly, both the comic strip and film developed almost at the same time after centuries of attempts to bring the illusion of motion to the static image. In 1906, one of the pioneer movies by Edwin Porter of the Edison Company was based on the early strip, *Dreams of a Rarebit Fiend* by Winsor McCay. McCay was himself a pioneer in both the film (*Gertie the Dinosaur*) and comic strip (*Little Nemo*). Although the comic strip and the sequential narrative evolved from earlier forms, all their elements had yet to be combined to create the genre that has proved to be one of singular longevity and richness.

The comic strip has played a vital role in the history of America. It has made a unique contribution—the significance of which has not been fully realized. More than any other medium of expression, with the possible exception of film, the American cartoon may indeed have had the most profound influence on American culture.

The concept of the picture-story, which Rodolphe Topffer first realized in 1827, enlarged the resources of the graphic medium. It appropriated from verbal language the property of developing time, which gave the visual arts a fourth dimension of incalculable potential. This illusion of time, created by a chronological sequence of images (one frame essential to the next, each frame truly growing out of the one before and impelling a further image as a result), gives the comic strip its unique dynamics. The strip is meant to be experienced for a few seconds or minutes at daily or weekly intervals. This time element is an essential ingredient. The repetition and constant renewal, the growth of the artist and reader together, provide a cumulative force of great power. Each episode is part of a larger work, a continuum without end. It is, truly, a living art form.

One can, of course, cite precursors of the narrative art throughout mankind's history: from cave drawings at Altamira, Spain; Egyptian hieroglyphics; Greek friezes, pre Columbian art, the Trajan Column, and Japanese scrolls, to the Bayeux tapestry; and the *Image d'Epinel*. However, from the 16th century onward, numerous artists, notably William Hogarth, Thomas Rowlandson, James Gillray and Gustave Doré, made notable contributions to the development of today's pictorial narrative. Rowlandson's *Doctor Syntax* was, perhaps the first regular cartoon character—one of the essential elements of the comic strip which have been evolving for centuries in many societies, seemingly waiting for the right combination of people, place, and time.

The catalyst was the bitter newspaper rivalry in the late 1800s between the giants of the press Joseph Pulitzer and William Randolph Hearst. The war was soon waged in a kaleidoscope of color (the origin of the term "yellow journalism") with the introduction of the color press. One result was the cartoon *Down in Hogan's Alley* by R.F. Outcault in Pulitzer's *New York World* in 1895. The setting was the city's slums—squalid tenements, and backyards filled with stray animals, tough characters, and various ragamuffins. One of the urchins was a flap-eared, bald-headed child with an Asian face and a quizzical yet knowing smile. He was dressed in a long, dirty nightshirt, which Outcault often used as a placard to comment on the cartoon itself, an analogous role to that of the *Chorus* in early Greek theater.

Although the urchin had appeared in various colors, the printers, experimenting with yellow ink, arbitrarily chose his nightshirt as a test area in one episode. The yellow was a success, and so was the *Yellow Kid*, as he soon became known. The early episodes were in one tableau, but Outcault soon employed the sequential narrative that became the characteristic structure of the comic strip. The form was further refined in *The Katzenjammer Kids* by Rudolph Dirks in 1897, with expanded use of speech balloons, framing and the limited time sequence. Thus, an indigenous American art form was born, and its authors and graphic artists the most widely viewed in the world.

Hundreds of millions of readers every day throughout the world experience the intimate relationships the comics provide. Cartoons not only reflect life, they help mold it. They form a record of life in the United States. Cartoons have set the style for clothes, coiffure, food, manners, and mores. They have become Broadway shows, motion pictures, radio and TV series, popular songs, books, and toys. Even in its infancy, the comics influenced the other arts. Victor Herbert wrote the score for a 1908 musical comedy based on *Little Nemo*, and the classic strip *Krazy Kat* was translated into a ballet by John Alden Carpenter in 1922.

Our language has been permeated with comic idiom. Some words have become so much a part of our speech that the origin has been forgotten. Popular comic idiom include, "Hot dog," "jeep," "baloney," and "Rube Goldberg contraption" (now a dictionary term). The code word for the Allied Forces on D-Day was "Mickey Mouse" and the password for the Norwegian underground was "The Phantom." Foods have been popularized in the comics: *Wimpy's* hamburgers, *Dagwood*'s sandwiches, and *Jiggs*' corned beef and cabbage. The comics have influenced fashion since the turn of the century when American boys affected (or more accurately, were afflicted with) the *Buster Brown* haircut and the outfit.

Many strips themselves have been inspired by other literary works. *Tarzan*, of course, was adapted from the novels of Edgar Rice Burroughs. Philip Nowlan drew upon his own story, *Armageddon 2419*, in creating *Buck Rogers*. *Bringing Up Father* was derived from a play, *The Rising Generation*. Chester Gould credits his conception of *Dick Tracy* to Sir Arthur Conan Doyle's *Sherlock Holmes*. Gould's grotesque gallery is in the tradition of literature dating back to the horrific masks of Greek comedy and the works of Victor Hugo, Edgar Allan Poe, and others who elevated the grotesque, the bizarre, and the ugly to art. Other features, particularly in the comic books, have drawn upon mythology and legends, such as *Thor*, *Hercules*, and *King Arthur*.

Since the birth of the comic strip and the pioneer cartoonist-printers, there has been a continuous interplay with the fine arts. To ignore one form is to not fully understand the other. George Luke, who also drew *The Yellow Kid*, was a prominent painter of the Ash Can School, as was John Sloan, who also drew a weekly cartoon feature. Lionel Feininger, the noted Cubist painter, created two strips in Germany for the *Chicago Tribune* in 1906. His prismatic canvases and muted hues are reflected in his cartoons. Winsor McCay used the intensity of impressionistic color and electric juxtapositions to heighten the fantasy of *Little Nemo*. Feininger, the painter, was always grateful to Feininger, the cartoonist: "Far be it from me to underrate those important years as a comics draftsman, they were my only discipline."

This cross-pollination is seen between the characteristics of Art Nouveau and Art Deco, which developed at the time of the creation of the comic strip, and in the work of McManus and McCay. Noel Sickles and Milton Caniff brought the art of Chiaroscuro to the comics. Other influences are discernible, such as impressionism in the work of Caniff; abstract expressionism in Cliff Sterrett's *Polly and Her Pals*; and romantic classicism in the art of Burne Hogarth and Hal Foster. Surrealism, Pop, and Op Art have exerted their influences as well. Stan Drake (*Heart of Juliet Jones*) and Leonard Starr (*On Stage*) introduced a form of photographic realism in the 1950s. This New Realism evolved from the romanticism of Foster and Hogarth and the Caniff-form of impressionism. It paralleled the development of *cinema verité* and the trend of super, hard-focus realism in painting.

Numerous painters have in turn recognized the potential of the cartoon idiom and iconography and found the comics a rich source of inspiration, reflecting the deep cultural absorption of its imagery. Comics iconography is seen in the works of Jasper Johns (*Alley Oop*), Andy Warhol (*Dick Tracy*), Roy Lichtenstein (*Mickey Mouse*), Robert Rauchenberg (*Popeye*) and many others. In 1975 I served as special consultant to *CARTOON*, at the John F. Kennedy Center in Washington, the largest exhibition of American cartooning ever held. In one section we attempted to demonstrate the pervasive influence of the comics in our culture. On one wall we placed the Mel Ramos painting, *The Joker* (then valued at $150,000), and on the facing wall the original of the *Detective Comics* cover I drew in 1941 featuring *The Joker* (for which, even now, I am ashamed to say how much I was paid).

Masters of the medium have blended the art of the two disciplines—pictures and words—into a seemingly seamless whole. In this sophisticated balance was created a comics vocabulary and iconography with the ability to create a sense of time, space, sound, and emotion. America seemed to have an inexhaustible reservoir of comic geniuses: George Herriman, whose *Krazy Kat* was described by Gilbert Seldes as the most amusing, fantastic, and satisfactory work of art produced in America; Rube Goldberg and his one-man insurrection against the tyranny of the machine with his wildly complex contraptions that accomplish trivial ends; Milt Gross, with his extravagant creations such as *Count Screwloose from Toulouse*; Billy DeBeck and his depiction of the born loser in *Barney Google*; Frank Willard, with his lovable menage of lowbrows in *Moon Mullins*; Elzie Segar, whose fantasy of *Thimble Theater Starring Popeye* was peopled with a Dickens-like cast of splendid buffoons. All contributed perceptive comic portraits of American life. Bill Mauldin's *Up Front*, George Baker's *Sad Sack*, and Mort Walker's *Beetle Bailey* continued the American tradition of the soldier's healthy irreverence for military authority. Percy Crosby in *Skippy*, Charles Schulz in *Peanuts*, and Bill Watterson in *Calvin and Hobbes* brought an adult sophistication with philosophical insight to the children's strip.

Social satire in the tradition of Jonathan Swift and Mark Twain came to the comics in 1934 with Al Capp's *Li'l Abner*, and is best exemplified in the episodes with the *Schmoos* (who supply all our material needs) and the *Kigmies* (epitomes of masochism who release all human aggression), both of which posed grave threats to the establishment. Although Harold Gray's *Little Orphan Annie* (1924) gave voice to its creator's rightist philosophy, it was Walt Kelly who contributed a new dimension of political allegory in *Pogo*. Following this tradition were Pulitzer Prize winners Jules Feiffer, who enlarged the scope of the comics in 1956 with literary cartoons of radical politics and vignettes of psychological torment in *Feiffer*, and Garry Trudeau whose *Doonesbury* debuted in 1970 with a brilliant blend of political/social satire that has outgrown cult status to become a fixture of the innovative mainstream.

The beginnings of the adventure strip and story continuity appeared as early as 1906 with the work of Charles Kahles, one of the most inventive of the early cartoonists. His *Hairbreadth Harry*, the first strip without a distinct ending each week, introduced a suspense situation for each following episode—a device that extended the story potential of the comic strip. The "cliffhanger," the final panel of impending danger, proved to be an essential technique in a modern adventure strip, as well as the movie serial that it predated by several years.

While some other early strips adopted a story line, notably *The Gumps*, essentially the era of the adventure strip had not yet really begun. One of the earliest and most influential contributors to its evolution was Roy Crane, who created *Wash Tubbs* in 1924. Crane strongly influenced his contemporaries and became one of the finest storytellers the medium has produced. The introduction of two epic strips (coincidentally on the same day, January 7, 1929) established the adventure genre in the comics—*Tarzan* and *Buck Rogers*. *Tarzan* was illustrated by two brilliant and diverse talents: Hal Foster, who went on to create *Prince Valiant*, which established him as one of the masters of the art; and Burne Hogarth, whose command of classic composition and dynamic movement of form and line brought the comics to another plateau of achievement.

In a unique departure from comic dogma, Frank King's *Gasoline Alley* had its characters grow up, day by day from 1921, along with generations of its readers. Chester Gould's *Dick Tracy* (1931), who Ellery Queen called the world's first procedural detective in fiction, also made a radical departure. When the first character to be gunned down in the funnies occurred in the first week of *Tracy*, the "comics" became a misnomer; they were no longer just romantic or funny. Gould pioneered a new, hard-hitting realism dealing with contemporary themes.

Two strips debuted in 1934 which were to further the development of adventure continuity, *Flash Gordon* and *Terry and the Pirates*. Alex Raymond proved to be one of the most brilliant creators of illustrative fantasy in *Flash Gordon*. Frederico Fellini describes the strip's hero with profound affection: "When I think of it, it seems as though he actually existed. At times in my films, I seek to find the color and verve of *Flash Gordon* and his world."

In Milton Caniff's *Terry and the Pirates* (1934) all of the techniques of storytelling and of the visual-verbal experience fused and a classic style emerged. Caniff integrated the narrative and its visual expression into a uniform aesthetic balance utilizing so-called film techniques: long, medium, close-up and angle shots; cross-cuts; and establishing shots to set the scene or introduce characters. The strip and film both utilize a linear progressive series of pictures to tell a story. The comics, however, used the close-up before D.W. Griffith "invented" it, and notable filmmakers such as Fellini, Orson Welles, and Alain Resnais have adapted important techniques of the comics in their films.

Though having a common heritage, the comic strip, comic book and graphic novel have their own idiosyncratic development and each has evolved its own unique vision and symbolism. Innovators have enlarged the genre's potential by changing the structure, as well as employing new narrative and visual techniques. Together, the various strands of cartoon art should be viewed as a distinct, but logical, development in the long history of narrative art.

The origin of the comic book can be traced to the English 19th century penny dreadfuls—adventure stories with an illustrated cover. They were followed at the turn of the century by children's books in series with occasional illustrations such as *The Rover Boys* and *Tom Swift*. The comic book's immediate literary predecessors were the pulps, which began in the mid-1800s with romanticized versions of *Buffalo Bill*, *Wyatt Earp* and other folk heroes and reached their peak of popularity in the 1920s and 1930s. Such titles as *Doc Savage*, *The Shadow*, *Weird Tales*, and *Black Mask* first featured masked heroes à la *Scarlet Pimpernel*, in addition to science fiction, detective, and western tales written by Isaac Asimov, Dashiell Hammett, Zane Grey and other notable writers of popular fiction.

The comic book, which began with reprints of comic strips, came into its own in 1939 with Joe Shuster and Jerry Siegel's *Superman* and the following year with Bob Kane and Bill Finger's *Batman*. The superhero—and the supervillain with the addition of the *Joker*—became the essential narrative framework for the next half century and the present. As did the comic strip, the comic book somehow found a pool of exceptional talent, writers and artists, eager to fill the pages of the flood of new titles in the wake of the success of *Superman* and *Batman*, and beginning with *Mad* magazine in 1952, great satirists and caricaturists, including Jack Davis, Mort Drucker, Harvey Kurtzman, and Wally Wood. They include C.C. Beck, Charles Biro, Will Eisner, Jack Kirby and Joe Simon, Joe Kubert, Stan Lee, Mort Meskin, Alex Toth, and Mort Weisinger. In the following decades, comic books were replenished by successive generations of exceptional artists and storytellers, including, currently, John Byrne (*Fantastic Four*), Todd McFarlane (*Spawn*), Walt Simonson (*Thor*), and Mike Mignola (*Bram Stoker's Dracula*).

Cartoonists have traditionally revolted against accepted values. Not being part of the establishment has freed them to be experimental and as outrageous, and even tasteless, as they wish. The *avant garde* and underground art of one day is often co-opted by society the next. This is evidenced in the counter culture comics, or comix, as they are often distinguished from mainstream comics, exemplified by the work of Robert Crumb and Gilbert Shelton in the 1960s. Seen in such magazines as *Zap* and *Bijou*, many self-published, they defied all conventions and dealt with the dark side, often pornographic and scatological. They were also original, raucous, and often hilariously funny.

Although the comic strip sustained audiences for a century, its inherent limitation—relatively minute daily doses—has been exacerbated in the last decade due to further restrictions in newspaper space and competition from television, as well as the resurgence of the comic book and the growth of the graphic novel. The graphic novel, essentially a comic book but with fine color reproduction on coated stock (selling from $15 to $45) and with the space for both extensive art and full length novels, has attracted a new generation of artists and writers as well as a new audience nurtured by the comic strip and traditional comic book. It is a form of sequential narrative pioneered in Europe by George Remi (Hergé) with *Tintin* and René Goscinny and Albert Uderzo with *Asterix*, followed by such exceptional creators as Jean (Moebius) Giraud, Phillipe Druillet, and Hugo Pratt. The French were perhaps the first to attract adult readers and treat the art seriously. The comics have been reviewed in *Le Monde*, and extolled by such affectionados as literary critic Andre Maroux and filmmaker Alain Resnais. Magazines and festivals, even exhibitions at the Louvre, are devoted to the examination of the art form.

The American pioneers of the genre include the brilliant Eisner (*The Spirit*), who beginning with *A Contract With God* in 1978, explored the potential of the graphic novel and Frank Miller's *Dark Knight* which revolutionized *Batman*. Art Spiegelman's shattering work *Maus* (which earned him a special Pulitzer Prize), confirmed once and for all that serious subjects such as the holocaust can be dealt with in a cartoon. The creators of the so-called "New Comics" of the 1980s and 1990s—a new generation of counterculture comix, often sexual and violent, intensely personal and autobiographical—include Harvey Pekar, Lynda Barry, Nicole Hollander, Mary Fleener, and Matt Groening.

Exceptional creators in disparate cultures throughout the world have adopted the form, notably Eduardo Rius in Mexico, Alberto Breccia in Uruguay, Lorenzo Mallotti in Italy and Enki Bilil in Yugoslavia. In Japan the popularity of comics (*manga*) and the graphic novel has reached phenomenal proportions—some titles sell up to 5 million copies per week. The idiosyncratic and stylistic nuances found in Japanese comics have roots in 18th century Hokusai prints, Samurai Warriors and Kabuki Theater. Rakuten Kitazawa pioneered the first serialized strip in 1902. Osama Tezuka, creator of the series *Phoenix* and *Astro Boy*, introduced the modern sequential narrative and was accorded the supreme Japanese accolade of "*Manga No Kamisama*" (God of the Comics). Another leading artist is Ishinomori Shotaro, author of *Hotel*, which explored the nature of contemporary Japanese society, and other popularly acclaimed works. In 1986 he introduced the so-called "informational comic" in *The Manga Introduction to the Japanese Economy* (published in the West as *Japan, Inc.*) which became an overnight best seller.

The weekly manga, running 200 pages or more, are often erotic, sentimental, and violent, exploding in a wide range of sound, mood, rhythm, and content. The length often allows for a unique sense of spaciousness and sequences of cinematic-like slow motion not normally seen in the West. Among the first Japanese graphic novels successfully translated in the West was the semi-autobiographical *Barefoot Gen* in which Keiji Nakazawa recounts his experience in this dramatic and harrowing tale of a Hiroshima survivor.

The comic arts are now being given serious study worldwide. For example, one can obtain a Doctorate in Comics at the University of São Paulo. In Angoulême

(France), Brussels, London, Ottawa, and Omiya (Japan) museums have been built for the preservation and study of the comics. The International Museum of Cartoon Art, a magnificent new 15 million dollar structure, is soon to open in Boca Raton, Florida. I am honored to contribute to this exhaustive and much needed bibliography by John Lent who has written many learned and insightful studies of world comics. He is uniquely qualified to undertake this monumental task. Anyone who writes, draws, studies, reads, enjoys and loves the comics is in his debt.

Jerry Robinson, president and editorial director of Cartoonists and Writers Syndicate, is well known in many art-related capacities. As an award-winning cartoonist, he created the first supervillain, "The Joker," while drawing *Batman* in its formative years, as well as the strips, "Life with Robinson," "still life," "Jet Scott," and "Flubs and Fluffs," among others. He is also noted as a film director and writer, author of about 30 books, teacher, illustrator, and curator of exhibitions. Robinson has served as president of both the American Association of Editorial Cartoonists and the National Cartoonists Society.

1

Comic Books and Strips

RESOURCES

Bibliographies, Dictionaries, Encyclopedias

1. "Additions to the Krigstein Bibliography." *Squa Tront*. No. 9, 1983, p. 62.

2. "Alex Toth—A Bibliography." *Robin Snyder's History of the Comics*. July 1991, p. 79.

3. "An Annotated Carl Barks Bibliography." *The Barks Collector*. July 1981, p. 19.

4. Bails, Jerry. *The Who's Who of American Comic Books*. St. Claire Shores, Michigan: Jerry Bails, 1973-1976. Vol. I, A-F; Vol II, G-M; Vol. III, N-S; Vol. IV, T-Z plus Addenda.

5. Bails, Jerry. *The Who's Who of American Comic Books*. 2d ed. St. Claire Shores, Michigan: Jerry Bails, 1986-. Serially as Vol. II of Bails' *The Panelologist*.

6. Barrier, Mike. "Comic Book Books." *Comics Journal*. January 1986, pp. 85-88, 90.

7. Budiansky, Bob, Ian Akin, and Brian Garvey. *Transformers Universe*. New York: Marvel Comics, 1987. 128 pp.

8. Castelli, Alfredo. "Bibliografia Orientativa di Walt Disney in USA." *Guida a Topolino*. November 1966, pp. 34-36.

9. "Comics." In *Encyclopedia Americana*, Vol. 7, p. 362. New York: 1951.

10. "Comic-Strips." In *Encyclopedia Brittannica*, Vol. 4, pp. 870B-872. London: 1961.

11. Crawford, Hubert H. *Crawford's Encyclopedia of Comic Books*. Middle Village, New York: Jonathan David Publishers, 1978.

12. Day, David. *An Encyclopedia of Monsters and Imaginary Beings Created by Edgar Rice Burroughs. The Burroughs Bestiary*. London: New English Library, 1978.

13. Dippie, Brian W. and Paul A. Hutton. *The Comic Book Custer: A Bibliography of Custeriana in Comic Books and Comic Strips*. Publication No. 4, Brazos Corral of the Westerners, 1983.

14. "Directory of Comics Scholars." *Comic Art Studies*. December 2, 1992, pp. 9-14.

15. Fiore, Robert. "A Selected Bibliography: Comics, Comics Everywhere." *Print*. November-December 1988, pp. 172, 181-182, 184.

16. Fleischer, Michael L. *Batman*. The Encyclopedia of Comic Book Heroes. Vol. 1. New York: Collier Books, 1976. 387 pp.

17. Fleischer, Michael L. *The Great Superman Book*. The Encyclopedia of Comic Book Heroes. Vol. 3. New York: Warner Books, 1978. 512 pp.

18. Fleischer, Michael L. *Wonder Woman*. The Encyclopedia of Comic Book Heroes. Vol. 2. New York: Collier Books, 1976. 253 pp.

19. Gale, Carole F. "An Annotated Bibliography of Books and Articles on the Modern American Comic Book, 1940-Spring 1972." Masters research paper, Library Science, Kent State University, 1972.

20. Garvin, John. "A Shakespeare Comics Bibliography/Catalog." *Comic Art Collection*. December 2, 1989, pp. 4-7.

21. Goulart, Ron. "The Encyclopedia of Golden Age Heroes." *Comics Buyer's Guide*. Continuing series, 1983-1985.

22. Goulart, Ron, ed. *The Encyclopedia of American Comics, 1897 to the Present*. New York: Facts on File, 1990.

23. Gruenwald, Mark. *The Official Handbook of the Marvel Universe*. New York: Marvel Comics Group, 1983. 384 pp.

24. Gruenwald, Mark. *The Official Handbook of the Marvel Universe*. New York: Marvel Comics, 1985-. 64 pp. each. Issue #9 in 1987.

25. Gruenwald, Mark and David Iofvers. *The Complete Justice League of America Reader*. New York: Marvel Comics Group, 1973. 22 pp.

26. Gruenwald, Mark and Peter Sanderson. *The Official Handbook of the Marvel Universe*. New York: Marvel Comics Group, 1986-1987. 7 vols.

27. Harwood, John and Allen Howard. "Tarzan Encyclopedia." *The Burroughs Bulletin*. January 1975.

28. Horn, Maurice, ed. *The World Encyclopedia of Cartoons*. New York: Chelsea House, 1980. 676 pp.

29. Horn, Maurice, ed. *The World Encyclopedia of Comics*. New York: Chelsea House, 1976.

30. "A Krigstein Bibliography." *Squa Tront*. No. 6, 1975, pp. 49-52.

31. Lowery, Larry. *The Collector's Guide to Big Little Books and Similar Books*. Danville, California: Educational Research and Applications Corp., 1981. 378 pp.

32. Mannes, Marya. "Comics." In *Encyclopedia Americana*. Vol. 7, pp. 361-362 e. New York: 1959.

33. "'New Finds/Updates to the Kelly Bibliography." *Fort Mudge Most*. April 1988, pp. 16-18.

34. Resnais, Alain and Alain Tercinet. "Bibliographie de Dick Tracy." *Giff-Wiff* (Paris). No. 21, 1966.

35. Richardson, Darrell C. *J. Allen St. John: An Illustrated Bibliography*. Memphis, Tennessee: Privately printed; distributed by Mid-American Publishers, 1991. 111 pp.

36. Rifas, Leonard. "A Bibliography of Articles About Comic Books and Strips Which Are Cited or Abstracted in Reference Indices." Unpublished paper. March 1989.

37. Rovin, Jeff. *The Encyclopedia of Superheroes*. New York: Facts on File, 1985. 443 pp.

38. Rovin, Jeff. *The Encyclopedia of Super Villains*. New York: Facts on File, 1987. 416 pp.

39. Scott, Randall W. *Comic Books and Strips*. Phoenix, Arizona: Oryx Press, 1988.

40. "Supplement to the Krigstein Bibliography." *Squa Tront*. No. 7, 1977, p. 50.

41. Thompson, Don. "Dan Noonan Bibliography." *Graphic Story Magazine*. No. 9, 1968, pp. 18-19.

42. Thompson, Don and Dick Lupoff. *All in Color for a Dime*. New Rochelle, New York: Arlington House, 1970.

43. Wein, Len. *Who's Who, the Definitive Directory of the DC Universe*. New York: DC Comics, 1984-1987. 26 issues, 32 pp. each.

44. Willits, Malcom. "A Bibliography of the Mickey Mouse Comic Strips." *Vanguard*. No. 2, 1968, pp. 35-36.

45. Zelenetz, Alan. *The Official Handbook of the Conan Universe*. New York: Marvel Comics Group, 1986. 32 pp.

Catalogues, Collections

46. "Colorado Department of Revenue Has a Collection of 90,000 Seized Comic Books for Sale." *Comics Buyer's Guide*. March 26, 1993, p. 6.

47. "Fantagraphics Catalogue." *Comics Interview*. No. 92, 1991, pp. 19-50.

48. Gabbard, Dana. "Fredric Wertham Papers Located." *Comics Buyer's Guide*. February 8, 1991, p. 48.

49. Gifford, Denis. *American Comic Strip Collections. 1884-1939: The Revolutionary Era*. New York: G.K. Hall, 1990.

50. "New Collection Announcement." *Popular Culture in Libraries*. 1:1 (1992), pp. 127-128.

51. Scott, Randy. "The International Comics Collection." *Comic Art Studies*. May 2, 1992, p. 8.

52. State Historical Society of Wisconsin. *Box Inventory to Comic Literature in the August Derleth Collection*. Madison, Wisconsin: 197?. 36 pp.

53. "Student Presents Collection to Alma Mater; Ohio State University Receives Exhibit of Original Newspaper Cartoons." *Hobbies*. January 1942, p. 9.

54. "Syndicate Contributes 60 Years of Original Art to OSU." *Comics Journal*. March 1993, p. 33.

55. University of Chicago Library. *Comic Book Collection*. 23 leaves. Photocopy. Inventory of a collection of approximately 2,300 comic books at University of Chicago Library.

56. Willis, Steve. *Folkomix, a Catalog of Underground, Newave, and Small Press Comix in the Washington State University Rare Books Collection.* 2nd. Rev. Ed. Pullman, Washington: Morty Dog Publishing House, 1985. 110 pp.

57. Willis, Steve. *Folkomix, Supplement 1.* Pullman, Washington: Morty Dog Publishing House, 1985. 44 pp.

58. Willis, Steve. *Folkomix, Supplement* 2. Pullman, Washington: Morty Dog Publishing House, 1986. 77 pp.

59. Winchester, Mark D. "Comic Strip Theatricals in Public and Private Collections: A Case Study." *Popular Culture in Libraries.* 1:1 (1992), pp. 67-75.

60. *The Year's Work in Comic Indexing.* East Lansing, Michigan, 1977/78-. (An index to Amateur Press Alliance for Indexing and to most comics indexes in the Michigan State University collection).

Checklists, Guides

61. Bails, Jerry. *The Collector's Guide: The First Heroic Age.* Detroit, Michigan: Panelologist Publication, 1969. 70 pp.

62. Ball, Dean. *Superman 1980.* Wenatchee, Washington: 1979. 50 pp.

63. Benson, John. "The Complete Guide to EC Comics." *Squa Tront.* No. 9, 1983.

64. Brown, Gary. *Magnus, Robot Fighter.* Miami, Florida: 1978, 10 pp.

65. Brown, Gary. *Space Family Robinson Lost in Space.* Miami, Florida: 1977. 9 pp.

66. Brown, Gary. *Turok and the Sons of Stone.* Miami, Florida: 1978. 29 pp.

67. "Chronological List of Key Comic Books for Period 1933-1943." In *The Comic Book Price Guide 1985-86*, edited by R.M. Overstreet, pp. A-28 - A-50. Cleveland, Tennessee: 1985.

68. Collier, J. "The Hands of Shang-Chi, Master of Kung Fu Checklist." *Amazing Heroes.* June 1982, pp. 53-59.

69. "Comics Publishers." In *Comics Buyer's Guide 1993 Annual*, pp. 77-92. Iola, Wisconsin: Krause, 1992.

70. Drew, Bernard A. "A Roundup of Cowboys in PB Book Series... 1933 to 1984." *Comics Buyer's Guide.* September 28, 1984, pp. 52, 54, 56.

71. Fiene, Don. *R. Crumb Checklist of Work and Criticism*. Cambridge, Massachusetts: Boatner Norton Press, 1981. 170 pp.

72. "50th Anniversary Checklist: DC Comics Titles, 1935-Present." *Comics Buyer's Guide*. September 6, 1985, pp. 22, 24, 28, 30.

73. Fishburn, Katherine. *Women in Popular Culture: A Reference Guide*. Westport, Connecticut: Greenwood Press, 1982. Chapter 6, "Women in Advertising, Fashion, Sports, and Comics," pp. 186-189.

74. Gerber, Ernst and Mary. *The Photo-Journal Guide to Comic Books*. Minden, Nevada: Gerber Publishing Co., 1990.

75. Goulart, Ron. "A Reader's Guide to Golden Age Comics 'Movie Comics.'" *Comics Buyer's Guide*. February 1, 1991, pp. 50, 52, 55.

76. Highsmith, Doug. "Comic Books: A Guide to Information Sources." *RQ*. Winter 1987, pp. 202-209.

77. Hudgeons, Thomas E., ed. *The Official 1981 Price Guide to Comic and Science Fiction Books*. 4th Ed. Orlando, Florida: House of Collectibles, 1981. 437 pp.

78. Hudgeons, Thomas E., ed. *The Official Price Guide to Comic Books*. Orlando, Florida: House of Collectibles, 1983-.

79. Humphrey, M. Clark. "A Pogo Checklist." *Comics Journal*. February 1991, pp. 56-57.

80. *Illustrated Checklist to Underground Comix*. Cambridge, Massachusetts: Archival Press, 1979. 127 pp.

81. Kennedy, Jay. *The Official Underground and Newave Comix Price Guide*. Cambridge, Massachusetts: Boatner Norton Press, 1982. 273 pp.

82. Leiffer, Paul and Hames Ware. "American Comic Strips: A Chronological Listing." *Comics Buyer's Guide*. October 26, 1984, pp. 20, 24; November 9, 1984, pp. 28, 30; April 5, 1985, pp. 50, 52, 54; February 14, 1986, p. 18; June 6, 1986, p. 18.

83. Mintz, Lawrence E., ed. *Humor in America: A Research Guide to Genres and Topics*. Westport, Connecticut: Greenwood, 1988. 251 pp. Includes M. Thomas Inge, "The Comics."

84. Mougin, Lou. *Tarzan*. Graham, Texas: 1980-1981. 54 pp.

85. Mullaney, Dean. *Gene Colan Marvel Checklist*. Philadelphia, Pennsylvania: Eclipse Enterprises, 1978. 12 pp.

86. Murray, Will. "Doc Savage at Bantam Books." *Comics Buyer's Guide*. February 12, 1993, pp. 87, 90.

87. Murray, Will. "Street and Smith's 'Doc Savage Magazine.'" *Comics Buyer's Guide*. February 12, 1993, pp. 86-87.

88. Nigro, Rocco. "The Daredevil Checklist." *Daredevil Chronicles*. February 1982, pp. 43-46.

89. Norwood, Rick. "The Great Adventures: The Best Story Strip Reprints and Where To Find Them." In *Comics Buyer's Guide 1993 Annual*, pp. 66-76. Iola, Wisconsin: Krause, 1992.

90. Patten, Fred. "Lists." *Minnesota Cartoonist*. September 19, 1990, pp. 2-3. (Of comic book publishers, publications, syndicates, etc.).

91. Resnick, Michael. *Official Guide to the Fantastics*. Florence, Alabama: House of Collectibles, 1976. 212 pp.

92. Resnick, Michael. *The Official Price Guide to Comic and Science Fiction Books*. 3rd Ed. Orlando, Florida: House of Collectibles, 1979. 422 pp.

93. Richardson, Darrell C. *A St. John Checklist*. West Kingston, Rhode Island: Donald M. Grant, 1964.

94. Sabatini, Beppe. "Guide to Marvel Reprints. Part 1: Amazing Adventures to Amazing Spider-Man." *Amazing Heroes*. August 1982, pp. 50-52.

95. Taylor, Dan. "Marvel Comics Checklist for September." *The Collector's Club Newsletter*. September 1980, pp. 20-21.

96. "TFN Checklist." *Fans-Zine*. Spring-Summer 1979, p. 25. (Of superheroes).

97. Thompson, Don and Maggie, eds. *Comics Buyer's Guide 1993 Annual*. Iola, Wisconsin: Krause Publications, 1992. 96 pp.

98. Torcivia, Joe. *Mickey Mouse Checklist*. Westbury, New York: 1983. 32 pp.

99. Von Bernewitz, Fred and Joe Vucenic. *The Full Edition of the Complete E.C. Checklist*. Rev. Ed. Los Alamos, New Mexico: Wade M. Brothers, 1974.

100. Watt-Evans, Lawrence. "A Reader's Guide to Pre-Code Horror Comics." *Comics Buyer's Guide*. Part 7, April 13, 1984, pp. 44-47; Part 9, May 11, 1984, pp. 24-25; Part 10, June 1, 1984, p. 30; Part 13, August 17, 1984, pp. 20, 22, 24; Part 15, December 14, 1984, pp. 22, 24, 26; Part 16, December 28, 1984, pp. 20, 22; Part 18, February 1, 1985, pp. 30, 32, 34, 36, 46; Part 19, February 15, 1985, pp. 20, 24; Part 20, March 1, 1985, pp. 20, 22, 24, 26, 28.

101. Wiener, Robert K., ed. *The Archival Press Inc. Illustrated Checklist to Underground Comix*. Cambridge, Massachusetts: Archival Press, 1979. 127 pp.

102. Worden, Mark. *The Carl Barks Checklist*. Ann Arbor: Michigan, 1981?. 67 pp.

Fanzines and Fans

103. Bails, Jerry. "TCR History." *Comic Reader*. No. 147 (Super Summer 1977), p. 19.

104. Benson, John. "The E.C. Fanzines. Part One: The Gelatin Years." *Squa Tront*. No. 5, 1974, pp. 38 +.

105. Benson, John. "The EC Fanzines. Part Two: Potrzebie Bounces." *Squa Tront*. No. 7, 1977, pp. 36-39, 42.

106. Benson, John. "The EC Fanzines. Part 3: The Dallas Connection." *Squa Tront*. No. 8, 1978, pp. 3-5.

107. Benson, John. "The EC Fanzines. Part 4: Bibliographics." *Squa Tront*. No. 8, 1978, pp. 6-9.

108. Bertges, Jim. "The Zine Fan." *Comics Buyer's Guide*. Continuing column reviewing fanzines; from at least early 1980s.

109. Bethke, Marilyn. "*The Comic Reader*: Comics Fandom's Oldest Newszine." *Comics Journal*. October 1978, pp. 56-57.

110. Bethke, Marilyn. "The Comics Journal." *Comics Journal*. Summer 1979, pp. 120-121, 131.

111. Brennan, T. Casey. "The Spirit of Comics Fandom." *Amazing Heroes*. June 1982, p. 73.

112. Castelli, Alfredo. "Le Fanzines di Tarzan." *Comics Club* (Milan). No. 1, 1967, p. 44.

113. Curtis, Paul. "Fanzine Guide." *Comics Buyer's Guide*. September 20, 1985, pp. 24, 26.

114. Decker, Dwight R. "Some Opinionated Bastards." *Comics Journal*. August 1981, p. 107. (*FCA/SOB*).

115. Dushkind, Paul. "Hogarth and Crimmer's: An Exercise in Academic Futility." *Comics Journal*. February 1977, pp. 47-48.

116. "The Fandom Zone." *Comics Feature*. June 1980, pp. 29-36; September 1980, pp. 43-53.

117. Gelb, Jeff and Bill Schelly. "Fandom's Founders: Biljo White." *Comics Buyer's Guide*. January 1993, pp. 80-81.

118. Greim, Martin L. *Comic Crusader Storybook*. Dedham, Massachusetts: n.d. 164 pp.

119. Groth, Gary. "Black and White and Dead All Over." *Comics Journal*. July 1987, pp. 8-12.

120. Groth, Gary. "On Ethics and Fanzines." *Comics Journal*. December 1977, pp. 8-9.

121. Grove, T.W.M. "F.P.O." *Comics Buyer's Guide*. January 15, 1993, p. 64.

122. Hopkins, Harry A., ed. *Fandom Directory*. Langley AFB, Virginia: Fandom Computer Services, 1980. 304 pp. (Includes "Forward" [sic], glossary, fanzine index, conventions, convention index, international listing, "Why Do People Collect Comics?" "Why Publish?" and fan club listing).

123. Horak, Carl. "A Strip Fanzine History." *The Funnie's Paper*. November 1985, pp. 15-17.

124. "Indiana Joan." *Comics Feature*. June 1983, pp. 43-46.

125. Jensen, Jeff. "POW! How Comic Magazines Are Riding High." *Advertising Age*. March 8, 1983, p. 33.

126. Johnson, Glen D. "TCR History." *The Comic Reader*. September 1977, pp. 18-20.

127. Kujava, Sam. "The Triumph of Comic Freedom." *Comics Feature*. January-February 1984, pp. 53-55.

128. Light, Alan. "Through Time and Space with Buyer's Guide." *Comics Buyer's Guide*. January 15, 1993, pp. 25, 28.

129. "Lo! The Letterhacks!" *Comics Interview*. No. 107, 1992, pp. 42-46, 49-50, 52-53.

130. Mayerson, Mark. "The Rocky Road for Fans and Pros." *Comics Journal*. September 1981, pp. 6-7.

131. Pachter, Rich. "Fans on the Street." *Comics Interview*. No. 108, 1992, pp. 26-47.

132. Pack, Jim. "Sound Effects from the Editor." *The Comicist*. September 1990, p. 3.

133. Parker, Ron. "The EC Fanzines. Part 5: A Legend in Its Time." *Squa Tront*. No. 9, 1983, pp. 13-20.

134. Norwood, Rick. "Publications for Strip Collectors." *Comics Buyer's Guide*. October 28, 1983, pp. 49-50.

135. Schwartz, Ron. "The Funnie's Paper Index." *The Funnie's Paper*. May 1985, pp. 3-4.

136. Sienkiewicz, Bill. "Obsessed by Obsession." *Society of Strip Illustration Newsletter*. April 1989, pp. 3-5.

137. "Slave Labor Debuts Trade Journal." *Comics Journal*. November 1986, p. 16.

138. "TCR History: Mark Hanerfeld." *Comic Reader*. November 1977, pp. 11-14.

139. Thomas, Kenn. "Whither Fandom?" *Whizzard*. February 1981, pp. 20-21.

140. Thomas, Roy. "The Altered Ego: A Final Bow." *Alter Ego*. No. 11, 1978, p. 2.

141. Thompson, Don and Maggie. "Editorial." *Comics Buyer's Guide*. January 15, 1993, p. 4.

142. Thompson, Don and Maggie. "Fandom Exposed!" *Comics Feature*. September-October 1981, pp. 110-111.

143. Thompson, Don and Maggie. "Getting Together: Fandom Origins." *Comics Feature*. September-October 1981, pp. 105-107.

144. "United Fanzine Organization Checklist." *Comics Journal*. April 1978, p. 16.

145. Wertham, Frederic. *The World of Fanzines*. Carbondale, Illinois: Southern Illinois University Press, 1973.

146. White, Ted. "Fandom Origins." *Comics Feature*. June 1980, pp. 30-31.

147. Yronwode, Cat. *Arcade, the Comics Revue*. Birch Tree, Missouri: Yronwode (1979). 5 pp. (Contents of *Arcade* described in detail, with cross-index to artists and writers).

Indices

148. Austin, Alan. *DC Index*. London, 1974-. Vol. 1, A-I, 60 pp.

149. Bails, Jerry B. *An Authoritative Index to All Star Comics*. Glendale: 1964. 14 pp.

150. Bails, Jerry B. and H. Keltner. *An Authoritative Index to DC Comics*. Detroit, Michigan: 1963. 32 pp.

151. Beahm, George W., ed. *Vaughn Bode Index*. Newport News, Virginia: Distributed by C.W. Brooks jr., 1976. 64 pp.

152. Becattini, Alberto and Luca Boschie. *Disney Index*. Firenze, Italy: Al Fumetto, 1984. 64 pp. (Newspaper strips).

153. Black, William. *The Fox Features Phantom Lady Comic Book Index*. Longwood, Florida: Paragon Publications, 1979. 34 pp.

154. Bray, Glenn. *The Illustrated Harvey Kurtzman Index, 1939-1975*. Sylmar, California: Glenn Bray, 1976. 120 pp.

155. Brenner, Bruce. "Frazetta and Krenkel Index." *Qua Brot*. 1, 1985, pp. 52-65.

156. Brunner, Frank. *After Image*. Artist Index Series, Vol. 2. The Brunner Mystique, Vol. 2. Boulder Creek, California: S.R. Johnson, 1978. 52 pp.

157. Brunner, Frank. *The Brunner Mystique*. Artist Index Series, Vol. 1. Boulder Creek, California: S.R. Johnson, 1976. 32 pp.

158. Dellinges, Al. *Fiction House: A Golden Age Index of Planet Comics*. San Francisco, California: 1978. 40 pp.

159. "The Doom Patrol Index." *Best of Amazing Heroes*. No. 1, 1982, pp. 100-103.

160. Fisher, George T. *The Classic Comics Index*. Including References to *World Around Us*, Classic Special Issues, Classic Juniors. Nottingham, Hew Hampshire: Thomas Fisher Publishing, 1986. 53 pp.

161. Gafford, Carl. *Eclipso's Amazing Index*. Staten Island, New York: 1986. 8 pp.

162. Gafford, Carl. *The Flash Index*. Staten Island, New York: 1985. 24 pp.

163. Hegeman, Tom. *An Index to Articles Appearing in the Menomonee Falls Gazette and the Menomonee Falls Guardian*. Oneonta, New York: 1979. 23 pp.

164. Hill, Michael. *The Timely Index*. London: 1983-1984. 3 Vols.

165. "Justice Society Index." *Best of Amazing Heroes*. No. 1, 1982, pp. 32-34.

166. "The Justice Society of America Index." *Amazing Heroes*. August 1981, pp. 48-52.

167. Keltner, Howard. *Howard Keltner's Index to Golden Age Comic Books*. St. Claire Shores, Michigan: Jerry Bails, 1976.

168. Kozak, Darryn J. *Charlton Comics' Ghostly Haunts*. Indexed, No. 1. New Brighton, Minnesota: 1986. 25 pp.

169. Kozak, Darryn J. *Charlton Comics' Monster Hunters*. Indexed, No. 2. New Brighton, Minnesota: 1987. 15 pp.

170. Kubert, Joe. *Joe Kubert, a Golden Age Index*. San Francisco, California: A. Dellinges, 1978. 120 pp.

171. Lynch, Dennis. *Lynch's Index to Warren Comics*. Cedar Rapids, Iowa: 1981. 161 pp.

172. McAdams, Mindy. "The Swamp Thing Index." *Amazing Heroes*. May 1982, pp. 44-45.

173. McGeehan, John and Tom. "Index to Walt Disney's Comics and Stories." *Guida a Topolino*. November 1966, pp. 30-33.

174. *The Marvel Comics Index*. Toronto: G and T Enterprises, 1976-.

175. Mougin, Lou. *The All-Star Index*. Guerneville, California: Independent Comics Group, 1987-.

176. Mougin, Lou and Mark Waid. *The Official Crisis on Infinite Earths Cross-Over Index*. Guerneville, California: Independent Comics Group, 1986. 32 pp.

177. Mullaney, Dean. *The Steve Gerber Index*. An Eclipse Enterprises Production. Philadelphia, Pennsylvania: 1978. 13 pp.

178. Murray, Doug. *The Neal Adams Index*. Frankensteve Productions, 1974. 28 pp.

179. Olshevsky, George. *The Amazing Spider-Man*. The Marvel Comics Index, Vol. 1, No. 1. Toronto: G and T Enterprises, 1976. 79 pp.

180. Olshevsky, George. *The Avengers, Defenders and Captain Marvel*. The Marvel Comics Index, Vol. 1, No. 3. Toronto: G and T Enterprises, 1976. 116 pp.

181. Olshevsky, George. *Conan and the Barbarians*. The Marvel Comics Index, Vol. 1, No. 2. Toronto: G and T Enterprises, 1976. 96 pp.

182. Olshevsky, George. *Daredevil, Also Featuring Black Panther, Shanna, Black Goliath, Human Fly, and Dazzler*. The Marvel Comics Index, Vol. 1, No. 9B. San Diego, California: G. Olshevsky and T. Frutti, 1982. 113 pp.

183. Olshevsky, George. *The Fantastic Four and the Silver Surfer*. The Marvel Comics Index, Vol. 1, No. 4. Toronto: G and T Enterprises, 1977. 100 pp.

184. Olshevsky, George. *Heroes from Strange Tales*. The Marvel Comics Index, Vol. 1, No. 6. Toronto: G and T Enterprises, 1977. 96 pp.

185. Olshevsky, George. *Heroes from Tales of Suspense*. Book 1. The Marvel Comics Index, Vol. 1, No. 8A. Toronto: G and T Enterprises, 1979. 104 pp.

186. Olshevsky, George. *Heroes from Tales of Suspense*. Book 2. The Marvel Comics Index, Vol. 1, No. 8B. Toronto: G and T Enterprises, 1978. 100 pp.

187. Olshevsky, George. *Heroes from Tales To Astonish*. Book 1. The Marvel Comics Index, Vol. 1, No. 7A. Toronto: G and T Enterprises, 1978. 96 pp.

188. Olshevsky, George. *Heroes from Tales To Astonish*. Book 2. The Marvel Comics Index, Vol. 1, No. 7B. Toronto: G and T Enterprises, 1978. 96 pp.

189. Olshevsky, George. *The Mighty Thor*. The Marvel Comics Index, Vol. 1, No. 5. Toronto: G and T Enterprises, 1977. 96 pp.

190. Olshevsky, George. *The Official Marvel Index to Marvel Team-Up Featuring Spider-Man*. New York: Marvel Comics Group, 1986-.

191. Olshevsky, George. *The Official Marvel Index to the Amazing Spider-Man*. New York: Marvel Comics Group, 1985-.

192. Olshevsky, George. *The Official Marvel Index to the Avengers*. New York: Marvel Comics, 1987-.

193. Olshevsky, George. *The Official Marvel Index to the Fantastic Four*. New York: Marvel Comics Group, 1985-.

194. Olshevsky, George. *The Official Marvel Index to the X-Men*. New York: Marvel Comics, 1987-.

195. Olshevsky, George. *The X-Men, Also Featuring Ghost Rider, Champions, Black Goliath, and Dazzler*. The Marvel Comics Index, Vol. 1, No. 9A. San Diego, California: G. Olshevsky and T. Frutti, 1981. 112 pp.

196. Reed, Gene. *Adventures of Rex the Wonder Dog Index*. Huntsville, Alabama: 1982. 14 pp.

197. Reed, Gene. *All-Star Western*. Huntsville, Alabama: 1982. 18 pp.

198. Reed, Gene. *Archie Adventure Series Index*. Huntsville, Alabama: 1978. 16 pp.

199. Reed, Gene. *The Atom and Hawkman*. Huntsville, Alabama: The Comic Library, 1973. 10 pp.

200. Reed, Gene. *The Brave and the Bold*. Huntsville, Alabama: 1983. 26 pp.

201. Reed, Gene. *Dale Evans Comics*. Huntsville, Alabama: 1981. 6 pp.

202. Reed, Gene. *DC Giant Comics Index*. Huntsville, Alabama: 1978-. 3 Parts.

203. Reed, Gene. *DC Reprint Series Index*. Huntsville, Alabama: 1980. 20 pp.

204. Reed, Gene. *DC Special Series*. Huntsville, Alabama: 1983. 7 pp.

205. Reed, Gene. *DC Story Index 1935-1974*. Huntsville, Alabama: 1975. 234 pp.

206. Reed, Gene. *Gang Busters Index*. Huntsville, Alabama: 1984. 19 pp.

207. Reed, Gene. *Lois Lane Index*. Huntsville, Alabama: 1977. 19 pp.

208. Reed, Gene. *Mary Marvel Index*. Huntsville, Alabama: 1985. 7 pp.

209. Reed, Gene. *Metal Men Index*. Huntsville, Alabama: 1978. 8 pp.

210. Reed, Gene. *Phantom Stranger Index*. Huntsville, Alabama: 1978. 9 pp.

211. Reed, Gene. *Shazam Index*. Huntsville, Alabama: 1982. 7 pp.

212. Reed, Gene. *Showcase Index*. Huntsville, Alabama: 1983. 11 pp.

213. Reed, Gene. *The Superboy Index*. Huntsville, Alabama: 1981. 40 pp.

214. Reed, Gene. *Superman's Pal, Jimmy Olsen Index*. Huntsville, Alabama: 1980. 18 pp.

215. Reed, Gene. *The Tabloids*. Huntsville, Alabama: 1982. 19 pp.

216. Reed, Gene. *T.H.U.N.D.E.R. Agents*. Huntsville, Alabama: 1978. 12 pp.

217. Satin, Allan D. *A Doonesbury Index: An Index to the Syndicated Daily Newspaper Strip "Doonesbury" by G.B. Trudeau, 1970-1983*. Metuchen, New Jersey: Scarecrow Press, 1985. 269 pp.

218. Scott, Randall W. *Beowulf Dragon Slayer*. Preserved Context Indexes to Serial Fiction, No. 1. East Lansing, Michigan: 1978. 15 pp.

219. Scott, Randall W. *Index to Wonder Woman (a Ms. Book)*. New York: 1977. 9 pp.

220. Scott, Randall W. *Moby Dick Comics*. Preserved Context Indexes to Serial Fiction, No. 3. East Lansing, Michigan: 1979. 13 pp.

221. Scott, Randall W. *Rima of Green Mansions*. Preserved Context Indexes to Serial Fiction, No. 2. East Lansing, Michigan: 1978. 8 pp.

222. Scott, Randall W. *Seduction of the Innocent Index*. East Lansing, Michigan: 1978. 10 pp.

223. Scott, Randall W. *A Subject Index to Comic Books and Related Material*. East Lansing, Michigan: Michigan State University Libraries, 1975. 37 pp.

224. Steele, Henry. *Fiction House, a Golden Age Index*. San Francisco, California: A. Dellinges, 1978. 62 pp.

225. Steele, Henry. *Quality Comic Group, a Golden Age Index*. San Francisco, California: A. Dellinges, 1978. 46 pp.

226. Sundahl, Steve. *A New Marvel Super Hero Index*. Pontiac, Michigan: 1973. 46 pp.

227. "The Teen Titans Index." *Best of Amazing Heroes*. No. 1, 1982, pp. 80-84.

228. Thompson, Steve. *Walt Kelly and Pogo, a Bibliography and Checklist*. 4th Ed. Richfield, Minnesota: Spring Hollow Books, 1987. 91 pp.

229. Thompson, Steve. *The Walt Kelly Collector's Guide. A Bibliography and Price Guide*. Richfield, Minnesota: Spring Hollow Books, n.d. (1988?). 192 pp.

230. Tiefenbacher, Michael. *All-American Men of War*. Menomonee Falls, Wisconsin: 1980. 14 pp.

231. Tiefenbacher, Michael. *All-American Western*. Menomonee Falls, Wisconsin: 1983. 11 pp.

232. Tiefenbacher, Michael. *Aquaman*. Menomonee Falls, Wisconsin: 1981. 6 pp.

233. Tiefenbacher, Michael. *Big Town*. Menomonee Falls, Wisconsin: 1982. 22 pp.

234. Tiefenbacher, Michael. *Blackhawk, Challengers of the Unknown, Sea Devils*. Menomonee Falls, Wisconsin: 1981. 24 pp.

235. Tiefenbacher, Michael. *Ghosts*. Menomonee Falls, Wisconsin: 1979. 11 pp.

236. Tiefenbacher, Michael. *G.I. Combat*. Menomonee Falls, Wisconsin: 1979. 22 pp.

237. Tiefenbacher, Michael. *Hopalong Cassidy*. Menomonee Falls, Wisconsin: 1981. 8 pp.

238. Tiefenbacher, Michael. *House of Mystery*. Menomonee Falls, Wisconsin: 1977. 31 pp.

239. Tiefenbacher, Michael. *House of Secrets*. Menomonee Falls, Wisconsin: 1977. 20 pp.

240. Tiefenbacher, Michael. *My Greatest Adventure*. Menomonee Falls, Wisconsin: 1978-1979. 16 pp.

241. Tiefenbacher, Michael. *Mystery in Space*. Menomonee Falls, Wisconsin: 1983. 22 pp.

242. Tiefenbacher, Michael. *The Official Hawkman Index*. Guerneville, California: Independent Comics Group, 1986-.

243. Tiefenbacher, Michael. *Our Army at War*. Menomonee Falls, Wisconsin: 1980. 37 pp.

244. Tiefenbacher, Michael. *Our Fighting Forces*. Menomonee Falls, Wisconsin: 1979. 22 pp.

245. Tiefenbacher, Michael. *Rip Hunter, Time Master*. Menomonee Falls, Wisconsin: 1980. 5 pp.

246. Tiefenbacher, Michael. *The Sinister House of Secret Love*. Menomonee Falls, Wisconsin: 1979. 4 pp.

247. Tiefenbacher, Michael. *Star Spangled War Stories*. Menomonee Falls, Wisconsin: 1980. 30 pp.

248. Tiefenbacher, Michael. *Strange Adventures*. Menomonee Falls, Wisconsin: 1984. 45 pp.

249. Tiefenbacher, Michael. *The Superman Family*. Menomonee Falls, Wisconsin: 1981. 13 pp.

250. Tiefenbacher, Michael. *Tales of the Unexpected*. Menomonee Falls, Wisconsin: 1978. 25 pp.

251. Tiefenbacher, Michael. *Television and Comics*. Menomonee Falls, Wisconsin: 1980. 11 pp.

252. Tiefenbacher, Michael. *Tomahawk*. Menomonee Falls, Wisconsin: 1982. 22 pp.

253. Tiefenbacher, Michael. *Weird Mystery Tales*. Menomonee Falls, Wisconsin: 1979. 4 pp.

254. Tiefenbacher, Michael. *Weird War Tales*. Menomonee Falls, Wisconsin: 1979. 12 pp.

255. Tiefenbacher, Michael. *Western Comics*. Menomonee Falls, Wisconsin: 1983. 9 pp.

256. Tiefenbacher, Michael. *The Witching Hour*. Menomonee Falls, Wisconsin: 1978. 14 pp.

257. Von Bernewitz, Fred. *The Full Edition of the Complete E.C. Checklist*. Los Alamos, New Mexico: Wade M. Brothers, 1970. 171 pp.

258. Waid, Mark and Andrew MacLaney. *The Official Legion of Super-Heroes Index*. Guerneville, California: Independent Comics Group, 1986-.

259. Ward, Murray R. *Doom Patrol, the Official Index*. Guerneville, California: Independent Comics Group, 1986. 2 vols.

260. Ward, Murray R. *The Official Justice League of America Index*. Guerneville, California: Independent Comics Group, 1986-.

261. Ward, Murray R. *The Official Teen Titans Index*. 5 Vols. Guerneville, California: Independent Comics Group, 1985-1986.

262. Wermers, Bernie. "Dick Tracy Index 'BLB's.'" *New Comic News*. September-October 1967, p. 3.

263. Wormstedt, Bill. "An Index to The Rose and The Thorn." *Robin Snyder's History of the Comics*. July 1991, p. 76.

264. Yronwode, Catherine. *Deities, Powers and Forces*. The Lesser Book of the Vishanti, Chapter 2. Return from Reality, No. 3. Willow Springs, Missouri: Fly By Nite Grafiks, 1979. 4 pp.

265. Yronwode, Catherine. *Shade, the Changing Man*. Return from Reality, No. 2. Willow Springs, Missouri: 1979. 4 pp.

266. Yronwode, Catherine. *The Spirit Checklist*. ca. 1980. 55 pp.

Periodical Directory

267. *Alter Ego*. Fanzine, edited by Jerry Bails and Roy Thomas, credited with renewing interest in superhero comics. One of first fanzines; 11 issues between 1961-1969, 1978.

268. *Amazing Heroes*. Twice monthly. News, articles, interviews, checklists, reviews, histories of superheroes. Fantagraphics, 7563 Lake City Way N.E., Seattle, Washington 98115. 1981-.

269. *Amazing World of DC Comics*. Bi-monthly featuring reviews, interviews, histories, and stories about DC Comics. Reprinted dailies from September 14, 1970, to January 2, 1971. National Periodical Publications, P.O. Box 116, Radio City Station, New York, New York 10019. Started 1974; ceased 1978 after 17 numbers.

270. *Annie People*. Bi-monthly newsletter dealing with "Little Orphan Annie" strip, but especially "Annie" Broadway show and movie. Jon Merrill, Cedar Knolls, New Jersey. Since 1983.

271. *Arcade, the Comics Revue*. Specialized fan periodical published in 1970s by Cat Yronwode, Star Route 3, Birch Tree, Missouri 65793.

272. *The Archie Fan Magazine*. "Six monthly issues" by Mary Smith, 185 Ashland St., Holliston, Massachusetts 01746. No. 14, November 1991.

273. *Art? Alternatives*. Published quarterly by OB Enterprises, Suite 2305, 450 Seventh Ave., New York, NY 10123-0101. Alternative art forms, including underground comix. Started 1992.

274. *The Barks Collector*. Published quarterly by Bear Mountain Enterprises and Oak Tree Press, P.O. Box 616, Victoria, Virginia 23974. Fanzine about Carl Barks' work and life.

275. *The Best of the Tribune Co.* Four issues in 1985-86, each reprinting long runs of strips, such as "On Stage," "Dick Tracy," "Tales of the Green Beret," and "Little Orphan Annie." Continued as *Thrilling Adventure Stories*, Dragon Lady Press, Toronto, Canada. 1986-.

276. *Big Little Times*. Bi-monthly of Big Little Book Collectors of America, Danville, California. Edited by Larry Lowery; deals with history and collecting of Big Little Books. 1982-.

277. *Breaking In*. Monthly devoted to the aspiring comic strip professional hoping for syndication. Articles, tips, interviews, tools of trade, debuts of newly syndicated strips, and showcases of promising work. P.O. Box 89147, Atlanta, Georgia, 30312. Premiere issue 1992.

278. *Buried Treasure*. Irregularly published periodical reprinting old comic book stories. Pure Imagination, New York, New York. 1986-.

279. *Burroughs Bulletin*. Fanzine published for fans of Edgar Rice Burroughs in 1960s. Kansas City, Missouri.

280. *The Buyer's Guide for Comic Fandom*. A weekly newspaper of advertising and articles; started as monthly by Alan Light. Dyna Pubs Enterprises, East Moline, Illinois. 1971-1983. Continued as *Comics Buyer's Guide*.

281. *Buz Sawyer Quarterly*. Reprints Roy Crane's daily strip, "Buz Sawyer." Dragon Lady Press, Toronto, Canada. 1986-.

282. *Caniffites*. More than 40 numbers portraying and discussing Milton Caniff and his works. 1310 108th Ave. S.W., Calgary, Alberta, Canada T2W 0C6.

283. *CAPA-alpha*. Started 1964 by Jerry Bails as cooperative fanzine for members who wrote about comics. Monthly of Comicdom's Amateur Press Association.

284. *C.B.S. Journal*. Published in mimeograph form in 1967 by Jimmy Reyna, 725 NW 3rd St., Tulia, Texas 79088.

285. *Chapters*. Published monthly by Trident Publications, 4 Brattle St., Rm. 306, Cambridge, Massachusetts 02138. "Named after the old movie serials, whose segmented storytelling, inspired, in part, the flowering of the continuity comic strip genre." Contains vintage U.S. strips. 1980, only six numbers.

286. *City Limits Gazette*. Published every two weeks by *City Limits Gazette*, P.O. Box 390, McCleary, Washington 98557-0390. Forum for alternative, small-press, and self-published comics. Eight pages of news, letters, promotionals, announcements, review columns, interviews, and opinion articles. Fifteen numbers, 1980-1986.

287. *Classic Adventure Strips*. Bi-monthly published by Dragon Lady Press, Toronto, Canada; reprints complete vintage comic strips. 1985-.

288. *The Classics Collector*. Quarterly promoting hobby of collecting *Classics Illustrated* comics, art, memorabilia worldwide. Articles, profiles, news. Malan Classical Enterprises, 7519 Lindbergh Dr., St. Louis, Missouri 63117. No. 10 in 1990. Formerly *Worldwide Classics Newsletter*.

289. *The Collector*. Irregularly published fanzine on comics. About 60 pages of editorials, articles, illustrations, interviews, articles, letters. 1535 Oneida Drive, Clairton, Pennsylvania 15025. No. 27, Winter 1973.

290. *The Collector's Club Newsletter*. Monthly, mimeographed newsletter dealing with history, interviews, news about strips and comic books. Mat Kramer, 88 Many Levels Rd., White Bear Lake, Minnesota 55110. 1970s.

291. *Collector's Dream*. Published by George Olshevsky, G and T Enterprises, 260 Wellesley St. E. # 2203, Toronto M4X 1G6, Canada. For comic collectors around world. Interviews, articles, listings. 1970s.

292. *The Collectors Guide*. Monthly on all types of collecting, including comics. P.O. Box 160, Drexel Hill, Pennsylvania 19026. Started December 1992.

293. *Comic Art*. Fanzine covering both comic books and comic strips, started in 1961 by Don and Maggie Thompson.

294. *Comic Art Collection*. Quarterly to facilitate communication about comic art collection at Michigan State University. Articles, lists from other collections too. Randall W. Scott, editor, Russel B. Nye Popular Culture Collection, Michigan State University, East Lansing, Michigan. 1979-. Continues as *Comic Art Studies*.

295. *Comic Book Collector*. Monthly for "novice" and "expert" in comics collecting, with articles, letters, cards, price guides, history. Started January 1993 by Century Publishing, 155 E. Ames Ct., Plainview, New York 11803.

296. *The Comic Book Marketplace*. Published from P.O. Box 180900, Coronado, California 92178-0900. Frequency unknown. Includes many advertisements, prices, articles, and columns on collectibles and the historical and current aspects of comic books. Beginning in 1990 or 1991.

297. *Comic Book Newsletter*. Monthly devoted to small press comics with news, reviews, and how-to articles. One of publications of James Pack, P.O. Box 233, Loveland, Ohio 45140.

298. *The Comic Book Price Guide*. Annual since 1970, including price lists, articles on status of comics, special themes. Published by Overstreet Publications, Inc., 780 Hunt Cliff Dr., N.W., Cleveland, Tennessee 37311. Title changed to *The Official Overstreet Comic Book Price Guide* with 17th edition, 1987-1988.

299. *Comic Book Trader*. Published only few issues in 1987. Greenlee Publications, Box 13044, Whitehall, Ohio 43213.

300. *Comic Chronicles*. Club zine of Eau Claire Comics Club, 440 Garfield, Eau Claire, Wisconsin 54701. Articles, indices, criticism, opinion on all aspects of comics fandom.

301. *Comic Informer*. Bi-monthly with interviews, columns, fanzine reviews, showcases on comics. 6620 Harwin Suite 240, Houston, Texas 77036. 1982-.

302. *The Comicist*. Published for small press comics by Rocket Graphics. P.O. Box 233, Loveland, Ohio 45140.

303. *The Comic Reader*. Monthly review and checklist of coming comics from all US comics companies. 32 pp. Street Enterprises, P.O. Box 255, Menomonee Falls, Wisconsin 53051. 1961-1984; 219 numbers.

304. *Comic Relief*. Monthly by Page One Publishers, 2834 F Street, Eureka, California 95502. Features "This Month in Cartoons," "Strips and Panels," and "Columns." Fourth year, No. 31, January 1992.

305. *Comics Arena*. Published 12 times yearly, beginning July 1992. History, reviews, interviews, news, letters about comic books. 264 Main St., Florence, Kentucky 41042.

306. *Comics Business*. Monthly started in July 1987 with information about comics and animation as businesses—tax tips, markets, publisher's reliability charts, etc. P.O. Box 3185, Thousand Oaks, California 91359.

307. *The Comics Buyer's Guide*. Originally *The Buyer's Guide for Comic Fandom*. Present title after 1983. Weekly about comic book industry news, advertising, commentary, reviews. Published by Krause Publications, 700 E. State St., Iola, Wisconsin 54990.

308. *Comics Career Newsletter*. Monthly magazine for amateur comics writers and artists. Published by Kirk Chritton, 2012 W. Ash, M-10, Columbia, Missouri 65203.

309. *Comics Collector*. Published quarterly by Krause Publications, 700 E. State St., Iola, Wisconsin 54990. Interviews, articles, reviews, price guides about comic books and collecting. Started 1983.

310. *Comics Feature*. Published six times yearly. News and articles about comic books. New Media Publishing, 1518 East Fowler Ave., Tampa, Florida 33612. Begun in 1980.

311. *Comic Shop News*. Weekly newsletter available gratis at comic shops. Includes "Quickshots" of news of the comic book industry, top selling lists, interviews, and previews of new books. 2339 Milstead Circle, Marietta, Georgia 30066.

312. *Comics Interview*. Monthly. About four or five in depth interviews each issue with comic book artists, writers, inkers, colorists, shop owners, and fans. Fictioneer Books, Suite 301, 234 Fifth Ave., New York, New York 70001. 1983-.

313. *The Comics Journal*. Published monthly (except February, April and June) by Fantagraphics, 7563 Lake City Way N.E., Dept. CJ154, Seattle, Washington 98115. Over 100 pages. Editorial, news, letters, critiques, feature articles, columns, in-depth interviews, advertising. More recently, some emphasis on international comic art. First 32 issues before January 1977, called *Nostalgia Journal*, devoted to advertising for various collecting hobbies.

314. *Comics Retailer*. Monthly of business management for the comics industry. Features on computerizing a comics store, ethics in comics industry, Marvel financial report, columns, news, book reviews, licensing information. Krause Publications, 700 East Main St., Iola, Wisconsin 54990-0001. Since April 1992.

315. *Comics Revue*. Monthly published by Fictioneer Books, Suite 301, 234 Fifth Ave., New York, New York 10001. About 50 pages of popular comic strips each

issue. Reprinted daily strips from February 13, 1984 to March 6, 1986, from June 4, 1990 to date. First 10 numbers, 1983-1985, called *Comics Review*.

316. *Comics Scene*. Six times yearly since 1981. Interviews, articles, reviews about U.S. comics; some foreign. Sometimes titled *Starlog Presents Comics Scene*. Also supplemented by *Spectacular* issues. Comics World Corp., 475 Park Ave. South, New York, New York 10016.

317. *Comics Score Board*. Published by Heroes World Distribution, 961 Route 10, East Rutherford, New Jersey 07869. About 100-112 pages of prices and descriptions of comic books by company.

318. *Comics Strip News*. Weekly of Quality Art Productions, 200 Queen St. West, Toronto, Canada. Reprints old and contemporary comic strips.

319. *Comics Values Monthly*. Published monthly by Attic Books, 15 Danbury Rd., Ridgefield, Connecticut 06877. Articles, lists of top 100 comics, catalog of comics values.

320. *The Comic World*. Comics-slanted fanzine produced bi-monthly. Claims to be oldest comic book fanzine "still published by its original editor, dating back to 1961!!!" Yet, Vol. 1, No. 21 was November 1979. Overviews of comics series, mainly Golden Age. Robert Jennings, RFD 2, Whiting Rd., Dudley, Massachusetts 01570.

321. *Counter Media*. Devoted to underground, counterculture, and alternative publications from 1960s on. Much on comics. Box 6822, Portland, Oregon 97228.

322. *Crimmer's, The Harvard Journal of Pictorial Fiction*. Continues *The Harvard Journal of Pictorial Fiction*. One issue of each, 1974 and 1975. Interviews and articles on comics and film. Published by Harvard University Comics Society and T. Durwood. Continued as *Crimmer's, The Journal of Narrative Arts*; one issue in 1976 by T. Durwood, New York.

323. *The Daredevil Chronicles*. First published February 1982 by FantaCo Enterprises, Inc., 21 Central Ave., Albany, New York 12210. Promotes Marvel Comics Group book *Daredevil*, with portfolios, articles, interviews.

324. *Diktomania*. Published by Aardvark Comics, P.O. Box 110, Weedsport, New York 13166. Dedicated to work and life of comics artist Steve Ditko. Early 1980s.

325. *Dreamline*. Published 10 times yearly. Interviews, reviews, features on history and present status of comic books. Superlinea, 310 Niska Rd. #610, Downsview, Ontario M3N 2S3 Canada. 2:6, March 1982.

326. *EC Classic Reprints*. Twelve numbers, 1973-1975. Color facsimiles of E.C. comics from 1950s. East Coast Comix, Great Neck, New York.

327. *EC Classics*. Color reprints of E.C. comics stories of 1950s. R. Cochran, West Plains, Missouri. 1985-.

328. *EC Fan Bulletin*. Published in 1950s; short-lived. Showed interest for William Gaines' E.C. titles. Others in same genre of that time were *The EC Fan Journal*, *EC Scoop*, *Concept*, *The EC World Press*, *Hoohah*.

329. *Famous First Edition*. Eight issues between 1974 and 1978; large-size facsimile reprints of first issues of comic books. National Periodical Publications, New York, New York.

330. *Fandom Annual*. First published in 1967 by SFCA, 9875 SW 212 St., Miami, Florida, by G.B. Love. Much history and critiquing of comic books.

331. *Fandom Directory*. Annual listing of fan clubs, individuals, publications, conventions, retail stores, and libraries in all aspects of comics. Fandata Computer Services, Springfield, Virginia. 1979-.

332. *Fandom Times*. Published by FTO Publications, 19129 136th Ave., Apt. B, Ninica, Michigan 49448. Newszine concerned with current events in fan publishing. Profiles, interviews with creators of small comics. Early 1980s.

333. *The Fans of Central Jersey*. Newsletter of Fans of Central Jersey, 262 Garner Rd., North Brunswick, New Jersey 08902. Interviews, club news, comics news. Late 1970s.

334. *Fantasy Comics*. First comic book fanzine regularly issued; lasted 6 to 12 numbers beginning in early 1953. Science fiction comics. Published by James Taurasi.

335. *Favorite Funnies*. Twelve issues reprinting adventure strips, 1912-1945. DynaPubs, East Moline, Illinois. 1973.

336. *FCA and Me, Too!* Irregularly published as newsletter of Fawcett Collectors of America and Magazine Enterprise comics at 301 East Buena Vista Ave., North Augusta, South Carolina 29841. Continues after 1986 a newsletter started in 1973 as *FCA Newsletter*.

337. *Flashback*. Thirty-eight numbers, 1971-1976, reprinting Golden Age (1940s) comic books. DynaPubs, East Moline, Illinois.

338. *Foom Magazine*. Interviews, previews, news of Marvel Group. Marvel Comics Group, 575 Madison Ave., New York, New York 10022. About 1974.

339. *The Fort Mudge Most.* Regularly published every two months for Pogophiles. Published and edited since No. 3 (1988) by Steve Thompson, 6908 Wentworth Ave. So., Richfield, Minnesota 55423. Articles on Walt Kelly and aspects of "Pogo," letters, etc. Index for Nos. 1-24 published. Originally published as *The Fort Mudge Moan* in 1984.

340. *Four-Color Magazine.* Monthly of interviews, news, articles, letters and reviews covering comics industry. Paragon Q, P.O. Box 1146, Maplewood, New Jersey 07040. 1986-.

341. *Fred Greenberg's Omnibus.* A one-man project, consisting of interviews, articles, "freditorials" about comics industry. Fred Greenberg, 69 Morris Ave., Morristown, New Jersey 07960. Started February 1978.

342. *The Funnie's Paper.* "Comic strip fanzine" started March 1983. Every month except June, July, and August. Information on history of strips, artists, museums, characters. 2080 McGregor Blvd., Fort Myers, Florida 33901.

343. *Gizmo!* Stripzine with top cartoonists' works. 1970s.

344. *Golden Funnies.* Weekly started in 1973; reprinted newspaper adventure comic strips, 1915-1945. Title changed to *Vintage Funnies*, 1973-1975; 85 numbers published. DynaPubs, East Moline, Illinois.

345. *Gosh Wow!* Fanzine of 1960s.

346. *Graham Backers.* Fanzine devoted to work of artist Graham Ingels. Published in 1950s.

347. *Heroic Fantasy.* Published quarterly, beginning in February 1984, by Heroic Fantasy Publications, 110 East 236th Street, New York, New York 10470. Highlights work of a comic book artist in each issue, as well as other pages of fantasy comics.

348. *The Hollywood Eclectern.* Fanzine concerning U.S. strip, "Little Lulu." Articles, letters. Ed Buchman, P.O. Box 4215, Fullerton, California 92634. First issue, "Halloween 1992." Approximately thrice yearly.

349. *Honk!* Bi-monthly of comics strips and stories by various artists, interviews of artists. Fantagraphics, 7563 Lake City Way NE, Dept. CJ154, Seattle, Washington 98115.

350. *Hoohah.* Published in 1980s for EC fans by Ron Parker, 324 Warwick Ave., Suite 401, Oakland, California 94610.

351. *Infinity.* Published in early 1970s [?]. Editors, Adam Malin and Gary Berman. Interviews with comic book artists, portfolios, viewpoints.

352. *Inside Comics*. Four issues in 1974 with articles and interviews. Galaxy News Service, New York, New York.

353. *It's a Fanzine*. Published by Gene Kehoe, 3405 Woodland Ave., #90 D, West Des Moines, Iowa 50265. Covers comics field with articles of historical and contemporary importance. Early 1980s.

354. *Johnny Hazard Quarterly*. Reprints Frank Robbins' "Johnny Hazard" comic strips. Dragon Lady Press, Toronto, Canada. 1986-.

355. *Kitchen Sink Pipeline*. Monthly newsletter describing comics stories published by Kitchen Sink Press, No. 2 Swamp Rd., Princeton, Wisconsin 54968. No. 67, March 1991.

356. *LOC*. Bi-monthly of historical and contemporary aspects of comics. First issue carried articles on collecting, future new "X-Men," "Wonder Woman," "Titans," "Ms. Marvel," "Fu Manchu," "comics over-writing," women's reading of comics. New Media Publishing Co., 12345 Starkey, Largo, Florida 33543. January 1980-.

357. *Marvel Age*. Monthly "Official Marvel News Magazine" of information and previews. Marvel Comics Group, 387 Park Ave., South, New York, New York 10016. 1983-.

358. *Marvel Age Annual*. Discusses status of each "Marvel" strip. Marvel Comics Group, 387 Park Ave., South, New York, New York 10016. 1985-.

359. *Marvel Requirer*. Eight-page newsletter promoting Marvel titles on sale each month. 387 Park Ave., South, New York, New York 10016.

360. *Masquerader*. Magazine published in Pontiac, Michigan, in mid-1960s; dealt with comics.

361. *Media Sight*. Fanzine with comic strips, episode guides, book reviews, and column of "Firsts," with much trivial information about comics. 4146 Marlaine Dr., Toledo, Ohio 43606. 1983.

362. *The Menomonee Falls Gazette*. First published December 13, 1971, by Jerome Sinkovec, N85 W 16505 Mary Court, Menomonee Falls, Wisconsin 53051. Weekly that reprinted U.S. and some foreign strips, as well as letters, promos, news. 232 issues until demise in 1978.

363. *The Menomonee Falls Guardian*. Published weekly, reprinting humor comic strips. Articles also. Street Enterprises, N88 W 17015 Main St., Menomonee Falls, Wisconsin 53051. Michael L. Tiefenbacher, editor. 146 issues between 1973-1976.

364. *Milton Caniff's Steve Canyon*. Irregular publication of Kitchen Sink Press, 4 Swamp Rd., Princeton, Wisconsin 54968; reprints "Steve Canyon" daily and Sunday strips. 1983-.

365. *Model & Toy Collector Magazine*. Published and edited by Bill Bruegman, features comics occasionally. Summer 1990 "Dick Tracy Special" included features, articles, photos.

366. *The National EC Fan-Addict Club Bulletin*. Established by William Gaines in 1950s.

367. *Near Mint*. Published irregularly by Al Dellinges, P.O. Box 34158, San Francisco, California 94134. Devoted to comic art, movies. Profiles, sketchbooks, interviews, drawings. First issue 1980.

368. *The New Comic News*. First published September-October 1967 as revival of *Comic News* and, before that, *Fantastic Comics*, all done by Bruce H. Williams. Mimeographed fanzine with short articles, indices, listings, advertisements. 8426 W. Christiana Ave., Skokie, Illinois 60076.

369. *N.I.C.E. News Monthly*. Stands for New Issues Comics Express, a club for collectors who want to have mail order subscriptions to comics from one or more publishers. Mainly promotionals for merchandise of Mile High Comics, but also historical articles and listings. Mile High Comics, 2151 W. 56th St., Denver, Colorado 80221. No. 39, July 1989.

370. *The Okefenokee Star*. First published Winter 1977 by Swamp Yankee Studios, P.O. Box 2311, Bridgeport, Connecticut 06608. Articles, drawings, interviews about Walt Kelly and his "Pogo" strip. Seven issues until 1982.

371. *Overstreet's Price Update*. Started in mid-1980s as supplement to *The Comic Book Price Guide*. Almost entirely listing of books with grades and prices, plus letters and column on "What's hot, what's not." Published by Overstreet Publications, Inc., 780 Hunt Cliff Dr., N.W., Cleveland, Tennesee 37311.

372. *Panels*. Occasional magazine on comic art. No. 1 in Summer 1979; No. 2, Spring 1981. Well-researched articles, interviews, reviews; important artists such as Will Eisner and Carl Barks discuss their careers. John Benson, 205 W. 80th St., #2E, New York, New York 10024.

373. *Pogo Is Back!* Published by Entertainment Art Co., 47 Euclid Ave, Stamford, Connecticut 06902. Mainly promotional material for Pogo books and paraphernalia published or sold by Entertainment Art.

374. *Potrzebie*. Mimeographed EC fanzine of 1954 started by Bhob Stewart.

375. *Previews*. Published monthly by Diamond Comic Distributors, 181 Route 46 West, Lodi, New Jersey 07644. Includes previews of comics, trading cards, and games; interviews; price guides, and Marvel highlights. Since 1990.

376. *Princessions*. Published with information about women in the fantasy field by Foster Publications, P.O. Box 6783, San Jose, California 95150-6783. In mid-1980s.

377. *Qua Brot*. Irregular publication about E.C. Comics. Interviews, indices, folios. Kyle Hailey, Box 194, Somerville, Massachusetts 02143. 1985-.

378. *Retail Express*. Subtitled, "Profitable Answers for the Fantasy Retailer"; first appeared Summer 1987 as semi-monthly giving considerable attention to comics. 324 Main St., Norwalk, Connecticut 06851.

379. *Robin Snyder's History of the Comics*. Quarterly magazine to produce a working oral history of comic books "by those who were there." First published in December 1989 as a newsletter, the periodical now has 24 pages. 255 N. Forest #405, Bellingham, Washington 98225-5833.

380. *Rocket's Blast Comic Collector*. Among oldest of comic fanzines, 1961 to 1982. Published by James Van Hise of S.F.C.A., 6351 S.W. 43 St., Miami, Florida 33155. 153 issues.

381. *Small Press Comics Explosion*. Published bi-monthly as "cornerstone of the self publishing revolution." Included news, art tips, reviews, tools of trade, etc. Started in 1985. Cat Graphics, 45 Wilcox St., Rochester, New York 14607.

382. *Squa Tront*. Irregular magazine about comics; No. 3, 1969, No. 9, 1983. Articles about E.C. artists and stories; historical and reminiscent. John Benson, 205 W. 80th St., #2E, New York, New York 10024.

383. *Standard Comics*. Reprints stories from Standard Publishing comic books of 1950s. Pure Imagination, New York, New York. 1985-.

384. *The Stanley Steamer*. Fanzine related to U.S. strip, "Little Lulu." Published by Jon Merrill, 517 North Fenwick St., Allentown, Pennsylvania 18103. Run of 60 issues over 10 years ended 1992.

385. *Telegraph Wire*. Newsletter for the Comics and Comix shops or Northern California. 2461 Telegraph Ave., Berkeley, California 94704. Early 1980s.

386. *Tetragrammaton Fragments*. Official newsletter of United Fanzine Organization, 315 E. 5th St. #4-A, New York, New York 10003. Monthly formed in 1970. Official business of UFO, reviews of fanzines, etc.

387. *Transformation*. Fanzine "Published whenever we get around to it" by TR, 14349 Arlee Ave., Norwalk, California 90650. Late 1960s.

388. *Vot Der Dumboozle?* Mimeographed, infrequent publication of James Lowe, 403 E. Georgia St., Tallahassee, Florida 32301. Devoted to examining the life, work, and times of Harold H. Knerr, cartoonist of "Katzenjammer Kids." First issue, late 1987.

389. *W.A.P.! (Words and Pictures)*. Monthly for freelance comics professionals, designed to air their gripes and discuss issues affecting their livelihood. Frank Miller and Stever Gerber, 1879 E. Orange Grove Blvd., Pasadena, California 91104. April 1988-1991, 9 issues.

390. *Whizzard*. Quarterly of interviews, articles, and features about comic books. No. 14 appeared February 1981. No. 14 articles cited in this volume; No. 12 included interviews with Jim Starlin, Walt Simonson, Michael Golden, Mike Nasser; No. 10, Phil Farmer, Isaac Asimov. Edited and published by Marty Klug, 5730 Chatport Rd., St. Louis, Missouri 63129.

391. *Will Eisner's Spirit Magazine*. Periodical concerned with reprinting "The Spirit." Title changes: *The Spirit* to *Will Eisner's The Spirit* to *Will Eisner's Spirit Magazine*. Published by Warren (New York) and Kitchen Sink (Princeton, Wisconsin). Forty-one numbers, 1974-1983.

392. *Xero*. Fanzine started by Dick Lupoff in 1960. Mainly science fiction. Had first installment of series called "All in Color for a Dime," which discussed comic books of the 1930s and 1940s, and later became a book.

393. *The Yellow Kid Notes: The Official Newsletter of the Yellow Kid Society*. Vol. 1, No. 1 (March 1989). Richard D. Olson, editor.

394. *Zine*. First issued November 1992 for small press comics enthusiasts. Protoplasm Press, P.O. Box 2230, University, Mississippi 38677-2230.

GENERAL STUDIES

395. "Adult America's Interest in Comics." *Puck, the Comic Weekly*. December 1948, p. 19.

396. "Adult Interest in Comic Reading." New York: Steward Dougal and Associates, 1947.

397. "Airborne Crime." *Newsweek*. August 23, 1943, pp. 42-43.

398. "America Reads the Comics." *Puck, the Comic Weekly*. January 1954, p. 24.

399. "Apology for Margaret." *Time*. January 11, 1943, pp. 70-71.

400. Arnold, Henry. "Some Comments on Comics." *The Cartoonist*. February 1967, pp. 29-33.

401. "Association of Comics Publishers." *Advertising and Selling*. July 1947, p. 102.

402. Barlow, Tany. "We're All in the Same Boat." *New York Herald Tribune*. November 23, 1948.

403. Bertieri, Claudio. "La Storia del'America in Strisce." *Il Lavoro* (Genoa). April 28, 1966.

404. Bertieri, Claudio. "Twiggy and Comics." *Photographia Italiana* (Milan). No. 129, 1968.

405. Bester, Alfred. "King of Comics." *Holiday*. June 1958.

406. Bowie, P. "Coiffures Are Not Comic." *Colliers*. January 1948, pp. 58-59.

407. Caniff, Milton. "Don't Laugh at the Comics." *Cosmopolitan*. November 1958, pp. 43-47.

408. Chamberlain, John. "Low, Jack and Game." *New Republic*. August 23, 1939, pp. 80-81.

409. "Comic Realities." *Newsweek*. November 23, 1970, pp. 98-99B.

410. Carrick, Bruce R. "Comics." *Saturday Review of Literature*. June 19, 1948, p. 24.

411. Cavallone, Bruno. "Uno Specchio per Alice." *Linus*. No. 33, 1967, pp. 1-7.

412. "Chance To Chuckle." *Newsweek*. May 12, 1958, p. 64.

413. "Comics." In *Das Amerikabuch für die Jugend*, pp. 428-431. Cologne: S. Heuft KG, 1953.

414. "The Comics." *Life*. September 25, 1944.

415. "The Comics." *Newsweek*. July 23, 1945, p. 76.

416. "Comics." *Newsweek*. August 6, 1945, pp. 67-68.

417. "The Comics." *New York Herald Tribune*. June 12, 1949.

418. "Comics To Stir (Sob!) Memories at Home." *New York Times*. October 12, 1963.

419. "Comic Strip Down. Comic-Strips and Comic-Books in the U.S." *Time*. March 14, 1955, p. 34.

420. Cort, D. "Comics Etc." *Commonweal*. July 9, 1965, pp. 503-505.

421. "Cushlamochree." *Newsweek*. October 4, 1943, p. 192.

422. Dawson, Margaret C. *Comic Project, Report of Preliminary Study*. New York: National Social Welfare Assembly, 1951.

423. De Giacomo, Franco. "Il Caso Robinson." *Linus*. No. 32, 1967, pp. 1-5.

424. De Turris, Gianfranco and S. Fusco. "The Stupid New Orleans Jac Band." *Linus*. No. 27, 1967, pp. 63-66.

425. Dibert, George C. and C. Earl Pritchard. "Greater Leisure." *People*. May 1937, pp. 11-13.

426. Doty, Roy. "Wordless Workshop." *Popular Science*. 169:3 (1956), pp. 218-219.

427. Dunn, Robert. "Future: Bob Predicts." *The Cartoonist*. Special Number, 1966, pp. 38-40.

428. "Fact and Fiction." *Newsweek*. January 23, 1956, p. 2.

429. "First Stone." *Time*. December 22, 1947, p. 62.

430. Funk, Ray. "Rap with Ray." *Near Mint*. October 1982, pp. 20-23.

431. Hanscom, Sally. "Color Them Suburban." *The World of Comic Art*. 1:3 (1966/1967), pp. 42-47.

432. Hegerfors, Sture. "Styrkta av Mistelsoppa Bekrigar Gallerna USA." *Expressen* (Stockholm). April 20, 1967.

433. Horn, Maurice. "Comics USA." *Tintin*. July 28-August 25, 1970.

434. Horn, Maurice. "La Nouvelle Vague Américaine." *Tintin*. Nos. 1-3, 1973.

435. Horn, Maurice. "Preface." *Scarlett Dream*. Paris: Le Terrain Vague, 1967.

436. Inge, M. Thomas. "What's So Funny about the Comics?" *Amerikastudien/American Studies*. 30 (1986), pp. 213-218. Also in Arthur P. Dudden, ed. *American Humor*. New York: Oxford University Press, 1987, pp. 76-84.

437. Jackson, C.E. "The Comics." *Newsweek*. November 22, 1954, p. 6.

438. Kaselow, Joseph. "Nothing To Laugh at." *New York Herald Tribune*. December 16, 1956, p. 35.

439. Kurtzman, Harvey. *History of Comic Art from Argh to Zap*. New York: Nostalgia Press, 1973.

440. Lardner, J. "What We Missed." *Newsweek*. December 21, 1953, p. 80.

441. Lieberman, Joseph. "Comic Heaven." *Asahi Weekly*. March 14, 1993, p. 5.

442. "The Light Side of Darkness." *Newsweek*. September 22, 1986, p. 79.

443. "Little Man, What Now?" *Newsweek*. June 16, 1952, p. 41.

444. Lochte, Richard S. "The Comics." *Chicago Daily News*. January 27, 1968.

445. MacLeod, John. "Commentary on Comics." *Comicist*. July 1990, pp. 6-7.

446. McLuhan, Marshall. "The Comics." In *The Pop Culture Tradition*, edited by E.M. White, pp. 89-94. New York: Norton, 1972.

447. "The Maddest Comedy on the Boards." *Jem*. 8:6 (1967), pp. 10, 12, 16.

448. Marker, Chris. *L'Amérique Rêve*. Paris: Éditions du Seuil, 1961.

449. Morton, Charles W. "Accent on Living." *Atlantic Monthly*. 197:3 (1956), pp. 90-91.

450. "Mr. O'Malley, Ph.D." *Newsweek*. September 30, 1946, p. 89.

451. "New York Spielt Verrückt." *Der Stern*. No. 38, 1966.

452. "New York Wehrt Sich Gegen Comic-Serien." *Frankfurter Rundschau*. July 2, 1955.

453. "The Old Folks Take It Harder Than Junior." *Colliers*. July 9, 1949, p. 74.

454. "The Other Cruikshank." *The World of Comic Art*. 1:2 (1966), pp. 24-25.

455. Pascal, David. "10 Millions d'Images." *Newsletter*. June 1966, pp. 17-21.

456. Peltz, Hans D. "Comics." *Es* (Hamburg). No. 5, 1968, p. 44f.

457. Pivano, Fernanda. *America Rossa e Nera*. Milan: Feltrinelli, 1964.

458. "Raven Nevermore." *Newsweek*. November 3, 1941, p. 56.

459. Reilly, Maurice T. "The Payoff Is at Drawing Board." *The Cartoonist*. Autumn 1957, pp. 4, 6, 34.

460. Renaud, Hubert. "BD Américaine de l'An 2000. De la Confusion Naît la Richesse." *Le Quotidien de Paris*. January 22, 1992, pp. xii-xiii.

461. Rivière, François. "L'Amérique pour Rire de Rock Derby et Ses Amis." *Cahiers Universitaires* (Paris). No. 17, 1972.

462. Rodríguez Arbesú, Faustino. "Sombros." *El Wendigo*. May 1984, pp. 31-35.

463. Rodríguez, Faustino. "Una Forma Diferente de Mirar Viejos Mitos." *El Wendigo*. No. 50, 1990, p. 14.

464. Rifas, Leonard. "From Tyrant to Democrat: Gorbachev in Comics." *Reflex*. July/August 1990, pp. 16-17.

465. Sailer, Anton. "Adamsons Verrückte Abenteuer." *Quick*. 1970, pp. 71-72.

466. Sambonet-Bernacchi, Luisa. "America." *Sgt. Kirk*. No. 16, 1968, pp. 20-22.

467. Robinson, Jerry. *The World's Greatest Comics Quiz*. New York: Grosset and Dunlap, 1978. 181 pp.

468. Roy, Claude. *Clefs pour l'Amérique*. Paris: Gallimard, 1947.

469. Seidman, David. "The Comics Editor's Desk." *Cartoonist PROfiles*. June 1989, pp. 34-38; September 1989, pp. 28-31.

470. Sheridan, Martin. "This Serious Business of Being Funny." *St. Nicholas*. December 1937, pp. 21-23.

471. Siegfried, Joan C. *The Spirit of the Comics*. Philadelphia, Pennsylvania: Institute of Contemporary Art, University of Pennsylvania, 1969.

472. "Silent Sport." *Newsweek*. March 27, 1950, p. 33.

473. Sitter, Albert J. "Manuring Cartoons Speak Lucidly." *Newsletter*. June 1966, p. 29.

474. Smith, G.P. "The Plight of the Folklore in the Comics." *Southern Folklore Quarterly*. 16, 1952, pp. 124-127.

475. Solis-Cohen, Lita. "Comic-Art Sale Puts Mickey on Madison." *Philadelphia Inquirer*. January 31, 1988, p. 5-F.

476. Stanley, John and Mal Whyte. *The Great Comics Game*. Los Angeles, California: Price Stern Sloan Publisher Inc., 1966.

477. Strnad, Jan. "Comics Writer Solos: Does Not Crash." *Comics Journal*. October 1981, pp. 111-113, 119.

478. "Stuff of Dreams." *Time*. December 1, 1947, p. 71.

479. Thomas, Kay. "Chatter!" *New York Daily News*. May 11, 1965.

480. Thompson, Maggie. "Comics Lexicon." *Comics Collector*. Summer 1984, pp. 55-57.

481. "Universitality of Comics." *King Features Syndicate Report*. January 16, 1962.

482. Vogel, Bertram. "Fun in Any Language." *Redbook*. February 1948, p. 7.

483. "Vulnerable Funnyman." *New Yorker*. December 25, 1948, pp. 13-15.

484. Waugh, Coulton. *The Comics*. Westport, Connecticut: Hyperion Press, 1974. 360 pp. Reprint of 1947 edition.

485. Wigand, Rolf. "Toward a More Visual Culture Through Comics." In *Comics and Visual Culture: Research Studies from Ten Countries*, edited by Alphons Silberman and H.-D. Dyroff, pp. 28-59. Munich: K.G. Saur, 1986.

486. Wilkes, Paul. "You May Be Laughing at Yourself?" *The Cartoonist*. October 1966, pp. 45-47.

487. "Writers." *Comics Journal*. July 1984, pp. 57-65.

488. "Your Friends—The Comics." *New York Sunday Herald Magazine*. March 10, 1957.

ARTISTIC ASPECTS

489. "Comic Strip Art To Benefit USO." *New York World Telegram*. May 11, 1965.

490. Dunn, William. "The Funnies As Fine Art." *Cartoonist PROfiles*. September 1981, pp. 92-97. Reprinted from *Detroit News Magazine*, March 22, 1981.

491. Erwin, Ray. "Newspaper Comics in Pop Art Show." *Editor and Publisher*. May 8, 1965.

492. Feiffer, Jules. "Pop-Sociology." *New York* (*Herald Tribune*). January 9, 1966, p. 7.

493. Fiore, R. "Art in the Hands of Ribbon Clerks." *Comics Journal*. December 1986, pp. 9-10.

494. Gold, Mike. "Death of an Artform." *The Funnie's Paper*. March 1984, p. 5.

495. Gowans, Alan. "America's Best: Cartooning and Comic Strips As American Art Forms." *The Festival of Cartoon Art*. Catalogue of exhibition at Ohio State University, Columbus, Ohio, October 1983, pp. 3-10.

496. Gowans, Alan. *The Unchanging Arts*. Philadelphia, Pennsylvania: Lippincott, 1971. 433 pp.

497. Harvey, Robert C. "The Aesthetics of the Comic Strip." *Journal of Popular Culture*. Spring 1979, pp. 640-652.

498. Henry, G. "Pop Pop Pop; Exhibition at the Graham Gallery, Manhattan." *New Republic*. April 8, 1972, p. 18.

499. Herdeg, Walter. *The Art of the Comic Strip*. Zurich: Graphis Press, 1972. 126 pp.

500. Loring, John. "Graphic Arts: Comic Strip Pop." *Arts Magazine*. September 1974, pp. 48-50.

501. "Newspaper Art." *Editor and Publisher*. 67:20 (1934), p. 12-17.

502. "Pop! Goes the Poster, Pop-Art Portraits of Comic-Book Features." *Newsweek*. March 29, 1965, p. 72.

503. Rogow, Lee. "Can the Comic Strip Be Art?" *Saturday Review of Literature*. Spring 1950.

504. Rublowsky, John and Kenneth Heyman. *Pop Art*. New York: Basic Books, 1965.

505. "San Diego Jack Kirby Panel Spotlights Art Controversy." *Comics Journal*. September 1986, p. 11.

506. Seldes, Gilbert. "Golla, Golla, the Comic Strip's Art." *Vanity Fair*. May 1922.

Lichtenstein, Roy

507. Alloway, Lawrence. *Roy Lichtenstein*. New York: Abbeville Press, 1983.

508. "Bericht über Roy Lichtenstein." In *Roy Lichtenstein, Ausstellungsprospekt, Berner Kunsthalle* Berne, July 8-September 10, 1967, p. 10.

509. Berner, Horst. "Comics in der Pop-Art: Roy Lichtenstein." *Comixene*. 7:32 (1980), pp. 13-16.

510. Boime, Albert. "Roy Lichtenstein and the Comic Strip." *Art Journal*. Winter 1968-1969, pp. 155-159.

511. Coplans, John. *Roy Lichtenstein*. New York: Praeger, 1972. 199 pp.

512. Levin, Bob. "Why Roy Lichtenstein Is a Greater Artist Than Ghastly Ingels." *Comics Journal*. April 1990, pp. 3-6.

513. Lichtenstein, Roy and David Pascal. "Pop Art et Comic Books." *Giff-Wiff*. 20, 1966, pp. 6-15.

514. "Lichtenstein—Mythos von Mickey." *Der Spiegel*. No. 51, 1967.

515. Moreira, Julio. "Roy Lichtenstein. Uma Arte Conceptual." *Journal do Fundao* (Lisbon). Supplement "E Etc." January 28, 1968.

516. Netter, Maria. "Comics und Abstraktion (Roy Lichtenstein-Ausstellung)." *Die Weltwoche* (Berne). March 1, 1968, p. 29.

517. Rosenblum, Robert. "Lichtenstein-Roy Lichtenstein." *DISKUS* (Frankfurt). No. 7, 1963, p. 10.

518. Sterckx, Pierre. "La Loupe ou l'Éponge." *Les Cahiers de la Bande Dessinée* (Grenoble). 69, 1986, pp. 77-80.

519. Strelow, Hans. "Ein Klassiker des Comic. Zu Einer Roy Lichtenstein—Ausstellung in Amsterdam." *Die Zeit* (Hamburg). 22:47 (1967), p. 19.

CHILDREN

520. Alsop, Ronald. "Comics Publishers Woo Kids With Top Dog and the Pope." *Wall Street Journal*. October 10, 1985, p. 37.

521. Arbuthnot, M.H. "Children and the Comics." *Elementary English Review*. March 1947, pp. 171-182.

522. "Are Comics Fascist? Are They Good for Children?" *Time*. October 22, 1945, pp. 67-68.

523. "Are the Comics Harmful Reading for Children?" *Coronet*. August 1944, p. 179.

524. "Attack on Juvenile Delinquency." *National Education Association Journal*. December 1948, pp. 632 +.

525. Bakwin, Ruth M. "The Comics." *Journal of Pediatrics*. 42:5 (1953), pp. 633-635.

526. Bakwin, Ruth M. "Effect of Comics on Children." *Modern Medicine*. September 1953, pp. 192-193.

527. "Bane of the Bassinet: Radio Debate in Town Hall." *Time*. March 15, 1948, p. 70.

528. Bechtel, Louis S. "The Comics and Children's Books." *Horn Book*. July 1941, pp. 296-303.

529. Bender, Lauretta. "The Psychology of Children's Reading and the Comics." *Journal of Educational Sociology*. December 1944, pp. 223-231.

530. Bender, Lauretta and Reginald Lourie. "The Effect of Comic Books on the Ideology of Children." *American Journal of Orthopsychiatry*. July 1941, pp. 540-550.

531. Bent, Silas and Chester Gould. "Are Comics Bad for Children? Yes! No!" *Rotarian*. March 1940, pp. 18-19.

532. Brown, John M. "The Case Against the Comics." *Saturday Review of Literature*. March 20, 1948, pp. 31-32.

533. Brumbaugh, Florence N. "Stimuli Which Cause Laughter in Children." Ph.D. dissertation, New York University, 1939.

534. Brumbaugh, Florence N. and Frank T. Wilson. "Children's Laughter." *Journal of Genetic Psychology*. 1940, pp. 3-29.

535. Butterworth, Robert F. and George C. Thompson. "Factors Related to Age-Grade Trends and Sex Differences in Children's Preferences for Comic Books." *Pedagogical Seminary and Journal of Genetic Psychology*. March 1951, pp. 71-96.

536. Buzzatti, Dino. "1952: Strips, Tomb of Infantile Imagination." *General Report on the Literacy Aspects of the Periodical Press for the Young. Press, Cinema and Radio for the Young* (New York). March 19, 1952, pp. 3-5.

537. "Cain Before Comics." *Saturday Review of Literature*. July 24, 1948, pp. 19-20.

538. Capp, Al. "The Case for the Comics." *Saturday Review of Literature*. March 1948, pp. 32-33.

539. "Cartoon's Magazine for Children Big Success." *Publisher's Weekly*. March 8, 1941, p. 1127.

540. "Cause of Delinquency." *Science News Letter*. May 1, 1954, p. 275.

541. *Children and Comic Magazines: The Answers to Many Questions Parents and Teachers Are Asking*. New York: Superman D.C. Publications, 1941(?).

542. "Children Escape Terrors of Life in Comics." *Science News Letter*. January 7, 1950, p. 2.

543. Christ, J.K. "Horror in the Nursery." *Colliers*. March 27, 1948, pp. 22-23.

544. Clifford, D. "Common Sense About Comics." *Parents Magazine*. October 1948, pp. 30-31; *Reader's Digest*. November 1948, pp. 56-57.

545. "Comic Books and Delinquency." *America*. April 24, 1954, p. 86.

546. "Comic Books and Juvenile Delinquency." Interim Report of the Committee on the Judiciary Pursuant." Washington, D.C.: Government Printing Office, No. 62, 1955.

547. "Comic Books and Your Children; the-Debate-of-the-Month." *Rotarian*. February 1954, pp. 26-27+. "Discussion," August 1954, p. 53.

548. "Comic Books Vs. Cavities." *Dixie Times* (Picayune States Roto Magazine). February 19, 1956, p. 15.

549. "The Comics." *Parents Magazine*. October 1950.

550. "Comics." *Parents Magazine*. August 1954.

551. "Comics Again." *Parents Magazine*. October 1953.

552. "The Comics—Aha!" *Saturday Review of Literature*. July 17, 1948, p. 19.

553. "Comics Books and Character; Summary of Three Surveys." *School and Society*. December 6, 1947, p. 439.

554. "Comics... a Force for Good." *Huber News*. July-August 1950, pp. 3-6.

555. "Comics for Kids." *Time*. September 30, 1940, p. 38.

556. "Comics Good for Children?" *Parents Magazine*. November 1952.

557. "Comics: A Guide for Parents and Teachers." *Spectator*. December 30, 1955, p. 899.

558. "The Comics—Very Funny." *Saturday Review of Literature*. August 21, 1948; September 25, 1948, p. 22.

559. "The Comics: What Books for Children." In *The Comics*. New York: Doubleday-Doran, 1941.

560. "Comics Woes." *Time*. April 20, 1942, p. 62.

561. Conrad, Adelaide K. "A Survey of Children's Reactions to the 'Comics.'" Ed.M. thesis, Temple University, 1941. 78 pp.

562. Conway, Robert. "Children Rate the Comics; Some Sixth Grader Opinions." *Parents Magazine*. March 1951, pp. 48-49 +.

563. "Crime Against American Children; Comic Supplement of the Sunday Paper." *Ladies' Home Journal*. January 1909, p. 5.

564. Cutright, Frank, jr. "Shall Our Children Read the Comics? Yes!" *Elementary English Review*. May 1942, pp. 165-167.

565. "Dirt and Thrash That Kids Are Reading." *Changing Times*. November 1954, pp. 25-29; Discussion, February 1955, p. 48.

566. Dottin, Mireille. "L'Enfant dans Deux Bandes Dessinées Américaines du Début du Siècle." *Cahiers de Littérature Générale et Comparée* (Aix-en-Provence). 3/4, 1978, pp. 119-136.

567. Eisenberg, Azriel L. *Children and Radio Programs*. New York: Columbia University Press, 1966. 81 pp.

568. Ellsworth, Whitney. "Are the Comics a Part of a Child's Life?" *Newsdealer*. July 1951, p. 11.

569. Fagan, Tom. "Thoughts of Youth... Long Thoughts." *The Golden Age*. No. 2, 1959, pp. 15-33.

570. Field, Walter. *A Guide to Literature for Children*. New York: Grimm and Co., 1928.

571. Fisher, Dorothy C. "What's Good for Children?" *Christian Herald*. May 1944, pp. 26-28.

572. Foster, F. Marie. "Why Children Read the Comics." *Book Against Comics, Bulletin of the Association for Arts in Childhood* (Chicago). 1942, pp. 7-14.

573. Frank, Josette. "Chills and Thrills in Radio, Movies, and Comics: Some Psychiatric Opinion." *Child Study*. February 1948, pp. 42-46.

574. Frank, Josette. *Comics, Radio, Movies—and Children*. New York: Public Affairs Committee, No. 148, 1949. 32 pp.

575. Frank, Josette. "Comics, TV, Radio and Movies—What Do They Offer to Children?" *Public Affairs Pamphlet* (New York). No. 48, 1955.

576. Frank, Josette. *The Comics, What Books for Children*. New York: Doubleday-Doran, 1941.

577. Frank, Josette. "Let's Look at the Comics." *Child Study*. April 1942, pp. 76-77, 90-91.

578. Frank, Josette. "Looking at the Comics." *Child Study*. Summer 1943, pp. 112-118.

579. Frank, Josette. "The Role of Comic Strips and Comic Books in Child Life." *Supplementary Educational Monographs*. December 1943, pp. 158-162.

580. Frank, Josette. "Some Questions and Answers for Teachers and Parents." *Journal of Educational Sociology*. December 1949, pp. 206-214.

581. Frank, Josette. *Your Child's Reading Today*. Garden City, New York: Doubleday, 1952.

582. "Funny Strips: Cartoon-Drawing Is Big Business, Effects on Children Debated." *Literary Digest*. December 12, 1936, pp. 18-19.

583. Garrison, J.W. and Katherine Shippen. "Billy Reads the Comics." *Woman's Home Companion*. December 1942, p. 98.

584. Gilbert, James. *A Cycle of Outrage: America's Reaction to the Juvenile Delinquent in the 1950s*. New York: Oxford University Press, 1986.

585. Goulart, Ron. *The Assault on Childhood*. Los Angeles, California: Sherbourne Press, 1969.

586. Gourley, Myrtle H. "A Mother's Report on Comic Books." *National Parent-Teacher*. December 1954, pp. 27-29.

587. Gruenberg, Sidonie M. "Comics: Their Power and Worth." *Teacher's Digest*. March 1945, pp. 51-54.

588. Gruenberg, Sidonie M. "The Comics." *Encyclopedia of Child Care and Guidance*. New York: Doubleday, 1954.

589. Gruenberg, Sidonie M. "New Voices Speak to Our Children." *Parents Magazine*. June 1941, p. 23.

590. Grumette, Jesse. "Investigation into the Newspaper Reading Tastes and Habits of High School Students." *High Points*. December 1937, pp. 5-10.

591. Harms, Ernst. "Comics for and by Children." *New York Times Magazine*. September 24, 1939, pp. 12-13.

592. Henry, Harry. "Measuring Editorial Interest in Children's Comics." *Journal of Marketing*. 17:14 (1953), pp. 372-380.

593. Hill, G.E. "Children's Interest in Comic Strips." *Educational Trends*. 1 (1939), pp. 11-15.

594. Hill, G.E. "How Much of a Menace Are the Comics?" *School and Society*. November 15, 1941, p. 436.

595. Hill, G.E. and M.E. Trent. "Children's Interest in Comic Strips." *Journal of Educational Research*. September 1940, pp. 30-36.

596. Hoult, T.F. "Comic Books and Juvenile Delinquency." *Sociology and Social Research*. 33 (1949), pp. 279-284.

597. Hutchinson, B.D. "Comic Strip Violence, 1911-66." *Journalism Quarterly*. 46:2 (1969), pp. 358-362.

598. "Irate Parent Sues Over Comic." *Comics Journal*. August 1986, p. 10.

599. "It's Humor Children Want in Comic Books." *Science News Letter*. June 16, 1951, p. 376.

600. Jenkins, Arthur. "Comics Characters and Children." *Literary Digest*. March 10, 1934, p. 47.

601. Johnson, B.L. "Children's Reading Interests As Related to Sex and Grade in School." *School Review*. April 1932, pp. 257-272.

602. Johnson, Ferd. "Waifs of the Sunday Page." *The World of Comic Art*. Fall 1966, pp. 47-49.

603. Johnson, Nicholas. "What Do Children Learn from War Comics?" *New Society*. July 7, 1966, pp. 7-12.

604. "Juvenile Delinquency: Crime Comics." *Congressional Digest*. December 1954, p. 293.

605. Kahn, Albert E. "Comics, TV and Your Child." *Masses and Mainstream*. June 1953, pp. 36-43.

606. Kahn, Albert E. *The Game of Death: Effects of the Cold War on Our Children*. New York: Cameron and Kahn, 1953.

607. Kelly, O. "Newspapers Start Giving Comics Back to Kids." *U.S. News and World Report*. September 17, 1984, pp. 52-53.

608. Kessel, Lawrence. "Kids Prefer Real Heroes on the Air." *Variety*. January 1, 1944, p. 23.

609. "Kiddies Like the Funnies." *Broadcasting-Telecasting*. December 10, 1951, p. 38.

610. Kinneman, Fleda C. "Comics and Their Appeal to the Youth of Today." *English Journal*. June 1943, pp. 331-335.

611. Leacock, Stephen. "Soft Stuff for Children." *The Rotarian*. October 1940, pp. 16-17.

612. Leaf, M. "Lollipops or Dynamite?" *Christian Science Monitor Magazine*. November 13, 1948, p. 4.

613. Legman, Gershon. *Love and Death: A Study in Censorship*. New York: Hacker Art Books, 1963 [1949]. 95 pp.

614. Leiberman, Irving. "How Harmful Are Your Child's Comic Book?" *Liberty*. March 1955, pp. 18-19.

615. "Let Children Read Comics, Science Gives Its Approval." *Science News Letter*. August 23, 1941, p. 124.

616. Lewin, Herbert S. "Facts and Fears About the Comics." *Nation's Scholars*. July 1953, pp. 46-48.

617. "Looking at the Comics." *Our Sunday Visitor*. January 2, 1944.

618. Mannes, Marya. "Junior Has a Craving." *New Republic*. February 17, 1947, pp. 20-23.

619. Markey, Morris. "The Comics and Little Willy." *Liberty*. August 24, 1940, p. 9.

620. Martin, Kingsley. "Sadism for Kids." *New Stateman and Nation*. September 25, 1954.

621. Mary Clare, Sister. "Comics: A Study of the Effects of Comic Books on Children Less Than Eleven Years Old." *Our Sunday Visitor*. 1943. 40 pp.

622. Milton, Jenny. "Children and the Comics." *Childhood Education*. October 1939, pp. 60-64.

623. Morrissey, Richard H. "Kid Stuff." *Comics Journal*. September 1981, pp. 258-263.

624. Newton, Myrtle C. "Certain Third Grade Children and the 'Comics.'" Ed.M. thesis, Temple University, 1943. 55 pp.

625. North, Sterling. "The Antidote for Comics." *National Parent Teacher*. March 1941, pp. 16-17.

626. North, Sterling. "The Creative Way Out." *National Parent Teacher*. November 1941, pp. 14-16.

627. North, Sterling. "Good Project for Local Associations: Antidote to the Comic Magazine Poison." *Journal of the National Education Association*. December 1949, p. 158.

628. North, Sterling. "A Major Disgrace." *Childhood Education*. October 1940.

629. North, Sterling. "A National Disgrace." *Chicago Daily News*. May 8, 1940.

630. North, Sterling. "National Disgrace and a Challenge to American Parents." *Childhood Education*. October 1940, p. 56.

631. Ochs, Malcom B. "Sunday Comics Reach Widest Teen Market." *Editor and Publisher*. April 22, 1967, p. 26.

632. "Opposition to the Comics; Report Prepared for United States Conference of Mayors." *School Review*. March 1949, pp. 133-134.

633. Pallenik, M.J. "A Gunman in Town! Children Interpret a Comic Book." *Studies in Visual Communication*. 3:1 (1977), pp. 38-51.

634. Penny, E.J. "Are Comics Bad for Children?" *Rotarian*. May 1940, p. 2.

635. Peppard, S. Harcourt. "Science Contributes: Children's Fears and Fantasies, and the Movies, Radio and Comics." *Child Study*. April 1942, pp. 78-79.

636. Pumphrey, George H. *What Children Think of Comics*. New York: Epworth Press, 1964. 48 pp.

637. Ramsey, B. "The Effect of Comics on Children." *American Journal of Psychology*. 1943.

638. Reynolds, George R. "The Children's Slant on Comics." *School Executive*. September 1942, pp. 17-18.

639. Richards, Edmond. "Kiddies Know Best." *Sunday Review of Literature*. May 1, 1948, p. 21.

640. "The Role of Comic Strips and Comic Books in Child Life." *Supplementary Educational Monographs*. December 1943, pp. 158-162.

641. Rose, Arnold M. "Mental Health Attitudes of Youth As Influenced by a Comic Strip." *Journalism Quarterly*. Summer 1958, pp. 342-353.

642. Sampsell, B. "They Pick Their Books with Care." *Parents Magazine*. November 1950, pp. 48 +.

643. Saunders, Buddy. "Drawing the Line." *Comics Journal*. October 1990, pp. 109-122.

644. Schultz, G.D. "Comics, Radio, Movies; What Are They Doing to Our Children?" *Better Homes and Gardens*. November 1945, pp. 22-23.

645. Schultz, Henry E. "Censorship or Self-Regulation?" *Journal of Educational Sociology*. December 1949, pp. 215-224.

646. "Selling the Youth Market." *Business Week*. October 4, 1947, p. 5.

647. Smith, Helen. "Comic Books in Our House!" *Wilson Library Bulletin*. December 1945, p. 290 +.

648. Smith, S.M. "Friends of the Family, the Comics." *Pictorial Review*. January 1935, pp. 24-25.

649. Southard, R.S.J. "Parents Must Control the Comics." *St. Anthony Messenger*. May 1944, pp. 3-5.

650. Strang, R. "Why Children Read Comics." *Elementary School Journal*. 1942/1943, pp. 336-342.

651. Stuart, N.G. "We Let Our Kids Read Comic Books." *Reader's Digest*. July 1964, pp. 124-126.

652. Swartz, John A. "The Anatomy of the Comic Strip and the Value World of Kids." Vols. 1-2. Doctorial dissertation, Ohio State University, 1978.

653. Tan, Alexis S. and Kermit J. Scruggs. "Does Exposure to Comic Book Violence Lead to Aggression in Children?" *Journalism Quarterly*. Winter 1980, pp. 579-583.

654. Thompson, D. "There Was a Child Went Forth." *Ladies' Home Journal*. September 1954, pp. 11 +.

655. Thrasher, Frederick. "The Comics and Delinquency—Cause or Scapegoat." *Journal of Educational Sociology*. December 1949, pp. 195-205.

656. Thrasher, Frederick. "Do the Crime Comic Books Promote Juvenile Delinquency?" *Congressional Digest*. December 1954, pp. 302-305.

657. Truck, Walter. "Nicht Mehr nur für Kids." *ICOM-INFO*. February 1990, pp. 18-23.

658. Van Tubergen, Norman and Karen Friedland. "Preference Patterns for Comic Strips Among Teenagers." *Journalism Quarterly*. Winter 1972, pp. 745-750.

659. Walp, R.L. "Comics, As Seen by the Illustrators of Children's Books." *Wilson Library Bulletin*. October 1951, pp. 153-157 +.

660. Weber, Bob, jr. "Comics for Kids." *Cartoonist PROfiles*. December 1989, pp. 73-76.

661. Wertham, Frederic. "Are Comic Books Harmful to Children?" *Friends Intelligencer*. July 10, 1948.

662. Wertham, Frederic. "The Betrayal of Childhood: Comic Books." Annual Conference of Correction, American Prison Association, New York, 1948.

663. Wertham, Frederic. "Comic Books, Blueprints for Delinquency." *Reader's Digest*. May 1954, pp. 24-29.

664. Wertham, Frederic. "Horror in the Nursery." *Colliers*. March 27, 1948.

665. Wertham, Frederic. "What Your Children Think of You." *This Week*. October 10, 1948.

666. "What Shall Our Policy Be?" *Scholastic*. November 17, 1941, p. 3.

667. "Why Children Read Comics." *Science Digest*. March 1950, p. 37.

668. "Who Reads the Comics?" *Senior Scholastic*. May 17, 1948, p. 3.

669. Wilson, E.J. "Comic Books in Whose House? Reply to H. Smith." *Wilson Library Bulletin*. February 1946, p. 432.

670. Wilson, Frank T. "Reading Interest of Young Children." *Journal of Genetic Psychology*. June 1941, pp. 363-389.

671. Winn, Marie. "What Became of Childhood Innocence?" *New York Times Magazine*. January 25, 1981, pp. 14-17.

672. Witty, Paul A. "Books Versus Comics." *Bulletin of the Association for Arts in Childhood*. 1942.

673. Witty, Paul A. "Children's Interest in Reading the Comics." *Journal of Experimental Education*. December 1941, pp. 100-104.

674. Witty, Paul A. "Comics, TV, and Our Children." *Today's Health*. February 1955, pp. 18-21; *Science Digest*. June 1955, p. 33.

675. Witty, Paul A. *Your Child and Radio, TV, Comics and Movies*. Chicago: Science Research Associates, 1953. 48 pp.

676. Wolf, A.W.M. "TV, Movies, Comics, Boon or Bane to Children." *Parents Magazine*. April 1961, pp. 46-48 +.

677. Wolfe, Katherine M. and Marjorie Fiske. "The Children Talk About Comics." In *Communications Research, 1948-1949*, edited by Paul F. Lazarsfeld and Frank N. Stanton, pp. 3-50. New York: Harper and Brothers, 1949.

678. "Woo for the Kiddies." *Time*. April 20, 1959, p. 53.

679. Zurier, Rebecca. "Hey Kids: Children in the Comics and the Art of George Bellows." *The Print Collector's Newsletter*. January/February 1988, pp. 196-203.

COLLECTING

680. "Always Another Rainbow." *The Comic Book Marketplace*. No. 3, pp. 10-13.

681. "Are You Missing These Great Comics?" *Comics Collector*. Winter 1985, pp. 19-23.

682. "Back-Issue Sales on Comics Slacken; Dealers Blame Recession, Comics Glut." *Comics Journal*. October 1984, pp. 16-17.

683. Benton, Mike. *Comic Book Collecting for Fun and Profit*. New York: Crown Publishers, 1985. 149 pp.

684. Benton, Mike. "Fun and Profit." *Comics Feature*. May 1986, pp. 8-9, 58.

685. Benton, Mike. "Fun and Profit: Hot Comics: A Critical View." *Comics Feature*. October 1986, pp. 22-25.

686. Benton, Mike. "Fun and Profit: Organizing Your Collection." *Comics Feature*. January 1986, pp. 22-23, 47.

687. Benton, Mike. "Fun and Profit: Reprints." *Comics Feature*. May 1987, pp. 20-25.

688. Benton, Mike. "What Comics Should You Collect?" *Comics Collector*. Fall 1984, pp. 62-64.

689. Benton, Mike. "Where Do Comic Book Prices Come From?" *Comics Features*. February 1987, pp. 46-49.

690. Biggers, Cliff. "Collectors Snub Independents, Seek Out Silver Age Comics." *Comics Buyer's Guide*. October 6, 1989, p. 82.

691. Bissette, Steve. "The Olde Bookdeal'r: Gud Boox." *Comics Feature*. June 1983, pp. 73-79.

692. "The Book Nook." *Comics Interview*. October 1984, pp. 67-75.

693. Brancatelli, Joe. "Superman: The Real Comic Art Rip-Off." *Inside Comics*. Spring 1974, pp. 12-16.

694. Burbey, Mark. *The Marvel Guide to Collecting Comics*. New York: Marvel Comics Group, 1982. 16 pp.

695. Carlson, Raymond. *A Guide to Collecting and Selling Comic Books*. New York: Pilot Books, 1976.

696. Carter, Gary M. "The Relative Rarity and Demand of Showcase 1-40." *Comic Book Marketplace*. No. 3, pp. 18-21.

697. Caruba, David. "You Can Make New Friends and Improve Your Collection, If You... Organize a Comics Club." *Comics Collector*. Summer 1984, pp. 52-54.

698. Clark, Calvin L. "Kryptonian Kollectibles." *Comics Collector*. Spring 1983, pp. 56-57.

699. Coddington, Gary. "Collecting Superman." *Comics Buyer's Guide*. March 18, 1988, p. 18.

700. "Collector's Item." *Cartoonist PROfiles*. September 1977, p. 34.

701. "Collezionismo Americano." *La Borsa del Fumetto*. No. 1, 1979, p. 4.

702. "Color Guide to Defects." *Comics Collector*. Spring 1984, p. 75.

703. "Comics in Your Future." *Comics Buyer's Guide*. April 15, 1988, pp. 22-34; November 27, 1992, pp. 100-103, 111. Continuing column.

704. Crouch, William and Lawrence Doucet. *The Authorized Guide to Dick Tracy Collectibles*. Radnor, Pennsylvania: Wallace-Homestead Book Company, 1990. 162 pp.

705. "'Death of Superman' Art for Sale." *Comics Buyer's Guide*. December 18, 1992, p. 40.

706. Deitcher, D. "Comic Conoisseurs." *Art in America*. February 1984, pp. 101-106.

707. Desris, Joe. "Toys, Comics, and Collectors." *Comics Buyer's Guide*. September 12, 1986, pp. 32, 34, 36-37, 39.

708. Devon, R.S. "Comics Collector Number One: A. Derleth." *Hobbies*. June 1945, p. 126.

709. Doucet, Larry. "Collecting Dick Tracy." *Collectors' Showcase*. November/December 1988.

710. Ebert, Roger. "A Comeback (Sock!) for Comic Books (Pop!)." *Fandom Annual*. 1967, pp. 55-57.

711. Edwards, Jerry. "Experts on Misinformation." *Comics Buyer's Guide*. December 11, 1992, p. 44.

712. Fagan, Tom. "Supersnip—The Boy with the Most Comic Books in America." *Fandom Annual*. 1967, pp. 32-35.

713. Fritz, Steve. "How To Make Money in Comics." *Comic Book Collector*. January 1993, pp. 10-12.

714. Gillis, Peter B. "Some Good Reasons To Eventually Burn Your Comic Collection." *LOC*. January 1980, pp. 56-60.

715. Greenberg, J. "Investments That Are More Than Kid Stuff." *Money*. April 1982, pp. 170-172.

716. Griffith, Rob. "Forgotten Marvels." *Comics Buyer's Guide*. December 18, 1987, pp. 38-40.

717. Halegua, Richard. "Comic Art." *Collector's Showcase*. August 1992, pp. 32, 34.

718. Halegua, Richard. "Comic Convention." *Collector's Showcase*. November 1992, pp. 44-45.

719. Halegua, Richard. "The Search for the Grail: Silver Age DC Art." *Collector's Showcase*. February 1992, pp. 34-37.

720. Hamill, Pete. "A Comic Collector's First and Only Love." *Near Mint*. April 1981, pp. 23-24.

721. "He Regards Comic Strips As Priceless Art Treasures." *Miami Herald Sunday*. December 13, 1970.

722. Hix, Hubert E. "Fling Your Comic Books." *Comics Collector*. Winter 1986, pp. 30-31.

723. Howard, D.W. and Ralph Roberts. "Collectible Comics: Toy-Related Comics." *Comics Buyer's Guide*. October 26, 1984, pp. 32, 34.

724. "How Can I *Find* Direct-Market Comics?" *Comics Collector*. Summer 1985, p. 28.

725. "How To Collect Marvel Comics." *Foom*. No. 11, 1975, pp. 22-23.

726. Inge, M. Thomas. "Collecting Comic Books." *American Book Collector*. March-April 1984, pp. 3-15.

727. Kaonis, Donna C. "Steve Geppi, Comics King." *Inside Collector*. July/August 1991, pp. 41-46.

728. Kochanek, Pat. "The Ultimate Pedigree." *Comic Book Marketplace*. No. 3, pp. 26-29.

729. Korkis, Jim. "Books Are Growth Area for Toy Stores." *Comics Business*. September 1987, p. 18.

730. Krause Publications. *The Guide to Comics Collecting*. 3rd Ed. Iola, Wisconsin: Krause Publications, 1986. 28 pp.; 4th ed, 1989. 28 pp.

731. Krolik, Joseph. "Some Opinions on Comic Investing." *Collector's Dream Magazine*. 1:2, pp. 26-27.

732. Kupperberg, Paul. "Comic Collecting: Hints for a New Hobbyist." *Amazing World of DC Comics*. February 1976, pp. 38-40.

733. Laganga, Maria L. "Golden Age Comics Are Raking in the Gold." *Near Mint*. October 1982, pp. 32-33.

734. Leiter, Maria. *Collecting Comic Books*. Boston, Massachusetts: Little, Brown, 1983. 162 pp.

735. Levin, Bob. "Missing: The Search for Zap #0." *Comics Journal*. February 1993, pp. 73-76.

736. Main, J.R. "The Mini Series Market." *Comics Collector*. Spring 1983, pp. 16-17.

737. Malone, Judy. "A Precise Hobby: June Stratton's Applique Comics." *Cartoonist PROfiles*. March 1975, p. 47.

738. Maxwell, G.T. "This Cartoon Collector Really Collects." *Hobbies*. September 1942, pp. 8-9.

739. May, Carl. "Discovering Gordon Campbell." *The World of Comic Art*. Winter 1966/1967, pp. 32-37.

740. Merrihue, Jeff, David Casner, and Geoff Steadman. *A Collectors Guide to the Artists*. Belmont, Massachusetts: 1977. 104 pp.

741. Metzger, Kim. "Now You Can Collect 'Dangermouse.'" *Comics Collector*. Fall 1985, p. 10.

742. Metzger, Kim. "The $38,000 Comic Book." *Comics Collector*. Summer 1985, p. 74.

743. Metzger, Kim. "You, Too, Can Be a Super-Hero." *Comics Collector*. Summer 1985, pp. 48-49.

744. "The Most Valuable Comics, Silver Age to the Present." In *Comics Buyer's Guide 1993 Annual*, pp. 28, 30, 32, 34, 36, 38. Iola, Wisconsin: Krause, 1992.

745. Neilson, Adam. "Four for $1." *Comics Collector*. Spring 1983, pp. 64-65.

746. Nichols, John. "Transcontinental Ducks." *The Barks Collector*. July 1981, pp. 20-24.

747. Nuhn, R. "The Earliest Comic Books 1897 to 1930." *Hobbies*. November 1982, pp. 30-33.

748. "On the Scene at Sotheby's Auction." *Comics Journal*. February 1992, pp. 20-21.

749. "Original Walt Kelly Pogo Artwork." *Pogo Is Back*. 3:1 (1992), p. 2.

750. Overstreet, Bob. "Bill Gaines EC Time Vault Is Opened." *The Comic Book Marketplace*. No. 3, p. 37.

751. Overstreet, Robert M. *Comic Book Collecting, a Valuation Guide*. Cleveland, Tennessee: Overstreet, 1984. 64 pp.

752. Peck, John. "A Comix Cavalcade." *Fusion*. June 25, 1970.

753. "Photo Grading Guide." *Comics Collector*. Spring 1983, pp. 70-71. Continuing feature.

754. *Popeye, The Collectible*. Iola, Wisconsin: Krause Publications, 1990.

755. Puckett, David. "Selling Your Comic Book Collection." *Comics Collector*. Fall 1984, pp. 59-61.

756. Rogers, V. Cullum. "Laughing Stock: Bill the Booky's Funny Business." *Spectator* (Raleigh, North Carolina). March 28, 1991, pp. 5-6.

757. Sabatini, Beppe. "How To Buy Your New Comics." *Comics Scene*. July 1982, pp. 30-31.

758. Scarlett, Harold. "Comics Collector." *Fandom Annual*. 1967, p. 54.

759. Siegel, Howard P. "Comic Collector's Comments." *RBCC*. No. 119, 1975, pp. 34-35.

760. "Speculating on 'Hot Titles': A Risky Business?" *Comics Collector*. Summer 1984, pp. 24-25.

761. Spragins, E. "When the Price—or the Addams—Is Right." *Forbes*. July 5, 1982, pp. 148 +.

762. Stuempfig, Julie. "Who Buys Comic Books?" In *Comics Buyer's Guide 1993 Annual*, pp. 44-46. Iola, Wisconsin: Krause, 1992.

763. Sulipa, Doug. "The Comicollector." *Comics Feature*. June 1980, pp. 52-53.

764. Tamn, Stephen. "There's Gold in Comics: I Dreamt the Dollar Collapsed and the Medium of Exchange Was Old Comic Books." *Before I Get Old*. April 1987, p. 23.

765. Thau, Richard. "When the Past Is Precious." *Magazine Week*. October 26, 1992, pp. 23-24.

766. Thompson, Don and Maggie. "A Guide for the Seventies." *Comics Feature*. November 1982, pp. 52-54.

767. Thompson, Don and Maggie. "It Was Comics Time!" *Comics Feature*. January 1981, pp. 37-39.

768. Thompson, Don and Maggie. "'Paleolithic Fandom.'" *Comics Feature*. November 1980, pp. 22-23.

769. Thompson, Don and Maggie. "'Your Money or Your Love' Or 'When Is a Hobby Not a Hobby?'" *LOC*. January 1980, pp. 53-55.

770. Thompson, Maggie. "Little Ms. Moppet." *Comics Collector*. Winter 1984, pp. 67-72.

771. Thompson, Maggie. "Little Ms. Moppet, Part II." *Comics Collector*. Spring 1984, pp. 67-71.

772. Thompson, Maggie. "Old Comics for $5 Each? Go Fiche!" *Comics Buyer's Guide*. August 11, 1989, pp. 60, 20.

773. "3-D Comics: The Third Dimension." *Comics Collector*. Winter 1986, pp. 26-29.

774. Tiefenbacher, Mike. "Stuck in the '60s: Collectors' First Aid." *Comics Buyer's Guide*. August 16, 1991, pp. 24, 26, 28.

775. Towle, L.H. "Zap! Pow! Profit from Appreciating Comics!" *Money*. July 1988, p. 28.

776. Ward, Murray. "Sacred Identities." *Collector's Dream Magazine*. Spring 1978, pp. 47-48.

777. Watt-Evans, Lawrence. "Lost in the Mists: Comics That Don't Exist." *Comics Collector*. Winter 1986, pp. 70-71.

778. "Who Wants Back Issues?" *New York Times*. February 17, 1991.

779. Wilcox, John. "Let's Go Collecting." *Comics Collector*. Spring 1983, pp. 62-63.

780. Wooley, John. "A Guide to Collecting Funk Comics." *Collector's Dream*. No. 5, 1978.

781. "Wow! There's a Kaboom in Old Comic Books." *Changing Times*. January 1972, p. 36.

EDUCATION and CULTURE

782. Altman, Mark. "Classroom Comics." *Comics Scene*. No. 10, 1989, pp. 50-51, 66.

783. Andrews, Mildred B. "Comic Books Are Serious Aids to Community Education." *Textile World*. May 1953, pp. 145, 222.

784. Andrews, S.M. "So This Is Education!" *Teacher's Digest*. 6, 1946, pp. 52-53.

785. Arlin, Marshall and Garry Roth. "Pupil's Use of Time While Reading Comics and Books." *American Educational Research Journal*. Spring 1978, pp. 201-206.

786. Armstrong, D.T. "How Good Are the Comic Books?" *Elementary English Review*. December 1944, pp. 283-285.

787. "As Barry Jenkins, Ohio '69, Says: A Person Has To Have Intelligence To Read Them." *Esquire*. September 1966, pp. 116-117.

788. "Athelstan's World; No-Nonsense Science Strip." *Newsweek*. February 18, 1963, p. 86.

789. Bakjian, M.J. "Kern Avenue Junior High Uses Comics As a Bridge." *Library Journal*. April 1, 1945, pp. 291-292.

790. Bishop, M. "From Comic to Classic." *Wilson Library Bulletin*. April 1954, p. 696.

791. Blakely, W. Paul. "A Study of Seventh Grade Children's Reading of Comic Books As Related to Certain Other Variables." Ph.D. dissertation, University of Iowa, 1957.

792. Blanchard, M. Gervase. "An Evaluation from the Catholic View-point of Comics Read by Fourth, Fifth, and Sixth Grade Parochial-School Children in the United States." Ph.D. dissertation, Fordham University, 1948.

793. Bothwell, A. "Who Reads the Comics?" *Library Journal*. September 15, 1947, p. 1263.

794. Bottrell, H.R. "Reading the Funny Paper Out Loud." *English Journal*. December 1945, p. 564.

795. Brady, Margaret E. "Comics, To Read or Not To Read." *Wilson Library Bulletin*. 24:9 (1950), pp. 662-667.

796. Brown, James W. "Comics in the Foreign Language Classroom: Pedagogical Perspectives." *Foreign Language Annals*. February 1977, pp. 18-25.

797. Brown, J.M. "Knock, Knock, Knock! Comic-Book Edition of MacBeth." *Saturday Review*. July 29, 1950, pp. 22-24. "Discussion," September 2, 1950, p. 26.

798. Burton, Dwight L. "Comic Books: A Teacher's Analysis." *Elementary School Journal*. October 1955, pp. 73-75.

799. "Can the Rest of the Century Be Salvaged? Five Overwhelming Answers." *Esquire*. October 1968, pp. 135-139.

800. Carr, Patrick. "Can Comic Books be Used in Education?" *Education*. September 1958, pp. 57-61.

801. Center, Stella S. "Survey of Reading in Typical High Schools of New York City." *Monograph No. 1* (New York City Association of Teachers of English). 1936, p. 76.

802. "Classic Comics Sell a Hundred Million." *Publishers Weekly*. March 23, 1946, p. 1736.

803. "Comic Books and Characters. Summary of Three Surveys." *School and Society*. December 1947, p. 439.

804. "Comic Books Boosted As Mental Health Aid!" *New York World Telegram and Sun*. April 10, 1956.

805. "Comic Cartoon Used To Study Mentally Ill." *Science News Letter*. July 28, 1956, p. 56.

806. "The Comics." *The Library Association Record.* 54:7 (1952), pp. 9-10, 12.

807. "Comics Are Serious Business Here." *Cartoonist PROfiles.* December 1983, pp. 71-73.

808. "The Comics Evaluated." *Acolyte.* January 1944, p. 22.

809. "Comics to Classics." *Journal of Education.* December 1956, pp. 511-512.

810. "Comic Strip Explains Atomic Energy." *Des Moines Sunday Register.* October 24, 1948.

811. "Comic Strip Language." *Time.* June 21, 1943, p. 96.

812. Commer, Anne and Paul A. Witty. "Reading the Comics in Grades 7 and 8." *Journal of Educational Psychology.* March 1942, pp. 173-182.

813. "Confessions and Comics (Comics and Sex Education)." *Time.* January 3, 1972, p. 34.

814. Cooper, Faye. "Funny Paper Art." *School Art Magazine.* January 1937, pp. 316-318.

815. Cooper, Faye. "Use Comic Magazines As a Learning Tool." *School Management.* March 1947, p. 21.

816. Cusumano, Ben. "Comics and Education." *High Point.* October 1957, pp. 5-17.

817. Darrow, B.H. "Who Teaches Our Children in Their Spare Time?" *High School Teacher.* June 1935, pp. 182-183.

818. Denecke, Lena. "Fifth Graders Study the Comic Books." *Elementary English Review.* January 1945, pp. 6-8.

819. Dias, E.J. "Comic Books—A Challenge to the English Teacher." *English Journal.* March 1946, pp. 142-145.

820. Dorrell, Larry D. "Why Comic Books?" *School Library Journal.* 34 (1987), p. 31.

821. Dorrell, Larry D. and Carey T. Southall. "Captain America: A Hero for Education." *The Clearing House.* May 1982, pp. 397-399.

822. Drachman, J.S. "Prospectus for an American Mythology." *English Journal* (High School Edition). December 1930, pp. 781-788.

823. Drummond, William H. "Comic Book Reading in the Secondary Schools of a Rural Community." Masters thesis, Leland Stanford Junior University, 1948.

824. Eble, Kenneth E. "Our Serious Comics." *The American Scholar*. Winter 1958/1959.

825. "Education by the Comic Strip." *American Weekly*. June 11, 1944, p. 20.

826. "Educator in Orbit: Our New Age." *Time*. August 3, 1959, p. 74.

827. Eisner, W. "Comic Books in the Library." *Library Journal*. October 15, 1974, pp. 2703-2707.

828. Elkins, Roger H. and Christian Bruggemann. "Comic Strips in the Teaching of English as a Foreign Language." Paper presented at Conference on Teaching of English, Kassel, West Germany, 1971.

829. Ellman, Neil. "Comics in the Classroom." *Audiovisual Instruction*. May 1979, pp. 24-25.

830. "Even Economics Can Be Fun." *Business Week*. December 16, 1950, pp. 41-42.

831. Fine, Benjamin. "Grammar with Jive to It." *New York Times Magazine*. January 2, 1944, pp. 10-11.

832. Fischer, Herve. "Phonetic Writing and Pictograms in Comic Strips. Ecriture Phonetique et Pictogrammes dans les Bandes Dessinees." *Communications*. 9:2-3 (1983), pp. 191-200.

833. Fleece, Jeffrey. "A Word-Creator." *American Speech*. February 1943, pp. 68-69.

834. Frank, Josette. "People in the Comics." *Progressive Education*. January 1942, pp. 28-31.

835. Frank, Josette. "What's in the Comics?" *Journal of Educational Sociology*. December 1944, pp. 214-222.

836. Gallyer, Lucilla. *A Report of Comic Book Reading By Pupils of Grades IV-VII*. Salt Lake City, Utah: Forest School, 1951.

837. Gay, R.C. "A Teacher Reads the Comics." *Harvard Educational Review*. March 1937, pp. 198-209.

838. Gordon, Sol. "Sex Ed Via Comics." *Playboy*. No. 12, 1972.

839. Gray H. "Leapin' Lizards, Look Who's Using the Comics!" *Media Decisions*. 12, 1977, p. 133.

840. Gray, W.S. "Issues Relating to the Comics." *Elementary School Journal*. May 1942, pp. 641-654.

841. Green, I. "The Comics Can Do It Better." *Nation's School*. September 1947, p. 30.

842. Hadad, Herb. "Pow! Comics in the Classroom." *New York Times*. December 8, 1991, p. 10.

843. Haggard, E.A. "A Projective Technique Using Comic Book Characters." *Character and Personality*. 10 (1942), pp. 289-293.

844. Hallanbeck, Phyllis N. "Remediating with Comic Strips." *Journal of Learning Disabilities*. January 1976, pp. 11-15.

845. Hall-Quest, A.L. "Our Comic Culture." *Education Forum*. November 1941, pp. 84-85.

846. Harris, Sidney. "Science Can Be Fun!" *Cartoonist PROfiles*. June 1990, pp. 66-73.

847. Harrison, E. "Comics on Crusade." *New York Times Magazine*. November 1, 1959, pp. 68-69 +.

848. Heisler, Florence. "Comparison of Comic Book and Non-Comic Book Readers of the Elementary School." *Journal of Educational Research*. February 1947, pp. 458-464.

849. Henne, Frances E. "Comics Again." *Elementary School Journal*. March 1950, p. 372.

850. Henne, Frances E. "Comics in Graduate Library School of The University of Chicago." *Elementary School Journal*. April 1950.

851. Higgins, Mildred M. "Adult Literary Responses to Comic Strip Narratives Among Inmates of a Correctional Institution." Ph.D. dissertation, Florida State University, 1969.

852. Hill, G.E. "Taking the Comics Seriously." *Childhood Education*. May 1941, pp. 413-414.

853. Hill, G.E. "Word Distortions in Comic Strips." *Elementary School Journal*. May 1943, pp. 520-525.

854. Hill, Louise D. "The Case for the Comics." *School Executive*. December 1944, pp. 42-44.

855. Hodgins, A. "How I Teach During the First Week of Schooling Drugstore Cowboys." *Senior Scholastic*. September 22, 1955, pp. 13T-14T.

856. Houle, C.O. "Safety in Comic Strips." *Elementary School Journal*. October 1948, pp. 67-68.

857. Hutchinson, Katherine H. "Comics in the Classroom." *Puck*. University of Pittsburgh, 1947.

858. Hutchinson, Katherine H. "An Experiment in the Use of Comics As Instructional Material." *Journal of Educational Sociology*. December 1949, pp. 236-245.

859. "I Fumetti Intellettuali Distrussero McCarthy?" *L'Espresso* (Milan). May 10, 1959.

860. "In Answer to Many Attacks." *English Journal*. April 1949, p. 236.

861. "In Defense of Comics." *Newsweek*. September 27, 1954, p. 30.

862. Inge, M. Thomas. *Comics in the Classroom*. For the Smithsonian Institution Traveling Exhibition Service. Washington, D.C.: Smithsonian Institution, 1989. 18 pp.

863. Jones, Ruth M. "Competing with the Comics." *Wilson Library Bulletin*. 23:10 (1949), p. 782.

864. Kandel, I.L. "Challenge of Comic Books." *School and Society*. April 5, 1952, p. 216.

865. Kandel, I.L. "Comics to the Rescue of Education." *School and Society*. May 20, 1950, pp. 314-315.

866. Katz, B. and A.E. Prentice. "Comics Scene: Magazines in the Library." *Library Journal*. January 1, 1968, p. 59.

867. Kempe, M. "Comic Books." *Senior Scholastic* (Teacher's ed.). April 26, 1950, p. 16.

868. Kenney, H.C. "Comics for Education." *Christian Science Monitor*. October 8, 1952.

869. Kessel, Lawrence. "Some Assumptions in Newspaper Comics." *Childhood Education*. 14 (1938), pp. 349-353.

870. Kris, I. "Ego Development and the Comic." *International Journal of Psychoanalysis*. 19 (1938), pp. 77-90.

871. Lee, Harriet E. "Discrimination in Reading." *English Journal*. 31, pp. 677-678.

872. Lee, Wendi. "Comics in the Classroom." *Uncle Jam Quarterly*. Summer 1990, p. 4.

873. Lehman, H.C., and P.A. Witty. "The Compensatory Function of the Sunday Funny Paper." *Journal of Applied Psychology*. June 1927, pp. 202-211.

874. Logasa, Hannah. "The Comics Spirit and the Comics." *Wilson Library Bulletin*. November 1946, pp. 238-239.

875. Loizeaux, M.D. "Talking Shop." *Wilson Library Bulletin*. November 1946, p. 243; November 1948, p. 257; June 1954, p. 884; April 1955, p. 651.

876. Lunn, Mervel S. and Ruth R. Davis. "Comic Strip—a Combination of Verbal and Nonverbal." *The Instructor*. January 1967, pp. 90-91.

877. "MacBeth or Local Thane Makes Good." *Sunday Review of Literature*. December 2, 1950, pp. 13-14.

878. McCarthy, M. Katherine and Marion W. Smith. "The Much Discussed Comics." *The Elementary School Journal*. October 1943, pp. 97-101.

879. McCarthy, M. Katherine and Marion W. Smith. "Those Horror Comics." *Teacher's Digest*. January 1947, pp. 44-46.

880. McGuff, M.B. "The Comics." *Library Journal*. April 1, 1968, p. 1390.

881. McIntire, G.L. "Not So Funny Funnies." *Progressive Education*. February 1945, pp. 28-30.

882. Makey, H.O. "Comic Books: A Challenge." *English Journal*. December 1952, pp. 547-549.

883. Malter, Morton S. "Content of Current Comic Magazines." *Elementary School Journal*. May 1952, pp. 505-510; *Journal of Social Psychology*. 1953.

884. "Mental Hygiene Takes to the Comics." *American Journal of Public Health*. January 1951, p. 102.

885. Meyer, Ron and Joyce Buckner. "Superheroes and Summer Reading." *Instructor*. May 1980, p. 83.

886. Miner, M.E. "Charlie Brown Goes to School." *English Journal*. November 1969, pp. 1183-1185.

887. Mulberry, Harry M. "Comic Strips and Comic Books?" *Supplementary Educational Monographs*. December 1943, pp. 163-166.

888. Munger, E.M. "Preferences for Various Newspaper Comic Strips As Related to Age and Sex Differences in School Children." Thesis, Ohio State University, 1939. 65 pp.

889. Murphy, T.E. "For the Kiddies To Read, Hartford, Conn." *Reader's Digest*. June 1954, pp. 5-8.

890. Newcomb, Robert and Mary Simmon. "A Comic Booklet Tackles Inflation." *Advertising Age*. September 17, 1951. p. 75.

891. Notarangelo, Gabriella and Daniela Schipani. "Comics in Class." *MET. Modern English Teacher* (London). 13:4 (1986), pp. 33-35.

892. "O.K. You Passed the 2-S Test; Now You're Smart Enough for Comic Books." *Esquire*. September 1966, pp. 114-115.

893. "People in the Comics." *Progressive Education*. January 1942, pp. 28-31.

894. Pincus J. "Advice for the Lifelorn." *Seventeen*. April 1988, p. 164.

895. Pope, Dean. "Comics Craze Covers Campus." *Philadelphia Inquirer*. March 17, 1966.

896. Pope, Dean. "ZAP! POW! Comics Sweep Princeton." *Philadelphia Inquirer*. March 17, 1966.

897. Prentice, A.E. "Comics Scene; Magazines in the Library." *Library Journal*. January 1, 1968, p. 59.

898. Pumphrey, George H. "Comics." *The School Librarian*. 6:5 (1953), p. 310.

899. Punke, Harold H. "The Home and Adolescent Reading Interest." *School Review*. October 1937, pp. 612-620.

900. "Reading the Comics—A Comparative Study." *Journal of Experimental Education*. December 1941.

901. "Results of Comic Book Surveys." *California Journal of Secondary Education*. April 1948, p. 244.

902. Richie, Rose J. "The Funnies Aren't Just Funny—Using Cartoons and Comics To Teach." *The Clearing House*. November 1979, pp. 125-128.

903. Roberts, Thomas J. "What About the Comic Strips?" *GSE: The Graduate of English*. 2:4 (1959), pp. 2-10.

904. Robinson, Edward J. and David M. White. *An Exploratory Study of Attitudes of Children in Grades 3 Through 9 Toward the Comic Strips*. Boston: Report No. 4, Communications Research Center, Boston University, 1962.

905. Robinson, Edward J. and David M. White. *An Exploratory Study of Attitudes of More Highly Educated People Toward the Comic Strip*. Boston: Communications Research Center, Boston University, 1960.

906. Robinson, Edward J. and David M. White. "An Exploratory Study of the Attitudes of More Highly Educated People Toward the Comic Strip." *Audio-Visual Communication Review*. September 1960, pp. 284 +.

907. Robinson, S.M. "Schools, Mass Media and Delinquency." *School and Society*. February 27, 1960, pp. 99-102.

908. Rosencrans, L.L. "What About Comics?" *Instructor*. May 1945, p. 25.

909. "Safety in Comic Strips." *Elementary School Journal*. October 1948, pp. 67-68.

910. Saltus, Elinor C. "Comics Aren't Good Enough." *Wilson Library Bulletin*. 26:5 (1952), pp. 382-383.

911. "Santa Barbara School Fights Comics with Paperbounds." *Publishers Weekly*. 166:25 (1954), p. 3231.

912. Saunders, A. "No Pictorial Cliches: Library in a Comic Strip." *Library Journal*. January 15, 1954, pp. 97-102.

913. Schramm, Wilbur and David M. White. "Age, Education and Economic-Status: Factors in Newspaper Reading." *Journalism Quarterly*. 26 (1949), pp. 149-166.

914. "Seriocomics: Marx for Beginners." *Time*. April 2, 1979, p. 87.

915. "Shame on Teacher." *Newsweek*. March 14, 1955, p. 94.

916. Shenker, Israel. "The Great Eggplant Grows into a Popular Academic Success." *New York Times*. August 17, 1971.

917. Shute, N. "Scientists Meet Their Alter Ego on 'The Far Side.'" *Smithsonian*. April 1984, pp. 112-114 +.

918. Smith, Elmer R. "Comic Strips 'Sell' School Library Books." *Clearing House*. September 1937, p. 11.

919. Smith, Ethel. "Reading the Comics in Grades 7 and 8." *Journal of Educational Psychology*. March 1942, pp. 173-182.

920. Smith, L.C. "Comics As Literature." Greeley, Colorado: Colorado State College of Education, 1938.

921. Sones, W.W.D. "Comics Books Are Going to School." *Progressive Education*. April 1947, pp. 208-209.

922. Sones, W.W.D. "Comic Books As Teaching Aids." *The Instructor*. April 1942, pp. 14, 55.

923. Sones, W.W.D. "Comics and Instructional Method." *Journal of Educational Sociology*. December 1944, pp. 232-240.

924. Sones, W.W.D. "Comics in the Classroom." *The School Executive*. October 1943, pp. 31-32, 82.

925. Southard, Ruth. "Superman Grabs Chance To Teach Grammar." *America*. June 9, 1945, pp. 196-197.

926. "Speaking of Pictures, The Democrats Make U.S. Political History and Rewrite It With Comic Books." *Life*. September 25, 1950, pp. 14-16.

927. Staunton, Helen. "Comic Characters Invade the Classroom." *Editor and Publisher*. March 6, 1948.

928. Stempel, Guido III. "Comic Strip Reading: Effect of Continuity." *Journalism Quarterly*. Summer 1956, pp. 366-367.

929. Stevens, John D. "College Students Rate the Comics." *Journalism Quarterly*. Spring 1973, pp. 158-159.

930. "Superman Goes to College." *Esquire*. September 1964, pp. 106-107.

931. Taff, Thomas G. "Motivation: Batman to the Rescue." *Grade Teacher*. March 1968, pp. 112, 114.

932. Taylor, Millicent J. "Comics Go to School." *Christian Science Monitor Weekly Magazine Section*. October 14, 1944, pp. 8-9.

933. "Teachers Urged To Combat 'Horror' Comics." *The Manchester Guardian*. November 12, 1954.

934. "Teaching by Comic Technique." *Nation's Business*. August 1952, pp. 77-79; March 1967, p. 27.

935. Terdoslavich, William. "Comics Are Serious Business Here." *Dover Daily Advance*. November 8, 1983.

936. Thomas, James L. *Cartoons and Comics in the Classroom: A Reference for Teachers and Librarians*. Littleton, Colorado: Libraries Unlimited, Inc., 1983. 181 pp.

937. Thomas, Margaret K. "Superman Teaches School in Lynn, Mass." *Magazine's Digest*. April 1944, pp. 5-7.

938. Thompson, Lovell. "How Serious Are the Comics?" *Atlantic Monthly*. September 1942, pp. 127-129.

939. Thorndike, Robert L. "Words and the Comics." *Journal of Experimental Education*. December 1941, pp. 110-113.

940. Tuttle, F.P. "Educative Value of the Comic Strip." *American Childhood*. March 1938, pp. 14-15.

941. Tysell, Helen Tr. "Character Names in the Comic Strips." *American Speech*. April 1934, pp. 158-160.

942. Tysell, Helen Tr. "The English of the Comic Cartoon." *American Speech*. February 1935, pp. 43-55.

943. "Ubiquitous Comics." *National Education Association Journal*. December 1948, p. 570.

944. Urbani, Trudy. "Fun, Funny, Funnies." *Teacher*. September 1978, pp. 60-62.

945. Urell, Barbara. "They Call That Reading." *Teacher*. January 1976, pp. 64-68.

946. Vacca, Carlo. "Comic Books As a Teaching Tool." *Hispania*. 12 (1959), pp. 291-292.

947. Vigus, Robert. "The Art of the Comic Magazine." *Elementary English Review*. May 1942, pp. 168-170.

948. Vrsan, F.W. "Comics Vs. Good Literature." *Grade Teacher*. October 1947, p. 14.

949. Waite, C.A. "Language of the Infant's Comic Papers." *School Librarian*. July 1968, pp. 140-145.

950. Waite, C.A. "What's in the Comics?" *School Librarian*. December 1964, pp. 254-256.

951. Walp, R.L. "Comics, As Seen by the Illustrators of Children's Books." *Wilson Library Bulletin*. 26:2 (1951), pp. 153-157, 159.

952. Walter, M.S. "Content of Current Comic Magazines." *School*. 52 (1952), pp. 505-510.

953. Wertham, Frederic. "Comics and Education: A Reply." *High Point*. October 1957, pp. 18-22.

954. "What About the Comics?" *Illinois Libraries*. 28 (1958), pp. 192-203.

955. "What Makes You Think So? Propaganda in the Comic Strips." *Scholastic.* May 20, 1940, pp. 34 +.

956. "What's in the Comic?" *Journal of Educational Sociology.* December 1944, pp. 214-222.

957. White, Blanchard. "Beware of the Comics." *Alabama School Journal.* November 1947, p. 10.

958. "Who Reads the Comics?" *Scholastic.* May 17, 1948, p. 3.

959. Williams, Arnold. "Hamburger Progeny." *American Speech.* April 1939, p. 154.

960. Wilson, Richard C. and Edward J. Shaffer. "Reading Comics To Learn." *The Elementary School Journal.* November 1965, pp. 81-82.

961. Witty, Paul A. "Reading the Comics—A Comparative Study." *Journal of Experimental Education.* December 1941, pp. 105-109.

962. Witty, Paul A. "Reading the Comics in Grades 4, 5, and 6. *Journal of Experimental Education.* December 1941.

963. Witty, Paul A. "Some Observations From the Study of the Comics." *Books Against Comics.* (Bulletin of the Association for Arts in Childhood). 1942, pp. 1-6.

964. Witty, Paul A. "Those Troublesome Comics." *National Parent Teacher.* January 1942.

965. Witty, Paul A. and Anne Coomer. "Reading the Comics in Grades IX-XII." *Educational Administration and Supervision.* May 1942, pp. 344-353.

966. Witty, Paul A. and H.C. Lehmann. "The Compensatory Function of the Sunday Funny Paper." *Journal of Applied Psychology.* June 1927, pp. 202-211.

967. Witty, Paul A. and R.A. Sizemore. "Reading the Comics: A Summary of Studies and an Evaluation." *Elementary English.* 31 (1954), pp. 501-506.

968. Witty, Paul A. and Robert A. Sizemore. "Reading the Comics: A Summary of Studies and an Evaluation III." *Elementary English.* February 1955, pp. 109-114.

969. Witty, Paul A., Ethel Smith, and Anne Coomer. "Reading the Comics in Grades VII and VIII." *Journal of Educational Psychology.* March 1942, pp. 173-182.

970. Wolfe, Katherine. "The Children Talk About Comics." In *Communication Research.* pp. 3-50. New York: Harper and Bros., 1949.

971. Wood, Auril. "Jimmy Reads the Comics." *Elementary School Journal*. October 1950, pp. 66-67.

972. "Word Distortions in Comic Strips." *Elementary School Journal*. May 1943, pp. 520-525.

973. "A Word from Batman. Comic Strip Characters and a Computer Spice Study for Young Readers." *Christian Science Monitor*. May 16, 1970, p. 8.

974. Wright, Ethel C. "A Public Library Experiment with the Comics." *The Library Journal*. October 15, 1943, pp. 832-835.

975. Wright, Gary. "The Comic Book—A Forgotten Medium in the Classroom." *The Reading Teacher*. November 1979, pp. 158-161.

976. Wright, Helen M. "Down to Brass Tacks on the Comics." *Library Journal*. January 1, 1944, p. 2.

977. Yuill, L.D. "Case for the Comics." *School Executive*. December 1944, pp. 42-44.

978. Zamchick, D. "Comic Books." *English Journal*. February 1952, pp. 95-97.

979. Zimmerman, T.L. "What To Do About Comics." *Library Journal*. September 15, 1954, pp. 1605-1607.

980. Zorbaugh, Harvey. "The Comics! Good Influence or Bad?" *Read*. September 1944, pp. 83-85.

981. Zorbaugh, Harvey. "The Comics—Where They Stand." *Journal of Educational Society*. December 1944, pp. 196-203.

982. Zorbaugh, Harvey. "Our Changing World of Communication—The Comics, Mass Medium of Communication." *Rho Journal*. April 1950.

983. Zorbaugh, Harvey. "What Adults Think of Comics As Reading for Children." *Journal of Educational Sociology*. December 1949, pp. 225-235.

Culture

984. Berger, Arthur A. "Comics and Culture." *Journal of Popular Culture*. Summer 1971, pp. 164-178.

985. Buhle, Paul. "The New Comics and American Culture." In "Literature in Revolution." Special issue of *Tri-Quarterly* (Evanston, Illinois). Winter/Spring 1972, pp. 367-411.

986. Buhle, Paul, ed. *Popular Culture in America.* Minneapolis, Minnesota: University of Minnesota Press, 1987. 288 pp. "Surrealism in the Comics I and II: Krazy Kat and Dick Tracy," by Franklin Rosemont; "As the Artist Sees It: Interviews with Comic Artists," by R. Crumb and Bill Griffith.

987. "Comic Culture." *Time.* December 18, 1944, pp. 86-87.

988. Davidson, Sol. "Culture and the Comic Strip." Ph.D. dissertation, New York University, 1959. 1,013 pp.

989. Gruenberg, Sidonie M. "Comics As a Social Force." *Journal of Educational Sociology.* December 1944, pp. 204-213.

990. Haugaard, Kay. "Comic Books: Conduits to Culture?" *The Reading Teacher.* 27:1 (1973), pp. 54-55.

991. Inge, M. Thomas. *Comics As Culture.* Jackson, Mississippi: University Press of Mississippi, 1990.

992. Inge, M. Thomas. "Comics As Culture." In *The Creative Step: An Inquiry into the Arts*, edited by Carl E. Rollyson and Hope E. Palmer, pp. 28-33. Detroit, Michigan: University Studies, Weekend College, Wayne State University, 1977. Also in *VSU Magazine.* August 1975, pp. 2-7.

993. Inge, M. Thomas, ed. "The Comics As Culture." *Journal of Popular Culture.* Spring 1979, pp. 631-639.

994. Kandel, I.L. "Fiddling During the Emergency, Are Comic-Books Contributary Factors to American Culture?" *School and Society.* February 10, 1951, pp. 88-89.

995. Kandel, I.L. "Threat to International Cultural Relations." *School and Society.* March 26, 1949, p. 220.

996. Mattingly, Ignatius G. "Some Cultural Aspects of Serial Cartoons, Or Get a Load of Those Funnies." *Harper's.* December 1955, pp. 34-39.

Literacy, Reading

997. Benenson, Joel. "Teacher Uses Comic Approach To Teach Children Reading." *Gannett Suburban Newspapers.* May 5, 1984.

998. Brumbaugh, Florence N. "Comics and Children's Vocabularies." *Elementary English Review.* February 1939, pp. 63-64.

999. "Comics As Remedial Reading Tool!" *Cartoonist PROfiles*. No. 23, 1974, pp. 48-52.

1000. Edwards, N. "Comics Lend a Hand in Remedial Reading." *Elementary School Journal*. October 1950, pp. 66-67.

1001. Guthrie, John T. "Comics." *The Reading Teacher*. December 1978, pp. 376-378.

1002. Hill, G.E. "Relation of Children's Interest in Comic Strips to the Vocabulary of These Comics." *Journal of Educational Psychology*. January 1943, pp. 48-54.

1003. Hill, G.E. "Vocabulary of Comic Strips." *Journal of Educational Psychology*. February 1943, pp. 77-87.

1004. "Nancy Leads Literacy Program in Arizona." *CAPS*. February 1992, p. 16.

1005. Ross, C.S. "Comic Book in Reading Instruction." *Journal of Education*. April 1946, pp. 121-122.

1006. Sanders, Betty. "Mad Magazine in the Remedial English Class." *English Journal*. February 1970, pp. 226-267, 272.

1007. Shaffer, Edward J. "Pupil Dictated Captions and Prose for Familiar Comics and Cartoons As a Stimulus for Reading in Grade One." Ph.D. dissertation, Florida State University, Tallahassee, 1965.

1008. Sperzel, E.Z. "Effect of Comic-Books on Vocabulary Growth and Reading Comprehension." *Elementary English Review*. February 1948, pp. 109-113.

1009. Swain, Emma H. "Using Comic Books To Teach Reading and Language Arts." *Journal of Reading*. December 1978, pp. 253-258.

1010. Waller, Elinor R. "The Place of the Comics in the Reading Program." *Washington Educational Journal*. May 1945, pp. 179-180.

Religion

1011. "Biblical Comic Books." *Newsweek*. August 3, 1942, pp. 55-56.

1012. "Captain Wojtyla!" *Commonweal*. October 22, 1982, p. 549.

1013. Clapp, R. "A Cartoonist Deals with the Faith in the Funnies." *Christianity Today*. March 19, 1982, pp. 42-44.

1014. "Comic Book Scriptures." *Newsweek*. October 16, 1944, p. 88.

1015. Haines, A.B. "Christian Comic Books." *Christianity Today*. January 20, 1982, pp. 47-48.

1016. Lawing, J.V., jr. "No More Than Roast Beef: Jubiles, an Oversized Adult Christian Comic Book." *Christianity Today*. October 24, 1975, p. 18.

1017. Lynch, Norman. "Bible Story Cartoons." *Cartoonist PROfiles*. December 1979, pp. 29-35.

1018. Neal, Jim. "Dennis the Menace To Teach Children Prayers." *Comics Buyer's Guide*. March 19, 1993, p. 52.

1019. "Old Testament in Comics." *Newsweek*. August 3, 1942.

1020. "Religion in the Comics... The New Thing." *Publisher's Weekly*. September 26, 1977. pp. 71-72.

1021. Savramis, Demosthenes. "Religion and Comic Strips: Tarzan and Superman As Saviors. Religion et bande dessinees: Tarzan et Superman sauveurs." *Social Compass*. 34:1 (1987), pp. 77-86.

1022. Sparks, Andrew. "Teaching Sunday School with the Comics." *The Atlantic Journal Magazine*. February 9, 1947, p. 10.

EROTICISM, PORNOGRAPHY, SEX

1023. Beck, Henry. "Sex and Breasts and Comic Books." *Village Voice*. July 14, 1987, pp. 42-43, 45.

1024. Bocage, Angela. "Define the Terms, Dismiss the Dregs, and Enjoy the Results." *Comics Journal*. July 1991, pp. 3-4.

1025. Brannigan, Augustine. "Is Obscenity Criminogenic?" *Society*. July-August 1987, pp. 12-19.

1026. Collier, James L. "Learning About Sex in Mickey Mouse Land." *The Village Voice*. July 6, 1967, pp. 9-10, 22.

1027. Dines-Levy, Gail and Gregory W.H. Smith. "Representations of Women and Men in *Playboy* Sex Cartoons." In *Humour in Society: Resistance and Control*, edited by Chris Powell and George Paton, pp. 234-259. New York: St. Martin's Press, 1988.

1028. Daley, Bill. *Dirty Comics*. King Productions, n.d. 131 pp.

1029. Geerdes, Clay. "The New Dirty Comics." *Hustler*. April 1976, pp. 68-74.

1030. Gilmore, D.H. *Sex in Comics: A History of the Eight Pagers*. 4 Vols. San Diego, California: Greenleaf Classics, Inc., 1971.

1031. Groth, Gary. "Confessions of a Smut Peddler." *Comics Journal*. July 1991, pp. 5-7.

1032. Grover, Jan. "Safer Sex Guidelines." *Jump/Cut*. No. 33, 1988, pp. 118-122.

1033. Harvilicz, Helena G. "'You're Busted, Creep': An Interview with Donald 'Anton Drek' Simpson." *Comics Journal*. July 1991, pp. 100-110.

1034. Horn, Maurice. "Sex in the Comics." *Playboy*. March 1985.

1035. Jennings, Michael. *A Treasury of Dirty Little Comics*. New York: Valiant, 1972.

1036. Klonsky, M. "Comic Strip-Tease of Time." *American Mercury*. December 1952, pp. 93-99.

1037. Kluger, Richard. "Sex and the Superman." *Partisan Review*. 13 (1966), pp. 111 ff.

1038. Kreiner, Rich. "Kitty Porn: An Interview with Reed Waller and Kate Worley." *Comics Journal*. July 1991, pp. 93-99.

1039. Kurtzman, Harvey. "@&%#!! Or, Takin' the Lid Off the Id." *Esquire*. June 1971, pp. 128-136.

1040. Layne, Gwendolyn. "Mum's the Word: Sexuality in Victorian Fantasy Illustrated (and Beyond)." In *Eros in the Mind's Eye*, edited by Donald Palumbo, pp. 59-74. New York: Greenwood, 1986. 290 pp.

1041. Levin, Bob. "'Yes, Yes,' She Panted. On the Censorship of Pornography." *Comics Journal*. July 1991, pp. 62-70.

1042. Mahogoff, Jack and Hugh G. Rection. "Porn Comics." *Comics Journal*. July 1991, pp. 43-47.

1043. Moscowitz, David. "From the Other Side of the Fence: Comics and Pornography." *Comics Journal*. July 1991, pp. 125-128.

1044. Palmer, C. Eddie. "Filthy Funnies, Blue Comics, and Raunchy Records: Dirty Jokes and Obscene Language as Public Entertainment." In *Sexual Deviancy in Social Context*, edited by C.D. Bryant. New York: New Viewpoints, 1977.

1045. Palmer, C. Eddie. "Pornographic Comics: A Content Analysis." *Journal of Sex Research*. November 1979, pp. 285-298.

1046. Parkinson, Robert E. "Carnal Comics." *Sexscope*. 1:3, 1:4 (n.d.).

1047. Pfouts, Chris. "You Can't Preach from a Tijuana Bible." *Art? Alternatives*. April 1992, pp. 27-29.

1048. Raymond, Otis. *An Illustrated History of Sex Comic Classics*. New York: Comic Classics, 1972. 223 pp.

1049. Rodi, Rob. "Was It Bad for You, Too?" *Comics Journal*. December 1991, pp. 33-36.

1050. Rymarkiewicz, Wencel. *A Scientific Study of Hot Little Comics*. Vols. 1, 2. California: Monogram, 1972.

1051. Strickland, Carol. "The Rape of Ms. Marvel." *LOC*. January 1980, pp. 61-65.

1052. "Strip Érotique de l'An 4000 pour Jane Fonda." *Cine Revue* (Brussels). July 20, 1967, p. 9.

1053. Sullivan, Darcy. "The Most Honest Sex Comics." *Comics Journal*. July 1991, pp. 49-52.

1054. Welz, Larry. "Cherry, Me and Censorship; Or No Flies on Me." *Gauntlet*. No. 2, 1992, pp. 135-141.

1055. "Who's More Exploitive?" *Comics Journal*. February 1992, p. 15.

ETHNICITY, MINORITIES, RACISM

1056. "ANIA Attacks DC and Milestone." *Comics Journal*. November 1992, p. 14.

1057. "ANIA—The Association of Black Comic-Book Publishers." *Comics Buyer's Guide*. February 26, 1993, p. 28.

1058. "ANIA—The Heroes." *Comics Buyer's Guide*. February 26, 1993, pp. 30, 34.

1059. "Backwords' 'Jewish Question.'" *Comics Journal*. October 1991, p. 24.

1060. Boyd, Robert. "Racist Murder As Entertainment." *Comics Journal*. February 1990, pp. 3-4.

1061. Burma, John H. "Humor As a Technique in Race Conflict." *American Sociological Review*. December 1946, pp. 710-711.

1062. Carter, Kevin L. "Hip-Hop Heroes." Philadelphia *Inquirer Magazine*. November 15, 1992, pp. 20-26.

1063. "Charlie Brown's New Pal." *Newsweek*. July 29, 1968, pp. 66-67.

1064. "Comics To Promote Black Superheroes." *Penstuff*. January 1993, p. 3.

1065. "Don't Forget the Motor City." *Comics Journal*. July 1993, p. 91.

1066. "Dismantler of Black Stereotypes." *Comics Journal*. April 1993, p. 24. (Alden Spurr McWilliams).

1067. Dorf, Shel. "Herb and Jamaal by Stephen Bentley." *Cartoonist PROfiles*. June 1991, pp. 20-30.

1068. "The First Gay Superhero—Not." *Comics Journal*. February 1992, pp. 12-13.

1069. "Friday Foster." *New Yorker*. March 21, 1970, pp. 33-34.

1070. "*Gasoline Alley* Is Charged with Racism." *Comics Journal*. November 1991, p. 27.

1071. Groth, Gary. "Nabile Hage: 'I Will Always Speak Out.'" *Comics Journal*. July 1993, pp. 39-46.

1072. Groth, Gary. "Spin Controlling Racist Comics." *Comics Journal*. February 1990, pp. 5-6.

1073. Groth, Gary. "Strategies of Self-Deception." *Comics Journal*. July 1990, pp. 7-10.

1074. Hardy, Charles and Gail F. Stern, eds. *Ethnic Images in the Comics*. Exhibition in the Museum of the Balch Institute for Ethnic Studies, September 15-December 20, 1986. Philadelphia: Balch Institute, 1986. 51 pp.

1075. "Hopi Leaders Protest NFL SuperPro." *Comics Journal*. March 1992, p. 20.

1076. "Is Mr. Dithers a Bigot?" *The Quill*. November 1988, p. 23.

1077. Jesuele, Kim. "Jump Start by Robb Armstrong." *Cartoonist PROfiles*. December 1990, pp. 12-19.

1078. Jones, Steven L. "From 'Under Cork' to Overcoming: Black Images in the Comics." In *Ethnic Images in the Comics*, edited by Charles Hardy and Gail Stern, pp. 21-30. Philadelphia, Pennsylvania: Balch Institute, 1986. Reprinted, *Nemo*. December 1987, pp. 16-21; *Black Ink*, pp. 5-15, San Francisco, California: Cartoon Art Museum, 1992.

1079. Joyner, Samuel. "My Life As an African-American Cartoonist." *Comics Journal*. May 1992, pp. 102-107.

1080. "The King's Tagalog." *Newsweek*. July 28, 1952, p. 75.

1081. Klotman, Phyllis R. "Racial Stereotypes in Hard Core Pornography." *Journal of Popular Culture*. Summer 1971, pp. 221-235.

1082. Leyland, Winston, ed. *Meatmen: An Anthology of Gay Male Comics*. San Francisco; California: G.S. Press, 1986. 191 pp.

1083. Mangels, Andy. "Out of the Closet and into the Comics. Gays in Comics." *Amazing Heroes*. July 1988, pp. 47-66.

1084. Marmel, Steve. "Stereotyping in the Comics." *Comics Buyer's Guide*. September 16, 1983, p. 39.

1085. Marty, M.E. "Discrimination Isn't Comic." *Christian Century*. February 22, 1989, p. 215.

1086. Neal, Jim. "Campus Comic Strip Stirs Racial Furor." *Comics Buyer's Guide*. July 2, 1993, p. 22.

1087. Neal, Jim. "Study Group Says Bugs Bunny Is Gay." *Comics Buyer's Guide*. March 12, 1993, p. 22.

1088. "Negro Heroes; A New Comics Publication." *School and Society*. June 19, 1948, p. 457.

1089. Norman, Tony. "Ho Che Anderson." *Comics Journal*. July 1993, pp. 85-90.

1090. Norman, Tony. "Mile Stone: 'This is a Beginning, Not a Fad." *Comics Journal*. July 1993, pp. 67-69, 71-77.

1091. Norman, Tony. "Seitu Hayden: 'Stories About People, Just Regular People.'" *Comics Journal*. July 1993, pp. 53-57, 59-60.

1092. Norman, Tony. "Sims Brothers." *Comics Journal*. July 1993, pp. 93-99, 101.

1093. Norman, Tony. "Stan Shaw." *Comics Journal*. July 1993, pp. 33-38.

1094. Onli, Turtel. "The Black Age of Comics." *Comics Buyer's Guide*. February 26, 1993, p. 28.

1095. Perkins, William E. and Steven Heller. "Dirty Pictures (African and Jewish Americans Share the Bitter Legacy of Being the Most Stereotyped People in the Melting Pot)." *Print*. March/April 1991, pp. 104-113.

1096. Pierce, Ponchitta. "What's Not So Funny about the Funnies." *Ebony*. November 1966, pp. 48-56.

1097. "Quincy by Ted Shearer." *Cartoonist PROfiles*. September 1971, pp. 34-43.

1098. "Redrawing the Color Line, Integrated Comic-Strip." *Newsweek*. February 1965, p. 45.

1099. Rosendahl, Peter J. *Han Ola og han Per*. Northfield, Minnesota: The Norwegian-American Historical Association, 1984. 165 pp.

1100. Rosendahl, Peter J. *Han Ola og han Per*. Ed. Joan N. Buckley and Einar Haugen. Vol. 1. Oslo: Universitetsforlaget, 1984. Vol. 2. Iowa City, Iowa: University of Iowa Press, 1988.

1101. "Sketchbook: Grass Green." *Comics Journal*. July 1993, pp. 108-111.

1102. Stevens, John D. "Bungleton Green: Black Comic Strip Ran 43 Years." *Journalism Quarterly*. Spring 1974, pp. 122-124.

1103. Stevens, John D. "Reflections in a Dark Mirror: Comic Strips in Black Newspapers." *Journal of Popular Culture*. Summer 1976, pp. 239-244.

1104. Stevens, John D. "Reflections in a Dark Mirror: Comic Strips in Black Newspapers." Presented at Third Annual Convention, Popular Culture Association, Milwaukee, Wisconsin, April 1974.

1105. Thibodeau, Ruth. "From Racism to Tokenism: The Changing Face of Blacks in *New Yorker* Cartoons." *Public Opinion Quarterly*. Winter 1989, pp. 482-494.

1106. Triptow, Robert, ed. *Gay Comics*. New York: Plume, 1989.

1107. Winbrush, Jeffrey. "The New Black Era of Comics." *Comics Journal*. July 1993, pp. 79-83.

1108. Witty, Paul A. and Dorothy Moore. "Interest in Reading the Comics Among Negro Children." *Journal of Educational Psychology*. May 1945, pp. 303-308.

Brandon, Brumsic, jr.

1109. Brandon, Brumsic, jr. "Luther." *Cartoonist PROfiles*. March 1986, pp. 20-25.

1110. Brandon, Brumsic, jr. *Luther's Got Class*. New York: Paul S. Erikkson, 1976.

1111. Brandon, Brumsic, jr. "The Serious Side of Cartooning." *Crisis*. 88 (1981), pp. 476-478.

Harrington, Oliver W.

1112. Harrington, Oliver W. *Bootsie and Others: A Selection of Cartoons by Ollie Harrington*. New York: Dodd, Mead, 1958. Unpaginated.

1113. Harrington, Oliver W. "How Bootsie Was Born." *Freedomways*. 3 (1963), pp. 518-524. Reprinted. John Henry Clarke. *Harlem USA*, pp. 72-79. New York: Collier, 1971.

1114. Harrington, Oliver W. "Like Most of Us Kids." *Freedomways*. 16 (1976), pp. 255-257.

1115. Harrington, Oliver W. "Look Homeward Baby." *Freedomways*. 13 (1973), pp. 135-143.

1116. "Bids Negro Fight for Place in Art." *New York Times*. November 25, 1946, p. 32.

1117. Ransom, Llewellyn. "PV's Art Editor Ollie Harrington, Creator of 'Bootsie' and 'Pee Wee,' Enjoyed Life, Despite Setbacks." *People's Voice*. August 8, 1942, p. 4.

1118. Smythe, Hugh H. "Bootsie and Others." *Journal of Human Relations*. Summer 1959, pp. 592-594.

Turner, Morrie

1119. "Black and White by Morrie Turner." *Cartoonist PROfiles*. No. 6, 1970, pp. 36-42.

1120. Ericsson, Mary K. "Morrie." *WittyWorld*. Spring 1988, pp. 9-11.

1121. Ericsson, Mary K. *Morrie Turner*. Chicago: Childrens Press, 1986, 111 pp.

1122. "Morrie Turner." *Cartoonist PROfiles*. December 1987, pp. 66-67.

1123. "Morrie Turner: Wee Pals." *Newsletter*. October 1966, p. 20.

1124. Robinson, L. "Cartoonist with a Conscience: M. Turner's Multiracial Comic Characters." *Ebony*. February 1973, pp. 31-34 +.

1125. Turner, Morrie. *Freedom Is...Featuring Wee Pals*. Valley Forge, Pennsylvania: Judson Press, 1970.

1126. Turner, Morrie and Jacqueline Low. *Bow Bells*. Belmont, California: Fearon, 1972.

1127. Turner, Morrie and Jacqueline Low. *Grandma Cigar*. Belmont, California: Fearon, 1972.

1128. Turner, Morrie and Jacqueline Low. *Messing Up*. Belmont, California: Fearon, 1972.

1129. Turner, Morrie and Jacqueline Low. *Pike's Peak Pack*. Belmont, California: Fearon, 1972.

1130. Turner, Morrie and Jacqueline Low. *Ser un Hombre*. Belmont, California: Fearon, 1972.

1131. Turner, Morrie and Jacqueline Low. *The Vandals*. Belmont, California: Fearon, 1974.

HUMANISM, SOCIAL CONSCIOUSNESS, RELEVANCY

1132. "AIDS Comics Update." *Comics Journal*. July 1991, p. 17.

1133. "Archie Comics Launches a Campaign To Help Fight AIDS." *Comics Buyer's Guide*. January 15, 1988, pp. 1, 3.

1134. Beiswinger, George L. "More Involvement in Charitable Matters." *Editor and Publisher*. February 21, 1987, pp. 52-53.

1135. Braun, Saul. "Shazam! Here Comes Captain Relevant." *New York Times Magazine*. May 2, 1971, pp. 32-55.

1136. Bruning, Fred. "Yikes! Real Life in the Funnies." *New York Newsday*. May 4, 1993, pp. 56-57, 81.

1137. "Comical Protest Is Strummed up by Joanie Phoanie." *Minneapolis Tribune*. January 11, 1967.

1138. "Comic Books for Workers Do a Job of Employer House Organ." *Printer's Ink*. November 13, 1942, p. 56.

1139. "Comic Book To Aid Ethiopia." *Comics Buyer's Guide*. April 19, 1985, p. 1.

1140. "'Comics F/X' Gives Away 'AIDS News' Comic Book." *Comics Buyer's Guide*. December 1988.

1141. Decker, Dwight R. "Propaganda Comics: Two Views." *Comics Journal*. February 1985, pp. 93-97.

1142. Des Pres Terrence. "Holocaust Laughter?" In *Writing and the Holocaust*, edited by Berel Lang, pp. 216-233. New York: Holmes and Meier, 1988. 301 pp.

1143. "Fascism in the Funnies: In Little Orphan Annie, H. Gray Continues His Attack Upon the New Deal." *New Republic*. September 18, 1935, p. 147.

1144. "Fleagle and Friends." *Cartoonist*. June 1977, pp. 82-85.

1145. Graham, Helen C. "Comic Show To Support March of Dimes." *Comic Book Trader Quarterly*. Fall 1987, p. 1.

1146. Groeneveld, K. "Marvel Comics Supports Blood Drive." *Comic Book Retailer*. Winter 1988, p. 1.

1147. Hall, D. "Comic Reality." *Omni*. January 1988, pp. 20 +.

1148. Hess, John, *et al*. "Representing AIDS." *Jump/Cut*. No. 33, 1988, pp. 116-117.

1149. "How the National Social Welfare Assembly Uses Comics To Bring Socially Constructive Messages to American Youth." *Report of the National Social Welfare Assembly* (New York). 1956, p. 8.

1150. Jones, Bill. "Truth, Justice, and the Comics or, MoMa to NY: Drop Dead (High & Low, Museum of Modern Art, New York: traveling exhibit)." *Arts Magazine*. December 1990, pp. 72-74.

1151. Kandel, I.L. "Threat to International Cultural Relations." *School and Society*. March 26, 1949, p. 220.

1152. Kassarjian, Harold H. "Social Values and the Sunday Comics: A Content Analysis." In *Advances in Consumer Research*, Vol. 10, edited by Richard P. Bagozzi and Alice M. Tybout, pp. 434-438. Ann Arbor, Michigan: Association for Consumer Research, 1983.

1153. Kunzle, David. "Self-Conscious Comics." *New Republic*. July 19, 1975, pp. 26-27.

1154. Latona, Robert. "The Pride of the Navy." *Vanguard*. No. 1, 1966, pp. 4-24.

1155. Lent, John A. "The Seriously Funny Art of Comics." *Group Media Journal*. 7: 3/4 (1988), pp. 3-5.

1156. Luciano, Dale. "Trapped by Life: Pathos and Humor Among Mice and Men." *Comics Journal*. December 1986, pp. 43-49, 52.

1157. McAllister, Matthew P. "Comic Books and AIDS." *Journal of Popular Culture*. Fall 1992, pp. 1-24.

1158. MacDonald, Heidi. "Archetype Meets Angst." *Comics Journal*. July 1982, pp. 35-39.

1159. "Marvel Offers Spider-Man Comic Book To Benefit U.S. Committee for UNICEF." *Comics Buyer's Guide*. December 4, 1992, p. 67.

1160. Metzger, Kim. "Teen Titans Fight Drugs." *Comics Collector*. Spring 1984, pp. 31-32.

1161. Monaco, Steve. "Exploiting Social Relevancy: A Waste of Trees." *Comics Journal*. September 1987, pp. 121-122.

1162. Ozorio, P. "Cartoon Heroes Needn't Smoke!" *World Health*. January/February 1986, p. 9.

1163. Parachini, A. "Social Protest Hits the Comic Pages." *Columbia Journalism Review*. November 1974, pp. 4-7.

1164. Pekar, Harvey. "American Slander: Serious Funnybooks." *Comics Journal*. February 1991, pp. 109-111.

1165. Pekar, Harvey. "The Potential of Comics." *Comics Journal*. July 1988, pp. 81-88.

1166. "Reaction to Animal-Testing Series." *Editor and Publisher*. January 21, 1989, p. 66.

1167. Rifas, Leonard. "AIDS Educational Comics." *Reference Services Review*. 19:2 (1991), pp. 81-87.

1168. Robeznieks, Andis. "The Comic Side of Vegetarianism." *Vegetarian Times*. November 1987, pp. 28-32.

1169. Rodi, Rob. "Bigot-Bashing." *Comics Journal*. January 1989, pp. 43-46.

1170. Rose, Arnold M. "Mental Health Attitudes of Youth As Influenced by a Comic Strip." *Journalism Quarterly*. Summer 1958, pp. 333-342.

1171. Rose, Charles R. "Safety Posters Ride the Bus." *The Instructor*. September 1964, p. 123.

1172. Sanderson, Peter. "Strip AIDS USA: The Making of a Benefit Book." *Amazing Heroes*. July 1988, pp. 67-68.

1173. "Spider-Man Battles Emotional Abuse." *Children Today*. May-June 1988, pp. 2-3.

1174. Spiegelman, Art. "Commix: An Idiosyncratic Historical and Aesthetic Overview." *Print*. November-December 1988, pp. 61-73.

1175. Spiggle, Susan. "Measuring Social Values: A Content Analysis of Sunday Comics and Underground Comix." *Journal of Consumer Research*. June 1986, pp. 100-113.

1176. Stangroom, Howard W. "AARGH! Protests Anti-Gay Legislation." *Comics Buyer's Guide*. March 25, 1988.

1177. "Survey: AIDS Comics." *Itchy Planet*. Spring 1988, p. 3.

1178. "Taking the Smoke Out of the Heroes of Comic Books." *World Health*. October 1983, p. 30.

1179. Thomas, Roy, *et al*. "Relevancy in Comics." *Comics Journal*. November 1981, pp. 52-66.

1180. Thompson, Maggie. "Archie's AIDS Posters Available to Shops." *Comics Buyer's Guide*. March 11, 1988, p. 20.

1181. Toner, M. "Mark Trail: Comic With a Cause." *National Wildlife*. February-March 1988, pp. 14-17.

1182. Tucker, Ken. "Cats, Mice and History—The Avant-Garde of the Comic Strip." *New York Times Book Review*. May 26, 1985, p. 3.

1183. Tucker, Ken. "The Comic Image: Not Just for Laughs." *Philadelphia Inquirer*. November 26, 1989, pp. I-1, I-4.

1184. Van Gelder, Lawrence. "Comic Book Industry To Allow Stories on Narcotics." *New York Times*. April 16, 1971.

1185. Vlamos, J.F. "The Sad Case of the Funnies: Comic Strips Have Gone He-Man, Haywire and Hitlerite." *American Mercury*. April 1941, pp. 411-416.

1186. Walters, Nolan. "'Doonesbury' To Urge Calls to White House." *Philadelphia Inquirer*. April 30, 1987, p. 8-D.

1187. Weinberg, Nancy and Rosina Santana. "Comic Books: Champions of the Disabled Stereotype." *Rehabilitation Literature*. November-December 1978, pp. 327-331.

1188. Witek, Joseph. *Comic Books As History. The Narrative Art of Jack Jackson, Art Spiegelman, and Harvey Pekar*. Jackson, Mississippi: University Press of Mississippi, 1990. 164 pp.

Callahan, John

1189. Baker, Mike. "Disturbing Images: The Cartoons of John Callahan." *Gauntlet*. No. 3, 1992, pp. 106-109.

1190. Callahan, John. "Welfare Hell." *Utne Reader*. March/April 1993, pp. 104-106.

MOVIES, TELEVISION, RADIO

1191. "Adam West, the Most Charming Scoundrel." *Motion Picture*. June 1966.

1192. Allstetter, Rob. "Fantastic Four Movie Aims High on a Low Budget." *Comics Buyer's Guide*. February 26, 1993, pp. 36, 40.

1193. Ardmore, Jane. "Batman and the Blonde Secretary." *Screenland*. July 1966.

1194. "*Arkham Asylum* Threatened by Concern for *Batman* Film." *Comics Journal*. March 1989, p. 19.

1195. Arnott, Duane S. "Dick Tracy: The Lost Casebook." *Comics Scene*. December 1990, pp. 57-60.

1196. Balling, Fredda. "Secrets of Batman's Other Family." *Movie Mirror*. October 1966.

1197. Baquedano, José J. "Supermanismo en el Cine." *Cuto* (San Sebastian). No. 2-3, 1967, pp. 65-67.

1198. Barbour, Alan G. *The Serials of Columbia*. New York: Screen Facts Press, 1967. 68 pp.

1199. Barbour, Alan G. *The Serials of Republic*. New York: Screen Facts Press, 1965.

1200. Barclay, Dorothy. "Comic Books and TV." *New York Times Magazine*. March 5, 1950, p. 43.

1201. "The Batboom." *Time*. March 11, 1966.

1202. "Batman and Robin from Comic Strip to Movie Screen." *Screen Thrills Illustrated*. No. 4, 1963, pp. 10-15; No. 5, 1963, pp. 12-16.

1203. "Batman and Robin Lost!" *Teen Screen*. May 1966.

1204. "Batman: Craziest, Whackiest Send-up of Them All." *Photoplay*. February 1967.

1205. "Batman-Film-Ankündigung." *Neues vom Film. 2. Deutsches Fernsehen (ZDF).* February 4, 1967.

1206. "Batman's Most Intimate Secrets." *Screen Parade.* August 1966.

1207. Becker, Joyce. "The Green Hornet Sees Red." *Movieland.* November 1966.

1208. Beckerman, Howard. "The Superman Story." *Filmmakers Newsletter.* February 1976, pp. 54-55.

1209. "Behind the Scenes on Batman: The Movie." *Speakeasy.* February 1989, pp. 30-32.

1210. "Behind the Scenes with Fu Manchu." *Castle of Frankenstein.* No. 8, 1966, pp. 12-13.

1211. "Behind the Shadow Mask." *Screen Thrills Illustrated.* No. 4, 1963, pp. 28-29.

1212. Behlmer, Rudy. "The MGM Tarzans." *Screen Facts.* No. 15, 1967, pp. 44-61.

1213. Behlmer, Rudy. "The Saga of Flash Gordon." *Screen Facts.* No. 10, 1967, pp. 53-63.

1214. Bertieri, Claudio. "Tutto James Bond e Quelcosa di Più." *Il Lavoro.* May 12, 1966.

1215. "Books into Films; Movies Based on Characters Out of the Funnies." *Publisher's Weekly.* May 31, 1947, p. 2718.

1216. Borie, Marcia. "Batman Bonus." *Motion Picture.* May 1966.

1217. Buchman, Chris. "The Television Scene." *Films in Review.* November 1985, pp. 559-564.

1218. *Charlie Brown, A Boy for All Seasons: 20 Years on Television.* New York: Museum of Broadcasting, 1985. 46 pp.

1219. Chute, David. "The Great Frame Robbery." *Film Comment.* September-October 1982, pp. 13-17.

1220. Colbert, William. "The Lowdown on the Green Hornet." *Screen Parade.* December 1966.

1221. Coleman, Earle J. "The Funnies, the Movies and Aesthetics." *Journal of Popular Culture.* Spring 1985, pp. 89-100.

1222. "Comico News: The Grendel Movie." *Comics Journal.* September 1986, p. 26.

1223. "Comics and TV." *Time*. November 26, 1943.

1224. "Comic Screen." *Comics Scene*. February 1990, pp. 68-69.

1225. "Conan Movie Review." *Comics Scene*. July 1982, pp. 34-36, 62.

1226. Connor, Edward. "The First Eight Serials of Columbia." *Screen Facts*. No. 7. 1964, pp. 53-62.

1227. Connor, Edward. "Oriental Detectives on the Screen." *Screen Facts*. No. 8, 1964, pp. 30-39.

1228. Conquet, André. "Comics, Cinéma et Télévision aux Etats-Unis." *Educateurs* (Paris). October 1954, pp. 339-407.

1229. "Continued Next Week." *Screen Thrills Illustrated*. No. 1, 1962, pp. 16-29.

1230. D'Angelo, Carr. "Batman Take One." *Comics Scene*. No. 3 (Vol. 3, #14), pp. 11-16.

1231. Decker, Dwight R. "Superman: The Movie Review." *Comics Journal*. March 1979, pp. 46-53.

1232. DeMarco, Mario. *The Red Ryders of the Screen, Radio, TV and Comics*. N.P. 1986? 100 pp.

1233. Dempsey, Jimmy. "Great Old Time Radio Premiums." In *The Comic Book Price Guide 1983-84*, edited by R.M. Overstreet, pp. A-62 - A-63. Cleveland, Tennessee: 1983.

1234. "Dennis the Menace Film Planned." *CAPS*. September 1991, p. 11.

1235. "'Dick Tracy' Seen As Risky Business." *Variety*. May 30, 1990, pp. 41, 44.

1236. "Dick Tracy Som Film." *Seriejournalen*. September 1990, pp. 21-22.

1237. Dietz, Lawrence. "The Caped Crusader and the Boy Wonder." *New York Herald Tribune*. January 9, 1966, p. 20.

1238. Dixon, Ken. "The Screen Tarzan." *Oprian*. 1:1 (1965), pp. 54-58.

1239. Dorf, Shel. "Little Orphan Annie Goes to Hollywood." *Comics Journal*. September 1982, pp. 6-7.

1240. Dosch, Andreas. "Dracula." *ICOM*. January 1993, pp. 52-53.

1241. Edgerton, Lane. "The Actor Who Lives in Fear of Batman." *Silver Screen*. June 1966.

1242. Eisner, Joel. *The Official Batman Batbook*. Chicago, Illinois: Contemporary Books, 1986. 171 pp.

1243. Eller, Claudia. "'Tracy' Cost Put at $101 Mil." *Variety*. October 22, 1990, pp. 3, 10.

1244. Essoe, Gabe. *Tarzan of the Movies*. New York: Citadel Press, 1968; 2nd Ed., 1972.

1245. Fiore, R. "Beauty and the Beast, Hook, the World of Charles Addams." *Comics Journal*. February 1992, pp. 36-39.

1246. "Flash Gordon's Flight for Life." *Fantastic Monsters of the Film*. 1:1 (1965).

1247. "Flicks in the Future." *Screen Thrills Illustrated*. No. 2, 1962, pp. 7-11.

1248. "Flying and Fighting Heroes." *Screen Thrills Illustrated*. No. 9, 1964, pp. 34-41.

1249. Francis, Terry. "Batman Adam West Says: 'I'm Only Half a Man.'" *TV Radio Mirror*. June 1966.

1250. Frezza, Gino. *L'Immagine Innocente. Cinema e Fumetto Americani delle Origini. Da Swinnerton a Feininger (1892-1907). David Wark Griffith (1908-1931).* Preface by Emilio Garroni. Rome: Casa Editrice Roberto Napoleone S.r.l., 1978.

1251. "From Tarzan to Lion Man." *Screen Thrills Illustrated*. No. 4, 1963, pp. 7-9.

1252. "'Funny Papers'—CBS-TV Network Special." *Cartoonist PROfiles*. September 1971, pp. 58-73.

1253. Gehl, Ray. "Comic Strip???? on Radio." *Cartoonist PROfiles*. December 1984, pp. 14-17.

1254. Gent, George. "The Love to Be Mean to Batman." *New York Times*. May 1, 1966.

1255. "Gespräch mit Robert Altman über 'Popeye.'" *Comic Forum* (Vienna). 3:12 (1981) p. 38.

1256. "Globe Cartoon Dennis Comes to Life on TV." *Boston Globe*. October 4, 1959, p. 65.

1257. "Great Scott!! The Comics Invade Hollywood!" *U.S. News and World Report*. March 26, 1979, p. 62.

1258. "The Green Hornet's Buzz Bomb." *Movie Mirror*. October 1966.

1259. Gregory, James. "Batman's Mad for Mia Farrow." *Screenland*. June 1966.

1260. Gross, Edward. "Able To Change the Course of Mighty Mouse." *Comics Scene*. February 1990, pp. 53-56.

1261. Haigh, Peter S. "Blaise, Batman, Blondie and Co." *Film in Review* (London). April 1966.

1262. Harmon, Jim. "Shadow Strikes Back." *Fantastic Monsters of the Films*. 1:6 (1967), pp. 47-48.

1263. Harvey, R.C. "Comics Aren't Film and Other Vicey Verses." *Comics Journal*. September 1983, pp. 80-86.

1264. Haydock, Ron. "The Cliff-Hanging Adventures of Captain America." *Fantastic Monsters of the Films*. No. 0, 1965, pp. 25-28.

1265. Hegerfors, Sture. "Jättesatsning pa Broadway: Stalmannen som Musical." *Göteborgs-Tidningen*. March 18, 1966.

1266. Hegerfors, Sture. "Roligaste Serien: Serie—Parodin." *Göteborgs—Posten*. November 23, 1959.

1267. Hoffman, Eric L. "Comics on Film. Superman—The Columbia Serials, Part Two." *Comics Feature*. May 1987, pp. 40-45.

1268. "Holy Batmania." *Movie Screen Yearbook*. No. 15, 1966.

1269. "Holy Popcorn. Is Batman Doomed?" *Teen Screen Yearbook*. August 1966.

1270. Horn, Maurice. "Les Héros des Bandes Dessinées à la Télévision Américaine." *Giff-Wiff*. No. 10, 1965, p. 27.

1271. Howard, John. "I'm Not Flabby." *Movieland*. May 1966.

1272. Ivie, Larry. "The Controversy of Frankenstein." *Monsters and Heroes*. No. 1, 1967, pp. 8-11.

1273. Ivie, Larry. "From Comic to Film." *Monsters and Heroes*. No. 1, 1967, pp. 22-27.

1274. Ivie, Larry. "Heroes of Radio." *Monsters and Heroes*. No. 1, 1967, pp. 18-21.

1275. Ivie, Larry. "Jonny Sheffield, Filmland's Son of Tarzan." *Monsters and Heroes*. No. 1, 1967, pp. 40-49.

1276. Ivie, Larry. "The Three Faces of Captain Video." *Monsters and Heroes*. No. 3, 1967, pp. 26-34.

1277. Key, Theodore. "Hazel and TV." *The Cartoonist*. March 1968, pp. 9-11.

1278. "Killer Ailler Ape." *Fantastic Monsters of the Film*. 1:1 (1965).

1279. Kinnard, Roy. *Comics Come Alive*. Metuchen, New Jersey: Scarecrow Press, 1991, 237 pp.

1280. Kunzle, David. "Comic Strip and Film Language." *Film Quarterly*. Autumn 1972, pp. 11-23.

1281. Lahue, Kalton C. "E.R.B. and the Silent Screen." *E.R.B. Dom*. Nos. 20 and 21, 1967, pp. 3-16 and 2-17.

1282. "The Lone Ranger Story." *Screen Thrills Illustrated*. No. 10, 1965, pp. 6-13.

1283. Lowry, Brian. "It's a New 'Bat' Time for Same 'Bat' Channel." *Variety*. November 30, 1992, p. 51.

1284. Luciano, Dale. "Flash Gordon; Opulent, Orgiastic Camp Versus Pop Mythology." *Comics Journal*. September 1981, pp. 325-326.

1285. Luciano, Dale. "Robert Altman's Hyperkinetic Comic Strip—Musical—Movie." *Comics Journal*. September 1981, pp. 321-325.

1286. Luciano, Dale. "Superman III: Synthetic Jumble of a Movie at the Character's Expense." *Comics Journal*. October 1983, pp. 99-100.

1287. Maartens, Alf. "Flash Gordon. Der Film-Der Comic." *Comixene* (Hanover). 8:36 (1981), pp. 56-59.

1288. McGrath, Ron. "A Marvelous TV Season." *The World of Comic Art*. 1:3 (1966/1967), pp. 18-21.

1289. "Matinee Idol." *Fantastic Monsters of the Film*. 1:1 (1965).

1290. Matranga, Stuart. "Look What's in the Movies." *Comics Scene*. January 1981, pp. 20-22.

1291. Moser, Leopold. "Film and Comics." *Comic Forum* (Vienna). 4:16 (1982), pp. 17-18. ("Little Orphan Annie").

1292. Moser, Leopold. "Film and Comics: Conan-Der Barbar. Robin Hood. 2 Neue Bücher über den Zeichentrickfilm. Film and Comics—Comics and Film." *Comic Forum* (Vienna). 4:15 (1982), pp. 32-34.

1293. Moser, Leopold. "Film and Comics: Heavy Metal-Der Film. Ein Comicmagazin Wird Lebendig." *Comic Forum* (Vienna). 4:13 (1982), pp. 32-34.

1294. Moser, Leopold and Hans Langsteiner. "Film and Comics: Conan, Popeye." *Comic Forum* (Vienna). 3:12 (1981), p. 39.

1295. "Movies Option 'Grendel.'" *Comics Buyer's Guide*. September 12, 1986, p. 1.

1296. Murphy, Stan. "Adam West Says: My Girls' Gangster Lover Tried To Kill Me." *Screenland*. May 1966.

1297. Murray, Will. "Doc on Radio." *Comics Buyer's Guide*. March 26, 1993, p. 54.

1298. Murray, Will. "Marvel and the Movies." *Comics Scene Spectacular*. 1989, pp. 8-11.

1299. Murray, Will. "Remember the Doc Savage Movie Disaster?" *Comics Buyer's Guide*. March 26, 1993, pp. 54, 58.

1300. Neal, Jim. "TV Resurrects Movie Serials." *Comics Buyer's Guide*. April 23, 1993, pp. 36, 40.

1301. "Nemesis of the Underworld." *Screen Thrills Illustrated*. No. 8, 1964, pp. 7-11.

1302. "Neue Fernsehsprache 1967: Batman." *Hamburger Morgenpost*. December 29, 1966.

1303. Noglows, Paul. "Comic-Book Heroes Flex Megapic Muscle." *Variety*. November 30, 1992, pp. 1, 107-108.

1304. O'Neill, Patrick D. "Panels and Frames: The Relationship Between Film and Comics...." *Comics Scene*. September 1982, pp. 41-44, 46.

1305. "Peng-Batman Kommt." *Hamburger Morgenpost*. February 1, 1967.

1306. "The Phantom. A King of the Comics Became a King of the Serial." *Screen Thrills Illustrated*. No. 6, 1963.

1307. Pirani, Adam. "Batman's Armorer." *Comics Scene Spectacular*. 1989, pp. 12-47.

1308. "Popeye. Der Seemann Mit dem Harten Schlag." *Comic Forum* (Vienna). 3:12 (1981), pp. 32, 37.

1309. Price, Bob. "The Dick Tracy Story." *Screen Thrills Illustrated*. No. 1, 1962, pp. 52-59.

1310. Price, Bob. "The Men Behind the Mask of Zorro." *Screen Thrills Illustrated*. No. 9, 1964, pp. 7-15.

1311. Price, Bob. "Serial Queens." *Screen Thrills Illustrated*. No. 3, 1963, pp. 12-18.

1312. Price, Bob. "Shazam!" *Screen Thrills Illustrated*. No. 2, 1962, pp. 12-19.

1313. Prosperi, Pierfrancesco. "Wow! The Batmobile." *Sgt. Kirk*. No. 5, 1967, pp. 58-61.

1314. Prosperi, Pierco. "Componenti S.F. nei Film di James Bond." *Oltre il Cielo* (Rome). No. 140, 1967, p. 211.

1315. Reed, Leslie. "Robin the Boy Wonder, on and off Screen." *Hit Parade*. July 1966.

1316. "The Return of Batman." *Newsweek*. December 20, 1965.

1317. "The Return of Captain America." *Screen Thrills Illustrated*. No. 7, 1964, pp. 20-25.

1318. Rifas, Leonard. "Superman and the Amusing Nuclear Man." *Comics Journal*. December 1987, pp. 9-10.

1319. "Robin and Batman." *Time*. August 30, 1971, p. 38.

1320. Rodman, Howard A. "They Shoot Comic Books, Don't They?" *American Film*. May 1989, pp. 34-39.

1321. Rodríguez Arbesú, Faustino. "Hitchcock y Yo." *El Wendigo*. No. 50, 1990, p. 12.

1322. Roland, Leila. "Batman's Hidden Children." *Silver Screen*. July 1966.

1323. Roux, Antoine. "Analyse: Ciné et B.D.: Steve Canyon." *Le Noveau Bédésup*. 35, 1985, pp. 38-39.

1324. "The Saga of Superman, Part I-III." *Screen Thrills Illustrated*. No. 1, 1962, pp. 30-37; No. 2, 1962, pp. 42-48; No. 3, 1963, pp. 52-57.

1325. Saltzman, J. "Hollywood's Comic Strip Mentality." *USA Today*. January 1981, p. 33.

1326. Scapperotti, Dan. "Able To Soar Higher Than a Bird." *Comics Scene*. February 1990, pp. 40-44.

1327. Schoell, William. *Comic Book Heroes of the Screen*. Secaucus, New Jersey: Carol Publishing Group, Citadel Press, 1991. 239 pp.

1328. Schöler, Franz. "Männer, die Zusammenhalten. Ein Comics-Held im Film. Zur Aufführung von 'Batman' in Deutschland." *Film* (Hanover). 4:1 (1966) pp. 6-10.

1329. Schwartz, Howard. "Bat-matography, or Capturing Batman on Film." *American Cinematographer*. June 1966, pp. 384-387, 419.

1330. Shapiro, Marc. "Directing Rocketeer." *Comics Scene*. October 1991, pp. 45-48, 60.

1331. Sherman, Sam. "The Case Charlie Chan Lost." *Screen Thrills Illustrated*. No. 6, 1963.

1332. Silver, Rosalind. "Comics and Culture: Cartoonists' Role As TV Critics." *Media and Values*. Fall 1992, pp. 4-7.

1333. Skow, John. "Has TV Gone Batty?" *New York Post*. May 7, 1966.

1334. Sloane, Allyson. "I Like To Make Love! Batman Tells All!" *Movieland*. June 1966.

1335. Spillman, Susan. "Big Gamble for Beatty and Disney." *USA Today*. May 11-13, 1990, pp. 1-2.

1336. Spock, Benjamin. "TV, Radio, Comics and Movies." *Ladies' Home Journal*. April 1960, p. 61.

1337. Stazer, Tom. "Watched Any Good Comics Lately?" *Comic Informer*. January-February 1983, pp. 31-36.

1338. Stephens, Lynne. "Able To Bend in His Bare Hands." *Comics Scene*. February 1990, 45-47.

1339. "Steve Canyon: New TV Star." *Flying*. September 1958, p. 46.

1340. Stevens, Bill. "Batman As He Really Is." *Screen Parade*. October 1966.

1341. Stewart, Bhob. "Horror on the Air." *Castle of Frankenstein*. No. 6, 1965, pp. 44-48.

1342. "A Sudden Superbatmad Looniness." *Life*. May 16, 1966.

1343. "Super-Batman Kommt." *Quick* (Munich). October 2, 1966.

1344. "Superheroes in Primetime." *Speakeasy*. April 1990, p. 13.

1345. "Superman - der Film." *Comic Forum* (Vienna). 6:23 (1984), pp. 28-29.

1346. "Tagneserier som Råmateriale for Hollywood." *Serieskaberen*. December 1989, p. 11.

1347. "Tarzan Comes to TV, Lion Sommer Spectacular." *Epic* (London). 1957.

1348. "Tarzan 1962." *Screen Thrills Illustrated*. No. 3, 1963, pp. 19-23.

1349. "The 13 Faces of Tarzan." *Screen Thrills Illustrated*. No. 1, 1962, pp. 4-9.

1350. Tiefenbacher, Mike. "Dell/Gold Key Movie Adaptations." *Comics Buyer's Guide*. August 16, 1991, pp. 28, 30, 32, 74.

1351. Traini, Rinaldo and Sergio Trinchero. "L'America Ride (Amaro) di 007." *Il Travaso* (Milan). May 22, 1965.

1352. Wagenknecht, Edward. *The Movies in the Age of Innocence*. Norman, Oklahoma: University of Oklahoma Press, 1962. 280 pp.

1353. Wagner, Charles A. "1954's TV Adventures of Superman: Episode #56." *Comics Buyer's Guide*. March 18, 1988, p. 30.

1354. Wagner, Charles A. "TV's 1953 Adventures of Superman: Epsidode #70 'Topsy Turvy.'" *Comics Buyer's Guide*. October 13, 1989, pp. 65-66.

1355. Walker, Mort. "Beetle Bailey—The All-American Musical." *Cartoonist PROfiles*. June 1988, pp. 15-17.

1356. "William Hopalong Cassidy Boyd." *Screen Thrills Illustrated*. No. 5, 1963, pp. 35-37.

1357. Witty, Paul A. "Comics and Television: Opportunity or Threat?." *Today's Health*. October 1952, pp. 18-19, 53.

1358. "Wo Helden Noch Helden Sind. 'Superman' und 'Phantom': Comic-Strips Beeinflussen Italienische Filme." *Die Welt* (Hamburg). July 17, 1965.

1359. "X-Men on TV." *Comics Interview*. No. 58, 1988, pp. 5-7, 9-11, 13-15, 17.

1360. York, Cal. "Batman, Unmasked." *Photoplay*. April 1966.

1361. Zanotto, Piero. "Mandrake in Film." *Il Gazzettino* (Venice). April 21, 1965.

PROFESSIONS

1362. Bainbridge, John. "Significant Sig and the Funnies." *New Yorker*. January 8, 1944, pp. 25-32.

1363. "Business Takes Comics Seriously." *Business Weekly*. October 9, 1948, p. 56.

1364. Carter, Henry. "Chemistry in the Comics." *Journal of Chemical Education*. December 1988, January 1989.

1365. Clarke, Gerald. "The Comics on the Couch." *Time*. December 13, 1971, pp. 70-71.

1366. "Flying Made Easy." *Newsletter*. May 8, 1944.

1367. Hochstein, Rollie. "Her Boss Is in the Funny Papers." *Today's Secretary*. October 1955.

1368. "Medicine." *Newsweek*. November 27, 1950, p. 76.

1369. "Mental Hygiene Takes to the Comics." *American Journal of Public Health*. January 1951, p. 102.

1370. Musial, Joseph W. "Comic Books and Public Relations." *Public Relations Journal*. November 1951.

1371. Scharff, Monroe B. "American Newspaper Comics: Even the Funnies Have Serious Public Relations." *Public Relations Journal*. May 1964.

1372. Schmidt, Carl F. "An Ad Exec Reins It Up the Flagpole." *Newsletter* (Newspaper Comics Council, New York). 1965.

VIOLENCE CONTROVERSY

1373. "About the Horror Comics." *New York Herald Tribune*. September 27, 1954.

1374. Anttonen, E.J. "On Behalf of Dragons: Need To Combat the Comics." *Wilson Library Bulletin*. March 1941, pp. 567, 595.

1375. "Are Comics Horrible?" *Newsweek*. May 3, 1954, p. 60.

1376. Arnold, Arnold. *Violence and Your Child*. New York: Award Books, 1969.

1377. Aronson, J. "What's Funny About Funnies?" *Scholastic*. March 26, 1938, pp. 18E-19E.

1378. "Back to the Crypt." *Speakeasy*. February 1990, p. 16.

1379. Baer, M.F. "Fight on Bad Comic Books." *Personnel and Guidance Journal*. December 1954, p. 192.

1380. "Ban of the Week." *Time*. November 21, 1938, p. 52.

1381. Barclay, D. "That Comic Book Question." *New York Times Magazine*. March 20, 1955, p. 48.

1382. Beck, C.C. "Sex and Violence in Comics." *Comics Journal*. September 1987, p. 128.

1383. Benson, John. "The Transcripts: 1972 EC Convention, the Horror Panel." *Squa Tront*. No. 8, 1978.

1384. Berenberg, Samuel R. "Horrors a Dime Can Buy." *American Home*. June 1949, pp. 56-57, 131.

1385. "The Boy Who Read Horror Comics." *Spectator* (New York). March 11, 1955, p. 304.

1386. Brady, M.E. "Comics, To Read or Not To Read." *Wilson Library Bulletin*. May 1950, pp. 662-667.

1387. Brothers, Joyce. "Violence in Comics." *Cartoonist PROfiles*. 1:1 (1969), pp. 50-52.

1388. Brown, J.M. and Al Capp. "Case Against and for the Comics." *Saturday Review of Literature*. March 20, 1948, pp. 31-33.

1389. Caplin, E.A. "Horrors a Dime Can Buy." *American Home*. November 1949, p. 26.

1390. Carnell, R. "Clean Up the Comic Book Badlands, Now." *Parent's Magazine*. December 1977, pp. 8 +.

1391. Cary, J. "Horror Comics." *Spectator*. February 18, 1955, p. 177.

1392. "Case Against and For Comic Books." *Unesco Courier*. February 1949, p. 12.

1393. "The Challenge of Comic Books." *School and Society*. April 5, 1952, p. 216.

1394. Chaykin, Howard, Gary Groth, Gil Kane, and Walt Simonson. "Debate: Values in Comics." *Comics Journal*. June 1985, pp. 73-81.

1395. "Child's Garden of Reverses." *Time*. March 3, 1958, p. 58.

1396. Collings, James L. "Al and Mel Convinced a Skeptical Editor." *Editor and Publisher*. December 3, 1955, p. 62.

1397. "Comic Battlefront." *Time*. March 2, 1962, pp. 39-40.

1398. "Comic Book Cease-Fire?" *America*. March 5, 1955, p. 580.

1399. "Comics Deride Crime." *New York Times*. November 22, 1957.

1400. "The Comics Discussion, Michigan Record." *Albion*. January 13, 1951, p. 2.

1401. "Crime and Comics." *Newsweek*. June 21, 1954, p. 1.

1402. "Crime and Punishment." *Time*. January 4, 1960, pp. 43-44.

1403. Dale, R. "Comics for Adults." *New Republic*. December 7, 1953, p. 21.

1404. "Das Problem der Comics in den USA." *Welt und Wort*. 11, 1955, pp. 382-383.

1405. "Das Problem der Comics in den Vereinigten Staaten." *Jugendliteratur* (Munich). 1, 1956, pp. 42-44.

1406. "Deathless Dear." *Time*. October 19, 1942, p. 94.

1407. Deland, Paul S. "Battling the Crime Comic To Protect Youth." *Federal Probation* (New York). 19 (1955), pp. 26-30.

1408. "Depravity for Children: 10 Cents a Copy!" Pamphlet from *Hartford Courant*. In Records of the Subcommittee on Juvenile Delinquency, Box 167, National Archives.

1409. "Dior (Horror) Look." *Time*. January 10, 1955, p. 38.

1410. Edelstein, Alex S. and Jerome L. Nelson. "Violence in the Comic Cartoon." *Journalism Quarterly*. Summer 1969, pp. 355-358.

1411. Emery, James N. "Those Vicious (?) Comics." *Teacher's Digest*. September 1944, pp. 32-34.

1412. "Fighting Gunfire with Fire." *Newsweek*. December 20, 1948, p. 54.

1413. Foster, F. Marie. "Books of Fun and Adventure As Substitutes for Comics." *Books Against Comics, Bulletin of the Association for Arts in Childhood* (New York). 1942, pp. 15-16.

1414. Frakes, Margaret. "Comics Are No Longer Comic." *Christian Century*. November 4, 1942, p. 1349.

1415. "The Friendly Home-Wrecker." *Time*. February 16, 1953, p. 84.

1416. "Full Report ASNE Comics Panel Discussion. What About Your Comics?" *Bulletin of the Newspaper Comics Council*. September 1955, pp. 6-11.

1417. Gaines, M.C. "Good Triumphs Over Evil—More About the Comics." *Print*. Autumn 1942, pp. 1-8.

1418. Gardiner, H.C. "Comic Books: Cultural Threat?" *America*. June 19, 1954, pp. 319-321.

1419. Gardiner, H.C. "Comic Books: Moral Threat?" *America*. June 26, 1954, pp. 340-342.

1420. Giammanco, Roberto. "Alcuni Osservazioni sui Comics Nella Società Americana." *Quaderni di Communicazioni di Massa* (Rome). No. 1, 1965, pp. 52-58.

1421. Gleason, L. "In Defense of Comic Books." *Today's Health*. September 1952, pp. 40-41 +.

1422. "Good and Bad Comics." *Scholastic*. January 4, 1950, p. 12.

1423. Graalfs, Marilyn. "Violence in the Comic Books." In *Violence and the Mass Media*, edited by Otto N. Larsen, pp. 95 +. New York: Harper and Row, 1968.

1424. Harker, Jean Gray. "Youth's Librarians Can Defeat Comics." *Library Journal*. December 1, 1948, pp. 1705-1707.

1425. Haviland, Virginia. "Das Problem der Comics in den USA." *Jugendliteratur* (Munich). 1, 1956, pp. 42-44; *Welt und Wort*. 11 (1955), pp. 382-383.

1426. Hickey, M. "Mothers Enforce Cleanup of Comics, North Platte, Neb." *Ladies' Home Journal*. January 1957, pp. 19-20 +.

1427. "Horror Comics." *Spectator* (New York). February 25, 1955, pp. 208, 220.

1428. "Horror Comics." *Time*. May 3, 1954, p. 78; May 16, 1954, p. 50; Reply, C.K. Whitehill, May 24, 1954, p. 10.

1429. "Horror Comics for the Lords." *Economist*. February 19, 1955, p. 515.

1430. "Horror on the Newsstands." *Time*. September 27, 1954, p. 77.

1431. Hoult, T. and L. Hoult. "Are Comic Books a Menace?" *Today's Health*. June 1950, pp. 20-21 +.

1432. "How About the Comics? Town Meeting Tackles the Comics." *Newsweek*. March 15, 1948, p. 56.

1433. "How Much Gore?" *Newsweek*. February 13, 1956, p. 62.

1434. Hutchinson, Bruce D. "Comic Strip Violence, 1911-66." *Journalism Quarterly*. Summer 1969, pp. 358-362.

1435. "In Defense of Comics." *Newsweek*. September 27, 1954, p. 30.

1436. Inglis, R.A. "Comics Book Problem." *American Mercury*. August 1955, pp. 117-121.

1437. Johnson, Ruth I. *The Truth About Comic Books*. Lincoln, Nebraska: Back to the Bible Publishers, 195?.

1438. Johnston, W. "Curing the Comic Supplement." *Good Housekeeping*. July 1910, p. 81.

1439. Jones, Adam. "Men on the Margin." *Content*. August 1992, pp. 7-11, 14-16.

1440. Kihss, Peter. "No Harm in Horror, Comics Issuer Says." *New York Times*. April 22, 1954, p. 1.

1441. Kunitz, S.J. "Comic Menace." *Wilson Library Bulletin*. June 1941, pp. 846-847.

1442. Lardner, J. "How To Lick Crime." *Newsweek*. March 7, 1955, p. 58.

1443. Leaf, M. "Lollipops or Dynamite?" *Christian Science Monitor Magazine*. November 13, 1948, p. 4.

1444. "Librarian Named on Comics Advisory Committee." *Library Journal*. January 1, 1949, p. 37.

1445. Linton, C.D. "Tragic Comics." *Madison Quarterly*. January 1946, pp. 1-6.

1446. Littledale, C.S. "What To Do About the Comics." *Parent's Magazine*. March 1941, pp. 27-67.

1447. Long, Bruce and Bill Kropfhauser. "700 Club Attacks Comics." *Comics Buyer's Guide*. October 19, 1984, p. 1.

1448. Lynn, Gabriel. "The Case Against the Comics." *Timeless Topix* (St. Paul). 1943.

1449. McGuire, Dave. "Another View of Comic Book Control." *American City*. January 1949, p. 101.

1450. Machen, J.F. "De-composing the Classics: The Case Against the Comic Books." *Alabama School Journal*. March 1945, pp. 9-10.

1451. Melcher, F.G. "Comics Under Fire." *Publisher's Weekly*. December 18, 1948, p. 2413.

1452. Mercer, Marilyn. "The Only Read Middle-Class Crimefighter." *New York Sunday Herald Tribune Magazine*. January 9, 1966, p. 8.

1453. Mitchell, Steven. "Evil Harvest: Investigating the Comic Book, 1948-1955." Master's thesis, Arkansas State University, 1982.

1454. Mitchell, Steven. "The Red-Hot Thrill: The Comic-Book Crisis of 1948." *Comics Buyer's Guide*. Part I, June 21, 1985, pp. 26+; Part II, June 28, 1985, p. 32+.

1455. Mooney, Linda A. and Carla Marie Fewell. "Crime in One Long-Lived Comic Strip: An Evaluation of Chester Gould's 'Dick Tracy.'" *American Journal of Economics and Sociology*. January 1989, pp. 89-100.

1456. "Mothers Enforce Cleanup of Comics." *Ladies' Home Journal*. January 1957, pp. 19-20.

1457. Motter, A.M. "How To Improve the Comics." *Christian Century*. October 12, 1949, pp. 1199-2000.

1458. "Much Gore?" *Newsweek*. February 13, 1956, p. 62.

1459. Mühlen, Norbert. "Comic-Books als Sorgenkinder, ein Brief aus Amerika." *Der Monat* (Berlin). 1:7 (1949), pp. 86-89.

1460. Mühlen, Norbert. "Comic Books and Other Horrors: Prep School for Totalitarian Society?" *Commentary*. January 1949, pp. 80-87; March 1949, pp. 293-295.

1461. Murphy, T.E. "Face of Violence." *Reader's Digest*. November 1954, pp. 54-56.

1462. Neal, Jim. "Comic Books Take on Street Realism, Violence." *Comics Buyer's Guide*. April 7, 1993, p. 30.

1463. "No More Werewolves." *Newsweek*. November 8, 1954, p. 55. "Reply," by C.E. Jackson, jr., Novebmer 22, 1954, p. 6 +.

1464. "Not So Funny." *Time*. October 4, 1948, p. 46.

1465. O'Brien, Dan. "And the Chairman Has the Final Word." *Newsletter*. 1965.

1466. "On Behalf of Dragons: Need To Combat the Comics." *Wilson Library Bulletin*. March 1941.

1467. "1848320 of Them." *Time*. July 3, 1939, p. 30.

1468. Ong, Walter J. "The Comics and the Super State: Glimpses Down the Back Alleys of the Mind." *Arizona Quarterly*. Autumn 1945.

1469. "Opposition to the Comics: Report Prepared for U.S. Conference of Mayors." *School Review*. March 1949, pp. 133-134.

1470. "Passing the Buck." *Time*. June 30, 1958, p. 42.

1471. Pierallini, Giulio. "L'Odisea Sadomasochista da Ercole a James Bond." *Il Lavoro* (Genoa). May 5, 1966, p. 3.

1472. "Puddles of Blood." *Time*. March 29, 1948, pp. 66 +. Also in *Etude*. October 1948, p. 594.

1473. "Real Danger of Some Comics." *Science Digest*. April 1948, p. 29.

1474. Rea, Steven. "Dick Tracy, Copycat Crimestopper." *Philadelphia Inquirer*. May 22, 1990, pp. C-1, C-4.

1475. Ryan, J.K. "Are the Comics Moral?" *Forum*. May 1936, pp. 301-304.

1476. Saltus, Elinor C. "The Comics Aren't Good Enough." *Wilson Library Bulletin*. January 1952, pp. 382-383.

1477. Sandburg, Carl. "Cartoons? Yes." *The Cartoonist*. Summer 1957, pp. 3-4, 27.

1478. "Scary Comics Are Scared." *America*. September 25, 1954, p. 606.

1479. Schultz, H.E. "Comics As Whipping Boy; Summary of Address." *Recreation*. August 1949, p. 239.

1480. Sisk, J.P. "Sound and Fury, Signifying Something; Attempts To Control Comic-Book Publishers." *America*. March 10, 1956, pp. 637-638.

1481. Spock, Benjamin. "Television, Radio, Comics and Movies." *Ladies' Home Journal*. April 1960, pp. 61 +.

1482. Strnad, Jan. "Comic Book Morality: The Impending Crisis." *Comics Scene*. July 1983, pp. 30-31.

1483. Sturges, F.M. "Comics, They Are Called." *Christian Science Monitor Magazine*. August 6, 1949, p. 12.

1484. Swabey, M.C. "The Comics Nonsense." *Journal of Psychology*. September 1958, pp. 819-833.

1485. "Testimony in Comic Printing Case Ends." *Editor and Publisher*. July 29, 1967, p. 48.

1486. Thompson, B.J. "After You Buy the Book." *Catholic World*. December 1946, pp. 248-249.

1487. "To Burn or Not To Burn?" *Senior Scholastic*. February 2, 1949, p. 5.

1488. "Too Harsh in Putting Down Evil: Violence in the Dick Tracy Strip." *Time*. June 28, 1968, p. 42.

1489. Towne, Charles L. "Hartford Is Aroused by Comic Book Expose." *Editor and Publisher*. April 10, 1954, p. 11.

1490. Twomey, John E. "The Anti-Comic Book Crusade." Masters thesis, University of Chicago, 1955.

1491. "Unfinished Comic Crusade." *America*. December 14, 1963, p. 759.

1492. Vlamos, James F. "The Sad Case of the Funnies." *The American Mercury*. April 1941, pp. 411-416.

1493. "What About the Comic Books?" *Christian Century*. March 30, 1955. p. 389; Reply, R. Lee, May 11, 1955, p. 569.

1494. "What Comic Books Pass Muster? Report on the St. Paul and Cincinnati Investigations." *Christian Century*. December 28, 1949, pp. 1540-1541.

1495. "What Is the Solution for Control of the Comics." *Library Journal*. February 1, 1949, p. 180.

1496. "What's Wrong with the Comics?" *Town Meeting*, Bulletin of "Town Meeting of the Air." March 2, 1948, pp. 1-23.

1497. Williams, Gweneira. "They Like It Rough (In Defense of Comics)." *Library Journal*. March 1, 1942, pp. 204-206.

1498. Williams, Gweneira. "Why Not Give Them What They Want." *Publisher's Weekly*. April 18, 1942, pp. 1490-1496.

1499. Winnet, Nochem. "A Judge Looks at... Comics, Movies and Radio." *Parent's Magazine*. October 1949, pp. 39, 70.

1500. Zimmerman, Thomas L. "What To Do About Comics." *Library Journal*. September 15, 1954, p. 1607.

Codes and "Cleanup"

1501. "Anti-Comics Law Proposed in New York, Industry Code Debated." *Publisher's Weekly*. 167:10 (1955), p. 1388.

1502. "Code for Comics." *New Statesman*. January 8, 1955.

1503. "Code for Comics." *Scholastic Life*. November 1948, p. 12.

1504. "Code for Comics." *Time*. November 8, 1954, p. 60.

1505. "Code for the Comics; Comic-Book Publishers' Cleanup Campaign." *Time*. July 12, 1948, p. 62.

1506. "Code Seal of Approval Appears on Comics Books." *Library Journal*. 80:4 (1955).

1507. "Comic Book Clean-Up." *Senior Scholastic.* March 16, 1955, pp. 22-23.

1508. "Comic Book Code." *New York Times.* April 16, 1971, p. 34; June 2, 1971, p. 57.

1509. "Comic-Book Czar and Code." *America.* October 2, 1954, pp. 2-3.

1510. "Comic Book Czar Resigns." *America.* June 23, 1956, pp. 295-296.

1511. "Comic Book Industry Organizes To Enforce Ethical Standards." *Library Journal.* October 15, 1954, p. 1967.

1512. "Comic Book Publishers Promise Reforms." *Christian Century.* November 10, 1954, p. 1357.

1513. "Comic Publishers Organize To Improve Standards." *Publisher's Weekly.* June 14, 1947, p. 2941.

1514. "Comics Book Industry Organizes To Enforce Ethical Standards." *Library Journal.* October 15, 1954, pp. 1967 +.

1515. Comics Magazine Association of America Inc. *Facts About Code Approved Comic Magazines.* New York: 1963. 31 pp.

1516. "Comics Publishers Institute Code, Appoint 'Czar.'" *Publisher's Weekly.* 166:13 (1954), p. 1386.

1517. "Comic Publishers Release Terms of Self-Censoring Code." *Publisher's Weekly,* 166:20 (1954).

1518. "Corrected Comic Code." *New York Times.* February 4, 1971, p. 37.

1519. "'Czar' Says Comic Books Have Been 70% Purged." *New York Herald Tribune.* December 29, 1954.

1520. "Distributors Promise Comic-Book Cleanup." *Los Angeles Times.* November 1954.

1521. *Facts About Code-Approved Comics Magazines.* New York: Comics Magazine Association of America, 1959.

1522. "First 'Seal of Approval' Comics Out This Month." *Publisher's Weekly.* 167:3 (1955), p. 211.

1523. "Horror Comic Code." *The Manchester Guardian.* December 10, 1954.

1524. Murphy, T.E. "Progress in Cleaning up the Comics." *Reader's Digest.* February 1956, pp. 105-108.

1525. "New York Officials Recommend Code for Comics Publishers." *Publisher's Weekly*. February 19, 1949, pp. 977-978.

1526. "Progress in Comic Book Cleanup." *America*. October 30, 1954, p. 114. "Discussion." November 13, 1954, pp. 196, 308; December 11, 1954, p. 56.

1527. "Proposed Ban on Crime Comics." *The Manchester Guardian*. January 1, 1955.

1528. "Publishers of Comics Take on a Czar for the Industry." *Publisher's Weekly*. 166:13 (1954), p. 1389.

1529. "Purified Comics: Association of Comics Magazine Publishers Standards." *Newsweek*. July 12, 1948, p. 56.

1530. Smith, R.E. "Publishers Improve Comic Books." *Library Journal*. November 15, 1948, pp. 1649-1653.

1531. Twomey, John E. "The Citizen's Committee and Comic-Book Control: A Study of Extragovernmental Restraint." *Law and Contemporary Problems*. Durham, North Carolina: West Publishing Co., 1955.

1532. Varah, Chad. "Progress in Cleaning up the Comics." *Reader's Digest*. July 1956, pp. 66-70.

1533. Walker, R.J. "Cleaning Up the Comics." *Hobbies*. February 1955, p. 57.

1534. Weisinger, M. "How They're Cleaning Up the Comic Books." *Better Homes and Gardens*. March 1955, pp. 58-59.

Legislative Actions

1535. "ABPC Memo Urges Veto of Fitzpatrick 'Comics' Bill." *Publisher's Weekly*. 167:16 (1955), p. 1860.

1536. "Comic Book Hearing to Start Tomorrow." *New York Times*. April 20, 1954, p. 32.

1537. "Comics Censorship Bill Passes New York Senate." *Publisher's Weekly*. March 5, 1949, p. 1160.

1538. "Comics Censorship Bills Killed in Two States." *Publisher's Weekly*. April 30, 1949, p. 1805.

1539. "Dewey Vetoes Objectionable Comic Book." *Publisher's Weekly*. April 26, 1952, p. 1766.

1540. Feder, Edward L. *Comic Book Regulation.* Berkeley, California: Bureau of Public Administration, University of California, 1955. 59 pp.

1541. Greenberg, D.S. "Funnies on Capitol Hill." *Science.* March 10, 1967, p. 1222.

1542. Kihss, Peter. "Senator Charges 'Deceit' on Comics." *New York Times.* April 23, 1954, p. 29.

1543. Mitchell, Steve. "Superman in Disguise: The New York State Investigations." *Comics Buyer's Guide.* May 9, 1986, p. 28 +.

1544. "Municipal Control of Comic Books." *American City.* December 1948, p. 153.

1545. New York State Joint Legislative Committee. *Report of the Committee To Study the Publication of Comics* (Legislative Document No. 37 of 1955). Albany, New York: Williams Press, 1955.

1546. New York State. Legislature. Joint Legislative Committee To Study the Publication of Comics. *Report.* Albany: Williams Press, 1951. 82 pp.

1547. Nyberg, Amy K. "Ignoring the Evidence: The Senate Investigation of Comic Books in the 1950s." Paper presented at American Journalism Historians Association, Coeur d'Alene, Idaho, October 4-7, 1990.

1548. "Personal and Otherwise; Senate Crime Investigators' Report on Comic Books." *Harper's.* July 1951, pp. 6-8; "Discussion." September 1951, p. 16.

1549. "Senate Sub-Committee Holds Hearing on the Comics." *Publisher's Weekly.* No. 18, 1954, pp. 1903, 1906.

1550. Sheerin, J.B. "Crime Comics Must Go! Investigation by Senate Subcommittee on Juvenile Delinquency." *Catholic World.* June 1954, pp. 161-165.

1551. "State Laws To Censor Comics, Protested by Publishers." *Publisher's Weekly.* March 12, 1949, pp. 1243-1244.

1552. U.S. Conference of Mayors. *Municipal Control of Objectionable Comic Books.* Washington, D.C.: 1949.

1553. U.S. Congress. Senate Committee on the Judiciary. *Juvenile Delinquency: Comic Books, Motion Pictures, Obscene and Pornographic Materials, Television Programs.* Westport, Connecticut: Greenwood Press, 1969.

1554. U.S. Congress. Senate Sub-Committee. *Comic Books and Juvenile Delinquency. Interim Report.* Washington, D.C.: U.S. Government Printing Office, 1955.

1555. U.S. Congress. Senate. "Subcommittee to Investigate Juvenile Delinquency of the Committee on the Judiciary." 83rd Cong., 2nd sess. 1954.

Ratings

1556. "Annual Rating of Comic Magazines." *Parent's Magazine.* August 1955, pp. 48-50; July 1956, pp. 48-49.

1557. Murrell, J.L. "Annual Rating of Comic Magazines." *Parent's Magazine.* November 1952, pp. 48-49 +; October 1953, pp. 54-55 +; August 1954, pp. 48-49 +.

1558. Murrell, J.L. "Cincinnati Again Rates the Comics." *Parents' Magazine.* October 1950, pp. 44-45 +.

1559. Murrell, J.L. "Cincinnati Rates the Comic Books." *Parent's Magazine.* February 1950, pp. 38-39 +; *Publisher's Weekly.* March 4, 1950, p. 1204.

1560. Murrell, J.L. "How Good Are the Comic Books?" *Parent's Magazine.* November 1951, pp. 32-33 +.

1561. "The Ratings Debate: Violence and Sex in Comics: How Will Publishers Cope With It?" *Comics Journal.* October 1983, pp. 17-18.

Wertham, Dr. Frederic

1562. Bethke, Marilyn. "Conversation with Dr. Wertham." *Instant Gratification.* No. 1, 1979.

1563. Delaney, Mark. "A New Wertham, A Greater Nightmare." *Comics Journal.* December 1990, pp. 3-6.

1564. "Dell Quits MPA After Wertham's Blast at Comics." *Advertising Age.* November 23, 1953, p. 1.

1565. Denney, Reuel. "The Seduction of the Innocent." *New Republic.* May 3, 1954, p. 18.

1566. Erickson, Peter. "Seduction of the Innocent." *Comics Journal.* December 1989, p. 87.

1567. Gibbs, W. "The Seduction of the Innocent." *The New Yorker.* May 8, 1954, p. 134f.

1568. Harvey, R.C. "Wertham Revisited: Seduction in the Eighties." *Comics Journal.* March 1986, pp. 72-90.

1569. Hewetson, Alan. "Dr. Frederic Wertham—Mennesket bag 50-Ernes Tegneserie-hetz." *Serieskaberen.* March 1990, pp. 51-53.

1570. Hewetson, Alan and Frederic Wertham, M.D. "'Censorship Is Not Answer; It Is Not Even the Question.'" *Comics Journal.* December 1989, pp. 81-84.

1571. Mason, Bill. "The Secret: Gaines, Wertham and 'Seduction of the Ignorant.'" *Comics Journal.* October 1983, pp. 28-29.

1572. Mitchell, Steve. "Slaughter of the Innocents: Comic-Book Controversy Long Before Wertham." *Comics Buyer's Guide.* May 17, 1985, pp. 40, 42, 44, 52, 54, 58, 60, 62, 64.

1573. Moore, W. "The Seduction of the Innocent." *The Nation.* May 15, 1954, pp. 426-427.

1574. Morgan, J.E. "The Seduction of the Innocent." *National Education Association Journal.* November 1954, p. 473.

1575. Overholser, W. "The Seduction of the Innocent." *Saturday Review of Literature.* April 24, 1954, p. 16.

1576. Scholz, Carter. "Seduction of the Ignorant." *Comics Journal.* March 1983, pp. 43-53.

1577. Smith, L.E. "Protest Against Ad for Wertham Book." *Publisher's Weekly.* 165:12 (1954), p. 1399.

1578. Warshow, Robert. "Paul, the Horror Comics and Dr. Wertham." *Commentary.* 17:6 (1954), pp. 596-604.

1579. Warshow, Robert. "Paul, the Horror Comics, and Dr. Wertham." *Squa Tront.* No. 9, 1983, pp. 93-98.

1580. Wertham, Frederic. "Comics, Very Funny!" *Saturday Review of Literature.* May 29, 1948, pp. 6-7, 27-29. Also in *Reader's Digest.* August 1948, pp. 15-18.

1581. Wertham, Frederic. "The Curse of the Comic-Books! The Value Patterns and Effects of Comic Books." *Religious Education.* 49, 1954, pp. 394-406.

1582. Wertham, Frederic. "It's Still Murder." *Saturday Review of Literature.* April 9, 1955, pp. 11-12, 46-48.

1583. Wertham, Frederic. "Les 'Crime-Comic-Books' et la Jeunesse Américaine." *Les Temps Modernes* (Paris). No. 118, 1955.

1584. Wertham, Frederic. "The Psychopathology of Comic Books." *American Journal of Psychotherapy.* July 1948.

1585. Wertham, Frederic. "Reading for the Innocent." *Wilson Library Bulletin.* April 1955, pp. 610-613.

1586. Wertham, Frederic. *The Seduction of the Innocent*. New York: Holt, Rinehart and Winston, 1954.

1587. Wertham, Frederic. *Seduction of the Innocent*. Reviews in *National Education Association Journal*. November 1954, p. 473 (J.E. Morgan); *Nation*. May 15, 1954, p. 426-427 (W. Moore); *New Republic*, May 3, 1954, p. 18 (R. Denney); *New Yorker*, May 8, 1954, pp. 134 + (W. Gibbs); *Saturday Review*, April 24, 1954, p. 16 (W. Overholser).

1588. Wertham, Frederic. "The Seduction of the Innocent." *New Republic*. May 24, 1954, p. 22.

1589. Wertham, Frederic. *A Sign for Cain*. New York: Macmillan, 1966.

1590. Wertham, Frederic. "What Are Comic Books? (A Study for Parents)." *National Parent Teacher Magazine*. March 1949.

1591. Wertham, Frederic. "What Parents Don't Know About Comic Books." *Ladies' Home Journal*. November 1953, pp. 50-53. "Discussion." February 1954, p. 4.

1592. West, Mark I. "Frederic Wertham and His Comic Book Campaign." *Comics Journal*. December 1989, pp. 78-80.

WAR

1593. "Army Says Comics Boost R.O.T.C. Rolls." *New York Herald Tribune*. November 19, 1950, p. 16.

1594. Benson, John. "Is War Hell? The Evolution of an Artist's Viewpoint." *Panels*. Spring 1981, pp. 18-20.

1595. "Comics for Morale." *Business Week*. November 21, 1942, p. 45.

1596. "Comics Help, Army Finds." *New York Sunday News*. November 19, 1950.

1597. "Comics Used in Cold War." *New York Sun*. December 19, 1949.

1598. Coons, Hannibal and J.C. Mattimore. "The Fighting Funnies, Our Comic Strips Have Marched Off to War." *Colliers*. January 29, 1944, p. 34.

1599. Erwin, Ray. "Custer, Indians Fight Again in New Cartoon." *Editor and Publisher*. August 26, 1967, p. 43.

1600. "G.I.s and Miss Lace." *Newsweek*. May 8, 1944, p. 95.

1601. Greim, Martin, Bob Cosgrove, and James Steranko. "The Killer Skies: Fighting the Air War in Films, in Pulps, and in the Comics." *Mediascene*. January-February 1976, pp. 12-19.

1602. Hutchens, John K. "Tracy, Superman, *et al.* Go to War." *New York Times Magazine*. November 21, 1943, pp. 14, 42-43.

1603. Kash, Joanne. "When America Went to War, So Did the Comics!" *Reminisce*. January-February 1992, p. 19.

1604. Kreiner, Rich. "Being All They Can Be." *Comics Journal*. April 1989, pp. 57-61.

1605. "Laughs for a Warring World: U.S. Comics Circle the Globe." *Newsweek*. August 25, 1941, p. 46.

1606. Leab, Daniel J. "Cold War Comics." *Columbia Journalism Review*. Winter 1965, pp. 42-47.

1607. Lovece, Frank. "Darlin' Dick Ayers: War for a Career." *Comics Scene*. September 1983, pp. 48-50, 52.

1608. "Magazines for Soldiers." *Library Journal*. February 15, 1945, pp. 149-150.

1609. Monchak, Stephen J. "Readers Expected To Turn to Comics Humor for War Relief." *Editor and Publisher*. September 30, 1939, pp. 1, 23.

1610. Murray, Will. "The Immortal Fighting American." *Comics Scene*. February 1990, pp. 9-12, 66.

1611. "New Navy Recruiting Formula." *Newsweek*. July 28, 1941, pp. 46-47.

1612. "Pop Goes the War; Vietnam Story." *Newsweek*. September 12, 1966, pp. 66 +.

1613. Rifas, Leonard. "Adventure and Fantasy: The War in Comics." *Reflex*, September/October 1989, p. 11.

1614. Rifas, Leonard. "Comic Book Reflections on the Red Menace." *Comics Journal*. February 1991, pp. 45-47.

1615. "Star Wars in the Comics." *Amazing Heroes*. July 1982, pp. 40-53.

1616. "Tip for Whiskers." *Time*. July 20, 1959, pp. 52 +.

1617. "U.S. Comic Books and Nuclear War." *Itchy Planet*. Spring 1988, pp. 28-32.

1618. "War in the Comics." *Newsweek*. July 13, 1942, pp. 60-61.

1619. "The War Panel." *Squa Tront.* No. 8, 1978, pp. 31-36.

1620. Willson, David A. "The Comic Soldier." *Comics Journal.* July 1990, pp. 114-117.

WOMEN

1621. "Fräulein Stateside." *Newsweek.* March 17, 1952, p. 44.

1622. Goulart, Ron. "Wild Wild Women." *Comics Collector.* No. 51, 1985.

1623. Ironside, Virginia. "Holy Hooded Helpers—A Nostalgic View of Girl's Comics." *Cosmopolitan.* Autumn 1971, pp. 60-61.

1624. "Is There Love for Eros?" *Speakeasy.* November 1990, pp. 32-34.

1625. Jerome, Fiona. "Not in Front of the Children." *Speakeasy.* November 1990, pp. 43-45.

1626. Jerome, Fiona. "Who Are the Lost Girls?" *Speakeasy.* November 1990, pp. 37-39, 41.

1627. Klapper, Zina. "Female Funnies: Id Meets Raised Consciousness." *Mother Jones.* July 1978, p. 5.

1628. Knuttson, Magnus. "Amerikanische Frauen Packen die Comics an. Nachbemerkungen von Dr. Horst Schröder." *Comixene* (Hanover). 6:22 (1979), pp. 41-42.

1629. Lyvely, Chin and Joyce Farmer. "Women's Underground Comix." In *Official Underground and Newave Comix Price Guide*, edited by Jay Kennedy, pp. 28-30. Cambridge, Massachusetts: Boatner Norton Press, 1982.

1630. Macek, Carl. "Good Girl Art—An Introduction." In *Comic Book Price Guide.* 6th Ed. Cleveland, Tennessee: Overstreet, 1976.

1631. Müller-Egert, G. "Keine Fau für Mainzelmänner (Sind Mainzel-Mädchen Unmoralisch?)." *BILD*, March 23, 1968.

1632. "New Woman." *Cartoonist PROfiles.* December 1985, pp. 32-35.

1633. Pini, Wendy. "That Was Then—This Is Now." *Comics Buyer's Guide.* May 14, 1993, p. 32.

1634. Pini, Wendy. "Women, Comics, and Elfquest." *Comics Buyer's Guide.* May 14, 1993, pp. 27-28, 30, 32.

1635. Rodi, Rob. "Girls Just Wanna Survive." *Comics Journal*. April 1987, pp. 35-41.

1636. Segal, Danni. "The Trouble with Girls." *Fantazia*. No. 4, 1990, pp. 26-27.

1637. Shadoian, Jack. "Yuh Got Pecos! Doggone, Belle, Yuh're as Good as Two Men!" *Journal of Popular Culture*. Spring 1979, pp. 721-736.

1638. "Trina Robbins: 'Misty' Cartoonist Finds Girls Do Read Comics, Given a Chance." *Comics Buyer's Guide*. May 16, 1986, p. 32.

Cartoonists

1639. "Alison Marek: Author-Artist of 'Desert Streams' Tells Her Own Story." *Comics Buyer's Guide*. September 15, 1989, pp. 30, 32.

1640. Alley, Patricia W. "Hokinson and Hollander: Female Cartoonists and American Culture." In *Women's Comic Visions*, edited by June Sochen, pp. 115-138. Detroit, Michigan: Wayne State University, 1991.

1641. Bagge, Peter. "Aline Kominsky-Crumb." *Comics Journal*. December 1990, pp. 50-73.

1642. "Betty Swords." *Cartoonist PROfiles*. No. 19, 1973, pp. 36-45.

1643. Boatz, Darrel. "Geraldine Pecht and Gerry Giovinco." *Comics Interview*. No. 51, 1987, pp. 40-51.

1644. Boatz, Darrel. "Linda Stanley." *Comics Interview*. No. 59, 1988, pp. 46-55.

1645. Brandon, Barbara. "Where I'm Coming From." *Cartoonist PROfiles*. December 1992, pp. 10-17. (Barbara Brandon).

1646. Browning, N.L. "First Lady of the Funnies." *Saturday Evening Post*. November 19, 1960, pp. 34-35 +.

1647. Burbey, Mark. "The Fine Art of Comics—Carol Tyler Interview." *Comics Journal*. June 1991, pp. 90-102.

1648. Cantarow, Ellen. "Don't Throw That Old Diaphragm Away!" *Mother Jones*. June/July 1987, pp. 22-26, 43.

1649. Counts, Kyle. "Writer of the Beast." *Comics Scene*. April 1992, p. 53-56, 66. (Linda Woolverton).

1650. "Director: Lou Ann Merkle." *Comics Interview*. No. 53, 1987, pp. 45-57.

1651. Erwin, Ray. "Hilarious Housewife Writes, Draws Panel." *Newsletter*. March 1965, p. 13.

1652. Fox, Jo. "Lise Connell—The Grass Is Greener." *Cartoonist PROfiles*. March 1985, pp. 58-61.

1653. "Gloria Katz." *Comics Interview*. No. 38, 1986, pp. 50-55.

1654. Gregory, Roberta. "Lady Artist Comix." *Dynamite Damsels*. 1976, inside cover.

1655. Hegerfors, Sture. "Inga Barn för Diana Palmer." *Expressen* (Stockholm). October 1, 1966.

1656. "Interview: Gladys Briggs." *The Classics Collector*. February-March 1990, pp. 24-26.

1657. Jankiewicz, Pat. "Yvonne Craig." *Comics Interview*. No. 77, 1989, pp. 48-53.

1658. Jesuele, Kim. "Sherrie Shepherd's Francie." *Cartoonist PROfiles*. September 1991, pp. 18-25.

1659. "Jo Duffy." *Comics Interview*. September 1985, pp. 43-56.

1660. Kraft, David A. "Colorist: Adrienne Roy." *Comics Interview*. March 1984, pp. 74-77.

1661. Kraft, David A. "The Foom Interview." *Foom*. December 1976, pp. 8-14. (Marie Severin).

1662. Lim, C.T. "Excellent Adventures." *Big O Magazine*. May 1993, pp. 68-69. (Nina Paley).

1663. "Louise Simonson." *Comics Interview*. June 1984, pp. 61-73.

1664. Maier, Jürgen. "Good Girl Art und Gewalt der Fiction House-Comics." *Comixene*. 8:34 (1981), pp. 9-11.

1665. "Ms. Liz by Barbara Slate." *Cartoonist PROfiles*. June 1983, pp. 26-32.

1666. "Nicola Cuti, Charlton Publications Assistant Comics Editor." *Cartoonist PROfiles*. No. 20, 1973, pp. 4-12.

1667. Oliver, Jane J. "Special SPCE Spotlight on.... Jane Oliver." *Small Press Comics Explosion*. July 1986, pp. 14-15.

1668. Rifas, Leonard. "Cat Yronwode." *Comics Interview*. May 1985, pp. 47-63.

1669. Ringgenberg, Steve. "Sandy Plunkett." *Comics Interview.* November 1984, pp. 44-51.

1670. Robbins, Trina. "Hidden Treasure: Jackie Ormes Brought to Light." *Comics Journal.* July 1999, pp. 47-50.

1671. Robbins, Trina. "Women and the Comics." *Cartoonist PROfiles.* December 1983, pp. 40-45.

1672. Robbins, Trina. "Women Cartoonists of the Lost Planet (and Rangers, and Fight, and Jumbo...)." *Comics Buyer's Guide.* December 9, 1983, p. 56.

1673. Robbins, Trina and Catherine Yronwode. *Women and the Comics.* Guerneville, California: Eclipse Books, 1985. 127 pp.

1674. "Ruth Carroll." *Dibujantes* (Buenos Aires). No. 18, 1956, p. 25.

1675. Sanderson, Peter. "Diana Schutz and Bob Schreck." *Comics Interview.* No. 51, 1987, pp. 20-39.

1676. Saner-Lamken, Brian. "Jill Thompson: An Interview Calculated To Make Your Head Spin." *Comics Buyer's Guide.* June 25, 1993, pp. 26-28, 32, 34.

1677. Snead, Elizabeth. "'Bad Girl' Artists Break into Comics." *USA Today.* September 12, 1992, p. D-1.

1678. "Third Time the Charm for Elvira, Mistress of the Dark." *Comics Buyer's Guide.* March 19, 1993, pp. 34, 36.

1679. Thompson, Maggie. "Women in Comics." *Comics Collector.* No. 51 (1985).

1680. "Vivian Greene." *Cartoonist PROfiles.* March 1979, pp. 42-47.

1681. "Writer/Editor: Joyce Brabner." *Comics Interview.* No. 53, 1987, pp. 34-43.

1682. Zimmerman, D. Jon. "Power Pack: June Brigman." *Comics Interview.* March 1984, pp. 7-12.

Barry, Lynda

1683. Barry, Lynda. *Big Ideas.* Seattle, Washington: Real Comet Press, 1983. 126 pp.

1684. Barry, Lynda. *Everything in the World.* New York: Harper and Row, 1986. 95 pp.

1685. Barry, Lynda. *Girls and Boys.* Seattle, Washington: Real Comet Press, 1981. 93 pp.

1686. "Lynda Barry: Fascination with Adolescence." *Inquirer Magazine* (Philadelphia). January 6, 1991, p. 6.

1687. Powers, Thom. "Lynda Barry." *Comics Journal.* November 1989, pp. 60-75.

1688. Sullivan, Darcy. "Kids at the Abyss: Lynda Barry's *Come Over, Come Over.*" *Comics Journal.* February 1991, pp. 43-45.

Berger, Karen

1689. D'Angelo, Carr. "Karen Berger's Magic Kingdom." *Comics Scene.* No. 10, 1989, p. 57.

1690. "Karen Berger." *Comics Interview.* June 1985, pp. 40-61.

Brandon, Barbara

1691. Bruning, Fred. "Born to the Business." *New York Newsday.* May 4, 1993, p. 57.

1692. Robson-Scott, Markie. "New Strip on the Block." *The Jester.* April 1992, p. 12. Reprinted from *Guardian* (London). February 12, 1992.

Buell, Marjorie H.

1693. Collins, Glenn. "Marjorie Buell, 88, Pioneer Cartoonist of 'Little Lulu' Strip." *New York Times.* June 3, 1993. Also in *Newsweek.* June 14, 1993; *Cleveland Plain Dealer.* June 1, 1993.

1694. "Marjorie Henderson Buell Dies; Created 'Little Lulu.'" *Comics Buyer's Guide.* June 25, 1993, p. 6.

1695. "Marjorie Henderson Buell (1904-1993)." *Comics Journal.* July 1993, pp. 14-15.

1696. Tenan, Brad. "Marjorie Henderson Buell: A Loving Tribute." *Hollywood Eclectern.* June 1993, pp. 1-4.

Flenniken, Shary

1697. Boyd, Robert and Frank M. Young. "Shary Flenniken." *Comics Journal.* November 1991, pp. 54-78, 81-83.

1698. Hoffman, Pete. "A Phone Call from Shary." *Cartoonist PROfiles.* June 1990, pp. 36-42.

1699. Ringgenberg, S.C. "Of Mice and Ms: A Sip of Vintage Shary." *Comics Journal.* November 1991, pp. 84-85.

1700. "Sketchbook: Shary Flenniken." *Comics Journal*. October 1991, pp. 101-105.

Gregory, Roberta

1701. Cohen, Tyler. "Go Ahead and Bitch. A Feminist Perspective on Roberta Gregory's *Naughty Bits*." *Comics Journal*. April 1993, pp. 11-13.

1702. Ng, Sam. "Real Naughty: Roberta Gregory and Life in the Underground." *Big O Magazine*. April 1993, p. 72.

Guisewite, Cathy

1703. "Cathy by Cathy Guisewite." *Cartoonist PROfiles*. June 1977, pp. 34-36.

1704. "*Cathy* Comic Strip Dropped for 'Political Espousal.'" *Comics Journal*. January 1989, pp. 26-27.

1705. Guisewite, Cathy. *Another Saturday Night of Wild and Reckless Abandon*. Kansas City, Missouri: Andrews, McMeel and Parker, 1982. 128 pp.

1706. Guisewite, Cathy. *A Hand To Hold, an Opinion To Reject*. Kansas City, Missouri: Andrews, McMeel and Parker, 1987. 125 pp.

1707. Guisewite, Cathy. *The Cathy Chronicles*. Kansas City, Missouri: Sheed, Andrews, McMeel, 1978.

1708. Guisewite, Cathy. *Men Should Come with Instruction Booklets*. Kansas City, Missouri: Andrews, McMeel and Parker, 1984. 126 pp.

1709. Guisewite, Cathy. *A Mouthful of Breath Mints and No One To Kiss*. Kansas City, Missouri: Andrews, McMeel and Parker, 1983. 127 pp.

1710. Guisewite, Cathy. *Thin Thighs in Thirty Years*. Kansas City, Missouri: Andrews, McMeel and Parker, 1986. 125 pp.

1711. Guisewite, Cathy. *Wake Me Up When I'm a Size 5*. Kansas City, Missouri: Andrews, McMeel and Parker, 1985. 126 pp.

1712. Guisewite, Cathy. *What Do You Mean, I Still Don't Have Equal Rights?* Kansas City, Missouri: Andrews and McMeel, 1980.

1713. Harayda, J. "Talking with... Cathy Guisewite." *Glamour*. July 1978, pp. 84 +.

1714. Koris, S. "Cartoons Are No Laughing Matter for Cathy Guisewite." *People's Weekly*. July 5, 1982, pp. 90 +.

1715. Millner, C. "How Cartoonist Cathy Guisewite Makes Us Laugh at Life's Little Frustrations." *Seventeen*. May 1983, pp. 42-43.

1716. "Numerous Newspapers Drop or Move 'Cathy' Strips." *Editor and Publisher*. November 12, 1988, p. 41.

1717. Peter, L.J. "Sketches of Cartoon Cathy's Creator." *Human Behavior*. January 1979, pp. 68-69.

1718. Sperling, Dan. "Cathy Guisewite: She Cashes in on Her Insecurities—Comically." *USA Today*. October 30, 1986, p. 4D.

1719. Youngblood, Amy. "Cathy." *The Funnie's Paper*. October 1983, pp. 6-7.

Hollander, Nicole

1720. Eberle, Nance. "A Review of *I'm in Training To Be Tall and Blonde*." *Chicago*. June 1979, pp. 206 +.

1721. Gran, Martin. "Sylvia, by Nicole Hollander." *Cartoonist PROfiles*. March 1987, pp. 58-63.

1722. Hollander, Nicole. *Hi, This Is Sylvia*. New York: St. Martin's Press, 1983. 127 pp.

1723. Hollander, Nicole. *Ma, Can I Be a Feminist and Still Like Men?* New York: St. Martin's Press, 1980. 127 pp.

1724. Hollander, Nicole. *Mercy, It's the Revolution and I'm in My Bathrobe*. New York: St. Martin's Press, 1982. 127 pp.

1725. Hollander, Nicole. *My Weight Is Always Perfect for My Height, Which Varies*. New York: St. Martin's Press, 1982. 128 pp.

1726. Hollander, Nicole. *Never Tell Your Mother This Dream*. New York: St. Martin's Press, 1985. 125 pp.

1727. Hollander, Nicole. *Okay! Thinner Thighs for Everyone*. New York: St. Martin's Press, 1984. 128 pp.

1728. Hollander, Nicole. *Sylvia on Sundays*. New York: St. Martin's Press, 1983. 128 pp.

1729. Hollander, Nicole. *That Woman Must Be on Drugs*. New York: St. Martin's Press, 1981.

1730. Hollander, Nicole. *The Whole Enchilada, a Spicy Collection of Sylvia's Best*. New York: St. Martin's Press, 1986. 224 pp.

1731. Upton, Kim. "The Wit Behind the Wisdom of 'Sylvia.'" *The Funnie's Paper*. March 1984, pp. 8-10.

Kahn, Jenette

1732. Burton, Richard. "Interview." *Comic Reader*. No. 147 (Super Summer 1977), pp. 20-22, 27-28.

1733. Timmons, Stan. "Jenette Kahn." *Comics Journal*. December 1977, p. 54.

Kalish, Carol

1734. "Carol Kalish." *Comics Interview*. December 1984, pp. 57-73.

1735. "Carol Kalish, Marvel Executive, Dies Suddenly." *Comics Journal*. October 1991, p. 16.

1736. Groth, Gary. "Lies We Cherish: The Canonization of Carol Kalish." *Comics Journal*. November 1991, pp. 3-4.

Messick, Dale

1737. "Brenda Starr: A Pretty Nose for News." *The World of Comic Art*. Fall 1966, pp. 20-23.

1738. "Brenda Starr by Dale Messick." *Cartoonist PROfiles*. December 1972, pp. 4-11.

1739. "Brenda Starr, Reporter by Dale Messick." *Cartoonist PROfiles*. No. 15, 1972, p. 51.

1740. Browning, Norma L. "Brenda Starr: The Comics' Best-Dressed Woman." *Chicago Sunday Times*. October 25, 1954, p. 20.

1741. Johnson, F. "Brenda Starr's Toughest Assignment." *Ms*. December 1975, pp. 33-34 +.

1742. Messick, Dale. *Brenda Starr, Reporter*. Comic-Strip Preserves. 2 Vols. El Cajon, California: Blackthorne, 1986.

1743. Yakir, Dan. "Brenda Starr Reporter." *Comics Scene*. December 1990, pp. 61-64.

Nocenti, Ann

1744. "Ann Nocenti—The Guilty and the Innocent." *Speakeasy*. February 1989, p. 36.

1745. O'Neill, Patrick D. "Ann Nocenti." *Comics Interview*. No. 39, 1986, pp. 58-59.

Pini, Wendy

1746. Pini, Wendy. "Women, Comics, and Elfquest." *Comics Collector*. Fall 1985, pp. 17-20, 22-24.

1747. Wooley, John. "An Interview with Wendy Pini." *Comics Collector*. Fall 1985, pp. 24-27.

Robbins, Trina

1748. Lanyi, Ronald L. "Trina, Queen of the Underground Cartoonists: An Interview." *Journal of Popular Culture*. Spring 1979, pp. 737-754.

1749. "Neo-Nazi Threatens Trina Robbins." *Comics Journal*. October 1990, p. 8.

1750. Sherman, Bill. "Trina in the Mainstream." *Comics Journal*. September 1986, pp. 54-56.

1751. Sherman, Bill. "Trina Robbins." *Comics Journal*. July 1985, pp. 135-139.

1752. Sherman, Bill. "The Trina Robbins Interview." *Comics Journal*. Winter 1980, pp. 46-58.

1753. Sweeney, Bruce. "Meet Trina Robbins." *Comics Scene*. March 1983, pp. 48-52, 64.

1754. "Trina and the Underground." *Baycon* III Program Book. 1977, p. 31.

Seda, Dori

1755. Levin, Bob and Adele. "'I Don't Fuck My Dog.'" *Comics Journal*. November 1992, pp. 105-109.

1756. Sternbergh, Leslie. "Dori Seda... 'There's a Way.'" *Comics Journal*. November 1992, pp. 94-104.

1757. Sternbergh, Leslie. "...There's a Way': Dori Seda: An Appreciation." *Gauntlet*. No. 3, 1992, pp. 169-179.

Steinberg, Flo

1758. Salicrup, Jim. "Fabulous Flo Steinberg." *Comics Interview*. November 1984, pp. 59-75.

1759. "Gal Friday: Flo Steinberg." *Comics Interview*. November 1984, pp. 59-76.

Portrayals

1760. Brons, Ruth. "Ehefrauen in Funnies. Gedanken Einer Frau zum Frauenbild in Blondie, Hägar und Willi Wacker." *Comixene* (Hanover). 6:22 (1979), pp. 23-24.

1761. Brown, Judy. "Women-Bashing Comics: The Joke's on Us." *Mademoiselle*. 94: 4 (1988), p. 134.

1762. Carrillo, L. and T.A. Lyson. "The Fotonovela As a Cultural Bridge for Hispanic Women in the United States." *Journal of Popular Culture*. Winter 1983, pp. 59-64.

1763. Eisner, Will. "Women As They Are Portrayed in Comics." *Comics Collector*. Spring 1985, p. 32.

1764. "Funny Panel Guides Girl Characters." *Newsletter*. March 1965, p. 13.

1765. Grauerholz, Elizabeth, Larry E. Williams, and Robert E. Clark. "Women in Comic Strips: What's So Funny?" *Free Inquiry in Creative Sociology*. May 1982, pp. 108-111, 117.

1766. Howell, Richard. "Women in Terry and the Pirates: Part II." *Comics Feature*. November 1980, pp. 72-76; Part III, January 1981, pp. 71-74.

1767. Kalish, Carol B. "Why Women Don't Read Comics." *LOC*. January 1980, pp. 31-35.

1768. Kasserjian, Harold H. "Males and Females in the Funnies: A Content Analysis." In *Personal Values and Consumer Psychology*, edited by Robert E. Pitts, jr. and Arch G. Woodside, pp. 87-109. Lexington, Massachusetts: Lexington Books, 1984.

1769. "Lady Jane." *Time*. October 18, 1943, p. 38.

1770. Macek, Carl. "Women in Comics." In *The Comic Book Price Guide 1978-79*, edited by R.M. Overstreet, pp. A-54-A-75. Cleveland, Tennessee: Overstreet, 1978.

1771. O'Connell, Margaret. "How Superman Treats His Women." *Comics Feature*. November 1980, pp. 65-71; Part II, January 1981, pp. 58-66.

1772. Olson, Valerie V. "Garry Trudeau's Treatment of Women's Liberation in Doonesbury." Master's thesis, Michigan State University, 1979. 101 pp.

1773. Potkay, Catherine E., Charles R. Potkay, G.J. Boynton, and J.A. Klingbeil. "Perceptions of Male and Female Comic Strip Characters Using the Adjective Generation Technique (AGT)." *Sex Roles*. 8 (1982), pp. 185-200.

1774. Potkay, Charles R. and Catherine E. Potkay. "Perceptions of Female and Male Comic Strip Characters II: Favorability and Identification Are Different Dimensions." *Sex Roles*. 10:1/2 (1984), pp. 119-128.

1775. Rodi, Rob. "The Big Ladies Are So Funny." *Comics Journal*. May 1989, pp. 49-54.

1776. Saenger, Gerhart. "Male and Female Relations in the American Comic Strip." *Public Opinion Quarterly*. Summer 1955, pp. 195-205.

1777. Sanderson, Peter. "Amazons, Anarchy, and Androids." *Amazing Heroes*. October 15, 1984, pp. 27-37.

1778. Streicher, Helen W. "The Girls in the Cartoons." *Journal of Communication*. Spring 1974, pp. 125-129.

1779. Williams, Jeanne P. "All's Fair in Love and Journalism: Female Rivalry in *Superman*." *Journal of Popular Culture*. Fall 1990, pp. 103-112.

1780. Williams, Jeanne P. "The Evolution of Social Norms and the Life of Lois Lane: A Rhetorical Analysis of Popular Culture." Ph.D. dissertation, Ohio State University, 1986.

Sexism, Sex Role

1781. Blakely, M.K. "True or False: All Men Like To Girl-Watch, and Girls Don't Mind It." *Vogue*. January 1982, pp. 56-58 +.

1782. Brabant, Sarah. "Sex Role Stereotyping in the Sunday Comics." *Sex Roles*. 2:4 (1976), p. 331-337.

1783. Brabant, Sarah and Linda Mooney. "Sex Role Stereotyping in the Sunday Comics: Ten Years Later." *Sex Roles*. February 1986, pp. 141-148.

1784. Bryant, Anne. "Saturday Morning TV: No Girls Allowed." *Extra*. September-October 1991, p. 10.

1785. Cech, John. "Comic Books Foster Female Stereotypes." *USA Today Magazine*. December 1986, p. 15.

1786. Chavez, Deborah. "Perpetuation of Gender Inequality: A Content Analysis of Comic Strips." *Sex Roles*. July 1985, pp. 93-102.

1787. Chmaj, Betty E. "Fantasizing Women's Lib—Stereotypes of Women in Comic Books." In *Image, Myth and Beyond*, edited by Betty E. Chmaj, pp. 311-312. Pittsburgh, Pennsylvania: KNOW, Inc., 1972.

1788. Clark, Dennis. "Rap Box: Is Sexploitation Running Rampant in Small Press Comics?" *The Comicist*. November 1990, pp. 14-15.

1789. Crumb, Robert. "And Now, A Word to You Feminist Women." *Big Ass Comix*. No. 1.

1790. Glasberg, Ronald. "The Archie Code: A Study in Sexual Stereotyping As Reflective of a Basic Dilemma in American Society." *Journal of Popular Culture*. Fall 1992, pp. 25-32.

1791. Harvey, R.C. "Laughter with Captions." *Comics Journal*. November 1985, pp. 7-8 +.

1792. Harvey, R.C. "More Sexism in Comics." *Comics Journal*. January 1986, pp. 30-35.

1793. Matera, Fran. "Feminists and the Funnies." *Editor and Publisher*. October 24, 1987, pp. 68, 52.

1794. Mooney, Linda and Sarah Brabant. "Two Martinis and a Rested Woman: 'Liberation' in the Sunday Comics." *Sex Roles*. October 1987, pp. 409-420.

1795. Murphy, C. "Ms. Buxley?" *Atlantic*. December 1984, pp. 40 +.

1796. Schultze, Sydney. "Sex Roles in the Comics." Presented at Popular Culture Association, Montreal, Canada, March 1987.

1797. Thaber, B.J. "Gender Stereotyping in Comic Strips." In *Communication, Gender, and Sex Roles in Diverse Interaction Contexts*, edited by L.P. Stewart and S. Ting-Toomey, pp. 189-199. Norwood, New Jersey: Ablex, 1987.

1798. Thompson, Don. "Mort Walker Considers Changes in Miss Buxley." *Comics Buyer's Guide*. June 29, 1984, p. 24.

1799. Walker, Mort. *Miss Buxley: Sexism in Beetle Bailey?* Bedford, New York: Comicana Books, 1982. 95 pp.

Superheroines

1800. Bails, Jerry B. "Merciful Minerva: The Story of Wonder Woman." *Alter Ego*. No. 1, 1965, pp. 13-16.

1801. Basner, Naomi. "Sing a Song of She-Devils." *Foom*. June 1976, pp. 20-22.

1802. "Batgirl Kommt." *Funk-Uhr* (Hamburg). 1967, p. 31.

1803. Fossati, Franco. "Wonder Woman." *Siderea*. May 1966.

1804. "Comics Heroines Lauded in *Ms.*" *Comics Journal*. September 1991, p. 7.

1805. Counts, Kyle. "Batgirl Casebook." *Comics Scene*. No. 10, 1989, pp. 46-49, 65.

1806. Cuesta, Fernando. "La Dama de Lazo: El Retorno de Wonder Woman." *El Wendigo*. Winter 1988-1989, pp. 8-10.

1807. Glancy, Kathleen. "Catwoman Considered." *Comics Feature*. June 1983, pp. 48-51.

1808. Hartman, Thom. "Micra: Hi-Tech Heroine." *Amazing Heroes*. September 15, 1986, pp. 37-40.

1809. Howell, Richard. "Glimmers of Gold: Wonder Woman Under Jack C. Harris." *Comics Journal*. May 1979, pp. 30-33.

1810. Lee, Stan. *The Superhero Woman*. New York: Simon and Schuster,1977. 253 pp.

1811. Marston, William M. and Harry G. Peter. *Wonder Woman. A Ms. Book*. Intro. by Gloria Steinem. New York: Holt, Rinehart and Winston and Warner Books, 1972. 186 pp.

1812. Mayhew, Richard. "Female Villains in General—Part Two." *Collectors' Club Newsletter*. September 1980, p. 12.

1813. Metzger, Kim. "Girl and Supergirl." *Comics Collector*. Fall 1984, pp. 32-34, 36-45.

1814. Mills, Tarpe. *Miss Fury*. Cambridge, Massachusetts: Archival Press,1979. 62 pp.

1815. O'Connell, Margaret. "The Super-Heroine as Chaos-Bringer: Women and Power." *Comics Feature*. September-October 1981, pp. 77-81.

1816. Schnurrer, Achim and Riccardo Rinaldi. *Die Welt der Bilderfrauen. Von Barbarella bis Wonder Woman*. Heroldsbach: Edition Aleph, 1986.

1817. Shah, D.K. "Superwomen Fight Back!" *Newsweek*. March 20, 1978, p. 75.

1818. "Sisterhood of Steel: Myth or Reality?" *Comics Buyer's Guide*. April 15, 1988, p. 43.

1819. "Superwomen." *Seventeen*. July 1980, p. 61.

1820. Thompson, Kim. "Spider-Woman: Incest in the Marvel Family." *Comics Journal*. April 1978, pp. 51-53.

1821. Wagner, G. "Superman and His Sisters." *New Republic*. January 17, 1955, pp. 17-19.

1822. Ward, Murray R. "The Wonder Woman Who Wasn't." *LOC*. January 1980, pp. 19-28.

2
Comic Books

GENERAL STUDIES

1823. Adamo, Sue. "It's the Guy and Brad Show." *Comics Scene*. March 1982, pp. 58-61.

1824. Allwood, Martin S. *Comic Books in Geneva*. Geneva, New Jersey: N.I. Hobart Mass Communication Studies, 1950.

1825. "Among the Unlimitless Etha." *Time*. May 8, 1944, pp. 94-96.

1826. Anton, Uwe. "USA: Keine Enten, Wiele Helden." In *Comic-Jahrbuch 1986*, edited by Martin Compart and Andreas C. Knigge, pp. 275-288. Frankfurt: Ullstein GmbH, 1985.

1827. Arbesú, Faustino R. "Una Obra Maestra del Ritmo, Montaje y Movimiento." *El Wendigo*. Verano 1990, pp. 22-29.

1828. Arbesú, Faustino R. "Una Obra Maestra Dentro de un Subgénero del Comic." *El Wendigo*. No. 46, 1989, pp. 4-5.

1829. Arbesú, Faustino R. and Ramón Fermín. "Los Mejores del Mundo... Que No lo Son Tanto." *El Wendigo*. No. 52, 1991, pp. 12-13.

1830. Astor, David. "He Visits the Soviet Union and Far East." *Editor and Publisher*. December 5, 1987, pp. 54, 56.

1831. "Authority in the Comics." *Trans-Action.* December 1966, pp. 22-26.

1832. Ayers, Dick. "The AC Comics Gang at Orlandocon '91." *Cartoonist PROfiles.* June 1992, pp. 64-67.

1833. Bagge, Peter. "The Best Comics of the Late '70s." *Comics Journal.* December 1990, pp. 74-75.

1834. Bardini, Roberto and Horacio Serafini. "La 'Inocencia' de la Historieta." *Cambio* (México). October/November/December 1976, pp. 49-53.

1835. Barnette, Mark. "From the Other Side of the Tracts: Jack T. Chick's Pyramid Plan." *Comics Journal.* October 1991, pp. 89-94.

1836. Barrier, Michael. "Exaggerated Realism." *Comics Journal.* September 1985, pp. 107-110.

1837. Barrier, Michael and Martin Williams. *A Smithsonian Book of Comic-Book Comics.* New York: Smithsonian Institution Press and Harry N. Abrams, 1981. 336 pp.

1838. "Beauty and the Beast." *Comics Interview.* No. 73, 1989, pp. 4-23.

1839. Beck, C.C. "Are We Living in a Global Age and Don't Know It?" *Comics Journal.* April 1990, pp. 117-118.

1840. Beck, C.C. "The Bastards of the Art World." *Comics Journal.* January 1988, p. 120.

1841. Beck, C.C. "Degeneracy, Perversion, Depravity." *FCA/S.O.B.* April/May 1981, pp. 2-5.

1842. Beck, C.C. "Fiction." *FCA/S.O.B.* February/March 1982, p. 3.

1843. Beck, C.C. "A Letter from the Editor." *FCA/S.O.B.* June/July 1982, p. 3.

1844. Beck, C.C. "May We Have the Next Slide Please?" *Inside Comics.* 1:4 (1974-1975), p. 24.

1845. Beck, C.C. "Name Credit." *Comics Journal.* August 1986, p. 7.

1846. Beck, C.C. "True Art." *FCA/S.O.B.* December/January 1982, p. 8.

1847. Belk, Russell W. "Material Values in the Comics: A Content Analysis of Comic Books Featuring Themes of Wealth." *Journal of Consumer Research.* June 1987, pp. 26-42.

1848. Bell, Bob B. "Los Bros Magnificos." *Spin.* August 1988, p. 50.

1849. Berger, Arthur A. "Authority in the Comics." In *Games, Sports and Power*, edited by Gregory P. Stone, pp. 217-288. New Brunswick, New Jersey: Transaction Books, 1972.

1850. Bernard, Jami. "The Singing Slasher." *Comics Scene*. No. 10, 1989, pp. 21-24, 66.

1851. Bernstein, Mark. "Making the Dinosaur Evolve." *Comics Journal*. April 1986, pp. 86-88, 97.

1852. Bertieri, Claudio. "I Comics Nello Spettaculo USA." *Quaderni di Communicazioni di Massa* (Rome). No. 1, 1965.

1853. Bethke, Marilyn. "And Beneath All This Glitter and Tinsel... More Glitter and Tinsel." *Comics Journal*. March 1979, p. 30.

1854. Bethke, Marilyn. "Blurred Image." *Comics Journal*. November 1982, pp. 106-107.

1855. Bethke, Marilyn. "Comics Informer." *Comics Journal*. January 1983, pp. 99-100.

1856. Bethke, Marilyn. "On the Matter of Comic Books." *Comics Journal*. March 1979, p. 31.

1857. Biggers, Cliff. "Cliff's Notes." *Retail Express*. July 17, 1987, p. 6.

1858. Blackbeard, Bill. *Comics*. Boston, Massachusetts: Houghton Mifflin, 1973.

1859. Boyd, Robert. "Understanding Comics." *Comics Journal*. March 1993, p. 43.

1860. Braun, Saul. "Comics." *New York Times Magazine*. May 2, 1972.

1861. Brelner, M.A. "American Comics." *Library Association Record* (London). 54:12 (1952), p. 410.

1862. Brunner, Frank. "Farewell to Comics." *Comics Journal*. November 1979, pp. 49-51.

1863. Bull, Bart. "Comics." *Spin*. August 1988, pp. 40-43.

1864. Calisi, Romano. "Nei Fumetti lo Specchio della Società Americana." *Paese Sera* (Milan). September 22-24, 1964.

1865. Calzavara, Elisa. "Ancora Sui Comics USA." *Comics, Archivio Italiano della Stampa a Fumetti*. September 1996, pp. 27-28.

1866. Calzavara, Elisa. "Ancora Sui Comics USA." *Fantascienza Minore*. Sondsummer, 1967, pp. 52-54.

1867. Carlinsky, D. "Comeback of the Comic Books." *Seventeen*. August 1973, pp. 214-215 +.

1868. Cashwell, Peter. "Moonshine, Guns, Grits, and Crackers." *Comics Journal*. December 1987, pp. 53-54.

1869. Champigny, Robert. "Un Comic Américain." *Critique* (Paris). February 1957, pp. 124-135.

1870. Claremont, Chris. "The 1976 Irving Awards." *Foom*. December 1976, pp. 16-18.

1871. Clark, Douglas A. "World Without End, Amen." *Fantazia*. No. 4, 1990, p. 34.

1872. Clifton, John. "De-Elfing Comics." *Comics Journal*. April 1982, pp. 64-77.

1873. Clifton, John. "The Seven Deadly Cliches in Comics." *Comics Journal*. Winter 1980, pp. 59-64.

1874. Cochran, J.R. "Resuscitation." *Comics Journal*. August 1986, pp. 74-77.

1875. Collins, Nancy A. "Wedded Bliss: The State of Marriage in the Four-Color World." *Amazing Heroes*. June 15, 1984, pp. 43-49.

1876. "Comédie Humaine Amerikanisc." *Der Monat* (Berlin). 22:256 (1970), pp. 24-29.

1877. "Comic-Book." *The Nation*. March 19, 1949, p. 319.

1878. "Comic Book Confidential." *Serieskaberen*. June 1990, p. 15.

1879. "Comic Book Merry-Go-Round." *Comic World*. November 1979, pp. 23-24.

1880. "Comic Book Tells Check's Story." *New York Times*. October 1, 1958.

1881. "Comic Colors." *Newsweek*. April 24, 1950, p. 2.

1882. "Comic Mania." *Newsweek*. September 4, 1972, p. 75.

1883. "The Comics." *Journal of Popular Culture*. Summer 1971. (Section with work by Berger, Faust, Klotman, Mira, Sagarin, and Zlotnick).

1884. "Comics: An Introduction." *Print*. November/December 1988, pp. 59-172. (Eleven articles).

1885. "The Comics Break New Ground, Again." *New York Times*. January 24, 1992, p. A-28.

1886. "The Comics Glut of 1983." *Comics Journal*. November 1983, pp. 6-7.

1887. "Comics Library: Furriners." *Comics Journal.* January 1988, pp. 27-31.

1888. "Conte Vs. Loren (continued)." *Comics Journal.* February 1991, p. 18.

1889. Coogan, Pete. "Survey Results." *Comic Art Studies.* May 2, 1992, pp. 2-6.

1890. Cort, D. "Comics, Etc." *Commonweal.* July 9, 1965, pp. 503-505.

1891. Cruse, Howard. "Not Being There Yet." *Comics Scene.* July 1982, pp. 46-47, 52.

1892. Cuesta, Fernando. "Infierno en las Nubes." *El Wendigo.* No. 45, 1989, pp. 31-34.

1893. Cuesta, Fernando. "Slash Marand: Fundiendo la Nieve Purpura." *El Wendigo.* No. 50, 1990, pp. 41-42.

1894. Culhane, John. "Leapin' Lizards! What's Happening to the Comics?" *New York Times Magazine.* May 5, 1974, pp. 16-17 +.

1895. Dagilis, Andrew. "Uncle Sugar Vs. Uncle Charlie." *Comics Journal.* July 1990, pp. 62-84.

1896. Dahlen, Robert. "The Antares Circle: An Introduction." *Comics Buyer's Guide.* April 15, 1988, p. 3.

1897. Dale, R. "Comics for Adults." *New Republic.* December 7, 1953, p. 21.

1898. Dawson, Jim. "Blood and Irony." *Comics Journal.* April 1987, pp. 42-43.

1899. Dawson, Jim. "Hack, Hack, Hack." *Comics Journal.* March 1979, pp. 33-34.

1900. DeCandido, Keith R.A. "To Speak of Many Things." *Comics Journal.* November 1989, pp. 49-51.

1901. Decker, Dwight R. "The Best and Worst Comic Books." *Comics Journal.* January 1979, pp. 59-62.

1902. Decker, Dwight R. "Comics and Wrestling Update." *Amazing Heroes.* June 15, 1987, pp. 62-63.

1903. "Den Erwachsensen Leser im Visier." *ICOM-INFO.* February 1990, pp. 14-17.

1904. "Der Kampf Gegen die Comics in den USA und England." *Caritas* (Freiburg). 56, 1955, pp. 58-59.

1905. Deschaine, Scott. "Liquid Assets." *Comics Journal.* November 1985, pp. 81-84.

1906. Dickholtz, Daniel. "Hold Onto Your Seats!" *Comics Scene*. No. 3 (Vol. 3, Series #14), pp. 54-55, 60.

1907. Dooley, Michael. "Comics Fix To Print." *Comics Journal*. July 1988, pp. 67-71.

1908. "'Do You Want To Work in Mainstream Comics?'" *The Comicist*. February/ March 1991, pp. 13-14.

1909. Duveau, Marc. *Comics U.S.A.* Paris: Albin Michel, 1975.

1910. Edelman, Scott. "A Comic of One's Own." *Comics Journal*. April 1986, pp. 91-94.

1911. Edelman, Scott. "A Never-Ending Battle." *Comics Journal*. September 1985, pp. 104-106.

1912. Edelman, Scott. "Opportunity Knocked." *Comics Journal*. November 1985, pp. 100-102.

1913. Edelman, Scott. "With Great Power, But No Responsibility." *Comics Journal*. May 1986, pp. 109-112.

1914. Edwards, Don. "The Forbidden Fruit." *Qua Brot*. No. 1, 1985, pp. 8-13.

1915. Eisner, Will. *Comics and Sequential Art*. Forestville, California: Eclipse Books, 1986, 160 pp; Tamarac, Florida: Poorhouse Press, 1985.

1916. Engelhardt, Tom. "Ambush at Kamikaze Pass." In *American Media and Mass Culture: Left Perspectives*, edited by Donald Lazere, pp. 474-498. Berkeley, California: University of California Press, 1987.

1917. Epstein, Warren. "Professor Brings Credibility to Comics." *Tampa Tribune*. March 21, 1987, p. 10-F. (M. Thomas Inge).

1918. Faust, Wolfgang Max and R. Baird Shuman. "Comics and How To Read Them." *Journal of Popular Culture*. 5:1 (1971), pp. 194-202.

1919. Feiffer, Jules. "Pop Sociology." *New York Sunday Herald Tribune Magazine*. January 9, 1966, p. 6.

1920. Fermín Pérez, Ramón. "Una B Que No Es de Bondad." *El Wendigo*. No. 50, p. 36.

1921. Fiore, Robert. "The Pig Has It All Worked Out." *Comics Journal*. October 1981, pp. 8-9.

1922. Florez, Florentino. "Black Plot." *El Wendigo*. No. 52, 1991, pp. 4-5.

1923. Flórez, Florentino. "He Aquí la Cuestión." *El Wendigo*. Autumn/Winter 1989-1990, p. 12.

1924. Flórez, Florentino. "Incontinencia e Inconsistencia." *El Wendigo*. No. 51, 1991, pp. 32-33.

1925. François, E. "Le Mythe des Terres Lointaines dans la BD U.S." *Phénix*. No. 15, 1970.

1926. Free, Ken. "Pal-ul-don." *Oparian*. 1:1 (1965), pp. 25-33.

1927. Freeman, Gillian. *The Undergrowth of Literature*. London: Thomas Nelson and Sons, 1967.

1928. Fresnault-Deruelle, Pierre. "Les Comics Américains des Années 30/40 Avatar de l'Épopée." *Critique*. No. 284, 1972.

1929. Freund, Russell. "Jack the Footnote." *Comics Journal*. January 1987, pp. 35-36.

1930. Freund, Russell. "A Very Fine Pepper Jelly." *Comics Journal*. September 1987, pp. 45-48.

1931. Funk, Ray. "Rap with Ray." *Near Mint*. July 1982, pp. 30-35.

1932. "Generally Speaking." *Comics Journal*. July 1987, pp. 51-60, 62-66.

1933. Gilbert, Jonathan. "V—Die Ausserirdischen Besucher Kommen: Das Comic Magazin." *Watcher of the Unknown*. April 1988, pp. 48-50.

1934. Gilbert, Jonathan. "Von Jenseits des Grossen Teichs." *Watcher of the Unknown*. April 1988, pp. 66-70.

1935. Gillis, Peter B. "Guilty Fantasies." *Comics Feature*. July-August 1980, pp. 66-67; November 1980, pp. 77-78; January 1981, pp. 76-78.

1936. Gladstone, Jim. "Dog Boy's Bid Daddy." *City Paper* (Philadelphia). November 17-24, 1989, pp. 10-11.

1937. Goodwin, Archie and Gil Kane. "Die Comic-Books." *Graphis* (Zürich). 28:159 (1972-1973), pp. 52-61.

1938. Graalfs, M. "A Survey of Comic Books in the State of Washington." Unpublished Report, 1954. (Available Library Documents Section, University of Washington, Seattle, Washington).

1939. Goss, Tom. "Some Contemporary Comics and Their Creators: Personal Expression Vs. Mass Appeal." *Print*. November-December 1988, pp. 132-144.

1940. Goulart, Ron. *The Comic Book Reader's Companion.* New York: HarperCollins, 1993.

1941. Grabbe, Christian D. "Neglected Masterpieces." *Comics Journal.* April 1986, pp. 78-86.

1942. Greenberger, Robert. "Clearing the Clouds Away." *Comics Scene.* January 1981, pp. 46-49.

1943. Groensteen, Thierry. "Special USA. Situation de la BD Américaine." *Les Cahiers de la Bande Dessinée* (Grenoble). 66, 1985, pp. 42-46.

1944. Groth, Gary. "Catching Up." *Comics Journal.* February 1985, p. 6.

1945. Groth, Gary. "Comics and Their Critics." *Comics Journal.* June 1978, pp. 7-9.

1946. Groth, Gary. "Eclectic Banality." *Comics Journal.* August 1981, pp. 68-72.

1947. Groth, Gary. "An Explosion in a Cesspool." *Comics Journal.* July 1984, pp. 6-7.

1948. Groth, Gary. "Grouses About Louses." *Comics Journal.* August 1988, p. 5.

1949. Groth, Gary. "Paradise Lost." *Comics Journal.* March 1985, pp. 6-8, 112.

1950. Groth, Gary. "*Roboschlock 2*: Brought to You by Orion Consumer Products." *Comics Journal.* September 1990, pp. 7-8.

1951. Groth, Gary and Robert Fiore, eds. *The New Comics.* New York: Berkley Books, 1988.

1952. Groth, Gary and Kim Thompson. "Movin' Up and Movin' Out." *Comics Journal.* March 1979, p. 7.

1953. Gruenwald, Myron and Mark Gruenwald. *A Primer on Reality in Comic Books.* New York: Alternity Enterprises, 1977. 26 pp.

1954. Hanley, Alan J. "The Great Unknowns." *FCA/S.O.B.* October-November 1980, pp. 4-5.

1955. Harter, Maurice. "Words and Pictures." *Face Magazine.* January 29-February 11, 1992, pp. 6-7, 23.

1956. Harvey, R.C. "Keeping Score: Adding Abner to the Talley." *Comics Journal.* October 1988, pp. 121-126.

1957. Harvey, R.C. "Reruns and Revivals." *Comics Journal.* September 1983, pp. 122-123. ("Dick Tracy," "Kerry Drake," *et al.*).

1958. Harvey, R.C. "Scholars and the Comics." *Comic Art Studies*. December 2, 1992, pp. 5-8.

1959. Harvey, R.C. "A Short Look at a Long Run." *Comics Journal*. November 1986, pp. 47-52.

1960. Harvey, R.C. "Shreds and Patches." *Comics Journal*. August 1982, pp. 84-90.

1961. Harvey, R.C. and Heidi McDonald. "Leering or Laughing?" *Comics Journal*. April 1985, pp. 89-94.

1962. "Harvey Nominees Announced." *Comics Journal*. May 1992, pp. 16-17.

1963. Hegerfors, Sture. "Det Bottendaliga Toppen i USA Just Nu." *Göteborgs-Tidningen*. March 8, 1966.

1964. Heintjes, Tom. "The Negotiations." *Comics Journal*. February 1986, pp. 53-61.

1965. Heller, Steven. "Depressing Comics." *Print*. January-February 1989, pp. 143-144.

1966. Henahan, Donal. "The World (ZAP!) Goes POW!" *International Herald Tribune*. August 4-5, 1990.

1967. Hildick, E.W. *A Close Look at Magazines and Comics*. New York: Faber and Faber, 1972, 90 pp.

1968. Hofmann, Werner. "Die Kunst der Comic Strips. Hitlers Rache." *Merkur* (Stuttgart). 23:3 (1969), pp. 251-262.

1969. Hoops, Raymond. "A Comic Book on the Comics." *The World of Comic Art*. Summer 1967, pp. 48-50.

1970. "How Did You Become a Comics Professional?" *Comics Collector*. Winter 1986, p. 40.

1971. Hughes, Dave. "Tales from the Script." *Speakeasy*. April 1990, p. 23.

1972. Inge, M. Thomas. *The American Comic Book*. Columbus, Ohio: Ohio State University Libraries, 1985.

1973. Inge, M. Thomas. "Comic Books." In *Handbook of American Popular Literature*, edited by M. Thomas Inge, pp. 75-100. Westport, Connecticut: Greenwood, 1988.

1974. Inge, M. Thomas. "The Comics." In *Humor in America: A Research Guide to Genres and Topics*, edited by Lawrence E. Mintz, pp. 35-48. Westport, Connecticut: Greenwood, 1988.

1975. Inge, M. Thomas. "The Comics." *1989 Festival of Cartoon Art*. Columbus, Ohio: Ohio State University Libraries, 1989, pp. 15-44.

1976. Inge, M. Thomas. "The Comics and the American Language." *Inklings*. Summer 1976, pp. 3-4, 10.

1977. Inge, M. Thomas. "The Great Comics Revolution." *West Coast Review of Books*. November 1976, pp. 60-64.

1978. Inglis, R.A. "Comic Books Problems." *American Mercury*. August 1955, pp. 117-121.

1979. Jennings, Robert. "The Funny Book Racket." *The Comic World*. November 1979, pp. 18-22.

1980. Johnson, Kim H. "Together Again—For the First Time." *Comics Scene*. #3 (Vol. 3, Series #14), pp. 33-35, 44.

1981. Johnson, Kim H. "Who's on First Comics." *Comics Scene*. July 1983, pp. 51-54, 62.

1982. Johnson, Robin. "Just Ducky." *New York Review of Books*. June 26, 1986.

1983. "The Journal's Critics Disagree." *Comics Journal*. July 1981, pp. 24-31.

1984. Kane, Gil. "South of Olympus—Eyes Fixed on Comics." *Comics Journal*. January 1988, p. 115.

1985. Kane, Gil, Wendy Pini, Kenneth Smith, and Gary Groth. "Peer Pressure." *Comics Journal*. February 1986, pp. 69-74.

1986. "Killing the Comics." *Economist*. February 1955, p. 615.

1987. Knoblauch, Mary. "The Comic Craze." *Chicago's American Magazine*. July 31, 1966, pp. 8-9.

1988. Kreinz, Glória. "O Herói do Mês." *Boletim de HQ*. October 1991, p. 1.

1989. Kutsch, Thomas. "*Comics-Sociologically* Considered. *Comics-Soziologisch* Betrachtet." *Communications*. 6:1 (1980), pp. 43-57.

1990. Ladd-Smith, Henry. "Die Comics: Wesen, Herkunft und Entwicklung in den USA." *Handbuch der Publizistik*. 2:1 (1969), pp. 116-126.

1991. Lahman, Ed. "The New Trend." *Masquerader*. No. 6, 1964, pp. 8-9.

1992. Lamontagne, Christian. "Quelques Comics de San Francisco." *Le Temps Fou* (Montreal). No. 9, 1980, p. 52.

1993. Lanyi, Ronald L. "Comic Book Creativity As Displaced Aggression." Doctoral dissertation, University of California, Davis, 1977. 97 pp.

1994. Lee, R. "The Comics." *Christian Century*. May 11, 1955, p. 569.

1995. Lee, Stan. *Secrets Behind the Comics*. New York: Famous Enterprises, 1947.

1996. Levine, A. "Comic Books Are Winning New Respect." *U.S. News and World Report*. September 21, 1987, p. 69.

1997. Lewis, Robert. "He Doesn't Speak for Me." *Comics Feature*. No. 25, 1983, p. 4.

1998. Lin, Jennifer. "Pow! Bam! Comic Books Are Growing—and Growing Up." *Philadelphia Inquirer*. December 4, 1988, pp. 1-G, 9-G.

1999. Linton, C.D. "Tragic Comics." *Madison Quarterly*. 6 (1946), pp. 1-6.

2000. Lobdell, Scott. "Lords of the Ring." *Comics Scene*. No. 9, 1989, pp. 61-64.

2001. Lobdell, Scott. "Rent-a-Rex." *Comics Scene*. No. 3 (Vol. 3, Series #14), pp. 48-50.

2002. "Lobo on TV." *Comics Interview*. No. 99, 1991, pp. 4-9.

2003. Luciano, Dale. "Banal Poetics, Calculated Clunkiness, Live Rattles, and Small Press Bits." *Comics Journal*. August 1986, pp. 68-72.

2004. Lupoff, Richard and Don Thompson, eds. *All in Color for a Dime*. New Rochelle, New York: Arlington House, 1970.

2005. McCarron, Owen. "Cavalcade of Comics." *Cartoonist PROfiles*. September 1987, pp. 84-89.

2006. McCloud, Scott. *Understanding Comics*. Northampton, Massachusetts: Tundra, 1993. 220 pp.

2007. Macek, Carl. "For Those Who Know How To Look." In *The Comic Book Price Guide 1979-1980*, edited by R.M. Overstreet, pp. A-35-A-42. Cleveland, Tennessee: 1979.

2008. McKenzie, Roger. "Me and Rod—Sun-Running in the Twilight Zone." *Comics Journal*. March 1986, pp. 47-49.

2009. Manisco, Estella. "Se Muore un Eroe dei Fumetti, Piangono Milioni di Americani." *Il Messaggero* (Rome). June 11, 1954.

2010. Mantlo, Bill. "The Comics You Never Read About." *Comics Journal*. October 1978, p. 59.

2011. Mantlo, Bill. "And Still the Nazis March: Aryanman." *Comics Journal*. Summer 1979, pp. 134-136.

2012. Martínez, Rodolfo. "Un Retorno a la Grandeza." *El Wendigo*. No. 52, 1991, pp. 38-39.

2013. Mathiasen, Paw. "Hardboiled." *Seriejournalen*. March 1991, p. 34.

2014. Mehlhorn, H. "Freiwillige Selbstkontrolle für Comics in USA." *Der Neue Vertrieb*. 7:137 (1955), pp. 17-19.

2015. Mettler, Mike. "First Class." *Comics Feature*. No. 25, 1983, pp. 48-50.

2016. "Mister Rogers." *Comics Interview*. June 1984, pp. 74-77.

2017. Mitchell, W.B.J. "The Comics." *America*. December 11, 1954, p. 308.

2018. Miura, Setsuko. *Amerikan Komikkusu Eno Tabi* (A Trip to the American Comics). Tokyo: Tōjusha, 1981. 175 pp.

2019. Molina, Carlos. "En el Pais del Neon." *El Wendigo*. 14:43 (1988), pp. 19-20.

2020. Monaco, Steve. "March of the New Cartoonists." *Comics Journal*. January 1988, pp. 35-38.

2021. Monaco, Steve. "Sentimentality in the Mainstream." *Comics Journal*. November 1986, pp. 52-53, 56-58.

2022. Montalvo, Carlos, Jorge Vergara, Fernando Pérez, René Rebetez, and Ludolfo Paramio. *Ensayos Marxistas Sobre los 'Comics'* (Marxist Essays on the Comics). Bogota: Ediciones Los Comuneros, 1976 (?).

2023. Morrissey, Richard. "The Great Continuity Forum." *Comics Feature*. February 1981, pp. 67-71.

2024. Mougin, Lou. "Damn the Torpedoes." *Dreamline*. March 1982, pp. 15-25.

2025. Murray, Anne E. "Comic Book Draws on Gennifer Flowers' Past with Prez." *New York Post*. August 24, 1993, p. 7.

2026. Murray, Doug. "Flacks and Hacks at ACBA." *Inside Comics*. Spring 1974, pp. 26-29.

2027. Murray, Will. "Who Invented the Fortress of Solitude?" *Comics Buyer's Guide*. March 26, 1993, p. 50.

2028. Nelson, Roy P. "What the—?!! What's Happening to the Comics? Biff! Pow! 2 KO's Show Trend," *Los Angeles Times*. March 18, 1973, p. VI-4.

2029. "1993 Industry Award Nominees Announced." *Comics Journal*. May 1993, pp. 16-18.

2030. "The 1975 Irving Awards." *Foom*. No. 11, 1975, pp. 20-21.

2031. Nolan, Martin F. "New (Sob!) Trends in the Comics." *The Reporter*. December 29, 1966; April 29, 1968.

2032. "'Not Just for Kids Any More': Three Nationally Distributed Publications Take Notice of Comic Books." *Comics Journal*. August 1986, p. 16.

2033. Novinskie, Charles. "1963: An X-traordinary Year." In *San Diego Comic Convention 1993*, pp. 54-55. San Diego, California: 1993.

2034. Paetel, Karl O. "Die Amerikanischen Comics." *Deutsche Rundschau* (Baden-Baden). 80:6 (1954), pp. 564-566.

2035. Pasko, Martin. "Messages from a Curmudgeon." *Comics Scene*. No. 11, 1983, pp. 38-40.

2036. Pasko, Martin. "Victims of the Lie." *Comics Scene*. November 1982, pp. 21-24.

2037. Pasko, Martin, *et al*. "Forum." *Comics Journal*. September 1980, pp. 49-79.

2038. Patterson, W.D. "Mr. and Mrs. Comic America, SRL Reader Poll." *Saturday Review of Literature*. December 16, 1950, p. 33.

2039. Pekar, Harvey. "Power Trip in a Milk Truck." *Comics Journal*. September 1987, p. 42.

2040. Pekar, Harvey and Frank Stack. "Jack Dickens' Comic Kingdom." *American Splendor*. No. 12, 1987.

2041. Pérez, Juan J. and Norman Fernández. "El Extraño de dos Mundos." *El Wendigo*. No. 54, 1991, pp. 37-38.

2042. Pérez, Ramón F. "El Big Bang, Pero Menos." *El Wendigo*. No. 45, 1989, pp. 37-39.

2043. Pérez, Ramón F. "Hace 50 Años: El Nacimiento de un Mito." Program of Centro Cultural Campoamor, Oviedo, Spain, December 1988, p. 11.

2044. Phelps, Donald. "Word and Image." *Comics Journal*. April 1985, pp. 41-43.

2045. Piasecki, Wladislaw. "Le Problème des Comics Américains et les Bibliothèques Brittaniques." *Przeglad Biblioteczny* (Warsaw). 21 (1953), pp. 219-226.

2046. Piven, Leslie. "Funny Business." *Philadelphia Magazine*. October 1986, p. 21.

2047. "Plastic Forks." *Speakeasy*. December 1988, pp. 33-34, 36.

2048. Poh, Robbie. "Hardboiled Question." *Before I Get Old*. May 1987, p. 33.

2049. Prescott, Peter. "The Comic Book (Gulp!) Grows Up." *Newsweek*. January 18, 1988, pp. 70-71.

2050. Prezzolini, Guiseppe. "E'Nata in America la Passione dei Fumetti." *Il Tempo di Roma*. December 15, 1951.

2051. Queenan, Joe. "Drawing on the Dark Side." *New York Times Magazine*. April 30, 1989, pp. 32-34, 79, 86.

2052. Rebière, Michel. "Les Cases de l'Oncle Sam." *Charente Libre*. January 24, 1992, p. 24.

2053. Reynaldo, Randy. "Reassessing Comics." *Comics Journal*. August 1985, pp. 88-93.

2054. Rice, Charlie. "Bang, Bam, Whooof!" *This Week*. March 5, 1967, p. 13.

2055. Rifas, Leonard. "A Clean Mirror." *Comics Journal*. October 1990, pp. 42-43.

2056. Rodi, Rob. "Prestige Schmestige." *Comics Journal*. January 1988, pp. 32-34.

2057. Rodi, Rob. "Sexually Suspect." *Comics Journal*. September 1986, pp. 48-54.

2058. Rodi, Rob. "To the Heart of the Problem." *Comics Journal*. September 1991, pp. 43-44.

2059. Rodi, Rob. "A World-Saver and a Wanna-Be." *Comics Journal*. November 1989, pp. 52-55.

2060. Rodríguez Arbesú, Faustino. "Cuando la Sordidez Supera la Ternura." *El Wendigo*. Winter 1988-1989, pp. 13-14.

2061. Rose, Lloyd. "Comic Books for Grownups." *Atlantic*. August 1986.

2062. Sala, Paolo and Alfredo Castelli. "Storia del Fumetto Americano." *Comics-Bolletino di Comics-Club 104*. April 1, 1966.

2063. Schanes, Steve. "Hard-Working People." *Comics Journal*. January 1986, p. 97.

2064. Scholz, Carter. "Life on the First Tier." *Comics Journal.* August 1986, pp. 61-64.

2065. Scholz, Carter. "One for the Gipper." *Comics Journal.* January 1986, pp. 29-30.

2066. Scholz, Carter. "Raw Roots." *Comics Journal.* July 1981, pp. 34-36.

2067. Sherman, Bill. "Hedds and Feds." *Comics Journal.* May 1985, pp. 95-96.

2068. Sherman, Bill. "New Tales by an Old Hand." *Comics Journal.* September 1985, pp. 102-103.

2069. Sherman, Bill. "Schizzing in the Real World." *Comics Journal.* September 1980, pp. 90-91.

2070. Simpson, L.L. "Hall of Infamy." *Alter Ego.* No. 4, 1962, pp. 31-33.

2071. Simpson, L.L. "Hall of Infamy." *Fandom Annual.* 1967, pp. 11-12.

2072. Sirois, Al. "Windows." *Comics Journal.* December 1983, pp. 9-11.

2073. Skidmore, Max J. and Joey Skidmore. "More Than Mere Fantasy: Political Themes in Contemporary Comic Books." *Journal of Popular Culture.* Summer 1983, pp. 83-92.

2074. Smith, Jerry. "Comics Now." *Comics Arena.* July 1992, pp. 39-40.

2075. Smith, Kenneth. "Labyrinths of the Ordered Mind: A Reply to Fred Butzen." *Comics Journal.* September 1990, pp. 113-116.

2076. Smith, Kenneth. "On *The Incal.*" *Comics Journal.* April 1989, pp. 62-65.

2077. Smith, Kenneth. "Reduced Circumstances." *Comics Journal.* November 1989, pp. 56-59.

2078. Stevens, Carol. "Comics: An Introduction." *Print.* November-December 1988, pp. 59-60.

2079. Stewart, Bhob. "Ream-Walker." *Comics Journal.* September 1987, pp. 99-100.

2080. Strnad, Jan. "Babies, Ducks, and Asses." *Comics Journal.* May 1983, pp. 48-52.

2081. Strong, Rick. "A Hot Deal." *Alter Ego.* Autumn 1964, pp. 15-17.

2082. "Sunday at the Sunday Show." *Omnibus.* March 1978, pp. 14-15.

2083. Sutin, Lawrence. "Straight Talk About Comics." *Sky.* March 1986, pp. 58-64.

2084. Tebbel, John. "Who Says the Comics Are Dead?" *Saturday Review*. December 10, 1960, pp. 44-46.

2085. Thompson, Don and Dick Lupoff, eds. *The Comic-Book Book*. New Rochelle, New York: Arlington House, 1973; Carlstadt, New Jersey: Rainbow Books, 1977.

2086. Thompson, Don and Maggie. "Holy Heart Attack!" *Comics Feature*. December 1981, pp. 39-42.

2087. Thompson, Kim. "Another Relentlessly Elitist Editorial." *Comics Journal*. April 1980, pp. 6-7.

2088. Thompson, Kim. "Repaying the Debt." *Qua Brot*. No. 1, 1985, p. 3.

2089. Thompson, Kim. "Uncle Don (F)lies Again." *Comics Journal*. August 1988, p. 3.

2090. "Thought Balloons." *Comics Scene*. No. 9, 1989, pp. 48-50.

2091. Tompkins, Allan. "What's in a Name?" *Oparian*. 1:1 (1965), pp. 16-20.

2092. Toomey, Bob. "Vanishing Point." *Comics Journal*. March 1979, pp. 32-33.

2093. Trinchero, Sergio. "La Scoperta dell' America." *Hobby*. No. 3, 1967.

2094. "True-Life Comics." *Asiaweek*. June 30, 1993, p. 21.

2095. Tuckner, Howard M. "Unfunny Comic-Books Win Friends for Tennis." *New York Times*. October 21, 1956.

2096. "Two Little Nuns." *Newsweek*. January 22, 1951, p. 75.

2097. Tyree, Dan. "Dan T's Inferno." *Comics Buyer's Guide*. July 11, 1986, pp. 43-49. Continuing column.

2098. "USA-Neger Comics." *Bulletin: Jugend + Literatur*. No. 3, 1971, pp. 11-12.

2099. Uslan, Michael and Bruce Solomon. *The Pow! Zap! Wham! Comic Book Trivia Quiz*. New York: William Morrow, 1977.

2100. Vance, James. "Elite Comics." *Comics Interview*. No. 41, 1986, pp. 6-18.

2101. Vergara, Jorge. "Cómics y Relaciones Mercantiles." *Casa de las Américas* (Havana). March-April 1973, pp. 126-142.

2102. Via, Ed. "The Death of an Innovation." *Comics Journal*. September 1979, pp. 56-58.

2103. Ward, Murray R. "The Band That Time Forgot." *Comics Feature*. November 1980, pp. 43-53.

2104. Ward, Murray R. "Dept. of Un-Earth-ly Coincidence." *Collector's Dream Magazine*. 1:2, p. 23.

2105. Ward, Murray R. "Leftovers." *Dreamline*. March 1982, pp. 84-85.

2106. White, David M. "The Crazy World of Comics." *Media History Digest*. Fall 1985, pp. 2-7.

2107. White, Ted. "Blood and Thunder." *Comics Journal*. October 1984, pp. 20-22.

2108. Wiese, Ellen. *Enter: The Comics*. Lincoln, Nebraska: University of Nebraska Press, 1965.

2109. Wiese, Ellen. "Enter: The Comics." *Journal of Commerce*. 17:1 (1967), pp. 67-68.

2110. Windham, Ryder. "Comictopia: Scott McCloud's *Understanding Comics: The Invisible Art*." *Comics Journal*. May 1993, pp. 108-109.

2111. Woodring, Jim. "The Weirdo Difference." *Comics Journal*. December 1990, pp. 115-119.

2112. "World's Finest #300." *Comics Interview*. February 1984, pp. 7-13.

2113. "The World's Mightiest Waste of Time and Money." *FCA/S.O.B.* October/November 1981, p. 6.

2114. "The World's Mightiest Waste of Time and Money, Part 2." *FCA/S.O.B.* August/September 1981, p. 3.

2115. Zanotto, Piero. "I Fumetti Politico-Sociali Degli Stati Uniti." *La Nuova Sardegna*. March 21, 1967.

2116. Zanotto, Piero. "La Società Americana Specchiata nei Fumetti." *Tribuna del Mezzogiorno* (Messina). November 17, 1965.

2117. "Zap! Pow! Bang! Comics Grow Up!" In *Modern Mass Media*, edited by John C. Merrill, John Lee and Edward J. Friedlander, p. 151. New York: Harper and Row, 1990.

2118. Zilber, Jay. "Trufan Confessions." *Comics Feature*. November 1980, pp. 29-31.

Cards, Games, Toys

2119. Beck, Henry. "Topps Job." *Comics Scene*. December 1992, pp. 15-19.

2120. Butler, Don. "Comics Greats Contribute to Topps' Galaxy Cards." *Comics Buyer's Guide*. January 29, 1993, pp. 26-27.

2121. "Comic Strip Polls." *Life*. October 19, 1953, p. 82.

2122. Gray, Harold. *Little Orphan Annie Cut Out Doll and Dresses*. Sam Gabriel, n.d. Box of cutouts.

2123. Haring, Scott D. "From the Game Shelf." *Comics Retailer*. April 1992, p. 52.

2124. Harman, Kenny. *Comic Strip Toys*. Des Moines, Iowa: Wallace-Homestead, 1975. 119 pp.

2125. Kreiner, Rich. "Up from Bubblegum." *Comics Journal*. January 1993, pp. 42-48.

2126. MacDonald, Heidi D. "Toy Comics, Joy Comics." *Comics Journal*. July 1983, pp. 51-58.

2127. Noglows, Paul. "Marvel Taps Toy Tsar To Cash in on Comic Craze." *Variety*. April 26, 1993, p. 86.

2128. Perrin, Steve. "A Comics Feature Role-Playing Game." *Comics Feature*. October 1986, pp. 27-29.

2129. Perrin, Steve. "Games." *Comics Feature*. November-December 1984, pp. 12-13, 32-33.

2130. Perrin, Steve. "Games." *Comics Feature*. January-February 1985, pp. 8-9.

2131. Perrin, Steve. "Games." *Comics Feature*. February 1987, pp. 42-45.

2132. Perrin, Steve. "Games: What Is a Good Superhero Game? Part II." *Comics Feature*. January 1986, pp. 18-19, 40-41.

2133. "Politicians Blast *True Crime* Cards." *Comics Journal*. March 1992, p. 15.

2134. Robbins, Trina. *Paper Dolls from the Comics*. Forestville, California: Eclipse Comics, 1987. 32 pp.

2135. Sanders, Scott R. "Death Games: Toying with Murder and Mayhem." *Comics Journal*. December 1989, pp. 3-6.

2136. Schneider, Fred. "Super-Heroes in Miniature." *Amazing World of DC Comics*. February 1976, pp. 32-35.

2137. "Sparkle Plenty, the Daughter of B.O. Plenty and Gravel Gertie Becomes a Doll and Starts To Set Sales Records." *Life*. August 25, 1947.

2138. Stanley, John. *Great Comics Game*. Los Angeles, California: Price-Stern-Sloane-Inc., 1966.

2139. Stevens, John D. "Cut-Outs in Comics." *Cartoonist PROfiles*. No. 17, 1973, pp. 48-51.

Graphic Novels

2140. Byers, Reggie. *Shuriken Graphic Novel*. El Cajon, California: Blackthorne, 1987. 90 pp.

2141. Decker, Dwight R. and Allen Varney. "Two Comics-Related Novels." *Comics Journal*. July 1984, pp. 112-113.

2142. "The Graphic Novels from Bernd Metz." *B and W*. No. 1, 1990, pp. 53-57.

2143. "Graphic Novels Receive Bookstore Attention." *Comics Journal*. July 1987, p. 27.

2144. Levine, Beth. "Major Book Publishers To Enter Graphic Novel Market." *Comics Business*. August 1987, pp. 1, 3, 12.

2145. Levine, Beth. "Publishers Set Future Graphic Novels." *Comics Business*. August 1987, pp. 13-14.

2146. "New Publisher, New Artist, New Graphic Novel." *Comics Journal*. August 1992, p. 12.

2147. "Robotech Graphic Novel, from Cartoons to Print." *Cartoon Heroes*. Spring 1987, pp. 48-53.

2148. Spicer, Bill. "New Directions for the Graphic Story." *Fantasy Illustrated*. No. 7, 1967, pp. 42-44; *Graphic Story Magazine*. No. 8, 1967, pp. 34-37.

2149. Thornsjo, Doug. "A Graphic Novel: What Is—And What Isn't." *Comics Buyer's Guide*. November 30, 1984, pp. 76-78.

2150. Vogel, Henry. *Early Days of the Southern Knights*. New York: Fictioneer Books, 1986. 80 pp.

2151. Vogel, Henry and Butch Guice. *The Southern Knights Graphic Novel*. New York: Fictioneer Books, 1986. 64 pp.

HISTORICAL ASPECTS

2152. "Ace Harlem to the Rescue." *Time*. July 14, 1947, p. 75.

2153. "Adventures in Dreamland." *Time*. December 16, 1946, pp. 77-78 +.

2154. Barrier, Mike. "Graphic Innovations." *Comics Journal*. February 1986, pp. 91-94.

2155. Bean, R.I. "Comics Bogey." *American Home*. November 1945, p. 29.

2156. Beck, C.C. "Mr. Mind and the Monster Society of Evil." In *The Comic Book Price Guide 1985-86*, edited by R.M. Overstreet, pp. A-89-A-93. Cleveland, Tennessee: 1985.

2157. Benchley, Robert. "The Comics." *Literary Digest*. December 12, 1936, p. 18.

2158. Benson, John. "Qua Brot?" *Squa Tront*. No. 5, 1974, pp. 48-50.

2159. Benson, John. "The Wessler Stories." *Squa Tront*. No. 9, 1983, pp. 39-41.

2160. Benton, Mike. *The Comic Book in America: An Illustrated History*. Dallas, Texas: Taylor Publishing, 1990. 207 pp.

2161. Brennen, Casey T. "The Untold History of I.W. Comics." *Comics Journal*. June 1980, pp. 118-119.

2162. "A Brief History of Comic Books." *B and W*. No. 1, 1990, p. 10.

2163. Broughton, Roger. "Suppressed 'Lonely War' To Conclude 20 Years Later." *Comics Buyer's Guide*. July 20, 1990, p. 1.

2164. Broun, Heywood. "Wham! and Pow!" *New Republic*. May 17, 1939, p. 44.

2165. "The Camera Party." *Squa Tront*. No. 9, 1983, pp. 21-25.

2166. Collins, Max A. "Strip Search: Mickey Spillane and the Comics." *Comics Feature*. September-October 1984, pp. 24-28.

2167. "Comfort for Comics." *Newsweek*. January 9, 1950, p. 46.

2168. "Comic Book." *The Nation*. March 19, 1949, p. 319.

2169. "Comic-Coated History." *Newsweek*. August 5, 1946, p. 89.

2170. "Comics All Over the World." *Business Week*. June 8, 1946, p. 75.

2171. "Comics and Their Audience." *Publisher's Weekly*. April 18, 1942, pp. 1477-1479.

2172. "Comic Spirit and the Comics." *Wilson Library Bulletin*. November 1946, pp. 238-239.

2173. Cruse, Howard. "Abduction of a Mouse." *Comics Scene*. November 1982, pp. 46-48.

2174. Daniels, Les. *Comix: A History of Comic Books in America*. New York: Crown, 1971. 198 pp.

2175. Decker, Dwight R. "When Strikes the Senate." *Amazing Heroes*. June 1, 15, 1988.

2176. De Fuccio, Jerry. "Comic Command Performance No. 2." *Cartoonist PROfiles*. September 1975, pp. 28-37; No. 3, December 1975, pp. 28-34; No. 4, March 1976, pp. 38-43; No. 6, March 1977, pp. 76-84; No. 7, December 1977, pp. 68-75.

2177. Di Fazio, J.S. "A Content Analysis To Determine the Presence of Selected American Values Found in Comic Books During Two Time Periods, 1946-1950, 1966-1970." Ph.D. dissertation, University of Iowa, 1974.

2178. Dubberke, Ray. "Supersnipe: The Boy with the Most." *Comics Buyer's Guide*. April 5, 1985, pp. 56, 58, 60, 62.

2179. Edwards, Don. "The Forbidden Fruit." *Qua Brot*. 1, 1985, pp. 8-14.

2180. "Escapist Paydirt; Comic Books Influence Friends and Make Plenty of Money Too." *Newsweek*. December 27, 1943, pp. 57-58.

2181. Fiore, Robert. "'And Then Some Idiot Turned Out the Lights!'" *Comics Journal*. November 1980, pp. 47-54.

2182. "First Comic Book Awards." *America*. April 14, 1956, pp. 47-48.

2183. "540 Million Comics Published During 1946." *Publisher's Weekly*. September 6, 1947, p. 1030.

2184. Flessel, Creig. "Apples and Comic Books." *Robin Snyder's History of the Comics*. November 1990.

2185. Francis, Robert. "The Comic-Book Age." *American Legion Magazine*. October 1943.

2186. Frank, L.K. "Status of Comic Books." *New York Times Magazine*. February 6, 1949, p. 36.

2187. Frankes, Margaret. "Comics Are No Longer Comics." *Christian Century*. November 1942, pp. 1349-1351.

2188. Freidman, I.R. "Toward Bigger and Better Comic-'Mags.'" *Clearing House*. November 1941, pp. 166-168.

2189. Funk, Ray. "Rap with Ray." *Near Mint*. April 1981, pp. 20-22.

2190. Gaines, M.C. "Narrative Illustration: The Story of the Comics." *Print*. August 1942, pp. 25-38.

2191. Goldwater, John L. *Americana in Four Colors*. New York: Comics Magazine Association of America, 1974. 48 pp.

2192. Goulart, Ron. *The Adventurous Decade*. New Rochelle, New York: Arlington House, 1975. 224 pp.

2193. Goulart, Ron. *Over 50 Years of American Comic Books*. Lincolnwood, Illinois: The Mallard Press, 1991. 318 pp.

2194. Goulart, Ron. *Ron Goulart's Great History of Comic Books*. Chicago, Illinois: Contemporary Books, 1986. 314 pp.

2195. Goulart, Ron. "Some Comic Book Firsts." In *San Diego Comic Convention 1989* program book, p. 30. San Diego, California: San Diego Comic-Con Committee, 1989.

2196. Goulart, Ron. "That Gang of Mine, Part I." *Comics Buyer's Guide*. August 2, 1991, pp. 58-62-64.

2197. *Great American Comics: 100 Years of Cartoon Art*. Organized by Smithsonian Institution Traveling Exhibition Service and The Ohio State University Library for Communication and Graphic Arts. Columbus, Ohio: Ohio State University, 1990. 56 pp.

2198. Greene, W. "Comics Have Rules of Their Own." *Good Housekeeping*. September 1945, pp. 24 +.

2199. Guardineer, Fred. "Comic Command Performance No. 1." *Cartoonist PROfiles*. June 1975, pp. 26-33.

2200. Gubern, Roman. *El Lenguaje de los Comics*. Barcelona: Peninsula, 1974.

2201. "Half a Century in Comics." *Comics Journal*. September 1981, p. 15.

2202. Harvey, R.C. "Cold Blood and Weak Tea: Trips for Students and Historians." *Comics Journal*. August 1986, pp. 64-68.

2203. Harvey, R.C. "Reruns and Revivals." *Comics Journal*. December 1990, pp. 127-132.

2204. Harvey, R.C. "Shouts in the Street and Other Works of History." *Comics Journal*. April 1987, pp. 44-48.

2205. "Historian Finds Original Comic Book from 1906." *Comics Journal*. November 1992, pp. 13-14.

2206. Horak, Carl J. "Inside the Treasure Chest." *Comics Buyer's Guide*. May 7, 1993, pp. 47, 52.

2207. Hughes, Dave. "Wild Cards." *Speakeasy*. February 1990, pp. 52-53.

2208. Hutchinson, Don. "Those Mad, Mad, Mad Pulp Villains." *Collector's Dream Magazine*. 1:2, pp. 10-21.

2209. Inge, M. Thomas. "American Comic Books: A Brief History and State of the Art." *The World and I*. July 1992, pp. 560-577.

2210. Inge, M. Thomas. "A Chronology of the Development of the American Comic Book." In *The Comic Book Price Guide 1975*, edited by Robert M. Overstreet, pp. 27-31. Cleveland, Tennessee: Robert M. Overstreet, 1975.

2211. Inge, M. Thomas. "A Chronology of the Development of the American Comic Book." In *The Comic Book Price Guide. 1980-81*, edited by R.M. Overstreet, pp. A-41-A-45. Cleveland, Tennessee: 1981.

2212. "I Remember Comic-Books, Part I." *B and W*. No. 1, 1990, p. 9; Part II, No. 2, 1991, pp. 6-7.

2213. Ivie, Larry. *The History of the Comic-Book*. New York: Nostalgia Press, 1972. 250 pp.

2214. "Jekyll-Hyde of the Comics." *Squa Tront*. No. 5, 1974, p. 35.

2215. Johnson, Kim H. "Reluctant Flyer." *Comics Scene*. May 1992, pp. 13-16.

2216. Juanmarti, Jordi. "Gilgamesh II: El Héroe Quiere Ser Inmortal." *El Wendigo*. No. 52, 1991, pp. 8-10.

2217. Kahn, E.J. "Ooff! (Sob) Eep! (Gulp) Zowie!" *New Yorker*. November 29, 1947, pp. 45-58, December 6, 1947, pp. 46-50.

2218. Klingensmith, Grace. "The Old Comics Were More Real." *FCA/S.O.B*. August 1980, p. 5.

2219. Kurtzman, Harvey. *From Argh! to Zap! Harvey Kurtzman's Visual History of the Comics*. New York: Prentice-Hall, 1991. 96 pp.

2220. Lawson, Robert. "The Comics." *Chicago Tribune*. November 13, 1949.

2221. Lesser, Robert. *A Celebration of Comic Art and Memorabilia*. New York: Hawthorn Books, 1975.

2222. Malin, Adam. "The Phenomenon: 1965-1981." *Comics Scene*. January 1981, pp. 24-26.

2223. Mallow, Keith. "Where Have You Gone Herbie Popnecker?" *Comics Scene*. September 1982, pp. 48-49.

2224. Maloney, Russell. "The Comics." *Talks*. April 1948, pp. 18-19.

2225. Marston, W.M. "Why 100,000,000 Americans Read Comics." *American Scholar*. January 1944, pp. 35-44; April 1944, pp. 247-252.

2226. Miller, B.E. "At Long Last." *Horn Book*. July 1948, p. 233.

2227. Miller, Raymond. "Pocket Size Comics." *Fandom Annual*. 1967, pp. 36-42.

2228. Moliterni, Claude. "U.S.A. Comic-Books." In *Histoire Mondiale de la Bande Dessinée*, edited by Pierre Horay, pp. 233-244. Paris: Pierre Horay Éditeur, 1989.

2229. "More Friends for Comics." *Newsweek*. November 27, 1950, p. 50.

2230. "More Proof of Comics Power." *Printer's Ink*. September 10, 1948, p. 20.

2231. Mougin, Lou. "Jerry Grandenetti." *Comics Interview*. November 1984, pp. 53-58.

2232. Murray, Will. "Death Flight of the Doom Staffel." *Comics Scene*. February 1991, pp. 29-32.

2233. Murray, Will. "I Remember... Vandoom." *Comics Collector*. Spring 1984, pp. 34, 36-42.

2234. Murray, Will. "What Evil Lurked? The Shadow in Comics." *Comics Collector*. Summer 1984, pp. 33-34, 36-42.

2235. Murray, Will. "Who Was Klarkash Kenton?" *Comics Buyer's Guide*. December 4, 1992, p. 82.

2236. Myers, Greg W. "Flashback, 50 Years Ago." *Comics Buyer's Guide*. May 25, 1984, p. 1.

2237. "New Models." *Time*. February 7, 1944, pp. 71-72.

2238. Ng, Joe. "Lest They Be Forgotten: A Mudbath with Roy of the Rovers." *Before I Get Old*. July 1986, pp. 31-33.

2239. "Now Comics Have Gone Mad." *Squa Tront*. No. 5, 1974, pp. 36-37.

2240. Nye, Russel B. "Fun in Four Colors, the Comics." In *The Unembarrassed Muse: The Popular Arts in America*, New York: Dial Press, 1970. pp. 216-241.

2241. Olshevsky, George. "Beating Comic Book Inflation." *Collector's Dream Magazine*. 1:2, pp. 6-9.

2242. "Our Archives of Culture." *Newsweek*. July 12, 1954, p. 6.

2243. Pearson, Louise S. "Comics." *Saturday Review of Literature*. June 19, 1948, p. 24.

2244. "The Pioneers." *FCA/S.O.B.* October-November 1980, p. 3.

2245. "Pok! Ach! Pitooon!" *New Republic*. March 11, 1957, p. 7.

2246. Pringle, Henry F. "The Anatomy of Ballyhoo: A New Type of Magazine—Smutty or Smart?" *Outlook*. January 6, 1932.

2247. "Pulp for a Pulp." *The New Transformation*. No. 2, 1969, pp. 12-13.

2248. Reed, Gene. "Odds and Ends." *Dreamline*. March 1982, pp. 35-39.

2249. "Regarding Comic Magazines." *Recreation*. February 1942, p. 689.

2250. "Rootwild Remembered by Jim Jones." *The Collector*. Winter 1973, pp. 26-29.

2251. Santangelo, Tony. "40's Revisited." *Near Mint*. October 1982, pp. 36-39.

2252. Schiff, Jack. "Public Service." *Robin Snyder's History of the Comics*. July 1991, p. 75.

2253. Schiff, Jack and Gene Reed. "Reminisces of a Comic Book Editor." In *The Comic Book Price Guide 1983-84*, edited by R.M. Overstreet, pp. A-64-A-70. Cleveland, Tennessee: 1983.

2254. *75 Years of the Comics*. Intro. by Maurice Horn. Boston, Massachusetts: Boston Book and Art, 1971. 109 pp.

2255. Sewell, H. "Illustrator Meets the Comics." *Horn Book*. March 1948, pp. 136-140.

2256. Shutt, Craig. "1968: The Good, the Great, and the Goofy." *Comics Buyer's Guide*. January 1, 1993, pp. 60, 62, 64-65, 67.

2257. Snowden, George. "Panels in My Life." *Qua Brot*. No. 1, 1985, pp. 47-51.

2258. "Speaking of Pictures; The Democrats Make U.S. Political History, and Rewrite It with Comic Books." *Life*. September 25, 1950, pp. 14-16.

2259. Stark, Larry. "One Man's Opinion." *Squa Tront*. No. 7, 1977, pp. 40-41.

2260. Steranko, James. *The Steranko History of Comics*. Reading, Pennsylvania: Supergrahics, Vol. 1, 1970, 84 pp.; Vol. 2, 1972, 116 pp.

2261. Stoeckler, Gordon. "Comics." *Saturday Review of Literature*. June 19, 1948, p. 24.

2262. "T'aint Funny McGee!" *American Home*. January 1944, pp. 48-49.

2263. Thompson, Lovell. "How Serious Are the Comics?" *Atlantic*. September 1942, pp. 127-129.

2264. Thompson, Lovell. "Not So Comic; Craze for Comic-Strip Magazines." *Atlantic*. January 1941, pp. 105-107.

2265. Thompson, Maggie and Steve Bissette. "'1963' Think Comics Have Gone Too Far? This Is Meant To Bring Them Right Back!" *Comics Buyer's Guide*. December 11, 1992, pp. 26-27.

2266. "Truman's Life in Comic-Book." *New York Sunday News*. October 10, 1948.

2267. Weingroff, Rick. "Gift Comics." *Fandom Annual*. 1967, pp. 1-10.

2268. Whitehill, C.K. "The Comics." *Time*. May 24, 1954, p. 10.

2269. Wigransky, David P. "The Comics." *Saturday Review of Literature*. July 24, 1948.

2270. Wolfson, Martin. "The Comics." *Saturday Review of Literature*. June 19, 1948, p. 24.

2271. Wooley, Charles. *Wooley's History of the Comic Book, 1899-1936*. Lake Buena Vista, Florida: Charles Wooley, 1986. 48 pp.

2272. Zone, Ray. "Anaglyphs: A Survey of the 3-D Comic Books." In *The Comic Book Price Guide 1981-82*, edited by R.M. Overstreet, pp. A-44-A-54. Cleveland, Tennessee: 1981.

Periods

Pre-Golden

2273. "The Early Years Zumbrota, 1910-1925." *FCA/S.O.B.* June/July 1981, p. 7.

2274. Fresnault-Deruelle, Pierre. "Les Comics Américans des Années 30-40. *Critique* (Paris). 27 (1971), pp. 83-88.

2275. Gifford, Denis. *The American Comic Book Catalog: The Evolutionary Era, 1884-1939.* London: Mansell, ca. 1990.

2276. Glasser, Jean Claude. *Funnies: Les Quarante Premières Années de la Bande Dessinée Comique Américaine: 1895-1935.* Paris: Futuropolis, 1984.

2277. Goulart, Ron. "Before Superman. Part II: Popular Comics." *Comics Buyer's Guide.* June 17, 1983, pp. 92-96.

2278. Goulart, Ron. "Before Superman. Part III: The Funnies." *Comics Buyer's Guide.* July 29, 1983, pp. 20, 22.

2279. Goulart, Ron. "Before Superman. Part IV: Tip Top Comics." *Comics Buyer's Guide.* August 12, 1983, pp. 52, 54, 56, 58, 60-61.

2280. Goulart, Ron. "Before Superman. Part V: King Comics." *Comics Buyer's Guide.* September 16, 1983, pp. 40-42.

2281. Goulart, Ron. "Before Superman. Part VI: Super Comics." *Comics Buyer's Guide.* October 14, 1983, pp. 38-40.

2282. Goulart, Ron. "Before Superman. Part VII." *Comics Buyer's Guide.* November 4, 1983, pp. 14, 16, 18.

2283. Goulart, Ron. "Before Superman. Part VIII: Feature Funnies." *Comics Buyer's Guide.* January 6, 1984, pp. 20, 22-23, 26.

2284. Goulart, Ron. "Before Superman. Part IX: New Fun." *Comics Buyer's Guide.* April 6, 1984, pp. 24, 26, 28, 30.

2285. Goulart, Ron. "Before Superman: Part X: More Fun Comics." *Comics Buyer's Guide.* April 13, 1984, pp. 11-12, 14.

2286. Goulart, Ron. "Before Superman: Part XII: New Adventure Comics." *Comics Buyer's Guide.* November 23, 1984, pp. 52, 54.

2287. Goulart, Ron. "Funnies in the Thirties: Part 8: In Uniform." *Comics Buyer's Guide.* November 3, 1989.

2288. "The Guide to the First Heroic Age—From June 1938 to December 1946." *The New Transformation*. No. 2, 1969, pp. 9-11.

2289. Moore, Harold A. "The First Comic Book." *Newsletter*. October 1965, p. 9.

2290. Rodger, W. "Ancestors of the Comic Books." *Hobbies*. January 1975, pp. 140-141+.

2291. Vosburgh, J.R. "How the Comic Book Started." *Commonweal*. May 20, 1949, pp. 146-148. "Discussion." June 3, June 17, July 1, 1949, pp. 199, 244, 293.

2292. Weller, Hayden. "First Comic Book." *Journal of Educational Sociology*. December 1944, p. 195.

Golden

2293. Beck, C.C. "The Birth and Death of the Golden Age." *FCA/S.O.B.* October-November 1980, p. 9; December 1980/January 1981, p. 5; February/March 1981, p. 7.

2294. Benton, Mike. *Superhero Comics of the Golden Age. The Illustrated History*. Dallas, Texas: Taylor Publishing Co., 1992. 200 pp.

2295. Chambers, Jim. "Golden Age Extra." *Comic Book Collector*. January 1993, p. 22.

2296. Gold, Mike, ed. *The Greatest Golden Age Stories Ever Told*. New York: DC Comics, 1990.

2297. Goulart, Ron. "Golden Age Comic-Book Circulation." *Comics Buyer's Guide*. September 21, 1990, pp. 1, 3.

2298. Goulart, Ron. "Looking Back at the Golden Age: Centaur Days Part I." *Comics Feature*. September-October 1984, pp. 10, 59-62.

2299. Goulart, Ron. "Looking Back on the Golden Age." *Comics Feature*. January-February 1985, pp. 16-18.

2300. Goulart, Ron. "Looking Back on the Golden Age: The Blue Bolt." *Comics Feature*. October 1986, pp. 44-47.

2301. Goulart, Ron. "Looking Back on the Golden Age: Centaur Days Part 2." *Comics Feature*. November-December 1984, pp. 16-18, 40-42.

2302. Goulart, Ron. "Looking Back on the Golden Age: The Quality Gang (Part I)." *Comics Feature*. January-February 1984, pp. 44-49.

2303. Goulart, Ron. "Remembering the Golden Age: Before the War: Part II." *Comics Buyer's Guide*. February 5, 1993, pp. 28, 32.

2304. Goulart, Ron. "Remembering the Golden Age: This Is a Job for Adman." *Comics Buyer's Guide*. October 6, 1989, pp. 50, 52.

2305. Goulart, Ron. "Remembering the Golden Age: Welcome to the Club." *Comics Buyer's Guide*. August 4, 1989, p. 52.

2306. Goulart, Ron. "Remembering the Golden Age: Who Was That Masked Man (Part II). *Comics Buyer's Guide*. February 1, 1991, pp. 46, 48, 50, 52, 55.

2307. Goulart, Ron. "Remembering the Golden Age: Who Was That Masked Man? (Part III)." *Comics Buyer's Guide*. March 1, 1991, pp. 50, 54.

2308. Goulart, Ron. "Remembering the Golden Age: Who Was That Masked Woman?" *Comics Buyer's Guide*. May 3, 1991, pp. 54-55.

2309. Goulart, Ron, ed. *Comics. The Golden Age. The History of DC Comics. 50 Years of Fantastic Imagination*. Canoga Park, California: New Media Books, 1985. 100 pp.

2310. "Jerry Iger, Golden Age Editor." *Comics Journal*. December 1990, p. 15.

2311. Kudler, Harvey. "Golden Memories: First Impressions of Four Early Comic Books." *Comics Buyer's Guide*. May 7, 1993, pp. 39, 42.

2312. "Looking Back on the Golden Age." *Comics Feature*. May 1986, pp. 36-38.

2313. "The Marvel Family in the Golden Age." *FCA/S.O.B.* August 1980, p. 8.

2314. Miller, Raymond. "Wing Comics." *The Golden Age*. No. 2, 1967, pp. 1-6.

2315. O'Brien, Richard. "Golden Age Gleanings." *Comics Journal*. October 1974, p. 7; December 1974, p. 11; February 1975, p. 20; June 1975, p. 17; July 1975, p. 10; August 1975, p. 21; October 1975, p. 14; December 1975, p. 15; January 1976, p. 21.

2316. O'Brien, Richard. *The Golden Age of Comic Books, 1937-1945*. New York: Ballantine, 1977. 61 pp.

2317. Savage, William W., jr. *Comic Books and America, 1945-1954*. Norman, Oklahoma: University of Oklahoma Press, 1990. 151 pp.

2318. Seppi, Bob, ed. *The Golden Age Review*. St. Petersburg, Florida: Superlith, 1978. 96 pp.

2319. Thomas, Roy. "Looking Back on the Golden Age." *Comics Feature*. May 1987, pp. 50-54.

Silver

2320. Boerner, Brian C. "The Silver Age of Comics." *Comics Feature*. November 1980, pp. 34-41.

2321. Carter, Gary M. "The Silver Age... The Beginning." *The Comic Book Price Guide*. No. 20, 1990, pp. A-93-A-107.

2322. Chambérs, Jim. "Silver Bulletins." *Comic Book Collector*. January 1993, p. 23.

2323. Contarino, J. Keith. "When Was the Silver Age Anyway?" *Comic Book Marketplace*. No. 3, pp. 68-70.

2324. Jacobs, Will and Gerard Jones. *The Comic Book Heroes. From the Silver Age to the Present*. New York: Crown, 1985. 292 pp.

2325. Jacobs, Will and Gerard Jones. "Silver Age: Marvel Phase II." *Comics Feature*. January 1986, pp. 16-17, 44-46.

2326. Jacobs, Will and Gerard Jones. "Silver Age. Part I: The Marvel Age of Comics." *Comics Feature*. November-December 1984, pp. 43-51.

2327. Jacobs, Will and Gerard Jones. "The Silver Age. Bizarre Characters and Fantastic Weapons." *Comics Feature*. January-February 1985, pp. 10-11.

2328. Jones, Gerard. "Silver Age." *Comics Feature*. February 1987, pp. 50-54.

2329. Jones, Gerard. "Silver Age—Back to the Future." *Comics Feature*. May 1987, pp. 36-39.

2330. Morrissey, Richard and Murray R. Ward. "The Silver Age of Comics." *Comics Feature*. June 1980, pp. 21-26.

2331. Murray, Will. "Silver Age." *Comics Feature*. October 1986, pp. 50-54.

2332. Shutt, Craig. "Team-Ups Had a Personal Side in DC's Silver Age." In *Comics Buyer's Guide 1993 Annual*, pp. 54-64. Iola, Wisconsin: Krause, 1992.

2333. Van Hise, James. "Before the Silver Age." *Comics Feature*. May 1987, pp. 46-49.

2334. Ward, Murray R. "The Silver Age of Comics: Part III." *Comics Feature*. July-August 1980, pp. 30-36.

2335. Ward, Murray R. "The Silver Age of Comics Part IV." *Comics Feature.* September 1980, pp. 36-40.

Publishers

2336. Arbunich, Marty. "The Nedor Comics Group." *Fandom Annual.* 1967, pp. 18-28.

2337. Disbrow, Jay E. *The Iger Comics Kingdom.* El Cajon, California: Blackthorne, 1985. 95 pp.

2338. Fulop, Scott D. "Archie Comic Publications: The Mirth of a Legend." *Comics Buyer's Guide.* No. 21, 1991, pp. A-77-A-78.

2339. Gambaccini, Paul. "The History of Flash Comics." *Fandom Annual.* 1967, pp. 13-17.

2340. Isabella, Tony. "The Scarlotti Comics Group." *Comics Buyer's Guide.* May 6, 1983, p. 12.

2341. Miller, Raymond. "A History of ACE Publications." *Masquerader.* No. 6, 1964, pp. 4-7.

2342. Murray, Will. "Who Could Forget Mighty Comics?" *Comics Buyer's Guide.* May 3, 1991, pp. 55, 58, 60-62.

2343. Wooley, Chuck. "The Lost Comics Companies." *Comics Feature.* January 1981, pp. 67-70; December 1981, pp. 44-46.

2344. Wooley, Chuck. "The Lost Comics Companies—Eastern Color Printing Co." *Comics Feature.* September-October 1981, pp. 128-130.

2345. Wooley, Chuck. "The Lost Comics Companies: Jumbo Comics." *Comics Feature.* February 1981, pp. 92-95.

2346. Wooley, Chuck. "The Lost Comics Companies—Progressive Publishers." *Comics Feature.* January 1981, pp. 67-70.

ACG

2347. Murray, Edwin L. *The American Comics Group, a Sentimental Favorite.* Durham, North Carolina: 1978. 30 pp. plus 10 pp. supplement.

2348. Vance, Michael. "ACG: The Little Giant." *Comics Buyer's Guide.* September 1, 1989, pp. 44-45, 48.

2349. Vance, Michael. "ACG: The Little Giant: Dabbing in TrueVision and Super-Heroics." *Comics Buyer's Guide*. November 3, 1989, pp. 50-51.

2350. Vance, Michael. "ACG: The Little Giant. Kiss and Sell: The Romance Titles." *Comics Buyer's Guide*. October 6, 1989, pp. 52, 58.

2351. Vance, Michael. "ACG: The Little Giant. Laughing Matter, Part 2." *Comics Buyer's Guide*. March 25, 1988, p. 33.

2352. Vance, Michael. "ACG: The Little Giant, Part 5: Richard Hughes." *Comics Buyer's Guide*. June 10, 1988, p. 42.

2353. Vance, Michael. "ACG: The Little Giant: The Rest of the Gory." *Comics Buyer's Guide*. August 4, 1989, pp. 56, 60, 62.

DC

2354. Bridwell, E. Nelson. "Interview with Two Supermen." *Amazing World of DC Comics*. February 1976, pp. 13-17.

2355. Carter, Gary M. and Kent L. Carter. "DC Before Superman." In *The Comic Book Price Guide 1983-84*, edited by R.M. Overstreet, pp. A-72-A-86. Cleveland, Tennessee: 1983.

2356. DC Comics. *Fifty Who Made DC Great*. New York: DC Comics, 1985. 56 pp.

2357. Goulart, Ron, ed. *Year of the Bat: The History of DC Comics. Fifty Years of Fantastic Imagination*. Las Vegas, Nevada: Pioneer Books, 1989. 100 pp.

2358. "History of DC Comics." *Comics Buyer's Guide*. September 6, 1985, pp. 30, 32.

2359. "A History of DC Comics [by DC Comics]." In *Comics Buyer's Guide 1993 Annual*, pp. 39-42. Iola, Wisconsin: Krause, 1992.

2360. Shutt, Craig. "The Secret DC Silver Age Revival Plan for 1993!" *Comics Buyer's Guide*. April 2, 1993, pp. 98, 100.

2361. Tollin, Anthony. "Yesterday, Today and Tomorrow." *Amazing World of DC Comics*. February 1976, pp. 6-12.

EC

2362. Boatner, E.B. "Good Lord! Choke... Gasp... It's EC!" In *The Comic Book Price Guide 1979-80*, edited by R.M. Overstreet, pp. A-43-A-76. Cleveland, Tennessee: 1979.

2363. *The Complete EC Library*. 53 Vols. West Plains, Missouri: Russ Cochran Publisher, 1979-1989.

2364. Decker, Dwight R. "Muted Applause from Behind the Iron Curtain: EC Has the Last Laugh 30 Years Later." *Comics Journal.* December 1977, pp. 56-57.

2365. "The EC Writers." *Squa Tront.* No. 9, 1983, pp. 34-36.

2366. Fiore, Robert. "The Life, Death and Resurrection of EC Comics." *Comics Journal.* November 1980, pp. 47-53.

2367. Hill, Roger. "E.C.'s Death." *Squa Tront.* No. 3, 1969, pp. 52-59.

2368. Hunt, Leon. "EC on the Couch." *Comics Journal.* December 1989, pp. 54-63.

2369. Levin, Bob. "EC Comics." *Spin.* August 1988, pp. 44-45.

2370. Now, Michael. "Comics in the EC Mold or Just Moldy Comics." *Comics Journal.* June 1984, pp. 7-9.

2371. *Panic.* The Complete EC Library. 2 Vols. West Plains, Missouri: R. Cochran, 1984. (Reprints 1954-55 comic book *Panic.*)

2372. "The Secret EC Line." *Squa Tront.* No. 9, 1983, pp. 51-53.

2373. Spicer, Bill. "A Capsule History of E.C.'s 'Weird Science.'" *Fandom Annual.* 1967, pp. 29-31.

2374. Strzyz, Klaus. "EC Lives! Die Geschichte der EC-Comics." *Comixene. Das Comicfachmagazin.* 1 Teil, 8:34 (1981), pp. 4-9; 2 Teil, 8:35 (1981), pp. 14-17.

2375. "The Transcripts: 1972 EC Convention." *Squa Tront.* No. 8, 1978, pp. 21-30.

2376. Van Hise, James. *The EC Comics Story.* Canoga Park, California: Psi Fi Movie Press, 1987. 54 pp.

2377. Watt-Evans, Lawrence. "The EC Legend: A Brief History." *Comics Collector.* Winter 1984, pp. 40-46.

Fawcett

2378. "Golden Age Fawcett Artist." *FCA/S.O.B.* December 1981/January 1982, p. 3.

2379. Pierce, John. "Fawcett Comic Character Mary Marvel." *FCA/S.O.B.* October/November 1981, p. 3.

2380. Robbins, Ed. "Fawcett Golden Age of Comic Artists." *FCA/S.O.B.* August/September 1981, p. 5.

2381. Wego, Walter. "Were Fawcett Comics Art?" *FCA/S.O.B.* April/May 1981, p. 8.

Marvel

2382. Anton, Uwe. "25 Jahre Marvel Comics." In *Comic-Jahrbuch 1986*, edited by Martin Compart and Andreas C. Knigge, pp. 114-120. Frankfurt: Ullstein GmbH, 1985.

2383. Borchert, Karlheinz. "Marvel—ein Wandel Nach 20 Jahren?" *Comixene. Das Comicfachmagazin* (Hanover). 8:39 (1981), pp. 14-19.

2384. Daniels, Les. *Marvel: Five Fabulous Decades of the World's Greatest Comics.* New York: Harry N. Abrams, 1991. 287 pp.

2385. Griffith, Rob. "Forgotten Marvels." *Comics Buyer's Guide.* December 18, 1987, pp. 38-40.

2386. Lee, Stan. *Origins of Marvel Comics.* New York: Simon and Schuster, 1974. 254 pp.

2387. Lee, Stan. *Son of Origins of Marvel Comics.* New York: Simon and Schuster, 1975. 249 pp.

2388. "Marvel Turns 20." *Comics Scene.* January 1981, pp. 11-19.

2389. Olshevsky, George. "The Origin of Marvel Comics." In *The Comic Book Price Guide 1980-81*, edited by R.M. Overstreet, pp. A-46-A-73. Cleveland, Tennessee: 1981.

2390. Thomas, Roy. "One Man's Family. The Saga of the Mighty Marvels." *Alter Ego.* No. 7, 1964, pp. 18-27.

MLJ

2391. Goulart, Ron. "The MLJ Story: Part I." *Comics Collector.* Winter 1984, pp. 21-23.

2392. Goulart, Ron. "The MLJ Story, Part II. 'Top Notch Comics.'" *Comics Collector.* Spring 1984, pp. 18-20.

2393. Goulart, Ron. "The MLJ Story Part III. Pep." *Comics Collector.* Summer 1984, pp. 43-47.

2394. Goulart, Ron. "The MLJ Story—Part IV: Zip Comics." *Comics Collector.* Fall 1984, pp. 54-57.

2395. Keltner, Howard. "MLJ Leads the Way!" *Alter Ego.* No. 4, 1962, pp. 2, 9-18.

2396. Keltner, Howard. "MLJ Leads the Way!" *Fandom Annual.* 1967, pp. 43-52.

Warren

2397. Bissette, Steve. "Warren: R.I.P." *Comics Feature*. January-February 1984, pp. 13-17.

2398. Mougin, Lou. "Days of Fear and Terror at Warren." *Amazing Heroes*. May 1982, pp. 47-52.

Whitman

2399. Manesis, Dale. "A Listing of Big Little Books and Related Publications Printed by Whitman Publishing Company." United Printing Services, 1970. 23 pp.

2400. Molson, Francis J. "Films, Funnies and Fighting the War: Whitman's Children's Books in the 1940s." *Journal of Popular Culture*. Spring 1984, pp. 147-154.

2401. "Western Suspends Its Whitman Comics Line." *Comics Buyer's Guide*. May 18, 1984, p. 1.

2402. "Whitman: In Hiatus or Gone for Good?" *Comics Journal*. October 1984, pp. 14-15.

BUSINESS ASPECTS

2403. Anderson, Richard W. "Biff! Pow! Comic Books Make a Comeback." *Business Week*. September 2, 1985, pp. 59-60.

2404. Andreasen, Henrik. "Samlermani." *Seriejournalen*. December 1991, p. 17.

2405. Andreasen, Henrik. "USA-Nyt." *Seriejournalen*. September 1992, p. 12.

2406. "The Batglut Returns." *Comics Journal*. April 1990, pp. 104-116.

2407. "BatSummer Considered a Boon by Most." *Comics Journal*. November 1989, pp. 9-12.

2408. Batty, Ward. "A Funny Thing Happened on the Way to This Summer." *Comics Buyer's Guide*. June 19, 1987, pp. 32, 34, 38.

2409. "The Big Business of *Batman Returns*." *Comics Journal*. May 1992, p. 20.

2410. "Big Numbers To Debut in April." *Speakeasy*. February 1990, p. 9.

2411. Bloom, M.T. "Harvest Reaped in Comics; Reselling Used Newspapers." *Nation's Business*. June 1949, p. 86.

2412. Borax, Mark. "Hank Rose." *Comics Interview.* No. 48, 1987, pp. 55-62.

2413. Borax, Mark. "Michael Dobson." *Comics Interview.* No. 56, 1988, pp. 53-59.

2414. Borax, Mark. "Steve Schanes." *Comics Interview.* No. 54, 1988, pp. 33-39.

2415. Brabham, Dennis. "You Can't Judge a Book by Its Cover." *Comics Journal.* May 1993, pp. 7-8.

2416. Braun, S. "Comic Book Industry." *New York Times.* May 2, 1971, II, pp. 1, 32.

2417. "Comics a 'Penny Business.'" *Comics Journal.* September 1983, pp. 9-10.

2418. "Comics Business Faces Uncertain Future." *Comics Journal.* February 1991, pp. 15-17.

2419. "Comics Vs. Beer in St. Louis." *Comics Journal.* July 1991, p. 16.

2420. "Creator Vs. Corporate Ownership." *Comics Journal.* September 1990, pp. 101-106.

2421. "Crisis on Infinite Earths." *Comics Interview.* No. 26, 1985, pp. 6-25.

2422. Daglis, Andrew. "Money and... the Business and the Art of Comics." *Comics Journal.* April 1989, pp. 100-108.

2423. Friel, Jim. "Where Do Comic Books Come from, Daddy?" *Comics Collector.* Summer 1984, pp. 48-49.

2424. Furman, Nannette, *et al.* "What Can Industry Professionals Learn from the Recent Market Downturn?" *Comics Business.* July 1987, pp. 20, 22, 24-29.

2425. Groth, Gary. "Class Wars." *Comics Journal.* October 1992, pp. 3-4.

2426. Groth, Gary. "Comics: The New Culture of Illiteracy." *Comics Journal.* August 1992, pp. 3-6.

2427. Groth, Gary. "So Far, So Bad: The Schlockification of the Comics Market." *Comics Journal.* February 1991, pp. 5-10.

2428. Groth, Gary. "Tarnished Image." *Comics Journal.* March 1992, pp. 3-4.

2429. Harris, Jack C. "Michael Uslan and Ben Melnicker." *Comics Interview.* No. 77, 1989, pp. 55-67.

2430. "Harvey and Eisner Award Winners Announced." *Comics Journal.* October 1992, p. 17.

2431. Henry, Gordon M. "Bang! Pow! Zap! Heroes Are Back! After Decades in Decline, Comic Books are on the Rebound." *Time*. 128:14 (1986), p. 62.

2432. Herzog, Marty. "Neil Harris." *Comics Interview*. No. 54, 1988, pp. 41-51.

2433. Kraft, David A. "Dick Goldwater." *Comics Interview*. May 1983, pp. 47-52.

2434. Kraft, David A. "Gary Groth and Kim Thompson." *Comics Interview*. August 1984, pp. 48-69.

2435. Kreiner, Rich. "The Blockbuster Mentality." *Comics Journal*. July 1986, pp. 7-8.

2436. Lev, Michael. "Reaching Beyond the Ghouls and Gore for Major Payoffs." *New York Times*. February 17, 1991.

2437. McAllister, Matthew P. "Cultural Argument and Organizational Constraint in the Comic Book Industry." *Journal of Communication*. Winter 1990, pp. 55-71.

2438. McConnell, Kevin. "The House of Second-Hand Ideas." *Comics Journal*. August 1982, pp. 6-7.

2439. Mead, Ronald. "Comics Are Big Business." *Printing Magazine*. August 1947, p. 52.

2440. "*New York Times* Writes about Comics Industry." *Retail Express*. November 6, 1987, p. 8.

2441. "Novel Explores Comics Worlds." *Comics Journal*. September 1990, p. 19.

2442. Olbrich, David W. "Who Pays for a Free Market?" *Comics Business*. September 1987, pp. 5, 7.

2443. O'Neill, Patrick D. "Gary Berman and Adam Malin." *Comics Interview*. No. 56, 1988, pp. 49-51.

2444. O'Neill, Patrick D. "The Other Side: Does the 'Real World' Care?" *Comics Journal*. October 1983, pp. 20-21.

2445. O'Neill, Patrick D. "Steve Saffel and Pamela Rutt." *Comics Interview*. No. 55, 1988, pp. 43-49.

2446. Perry, George. "Inside the Wham! Zap! Pow! Business." *The Sunday Times Magazine*. November 26, 1967, pp. 64-65, 67, 69.

2447. "Personality Develops." *Comics Journal*. May 1992, pp. 20-21.

2448. Poh, Robbie. "Going Great Guns." *Before I Get Old*. January 1987, pp. 27-28.

2449. "Reprint Books: Classic Art or Retracings." *Comics Journal*. December 1991, pp. 20-21.

2450. "Rival Books of Public Domain Comic Strips." *Comics Journal*. September 1990, pp. 14-15.

2451. Schreck, Bob, *et al.* "What Is the Most Important Thing the Industry Must Do To Expand the Comics Audience?" *Comics Business*. August 1987, pp. 16-20.

2452. Smith, Mike and Ann Eagen. "More Sidelines and How To Get Them." *Comics Business*. September 1987, p. 10.

2453. "The State of the Comics Industry 1992." *Comics Journal*. March 1992, pp. 11-13.

2454. "The State of the Industry 1992-93." *Comics Journal*. February 1993, pp. 9-14.

2455. Strnad, Jan. "Business Is Service." *Comics Business*. August 1987, p. 4.

2456. Stuempfig, Julie. "Comics Professionals Speak Out on: Poor-Selling Titles." *Comics Buyer's Guide*. May 21, 1993, pp. 120, 122.

2457. Stuempfig, Julie. "State of the Industry: What Is a Comic Book?" In *Comics Buyer's Guide 1993 Annual*, pp. 42-44. Iola, Wisconsin: Krause, 1992.

2458. Stuempfig, Julie. "What Problems Do Comic Books Face?" In *Comics Buyer's Guide 1993 Annual*, pp. 50-53. Iola, Wisconsin: Krause, 1992.

2459. Swartz, J.E. "Comic Book Advertising: Directions and Implications for Research." *Southwestern Mass Communication Journal*. 1:2 (1985), pp. 35-42.

2460. Talley, Brian. "David Weaver." *Comics Interview*. July 1984, pp. 64-66.

2461. Tan, Stephen. "Growing Up To Catch Up." *Before I Get Old*. July 1986, p. 26.

2462. Tan, Stephen. "Looking Out for No. 1." *Before I Get Old*. March 1987, pp. 22-24.

2463. Tan, Stephen. "Price Wars." *Before I Get Old*. May 1987, pp. 31-32.

2464. Thompson, Maggie. "The Comics Industry: 1988." *Comics Buyer's Guide*. March 25, 1988, pp. 55-56, 58, 60.

2465. Thompson, Maggie. "The Comics Industry: 1989." *Comics Buyer's Guide*. March 31, 1989, pp. 58, 60, 62, 66, 68.

2466. Thornsjo, Doug. "The Licensing Game." *Comics Buyer's Guide*. December 7, 1984, pp. 20, 26, 28, 30, 32, 38.

2467. Underhill, Rod. "Steve Schanes." *Comics Interview*. No. 51 (1988), pp. 50-59.

Production

2468. "*Action Comics* To Be Published Weekly." *Retail Express*. November 6, 1987, p. 1.

2469. Adams, Neal and Doug Murray. "Why I'm on Strike Against National." *Inside Comics*. Spring 1974, p. 37.

2470. "*Amazing Heroes* Folding." *Comics Journal*. March 1992, p. 22.

2471. "Archie Comics Scraps Spectrum Comics Imprint." *Comics Journal*. September 1989, pp. 5-7.

2472. "Arrow Comics." *Comics Buyer's Guide*. March 18, 1988, p. 28.

2473. "Arrow Comics Returns." *Comics Journal*. January 1993, p. 29.

2474. "The Battle for *A Distant Soil*." *Comics Journal*. May 1986, pp. 7-12.

2475. "The Battle for Amazing, Wonder Color Titles." *Comics Journal*. April 1987, pp. 14-15.

2476. Bethke, Marilyn. "The New Kids on the Block: Amazing Heroes Comics Scene." *Comics Journal*. January 1982, pp. 110-111.

2477. Bethke, Marilyn. "New Media's Publishing Empire." *Comics Journal*. October 1982, pp. 154-159.

2478. "Caveat Creator." *Comics Journal*. February 1993, pp. 18-19.

2479. "Comics Companies Reborn in Chicago." *Comics Journal*. June 1991, pp. 9-10.

2480. "Comics Publishers." *Comics Buyer's Guide*. August 27, 1993, pp. 26-28, 30, 32, 34, 36, 40, 42, 44, 46, 48, 50, 56.

2481. "Comics Step Slowly into Computer Age." *Comics Journal*. February 1991, p. 20.

2482. "Comics Trade Press Expands This Summer." *Comics Journal*. July 1987, p. 25.

2483. "Continuity Comics Relaunched." *Comics Journal*. April 1993, p. 20.

2484. "Continuity To Publish 'Captain Power' Comic." *Comics Buyer's Guide*. April 15, 1988, p. 1.

2485. "Dark Horse Adapts 'Aliens' to Comics." *Comics Buyer's Guide*. December 18, 1987, pp. 1, 3.

2486. Darnall, Steve. "Topps Enters the Comic Book Market." *Comic Book Collector*. January 1993, pp. 14-15.

2487. "Declarations of Independents." *Comics Buyer's Guide*. August 30, 1991, pp. 20, 22, 24, 26, 28, 30, 34, 36, 38, 40, 42, 66, 68, 92.

2488. "Doran/WARP Dispute Now Settled." *Comics Journal*. August 1986, p. 17.

2489. "Eastman Buying *Heavy Metal*." *Comics Journal*. February 1992, p. 23.

2490. Eisner, Will. "The Alternative Comic Book Press." *Comics Journal*. September 1981, pp. 228-231.

2491. "Eternity's *Ex-Mutants* Starts Over, Spins Off New Titles." *Retail Express*. January 8, 1988, p. 11.

2492. "FAN Press: Mediascene Becomes Prevue." *Comics Journal*. April 1980, p. 19.

2493. "Fantagraphics Books: Prime Cuts." *Comics Journal*. September 1986, p. 27.

2494. "From Archie to Spidey to Anne." *New York Times*. February 17, 1991.

2495. Gorrell, Jeff. "Dell Comics Are Good Comics." *Rocket's Blast Comic Collector*. No. 119, 1975, pp. 32-33.

2496. Groth, Gary. "Gutlessness and Greed Run Rampant in the Trade Press." *Comics Journal*. July 1989, pp. 3-4.

2497. Groth, Gary. "House of No Shame." *Comics Journal*. February 1986, pp. 6-7.

2498. Groth, Gary. "Mainstream Comics Have at Best, Tenuous Virtues." *Comics Journal*. August 1992, pp. 89-100. (Alan Moore on the industry).

2499. Groth, Gary. "...That's the Spice of Life, Bud." *Comics Journal*. August 1992, pp. 45-54, 56-59, 61-66, 68-70. (Todd McFarlane on the industry).

2500. "*Heavy Metal* on Auction Block." *Comics Journal*. November 1989, p. 15.

2501. Heike, Mark G. "Paragon: The One and Only." *Comics Buyer's Guide*. December 18, 1992, p. 28.

2502. "Historic Comics Printer To Be Sold." *Comics Journal*. September 1991, p. 5.

2503. Julius, Lawrence F. "DC Vs Marvel: Which Is Better?" *Dreamline*. March 1982, pp. 12-13.

2504. Kreiner, Rich. "Brave New Whirl: A Survey of Iconographix Comics." *Comics Journal*. March 1993, pp. 109-112.

2505. Kuxhouse, Daryl. "Polish off the Second Bananas." *Penstuff*. June 1991, p. 3.

2506. "Look Mom! Suspends Publication." *Comics Journal*. October 1984, p. 19.

2507. Lucas, Mark. "Comics in 1993." In *San Diego Comic Convention 1993*, pp. 38-40. San Diego, California: 1993.

2508. Luciano, Dale. "High Profiles and Low Print Runs." *Comics Journal*. January 1988, pp. 40-48.

2509. McMeel, John P. "A Voice from the Heartland Alive and Well, Thank You." *Media Studies Journal*. Summer 1992, pp. 55-61.

2510. "Mainstream Media Courts Comic Book Artists." *Comics Journal*. November 1992, pp. 15-16.

2511. "Malibu Moves Ahead of DC in Comics Market." *Comics Journal*. August 1992, pp. 7-8.

2512. "Megaton Comics Suspends Publication; Blames Distributors, Low Orders." *Retail Express*. January 8, 1988, p. 4.

2513. "Mercy Killings; Street and Smith." *Time*. April 18, 1949, pp. 42+.

2514. "*National Lampoon* Cuts Back." *Comics Journal*. October 1991, p. 15.

2515. "A New Comics Publisher." *Comics Journal*. August 1982, p. 13.

2516. "Penguin Ceases Publication of Comics Albums." *Comics Journal*. February 1993, pp. 15-16.

2517. "Personality Buys *Amazing Heroes*." *Comics Journal*. February 1993, p. 21.

2518. "Phoenix Productions Rises from the Ashes of the Mass Press." *Comic Book Newsletter*. February 1988, p. 8.

2519. "Quality Look Predicted for Quality Comics with Quartuccio and Keenan." *Retail Express*. January 8, 1988, p. 13.

2520. "Re-introducing: Alpha Productions." *Comics Buyer's Guide*. April 9, 1993, pp. 100, 102.

2521. "Remco's Assets Assigned to Printer." *Comics Journal*. February 1993, p. 17.

2522. "Renaissance Comics Premieres Three." *Comics Journal*. September 1986, p. 28.

2523. "Renegade 'Refits' Publishing Strategy." *Comics Journal.* March 1989, pp. 17-18.

2524. "Revolutionary To Drop New Kids Issue." *Comics Journal.* October 1990, pp. 7-8.

2525. Rovin, Jeff. "How Not To Run a Comic Book Company." *Comics Journal.* February 1987, pp. 96-103.

2526. "School House Press Starts Year with Bang!" *Comic Book Newsletter.* January 1988, p. 5.

2527. Schultz, Adam. "Marvel Vs. DC: By the Numbers." In *Comics Buyer's Guide 1993 Annual*, pp. 16, 18, 20, 22. Iola, Wisconsin: Krause, 1992.

2528. "Shooter, Voyager Reach Agreement." *Comics Journal.* August 1993, pp. 18-19.

2529. Sloan, Dorothy. "What's Next from Mirage? A Talk with the Creators of Comics' Newest Universe." *Comics Buyer's Guide.* June 25, 1993, pp. 46, 50.

2530. Slutsker, Gary. "The Secret Is in the Repackaging." *Forbes*, June 15, 1987, pp. 230-231.

2531. Stradley, Randy. "Dark Horse Comics: From the Beginning." *Comics Buyer's Guide.* June 4, 1993, pp. 26-30.

2532. "Super Response for a Super Group." *Comics Collector.* Fall 1985, pp. 33-34.

2533. "Taboo #2 Finds Binder." *Comics Journal.* September 1989, pp. 7-8.

2534. Thompson, Don. "Malibu Introduces Its Super-Hero Ultraverse." *Comics Buyer's Guide.* March 26, 1993, pp. 26-28.

2535. Thompson, Kim. "... All They Have To Lose Is a Cog in a Wheel...." *Comics Journal.* August 1992, pp. 71-81, 83-87. (Chris Claremont on the industry).

2536. Thompson, Maggie. "Harvey Publications Sold." *Comics Buyer's Guide.* September 1, 1989, pp. 1, 20.

2537. Thompson, Maggie. "Voyager Announces New Valiant Projects." *Comics Buyer's Guide.* December 18, 1992, pp. 26-27.

2538. "'Total Eclipse' Is Guaranteed." *Comics Buyer's Guide.* March 18, 1988, p. 3.

2539. "Upshot Editor Forms Own Company." *Comics Journal.* September 1986, p. 23.

2540. "Valiant Promises Readers an Exceptional Summer." *Comics Buyer's Guide.* May 28, 1993, pp. 26-28.

2541. "*WAP!* Officially Laid to Rest." *Comics Journal*. June 1991, p. 18.

2542. "WARP Titles Now under Apple Aegis." *Comics Journal*. August 1986, p. 17.

2543. Young, Frank. "Comics Used To Be About Telling Stories...." *Comics Journal*. August 1992, pp. 114-119. (David Mazzucchelli on the industry).

Blackthorne

2544. "Blackthorne Audited." *Comics Journal*. August 1988, pp. 12-13.

2545. "Blackthorne Premieres New Titles." *Comics Journal*. September 1986, p. 26.

2546. "Blackthorne Struggles To Stay Afloat." *Comics Journal*. February 1990, pp. 7-8.

Charlton

2547. "Charlton: Back from the Dead." *Comics Journal*. September 1986, p. 22.

2548. "Charlton Comics Suspends Publication." *Comics Journal*. October 1984, p. 18.

2549. "Charlton Goes Down for the Count." *Comics Journal*. November 1985, pp. 10-11.

Comico

2550. "Comico, Blackthorne, Announce Difficulties." *Speakeasy*. April 1990, p. 11.

2551. "Comico Cancels Half Its Line." *Comics Journal*. April 1989, pp. 5-6.

2552. "Comico Files Chapter 11." *Comics Journal*. April 1990, pp. 11-12.

2553. "Comico Owes Printer $700,000." *Comics Journal*. December 1987, pp. 11-12.

2554. "Comico's Comeback." *Comics Journal*. December 1990, p. 8.

2555. "Comico Sold." *Comics Journal*. September 1990, pp. 9-10.

2556. "Comico Suspends Operations." *Comics Journal*. October 1990, p. 8.

2557. "Three Former Comico Titles Find New Homes." *Comics Journal*. May 1989, pp. 13-14.

2558. "Whither Comico?" *Comics Journal*. February 1991, p. 12.

DC

2559. Adams, Bob. "Dynamic DC Duo." *Publishing and Production Executive.* August 1993, pp. 10-12, 15.

2560. Berger, Thomas. "Impact Comics." *Seriejournalen.* March 1992, pp. 36-37.

2561. "Big Changes at DC Comics." *Comics Journal.* October 1992, p. 26.

2562. Choy, Larry. "DC Strut Their Stuff." *Before I Get Old.* January 1987, pp. 26-27.

2563. "DC Aims To Take a Bite Out of Comics with Piranha." *Comics Journal.* September 1987, pp. 13-14.

2564. "DC Allied with Milestone Media." *Comics Journal.* October 1992, pp. 26-27.

2565. "DC Announces Format Change 50¢—40 Page Books in June." *Comics Journal.* February 1977, pp. 8-10.

2566. "DC Changes Labeling Policy." *Comics Journal.* September 1987, pp. 11-12.

2567. "DC Changes Ownership Policy." *Comics Journal.* July 1988, p. 5.

2568. "DC Comics." *Comics Journal.* March 1979, pp. 17-18.

2569. "DC Comics: The Order Changeth... Again." *Comics Scene.* July 1982, p. 9.

2570. "DC Comics To Supervise Operations of 'Mad.'" *Comics Buyer's Guide.* December 25, 1992, p. 28.

2571. "DC Departs Sparta." *Comics Journal.* December 1991, p. 18.

2572. "DC Derring-Do." *Speakeasy.* April 1990, p. 15.

2573. "DC Hires Bob Wayne, Restructures Marketing Department." *Retail Express.* July 17, 1987, pp. 1, 12.

2574. "DC Skifter Tryk." *Seriejournalen.* March 1992, p. 13.

2575. "DC Softens *The Score.*" *Comics Journal.* April 1990, p. 12.

2576. "DC Sweeps Kirby Award Nominations." *Comics Journal.* July 1987, p. 26.

2577. "DC To Print, Distribute Comico." *Comics Journal.* January 1989, pp. 17-19.

2578. Harvey, R.C. "DC Is Dull Comics." *Comics Journal.* Winter 1981, pp. 113-123.

2579. "*History of DC Universe* Is Late." *Retail Express.* November 20, 1987, p. 1.

2580. Luscombe, Belinda. "DC Comics Switches Printing Facilities to Ronalds Printers in Montreal, Quebec." *Magazine Week News*. December 2, 1991, p. 11.

2581. Metzger, Kim. "Warner Loses $300 Million, But DC Makes a Profit." *Comics Buyer's Guide*. November 11, 1983, p. 1.

2582. Poh, Robby. "My Vote for DC." *Before I Get Old*. March 1987, pp. 27-28.

2583. Thompson, Maggie. "Time Warner: DC Comics Part of the World's Biggest Media Company." *Comics Buyer's Guide*. August 18, 1989, p. 3.

2584. "Time-Warner Merger Completed." *Comics Journal*. November 1989, pp. 15-17.

2585. "Warner Communications Announces Merger with Time Inc." *Comics Journal*. April 1989, pp. 10-12.

Disney

2586. De Giacomo, Franco. "Le Storie a Fumetti di Disney." *Linus*. No. 9, 1965.

2587. "Disney Comics Decimated." *Comics Journal*. October 1991, p. 17.

2588. "Disney Lets Gladstone License Lapse." *Comics Journal*. July 1989, pp. 13-15.

2589. "Disney To Publish Comics." *Comics Journal*. April 1990, p. 13.

2590. Dorfmüller, Vera. "Comics und Konsum (W. Disney)." *Aspekte—Aus dem Kulturleben, Sendung des 2. Deutschen Fernsehens (ZDF)*. December 7, 1971.

2591. Granacher, René. "Disney-Comics bei Gladstone Eingestellt." *ICOM-INFO*. February 1990, p. 58.

2592. "Taking the Mickey." *Speakeasy*. September 1990, pp. 41, 43.

2593. Thompson, Maggie. "Disney Revamps Line." *CAPS*. September 1991, pp. 19-20.

2594. West, Richard. "Once Again... What Has Happened to Disney's Comics?" *Duckburg Times*. December 15, 1981, pp. 10-13.

Eclipse

2595. "Artist Complains About Eclipse." *Comics Journal*. October 1992, p. 18.

2596. Baker, Mike. "The Eclipse True Crime Trading Cards Controversy." *Gauntlet*. No. 2, 1992, pp. 44-49.

2597. "Eclipse's Plans for 1983." *Comics Journal*. January 1983, pp. 11-12.

2598. "Eclipse To Release Acme Press Comics." *Speakeasy*. No. 81, 1987, p. 1.

2599. Freund, Russell. "A Timid 'Alternative.'" *Comics Journal*. June 1984, pp. 29-36.

2600. Greenberger, Robert. "Eclipse Rising." *Comics Scene*. March 1982, pp. 48-51.

2601. Joplin, Marlakan. "The Light and Shadow of Eclipse." *Comics Feature*. September-October 1981, pp. 66-68.

2602. Lustig, John. "Eclipse's World: How It Works, and Why." *Amazing Heroes*. No. 99, 1987, pp. 55-63.

2603. Nelson, Brien. "Eclipse Magazine—A Review of Its First Year." *Comics Feature*. November 1982, pp. 60-61.

2604. "Two Artists in Disputes with Eclipse Books." *Comics Journal*. August 1992, pp. 8-9.

First Comics

2605. "First Comics Acquires *Evangeline*." *Comics Journal*. September 1986, p. 23.

2606. "*First Comics* Pays Up." *Comics Journal*. August 1986, pp. 9-10.

2607. "First Comics Revives *Classics Illustrated* in January." *Comics Journal*. November 1989, p. 23.

2608. "First Drops Regular Comics." *Comics Journal*. December 1990, p. 11.

2609. "First Holding On." *Comics Journal*. July 1991, p. 11.

2610. "First Publishing and Dream Factory Merge into New Entertainment Conglomerate." *Comics Journal*. March 1993, pp. 27-28.

2611. "First Vs. Marvel and World Color." *Comics Journal*. September 1985, pp. 11-18.

Gladstone

2612. "Gladstone Partners Part Ways." *Comics Journal*. April 1991, p. 21.

2613. "Gladstone To Continue Disney Titles Through April '90." *Comics Journal*. November 1989, p. 17.

2614. "Gladstone To Publish *Dick Tracy*." *Comics Journal*. April 1990, pp. 15-16.

Image

2615. "Bye Bye Marvel; Here Comes Image." *Comics Journal*. February 1992, pp. 11-12.

2616. Cheah, Michael. "Sharper Image." *Big O Magazine*. July 1993, p. 11.

2617. "Image Comics Leaves Malibu Graphics, Establishes Itself As a 'Full-Service Company.'" *Comics Buyer's Guide*. December 11, 1992, p. 23.

2618. "Image Leaves Malibu, Becomes Own Publisher." *Comics Journal*. January 1993, p. 22.

2619. Thompson, Maggie. "Image Crosses Over with Valiant This Summer." *Comics Buyer's Guide*. February 10, 1993, pp. 26-27.

Kitchen Sink

2620. Butler, Don. "Kitchen Sink Completes Move." *Comics Buyer's Guide*. June 11, 1993, p. 49.

2621. "From the Heartland of America: An Interview with Krupp Comic's Denis Kitchen." *Comics Journal*. September 1981, pp. 211-225.

2622. Kitchen, Denis. "The Formation of Kitchen Sink and Krupp Comics." In *The Official Underground and Newave Comix Price Guide*, edited by Jay Kennedy, pp. 21-24. Cambridge, Massachusetts: Boatner Norton Press, 1982.

2623. "Kitchen Sink Continues To Reorganize." *Comics Journal*. July 1993, pp. 7-8.

2624. "Kitchen Sink Press Acquires Tundra." *Comics Buyer's Guide*. April 23, 1993, p. 26.

2625. "Kitchen Sink Press Buys Tundra Publishing." *Comics Journal*. April 1993, pp. 15-17.

2626. "KSP/Tundra: Who Owns What?" *Comics Journal*. August 1993, pp. 9-11.

Marvel

2627. Allstetter, Ron. "'Marvel Age' Continues To Change as Sales Rise." *Comics Buyer's Guide*. January 1, 1993, p. 26.

2628. Berger, Thomas. "Affald." *Seriejournalen*. March 1992, p. 15.

2629. Castelli, Alfredo and Paolo Sala. "Il Gruppo Marvel." *Linus*. No. 14, 1966, pp. 1-7.

2630. Clodius, Rainer. "Epic. Marvels Gescheiterte Comic-Revolution." *Comixene. Das Comicfachmagazin* (Hanover) 8:37 (1981) pp. 46-49.

2631. "Docu Probes Marvel's Impact." *Variety*. September 17, 1986, p. 83.

2632. "Does Marvel's High Output Help or Hurt Comics?" *Comics Buyer's Guide*. October 21, 1983, p. 1.

2633. Fermín Pérez, Ramón. "El Métoda Marvel." *El Wendigo*. No. 58, 1993, pp. 4-5.

2634. Greenberger, Robert. "Marvel Introduces New Contracts." *Comics Scene*. March 1982, pp. 18-19.

2635. Groth, Gary. "Marvel Crush Puny Artist." *Comics Journal*. August 1985, pp. 7-8.

2636. Groth, Gary. "Marvel's War with the Press." *Comics Journal*. January 1983, pp. 6-10.

2637. Groth, Gary. "What Made Jimmy Run?" *Comics Journal*. September 1987, pp. 5-6.

2638. Kalish, Carol. "Marvel Comics." *Comics Journal*. November 1982, pp. 102-104.

2639. "MacAndrews and Forbes Offers To Buy Up to 11 Million Shares of Marvel Stock." *Comics Buyer's Guide*. April 23, 1993, p. 22.

2640. "Marvel Acquires Fleer Corp." *Comics Journal*. October 1992, p. 27.

2641. "Marvel at a Glance." *Variety*. September 17, 1986, p. 82.

2642. "Marvel Comics Demands an End to *Megaton Man* Marvel Parodies." *Comics Journal*. January 1986, pp. 12-13.

2643. "Marvel Comics Zaps Up Its Readership Statistics." *Advertising Age*. July 17, 1978.

2644. "Marvel, Eclipse Ownership Titles." *Retail Express*. October 2, 1987, p. 1.

2645. "Marvel Establishes Press Policy." *Comics Journal*. October 1984, pp. 12-13.

2646. "Marvel Expands in 1984." *Comics Journal*. December 1983, pp. 15-17.

2647. "Marvel Follows DC to 50¢ Format." *Comics Journal*. April 1980, p. 11.

2648. "Marvel For Sale." *Comics Journal.* August 1988, pp. 14-15.

2649. "Marvel Gear Up for Summer." *Speakeasy.* April 1990, p. 19.

2650. "Marvel Gives Release Dates for Projects and Mini-Series in 1983." *Comics Journal.* No. 25, 1983, pp. 5-6.

2651. "Marvel Hopeful About 'Weird-World.'" *Comics Journal.* March 1979, pp. 10-13.

2652. "Marvel Magazines: Tomb of Dracula Cancelled New Back-Up Series in Howard the Duck." *Comics Journal.* April 1980, p. 12.

2653. "Marvel Meets with Distributors." *Comics Journal.* June 1988, pp. 13-14.

2654. "Marvel 1991: The Biggest Gets Bigger." *Comics Journal.* December 1991, pp. 13-15.

2655. "Marvel Raises Prices Selectively; 5 Titles Go Direct." *Retail Express.* November 6, 1987, pp. 1, 8.

2656. "Marvel Sells Stock, Breaks Sales Records." *Comics Journal.* July 1991, pp. 9-10.

2657. "Marvel's Folks Are Found on 500+ Products." *Variety.* September 17, 1986, p. 82.

2658. "Marvel's Horizon Expands with Push into New Territory." *Variety.* September 17, 1986, p. 83.

2659. "Marvel's New Incentives Plan." *Comics Journal.* July 1986, pp. 10-12.

2660. "Marvel Sold to New World Pictures." *Comics Journal.* December 1986, p. 11.

2661. "Marvel Stock Falls After Negative 'Barron's' Article." *Comics Retailer.* April 1992, pp. 24, 77.

2662. "Marvel Stock Price Takes a Fall." *Comics Journal.* February 1992, p. 23.

2663. Neal, Jim. "Marvel To Target Young Kids, Girls in 1993." *Comics Buyer's Guide.* January 1993, p. 68.

2664. "New Leaders at Marvel." *Comics Journal.* December 1990, p. 12.

2665. "New World Uses Marvel in Attempt To Buy Kenner." *Retail Express.* September 4, 1987, pp. 1, 14.

2666. "Publicity Campaign: Marvel Works To Increase Awareness of Comics." *Comics Buyer's Guide*. April 19, 1985, p. 40.

2667. "Reorganization at Marvel." *Comics Journal*. November 1982, pp. 7, 9.

2668. "Revlon Chairman Buys Marvel." *Comics Journal*. January 1989, p. 20.

2669. "Sales on Marvel's Miss Universe Line Mediocre, According to Many Retailers." *Comics Journal*. September 1986, p. 13.

2670. Strauss, Robert. "Marvel Productions." *Comics Feature*. January-February 1985, pp. 19-29.

2671. Sullivan, Darcy. "Marvel Comics and Kiddie Hustle." *Comics Journal*. August 1992, pp. 30-37.

2672. "20/20 Coverage of Marvel Neglects Mention of Kirby and Other Artists." *Comics Journal*. September 1986, p. 12.

2673. Van Hise, James. "Marvel's Mutant Universe." *Comics Feature*. May 1987, pp. 26-35.

2674. Weber, John. "Tom DeFalco." *Comics Buyer's Guide*. March 11, 1988, pp. 32, 34.

2675. Young, Frank. "I Can't Change Marvel. Who Could?" *Comics Journal*. August 1992, pp. 101-113. (Evan Dorkinon on the industry).

Neverending

2676. Isabella, Tony. "Neverending Battle Notes." *Comics Buyer's Guide*. March 18, 1988, p. 56.

2677. "Neverending Battle Ends." *Comics Journal*. August 1988, pp. 11-12.

2678. "Neverending Battle Inc.: A Chronology." *Comics Buyer's Guide*. March 18, 1988, p. 56.

NOW

2679. "Creators Accuse NOW of Non-Payment." *Comics Journal*. March 1989, pp. 5-15.

2680. "It's So Long for NOW." *Comics Journal*. February 1991, pp. 11-12.

2681. "NOW Suspends Publishing, Seeks Buyer." *Comics Journal*. December 1990, pp. 7-8.

Pacific

2682. Gelb, Jeff. "Pacific Comics." *Comics Scene*. May 1983, pp. 20-23.

2683. "The Pacific Comics Fallout." *Comics Journal*. May 1985, pp. 12-14.

Rip Off

2684. *The Best of the Rip Off Press*. 4 Vols. San Francisco, California: Rip Off Press, 1973-1987.

2685. Schutz, Diana. "Shelton, Gilbert, Fred Todd, and Don Baumgart: Rip Off Press: The Publishing Company That's a Little Like the Weather." *Comics Journal*. August 1984, pp. 59-83.

Distribution, Sales

2686. Andrews, Ed. "Quality Distributor Knowledge Is an Important Profit Factor." *Comics Business*. August 1987, p. 10.

2687. "Attracting Adventurous Customers: Seattle's Zanadu Comics." *Comics Journal*. February 1993, p. 31.

2688. "The Best Comics Shops in North America." *Comics Journal*. July 1992, pp. 88-96.

2689. "Big Fall Promotions from Big Two." *Retail Express*. August 7, 1987, pp. 1, 16.

2690. Biggers, Cliff. "Cliff's Notes: Dinosaur Dance of the Distributors." *Retail Express*. September 4, 1987, p. 4.

2691. "Black-and-White Explosion Slowing Down According to Comics Distributors." *Comics Journal*. February 1987, pp. 26-27.

2692. "The Black-and-White Market Rapidly Declining Say Industry Professionals." *Comics Journal*. April 1987, pp. 21-22.

2693. Bolle, S. "Comic Books Regain Their Readership—and Outlets." *Publisher's Weekly*. December 6, 1985, pp. 34+.

2694. "'Border Worlds' Rockets Up in Sales; No. 4 in January." *Kitchen Sink Pipeline*. October 1986, p. 2.

2695. Cardui, Vanessa. "Reorder Controversy Rages." *Retail Express*. July 17, 1987, pp. 1, 12.

2696. Carlson, K.C. "Comics Retailing 101." *Comics Retailer*. April 1992, pp. 10, 22.

2697. Carlson, K.C. "Setting Up Your Store." *Comics Retailer*. April 1992, pp. 42-46, 48, 50.

2698. Caruba, David. "How To Get the Post Office To Deliver Your *CBG*." *Comics Buyer's Guide*. February 8, 1985, p. 44.

2699. Colabuono, Gary. "Selling Comics." *Retail Express*. October 2, 1987, pp. 3, 6, 8, 14-17.

2700. "Comic Book Retailer Victim of Hate Crime." *Comics Journal*. November 1992, pp. 9-10.

2701. "Comic Book Sellers." *New York Times*. March 10, 1971, p. 57.

2702. "Comics As a Living." *Retail Express*. August 21, 1987, p. 2.

2703. "*Comic Shop News* Circulation at 50,500." *Retail Express*. August 7, 1987, p. 11.

2704. "Continuity Comics Acquire Newsstand Distribution." *Comics Journal*. November 1986, p. 14.

2705. "Cool Comics Shops." *Comics Journal*. August 1993, p. 93.

2706. Costa, Bruce G. "Suggested for Mature Retailers. Keep It Clean!" *Comics Retailer*. April 1992, pp. 66-69.

2707. "Distributor Finances Five Publishers." *Comics Journal*. April 1987, pp. 12-13.

2708. "Distributors Vow To Improve Reorder Service." *Comics Journal*. March 1992, p. 19.

2709. "ERCBRA and NCCDA Merge. Comic Book Retailers International Forms, Announces Plans." *Comics Journal*. November 1989, pp. 19-20.

2710. Friedman, Harry J. "Getting Tough." *Comics Retailer*. April 1992, p. 32.

2711. Friedman, Richard P. "Frankly, My Dear..." *Circulation Management*. September-October 1988, p. 50.

2712. Friedrich, Mike. "And Now the Good News: Mass-Market Comic Stores." *Comics Journal*. November 1989, p. 119.

2713. Friedrich, Mike. "The Trend Toward Distributor Consolidation." *Comics Journal*. April 1989, pp. 123-124.

2714. "Golden Age Comics Set New Sales Records." *Speakeasy*. April 1990, p. 12.

2715. Gottlieb, Gerald. "Some Old and New Friends on Cartoon Conoisseurs' Bookshelf." *New York Herald Tribune Book Review*. November 29, 1959, p. 6.

2716. Gray, Bob. "Computerizing a Comics Store." *Comics Retailer*. April 1992, pp. 70, 72.

2717. Gray, Bob. "Computerizing a Comics Store." *Comics Buyer's Guide*. Part 3, January 25, 1991, pp. 32, 34, 36; Part 4, February 1, 1991, pp. 20, 26, 30.

2718. Gray, Bob. "Maintain the Momentum." *Comics Retailer*. April 1992, p. 54.

2719. Groth, Gary. "Can Alternatives Sell?" *Comics Journal*. April 1991, pp. 7-11.

2720. Groth, Gary. "Comics Retailers and the Unfeasibility of Independent Titles." *Comics Journal*. March 1989, pp. 3-4.

2721. Groth, Gary. "What the Direct-Sales Market Has Wrought: Part One: Conventions and Awards." *Comics Journal*. September 1983, pp. 6-8.

2722. Groth, Gary. "What the Direct Sales Market Has Wrought. Part Two: The Comics Renaissance." *Comics Journal*. October 1983, pp. 8-11.

2723. Hagenauer, George. "How To Generate Publicity for Your Comics Store Through Public Service." *Comics Buyer's Guide*. August 7, 1987, pp. 26, 28, 32, 34, 36.

2724. "*Hero Comics* To Test Newsstand Distribution." *Comic Business*. July 1987, pp. 1, 3.

2725. Hibbs, Brian. "Ethics and the Comics Industry." *Comics Retailer*. April 1992, pp. 36-38, 40.

2726. "Increasing the Audience for Alternatives." *Comics Journal*. March 1993, p. 49.

2727. Kelley, Etna M. "Look Who's Buying Comics Now!" *Sales Management*. Part 1, February 15, 1951, p. 118; Part 2, March 1, 1951, p. 68.

2728. Kobylak, Wesley. "Taxman: Organizing Your Taxwise Dealership." *Comics Journal*. April 1977, pp. 14-16.

2729. Korkis, Jim. "Waldenbooks Open Children's Stores." *Comics Business*. July 1987, p. 14.

2730. Lent, John A. "Stores Won't Stock Cartoon Book." *Comics Journal*. October 1992, p. 27.

2731. Maple, Scott. "Behind the Counter." *Retail Express*. August 21, 1987, p. 6.

2732. "Marvel Aims for All Distributor Catalog Covers." *Comics Journal*. January 1993, p. 19.

2733. "Meet Dale Kanzler, Marvel Assistant Manager, Direct Sales/Administrative." *Retail Express*. November 6, 1987, p. 4.

2734. Myers, Greg W. "Comic-Book Circulation Figures." *Comics Buyer's Guide*. June 6, 1986, p. 44.

2735. Myers, Greg W. "Comic-Book Circulation Figures for 1983." *Comics Buyer's Guide*. March 30, 1984, p. 38.

2736. Myers, Greg W. "Comic Book Circulation Figures, 1988." *Comics Buyer's Guide*. July 21, 1989, p. 20.

2737. Neal, Jim. "McComics: Dream Factory Agreement Clears Way for Nationwide Chain of 100 Comics Stores Within Two Years." *Comics Buyer's Guide*. February 10, 1993, p. 6.

2738. "Newsstand Sales Struggle (Except Marvel's)." *Comics Journal*. September 1991, p. 11.

2739. O'Neill, Patrick D. "Stop 'Preaching to the Choir.'" *Comics Retailer*. April 1992, pp. 58, 61.

2740. O'Neill, Patrick D. "The Ups and Downs of Selling T-Shirts." *Comics Business*. September 1987, p. 30.

2741. Overstreet, Bob. "1983 Market Report." *The Comic Book Price Guide*. No. 14, 1984, pp. A-20-A-26.

2742. Overstreet, Bob. "1985 Market Report." *The Comic Book Price Guide*. No. 16, 1986, pp. A-17-A-24.

2743. Overstreet, Bob. "1986 Market Report." *The Comic Book Price Guide*. No. 17, 1987, pp. A-17-A-24.

2744. Overstreet, Bob. "1987 Market Report." *The Comic Book Price Guide*. No. 19, 1989, pp. A-17-A-23.

2745. Overstreet, Bob. "1988 Market Report." *The Comic Book Price Guide*. No. 19, 1989, pp. A-17-A-23.

2746. Overstreet, Bob. "1989 Market Report." *The Comic Book Price Guide*. No. 20, 1990, pp. A-19-A-27.

2747. Overstreet, Bob. "1990 Market Report." *The Comic Book Price Guide*. No. 21, 1991, pp. A-19-A-26.

2748. Pachter, Richard. "Promotion for Profit (and Fun)." *Retail Express*. August 21, 1987, p. 12.

2749. "Paying More for Less: Postal Problems and What You Can Do About Them." *Comics Buyer's Guide*. April 12, 1985, p. 3.

2750. Pendleton, Jennifer. "Manic Bat-Marketing Underway." *Variety*. April 20, 1992, pp. 3, 5.

2751. "Pied Piper Distributes Direct." *Comics Journal*. July 1987, pp. 21-22.

2752. "Regional Top Ten." *Retail Express*. September 4, 1987, p. 10; October 2, 1987, p. 10.

2753. "Retailer Association Forms." *Comics Journal*. July 1992, p. 19.

2754. "Retailers Speak Out." *Comics Journal*. July 1992, pp. 97-101.

2755. "*Retail Express* Interview: Mark Nevelow." *Retail Express*. September 4, 1987, pp. 11-13.

2756. "Retail Policies Debated at Dallas Con." *Comics Journal*. January 1989, pp. 22-24.

2757. Richardson, Wayne and Janine. "Learning the Four 'P's of Retail Marketing." *Comics Business*. July 1987, pp. 18-19.

2758. "Second Genesis Leaves Comics Distribution." *Comics Journal*. October 1990, p. 9.

2759. "Selling Comics: Gary Colabuono." *Retail Express*. October 2, 1987, pp. 3, 6, 8, 14-17.

2760. Sodaro, Robert J. "Witzend." *Comics Buyer's Guide*. November 16, 1984, p. 56.

2761. Strnad, Jan. "The Direct Sales Shops." *Comics Journal*. April 1986, pp. 6-7.

2762. Stuempfig, Julie. "Comics Professionals Speak Out On: Industry Demographics." *Comics Buyer's Guide*. February 10, 1993, pp. 38-44.

2763. Stuempfig, Julie. "How Big Is the Comic Book Market?" In *Comics Buyer's Guide 1993 Annual*, pp. 48-49. Iola, Wisconsin: Krause, 1992.

2764. Stuempfig, Julie. "How Is the Comic Book Market Divided?" In *Comics Buyer's Guide 1993 Annual*, pp. 49-50. Iola, Wisconsin: Krause, 1992.

2765. Stuempfig, Julie. "State of the Industry: Annual Comics Sales: $400-$500 Million." In *Comics Buyer's Guide 1993 Annual*, p. 44. Iola, Wisconsin: Krause, 1992.

2766. Stuempfig, Julie. "Who Sells Comic Books?" In *Comics Buyer's Guide 1993 Annual*, pp. 46-48. Iola, Wisconsin: Krause, 1992.

2767. "Sunrise Announces It May Not Pay Some Publishers Until July." *Comics Journal*. April 1987, p. 24.

2768. Thompson, Maggie. "What's the Direct Market and How Did It Get Here?" *Comics Collector*. Summer 1985, pp. 24-27.

2769. Tickal, Mike. "How To Discount." *Retail Express*. September 4, 1987, p. 2.

2770. "Who's Who at Comics Retailer." *Comics Retailer*. April 1992, pp. 8-9.

Bud Plant

2771. "Bud Plant Sells Out to Diamond." *Comics Journal*. August 1988, pp. 9-10.

2772. "The Bud Plant Story." *Comics Buyer's Guide*. July 19, 1985, p. 40.

2773. Groth, Gary. "In Defense of Bud Plant." *Comics Journal*. April 1985, p. 3.

2774. Plant, Bud. *Distribution in the Direct Market*. Grass Valley, California: 1984. 6 pp.

2775. Plant, Bud. "Distribution in the Direct Market." *Small Press Comics Explosion*. November 1986, pp. 46-49.

Capital City

2776. "Captial City Distribution: A History." *Comics Buyer's Guide*. April 29, 1988, p. 50.

2777. "Only 16 Publishers Ship 100% On-Time in July: Capital City." *Retail Express*. November 6, 1987, p. 10.

2778. "Ordering from Capital May Take More Capital." *Comics Journal*. July 1991, p. 12.

Diamond

2779. "Diamond Charges for Promo Flyers." *Comics Journal*. November 1991, p. 26.

2780. "Diamond Distributors Rejects *Slam Bang*." *Comics Journal*. November 1989, pp. 14-15.

2781. "Diamond Rejects 'Ant Boy.'" *Comics Journal*. August 1988, p. 16.

2782. Groth, Gary. "Flawed Diamond." *Comics Journal*. July 1992, pp. 3-4.

Glenwood

2783. "Four Publishers Sue Glenwood for Non-Payment." *Comics Journal*. July 1987, pp. 17-18.

2784. "Glenwood Distributors Declares Bankuptcy." *Comics Journal*. September 1987, p. 12.

2785. "Glenwood in Financial Crunch." *Comics Journal*. April 1987, p. 23.

GENRES

2786. "Bobbie Chase Talks About the 'Midnight Massacre.'" *Comics Buyer's Guide*. May 21, 1993, pp. 26-27.

2787. Boyd, Robert. "Two Post-Modern Comics." *Comics Journal*. January 1988, p. 39.

2788. "A Brief Overview of the Dell (Etc.) Little Lulu Comic Books." *Hollywood Eclectern*. June 1993, pp. 5-6.

2789. Cantey, Bill. "'Ghek,' a Look at One of Edgar Burroughs' Most Unusual Characters." *The Collector*. Winter 1973, pp. 12-14.

2790. Chambers, Jim. "Comic Book Underdog's [sic]." *Comic Book Collector*. January 1993, pp. 20-21.

2791. Dagilis, Andrew. "Pioneer Pillages and Plunders the Past." *Comics Journal*. January 1989, pp. 114-119.

2792. David, Peter. "Introduction to 'Sachs and Violets.'" *Comics Buyer's Guide*. September 10, 1993, pp. 28, 32.

2793. Dickholtz, Daniel. "The Dark Night of Saucy Jack." *Comics Scene*. No. 10, 1989, pp. 13-15.

2794. Enkemann, Jürgen, Claudia Franke, and Angela Lloyd. "Friedenserziehung im Englischunterricht. Raymond Briggs' Comic-Heft 'When the Wind Blows' als Unterrichtslektüre." *Englisch-Amerikanische Studien* (Cologne). 5:4 (1983), pp. 572-591.

2795. Fried, Lisa I. "*Spy* Mocks Candidates with Comic Book." *Magazine Week*. October 5, 1992, p. 13.

2796. Groth, Gary. "Through Kitsch-Colored Glasses. Ron Mann's *Comic Book Confidential*." *Comics Journal*. November 1989, pp. 5-7.

2797. Groth, Gary. "*WAP!*: The Sound of Bullshit Hitting the Wall or a Labor Union for Hacks?" *Comics Journal*. June 1988, pp. 3-6.

2798. Guzzo, Gary. "Interviews with Peter David on 'Sachs and Violets.'" *Comics Buyer's Guide*. September 10, 1993, pp. 27-28.

2799. "Is a Dinosaur Fad Ahead?" *Comics Business*. July 1987, p. 15.

2800. Jennings, Robert. "Black Knight." *The Comic World*. November 1979, pp. 7-10.

2801. Johns, T.L. "Charge of the Comandosaurs." *Comics Scene*. No. 10, 1989, pp. 29-32, 52.

2802. Johnson, Kim H. "Bullets, 'The Badger' and Baron." *Comics Scene*. No. 3, (Vol. 3, Series #14), pp. 45-47.

2803. Kempkes, Wolfgang. "Kann Man mit Comics Aufklären? Oder Batman in der Sprechblase von Mickymaus." In *Massenmedium Comics*, edited by Dieter Golombek and Reinhold Lehmann, pp. 38-43. Bonn: Bundeszentrale für Politische Bildung, 1976.

2804. Kubert, Joe. "Re: The Rose and the Thorn by RK and JK." *Robin Snyder's History of the Comics*. July 1991, p. 76.

2805. Lim, C.T. "Thought Balloon." *Big O Magazine*. March 1993, p. 62.

2806. McAvennie, Michael. "Raising Hellraiser." *Comics Scene*. No. 10, 1989, pp. 9-12, 60.

2807. MacDonald, Heidi. "Fight Scenes, Fight Scenes Everywhere... Nor Any Stop To Think." *Comics Journal*. December 1983, pp. 65-77.

2808. Martínez, Rodolfo. "De la Metafísica de Salón a la Carcajada." *El Wendigo*. No. 51, 1991, pp. 34-35.

2809. Mernit, Susan. "Modern Comix." *Express*. June-July 1989, pp. 16-20.

2810. Metzger, Kim. "Four-Color Comments." *Comics Buyer's Guide*. November 27, 1992, p. 48.

2811. Miller, Raymond. "Clue Comics." *The Golden Age*. No. 2, 1959, pp. 35-39.

2812. "New 'Xenozoic Tales' on Stands in February." *Kitchen Sink Pipeline*. October 1986, p. 1.

2813. Ng, Sam. "Heartaches over Heartbreak Comics." *Big O Magazine*. March 1993, p. 62.

2814. O'Neill, Patrick D. "Translating the Magic of Willow." *Comics Scene*. No. 3 (Vol. 3, No. 14), pp. 22-23.

2815. Ostertag, Hansjörg. *Mickey Maus und Superman. Comics als Lesestoff für Unsere Kinder?* Meiringen: Brügger, 1972.

2816. Pekar, Harvey. "Comics and Genre Literature." *Comics Journal*. July 1989, pp. 127-133.

2817. Sanderson, Peter. "Essay on the Tragi-Co(s)mic." *Comics Feature*. July-August 1980, pp. 59-63.

2818. Savramis, Demosthenes. "Tarzan & Superman und der Messias." In *Religion und Utopie in den Comics*. Berlin: Karin Kramer Verlag, 1985. Also in *Publik-Forum* (Frankfurt) 13:1 (1984), pp. 3-6.

2819. Stanley, John, *et al. The Little Lulu Library*. 18 Vols. Scottsdale, Arizona: Another Rainbow, 1985.

2820. Strnad, Jan. "Case Study: Jan Strnad on *Dr. Peculiar*." *Comics Journal*. October 1984, pp. 39-40.

2821. Thompson, Kim. "Death Warmed Over." *Comics Journal*. July 1982, pp. 50-52.

Alternative, Newave, Underground

2822. "Alternative Comics Publishers." *Comics Journal*. December 1978, pp. 15-16.

2823. "Alternative Comics Publishers." *Comics Journal*. March 1979, pp. 18-19.

2824. "American Underground-Comics." *Playboy*. December 1970.

2825. Arlington, Gary. "A Recollection." *The Official Underground and Newave Comix Price Guide*, edited by Jay Kennedy, p. 35. Cambridge, Massachusetts: Boatner Norton Press, 1982.

2826. Barrier, Mike. "On Comix." *Comics Journal*. November 1985, pp. 93-99.

2827. "Batman-Feber Rammer Alternative Udgivere." *Serieskaberen*. March 1990, pp. 12-13.

2828. Beck, C.C. "Comic Books for Grown-Ups." *Comics Journal*. December 1986, p. 7.

2829. *The Bijou/Apex Treasury of Underground Comics*. Princeton, Wisconsin: Kitchen Sink, n.d. 352 pp.

2830. Bisceglia, Jacques and Sylvie Brod. *Underground U.S.A.: La Bande Dessinée de la Contestation*. La Ferté-Milon, France: Corps 9, 1986.

2831. Boxell, Tim, ed. *Commies from Mars, the Red Planet*. San Francisco, California: Last Gasp, 1985. 151 pp.

2832. Boyd, Robert. "Mini-Malism: The Diazo Bros. Little-Read Book, *et al.*" *Comics Journal*. November 1992, pp. 44-45.

2833. Brackman, Jacob. "The International Comix Conspiracy." *Playboy*. December 1970, p. 195.

2834. Brummbär, Bernd. *Radical America Comix*. Frankfurt: Melzer-Verlag, 1971.

2835. Brummbär, Bernd. "Terror, Sex und Fritz the Cat. Die Kinderzeit der Comics Ist Vorbei. Amerikanische Anti-Comics Schocken die USA." *Underground*. June 1970, pp. 48-52.

2836. "Chambana Comix Club." *Comics Interview*. February 1985, pp. 63-75.

2837. Chute, David. "Comix of the '80s." *L.A. Weekly*. July 18, 1986, pp. 86-93.

2838. Curson, Nigel. "Underground." *Speakeasy*. December-January 1989-1990, pp. 44-47.

2839. Daniels, Les. "Comic Variations. Comics—Variationen. Variations de la Bande Dessinée." *Graphis* (Zürich) 28:159 (1972/1973), pp. 62-75.

2840. De Mott, B. "Darkness at the Mall." *Psychology Today*. February 1984, pp. 48-52.

2841. Donahue, Don. "A View from the Apex." In *The Official Underground and Newave Comix Price Guide*, edited by Jay Kennedy, pp. 31-32. Cambridge, Massachusetts: Boatner Norton Press, 1982.

2842. Donahue, Don and Susan Goodrick, eds. *The Apex Treasury of Underground Comics*. New York: Links, 1974. 192 pp.

2843. Erling, G. "Alternative Comix." In *The Official Underground and Newave Comix Price Guide*, edited by Jay Kennedy, pp. 36-38. Cambridge, Massachusetts: Boatner Norton Press, 1982.

2844. Estren, Mark J. "All in Color for Seventy-Five Cents." *Funnyworld*. Spring 1972, pp. 20-28.

2845. Estren, Mark J. *A History of Underground Comics*. New York: Quick Fox, 1974. 320 pp.; San Francisco, California: Straight Arrow, 1987.

2846. Fiore, Robert, Kim Thompson, and Gary Groth. "Comics in 1981: The Age of Alternatives." *Comics Journal*. April 1982, pp. 33-63.

2847. Fuchs, Wolfgang J. "USA: Newave Comics." In *Comic-Jahrbuch 1986*, edited by Martin Compart and Andreas C. Knigge, pp. 288-291. Frankfurt: Ullstein GmbH, 1985.

2848. Gantt, Barry. "Who Says Underground Comix Are Six Feet Underground?" *Cartoon Art Museum Newsletter*. Spring 1986, p. 3.

2849. Geerdes, Clay. "Newave 1980s: Comix in Revolution." *Fanfare*. Summer 1981, pp. 36-39.

2850. Geerdes, Clay. "The San Francisco Comix Scene." *Comics Journal*. April 1978, pp. 76-77, 79.

2851. Griffin, Rick. "Notes from the Underground!" *BLAB!* Summer 1986, pp. 24-25.

2852. Griffith, Bill. "A Sour Look at the Comix Scene." *Panels*. Summer 1979, pp. 28-29.

2853. Groth, Gary. "Grown-Up Comics: Breakout from the Underground." *Print*. November-December 1988, pp. 98-111.

2854. Hamilton, Kevin. "Comics—The New Adult Art Form." *Gauntlet*. No. 2, 1991, pp. 213-216.

2855. "In Search of Ralph Snart." *Four Color Magazine*. March 1987, pp. 36-41.

2856. Keeter, Steve. "Days of Small Press Past." *Small Press Comics Explosion*. May 1987, pp. 35-36.

2857. Kennedy, Jay. "Comix, Not Comics." In *The Official Underground and Newave Comix Price Guide*, edited by Jay Kennedy, pp. 11-15. Cambridge, Massachusetts: Boatner Norton Press, 1982.

2858. Kitchen, Denis. "Redefining the Undergrounds." *Comics Scene*. September 1982, pp. 30-31.

2859. Kitchen, Denis. "Staying Alive." *Comics Journal*. August 1984, pp. 84-85.

2860. Kreiner, Rich. "Strip Mining the Alternatives." *Comics Journal*. September 1990, pp. 3-5.

2861. Luciano, Dale. "Newave Comics Survey." *Comics Journal*. March 1985, pp. 51-78; April 1985, pp. 33-40; May 1985, pp. 80-84; June 1985, pp. 82-91; July 1985, pp. 197-213; August 1985, pp. 80-86; September 1985, pp. 91-98.

2862. Luciano, Dale. "Suckers and Survivors." *Comics Journal*. May 1985, pp. 46-47.

2863. Luciano, Dale. "Time, Effort, and Expense." *Comics Journal*. September 1987, pp. 49-62.

2864. Lynch, Jay, ed. *The Best of Bijou Funnies*. New York: Quick Fox, 1968.

2865. McCormick, Carlo. "Zap #12 (Zap Comix: Psychedelic Solution, New York)." *Artforum*. November 1989, pp. 149-150.

2866. Mad Peck. *Mad Peck Studios. A Twenty-year Retrospective*. Garden City, New York: Doubleday, 1987. Unpaginated.

2867. Miller, Michael. "Letter from the Berkeley Underground." *Esquire*. September 1965, pp. 85-161.

2868. Moliterni, Claude. "U.S.A Underground." In *Histoire Mondiale de la Bande Dessinée*, edited by Pierre Horay, pp. 245-248. Paris: Pierre Horay Éditeur, 1989.

2869. "*New York Times* Gives Boost to *American Splendor....*" *Comics Journal*. August 1986, pp. 14-15.

2870. Nik. "The Good, the Bad, the Stapled." *Zine*. November 1992, pp. 4-7.

2871. Pack, Jim. "From a Small Presser's Viewpoint." *Comicist*. August 1990, pp. 15-17.

2872. Pound, John. "Notes from the Underground." *BLAB!* Summer 1987, p. 66.

2873. Rifas, Leonard. "Underground Comix." In *Encyclopedia of the American Left*, edited by Mari Jo Buhle, *et al.* New York: Garland, 1990.

2874. Robbins, Trina. "Goodbye, Underground... I Don't Miss You at All." *FCA/S.O.B.* February/March 1981, p. 6.

2875. Rose, Lloyd. "Comic Books for Grown-Ups." *Atlantic*. August 1986, pp. 77-80.

2876. Rosenkranz, Patrick and Hugo Van Baren. *Artsy Fartsy Funnies*. Laren, New Hampshire: Holland: Paranoia, 1974. 79 pp.

2877. Sanders, Clinton R. "Icons of the Alternate Culture: The Themes and Function of Underground Comix." *Journal of Popular Culture*. Spring 1975, pp. 836-852.

2878. Sarill, William. "Conservation of Underground Comic Books." In *Official Underground and Newave Comix Price Guide*, edited by Jay Kennedy, pp. 39-44. Cambridge, Massachusetts: Boatner Norton, 1982.

2879. Schenkman, Joe. "Rat Roots." In *Official Underground and Newave Comix Price Guide*, edited by Jay Kennedy, p. 26. Cambridge, Massachusetts: Boatner Norton Press, 1982.

2880. Sherman, Bill. "Basix." *Comics Journal*. April 1977, pp. 29-30.

2881. Sherman, Bill. "The Black and White Room." *Comics Journal*. April 1987, pp. 144-145.

2882. Sherman, Bill. "Bring the Bad News." *Comics Journal*. June 1985, pp. 95-96.

2883. Sherman, Bill. "Dissent: Before the Bomb." *Comics Journal*. June 1980, pp. 78-79.

2884. Sherman, Bill. "Gasping Along." *Comics Journal*. December 1986, pp. 94-95.

2885. Sherman, Bill. "Harold Hedd Redux." *Comics Journal*. May 1982, pp. 126-128.

2886. Sherman, Bill. "It's Only Just Prices on Paper...." *Comics Journal*. July 1983, pp. 85-86.

2887. Sherman, Bill. "Lust Among the Ruins." *Comics Journal*. July 1981, pp. 82-85.

2888. Sherman, Bill. "Memories and Studebakers." *Comics Journal*. April 1980, pp. 71-72.

2889. Sherman, Bill. "Mod Cons and Urbanites." *Comics Journal*. January 1982, pp. 108-109.

2890. Sherman, Bill. "The Puzzling World of Howski Studios." *Comics Journal*. July 1984, pp. 109-111.

2891. Sherman, Bill. "Sex and the 60-Second Warning." *Comics Journal*. November 1982, pp. 109-110.

2892. Sherman, Bill. "Southern California Gets Me Down." *Comics Journal*. September 1982, pp. 86-87.

2893. Sherman, Bill. "Sympathy for the Ground Level." *Comics Journal*. November 1979, pp. 70-75.

2894. Sherman, Bill. "Turning in on Yourself." *Comics Journal*. December 1981, pp. 104-105.

2895. Sherman, Bill. "Underground Comics." *Comics Journal*. December 1977, pp. 58-59.

2896. Sherman, Bill. "Underground Comix: 'Only Lines on Paper: The Best and Worst Underground Comix.'" *Comics Journal*. February 1979, pp. 52-55.

2897. Sherman, Bill. "Whole Hog." *Comics Journal*. September 1981, pp. 296-297.

2898. Skidmore, Martin. "So-Called Critic." *FA*. October 1989, pp. 25-28.

2899. Snead, Elizabeth. "New Comics Draw Sophisticated Audience." *USA Today*. September 12, 1992, p. 5D.

2900. "Still the 'Artist's Artist.'" *Comics Journal*. May 1985, pp. 59-77.

2901. Strnad, Jan. "The Alternative Comics Cadaver Derby." *Comics Journal*. May 1985, pp. 49-57.

2902. Sweeney, Bruce. "Underground Station." *Comics Scene*. July 1982, p. 15; September 1982, p. 17; November 1982, p.15; May 1983, p.18; July 1983, p.18.

2903. Turner, Ron. "The Art That Wouldn't Die." In *The Official Underground and Newave Comix Price Guide*, edited by Jay Kennedy, pp. 33-34. Cambridge, Massachusetts: Boatner Norton Press, 1982.

2904. Ulla. "Brief aus New York." *Underground* (Frankfurt). No. 4, 1970, p. 35.

2905. "Undergrounds." *Comics Journal*. March 1979, p. 21.

2906. "Undergrounds: *Gen* Stops, *Omaha* Goes." *Comics Journal*. April 1982, p. 11.

2907. "Undergrounds: Going Down?" *Comics Journal*. March 1985, pp. 11-14.

2908. Wasserman, Jeffrey H. "Conversations with the Brother-in-Law of Underground Comix." *Inside Comics*. Summer 1974, pp. 16-25.

2909. Whiting, Jim. "Comix." *Art? Alternatives*. April 1992, pp. 14-16; October 1992, pp. 58-59.

2910. Williamson, Skip. "Notes from the Underground." *BLAB*. Summer 1986, p. 44.

2911. *Zap to Zippy: The Impact of Underground Comix. A Twenty-Five Year Retrospective*. Cartoon Art Museum, San Francisco, January 11 to April 7, 1990. San Francisco, California: Cartoon Art Museum, 1990. 32 pp. (Includes: Will Eisner, "Me and the Underground Comics," pp. 3-4; Bill Griffith, "Underground

Comics: Weird, Wacky and Over 21," pp. 5-10; Clay Geerdes, "Underground Comix at a Glance," pp. 11-13; Malcolm Whyte, "The Impact of Underground Comix," pp. 14-25).

Maus and *RAW*

2912. Benson, John. "Credit for 'Master Race.'" *Comics Journal.* January 1982, p. 21.

2913. Benson, John. "From Maus to Now." *Comics Journal.* June 1978, pp. 36-37.

2914. Benson, John, David Kasakove, and Art Spiegelman. "An Examination of 'Master Race.'" *Squa Tront.* No. 6, 1975, pp. 41-47.

2915. "Cat and Maus Games." *Before I Get Old.* December 1986, pp. 47-48.

2916. Cavalieri, Joey. "Slaughter on Greene Street." *Comics Journal.* August 1982, pp. 70-82.

2917. Dooley, Michael. "Cooking RAW." *Comics Journal.* April 1990, pp. 58-64.

2918. Gates, David. "The Light Side of Darkness." *Newsweek.* September 22, 1986, p. 79.

2919. Gopnik, Adam. "Comics and Catastrophe." *New Republic.* June 22, 1987, pp. 29-34.

2920. Grossman, Robert. "Mauschwitz." *The Nation.* January 10, 1987, pp. 23-24.

2921. Groth, Gary. "A Case of Complex Ignorance." *Comics Journal.* May 1992, pp. 3-4.

2922. Groth, Gary. "The *Maus* Fallacy." *Comics Journal.* December 1992, pp. 3-4.

2923. Luciano, Dale. "'Raw': Pataphysical Spirit and Graphic Possibilities." *Comics Journal.* July 1981, pp. 36-43.

2924. "Mad about the *Maus.*" *Comics Journal.* December 1991, p. 22.

2925. "*Maus* Receives Wave of Publicity; First Printing Sells Out." *Comics Journal.* November 1986, p. 14.

2926. Pekar, Harvey. "Maus and Other Topics." *Comics Journal.* December 1986, pp. 54-57.

2927. "Raw Magazine." *Comics Feature.* July 1980, pp. 49-56.

2928. Rodi, Rob. "Swine Song." *Comics Journal.* July 1990, pp. 39-40.

2929. Spiegelman, Art. *Maus, a Survivor's Tale*. New York: Pantheon Books, 1986. 159 pp.

2930. Spiegelman, Art. "Mauschwitz." *Esquire*. March 1987, pp. 67-69+.

2931. Weintraub, Judith. "Comic-Book Vision of the Holocaust." *Philadelphia Inquirer*. December 28, 1991, pp. 1-D, 10-D.

2932. Weschler, Lawrence. "Mighty 'Maus.'" *Rolling Stone*. November 20, 1986, pp. 103-105, 146-148.

Detective and Mystery

2933. Barr, Mike W. "Ellery Queen in the Comics: Sleuth Celebrates 60th Year, 50th in Comics." *Comics Buyer's Guide*. October 13, 1989, pp. 20, 27.

2934. *Crime SuspenStories*. The Complete EC Library. 5 Vols. West Plains, Missouri: R. Cochran, 1983.

2935. Cuervo, Javier. "Marvin. Un Detective Bajo las Luces de Hollywood." *El Wendigo*. May 1984, pp. 25-30.

2936. Goodwin, Archie and Walter Simonson. *Manhunter, the Complete Saga*. New York: Excalibur Enterprises, 1979. 85 pp.

2937. Goulart, Ron. "The Pulpwood Private Eyes." *Comics Buyer's Guide*. September 28, 1984, pp. 20, 22, 26.

2938. Goulart, Ron. "Remembering the Past: Gumshoes." *Comics Buyer's Guide*. August 4, 1989, pp. 54, 56.

2939. Horn, Maurice. "Charlie Chan." Introduction to *Charlie Chan's Adventures*. Papeete, Tahiti: Comics Stars in the World, 1976.

2940. Johnson, Kim H. "Detective Stories." *Comics Scene*. No. 13, 1990, pp. 14-18, 52.

2941. Jones, Bruce, April Campbell, and Brent Anderson. *Somerset Holmes*. Forestville, California: Eclipse Books, 1987. 128 pp.

2942. Karp, E. "Crime Comic Book Role Preferences." Ph.D. dissertation, New York University, 1954.

2943. Lardner, J. "How To Lick Crime." *Newsweek*. March 7, 1955, p. 58.

2944. Murray, Will. "The Man with The Shadow's Face." *Comics Buyer's Guide*. July 13, 1984, pp. 20, 22, 25.

2945. Roca, A. "El Hombre Libre por Exelencia. Un Elemento Básico de la Historia Gráfica Norte Americana: El Suspense." *Los Comics* (San Sebastian). February 1964.

2946. Shapiro, Marc. "Detective Comic." *Comics Scene*. No. 9, 1989, pp. 33-37.

Ms. Tree

2947. Beatty, Terry. "From the Drawing Board." *Comics Collector*. Fall 1984, pp. 12-17.

2948. Collins, Max A. "Watching the Detectives." *Amazing Heroes*. June 15, 1987, pp. 23-28, 30-41.

2949. Collins, Max A. and Terry Beatty. *The Files of Ms. Tree*, Vol. 1. Kitchener, Ontario: Aardvark-Vanaheim, 1984. 136 pp.

2950. Collins, Max A. and Terry Beatty. *The Files of Ms. Tree*, Vol. 2. North Hollywood, California: Renegade Press, 1985. 112 pp.

2951. Collins, Max A. and Terry Beatty. *The Files of Ms. Tree*, Vol. 3. Long Beach, California: Renegade Press, 1986. 120 pp.

007

2952. Angeli, Lisa. "007, Antenati e Pronipoti." *BIG* (Rome). No. 1, 1965.

2953. Bertieri, Claudio. "Da X-9 a 007 Si Perfeziona il Mito dell'Agente Segreto." *Il Lavoro Nuovo*. July 3, 1965.

2954. Traini, Rinaldo and Sergio Trinchero. "007 e Figlio dei Fumetti." *Le Ore*. May 1965.

Educational

2955. "Classic Comics Sell A Hundred Million." *Publisher's Weekly*. March 23, 1946, p. 1736.

2956. Cook, Margaret S. "Something Further Did Follow: More on Melville in the Comic Books." *Melville Society Extracts*. November 1983, p. 10.

2957. "EduComics Resumes Publication of Gen of Hiroshima." *Comics Journal*. July 1981, p. 18.

2958. "EduComics To Release Nakazawa's 'I Saw It.'" *Comics Journal*. July 1982, p. 16.

2959. Haufe, John. "National Lampoon: Classics Parodies." *The Classics Collector*. February-March 1990, p. 21.

2960. Heffelfinger, Charles. *The Classics Handbook*. 2nd. Ed. Tampa, Florida: 1980. 143 pp.

2961. "King Classics Update." *The Classics Collector*. February-March 1990, p. 13.

2962. Kroll, J. "How Much, Macbeth? Lay Off." *Newsweek*. September 13, 1982, p. 81.

2963. Malan, Dan. "Growing Pains and Pleasures." *Worldwide Classics Newsletter*. May 1989, pp. 16-18.

2964. Malan, Dan. "Masterpieces Illustrated—Non-Gilberton Classics." *Worldwide Classics Newsletter*. May 1989, pp. 26-29.

2965. Malan, Dan. "1989 Classics Market Analysis." *Worldwide Classics Newsletter*. May 1989, pp. 13-15.

2966. Malan, Dan. "Novel Insights." *Worldwide Classics Newsletter*. May 1989, p. 19.

2967. Malan, Dan. "Thriller Comics Library." *Worldwide Classics Newsletter*. May 1989, pp. 31-35.

2968. Mathiasen, Paw. "Classics Illustrated." *Seriejournalen*. March 1991, p. 33.

2969. "New Classics Series." *The Classics Collector*. February-March 1990, pp. 16-18.

2970. Richardson, Donna. "Classics Illustrated." *American Heritage*. May/June 1993, pp. 78-85.

2971. Rifas, Leonard. "Educational Comics: A Message in a Bubble." *Print*. November-December 1988, pp. 145-157+.

2972. Rifas, Leonard. "The Origins of Educomics." In *The Official Underground and Newave Comix Price Guide*, edited by Jay Kennedy, pp. 19-20. Cambridge, Massachusetts: Boatner Norton Press, 1982.

2973. "The Romance of Art and Literature." *The Classics Collector*. February-March 1990, pp. 14-15.

2974. Scholz, Carter. "Classics Lite." *Comics Journal*. February 1990, pp. 113-119.

2975. Schwartz, Delmore. "Masterpieces As Cartoons." *Comics Journal*. November 1991, pp. 91-96.

2976. Sheridan, Martin. *Classic Comics and Their Creators*. Arcadia, California: Post-Era, 1973. Reprint from 1942.

2977. Stredicke, Vic. "Comic-Book Series Draws from World's Great Literature." *Penstuff*. February 1990, p. 6.

2978. Sweeney, Bruce. "Undergrounds: Two New Books from Educomics." *Comics Journal*. March 1980, p. 20.

Funny Animal

2979. Angel, Bob, jr. "Ducksburg Revisited." *The Barks Collector*. March 1984, pp. 2-7.

2980. Cruse, Howard. "Ducks and a Legacy." *Comics Scene*. September 1982, pp. 22-23.

2981. Decker, Dwight R. "Rabbits in Clothes." *Comics Journal*. October 1982, pp. 135-138.

2982. Dorfman, Ariel and Armand Mattelart. *Walt Disneys "Dritte Welt." Massenkommunikation und Kolonialismus bei Micky Maus und Donald Duck*. Berlin: Basis Verlag, 1977.

2983. Duffield, Ted C. "Pogo, the Comic Book Star." *Okefenokee Star*. Summer 1977, p. 37.

2984. Gans, Grobian. *"Die Ducks: Psychogramm Einer Sippe."* Hamburg: Rowohlt, 1984.

2985. Gooch, Larry. "A Wind of the Spirit: Cultural Paths in Search of Transcendental Truths: As Evidenced by the Ducks and the Tralla Lallians." *The Barks Collector*. May 1985, pp. 11-20.

2986. Harvey, R.C. "A Cat Book for Comics Lovers." *Comics Journal*. July 1982, pp. 32-33, 35.

2987. Lock, Martin. "Dangermouse: Mouse in a Million." *Comics Collector*. Fall 1985, pp. 42-43.

2988. Nichols, John. "Fine Feathered Friends: The Disney Ducks, Part 2: Gyro Gearloose, an Interview." *The Barks Collector*. May 1985, pp. 1-10.

2989. Sodaro, Bob. "A Dog and His Boy." *Amazing Heroes*. June 15, 1984, pp. 26-32, 37-40, 42.

2990. Sperr, Monika. "Populärer Als die Kennedys: der Duck-Clan." *Twen* (Munich). 13:9 (1970), p. 132.

Donald Duck

2991. Barks, Carl. *Donald Duck and His Nephews*. Best Comics. New York: Abbeville Press, 1983. 190 pp.

2992. Barks, Carl. *Donald Duck in Frozen Gold*. The Best of Walt Disney Comics. Racine, Wisconsin: Western, 1974. 48 pp.

2993. Barks, Carl. *Donald Duck in the Ghost of the Grotto*. The Best of Walt Disney Comics. Racine, Wisconsin: Western, 1974. 48 pp.

2994. Barrier, Michael. "About 'Donald Duck' and Carl Barks." In *A Smithsonian Book of Comic-Book Comics*, edited by Michael Barrier and Martin Williams, pp. 197-223. New York: Smithsonian Institution Press, 1981.

2995. Blechen, Camilla. "Der Einzige Mensch: Donald Duck." *Frankfurter Allgemeine Zeitung*. January 13, 1970.

2996. Blitz, Marcia. *Donald Duck*. London: New English Library, 1980. Also: *Donald Duck. 50 Jahre und Kein Bißchen Leise*. Stuttgart: Unipart-Verlag, 1984.

2997. Bönisch, Max. "Die Sprache der Comics im Unterricht." *Kommunikation. Aspekte zum Deutschunterricht*, edited by Erich Wolfrum, pp. 225-266. Baltmannsweiler: Burgbücherei W. Schneider, 1975.

2998. "Donald Duck. Goede Dag, Meneer Duck." *Comic Forum* (Vienna). 7:28 (1985), pp. 40-43.

2999. "Donald Duck Hat Es Schon." *ADAC-Motorwelt* (Munich). No. 2, 1967, p. 6.

3000. "Donald Duck Hob Ein Schiff." *Der Stern* (Hamburg). No. 39, 1965.

3001. "Donald Duck Reist Mit." *Schöne Welt* (Munich). No. 8, 1971, p. 5.

3002. "Donald Duck Schlug die Wissenschaft." *Hamburger Morgenpost*. February 2, 1966.

3003. "Donald Inquiète les Specialistes." *L'Express* (Paris). March 8, 1965.

3004. Eberhart, Stephen. "Four Function Fowls." *The Barks Collector*. October 1984, pp. 12-22.

3005. Forytta, Claus. "Comics im Unterricht. Donald-Duck—Geschichten im 4. Schuljahr." *Diskussion Deutsch* (Frankfurt) 6:24 (1975), pp. 323-341.

3006. Forytta, Claus. *Donald-Duck-Geschichten. Materialien zur Unterrichtsplanung*. Bremen: Universität Bremen, 1980.

3007. Fuchs, Erika. "Haben Sie Eigentlich Etwas Gegen Donald Duck?" *Eltern* (Munich), January 5, 1970, pp. 50-53.

3008. Haertel, Volker. "Donald im Glück. Analyse Eines 'Micky Maus'—Titelblatts." *Anregung* (Munich), 1976, pp. 222-232.

3009. Jessen, Wolf. "Donald Duck in der Akademie. Eine Ausstellung von Comic Strips in Berlin." *Die Zeit* (Hamburg). January 9, 1970, p. 12.

3010. Klose, Werner. "Zwischen Hölderlin und Donald Duck." *Die Zeit* (Hamburg). No. 24, 1971, p. 54.

3011. O'Mealia, Phillip. "Donald Who? Why a Duck." *Comics Buyer's Guide*. March 1, 1991, pp. 54-55, 59.

3012. Schnurrer, Achim. "Donald Duck. Die Berühmteste Ente der Welt Feiert in Kürze Ihren Fünfzigsten Geburtstag!" *Comic Forum* (Vienna). 6:23 (1984), pp. 34-36, 38.

3013. Sharpe, Howard. "Donald Duck's Biggest Moments." *Liberty*. May 9, 1942.

3014. Stoeszinger, Jutta. "Donald Duck Ist der Größte-Comic Strips im Kreuzverhör." *Lippische Landeszeitung*. March 13, 1971.

3015. Strecker, Gabriele. "'Die Frau in Unserer Zeit'—Von Robinson zu Donald Duck. Eine Betrachung über Comic-Strips." *Rundfunkvortrag* (Hamburg). December 10, 1953.

3016. Swanson, Brent. "Donald Duck's Expense Account." *Duckburg Times*. December 15, 1981, p. 14.

3017. Wood, Daniel B. "Fifty Years Later, Donald Duck Is Still a Quack-up." *The Barks Collector*. October 1984, pp. 23-24. Reprinted from *Christian Science Monitor*. May 21, 1984, p. 1.

3018. Zimmer, Rainer. "Die Ducks." *Die Zeit* (Hamburg). No. 42, 1970, p. 27.

Scrooge McDuck

3019. Barks, Carl. *Uncle Scrooge and the Secret of the Old Castle*. Best Comics. New York: Abbeville Press, 1980. 30 pp.

3020. Barks, Carl. *Uncle Scrooge in Only a Poor Old Man*. The Best of Walt Disney Comics. Racine, Wisconsin: Western, 1974. 48 pp.

3021. Barks, Carl. *Walt Disney Uncle Scrooge*. Best Comics. New York: Abbeville Press, 1979. 213 pp.

3022. Blum, Geoffrey. "The Romance of Wealth." *Uncle Scrooge, Carl Barks Library, Set 3, Volume 1*, pp. 9-14. Scottsdale, Arizona: Another Rainbow, 1984.

3023. Boyd, Robert. "Uncle $crooge Imperialist." *Comics Journal*. October 1990, pp. 52-55.

3024. Chalker, Jack. *An Informal Biography of Scrooge McDuck*. Baltimore, Maryland: Mirage Press, 1974.

3025. Stewart, Fred. "Scrooge & 'the Raven.'" *The Barks Collector*. April 1981.

Mickey Mouse

3026. Becker, Hartmut. "Mickey Maus Zieht Minnie aus." *Comixene* (Hanover). 6:25 (1979), pp. 24-25.

3027. Busdorf, Hans-Jürgen. "Micky Maus—Geschichten in Ihrer Wirkung auf Schüler der 7." Hauptschulklassen. Haursarbeit zur 1. Lehrerprüfung, 1971.

3028. Büttner, Edgar. "Mickey Mouse Macht Mode." *Twen* (Munich). 12:9 (1970), pp. 54-63.

3029. "Comics: 'Micky Maus' Jünger Maos." *Der Spiegel*. No. 43, 1969, pp. 65, 67.

3030. Dela Potterie, Eudes. "Le Journal de Mickey, Répond-il a Son Programme Publicitaire?" *Educateurs* (Paris). No. 44, 1953, pp. 137-138.

3031. Facchini, G.M. and A. Baruzzi. "Dal Mondo di Topolino al Mondo di Paperino. Un'Importante Svolta del Fumetto Disneyano." *Quaderni di Communicazioni di Massa*. No. 1, 1965, pp. 89-92.

3032. Fossati, Franco. *Topolino: Storia del Topo Più Famoso del Mondo*. Milan: Gamma Libri, 1980.

3033. Freitag, Christian H. "Micky Maus—Literatur und Schüler." *Westermanns Pädagogische Beiträge* (Braunschweig). No. 6, 1971, pp. 332-334.

3034. Frémion, Yves. "Les Journaux: du Journal de Mickey à l'Echo des Savanes." *Magazine Littéraire* (Paris). 95, 1974, pp. 16-19.

3035. Grossmann, Robert. "50 Jahre Micky Maus." *Novum* (Munich). 49:11 (1978), pp. 4-11.

3036. Grünewald, Dietrich. "50 Jahre Micky Maus. Eine Methodische Anleitung zur Analyse von Disney-Comics." *Comixene* (Hanover). 5:21 (1978), pp. 19-24, 32.

3037. Hoffmann, Detlef. "Micky Maus im Lesebuch. Das Ende Eines Kulturkampfes." *Blätter des Bielefelder Jugend-Kulturringes* (Bielefeld). No. 240/241, 1970, pp. 201-211.

3038. Hoffman, Michael. "Was Kinder Durch Micki-Maus-Comics 'Lernen.'" *Westermanns Pädagogische Beiträge*. 22:10 (1970), pp. 497-507.

3039. Jacqmain, Monique. "*Topolino*. Maestro di Stile?" *Italiano d'Oggi. Lingua Letteraria e Lingue Speciali* (Trieste). 1974, pp. 237-248.

3040. Karasek, Hellmuth. "Auch Ich War Eine Micky Maus (Disney-World)." *Zeitmagazin* (Hamburg). November 26, 1971, pp. 4-8.

3041. Keller, Hans. "Mickey-Mouse Heftchen und Schundliteratur-Umtauschaktionen." *Jugendliteratur*. 2, 1956, pp. 595-596.

3042. Lob, Jacques. "Mickey Parodies." *Giff-Wiff*. No. 19, 1966, pp. 19-20.

3043. "Micky Maus Ist Prima." *Elternblatt* (Frankfurt). 20:8 (1970), pp. 24-25.

3044. "Micky Maus Stiftete Viele Preise." *Hör Zu* (Hamburg). No. 39, 1969, p. 143.

3045. "Mickey Mouse." *Der Stern*. No. 50, 1965.

3046. Piorkowski-Wühr, Irmgard. "Minni Maus, Klarabella und die Emanzipation. Mit Einer Einleitung von H. Jürgen Kagelmann." *Comixene* (Hanover). 6:22 (1979), pp. 45-46.

3047. Pourprix, Bernard. "Lecture Politique de Mickey." *Economie et Humanisme* (Lyon). 1971, pp. 69-78.

3048. Rhode, Werner. "Mickey Mouse Wird Aufgepumpt zur Kunst. Bilderbogen und Blasensprache. Die Berliner Akademie der Künste Zeigt Comic-Strips." *Kölner Stadtanzeiger* (Cologne). December 27/28, 1969, p. 6.

3049. Romer, Jean-Claude. "Les Mickey Mouse Cartoons." *Giff-Wiff*. No. 19, 1966, pp. 15-16.

3050. Strzyz, Klaus and Andreas C. Knigge. "30 Jahre Micky Maus." *Comixene*. (Hanover). 8:42 (1981), pp. 18-19.

3051. Wurm, Wolfgang. "Jugend-Micky Maus auf Abwegen." *Bayernkurier* (Munich). September 27, 1969, p. 13.

3052. Zanotto, Piero. "E'riapparso Topolino, l'Eroe di Walt Disney." *Il Lavoro*. October 8, 1966.

3053. Zanotto, Piero. "E'riapparso Topolino, l'Eroe di Walt Disney." *Il Piccolo*. November 13, 1966.

Horror

3054. Barlow, Ron and Bhob Stewart, eds. *Those Were the Terrible, Shocking, Sensational, Appalling, Forbidden, But Simply Wonderful Horror Comics of the 1950s*. Franklin Square, New York: Nostalgia Press, 1971. 200 pp.

3055. Benton, Mike. *Horror Comics: The Illustrated History*. Dallas, Texas: Taylor Books, 1991.

3056. "Blutrausch." *ICOM*. January 1993, pp. 54-55.

3057. Cary, J. "Horror Comics." *Spectator*. February 25, 1956, p. 220.

3058. Castelli, Alfredo. "Gli E.C. Horror Comics." *Comics Club*. No. 1, 1967, pp. 73-75.

3059. Cerdeirinha, Agnaldo. "Quadrinhos São um Terror!" *Boletim de HQ*. March-April 1992, pp. 4-5.

3060. Conça, Paulo. "Horrorismo." *Boletim de HQ*. March-April 1992, p. 3.

3061. D'Angelo, Carr. "Inside Arkham Asylum." *Comics Scene*. No. 10, 1989, pp. 53-56.

3062. de Suinn, Colin. "Necropolis Now." *Speakeasy*. October 1990, pp. 25-27.

3063. "Far-Out Fanfare and Infoomation!" *Foom*. Spring 1973, pp. 18-23.

3064. Fernández, Norman. "Frankenstein Desencadenado." *El Wendigo*. No. 59, 1993, pp. 36-37.

3065. Gafford, Carl. "Committee of Terror." *Baycon III Program Book*. 1977, pp. 9-11.

3066. Garrick, Joe. "Comic Horror." *How*. March-April 1987, pp. 80-89.

3067. Gilbert, Michael T. "Mr. Monster Attacks." *Comics Buyer's Guide*. November 27, 1992, pp. 26-28, 32.

3068. "Hamilton Ends Horror Comics." *Comics Journal*. February 1992, p. 17.

3069. *The Haunt of Fear*. The Complete EC Library. 5 Vols. West Plains, Missouri: R. Cochran, 1985.

3070. Hewetson, Alan. "May Days in Horror Comics." *Comics Journal*. March 1989, pp. 88-96.

3071. Kast, Paul. "The Ghoulunatic Photos." *Squa Tront*. No. 5, 1974, pp. 31-34.

3072. Johnson, Kim H. "Taste the Blood of Dracula." *Comics Scene*. No. 10, 1989, pp. 17-20, 60.

3073. Lobdell, Scott. "Call Him Doc Stearn... Mr. Monster." *Comics Scene*. No. 10, 1989, pp. 25-28, 60.

3074. "'Monsieur Gravedigger.'" *Cartoonist PROfiles*. December 1978, pp. 54-61.

3075. Shellenbarger, Shane. "Mythology in a Modern Era." In *San Diego Comic Convention 1993*, p. 86. San Diego, California: 1993.

3076. *Shock SuspenStories*. The Complete EC Library. 3 Vols. West Plains, Missouri: R. Cochran, 1985.

3077. *Tales from the Crypt*. The Complete EC Library. 5 Vols. West Plains, Missouri: R. Cochran, 1979.

3078. *The Vault of Horror*. The Complete E.C. Library. 5 Vols. West Plains, Missouri: R. Cochran, 1982.

3079. Warren, James, ed. *The Best of Creepy*. New York: Grosset & Dunlap, 1971. 158 pp.

3080. Watt-Evans, Lawrence. "A Brief History of Pre-Code Horror." *Comics Collector*. Spring 1984, pp. 46-49, 52-55.

3081. Watt-Evans, Lawrence. "Rayguns, Elves, and Skin-Tight Suits." *Comics Buyer's Guide*. December 23, 1983, pp. 24, 28, 30-31, 34, 36; April 27, 1984, pp. 26, 28, 30, 32; continuing column, early 1980s.

3082. Weidenbaum, Marc. "Read 'Em and Weep." *Pulse!* October 1992, pp. 87-88.

3083. Yarber, E. "Creature Comfort." In *San Diego Comic Convention 1993*, p. 70. San Diego, California: 1993.

Swamp Thing

3084. Bissette, Steve. "The Swamp Thing Papers Part I." *Comics Feature*. September-October 1984, pp. 8-9, 48-50.

3085. Bissette, Stephen. "The Swamp Thing Papers Part 2." *Comics Feature*. November-December 1984, pp. 14-15, 59-60.

3086. Burbey, Mark. "The Swamp Thing Section." *Comics Journal*. September 1984, pp. 45-99.

3087. "Character Profile: *Swamp Thing*." *Comics Scene*. January 1981, pp. 27-29.

3088. Fiore, Robert. "Drawing the Swamp." *Comics Journal*. June 1988, pp. 7-10.

3089. McAdams, Mindy. "The Swamp Thing That Was: Hero History." *Amazing Heroes*. May 1982, pp. 34-42.

3090. McConnell, Kevin C. "Definitive Vs. Derivative." *Comics Journal*. May 1982, pp. 48-51.

3091. Moore, Alan, Stephen Bissette, and John Totleben. *Saga of the Swamp Thing*. New York: DC Comics, 1987. 175 pp.

3092. "Swampy's New Look." *Before I Get Old*." March 1987, p. 25.

Jungle Adventure

3093. *Jerry Iger's Classic Jungle Comics*. El Cajon, California: Blackthorne, 1986. 70 pp.

3094. *Jerry Iger's Classic Sheena*. El Cajon, California: Blackthorne, 1985. 72 pp.

Ka-Zar

3095. Catron, Michael. "Ka-Zar Goes to Hell." *Best of Amazing Heroes*. No. 1, 1982, pp. 35-39.

3096. Luciano, Dale. "The Urbane Jungle Savage." *Comics Journal*. May 1981, pp. 103-104.

3097. Pierce, J.J. "Ka-Zar the Derivative." *Comics Journal*. December 1981, pp. 65-69.

Tarzan

3098. Barrett, Robert R. "'The Indian Is Not an Apache!' Paul Stahr (1883-1953)." *Burroughs Bulletin*. October 1992, pp. 15-18.

3099. Castelli, Alfredo. "Tarzan a Fumetti nei Quotidiani." *Comics Club* (Milan). No. 1, 1967, pp. 24-26.

3100. Donner, Wolf. "Tarzan: Psychogramm Einer Erfolgsfigur." *Die Zeit*. No. 7. February 12, 1971.

3101. Fuchs, Wolfgang J. "Zum Beispiel Tarzan. Ein Exkurs über die Heldenmultiplikation in Massenmedien." In *Comics im Medienmarkt, in der Analyse, im Unterricht*, edited by Wolfgang J. Fuchs, pp. 40-45. Opladen: Leske und Budrich, 1977.

3102. Harvey, R.C. "Foster's *Tarzan* and How It Grew." *Comics Journal*. April 1993, pp. 77-78, 80.

3103. Herner, Schmelz, Irene. *Tarzan, el Hombre Mito*. Sep/Setentas. 139. Mexico City: Secretaría de Educación Pública, 1974.

3104. Herner Schmelz, Irene. "Tarzán el Hombre Mito." *Revista Mexicana de Ciencia Política*. 19:74 (1973), pp. 29-35.

3105. Lacassin, Francis. *Tarzan ou le Chevalier Crispé*. Preface by Burne Hogarth. Paris: H. Veyrier, 1982; Paris: Union Génerale d'Editons, 1971.

3106. Leguebe, Eric. "Bataille d'Hernani pour Tarzan." *Arts* (Paris). March 2, 1966.

3107. Lémie, Claude and Robert Samuel. *L'Univers de Tarzan*. Paris: Bordas, 1976.

3108. Lorenz, Detlef. *Alles über Tarzan: Bücher, Filme, Comica*. Braunschweig: Ed. Corsar, 1982.

3109. Luz, Marco Aurélio. "Tarzan, o Homen-Macaco." *Revista de Cultura Vozes* (Petrópolis). September 1973, pp. 29-46.

3110. Nestle, Werner. "Materialien und Strukturskizze zu Einem Unterrichtsarrangement über den Comic 'Die Verschwörung.'" *Sonderpädagogik* (Berlin). 6:1 (1976), pp. 18-31.

3111. Pendleton, Thomas A. "Tarzan of the Papers." *Journal of Popular Culture*. Spring 1979, pp. 691-701.

3112. Re, Marzo. "Tarzan delle Scimmie." *Comics Club* (Milan). No. 1, 1967, pp. 21-23.

3113. Schiele, Joachim. *Tarzan, der Barfüssige Held*. Munich: Nüchtern, 1981.

3114. Schiele, Joachim. "*Tarzan*. Vom Letzten Urbild Eines Helden." *Comixene*. 8:39 (1981), pp. 4-9; 8:40 (1981), pp. 46-49.

3115. Spurlock, Duane. "'Where Have All the Fans Gone?' An Interview with Henning Kure." *Burroughs Bulletin*. January 1993, pp. 22-35.

3116. "Tarzan Issue." *Paperback Parade* (Brooklyn, New York). December 1988. Seven articles, 64 illustrations.

3117. "Tarzans Rückkehr auf den Büchermarkt." In Das Literarische Colloqium, 2. Deutsches Fernsehen (ZDF), July 28, 1971.

3118. "Tarzan: Thesen: Pro und Contra." *Bulletin: Jugend + Literatur* (Hamburg). No. 7/71, 1971, pp. 13-14.

3119. Taireja, Sanjay. "Taking Comics Seriously." *The Independent*. January 17, 1991.

3120. Woolsey, F.W. "Tarzan Swings Back." *Courier-Journal Magazine* (Louisville, Kentucky). January 15, 1984. (University of Louisville Burroughs Collection).

Rock and Roll

3121. "Cover Toons. Rock 'n' Roll Meets the Comics!" *Comics Journal*. May 1993, pp. 47-57.

3122. "Rock 'N Roll Comics: A Brief History." *Comics Buyer's Guide*. September 22, 1989, p. 48.

3123. Simon, J. "Rock and Roll Stars in Comic Books." *Rolling Stone*. August 10, 1978, p. 18.

Romance

3124. Bailey, Bruce. "An Inquiry into Love Comic Books: The Token Evolution of a Popular Genre." *Journal of Popular Culture*. Summer 1976, pp. 245-248.

3125. Breznick, Alan. "Love's Illusions I Recall." *Comics Scene*. September 1983, pp. 54-58.

3126. Carlson, Mark. "Romance Comics—The Forgotten Genre." *The Comic World*. November 1979, pp. 25-34.

3127. Howell, Richard E. "An End to Romance." *Comics Journal*. April 1980, pp. 30-32.

3128. Howell, Richard E., ed. *Real Love: The Best of Simon and Kirby Romance Comics: 1940s-1950s*. Forestville, California: Eclipse Books, 1988.

3129. "Love on a Dime." *Time*. August 22, 1949, p. 41.

3130. Mitchell, Steve. "The Best Is the Worst: Love, 'Classics,' and the ACMP." *Comics Buyer's Guide*. July 19, 1985, pp. 26+.

3131. Perebinossoff, Philippe. "What Does a Kiss Mean? The Love Comic Formula and the Creation of the Ideal Teen-age Girl." *Journal of Popular Culture*. Spring 1975, pp. 825-835.

3132. Sadler, A.W. "Love Comics and American Popular Culture." *American Quarterly*. 16 (1964), pp. 486-490.

3133. Scott, Naomi, ed. *Heart Throbs: The Best of DC Romance Comics*. New York: Simon and Schuster, 1979.

Science Fiction

3134. Benton, Mike. *Science Fiction Comics: The Illustrated History*. Dallas, Texas: Taylor Publishing Co., 1992.

3135. Compart, Martin. "Vom Traum zum Alptraum. Ein Historischer Überblick über die Amerikanischen SF-Comics." *Comixene*. 7:30 (1980), pp. 5-14.

3136. Disbrow, Jay. "My Ultimate Science Fiction Comic." *Comics Journal*. Summer 1979, pp. 100-103.

3137. Eizykman, Boris and Daniel Riche. *La Bande Dessinée de Science Fiction Américaine*. Paris: Albin Michel, 1976.

3138. Gross, Mitchell J. "Shattered Destinies." *Comics Scene*. No. 10, 1989, pp. 42-44, 52.

3139. Halliday, Andy. "Startrek Virtual Reality." *Comics Interview*. No. 118, 1993, pp. 5-8, 11-13.

3140. *Incredible Science Fiction*. The Complete EC Library. West Plains, Missouri: R. Cochran, 1982. 138 pp.

3141. Inge, M. Thomas. "Science Fiction in the EC Comic Books." *Questar*. Summer 1978, pp. 18-20.

3142. Olish, Cathy. "Shooting Down the Battlestar." *Whizzard*. February 1981, pp. 18-19.

3143. Scholz, Carter. "Radical Doubt: The Position of the Science Fiction Writer, Part 2." *Comics Journal*. October 1981, pp. 115-119.

3144. Scholz, Carter. "Science Fiction in the Comics." *Comics Journal*. July 1982, pp. 103-104.

3145. "The Science Panel." *Squa Tront*. No. 8, 1978, pp. 37-44.

3146. Seidman, David. "21st Century Comics." *Cartoonist PROfiles*. March 1989, pp. 68-71.

3147. Sherman, Sam. "Buck Rogers, Part 1-2." *Spacemen*. No. 5, 1962, pp. 34-42; No. 6, 1963, pp. 16-21.

3148. "The Space Patrol Returns." *Vanguard*. No. 2, 1968, pp. 12-15.

3149. Spicer, Bill. "Dawn of the Discs." *Comics Buyer's Guide*. Part I, September 7, 1984, pp. 20, 22; Part II, November 9, 1984, pp. 20, 22; Part III, December 7, 1984, pp. 60, 62.

3150. Spicer, Bill. "Dawn of the Discs, Part IV: To Mercury and Back with Bob Powell and Wally Wood." *Comics Buyer's Guide*. January 4, 1985, pp. 20, 22.

3151. Stallman, David. "A Space Cadet No More." *Comics Journal*. June 1980, pp. 8-9.

3152. *Star Trek, the Enterprise Logs*. 4 Vols. Racine, Wisconsin: Western, 1976-1977.

3153. Strnad, Jan and Richard Corben. "Return of the Mutant Planet." *Comics Journal*. August 1990, pp. 8-11.

3154. Uslan, Michael, ed. *Mysteries in Space, the Best of DC Science-Fiction Comics*. New York: Simon and Schuster, 1980. 251 pp.

3155. *Weird Fantasy*. The Complete E.C. Library. 4 Vols. West Plains, Missouri: R. Cochran, 1980.

3156. *Weird Science*. The Complete E.C. Library. 4 Vols. West Plains, Missouri: R. Cochran, 1978.

3157. *Weird Science Fantasy*. The Complete E.C. Library. West Plains, Missouri: R. Cochran, 1982. 242 pp.

3158. Weist, Jerry. "E.C. Science-Fiction Comics." *Squa Tront*. No. 3, 1969, pp. 6-24.

3159. Weldon, D. "They're Living Off Another Planet: Twin Earths." *Popular Science*. January 1953, pp. 132-135.

3160. Zilber, Jay. "UFO." *The Comic World*. November 1979, pp. 13-17.

Flash Gordon

3161. Barry, Dan and Harvey Kurtzman. *Flash Gordon*. Princeton, Wisconsin: Kitchen Sink Press, 1988. 136 pp.

3162. Castelli, Alfredo. "Il Nuovo Gordon Degli Albi King." *Comics*. No. 4, 1966, pp. 3-4.

3163. Ciment, Gilles. "Au Commencement, La Chute." *Les Cahiers de la Bande Dessinée* (Grenoble) 72, 1986, p. 24.

3164. "The Flushing of Flash." *Robin Snyder's History of the Comics*. July 1991, pp. 59-60.

3165. Masson, Pierre. "Flash Gordon ou la Recherche de la Profondeur." *Les Cahiers de la Bande Dessinée* (Grenoble). 72, 1986, pp. 20-23.

3166. Sterckx, Pierre. "Un Érotique de Glace." *Les Cahiers de la Bande Dessinée* (Grenoble). 72, 1986, pp. 25-26.

Superhero

3167. Allstetter, Rob. "U.N. Force." *Comics Buyer's Guide*. March 12, 1993, p. 22.

3168. "Avant-Vanguardists Inc." *FA*. October 1989, pp. 22-24.

3169. Baker, Ronald L. "Folklore Motifs in Comic Books of Superheroes." *Tennessee Folklore Society Bulletin*. December 1975, pp. 170-174.

3170. Balfour, Brad. "The New Superhero." *Spin*. August 1988, p. 49.

3171. Beck, C.C. "Comic Heroes in Ancient Times." *Comics Journal*. May 1985, p. 7.

3172. Benton, Mike. *Superhero Comics of the Silver Age: The Illustrated History*. Dallas, Texas: Taylor Publishing Co., 1991.

3173. Bishop, Derek G. "Return of the Mighty Crusaders." *Comics Collector*. Spring 1983, pp. 37-40.

3174. "Blood and T.H.U.N.D.E.R." *Comics Journal*. April 1985, pp. 7-13.

3175. Blythe, Hal and Charlie Sweet. "Formula and the Superhero." *Comics Journal*. July 1982, pp. 82-88.

3176. Boerner, Brian. "Bugging the Micronauts." *Comics Feature*. June 1980, pp. 58-60, 62-63.

3177. Brown, Slater. "The Coming of the Supermen." *New Republic*. September 2, 1940, p. 301.

3178. Byrne, John. "Da Un Punto di Vista Molto Personale." *Corto Maltese*. August 1988, pp. 84-86.

3179. Byrne, John and Nicola Cuti. *The Complete Rog 2000*. San Diego, California: Pacific Comics Distributors, 1982. 39 pp.

3180. "Camera Comics: Our Comic Book Heroes." *U.S. Camera*. August 1966, pp. 54-55.

3181. "Captain Midi Is Not Himself." *Time*. January 17, 1944, p. 77.

3182. Carter, Judy. "My Two Superheroes." *Redbook*. February 1981, pp. 74, 77, 114, 116.

3183. Cassen, Bernard. "Superman et Batman Ont Trente Ans. L'Âge d'Or de la Bande Dessinée en Amérique." *Le Monde* (Paris). October 11, 1967, p. 7.

3184. Catron, Michael. "A New Phase for Moon Knight." *Best of Amazing Heroes*. No. 1, 1982, pp. 49-53.

3185. Choy, Larry. "Larry Speaks." *Before I Get Old*. September 1986, pp. 60-61.

3186. Claremont, Chris, Frank Miller, and Josef Rubinstein. *Wolverine*. New York: Marvel Comics, 1987. 96 pp.

3187. Courtial, Gérard. *A la Rencontre des Super-Héros. De Neal Adams... aux X-Men*. Marseilles: Bédésup, 1985.

3188. Denney, R. "Great Comic-Book Heroes, comp. by Jules Feiffer." *Commentary*. May 1966, pp. 86-89.

3189. Dickholtz, Daniel. "Lacking Proper Adult Supervision." *Comics Scene*. August 1990, pp. 45-47, 60.

3190. Dickholtz, Daniel. "Murder Nearby the Cathedral." *Comics Scene*. October 1991, pp. 25-28.

3191. Dickholtz, Daniel. "The Strange and the Bold." *Comics Scene*. October 1991, pp. 19-24, 58.

3192. "Dissecting the Dazzler!" *Comics Feature*. November 1980, pp. 14-19.

3193. "Dr. Fate Reprint Series." *Comics Journal.* October 1984, pp. 18-19.

3194. Dunn, Deby. "A Review of Red Sonya." *Comics Feature.* No. 25, 1983, pp. 51-54.

3195. Feiffer, Jules. "The Great Comic Book Heroes." *Playboy.* October 1965, pp. 75-83.

3196. Feiffer, Jules, comp. *The Great Comic Book Heroes: The Origins and Early Adventures of the Classic Superheroes of the Comic Books—In Glorious Color.* New York: Bonanza Books, 1965.

3197. Freedland, Nat. "Super Heroes with Super Problems." *New York Sunday Herald Tribune Magazine.* January 9, 1966, pp. 14-15.

3198. Gafford, Carl and Franklin W. Maynard. "Happy Anniversary, Hero." *Amazing World of DC Comics.* February 1976, pp. 23-26.

3199. Gates, D. "Comic-Book Heroes to the Rescue." *Newsweek.* December 12, 1983, p. 27.

3200. Gehman, Richard B. "From Deadwood Dick to Superman." *Science Digest.* June 1949, pp. 52-57.

3201. Gemignani, Margaret. "What Happened to Hourman?" *Masquerader.* No. 2, 1962, p. 14.

3202. Gettmann, Patric. "Heavy Metal Oder: Wie die Comics Salonfähig Wurden." *Comic Forum. Das Österreichische Fachmagazin für Comicliteratur* (Vienna). 4:13 (1982), pp. 20-26.

3203. Goulart, Ron. "The Old Original Super-Heroes: Doll Man." *Comics Buyer's Guide.* March 5, 1993, pp. 100, 108.

3204. Goulart, Ron. "The Old Original Superheroes, Part VIII. Hawkman." *Comics Buyer's Guide.* November 20, 1987, pp. 46-47.

3205. Goulart, Ron. "The Old Original Super-Heroes: Silver Streak." *Comics Buyer's Guide.* February 3, 1989, pp. 21, 24.

3206. Goulart, Ron. "Super-Heroes and Horror." *Comics Buyer's Guide.* September 7, 1990, p. 46.

3207. "The Greatest Hero of Them All." *FCA/S.O.B.* October-November 1980, p. 8.

3208. "The Great Heroes Were All Losers." *FCA/S.O.B.* October-November 1981, p. 8.

3209. Green, Stuart. "The Changing Face(s) of Mr. X." *Speakeasy*. May 1989, pp. 51, 53.

3210. Gross, Theodore L. *Representative Men: Cult Heroes of Our Time*. New York: Collier-Macmillan, 1970.

3211. Guay, George. "The Life and Death of the Doom Patrol." *Best of Amazing Heroes*. No. 1, 1982, pp. 85-98.

3212. Guzzo, Gary. "Carl Potts Discusses Epic's 'Heavy Hitters' Line." *Comics Buyer's Guide*. March 19, 1993, pp. 26-28.

3213. Hansen, Neil A. "Testing Your Metal: Robocop vs. Terminator." *Comics Values Monthly*. September 1992, pp. 7-9.

3214. Harmetz, Aljean. "Superheroes' Battleground: Prime Time." *New York Times*. October 11, 1988.

3215. Harvey, R.C. "Super-Heroes on the Couch." *Comics Journal*. January 1986, pp. 78-82.

3216. "Hero With a Conscience." *Before I Get Old*. July 1987, pp. 33-34.

3217. Howell, Richard. "Fear City: Building a Town for Today." *Comics Buyer's Guide*. April 2, 1993, pp. 26-28.

3218. Inge, M. Thomas. "'A Hero in Our Eyes': Davy, Huck, Clark and Ollie." *The World and I*. November 1991, pp. 571-582.

3219. Jackson, Bruce. "Super-Heroes and Rock: The Unique Is Now Routine." *Comics Buyer's Guide*. October 14, 1983, pp. 59-60.

3220. Jankiewicz, Pat. "Vegetable Team-Up." *Comics Scene*. October 1991, 1991, pp. 14-17, 66. ("Flaming Carrot").

3221. Jefferson, David J. "Comic Book's Heroes and Villains Are Wearing Gray Hats Nowadays." *Wall Street Journal*. November 12, 1992, p. B-1.

3222. Jerome, Fiona. "Shock Story of the Year!" *Speakeasy*. November 1990, pp. 4-5.

3223. Johns, T.L. "Ragman Tales." *Comics Scene*. October 1991, pp. 29-32, 60.

3224. Johnson, Kim H. "Cool Blue Heroic Jazz." *Comics Scene*. April 1992, pp. 47-50.

3225. Johnson, Kim H. "Uncaged Again." *Comics Scene*. April 1992, pp. 9-11, 58.

3226. Johnson, Kim H. "Wild O.N.E.S." *Comics Scene*. December 1992, pp. 33-35, 52.

3227. Jones, R.A. "Flesh of Steel, Fist of Iron." *Amazing Heroes*. October 15, 1984, pp. 41-52.

3228. Kagan, Paul. "The Return of the Superhero: Comic Books Aim Beyond the Bubble-Gum Brigade." *The National Observer*. October 11, 1965.

3229. Kanalz, Hank. "Total Eclipse." *Comics Scene*. No. 3 (Vol. 3, Series #14), pp. 30-32, 44.

3230. Keltner, Howard. "The High Flying Hawkman." *Masquerader*. No. 2, 1962, pp. 4-7.

3231. Kida, Fred. *Valkyrie*. Park Forest, Illinois: K. Pierce, 1982. 80 pp.

3232. Klein, I. "Father of the Super-heroes?" *Cartoonist PROfiles*. December 1977, pp. 66-67.

3233. Klug, Marty. "Sabre." *Whizzard*. February 1981, pp. 10-11.

3234. Kraft, David A. *The Incredible Hulk, the Secret Story of Marvel's Gamma-Powered Goliath*. Milwaukee, Wisconsin: Ideals Publishing Corp., 1981. 64 pp.

3235. "Kung Foolishness." *Newsweek*. February 12, 1973, p. 51.

3236. Lahman, Ed. "The Superman Before the Time of Superman...Maximo." *Alter Ego*. No. 4, 1962, pp. 19-22.

3237. Lang, Jeffrey. "The Sleep of the Just: 'Sandman Mystery Theatre.'" *Comics Buyer's Guide*. March 26, 1993, p. 113.

3238. Lawrence, Lloyd. "Super-Villain Team-Up Returns." *Fans-Zine*. Spring-Summer 1979, p. 19.

3239. Leguebe, Eric. "Ronald Reagan Heros et Super-Heros de B.D." *Bédésup*. 4th Trimester, 1987, pp. 11-14.

3240. Lobdell, Scott. "The Better Part of *Squalor*." *Comics Scene*. No. 13, 1990, pp. 45-48, 67.

3241. "Los Comics Vietnik (Estudia Sobre las Parodias Politicas Realizadas en Norte-América a Base de los Super-hombres)." *SP* (Madrid). September 25, 1966.

3242. Luciano, Dale. "Stop! In the Name of the Carrot!" *Comics Journal*. July 1982, pp. 43-48.

3243. Lupoff, Dick. *The Big Nostalgia Book About the Comics, Heroes and Superheroes*. New York: Ace Books, 1970.

3244. Macchio, Ralph. "The Defenders Saga." *Foom*. Fall 1977, pp. 12-19.

3245. McGregor, Don. "Dragon Shade Is Waiting!" *Foom*. December 1976, pp. 18-21.

3246. "Making Light of the Shadow Universe." *Before I Get Old*. March 1988, pp. 21-22.

3247. "Man from U.N.C.L.E.: The Birds of Prey Affair." *Comics Buyer's Guide*. December 4, 1992, pp. 26-27.

3248. Mark, Norman. "The New Superhero (Is a Pretty Kinky Guy)." *Eye*. February 1969, pp. 40 ff.

3249. "The Marriage Between Heaven and Hell." *Fans-Zine*. Spring-Summer 1979, pp. 26-27, 44.

3250. Martin, Anya. "A Slow Descent into Total Malevolence." *Comics Scene*. April 1992, pp. 29-32, 52.

3251. Matranga, Stuart. "Superhero Scriptwriters." *Comics Scene*. March 1982, pp. 32-33, 36-37.

3252. Meyer, Ron and Joyce Buckner. "Superheroes and Summer Reading." *The Instructor*. May 1980, p. 83.

3253. Morrissey, Richard. "Dial H for Hero." *Best of Amazing Heroes*. No. 1, 1982, pp. 105-110.

3254. Mougin, Lou. "Forgotten Super-Heroes." *Comics Feature*. June 1983, pp. 83-85.

3255. Mougin, Lou. "Forgotten Super-Heroes: The Jack of Hearts." *Comics Feature*. 25, 1983, pp. 84-86.

3256. Mougin, Lou. "Go, Team, Go! Thirty Years of Team-Up Comics." *Comics Collector*. Winter 1985, pp. 34-39, 42-44.

3257. Mougin, Lou. "Twenty Years with a Thunder God." *Amazing Heroes*. July 1982, pp. 58-78.

3258. Muller, Georgene. "Thunder Agents: Do They Have a Fighting Chance?" *Comics Collector*. Spring 1983, pp. 66-67.

3259. Murray, Will. "Captain Future, Yesterday's Man of Tomorrow." *Comics Buyer's Guide*. November 11, 1983, pp. 60, 62, 64, 66.

3260. Murray, Will. "Listen to The Whisperer." *Comics Buyer's Guide*. August 1, 1986, p. 32.

3261. Murray, Will. "Where Hornets Swarm." *Comics Scene*. 9, 1989, pp. 39-42, 50.

3262. Ng Suat Tong. "Cerebus the Nihilist: Melmoth." *Comics Journal*. November 1992, pp. 35-37.

3263. "Nick Fury vs. S.H.I.E.L.D." *Comics Buyer's Guide*. December 18, 1987, p. 1.

3264. Niderost, Eric. "Arousing Aliens." *Comics Scene*. No. 3 (Vol. 3, Series #14), pp. 51-53, 66.

3265. "Of Werewolves and Musclemen." *Comics Arena*. July 1992, pp. 29-30.

3266. O'Neill, Patrick D. "Heroes of Another Day." *Comics Scene*. No. 13, 1990, pp. 53-55.

3267. "Our Comic-Book Heroes." *U.S. Camera*. August 1966, pp. 54-55.

3268. Pecora, N. "Superman/Superboys/Supermen: The Comic Book Hero As Socializing Agent." In *Men, Masculinity, and the Media*, edited by S. Craig, pp. 61-77. Newbury Park, California: Sage, 1992.

3269. Perigard, Mark A. "Death of the Superheroes." *Newsweek*. November 11, 1985, p. 15.

3270. Perrin, Steve. "What's Wrong with the Jaguar." *Masquerader*. No. 2, 1962, pp. 15-17.

3271. Phillips, Gene. "Heroes and Anti-Heroes in a Vulgar Valhalla." *Comics Journal*. April 1980, pp. 62-64.

3272. Pierce, John G. "Jimmy Olsen Vs. Billy Batson." *FCA and Me, Too! Newsletter*. Fall 1987, p. 6.

3273. Reed, Gene. "Justice Will Be Done! A Hero History of Captain Action." *Amazing Heroes*. March 1982, pp. 40-53.

3274. Richler, Mordecai. *The Great Comic Book Heroes and Other Essays*. Toronto: McClelland and Stewart, 1978.

3275. Roberts, Jeff. "Favorites." *Fans-Zine*. Spring-Summer 1979, pp. 36-38.

3276. Rodi, Rob. "The Big Three Get Smaller." *Comics Journal*. September 1987, pp. 42-44. (*Superman*, *Batman*, *Wonder Woman*).

3277. Rodríguez Arbesú, Faustino. "Hawkworld: Una Bella Historia de Denuncia." *El Wendigo*. No. 51, 1991, pp. 10-12.

3278. Rollin, Betty. "Return of the (Whoosh! There Goes One!) Superhero!" *Look*. March 22, 1966, pp. 113-114.

3279. Sanderson, Peter. "The Coming of the Night Force." *Amazing Heroes*. May 1982, pp. 26-32.

3280. Sanderson, Peter. "The Many Alternative Fates of the Phoenix." *Comics Feature*. July-August 1980, pp. 12-17.

3281. Savramis, Demosthenes. "Modern Man Between Tarzan and Superman. Der Moderne Mensch Zwischen Tarzan und Superman." *Communications*. 9:2-3 (1983), pp. 227-239.

3282. Schneider, Hal. "Green Force Five." *Cartoonist PROfiles*. March 1986, pp. 52-55.

3283. Schreiner, Dave. "Stage Settings: Struggling with Destiny." *The Spirit 26*. December 1986.

3284. Schumer, Arlen. "The New Superheroes: A Graphic Transformation." *Print*. November-December 1988, pp. 112-131.

3285. Seppi, Bob, ed. *The Magnificent Superheroes of Comics Golden Age*. St. Petersburg, Florida: Superlith, 1977. 128 pp.

3286. Shapiro, Marc. "Every Superhero's All-American." *Comics Scene*. August 1990, pp. 53-55, 66.

3287. Shapiro, Marc. "The Human Magnet." *Comics Scene*. May 1992, pp. 53-56.

3288. Shapiro, Marc. "The Punisher—Film Journal Entries." *Comics Scene*. No. 9, 1989, pp. 20-22, 24-27.

3289. Singer, David M. "Survival of the Fittest: *Or* Breathing New Life into Old Heroes." *Amazing Heroes*. September 1981, pp. 34-37.

3290. Skeates, Steve. "The Death of the Superheroes." *Comics Journal*. July 1979, pp. 34-39.

3291. Smith, David H. "Dr. Druid: Master of the Unknown." *Amazing Heroes*. June 15, 1987, pp. 57-61.

3292. Smith, Jerry. "On the Punisher: Are Three Titles Punishment Enough?" *Comics Arena*. July 1992, pp. 25-27.

3293. Sodaro, Robert J. "For Both Titans Teams, It's a Year of Big Changes." *Comics Buyer's Guide*. April 23, 1993, pp. 27-28.

3294. "Space Ghost." *Speakeasy*. No. 81, 1987, pp. 16-17.

3295. Stredicke, Victor. "Superheroes for Young and Old." *Cartoonist Northwest*. September 1990, pp. 6, 8.

3296. Sullivan, Darcy. "Biting the Fist That Feeds Them. Superhero Parodies." *Comics Journal*. April 1990, 53-57.

3297. Sullivan, Darcy. "The Politics of Super-Heroes." *Comics Journal*. June 1991, pp. 83-88.

3298. "Super Artists." *Amazing World of DC Comics*. February 1976, pp. 18-21.

3299. "Superfans and Batmaniacs." *Newsweek*. February 15, 1965, pp. 89-90.

3300. "Super Freaks; Comic Book Heroes." *National Review*. May 13, 1977, pp. 566-567.

3301. "Super Group. Fact File No. 1." *Comics Collector*. Spring 1983, p. 69.

3302. "Superman, Batman, Bond et Cie." *Formidable* (Paris). Supplement, No. 26, November 1967, pp. 6-7.

3303. Sutton, M.F. "So We Commemorate the Vegetable for Heroes." *Saturday Evening Post*. February 27, 1954, p. 108.

3304. Tan, Stephen. "HERO: More Than Just a Name." *Before I Get Old*. August 1986, p. 33.

3305. Thingvall, Joel. "Where Have All the Heroes Gone?" *FCA/S.O.B.* August/September 1981, p. 6.

3306. Thompson, Maggie. "New Universe: How and Why It Began." *Comics Buyer's Guide*. July 4, 1986, p. 3.

3307. Tobias, H. *Superman, Batman, Perry. Versuch Einer Analyse Moderner Abenteuer-Comics*. Bremen: Hausarbeit zur 1. Lehrerprüfung, 1970.

3308. Urbanek, Hermann. "Red Sonja." *Comic Forum* (Vienna). 7:29 (1985), pp. 39-43.

3309. Uslan, Michael and Bob Rozakis." It's a Bird, It's a Plane, It's Super-van." *The Amazing World of DC Comics*. September-October 1974, pp. 45-48.

3310. Valentino. *Normalman, the Novel*. San Jose, California: Slave Labor Books, 1987. 360 pp.

3311. Van Bockel, Jay. "Adam Warlock." *Fans-Zine*. Spring-Summer 1979, pp. 45-46.

3312. Van Gelder, Lindsay and Lawrence Van Gelder. "The Radicalization of the Superheroes." *New York*. October 19, 1970, pp. 36-43.

3313. Van Hise, James. "Alternative Thoughts: Some Exemplary Comics of Today." *LOC*. January 1980, pp. 29-30.

3314. Van Hise, James. *King Comic Heroes*. Las Vegas, Nevada: Pioneer Books, 1988. 98 pp.

3315. Van Hise, James. "Villains: Doctor Doom." *Comics Feature*. May 1987, pp. 12-19.

3316. Waldron, Lamar. "MICRA: Mind Controlled Remote Automaton." *Comics Buyer's Guide*. July 11, 1986, p. 28.

3317. Ward, Murray R. "One of the Good Ones." *Dreamline*. March 1982, pp. 40-46.

3318. Ward, Murray R. "The Super-Team Spirit." *Comics Feature*. January 1981, pp. 47-51; February 1981, pp. 82-85; December 1981, pp. 68-73.

3319. Way, Gregg. "Meet Dr. Solar." *Masquerader*. No. 2, 1962, pp. 9-10.

3320. "Whole Country Goes Super Mad." *Life*. March 11, 1966, pp. 22-23+.

3321. "Who's Who in the All-Star Squadron." *Amazing Heroes*. December 1, 1983, pp. 49-53.

3322. Wooley, John. "On the Funk Patrol." *Dreamline*. March 1982, pp. 48-55; 62-64.

3323. Zimmerman, Howard. "King Kull Lives!" *Foom*. June 1976, pp. 23-25.

DC

3324. Collier, J. "DC Conjures up a Gem of a Comic!" *Amazing Heroes*. February 1983, pp. 26-35.

3325. Harris, Jack C. "Costume Party Capers." *Amazing World of DC Comics*. February 1976, pp. 49-53.

3326. Kwok, Kenneth. "Getting an Impact." *Before I Get Old*. August 1991, p. 97.

3327. O'Neil, Dennis, ed. *Secret Origins of the Super DC Heroes*. New York: Warner Books, 1976. 239 pp.

3328. Wolfman, Marv and George Pérez. *History of the DC Universe*. 2 Vols. New York: DC Comics, 1986.

Marvel

3329. Berger, Arthur A. "Marvel Language: The Comic Book and Reality." *Etc.* June 1972, pp. 169-180.

3330. *The Best of Marvel Comics*. New York: Marvel Comics, 1987-.

3331. Blythe, Hal and Charlie Sweet. "Marvel's '60s Superheroes." *Amazing Heroes*. July 1982, pp. 54-56.

3332. Cook, Brian E. "The Rise and Fall of Richard Nixon and the Monsters from Marvel." *Comics Journal*. October 1979, pp. 76-79.

3333. Gallo, Miguel A. "Los Superheroes de la Marvel." *SNIF: El Mitín del Nuevo Cómic* (México). October 1980, pp. 76-81.

3334. Gärtner, Klaus H.J. "Marvel Comics Oder Klassenkampf von Oben." *Science Fiction Times* (Bremerhaven). 14:129 (1972), pp. 13-16.

3335. Gilroy, Dan. "Marvel Now $100-Million a Year Hulk." *Variety*. September 17, 1986, pp. 81, 92.

3336. Hansen, Neil A. "Marvel 2099: Days of Future Present." *Comics Values Monthly*. October 1992, pp. 11-13.

3337. "Heroes. 25th Anniversary of Marvel Comics. Special Section." *Comics Feature*. May 1986, pp. 15-26, 60.

3338. McEnroe, Richard S. "Why I Can't Write Comics in the Mighty Marvel Manner." *Comics Journal*. November 1986, pp. 102-104.

3339. "Marvel Comic Comments." *Fan's Zine*. Spring-Summer 1979, p. 8.

3340. Marvel Comics. *Marvel Masterworks*. New York: Marvel Comics, 1987-.

3341. "Marvel Comics." *Cartoonist PROfiles*. June 1980, p. 55.

3342. "A Marvelous Showing." *Comics Collector*. Fall 1985, pp. 30-32.

3343. "Marvel's Greatest Heroes: The Thing." *Foom*. April 1974, pp. 4-7.

3344. "Marvel Strikes Back." *Big O Magazine*. October 1992, p. 93.

3345. Palumbo, Donald A. "Adam Warlock: Marvel Comics' Comic Christ Figure." *Extrapolation*. Spring 1983, pp. 33-46.

3346. Palumbo, Donald A. . "Mighty Marvel's Cultural History Tours." *Amazing Heroes*. September 1981, pp. 39-48.

3347. Pérez, Ramón F. "No Todos los Días Nace un Universo." *El Wendigo*. No. 53, 1991, pp. 37-39.

3348. Salicrup, Jim. "Marvel Super Heroes Secret Wars." *Comics Interview*. August 1984, pp. 6-21.

3349. "Silver Age: A Brief Outline of Marvel Comics History." *Comics Feature*. May 1986, pp. 27-28.

3350. Thomas, Roy. "One Man's Family. The Saga of the Mighty Marvels." *Alter Ego*. No. 7, 1964, pp. 18-27.

3351. Van Hise, James. "Marvel's New Universe." *Comics Feature*. October 1986, pp. 32-38.

3352. Ward, Murray R. "Super-Team Spirit—The Avengers." *Comics Feature*. December 1981, pp. 68-72.

3353. Ward, Murray R. "The Super-Team Spirit: The Marvel Teams of the 1970's." *Comics Feature*. November 1982, pp. 71-80.

The Avengers

3354. Bethke, Marilyn. "On the Matter of Comic Books." *Comics Journal*. March 1979, p. 31.

3355. O'Neill, Patrick D. "The Avengers: Disassemble!?!" *Comics Scene*. No. 3 (Vol. 3, No. 14), pp. 17-22.

3356. Palumbo, Donald. "Comics As Literature: Plot Structure, Foreshadowing, and Irony in the Marvel Comics' Avengers Cosmic Epic." *Extrapolation*. Winter 1981, pp. 309-324.

3357. Van Hise, James. "The Avengers." *Comics Feature*. September-October 1984, pp. 5-7, 42-46.

Batman

3358. Andrae, Thomas. "Origins of the Dark Knight: A Conversation with Batman Artists Bob Kane and Jerry Robinson." *The Comic Book Price Guide*. No. 19, 1989, pp. A-71-A-93.

3359. Andreasen, Henrik. "Batman Vender Tilbage!" *Seriejournalen*. June 1992, p. 13.

3360. Appel, Kyra. "Batman, l'Homme Chauvesouris et Devenu l'Idole No. I des Américains." In *Cinémonde*. No. 1647, 1966.

3361. Augusto, Sergio. "Batman, Deus em Demonio?" *Jornal do Brasil.* February 17, 1967.

3362. Augusto, Sergio. "Novos Delírios em Gotham City." *Jornal do Brasil.* June 2, 1957.

3363. Barol, Bill. "Batmania." *Newsweek.* June 26, 1989, pp. 70-74.

3364. Barr, Mike W. "The First Fifty Years of the Batman." In *San Diego Comic Convention 1989* program, pp. 32-55. San Diego, California: San Diego Comic-Con Committee, 1989.

3365. "Batman." *Formidable* (Paris). November 1967, pp. 36-39.

3366. "'Batman' Amerikas Fledermausmensch Fliegt Manchmal Auch aus dem Programm." *Funk-Uhr* (Hamburg). No. 8, 1967.

3367. "Batman Blitz Returns." *Comics Retailer.* April 1992, pp. 11-12.

3368. "Batman Beeinflußt Nur Wenige Kinder." *Westdeutsche Allgemeine Zeitung* (Essen). February 24, 1972.

3369. *Batman from the 30s to the 70s.* Intro. by E. Nelson Bridwell. New York: Crown, 1971. 388 pp.

3370. "Batman Helps Gun Law Reform." *Comics Journal.* April 1993, p. 21.

3371. "Batman l'Homme Chauvesouris Est Devenue l'Idole No. 1 des Américains." *Cinemonde* (Paris). No. 1647, April 15, 1966.

3372. "Batman Returns—But This Time He's a Cartoon." *Penstuff.* September 1992, p. 6.

3373. "Batman Schlägt James Bond." *Welt am Sonntag* (Hamburg). January 12, 1967.

3374. "Batman Slug Fest." *Big O.* August 1991, pp. 82-83.

3375. "Batman-Tante Wacht." *Der Spiegel* (Hamburg). No. 39, 1966, p. 170.

3376. Bertieri, Claudio. "Batman: Eroe Disnezzato." *Il Lavoro* (Genoa). May 22, 1966.

3377. Bertieri, Claudio. "Una Vera Batmania." *Il Lavoro* (Genoa). February 24, 1967.

3378. Bethke, Marilyn. "The Death of Batman! No, Really! Honest! We're Not Kidding This Time!" *Comics Journal.* March 1979, pp. 35-36.

3379. Blackmore, Tim. "The Dark Knight of Democracy: Tocqueville and Miller Cast Some Light on the Subject." *Journal of American Culture*. Spring 1991, pp. 37-56.

3380. Charlton, Warwich. "Batman Batte Bond." *l'Europeo* (Rome). December 22, 1966, pp. 66-69.

3381. Chateau, René. "Bath Batman." *Lui* (Paris). November 1966.

3382. Cuervo, Javier. "'Batman Año Uno,' Esplendida Cosecha." *El Wendigo*. February-April 1988, pp. 15-17.

3383. DC Comics. *The Greatest Batman Stories Ever Told*. New York: DC Comics, 1988.

3384. DC Comics. *The Greatest Joker Stories Ever Told*. New York: DC Comics, 1989.

3385. "DC Restricts *Batman* Coverage." *Comics Journal*. May 1989, pp. 12-13.

3386. Dietz, Lawrence. "The Caped Crusader and the Boy Wonder." *New York Sunday Herald Tribune Magazine*, January 9, 1966, p. 20.

3387. "Englehart and Rogers: The Definitive Batman." *Comics Feature*. December 1981, pp. 58-64.

3388. Fernández, Norman and Germán Menéndez. "Batmanía, Épica y Otros Menesteres." *El Wendigo*. No. 57, 1992, pp. 32-33.

3389. Florez, Florentino. "Batman. Las Razones de la Locura." *El Wendigo*. February-April 1988, pp. 34-35.

3390. Fossati, Franco "Batman." *Fantascienza Minore*. Sondernummer, 1967, pp. 19-21.

3391. Fossati, Franco. "Batman." *SF Francese*. April 1966.

3392. Geerdes, Clay. "The Shadowy Origins of Batman: Human or Superhuman?" *WittyWorld*. Summer/Autumn 1989, pp. 30-33.

3393. Goulart, Ron. "Looking Back at the Golden Age: Batman." *Comics Feature*. January 1986, pp. 20-21, 47.

3394. Greere, Herb. "The Batman Cometh, or the Transmutation of Dracula by the Alchemy of Character Merchandising." *Penthouse*. 1:10 (1966), pp. 25-27.

3395. Groth, Gary. "Batshit." *Comics Journal*. May 1989, pp. 5-6.

3396. Harris, Jack C. "Batman II: The Sequel." *Comics Interview*. No. 77, 1989, pp. 68-70.

3397. Hauser, Olga. "Batman, Bueno o Malo para los Niños?" *Momento* (Caracas). February 26, 1957, pp. 18-25.

3398. Haydock, Ron. "The Exploits of Batman and Robin." *Alter Ego*. No. 4, 1962, pp. 23-30.

3399. Hegerfors, Sture. "Batman är Nog Bra... Men Inte Som Roman." *GT Söndags Extra* (Göteborg). August 6, 1967.

3400. "Holy Flypaper." *Time*. January 28, 1966, p. 38.

3401. "Is *Dark Knight* Fascistic?" *Comics Journal*. November 1986, pp. 9-10.

3402. Ivie, Larry. "The Four Faces of Batman." *Monsters and Heroes*. No. 1, 1967, pp. 28-32.

3403. Jankiewicz, Pat. "The Dark Knight Revised." *Comics Scene*. August 1990, pp. 48-52.

3404. Leonard, Tom. "Cliffhanger for the Caped Crusader." London *Sunday Times*. January 29, 1989.

3405. Levy, R. "Friend of Batman." *Duns Review and Modern Industry*. March 1966, pp. 51-52.

3406. Lim Cheng Tju. "Where's the Fun in Batman?" *Big O*. January 1991, pp. 80-81.

3407. McBride, Joseph. "'Batman' Swoops To Conquer." *Variety*. June 28-July 4, 1989, pp. 1, 2.

3408. Murray, Will. "The Ancestors of Batman." *Comics Buyer's Guide*. October 7, 1983, pp. 50, 52, 54.

3409. O'Neil, Denny. "The Year of The Bat." *Speakeasy*. February 1989, pp. 24-26.

3410. Ongaro, Alberto. "Tipi e Personaggi del Salone Internationale dei Fumetti: Batman e Co." *L'Europeo*. 1966.

3411. Paniceres, Ruben. "Batman: La Broma Asesina/Pasaporte a la Locura." Program of Centro Cultural Campoamor, Oviedo, Spain. December 1988, pp. 10-11.

3412. Pearson, Roberta E. and William Uricchio, eds. *The Many Lives of the Batman*. New York: Routledge, 1991. 213 pp.; London: British Film Institute, 1991. 288 pp.

3413. Phillips, Gene. "The Dark Knight Reborn." *Comics Journal.* February 1987, pp. 70-74.

3414. Pirani, Adam. "Paper Bats." *Comics Scene.* No. 9, 1989, pp. 28-31.

3415. Potter, Greg. "Bat Lash: Only the Good Die Young." *Comics Journal.* October 1984, pp. 110-113.

3416. Putzer, Gerald. "B.O. Blasts Off in Year of the Bat." *Variety.* January 3, 1990, pp. 1, 8.

3417. Reed, Gene. "Who Draws the Batman? An Investigative Report." *Comics Feature.* September 1980, pp. 54-57.

3418. "The Return of Batman." *Time.* November 26, 1965, p. 52.

3419. Rhode, Werner. "Batman in der Akademie." *Darmstädter Echo.* December 27, 1969.

3420. Richler, Mordecai. "Batman at Midlife or, the Funnies Grow Up." *New York Times Book Review.* May 3, 1987, p. 35.

3421. Romer, Jean-Claude. "Batman." *Midi-Minuit Fantastique* (Paris). No. 18-19, 1967, p. 101.

3422. Samuels, Stuart E. "Batmania." *Castle of Frankenstein.* No. 9, 1966, pp. 18-23.

3423. Schuster, Hal. *Comics Files Magazine Spotlight on Batman.* Canoga Park, California: Heroes Publishing, 1986. 66 pp.

3424. Sciacca, Thom. "Batman: The Comic Connection." *Variety.* June 28-July 4, 1989, pp. 6-7.

3425. Scott, Kenneth W. "Batman et la Camp." *Midi-Minuit Fantastique* (Paris). No. 14, 1966.

3426. Simpson, L.L. "Batman's Vogue Gallery." *Masquerader.* No. 6, 1964, pp. 19-21.

3427. Stelly, Gisela. "Groß Erhebt Sich Batman's Schatten über Gotham City." *Die Zeit* (Hamburg). October 20, 1967, p. 61.

3428. "Up Front." *Comics Interview.* No. 74, 1989, pp. 4-7.

3429. White, Frankie. "Batman un Mito Hecho Realidad." *Cineavance* (Mexico City). No. 105, 1966.

3430. Wolff, Michael. "Marvel Comics and The Batman." *Comic Informer*. January-February 1983, pp. 24-29.

Camelot 3000

3431. Greenberger, Robert. "Camelot 3000." *Comics Scene*. November 1982, pp. 33-38, 64.

3432. Sanderson, Peter. "A Special Preview of Camelot 3000." *Amazing Heroes*. August 1982, pp. 30-39.

Captain America

3433. "B'way May Be Whistling 'Captain America' Theme from Superhero Legiter." *Variety*. September 17, 1986, p. 84.

3434. Dorrell, Larry D. and Carey T. Southall. "Captain America: A Hero for Education." *The Clearing House*. May 1982, pp. 397-399.

3435. Goulart, Ron. "The Old Original Super-Heroes, Part XII: Captain America and the Super-Patriots." *Comics Buyer's Guide*. April 22, 1988, pp. 36-42.

3436. Hart, Ken. "Cap Thaws Out Again." *Comics Journal*. December 1980, pp. 64-67.

3437. Kraft, David A. *Captain America, the Secret Story of Marvel's Star-Spangled Super Hero*. Milwaukee, Wisconsin: Ideals Publishing Corp., 1981. 64 pp.

3438. MacDonald, Andrew and Virginia MacDonald. "Sold American: The Metamorphosis of Captain America." *Journal of Popular Culture*. Summer 1976, pp. 249-258.

3439. Murray, Will. "Project Captain America Declassified." *Comics Scene*. August 1990, pp. 56-59, 66.

Captain Marvel

3440. Beck, C.C. "Capt. Marvel and the Dailies." *FCA/S.O.B.* June 1980, pp. 6-7.

3441. Kanfer, S. "Captain Marvel on Capitalism." *New Republic*. February 25, 1985, pp. 28-30.

3442. McCarty. "The Old Captain Marvel Had Personality." *FCA/S.O.B.* August 1980, p. 6.

3443. Morrissey, Rich. "With One Magic Word... Shazam! In the 1970s, the Return of the Original Captain Marvel." *Comics Feature*. September-October 1981, pp. 132-139.

3444. Mougin, Lou. "Captain Courageous: A Hero History of Captain Marvel, Part I." *Amazing Heroes*. August 1982, pp. 40-49.

3445. Newton, Don. "The 'New' Capt. Marvel." *FCA/S.O.B.* August 1980, p. 3.

3446. Pierce, John. "Bring Back the Real Captain Marvel." *FCA/S.O.B.* August 1980, p. 4.

3447. Raboy, Mac. *Captain Marvel Jr. from Master Comics 27-42*. Special Edition Series, No. 3. East Moline, Illinois: Special Edition Publishers, 1975. 208 pp.

3448. *Shazam! from the Forties to the Seventies*. New York: Harmony Books, 1977. 352 pp.

3449. Smith, George, jr. "The Old Captain Marvel Was No Bargain." *FCA/S.O.B.* August 1980, p. 5.

3450. Sodaro, Robert J. "Death of a Hero." *Comics Collector*. Spring 1983, pp. 35-36.

3451. Weaver, Tom. "Cliffhanger Queen." *Comics Scene*. October 1991, pp. 49-52, 58.

Conan the Barbarian

3452. Dawson, Jim. "Hack Hack Hack." *Comics Journal*. March 1979, pp. 33-34.

3453. Dawson, Jim. "The Queen Is Dead... Finally." *Comics Journal*. October 1979, pp. 29-30.

3454. Gettmann, Patric. *Ein Kind der Zivilisationsmüdigkeit*. Conan der Barbar." *Comic Forum* (Vienna). 4:15 (1982), pp. 24-28.

3455. Gordo, Jose. "Conan: Unos Tanto y Otros Tan Poco o y Yo Que Hago Aqui?" *El Wendigo*. November 1982, pp. 6-7.

3456. McDonnell, David. "Conan the Merchandised." *Comics Scene*. July 1982, pp. 50-51, 64.

Daredevil

3457. Catron, Michael. "Devil's Advocate." *Best of Amazing Heroes*. No. 1, 1982, pp. 5-16.

3458. Cohn, Mitch, ed. *The Daredevil Chronicles*. Albany, New York: FantaCo Enterprises, 1982. 48 pp.

3459. Fernández, Norman. "Daredevil Born Again, Una Obra Maestra." *El Wendigo*. No. 45, 1989, pp. 40-42.

3460. Harvey, R.C. "McKenzie and Miller's Daredevil: Skillful Use of the Medium." *Comics Journal*. September 1980, pp. 92-94.

3461. Skerchock, John, III. "Bring Back the Bad Guys." *Daredevil Chronicles*. February 1982, pp. 30-31.

3462. Webb, Steve. "Daredevil: Birth of a Soap Opera." *Daredevil Chronicles*. February 1982, p. 33.

Doc Savage

3463. Farmer, Philip J. *Doc Savage*. Garden City, New York: Doubleday, 1973. 226 pp.

3464. "Man of Bronze: Doc Savage, Latest Hero." *Newsweek*. May 23, 1966, p. 118.

3465. Murray, Will. "Doc Savage at 60." *Comics Buyer's Guide*. February 12, 1993, pp. 22, 24.

3466. Murray, Will. "Doc Savage at Sixty." In *San Diego Comic Convention 1993*, pp. 44-46. San Diego, California: 1993.

3467. Murray, Will. "Doc Savage: The Man of Bronze Still Shines." *Comics Scene*. September 1983, pp. 41-45.

3468. Murray, Will. "Street and Smith's Doc Savage Comics." *Comics Buyer's Guide*. August 12, 1983, pp. 18, 20, 22, 24-25.

3469. Spicer, Bill. "Graphic Story Review: His Name Is...Savage." *Graphic Story Magazine*. No. 9, 1968, pp. 23-25.

Elektra

3470. Ang, Benjamin. "Benny's Guide to Elektra." *Before I Get Old*. September 1986, pp. 52-53.

3471. Juanmarti, Jordi and Javier Riva. "Elektra Lives Again: La Mona Se Viste de Seda." *El Wendigo*. No. 53, 1991, pp. 31-33.

3472. Sanderson, Peter. "Elektra-Shock Treatment." *Comics Journal*. January 1982, pp. 101-106.

3473. Yu, Wayne. "Elektra: The Lost Years." *Before I Get Old*. August 1986, pp. 38-41.

Elfquest

3474. Loubert, Deni. "Elfquest: What's On Tap for 1993." *Comics Buyer's Guide*. May 14, 1993, pp. 32, 38, 42.

3475. Loubert, Deni. "Team Elfquest." *Comics Buyer's Guide*. May 14, 1993, p. 42.

3476. Pini, Richard. "Elfquest Overview: 15 Years and What Do You Get?" *Comics Buyer's Guide*. May 14, 1993, pp. 46, 50.

3477. Stinnett, Conrad L. "Elfquest: Warp Graphics Reaches Its 15th Anniversary—with Plans for the Future." *Comics Buyer's Guide*. May 14, 1993, pp. 26-27.

Fantastic Four

3478. "Fantastic Four's Birthplace Named." *Comics Journal*. August 1986, pp. 16-17.

3479. Kraft, David A. *The Fantastic Four, the Secret Story of Marvel's Cosmic Quartet*. Milwaukee, Wisconsin: Ideals Publishing Corp., 1981. 64 pp.

3480. Murray, Will. "Return of the Fantastic Four." *Comics Collector*. Fall 1984, pp. 18-31.

3481. Noonchester, Ed. "When Titans Clash." *Foom*. Spring 1973, pp. 8-13.

3482. Van Hise, James. *The Fantastic Four Files*. Comics File Magazine No. 2, Canoga Park, California: Psi Fi Movie Press, 1986. 66 pp.

3483. Van Hise, James. "Heroes: The Fantastic Four." *Comics Feature*. January-February 1984, pp. 40-43.

3484. Ward, Murray R. "Super-Team Spirit: Fantastic Four." *Comics Feature*. September-October 1981, pp. 140-147.

Fu Manchu

3485. Mougin, Lou. "Fu Manchu and Son, Inc." *Amazing Heroes*. June 1982, pp. 40-52.

3486. Phillips, Gene. "The Assassination of Fu Manchu." *LOC*. January 1980, pp. 37-40.

Green Lantern

3487. Delany, Samuel. *Green Lantern and Green Arrow*. No. 1. New York: Paperback Library, 1972.

3488. Hughes, Bob. "In Brightest Day, in Blackest Night...." *Amazing Heroes*. October 1986, pp. 43-61.

3489. Kling, Bernt. "Die Rebellion der Grünen Laterne." *Science Fiction Times* (Bremerhaven). 14:129 (1972), pp. 34-37.

3490. Paul, George. "The Legend of the Original Green Lantern." *The Cartoonist*. No. 0, 1965, pp. 1-16.

3491. Van Hise, James. "Green Lantern." *Comics Feature*. January 1986, pp. 11-13, 37.

Justice League

3492. Fermín Peréz, Ramón. "Justice Inc: Una Historia Sorprendente." *El Wendigo*. No. 52, 1991, pp. 34-35.

3493. Thomas, Harry B. "In a League of Their Own." *The Comic Book Price Guide*. No. 20, 1990, pp. A-77-A-92.

3494. Ward, Murray R. "'...And Justice [League] for ALL!'" *Comics Feature*. November 1982, pp. 45-51.

3495. Ward, Murray R. "Super Team Spirit: Justice League of America." *Comics Feature*. September-October 1981, pp. 83-89.

Justice Society of America

3496. Bails, Jerry. "All Star Comics: The Justice Society of America." *Golden Age of Comics*. February 1984.

3497. Morrissey, Richard. "The Justice Society of America." *Amazing Heroes*. August 1981, pp. 34-47.

3498. Morrissey, Richard. "The Justice Society of America." *Best of Amazing Heroes*. No. 1, 1982, pp. 17-31.

Legion of Super-Heroes

3499. Flynn, Mike. "The Pendulum of Legion Fandom." *Comics Scene*. July 1982, pp. 16-18, 64.

3500. McPherson, Darwin. "Looking to the Future: New Life and New Direction for The Legion of Super-Heroes." *Comics Buyer's Guide*. January 8, 1993, pp. 26-28.

3501. Rapsus, Ginger. "The Legion of Super-Heroes." *Comics Buyer's Guide*. October 3, 1986, pp. 20, 22, 26, 30.

3502. "Their Name Is L.E.G.I.O.N." *Speakeasy*. December 1988, pp. 12-14.

Magnus Robot Fighter

3503. Brown, Gary. "Magnus Robot Fighter." *Comics Feature*. September 1980, p. 40.

3504. Holtsmark, Erling B. "Magnus Robot-Fighter. The Future Looks at the Present Through the Past." *Journal of Popular Culture*. Spring 1979, pp. 702-720.

3505. York, N.L. "Comic Book Luddite: The Saga of Magnus Robot Fighter." *Journal of American Culture*. Spring-Summer 1984, pp. 39-44.

Plastic Man

3506. Goulart, Ron. "The Old Original Super-Heroes: Plastic Man." *Comics Buyer's Guide*. October 21, 1988, pp. 20, 24, 26.

3507. Schröder, Horst. "Plastic Man. Der Verrückteste Superheld der Welt." *Comixene* (Hanover). 6:27 (1979), pp. 63-65.

Rocketeer

3508. "The Battle for the Rocketeer." *Comics Journal*. August 1986, p. 12.

3509. "Rocketeer." *Speakeasy*. August 1988, pp. 36-37, 39.

3510. Stevens, Dave. *The Rocketeer. An Album*. Guerneville, California: Eclipse Books, 1986. 70 pp.

3511. "Up, Up and Away." *Big O*. March 1989, p. 31.

Silver Surfer

3512. Cheah, Michael. "I Am Called the Silver Surfer." *Big O*. October 1988, p. 5.

3513. "Silver Surfer." *Speakeasy*. August 1988, pp. 24-31.

Spectre

3514. Goulart, Ron. "The Old Original Super-Heroes: Part II: The Spectre." *Comics Buyer's Guide*. April 24, 1987, pp. 22, 26.

3515. Thomas, Roy. "The Reincarnation of the Spectre." *Alter Ego*. No. 1, 1964, pp. 10-12.

Spider-Man

3516. Cline, Eddie. "Spider-Man." *Comics Feature*. September 1980, pp. 38-39.

3517. Courtial, Gérard. "Le Complexe d'Oedipe de Spiderman. (Une Interview Exclusive du Docteur Freud)." *Le Nouveau Bédésup*. (Marseilles). 29/30, 1984, pp. 39-42.

3518. Greenberger, Robert. "Spiderman and His Amazing Friends. Marvel Turns 20." *Comics Scene*. January 1981, pp. 11-18, 64.

3519. Mondello, S. "Spider-Man: Superhero in the Liberal Tradition." *Journal of Popular Culture*. Summer 1976, pp. 232-238.

3520. Navarro, Joe. "Brave New Web." *Comics Scene*. December 1992, pp. 11-14, 50.

3521. O'Neill, Patrick D. "An Arachnid's Anniversary." *Comics Scene*. March 1983, pp. 32-38.

3522. Palumbo, Donald A. "The Marvel Comics Group's Spider-Man Is an Existential Super-Hero; or 'Life Has No Meaning without My Latest Marvels!'" *Journal of Popular Culture*. Fall 1983, pp. 67-82.

3523. *The Spider-Man File*. Comics File Magazine. Canoga Park, California: Heroes Publishing, 1986. 56 pp.

3524. "Spidey's 30!" *Penstuff*. July 1992, p. 7.

3525. Stern, Roger, ed. *Spider-Man, The Secret Story of Marvel's World Famous Wall Crawler*. Milwaukee, Wisconsin: Ideals Publishing Corp., 1981. 64 pp.

3526. Van Hise, James. "Spider-Man." *Comics Feature*. January 1986, pp. 26-33, 51.

Sub-Mariner

3527. "Prince Namor, the Sub-Mariner." *Fan's-Zine*. Spring-Summer 1979, pp. 5-7.

3528. Van Hise, James. "Heroes: Prince Namor of Atlantis, The Sub-Mariner." *Comics Feature*. February 1987, pp. 18-23.

Superman, Superboy

3529. Alvarez Villar, Alfonso. "El Superman, un Mito de Nuestro Tiempo." *Diario de Mallorca*. October 6, 1966.

3530. Alvarez Villar, Alfonso. "Superman, Mito de Nuestro Tiempo." *Revista Española de la Opinion Publica* (Madrid). October-December 1966.

3531. *The Amazing World of Superman*. New York: National Periodical Publications, 1973. 64 pp.

3532. Andrae, Thomas. "From Menace to Messiah: The History and Historicity of Superman." In *American Media and Mass Culture*, edited by Donald Lazere, pp. 124-138. Berkeley, California: University of California Press, 1987.

3533. Ansón, Francisco. "Opiniones Sobre Algunos Numéros de Superman." *Estudios Psicologico y Medico* (Madrid). January 1965.

3534. Arski, Stefan. "Der Superman und der Rückanalphabetismus." *Nowa Kultura* (Warsaw). 3:2 (1952), p. 2.

3535. Asherman, Allan. "The Adventures of Superboy." *The Amazing World of DC Comics*. September-October 1974, pp. 10-13.

3536. Bastian, Hannelore. "'Birne und Superman.' Ein Unterrichtsversuch zum Thema 'Comics' in Einer 7. Klasse." *Diskussion Deutsch* (Frankfurt). 11:53 (1980), pp. 261-276.

3537. Beasley, Valeria. "Disowning the Superman Family." *Amazing Heroes*. July 1982, p. 82.

3538. Beck, C.C. "The Man of Steel." *Comics Journal*. November 1986, pp. 6-7.

3539. Bergman, Boris. "Arrghh, Woo, Grrhh, ou Superman dans la Société Américaine." *Bande à Part* (Paris). No. 5, 1967.

3540. Bertieri, Claudio. "Superman: Thirty Years of Fights." *Il Lavoro* (Genoa). June 14, 1968.

3541. Biamonte, S.G. "Gordon, Uomo Mascherato, Superman, l'Evasione in Pantofole." *Il Giornale d'Italia* (Rome). February 12, 1965.

3542. Born, Nicholas. "Superman Oder: Die Helden der Schweigenden Mehrheit." Konkret (Hamburg). April 8, 1971, pp. 60-62.

3543. Bourgeron, Jean-Pierre. "Superman et la Paraphrénie." *Giff-Wiff* (Paris). No. 22, 1966.

3544. Bourgeron, Jean-Pierre. "Superman et la Paraphrénie." *I Fumetti* (Rome). No. 9, 1967, pp. 35-39.

3545. Bourgeron, Jean-Pierre. "Superman y la Parafrenia." *Cuto* (San Sebastian). No. 2-3, 1967, pp. 31-33.

3546. Bradbury, Ray. "Superman. Oggi? Perché?" *Corto Maltese*. August 1988, pp. 50-83.

3547. Brown, Slater. "Coming of Superman." *New Republic*. September 2, 1940, p. 301.

3548. Burelbach, Frederick M. "Look! Up in the Sky! It's What's His Name." In *Names in Literature*, edited by Frederick M. Burelbach, pp. 105-117. Lanham, Maryland: University Press of America, 1987. 241 pp.

3549. Butler, Dick. "Superman Phenomenon Keeps Retailers Busy." *Comics Buyer's Guide*. December 11, 1992, p. 24.

3550. Cáceres, Germán. *Having a Talk with Clark Kent*. Buenos Aires: Editorial Fraterna S.A., 1988.

3551. Castelli, Alfredo. "Guia de Superman en USA." *Cuto* (San Sebastian). October 1967, pp. 27-30.

3552. Castelli, Alfredo. "Il Supermanismo, Ovvero i Miti della Civiltà delle Macchine." *Comics* (Milan). April 1, 1966.

3553. Castelli, Alfredo and Paolo Sala. "Da Superman a Nukla: I Magnifici Eroi dei Comic Books." *Comics*. Sondernummer, April 1966, pp. 6-12.

3554. Chan, Daniel. "Superman to the Fore." *New Sunday Times Sundate*. July 26, 1987, p. 17.

3555. Collins, Gail. "Life Without Superman? You'd Be Dead Wrong." *New York Newsday*. November 17, 1992, p. 3.

3556. "Das Abgründige in Mr. Superman." *Die Welt* (Hamburg). 20:16, 1966.

3557. DC Comics. *The Greatest Superman Stories Ever Told*. New York: DC Comics, 1987.

3558. "DC News: Superman Teams Named...." *Comics Journal*. September 1986, pp. 24-25.

3559. "DC Orders a Third Printing of 'Superman' #75." *Comics Buyer's Guide*. December 18, 1992, p. 22.

3560. Della Corte, Carlos. "Da Gulliver a Superman." *Il Caffe* (Milan). May 1957.

3561. Desris, Joe. "Superman: 1987." *Comics Buyer's Guide*. December 18, 1987, pp. 30-32.

3562. Dooley, Dennis and Gary Engle, eds. *Superman at Fifty: The Persistence of a Legend*. New York: Collier Books; Cleveland, Ohio: Octavia Press, 1987. 190 pp.

3563. Dorfman, Ariel and Manuel Jofré. *Superman y Sus Amigos del Alma*. Buenos Aires: Editorial Galerna, 1974.

3564. Downes, Harold. *The Superman Workbook.* New York: Juvenile Group Foundation, 1946.

3565. Eco, Umberto. "Der Mythos von Superman." In *Apokalyptiker und Integrierte. Zur Kritischen Kritik der Massenkultur. Aus dem Italienischen übersetzt von Max Looser*, edited by Ders, pp. 193-222. Frankfurt: S. Fischer Verlag, 1984.

3566. Eco, Umberto. "The Myth of Superman," pp. 107-124. In *The Role of the Reader.* London: Hutchinson, 1979.

3567. Eco, Umberto. "Il Mito di Superman e la Dissoluzione del Tempo." *Archivio di Filosofia* (Rome). No. 1-2, 1962.

3568. Eco, Umberto. "The Myth of Superman." *Communications.* 24 (1976), pp. 24-40.

3569. Eco, Umberto. "Superman Coltiva la Nostra Pigrizia." *Rassegna.* 39:2 (1962), pp. 51-54.

3570. Fermín Pérez, Ramón. "Por Enésima Vez, Que Conste." *El Wendigo.* No. 58, 1993, p. 38.

3571. Fine, Herbert S. [Jerry Siegel]. "The Reign of Superman." *Science Fiction: The Advance Guard of Future Civilization.* 1:3 (1933), p. 12.

3572. Fossati, Franco. "Superman." *Fantascienza Minore.* Sondernummer, 1967. pp. 45-47.

3573. Fossati, Franco. "Superman." *Sgt. Kirk.* No. 13, 1968, pp. 53-68.

3574. Fossati, Franco. "Superman, Un Discutible Campione Degli Oppressi." *Corriere Mercantile.* August 5, 1968.

3575. Freund, Russell. "Hit and Myth: Russell Freund on *Superman #400.*" *Comics Journal.* October 1984, pp. 29-34.

3576. Galloway, John T., jr. *The Gospel According to Superman.* New York and Philadelphia: A.J. Holman Co., 1973. 141 pp.

3577. Gasca, Luis. "Superman, Todo un Espectaculo." *Cuto* (San Sebastian). October 1967, pp. 57-61.

3578. Gorman, Tim. "Cleveland-Born Hero Returns." *Cleveland Plain Dealer.* June 16, 1988, special advertising supplement, 8 pp.

3579. Goulart, Ron. "The Events Leading to 'Superman.'" *Comics Buyer's Guide.* March 18, 1988, pp. 40, 42.

3580. Goulart, Ron. "The Old Original Super-Heroes: Part 1: Superman." *Comics Buyer's Guide*. April 17, 1987, pp. 40, 42, 44, 46.

3581. Goulart, Ron. "The Superman Revolution." *Comics Buyer's Guide*. March 18, 1988, p. 70.

3582. Gould, Kevin. "Back to the Future, Superman Style!." *Amazing Heroes*. June 15, 1987, pp. 42-46.

3583. Grossman, Gary H. *Superman, Serial to Cereal*. Big Apple Film Series. New York: Popular Library, 1976. 191 pp.

3584. Hansen, Neil A. "The Superman Evolution." *Comics Collector*. Spring 1983, pp. 42-49.

3585. "Icing the Man of Steel." *Philadelphia City Paper*. January 8, 1993, p. 6.

3586. Jacobs and Jones. "My Pal Superman: Superman's Literary Discoveries." *Comics Feature*. September-October 1984, pp. 19-23.

3587. Kahn, E.J. "Why I Don't Believe in Superman." *New Yorker*. June 29, 1940, pp. 64-66.

3588. Kanalz, Hank. "The Other Man Behind Superman." *Comics Scene*. No. 3, (Vol. 3, Series #14), pp. 36-41, 60.

3589. Kligfeld, Stanley. "Superman's In, Other Cartoon Heroes Pop Up As Supersellers for Business, Politicos." *Wall Street Journal*. May 20, 1952, p. 1.

3590. Kluger, Richard. "Sex and the Superman." *Partisan Review*. January 1966, pp. 111-115.

3591. Knilli, Friedrich. "'Der Wahre Jakob' Ein Linker Supermann? Versuch über die Bildsprache der Revolutionären Deutschen Sozialdemokratie." In *Comic-Strips: Geschichte, Struktur, Wirkung und Verbreitung der Bildergeschichten, Ausstellungskatalog der Berliner Akademie der Künste*, December 13, 1969-January 25, 1970, pp. 12-20. Berlin: 1970.

3592. Korkis, Jim. "The Superman Satires." *Amazing Heroes*. March 1982, pp. 54-55.

3593. Latona, Robert and Paul Leiffer. "El Superman de Ayer y el de Hoy, Visto por los Lectores Americanos." *Cuto* (San Sebastian). October 1967, pp. 34-35.

3594. Lengsfeld, Kurt. "Superman und Phantom Lady." *National-Zeitung* (Cologne). June 15, 1956.

3595. Lent, John A. "50 Years of Superman: The Triumphs, Trials, and Tribulations of Its Creators." *WittyWorld*. Autumn 1988, pp. 4-5.

3596. Lim, C.T. and Kevin Mathews. "Thought Balloon." *Big O Magazine*. January 1993, p. 62.

3597. McKee, Victoria. "Man of Steel's New Feet of Clay." *Society of Strip Illustration Newsletter*. June 1988, p. 8.

3598. McKee, Victoria. "Man of Steel's New Feet of Clay." *Sunday Times* (London). June 5, 1988.

3599. Maloney, Russell. "Forever Superman." *New York Times Book Review*. December 21, 1947.

3600. Martín, Antonio. "Superman, Folletín de Nuestro Tiempo." *Gaceta de la Press Española* (Madrid). August 15, 1967.

3601. Martínez, Antonio M. "Apuntes de Superman." *Cuto* (San Sebastian). No. 2-3, 1967, pp. 4-24.

3602. Martínez, Rodolfo. "Superman: Los Primeros Cien Numeros." *El Wendigo*. No. 54, 1991, pp. 41-42.

3603. Morrissey, Rich. "Superman II Forum." *Comics Feature*. December 1981, pp. 33-36.

3604. Nash, Bruce. *The Official Superman Quiz Book*. New York: Warner Books, 1978. 203 pp.

3605. Nordell, R. "Superman Revisited." *Atlantic Monthly*. January 1966, pp. 104-105.

3606. Nuñez, Vivian. "Superman Is Half a Century Old." *Granma Weekly Review*. September 11, 1988, p. 2.

3607. O'Connell, Margaret. "Superman's Other Loves." *Comics Feature*. January 1981, pp. 58-66.

3608. Ordway, Jerry. "Superman's Pal: Jerry Ordway." *Speakeasy*. February 1989, pp. 46, 48.

3609. Politzer, Heinz. "Mehr Goliath als David. Eine Analyse des 'Superman.'" *Tendenzen* (Munich). 1. Sonderheft, No. 53, 1968, pp. 190-191.

3610. Raju, Anand Kumar. "Up, Up and Away." *The Week* (New Delhi). November 15, 1992, pp. 54-59.

3611. Roca, Albert. "Los Comics Superman." *Realidad* (Rome). No. 4, 1964, p. 77.

3612. Romano, Carlin. "Insights into the Man of Steel." *Philadelphia Inquirer*. January 17, 1988, p. 3-I.

3613. Romer, Jean-Claude. "Superman." *Giff-Wiff* (Paris). No. 3, 1965, p. 5.

3614. Sala, Paolo. "Il Supermanismo, Ovvero i Miti della Civiltà delle Macchine." *Comics* (Milan). April 1966, p. 13.

3615. Sala, Paolo and Alfredo Castelli. "Da Superman a Nukla: I Magnifici Eroi dei Comic Books." *Comics*. Sondernummer. April 1966, pp. 6-12.

3616. Sala, Paolo and Alfredo Castelli. "Da Superman a Nukla: I Magnifici Eroi dei Comic Books." *Fantascienza Minore*. Sondernummer, 1966, pp. 8-11.

3617. Salzer, Michael. "'Superman' Gehört Zur Familie. Wie die Schweden mit Comics den Tag Beginnnen." *Die Welt* (Hamburg). February 23, 1966.

3618. Saner-Lamken, Brian. "Roger Stern: A Superman Mini-Interview." *Comics Buyer's Guide*. April 2, 1993, p. 22.

3619. Saner-Lamken, Brian. "Roger Stern Says Superman Is Most Sincerely Dead." *Comics Buyer's Guide*. January 15, 1993, pp. 34, 40.

3620. Seldes, Gilbert. "Preliminary Report on Superman." *Esquire*. November 1942, pp. 63, 153.

3621. Serrano, Eugenia. "Superman, Sandokan y....Anderson." *La Voz de España* (Madrid). 1965.

3622. Slifkin, Irv. "Superman's Greatest Hits." *Philadelphia Inquirer*. March 24, 1988, pp. 1-D, 7-D.

3623. Snook, Debbi. "Gee, Superman, He's More Than Jimmy." *Cleveland Plain Dealer*. June 17, 1988, pp. 27, 29.

3624. Snook, Debbi. "Here's to You, Superman." *Cleveland Plain Dealer*. June 17, 1988, pp. 26-27.

3625. Stuempfig, Julie. "The Effect of Superman's Death on the Comics Industry." *Comics Buyer's Guide*. June 11, 1993, pp. 36, 40, 44.

3626. Sullerot, Eveline. "Superman, le Héros Qui Nous Venge de Nos *Défaites*." *Arts* (Paris). October 26, 1966.

3627. Sullivan, Beryl K. "Superman Licked." *The Clearing House*. March 1943, pp. 428-429.

3628. "Superboy Returns to Comcs." *Comics Buyer's Guide*. October 13, 1989, pp. 1, 3.

3629. "Superman." *Comics Buyer's Guide*. December 4, 1992, pp. 72, 74.

3630. "Superman." *Time*. September 11, 1939, p. 56.

3631. "Superman Adopted." *Time*. May 31, 1948, p. 72.

3632. "Superman als Sozialist." *Süddeutsche Zeitung* (Munich). No. 295, 1969, p. 29.

3633. "Superman and the Atom Bomb." *Harper's Magazine*. April 1948, p. 355.

3634. "Superman at 50." *Variety*. July 8, 1987, pp. 27-47. (Dozens of articles, including "Superman" in Holland, Denmark, and England. Includes animation).

3635. "Superman Death Issue To Go to Second Printing." *Wall Street Journal*. November 20, 1992.

3636. "Superman Deathwatch." *Comics Journal*. November 1992, p. 20.

3637. *Superman: from the Thirties to the Eighties*. Intro. by E. Nelson Bridwell. New York: Crown, 1983. 384 pp.

3638. *Superman from the Thirties to the Seventies*. Intro. by E. Nelson Bridwell. New York: Crown Publishers, 1971. 386 pp.

3639. "'Superman' #75 Sales Exceed 4 Million Copies." *Comics Buyer's Guide*. December 25, 1992, p. 22.

3640. "*Superman #75* Sets Sales Records." *Comics Journal*. January 1993, p. 24.

3641. "Superman R.I.P." *Comics Journal*. October 1992, p. 26.

3642. "Superman's Back. Superman's Back." *Comics Buyer's Guide*. February 5, 1993, p. 26.

3643. "Superman Scores: Comic Magazines Become Big Business." *Business Week*. April 18, 1942, pp. 54-56.

3644. "Superman's Dilemma." *Time*. April 13, 1942, p. 78.

3645. "Superman Stymied." *Time*. March 11, 1940, pp. 46-47.

3646. "Superman War Wieder da." *Bild*. October 30, 1967, p. 10.

3647. "Superseding Superman; P-D Color Comics." *Newsweek*. July 19, 1948, pp. 51-53.

3648. "Supersuits: Right to Superman." *Newsweek*. April 14, 1947, p. 65.

3649. Sutton, Laurie S., ed. *The Great Superman Comic Book Collection*. New York: DC Comics, 1981. 199 pp.

3650. Swires, Steve. "Jimmy Olsen Grows Up." *Comics Scene*. No. 3 (Vol. 3, Series #14), pp. 42-44.

3651. Tamerin, Jane. "Would Superman Still Be Single If Lois Lane Had Worn Clothes Like This, Instead of Those Old Rags She Keeps on Wearing?" *New York* (*Herald Tribune*). January 9, 1966, pp. 18-19.

3652. Trabant, Jürgen. "Superman—Das Image Eines Comic-Helden." In *Visuelle Kommunikation*, edited by Hermann K. Ehmer, pp. 251-276. Cologne: DuMont Schauberg, 1971, 1973.

3653. Trabant, Jürgen. "Supermán: *La Imagen* de un Héroe de Cómic." *Miseria de la Comunicación Visual: Elementos para una Crítica de la Industria de la Conciencia*, edited by Hermann K. Ehmer, pp. 273-299. Barcelona: Editorial Gustavo Gili, 1977.

3654. "Unas Historietas Infantiles: los de Superman." *La Cordoniz* (Madrid). April 1, 1962.

3655. Urueña, Florentino. "Superman Versus 007." *Cuto* (San Sebastian). October 1967, p. 50.

3656. Van Gelder, Lawrence and Lindsay. "'Superman' au Viêt-nam. Les 'Comics' Américains se Politisent, les Illustrés Français Aussi." *Le Nouvel Observateur* (Paris). 313, 1970, pp. 40-41.

3657. Van Hise, James. "Heroes—Superman." *Comics Feature*. November-December 1984, pp. 6-7, 61-63.

3658. Van Hise, James. *The Superman Files*. Comics File Magazine No. 3. Canoga Park, California: Heroes Publishing, 1986. 58 pp.

3659. Vela Jimenez, Manuel. "La Triste Muerte de Superman." *Hoja del Lunes* (Barcelona). August 31, 1959.

3660. Von Zitzewitz, Monika. "Superman Mit Seele." *Die Welt* (Hamburg). October 17, 1966, p. 13.

3661. "Vuelve Superman, El Heroe de los Tebeos de Nuestra Juventud." *La Voz de Asturias*. March 30, 1966.

3662. Wagner, G. "Superman and His Sister; Excerpt from Parade of Pleasure." *New Republic*. January 17, 1955, pp. 17-19.

3663. Wainwright, David. "The Well-Tempered Superman: Less Is More." *Amazing Heroes*. June 15, 1987, p. 11.

3664. Waitman, Michael D. "Superman: Invulnerable to All but Kryptonite, Compassion, and Concupiscence." *Journal of Mental Imagery*. Fall 1984, pp. 87-98.

3665. Weber, John. "The Man of Steel's Hometown Pays Homage." *WittyWorld*. Autumn 1988, pp. 8-10.

3666. Wilson, Bill. "New Faces for the Boy of Steel." *Comics Scene*. No. 10, 1989, pp. 61-64, 66.

3667. Yronwode, Catherine. "Was 'Superman' Murdered?" *Comics Buyer's Guide*. May 7, 1993, pp. 22, 24.

3668. Zanotto, Piero. "Superman, Batman e Compagnie." *Il Gazzettino* (Venice). June 5, 1967.

Teenage Mutant Ninja Turtles

3669. Eastman, Kevin and Peter Laird. *Teenage Mutant Ninja Turtles*. First Graphic Novel, No. 9-10. 2 Vols. Chicago, Illinois: First Comics, 1986-1987.

3670. Freund, Russell. "Make the Heroes Turtles." *Comics Journal*. May 1985, pp. 37-41.

3671. "Hot Turtles." *Comics Collector*. Winter 1986, pp. 32-34.

3672. Tan, Joy. "Incredible! Great Kicks from Ninja Turtles." *Before I Get Old*. July 1986, pp. 34-.

3673. Van Hise, James. "Teenage Mutant Ninja Turtles." *Comics Feature*. February 1987, pp. 12-14.

Teen Titans

3674. Burkert, Tom. "Teen Titans." *Best of Amazing Heroes*. No. 1, 1982, pp. 69-78.

3675. Busiek, Kurt. "When Titans Clash—They Really Do!" *LOC*. January 1980, pp. 7-11.

3676. MacDonald, Heidi D. "DC's Titanic Success." *Comics Journal*. October 1982, pp. 46-51.

3677. Mougin, Lou. "Twenty Years with the Teen Titans." *Comics Collector*. Spring 1984, pp. 22-31.

Thor

3678. Beatie, Bruce A. "Wagner's 'Ring' and the Mighty Thor." Paper presented at Popular Culture Association, Montreal, Canada, March 28, 1987.

3679. Doherty, N. "Comics: Mercury and Atlas. Thor and Beowulf." *Clearing House*. January 1945, pp. 310-312.

3680. Fermín Pérez, Ramón. "'Thor' Vuelve a Ser un Dios." *El Wendigo*. March-April 1987, pp. 21-25.

3681. "Thor. Viewing Simonson's Thor—and Thor's Foe." *Comics Collector*. Summer 1984, pp. 18-21.

Ultraman

3682. Goldberg, Lee. "Ultraman." *Comics Scene*. April 1992, pp. 44-46.

3683. Jacobson, Sid. "Ultraman: Harvey Comics Returns to Super-Heroes in a Big Way." *Comics Buyer's Guide*. February 5, 1993, p. 27.

Vigilante

3684. Dagilis, Andrew. "Siren Song of Blood: The Rise of Bloodthirsty Vigilantes in Comics." *Comics Journal*. December 1989, pp. 89-94.

3685. Flórez, Florentino. "Quién Vigila al Vigilante?" *El Wendigo*. No. 42, 1988, pp. 4-6.

3686. Groth, Gary. "I Have a Hard Time with Vigilantes." *Comics Journal*. July 1986, pp. 70-104.

3687. Paniceres, Ruben. "El Otoño del Vigilante." *El Wendigo*. February-April 1988, pp. 26-30.

Watchmen

3688. Arbesú, Faustino Rodríguez. "Watchmen: El Comic de Autor... sin Pretenderlo." *El Wendigo*. No. 42, 1988, pp. 7-9.

3689. Moore, Alan and Dave Gibbons. *Watchmen*. New York: DC Comics, 1987. 413 pp.

The Wizard

3690. Bails, Jerry B. "The Wiles of the Wizard." *Alter Ego*. No. 1, 1965, pp. 8-9.

3691. Catalano, Frank. "We're Off To See the Wizard (Actually the Wizard Himself Is a Bit Off)." *Comics Journal*. June 1977, p. B-16.

X-Men

3692. Boatner, Charlie. "Changes in the X-Men." *Comics Journal*. May 1979, pp. 63-65.

3693. Eury, Michael. "X of a Kind: Super-Hero Deaths." *Amazing Heroes*. October 1986, pp. 63-88.

3694. Green, Roger, ed. *The X-Men Chronicles*. New York: FantaCo Enterprises, 1981. 32 pp.

3695. Johnson, Kim H. "X-O Manowar." *Comics Scene*. February 1991, pp. 25-28, 66.

3696. Kramer, Blair. "The X-Men Phenomenon." *Comic Book Collector*. January 1993, pp. 16-17.

3697. Sanderson, Peter. "The Secret of X-Appeal." *Comics Journal*. August 1982, pp. 62-67.

3698. Sanderson, Peter, jr. "Loc Ness: The Future X-Men." *LOC*. January 1980, pp. 48-52.

3699. Schuster, Hal, ed. *Critic's Choice File Looks at the X-Men*. Canoga Park, California: Heroes Publishing, 1987. 49 pp.

3700. Sodaro, Robert J. "A Portable Outline of X-Men's Careers." *Comics Collector*. Winter 1984, pp. 57-63.

3701. Sodaro, Robert J. "X-Men Evolution: Part 1." *Comics Collector*. Spring 1983, pp. 50-54.

3702. "The Third Generation of X-Men." *Comics Journal*. August 1982, pp. 56-60.

3703. Thompson, Maggie. "X-Men into X-Factor." *Comics Collector*. Winter 1986, pp. 18-24.

3704. "X-Factor." *Comics Interview*. No. 28, 1985, pp. 7-23.

3705. "'X-Factor' Plans." *Comics Scene*. No. 3 (Vol. 3, Series 13), pp. 18-21.

3706. "X Hits the Spot." In *Comics Buyer's Guide 1993 Annual*, pp. 8-10. Iola, Wisconsin: Krause, 1992.

3707. *The X-Men File, Sons of X-Men*. Comics File Magazine. Canoga Park, California: Psi Fi Movie Press, 1986. 53 pp.

3708. "X-Men Mark 30 Years." *Comics Buyer's Guide*. May 7, 1993, p. 28.

Teen

3709. Abel, B. "Focus on Teens in Comics." *Seventeen*. March 1978, pp. 54-55.

3710. Stokes, Carole. "Meet Marty Links: The Eternal Bobby Soxer." *Cartoon Art Museum Newsletter*. Spring 1986, p. 2.

3711. "Take It from Buzzy." *Time*. August 29, 1949, p. 46.

Archie

3712. Branch, Jeffrey C. "The Celebration That Was—Then Wasn't." *The Archie Fan Magazine*. November 1991, pp. 6-9.

3713. Branch, Jeffrey C. and Mary Smith. "Archie Comics News and Reviews." *The Archie Fan Magazine*. September 1992, p. 4.

3714. Philips, Adam. "Archie Comics in Review." *Comics Journal*. June 1985, p. 71.

3715. Philips, Adam. "Riverdale High Revisited." *Comics Journal*. June 1985, pp. 68-70.

3716. Phillips, Charles. *Archie: His First 50 Years*. New York: Abbeville, 1991. 128 pp.

3717. Pincus, J. "Advice for the Lifelorn [S. Prater Advises Archie Fans]." *Seventeen*. April 1988, p. 164.

3718. Uslan, Michael and Jeffrey Mendel, eds. *The Best of Archie*. New York: Putnam, 1980. 255 pp.

Katy Keene

3719. "John Lucas: The New Man in Katy Keene's Life." *Comics Buyer's Guide*. April 19, 1985, pp. 30, 32, 34, 36, 38.

3720. Leavitt, Craig. "Katy Keene: The Overstreet Connection." *The Comic Book Price Guide*. No. 14, 1984, pp. A-67-A-79.

3721. Rausch, Barbara A. "Katy Keene: Katy WHO?...Never Heard of Her." *The Comic Book Price Guide*. No. 14, 1984, pp. A-52-A-59.

War

3722. Cuervo, Javier. "Nam, Los Chicos No Tan Lejos de Casa." *El Wendigo*. 14:43 (1988), pp. 33-34.

3723. Darrigo, David. "Sgt. Rock, D.C.'s Unknown Superhero." *Dreamline*. March 1982, pp. 76-81.

3724. Ferraro, Ezio and Gianni Brunoro. "Sergente Fury Riposa in Pace." *Sgt. Kirk*. No. 16, 1968, pp. 58-65.

3725. "Green Berets and Pink Mongoose." *The Cartoonist*. January 1966, pp. 35-36.

3726. Harvey, R.C. "A Look at Battle Scenes in Comics." *Comics Journal*. September 1981, pp. 299-305.

3727. Huxley, David. "Naked Aggression: American Comic Books and the Vietnam War." In *Tell Me Lies About Vietnam: Cultural Battles for the Meaning of the War*, edited by Alf Louvre and Jeffrey Walsh. pp. 88-110. Milton Keynes; Philadelphia, Pennsylvania: Open University Press, 1988.

3728. Huxley, David. "Naked Aggression: American Comic Books and the Vietnam War." *Comics Journal*. July 1990, pp. 105-112.

3729. Huxley, David. "'The Real Thing': New Images of Vietnam in American Comic Books." In *Vietnam Images: War and Representation*, edited by Jeffrey Walsh and James Aulich, pp. 160-170. Hampshire, England: Macmillan Press, 1989.

3730. Miller, Russ. "Behind Enemy Lines, a Preface." *Gauntlet*. No. 2, 1991, p. 237.

3731. Murray, Will. "Pieces of the Rock." *Comics Scene*. No. 10, 1989, pp. 40-41.

3732. Pérez, Ramón Fermín. "Qué Viene NAM!" *El Wendigo*. No. 42, 1988, pp. 27-30.

3733. Rifas, Leonard. "The Forgotten War Comics: The Korean War and the American Comic Books." Master thesis, University of Washington, 1991. 294 pp.

3734. Rodríguez, Faustino. "Los Heroes de Papel y la II Guerra Mundial." *El Wendigo*. January 1984, pp. 5-13.

3735. Thomas, Harry B. and Gary M. Carter. "1941: Comic Books Go to War!" *The Comic Book Price Guide*. No. 21, 1991, pp. A-79-A-98.

3736. *Two-Fisted Tales*. The Complete EC Library. 4 Vols. West Plains, Missouri: R. Cochran, 1980.

3737. Uslan, Michael, ed. *America at War, the Best of DC War Comics*. New York: Simon and Schuster, 1979. 247 pp.

3738. Van Hise, James. "A Real American Hero." *Comics Feature*. Spring 1987, pp. 26-35. ("G.I. Joe").

3739. "Vietnam War Comic." *Variety*. September 17, 1986, p. 81.

Western Cowboy

3740. Horn, Maurice. *Comics of the American West*. South Hackensack, New Jersey: Stoeger, 1977. 224 pp.; New York: Winchester Press, 1977.

3741. Jackson, Jack. "The Good, the Bad, and the Foreign." *Comics Journal*. September 1991, pp. 50-62.

3742. *Lassie*. Racine, Wisconsin: Western, 1978. 224 pp.

3743. Oxstein, Walter H. "Cowpoke Cassidy Piles Sales High for Ninety Happy Manufacturers." *Wall Street Journal*. May 10, 1950, p. 1.

3744. Smith, Carl W. *Red Ryder and the Secret of the Lucky Mine*. Racine, Wisconsin: Whitman, 1947.

3745. Ward, Murray. "The Band That Time Forgot: The Marvel Western Heroes." *Comics Feature*. November 1980, pp. 42-53.

3746. Weaver, Tom. "The Wild Wild West." *Comics Scene*. August 1990, pp. 19-22, 60.

3747. Wildey, Doug. *Rio*. Norristown, Pennsylvania: Comico the Comic Company, 1987. 60 pp.

3748. "Wild-West-Bilderserie." *Der Neue Vertrieb* (Flensburg). 5:107 (1953), p. 420.

Lone Ranger

3749. Luciano, Dale. "Legend of Lone Ranger: A Nostalgic But Lackluster Revival." *Comics Journal*. August 1981, pp. 128-131.

3750. Murray, Will. "The Lone Ranger Rides the Pages of the Pulps." *Comics Buyer's Guide*. May 11, 1984, pp. 20, 22.

3751. Rothel, David. *Who Was That Masked Man? The Story of the Lone Ranger*. New York: A.S. Barnes, 1976.

3752. Scapperotti, Dan. "Then, You Are... Lone Ranger." *Comics Scene*. No. 9, 1989, pp. 43-46.

COMIC BOOK MAKERS and THEIR WORKS

3753. "The Adventures of Kevin Maguire." *Comics Scene*. May 1992, pp. 29-32.

3754. "Alex Kotzky." *Comics Interview*. No. 100, 1991.

3755. Allstetter, Rob. "Joe Quesada: 'X-Factor' Artist Considers Himself Lucky." *Comics Buyer's Guide*. April 9, 1993, p. 40.

3756. "The Amazing Spiderman: Tom DeFalco Gets Spidey Back in the Swing." *Amazing Heroes*. August 1981, pp. 54, 56, 58.

3757. "Andy Yanchus." *Comics Interview*. June 1983, pp. 33-34.

3758. Ang, Benjamin. "The Dave Ross Interview." *Before I Get Old*. December 1986, pp. 42-45.

3759. "Angus McKie." *Comics Interview*. No. 30, 1986, pp. 49-59.

3760. "Anthony Tollin." *Comics Interview*. April 1984, pp. 43-47.

3761. "Arnold Drake." *Comics Interview*. October 1984, pp. 5-17.

3762. "Art Director: Alex Wald." *Comics Interview*. No. 52, 1987, pp. 38-45.

3763. "Arthur Suydam." *Comics Interview*. December 1984, pp. 37-45.

3764. "Artist: Jack Abel." *Comics Interview*. No. 7, 1983, pp. 37-45.

3765. "Artist: Jean Giraud." *Comics Interview*. No. 75, 1989, pp. 78-85.

3766. "Artist John Beatty." *Comics Interview*. No. 72, 1989, pp. 35-45.

3767. "Artist: Mike De Carlo." *Comics Interview*. No. 7, 1983, pp. 29-33.

3768. "Artist Phil Zimelman." *Comics Interview*. No. 72, 1989, pp. 46-57.

3769. "Artist: Tod Smith." *Comics Interview*. No. 7, 1983, pp. 19-27.

3770. Ashford, Richard. "Aces High!" *Speakeasy*. September 1990, pp. 45, 47. (George and Scott Hampton).

3771. *Atlanta Comiccon*. Program Book. 1980. (Biographical sketches of Paul Gulacy, Mike Grell, George Perez, Bill Sienkiewicz, Walter Simonson, and Joe Orlando).

3772. Barker, Clive. "At the Threshold: Some Thoughts on the Razorline Imprint." *Comics Buyer's Guide*. July 2, 1993, pp. 26-27. Related stories, pp. 27-29, 32, 40, 42, 44.

3773. Batty, Ward. "Fred Hembeck: Interview with a Fan's Fan." *Amazing Heroes*. February 1983, pp. 50-57.

3774. Beck, C.C. "Ralph Daigh." *FCA/S.O.B.* February-March 1981, p. 3.

3775. Beck, C.C. "The Real Creators." *FCA/S.O.B.* October-November 1980, p. 6.

3776. Bell, John. "A New Day Dawning: An Interview with Dan Day." *Comics Journal*. September 1986, pp. 98-103.

3777. Berry, Michael. "Mental Mysteries." *Comics Scene*. October 1991, pp. 53-56, 60. (James Hudnall).

3778. "Bill Black." *Comics Interview*. No. 36, 1986, pp. 52-65.

3779. "Bill Campbell Interviews." *Comics Scene*. No. 20, 1991.

3780. "Bill Chadwick." *Comics Interview*. February 1983, p. 65.

3781. "Bill Liebowitz." *Comics Interview*. No. 38, 1986, pp. 56-65.

3782. "Bill Marks." *Comics Interview*. No. 40, 1986, pp. 50-65.

3783. "Bill Mumy and Miguel Ferrer." *Comics Interview*. No. 44, 1987, pp. 6-17.

3784. "Bill Woggon and Barb Rausch." *Comics Interview*. No. 45, 1987, pp. 22-33.

3785. Birmingham, Frederic A., *et al*. "A Portrait of Ray Kinstler." *Near Mint*. July 1982, pp. 1-15.

3786. Blanchard, Jim. "Retina Damage." *Art? Alternatives*. October 1992, pp. 21-30 (Jim Blanchard).

3787. Boatz, Darrel. "Daniel Greenberg." *Comics Interview*. No. 48, 1987, pp. 21-30.

3788. Boatz, Darrel. "Ray Winninger." *Comics Interview*. No. 48, 1987, pp. 31-39.

3789. Boatz, Darrel. "Sam Lewis and Greg Gordon." *Comics Interview*. No. 26, 1985, pp. 42-55.

3790. "Boaz Yakin." *Comics Interview*. No. 76, 1989, pp. 5-16.

3791. "Bob Chapman." *Comics Interview*. June 1985, pp. 63-67.

3792. "Bob Harras." *Comics Interview*. No. 62, 1988, pp. 4-15.

3793. "Bob Walters Portfolio, Part I." *Comics Journal*. April 1977, pp. 17-28.

3794. Borax, Mark. "Jules Engel." *Comics Interview*. No. 33, 1986, pp. 36-47.

3795. Borax, Mark. "Pander Bros." *Comics Interview*. No. 51, 1987, pp. 7-19.

3796. "Brent Anderson." *Comics Interview*. No. 30, 1986, pp. 30-47.

3797. Brett, Mark F. "The Insult That Made a Man Out of 'Mac.'" *Comics Journal*. September 1991, pp. 87-89.

3798. Briefer, Dick. *The Comic Book Art of Dick Briefer*. San Francisco, California: A. Dellinges, 1979. 32 pp.

3799. "Bruce Conklin." *Comics Interview*. No. 28, 1985, pp. 47-56.

3800. "Bruce D. Patterson." *Comics Interview*. No. 28, 1985, pp. 37-45.

3801. Burbey, Mark. "George Metzger." *Comics Journal*. December 1983, pp. 78-94.

3802. Burkett, Cary. "Remembering with Ross Andru and Mike Esposito." *Amazing World of DC Comics*. August 1977.

3803. Burton, Richard. "Interview: John D. Warner." *Comic Reader*. September 1977, pp. 11-13.

3804. Butler, Don. "Brandon Peterson." *Comics Buyer's Guide*. July 16, 1993, pp. 34, 38, 40.

3805. Campbell, Ramsey. "Ramsey Campbell Interview." *Comics Interview*. No. 27, 1985.

3806. Campiti, David. "The Executioner and His Secrets: An Interview with Don and Linda Pendleton." *Comics Buyer's Guide*. July 16, 1993, pp. 26-28, 32.

3807. "Carl Macek." *Comics Interview*. May 1985, pp. 30-45.

3808. "Carl Potts." *Comics Interview*. No. 63, 1988, pp. 20-27.

3809. "Carl Wessler: An EC Writer Revealed." *Squa Tront*. No. 9, 1983, pp. 37-38.

3810. "Cartoonist Deal Whitley, 35, Dies." *Comics Journal*. October 1992, p. 24.

3811. "CBM Spotlight on Bruce Hamilton." *The Comic Book Marketplace*. No. 3, pp. 44-47.

3812. Chadwick, Bill. "Letterer: Bob Pinaha." *Comics Interview*. March 1984, pp. 71-73.

3813. Chen, Mike. "X-Men. Andy Kubert." *Cartoonist PROfiles*. September 1993, pp. 26-34.

3814. Cherkas, Michael and John Sabljic. "The New Frontier." *Comics Buyer's Guide*. December 25, 1992, pp. 26-28. (Michael Cherkas, John Sabljic).

3815. Chesney, Lyle. "Mantlo Plays the Right Card." *Comics Journal*. December 1978, pp. 29-30. (Bill Mantlo).

3816. "Chris Warner." *Comics Interview*. No. 63, 1988, pp. 44-55.

3817. "Christy Marx." *Comics Interview*. April 1984, pp. 20-27.

3818. "Chuck Dixon." *Comics Interview*. No. 57, 1988, pp. 5-7, 9-11, 13, 15.

3819. "Collazo." *Comics Interview*. No. 57, 1988, pp. 34-35, 37, 39, 41.

3820. "Comic Book Editor for National." *Cartoonist PROfiles*. May 1970.

3821. "Comics Lose Three Creators." *Comics Journal*. February 1987, pp. 28-29.

3822. "Conversations in Steel." *Comic Scene*. December 1992, pp. 29-32. (Frank Miller, Walt Simonson).

3823. "Conversation with Bob Overstreet." *Collector's Dream Magazine*. Spring 1978, pp. 12-22, 26.

3824. "Conversation with Jackson Bostwick." *FCA/S.O.B.* August 1980, p. 7.

3825. Crumb, Robert and Bill Griffith. "As the Artist Sees It: Interviews with Comic Artists." In *Popular Culture in America*, edited by Paul Buhle, pp. 132-138. Minneapolis, Minnesota: University of Minnesota Press, 1987.

3826. Curson, Nigel. "Frank Miller, Dave Gibbons: Give Me Liberty, An American Dream." *Speakeasy*. June 1990, pp. 26-29, 31.

3827. Curson, Nigel. "Gerry Anderson." *Speakeasy*. December 1990-January 1991, pp. 26-27, 29.

3828. Curson, Nigel. "Spider-Man." *Speakeasy*. June 1990, pp. 45-47, 49.

3829. "D' Arc Tangent." *Comics Interview*. No. 7, 1983, pp. 7-17.

3830. "Darrell McNeil." *Comics Interview*. No. 47, 1987, pp. 35-38.

3831. "Dave Cockburn." *Comics Interview*. February 1985, pp. 25-27.

3832. "Dave Darrigo and Dave Ross." *Comics Interview*. No. 40, 1986, pp. 43-49.

3833. "David Singer." *Comics Interview*. February 1985, pp. 50-61.

3834. Davis, Vince and Bill Spicer. "Interview with Dan Noonan." *Graphic Story Magazine*. No. 9, 1968, pp. 12-17.

3835. "Dawn Geiger." *Comics Interview*. No. 67, 1989, pp. 44-52.

3836. Day, Gene. *Future Day*. Syracuse, New York: Flying Buttress Publications, 1979. 48 pp.

3837. "Dealer Profile on Bob Horn." *Omnibus*. March 1978, p. 17.

3838. "Defenders Dialogues." *Foom*. Fall 1977, pp. 8-11. (Roy Thomas, Steve Englehart, Len Wein, Steve Gerber, David Kraft).

3839. DeFreitas, Leo J. "Dave McKean." *Comics Journal*. January 1993, pp. 52-60, 63.

3840. De Fuccio, Jerry. "Cracked's Mike Ricigliano." *Cartoonist PROfiles*. December 1991, pp. 30-39.

3841. De Fuccio, Jerry. "Dean of Pulp Cover Artists—Rafael de Soto." *Cartoonist PROfiles*. June 1981, pp. 72-76.

3842. De Fuccio, Jerry. "Frank Borth Meets Spider Widow." *Cartoonist PROfiles*. June 1987, pp. 66-71.

3843. DeMarco, Mario. "Fred Gardineer, Golden Age Cartoonist." *Comics Buyer's Guide*. July 18, 1986, p. 40.

3844. "Dennis Mallonee." *Comics Interview*. No. 64, 1988, pp. 39-55.

3845. Deschaine, Scott. "Liquid Assets: An Examination of the Bizarre World of Rudy Palais." *Comics Journal*. November 1985.

3846. De Suinn, Colin. "Andy Helfer, Shadow of an Editor." *Speakeasy*. March 1990, pp. 28-29, 31.

3847. Dichiera, Sal. "Focus on Frank Brunner." *Baycon III Program Book*. 1977, pp. 22-23.

3848. "Dick Sprang." *Comics Interview*. No. 70, 1989, pp. 60-69.

3849. Disbrow, Jay. "Confessions of a Former Comic Book Artist." In *The Comic Book Price Guide 1978-79*, edited by R.M. Overstreet, pp. A-31-A-39. Cleveland, Tennessee: Overstreet, 1978.

3850. "Døde: Shuster og Gaines." *Seriejournalen*. September 1992, p. 12.

3851. Dodson, Jon. "A Moment with Ian Shires." *Comic Book Newsletter*. April 1988, p. 14.

3852. "Don and Maggie Thompson." *Comics Interview*. January 1985, pp. 67-76.

3853. Dorf, Shel. "Norman Maurer." *Comics Buyer's Guide*. November 23, 1984, pp. 20, 22, 26, 28, 30, 32, 42, 46.

3854. Dorf, Shel. "To Be, or Not To Be—an Actor or a Cartoonist: Scott Benefiel Interviewed." *Comics Buyer's Guide*. April 9, 1993, pp. 44, 52.

3855. Durrwachter, Jerry. "Paul Gulacy: Beyond the Shadow of Shang-Chi?" *Whizzard*. February 1981, pp. 4-9, 17.

3856. Dutter, Barry. "Rod Ramos." *Comics Interview*. No. 92, 1991, pp. 51-57.

3857. "E.C. Artist of the Issue." *Two Fisted Tales*. January/February 1952. (Jack Davis).

3858. "Editor: Byron Erickson." *Comics Interview*. No. 75, 1989, pp. 104-107.

3859. "Editor: Rick Oliver." *Comics Interview*. No. 52, 1987, pp. 23-27.

3860. "Editor: Tom Cook." *Comics Interview*. No. 70, 1989, pp. 72-76.

3861. Eisner, Will. "Will Eisner Interviews Chris Claremont, Frank Miller and Wendy Pini." *Comics Journal*. May 1984, pp. 87-96.

3862. "Ernie Colan." *Comics Interview*. July 1984.

3863. Evans, George. "Reed Crandall." *Squa Tront*. No. 3, 1969, pp. 42-51.

3864. "Fabian Nicieza Interview." *Comics Scene*. No. 27, 1992.

3865. Fermín Pérez, Ramón. "'La Otra Verdad'—El Extraño Caso del Dr. Lee y Mr. Kirby." *El Wendigo*. No. 53, 1991, p. 36.

3866. Fermín Pérez, Ramón. "Pesadillas Desenfocadas." *El Wendigo*. No. 57, 1992, pp. 12-13. (Mike Dringenberg).

3867. Fernández, Norman and Rodolfo Martínez. "El Sueño de la Razon." *El Wendigo*. No. 54, 1991, pp. 33-35.

3868. Ferrante, Tim. "Gray Morrow." *Comics Scene*. August 1990, pp. 24-28, 65.

3869. *Fifty Who Made DC Great*. New York: DC Comics, 1985. 56 pp.

3870. "Floyd Norman." *Comics Interview*. No. 44, 1987, pp. 21-23.

3871. "Frank Miller and Alan Moore Rule." *Amazing Heroes*. June 15, 1987, p. 13.

3872. Friedrich, Mike. "Gir/Moebius: An Interview with Jean Giraud." *Alter Ego*. No. 11, 1978, pp. 3-9.

3873. Friedwald, Will. "Rube Grossman: Forgotten Giant of DC's 'Funny Animals.'" *Comics Buyer's Guide*. October 7, 1983, pp. 70-72.

3874. Garriock, P.R. *Masters of Comic Book Art*. New York: Images Graphiques, 1978. 128 pp. (Will Eisner, Harvey Kurtzman, Frank Bellamy, Richard Corben, Barry Windsor-Smith, Jean Giraud, Philippe Druillet, Wallace Wood, Robert Crumb, Victor Moscoso).

3875. "Gary Berman and Adam Malin." *Comics Interview*. No. 56, 1988, pp. 49-51.

3876. Geary, Rick. *At Home with Rick Geary*. Intro. by Dale Luciano. Agoura, California: Fantagraphics Books, 1985. 102 pp.

3877. "Geof Darrow Interview." *Comics Scene*. No. 22, 1991.

3878. "George Delacorte, Founder of Dell Comics." *Comics Journal*. June 1991, p. 20.

3879. Gifford, Denis. "Martin Goodman." *The Jester*. August 1992, p. 5. Reprinted from *The Independent*. June 15, 1992.

3880. Gonick, Larry. "Master of the Universe." *Comics Feature*. September-October 1981, pp. 95-102.

3881. Goulart, Ron. *The Great Comic Book Artists*. 2 Vols. New York: St. Martin's Press, 1986, 1988.

3882. Green, Grass. "Destroying Idols: The Role of Satire and the Free Press in Comics: The Jay Lynch Interview." *Comics Journal*. February 1987, pp. 76-94.

3883. Greenberg, Fred. "The First Juan Ortiz Interview." *Omnibus*. March 1978, pp. 4-12.

3884. Greenberg, Fred. "Mark Pacella Interview." *Comics Buyer's Guide*. January 22, 1993, pp. 66, 70.

3885. Greenberger, Robert. "Mike Hernandez." *Comics Scene*. July 1983, pp. 48-49.

3886. Greenberger, Robert. "Rick Bryant." *Comics Scene*. November 1982, p. 16.

3887. "Greg Stafford." *Comics Interview*. No. 57, 1988, pp. 44-47, 49.

3888. "Greg Theakston." *Comics Interview*. February 1985, pp. 37-49.

3889. Grey, Zane. *King of the Royal Mounted*. Long Beach, California: T. Raiola, 1982. 72 pp.

3890. Groensteen, Thierry. "Quelques Auteurs Dont on Parole." *Les Cahiers de la Bande Dessinée* (Grenoble). 66, 1985, pp. 47-50. (Howard Chaykin, Steve Gerber, Jaime Hernandez, Frank Miller, Harvey Pekar).

3891. Grossman, Al. "The Legacy of Mac Raboy." *FCA/S.O.B.* June/July 1981, p. 5.

3892. Groth, Gary. "Life on the Fringe of Comics: An Interview with Ted White." *Comics Journal*. October 1980, pp. 56-81.

3893. Groth, Gary. "Thomas Radecki Interview." *Comics Journal*. December 1989, pp. 66-74.

3894. Groth, Gary. "Will Comics Creators Ever Grow Up?" *Comics Journal*. January 1984, pp. 7-9.

3895. Groth, Gary and Robert Fiore, eds. *The New Comics*. New York: Berkley Books, 1988. 324 pp.

3896. "Guests." In *San Diego Comic Convention 1989* program book. San Diego, California: San Diego Comic-Con Committee, 1989. (Forrest J. Ackerman, p.4; Bill Sienkiewicz, Paul Chadwick, p. 6; Gahan Wilson, Hernandez brothers, p. 8; Jerry Robinson, Michael Gross, p. 10; Ollie Johnston, Frank Thomas, Ron Goulart, p. 12; Greg Bear, Syd Mead, p. 14; Howard Cruse, Rick Geary, p. 16; Jack Kirby, p. 18; Fred Rhoads, Selby Kelly, p. 20).

3897. Gustafson, Jon. *Chroma, the Art of Alex Schomburg*. Poughkeepsie, New York: Father Tree Press, 1986. 108 pp.

3898. Hansen, Neil A. "The Men Behind the Man of Steel." *Comics Collector*. Spring 1983, pp. 20-26. (Curt Swan, Dick Giordano).

3899. Hansen, Neil A. "The Scene of Kelly Green." *Comics Collector*. Spring 1983, pp. 58-61 (Leonard Starr).

3900. Harper, Teresa and Bill. "War Correspondence: Simon and Kirby." *Comics Buyer's Guide*. February 1, 1985, p. 64.

3901. Harris, Jack C. "The Brave, Bold and the Batman: A Portrait of Artist Jim Aparo." *Comics Scene*. September 1982, pp. 50-54.

3902. Harvey, R.C. "Cartooning, Comix, Comics, the Classics, and the Kitchen Sink." *Cartoonist PROfiles*. March 1993, pp. 74-81.

3903. Hasted, Nick. "An Interview with V for Vendetta Artist David Lloyd." *Comics Journal*. April 1989, pp. 27-30.

3904. "Hello Neighbors, My Name Is Milton Knight, Jr. and...." *Comics Journal*. May 1985, pp. 92-94.

3905. Hessee, Tim. "The Pop Hollinger Story: The First Comic Book Collector/Dealer." In *Comic Book Price Guide 1982-83*, edited by R.M. Overstreet, pp. A-58-A-66. Cleveland, Tennessee: 1982.

3906. "He Thought He Retired! Mort Leav." *Cartoonist PROfiles*. December 1982, pp. 40-47.

3907. Hogarth, Burne. "I Remember Jack Cummings." In *San Diego Comic Convention 1989* program book, p. 90. San Diego, California: San Diego Comic-Con Committee, 1989.

3908. Horn, Maurice. "Dracula Lives!" Intro. to Fernando Fernandez. *Dracula*. New York: Catalan Communications, 1984.

3909. "Howard Mackie." *Comics Interview*. No. 92, 1991, pp. 4-9.

3910. "Howard Zimmerman." *Comics Interview*. No. 76, 1989, pp. 61-64.

3911. Howell, Richard. "An Interview with Don Heck." *Comics Interview*. November 1982, pp. 30-44.

3912. "Hugh Haynes Interviewed." *Comics Arena*. July 1992, pp. 20-27.

3913. "Hugo Gernsback: Godfather to Science-Fiction Comics." *The World of Comic Art*. June 1966, pp. 10-15.

3914. "Interview: David Batt." *The Classics Collector*. February-March 1990, pp. 27-29.

3915. "Interview Paul Mavrides." *Comixene* (Hanover). 8:41 (1981), pp. 8-9.

3916. "An Interview with Bill Dubay." *Near Mint*. April 1988, pp. 1-12.

3917. "An Interview with Boris Vallejo." *Comics Feature*. June 1981, pp. 14-20.

3918. "Jackson Gillis." *Comics Interview*. No. 60, 1988, pp. 4-13.

3919. Jankiewicz, Pat. "Face Value." *Comics Scene*. April 1992, pp. 38-42, 58. (Erik Larsen).

3920. Jankiewicz, Pat. "Wheels of Fire." *Comics Scene*. April 1992, pp. 12-16. (Mark Texeira).

3921. "Jay Lynch Sketchbook." *Comics Journal*. April 1993, pp. 89-93.

3922. "Jerry De Fuccio." *Qua Brot*. No. 1, 1985, pp. 33-38.

3923. "Jerry Perles." *Comics Interview*. No. 43, 1987, pp. 52-61.

3924. "Jim Bradrick." *Comics Interview*. No. 66, 1989, pp. 41-49.

3925. "Jim Galton." *Comics Interview*. February 1983, pp. 59-63.

3926. "Jim Novak." *Comics Interview*. February 1983, pp. 43-46.

3927. "Joe Italiano." *Comics Interview*. No. 47, 1987, pp. 55-63.

3928. "Joe Rubinstein." *Comics Interview*. No. 36, 1986, pp. 40-51; No. 37, 1986, pp. 54-63.

3929. "John Belfi." *Near Mint*. October 1982, pp. 14-19.

3930. "John Giunta." *Near Mint*. July 1982, pp. 16-29.

3931. "John Jackson on His Work in the Underground." *Comics Journal*. September 1982, pp. 75-84.

3932. Johns, T.L. "The Scribe Strikes!" *Comics Scene*. August 1990, pp. 13-17.

3933. Johnson, Kim H. "Heroic Ideals." *Comics Scene*. April 1992, pp. 25-28, 58. (Tom Veitch).

3934. Johnson, Kim H. "Shoot Outs." *Comics Scene*. December 1990, pp. 53-56, 68. (Jim Vance).

3935. Jones, Ken. "Paul Power." *Comics Interview*. No. 33, 1986, pp. 18-35.

3936. Jones, Ken. "Russ Heath." *Comics Journal*. September 1987, pp. 89-96.

3937. "Jon King." *Comics Interview*. March 1985, pp. 57-63.

3938. "Jose Luis Garcia Lopez." *Comics Interview*. June 1984, pp. 28-40.

3939. Juanmartí, Jordi and Javier Riva. "Mike Mignola, un Toque de Distinción." *El Wendigo*. No. 59, 1993, pp. 38-39.

3940. Juddery, Mark. "Artist: Glenn Lumsden." *Comics Interview*. No. 108, 1992, pp. 21-25.

3941. Kalish, Carol and Richard Howell. "Life Among the Mutants: The X-Men under Chris Claremont and John Byrne." *Comics Journal*. September 1979, pp. 59-75.

3942. Kanalz, Hank. "Wee Bit of Punishment." *Comics Scene*. February 1991, pp. 45-48, 66. (Cam Kennedy).

3943. "Kane and Chaykin." *Comics Journal*. July 1984, pp. 67-77.

3944. Kelly, John. "Drew Friedman." *Comics Journal*. July 1992, pp. 48-59, 61-62, 64-69, 71, 73-77, 79-83, 85-86.

3945. Kelly, John. "Idiot of the Savant-Garde: Doug Allen." *Comics Journal*. February 1993, pp. 78-88.

3946. "Ken Selig." *Comics Interview*. No. 44, 1987, pp. 41-61.

3947. "Kerry Gammill." *Comic Informer*. January-February 1983, pp. 7-15.

3948. "Kevin Eastman and Peter Laird." *Comics Interview*. September 1985, pp. 24-35.

3949. Kidson, Mike. "Creator Interview: Nick Cardy." *FA*. March 1989, pp. 16-18.

3950. Kirchner, Paul. *Realms*. New York: Catalan Communications, 1987. 80 pp.

3951. Knigge, Andreas C. and Klaus Strzyz. "Interview mit Michael Pierce." *Comixene* (Hanover). 8:40 (1981), pp. 49-50.

3952. Kraft, David A. "Batman—Legends of the Dark Knight." *Comics Interview*. No. 80, 1990, pp. 4-25.

3953. Kraft, David A. "Bob Larkin." *Comics Interview*. May 1983, pp. 33-35.

3954. Kraft, David A. "Department of InFOOMation." *Foom*. March 1977, pp. 18-29. (Steve Gerber, Roy Thomas, Archie Goodwin, Chris Claremont, Scott Edelman, David Kraft, Bill Mantlo, Jim Shooter).

3955. Kraft, David A. "Jan and Dean Mullaney." *Comics Interview*. March 1984, pp. 84-101.

3956. Kuxhouse, Daryl. "Phil Foglio: Putting the 'Funny' Back in Funny Books." *Penstuff*. May 1991, p. 3.

3957. Lane, Ed, ed. *The Art of Bob Powell*. San Francisco, California: Dellinges, 1978. 48 pp.

3958. Leguèbe, Eric. *Le Voyage en Balloon*. Marseilles: Bédésup, 1985. (Interviews with U.S. comic artists.)

3959. Leguèbe, Eric. *Voyage en Cartoonland*. Paris: S.E.R.G., 1977. (Interviews with U.S. cartoonists.)

3960. "Leslie Zahler." *Comics Interview*. January 1985, pp. 60-63.

3961. "Letterer: Joe Rosen." *Comics Interview*. No. 7, 1983, pp. 46-47.

3962. "Letterer: Willie Schubert." *Comics Interview*. No. 52, 1987, pp. 29-32.

3963. Littlefield, Andrew. "Mike McMahon Interview." *Comics Journal*. June 1988, pp. 81-85.

3964. Lucas, Mark. "Chris Bachalo." *Comics Interview*. No. 116, 1992, pp. 26-33, 35, 37-41, 43.

3965. Luciano, Dale. "AG-Man and a Drag Queen: Dale Luciano on *Anarcoma* and *Dick Tracy Feature Books*." *Comics Journal*. October 1984, pp. 41-43.

3966. Luciano, Dale. "Keeping the Comix Grapevine: An Interview with Clay Geerdes." *Comics Journal*. August 1985, pp. 85-90.

3967. Luciano, Dale. "Leonard Rifas: Before It's Too Late." *Comics Journal*. August 1984, pp. 87-109.

3968. Luciano, Dale. "Tales of the Zomoid: An Interview with Ray Zone." *Comics Journal*. September 1985, pp. 99-101.

3969. "Lynn Williams." *Comics Interview*. No. 47, 1987, pp. 26-33.

3970. McAvennie, Mike. "Youngblood." *Comics Scene*. April 1992, pp. 17-24, 66. (Rob Liefeld).

3971. Macchio, Ralph. "Department of InFOOMation." *Foom*. No. 15, 1976, pp. 16-29.

3972. Macchio, Ralph. "Department of InFOOMation." *Foom*. December 1976, pp. 22-29. (Archie Goodwin, Jack Kirby, Roy Thomas, John Warner, Len Wein, Marv Wolfman).

3973. McCormick, Carlo. "Interview with Joe Coleman." *Gauntlet*. No. 3, 1992, pp. 186-191.

3974. MacDonald, Heidi and Phillip D. Yeh. *Secret Teachings of a Comic Book Master. The Art of Alfredo Alcala*. Lompoc, California: Cartoonists Aeross America, 1993. 64 pp.

3975. MacGillivray, Cliff. "3-D Heroes." *Cartoonist PROfiles*. June 1986, pp. 54-59.

3976. Maddox, Mike. "Clive Barker: On the Beauty of the Beast." *Amazing Heroes*. December 1989.

3977. "The Man Behind the Covers Ron Dias." *The Comic Book Price Guide*. No. 17, 1987, p. A-84.

3978. "Marc Davis Interview." *Comics Scene*. No. 21, 1991.

3979. "Marc Silvestri." *Comics Interview*. No. 76, 1989, pp. 18-39.

3980. "Mark Bode Interview." *Comics Scene*. No. 24, 1991 or 1992.

3981. "Mark Hamlin." *Comics Interview*. April 1984, pp. 49-61.

3982. "Mark Wheatley Interview." *Comics Scene*. No. 23, 1991 or 1992.

3983. Maronie, Sam. "Joe Sinnott." *Comics Scene*. March 1982, pp. 14-17.

3984. "*Mars Attacks* Artist Norm Saunders Dead." *Comics Journal*. May 1989, pp. 18-20.

3985. Martin, Anya. "Radio City Mutant Haul." *Comics Scene*. February 1991, pp. 17-20, 60. (Mark Bodé).

3986. "Martin Goodman." *Comics Journal*. July 1992, p. 14.

3987. "Marvel Bullpen Profiles." *Foom*. April 1974, pp. 8-10. (Rich Buckler, Steve Gerber).

3988. Maschi, Bob. "Interview with Gary Gerani." *Comics Buyer's Guide*. April 16, 1993, pp. 28, 30.

3989. "Matt Jorgensen." *Comics Interview*. March 1985, pp. 65-75.

3990. McLaughlin, Shaun. "In with the New: R.A. Jones on Protectors, the Genesis Crossover, and Natural Light." *Comics Buyer's Guide*. September 17, 1993, pp. 27-28.

3991. McLaughlin, Shaun. "Pencilsaur for Hire." *Comics Buyer's Guide*. September 17, 1993, pp. 28, 32. (Leonard Kirk).

3992. McLaughlin, Shaun. "Riding a Roller Coaster: Charles Marshall Talks About Taking over 'Ex-Mutants.'" *Comics Buyer's Guide*. September 17, 1993, pp. 28, 30.

3993. Meglin, Nick. "The Days of Wine and Fleagles." *Squa Tront*. No. 3, 1969, pp. 38-41.

3994. Merlo, Carmela. "Joe Orsak and Tom Peyer." *Comics Interview*. No. 56, 1988, pp. 16-19, 21, 23-27.

3995. Metzger, Kim. "Brian Cosgrove: A Talk with the Director/Co-Producer of 'Dangermouse.'" *Comics Collector*. Fall 1985, pp. 36-41.

3996. "Michael Dobson." *Comics Interview*. No. 56, 1988, pp. 53-59.

3997. "Mike Higgins." *Comics Interview*. No. 29, 1985, pp. 37-51.

3998. "Mike Richardson and Randy Stradley." *Comics Interview*. No. 61, 1988, 34-51.

3999. "Mike Saenz." *Comics Interview*. March 1985, pp. 7-25.

4000. "Mike Teitelbaum." *Comics Interview*. February 1983, pp. 52-57.

4001. "Milton Grieff." *Comics Interview*. No. 43, 1987, pp. 43-51.

4002. Moldoff, Sheldon. "Autobiography: Whatever Happened to Shelly?" *Robin Snyder's History of the Comics*. July 1991, pp. 66-70.

4003. Monks, Joe. "Jae Lee." *Comics Buyer's Guide*. January 22, 1993, p. 22.

4004. "More Surprised Than Anybody... An Interview with Al Feldstein." *Squa Tront*. No. 9, 1983, pp. 3-9.

4005. Mougin, Lou. "Jerry Grandenetti." *Comics Interview*. November 1984, pp. 53-57.

4006. Mougin, Lou. "Writer: Mark Waid." *Comics Interview*. No. 118, 1993, pp. 37, 39-43, 45.

4007. "Murphy Anderson." *Comics Feature*. July 1981.

4008. Neal, Jim. "Kids Serenade Gene Autry on Star's 85th Birthday." *Comics Buyer's Guide*. December 11, 1992, p. 27.

4009. "Neil Vokes." *Comics Interview*. May 1985, pp. 21-29.

4010. "Nevelow Leaving Piranha." *Comics Journal*. February 1991, p. 13.

4011. Nicholls, Stan. "Conversations in Judgment." *Comics Scene*. May 1992, pp. 33-37. (Alan Grant, Simon Bisley).

4012. Nicholls, Stan. "Warped Imagination." *Comics Scene*. April 1992, pp. 33-37, 52. (Joe Bolton).

4013. "Norm Breyfogle Interview." *Comics Scene*. No. 21, 1991.

4014. "Nostalgia Lane: Jim McLoughlin, Raymond True." *The Classics Collector*. February-March 1990, pp. 32-33.

4015. "Novel Insights." *The Classics Collector*. February-March 1990, pp. 30-31.

4016. Oakley, Shane. "Ted McKeever." *FA*. October 1989, pp. 38-44.

4017. O'Connell, Margaret. "An Interview with Jack C. Harris." *Comics Journal*. April 1980, pp. 36-53.

4018. Offenberger, Rik. "Valentino Defends Image." *Comics Buyer's Guide*. March 27, 1992, pp. 1, 28.

4019. Ohlandt, Kevin. "Focus on the Future: The New Age of Artists." *Comics Values Monthly*. October 1992, pp. 16-19. (Greg Capullo, David Lapham, Jae Lee, Mark Pacella, Joe Quesada).

4020. "OK, Is Paul Ryan O'Connor Overworked?" *Comics Scene*. Vol. 9 (Vol. 4, Series 20), pp. 65+.

4021. Oldham, Stephen. "Joe Colquhoun." *Comics Interview*. November 1984, pp. 37-43.

4022. O'Neil, Dennis. "An Interview with Samuel R. Delany." *Comics Journal*. Summer 1979, pp. 37-44.

4023. O'Neill, Patrick D. "Alan Brennert Coming Full Circle." *Comics Scene*. September 1982, p. 18.

4024. O'Neill, Patrick D. "Artist: Karl Story." *Comics Interview*. No. 87, 1990, pp. 42-45, 47-49.

4025. O'Neill, Patrick D. "Randy Stradley." *Comics Interview*. No. 87, 1990, pp. 52-57.

4026. O'Neill, Patrick D. "Writer: John Arcudi." *Comics Interview*. No. 87, 1990, pp. 5-11.

4027. "Orlando Odyssey." *Qua Brot*. 1, 1985, pp. 15-18.

4028. "Parade of Idiots: Doug Allen/Gary Leib Sketchbook." *Comics Journal*. February 1992, pp. 97-101.

4029. Pastis, Steven D. "An Interview with Alfredo Alcala." *Collectors' Edition*. December 1986, pp. 12-13.

4030. "Pat Boyette." *BEM*. No. 36, 1982.

4031. "Pat Mills." *Comics Interview*. No. 36, 1986, pp. 9-23.

4032. "Paul Tallerday and Barbara Marker." *Comics Interview*. No. 47, 1987, pp. 39-54.

4033. Pegg, Robert. "The Addams Chronicles." *Comics Scene*. February 1991, pp. 49-52, 58. (Carole Thompson, Larry Wilson).

4034. "Peter B. Gillis." *Comics Interview*. September 1985, pp. 7-23.

4035. "Peter David." *Comics Interview*. No. 30, 1986, pp. 16-29.

4036. Pettus, David. "An Interview with Will Murray." *Comics Buyer's Guide*. February 12, 1993, pp. 90-92.

4037. Pfouts, Chris. "Spain: A Road Vulture in Full Flight." *Art? Alternatives*. April 1992, pp. 50-57. (Spain Rodríguez).

4038. "Phil Foglio." *Comics Interview*. May 1985, pp. 7-19.

4039. Plowright, Frank. "John Wagner and Alan Grant Interview." *Comics Journal*. June 1988, pp. 69-80.

4040. Power, Paul. "Dave Darrigo and Dave Ross." *Comics Interview*. No. 39, 1986, pp. 20-40.

4041. Pradarelli, Steve. "Creator of Characters." *Sumter* (South Carolina) *Item*. April 1, 1990, pp. 1C, 7C.

4042. "Production: Paul Guinan." *Comics Interview*. No. 52, 1987, pp. 33-37.

4043. "Publisher: Rick Obadiah." *Comics Interview*. No. 52, 1987, pp. 54-60.

4044. "Quasar: The Man Who Runs the Universe." *Speakeasy*. May 1989, pp. 32-33, 35.

4045. Reiche, Volker, Thomas M. Bunk and Klaus Strzyz. "Interview Gilbert Shelton." *Comixene* (Hanover). 8:41 (1981), pp. 4-7.

4046. "Reid Fleming's Back." *Comics Interview*. September 1986, p. 25.

4047. Reidy, Mike. "Todd Reis." *Comics Interview*. No. 41, 1986, pp. 57-62.

4048. "Remembering the Cosmic Visions of Rick Griffin." *Comics Journal*. October 1991, pp. 13-15.

4049. "Requiem for Lieuen." *Comics Journal*. November 1991, p. 31.

4050. "Retailer: Steve Sibra." *Comics Interview*. No. 74, 1989, pp. 52-58.

4051. "Richard Bruning and Bob Rozakis." *Comics Interview*. No. 45, 1987, pp. 48-59.

4052. "Richard Burton." *Comics Interview*. February 1984, pp. 43-51.

4053. Rifas, Leonard. "Don Lomax: An Interview with the Creator of *Vietnam Journal*." *Comics Journal*. July 1990, pp. 86-102.

4054. Ringgenberg, Steve. "Todd Klein." *Comics Interview*. May 1983, pp. 43-45.

4055. Rodi, Rob. "Some Masterworks (and Some Masters)." *Comics Journal*. June 1988, pp. 47-52.

4056. "Ron Randall." *Comics Interview*. No. 67, 1989, pp. 25-30.

4057. Saba, Arn. "Harold Fisher: Drawing Upon History." *Comics Journal*. September 1985, pp. 61-84.

4058. "Sal Buscema." *Comics Interview*. June 1985, pp. 24-39.

4059. "Sales Director: Kurt Goldzung." *Comics Interview*. No. 52, 1987, pp. 47-53.

4060. Salicrup, Jim. "Rick Parker." *Comics Interview*. No. 33, 1986, pp. 49-59.

4061. Sanderson, Peter. "The Frank Miller/Klaus Janson Interview." *The Daredevil Chronicles*. February 1982, pp. 9-27.

4062. Sanderson, Peter. "Lamar Waldron and Susan Barrows." *Comics Interview*. No. 49, 1987, pp. 6-25.

4063. Sanderson, Peter. "Ted Boonthanakit." *Comics Interview*. No. 49, 1987, pp. 26-33, 36-39.

4064. Sanderson, Peter, ed. *The X-Men Companion*. 2 Vols. Stamford, Connecticut: Fantagraphics Books, 1982. (Terry Austin, John Byrne, Chris Claremont, Dave Cockrum, Louise Jones, Roy Thomas, Len Wein).

4065. Schutz, Diana. "A Conversation with the Creator of 'Neil the Horse.'" *Comics Buyer's Guide*. February 17, 1984, pp. 20, 22, 24, 28.

4066. Schutz, Diana. "Tom Orzechowski." *Comics Interview*. May 1984, pp. 46-51; June 1984, pp. 53-59.

4067. Selbert, Kathy. "An Eternity Behind a Typewriter." *Comics Scene*. No. 9, 1989, pp. 65-68.

4068. Shaw!, Scott. "Mike Sekowsky—Comicdon's Unsung Jack-of-All-Styles." In *San Diego Comic Convention 1989* program book, pp. 88-89. San Diego, California: San Diego Comic-Con Committee, 1989.

4069. Sheridan, Martin. *Comics and Their Creatures*. Boston, Massachusetts: Hale, Cushman and Flint, 1972.

4070. Simon, Joe, with Jim Simon. *The Comic Book Makers*. New York: Crestwood/II Publications, 1990. 208 pp.

4071. "Sketchbook: Hunt Emerson." *Comics Journal*. November 1992, pp. 121-125.

4072. "Sketchbook: Mark Martin." *Comics Journal*. February 1993, pp. 97-101.

4073. Slifer, Roger. "Ernie Colon." *Comics Interview*. July 1984, pp. 47-63.

4074. Smeddy, Dan. "The Elementals: Bill Willingham." *Comics Interview*. November 1984, pp. 15-35.

4075. Smith, Beau. "Subscription Service/Retailer: Sherill and Bruce Ayers." *Comics Interview*. No. 35, 1986, pp. 46-58.

4076. Smith, Mary. "John L. Goldwater: The Founder of Archie Comics." *Comics Buyer's Guide*. August 2, 1991, pp. 62-65.

4077. Snowden, George. "Ray Bradbury—The Best of Two Worlds." *Qua Brot*. No. 1, 1985, pp. 27-32.

4078. "Spain Sketchbook." *Comics Journal*. October 1992, pp. 113-117. (Peter Spain).

4079. "Special SPCE Spotlight on Jay Kennedy." *Small Press Comics Explosion*. November 1986, pp. 27-30.

4080. Stack, Frank. "The Case of the Argentina Exiles." *Comics Journal*. January 1989, pp. 53-59.

4081. Stern, Roger. "Just a Barbarian from Missouri." *Baycon III Program Book*. 1977, pp. 13-15.

4082. "Steve MacManus and Alan McKenzie." *Comics Interview*. No. 58, 1988, pp. 18-23, 26-29, 31, 33-35, 37.

4083. "Steve Oliff." *Comics Interview*. February 1983, pp. 47-50.

4084. "Steve Ringgenberg." *Comics Interview*. No. 42, 1987, pp. 6-23.

4085. Sullivan, Darcy. "Too Silly for Comics?" *Comics Scene*. May 1992, pp. 39-44. (Don Simpson).

4086. Sumner, Andrew. "Vested Interest." *Speakeasy*. December-January 1990-1991, pp. 49, 51. (Charles Vess).

4087. "Terry Austin." *Comics Interview*. February 1983, pp. 39-41.

4088. Thingvall, Joel. "Sense of Wonder." *Dreamline*. March 1982, pp. 92-95.

4089. Thompson, Kim. "Maidens, Mutants, and Mages." *Amazing Heroes*. June 1982, pp. 29-38. (Paul Smith).

4090. Thompson, Maggie. "Byrne vs. Miller." *Comics Buyer's Guide*. July 17, 1983, pp. 6, 8, 10, 12, 14, 16.

4091. Thompson, Stephen. "Dan Vebber: A Look at the Boy Cartoonist of 'Adventure.'" *Comics Buyer's Guide*. December 25, 1992, pp. 32, 34. (Dave Vebber).

4092. Thorne, Frank. *A Display of Art Work by Frank Thorne*. San Francisco, California: Cartoonews, 1978. 60 pp.

4093. Thorpe, Dave. "Al Davison: Breaking Free." *Speakeasy*. April 1990, pp. 35, 37, 39.

4094. "Tim Sale and Jeph Loeb." *Comics Interview*. No. 99, 1991, pp. 34-47.

4095. "Tom and Mary Bierbaum." *Comics Interview*. February 1985, pp. 7-11.

4096. "Tom Condon." *Comics Interview*. December 1984, pp. 27-35.

4097. "Tom Ziuko." *Comics Interview*. February 1984, pp. 38-41.

4098. "Tony Isabella." *Comics Interview*. June 1983, pp. 47-55.

4099. "25th Anniversary of Marvel Comics. Special Edition—Interviews with Stan Lee, Jim Shooter, Jack Kirby, and Roy Thomas." *Comics Feature*. May 1986, pp. 29-35, 39-49.

4100. "Ty Templeton." *Comics Interview*. No. 66, 1989, pp. 34-39.

4101. Ugol, Donna. "Catching a Rising Star." *Comics Feature*. December 1981, pp. 74-76.

4102. Vance, James. "R.A. Jones." *Comics Interview*. No. 48, 1987, pp. 40-53.

4103. Vick, Edd. "Steve Gallacci—An Interview." *Penstuff*. November 1988, p. 3; December 1988, p. 3; January 1989, p. 3.

4104. Vinson, Stan. "J. Allen St. John." *The World of Comic Art*. Fall 1966, pp. 16-17.

4105. Ward, Bill. "The Man Behind Torchy." In *The Comic Book Price Guide 1978-79*, edited by R.M. Overstreet, pp. A-40-A-53. Cleveland, Tennessee: 1978.

4106. "Watchmen Round Table: Moore and Gibbons." *Comics Interview*. No. 65, 1988, pp. 24-67.

4107. "Wayne Boring." *Amazing Heroes*. February 15, 1984.

4108. "When Titans Clash (Stan Lee and Harlan Ellison)." *Comics Journal*. November 1985, pp. 86-92.

4109. Willette, Allen. *These Top Cartoonists Tell How They Create America's Favorite Comics*. Fort Lauderdale, Florida: Allied Publications Inc., 1964.

4110. "William Woolfolk." *Comics Interview*. No. 28, 1985, pp. 25-35; No. 29, 1985, pp. 6-15.

4111. "Willie Ito." *Comics Interview*. No. 38, 1986, pp. 47-49.

4112. Willis, Steve. *The Almost Complete Collected Morty Comix*. Irving, Texas: Jabberwocky Graphix, 1984. 23 pp.

4113. Wilson, Bill G. "Don Newton: A Portfolio of Western Illustrations." *The Collector*. Winter 1973, pp. 20-26.

4114. Wilson, Bill G. "An Interview with Gray Morrow." *The Collector*. Winter 1973, pp. 40-45.

4115. Windham, Ryder. "Peter Kuper." *Comics Journal*. May 1992, pp. 68-101.

4116. "Wm. Stout." *Comics Interview*. No. 74, 1989, pp. 26-51; No. 75, 1989, pp. 86-103; No. 76, 1989, pp. 42-60.

4117. "Writer and Artist: Kazuo Koike and Goseki Kojima." *Comics Interview*. No. 52, 1987, pp. 16-21.

4118. "Writer: Jim Lawrence." *Comics Interview*. No. 69, 1989, pp. 4-18.

4119. "Writer: Sam Hamm." *Comics Interview*. No. 70, 1989, pp. 6-29.

4120. "Writer Steven Grant." *Comics Interview*. No. 72, 1989, pp. 5-13.

4121. Yang, Samuel. "Eddie Campbell." *Comics Journal*. October 1991, pp. 58-88.

4122. Young, Frank. "Evan Dorkin." *Comics Journal*. August 1992, pp. 101-113.

4123. Zavisa, Christopher. *Satan's Tears, the Art of Alex Nino*. Detroit, Michigan: Land of Enchantment, 1977. 301 pp.

4124. Zilber, Jay. "Martin Pasko Interview." *Comics Journal*. December 1977, pp. 37-46.

4125. Zimmerman, Dwight J. "Al Weiss." *Comics Interview*. No. 33, 1986, pp. 6-17.

4126. Zimmerman, Dwight J. "Bill Oakley." *Comics Interview*. No. 54, 1988, pp. 27-32.

4127. Zimmerman, Dwight J. "Bob Hall." *Comics Interview*. No. 49, 1987, pp. 40-61.

4128. Zimmerman, Dwight J. "Buzz Dixon." *Comics Interview*. No. 37, 1986, pp. 37-53.

4129. Zimmerman, Dwight J. "Danny Crespi." *Comics Interview*. March 1984, p. 79-83.

4130. Zimmerman, Dwight J. "Ken Lopez." *Comics Interview*. No. 58, 1988, pp. 57-59.

4131. Zimmerman, Dwight J. "Larry Hama." *Comics Interview*. No. 37, 1986, pp. 18-25; No. 38, 1986, pp. 36-45.

4132. Zimmerman, Dwight J. "Mark Gruenwald." *Comics Interview*. No. 54, 1988, pp. 5-23.

4133. Zimmerman, Dwight J. "Willie Peppers." *Comics Interview*. No. 55, 1988, pp. 30-41.

4134. Zone, Ray. "An Interview with Big Daddy Roth." *Fanfare*. Summer 1983, pp. 44-50.

Adams, Neal

4135. Adams, Neal. *The Art of Neal Adams*. 2 Vols. Brooklyn, New York: S. Quartuccio, 1975-1977.

4136. Adams, Neal. "Jack Adler: Dinosaur?" *Comics Journal*. November 1981, pp. 8-9.

4137. Adams, Neal. *The Neal Adams Treasury*. Detroit, Michigan: Pure Imagination, 1976. 56 pp.

4138. "Cartoonist Wins ACBA Award." *Cartoonist PROfiles*. No. 15, 1972, p. 61.

4139. "Comic Book Comment—Conversation with Neal Adams (Pt. 3)." *Cartoonist PROfiles*. June 1972, pp. 11-13.

4140. "Conversation with Neal Adams—Part One." *Cartoonist PROfiles*. September 1971, pp. 6-17.

4141. "Conversations with Neal Adams—Part Two." *Cartoonist PROfiles*. December 1971, pp. 66-73.

4142. Dionnet, J.P. "Neal Adams." *Phénix*. No. 14, 1970.

4143. Frenzel, Martin. "Neal Adams." *Comic Forum* (Vienna). 8:32 (1986), pp. 41-47.

4144. Groth, Gary. "Neal Adams." *Comics Journal*. May 1982, pp. 68-114.

4145. Groth, Gary. "Neal Adams." *Comics Journal*. July 1985, pp. 73-78.

4146. Groth, Gary. "Neal Adams Interview." *Comics Journal*. December 1978, pp. 38-55.

4147. "Neal Adams Interview." *Comics Scene*. No. 27, 1992.

4148. "Opinion by Neal Adams." *Comics Journal*. November 1981, pp. 8-9.

4149. Potter, Greg. "Panel Progressions: Neal Adams." *Comics Journal*. Winter 1980, pp. 139-144.

4150. "Spotlight: Neal Adams." *Artsy*. No. 2, 1988, pp. 5-9.

Allard, Al

4151. Beck, C.C. "Conversation with Al Allard." *FCA/S.O.B.* April/May 1982, p. 7.

4152. Beck, C.C. "Conversation with Al Allard." *Minnesota Cartoonist*. December 12, 1990, p. 5.

Anderson, Murphy

4153. Carter, Gary M. "Murphy Anderson '...the Silver Age Legend....'" In *The Confident Collector*, edited by Jerry Weist, pp. 34-53. New York: Avon, 1992.

4154. "Classic Conversations: The Anderson Tapes—Part Two." *Comics Feature*. September-October 1981, pp. 150-154.

Ayers, Dick

4155. "Dick Ayers." *Cartoonist PROfiles*. September 1983, pp. 8-15; December 1983, pp. 60-65.

4156. "Dick Ayers: War for a Career." *Comics Scene*. September 1983, pp. 48-53.

Bagge, Peter

4157. Lim Cheng Tju. "Hateful Things: The Peter Bagge Interview." *Big O Magazine*. March 1993, pp. 63-65.

4158. Macrone, Michael. "Two Generations of Weirdos (Peter Bagge and Robert Crumb). *Comics Journal*. March 1986, pp. 50-71.

4159. Skidmore, Martin. "Interview: Peter Bagge." *FA*. March 1989, pp. 30-33.

4160. Sobocinski, Carole. "Peter Bagge!" *Comics Journal*. May 1993, pp. 58-67, 69-72, 74-76, 78-82, 84-88, 90-92, 94.

Baker, Kyle

4161. "Kyle Baker Sketchbook." *Comics Journal*. March 1993, pp. 122-126.

4162. Petersen, Poul. "Interview med Kyle Baker." *Seriejournalen*. June 1992, pp. 42-44.

Barks, Carl

4163. Barks, Carl. *The Carl Barks Library*. 30 Vols. Scottsdale, Arizona: Another Rainbow, 1983-.

4164. Barrier, Michael. *Carl Barks and the Art of the Comic Book*. New York: M. Lilien, 1981. 227 pp.

4165. "Carl Barks." *Comics Scene*. March 1982, pp. 41-47.

4166. Decker, Dwight R. "Carl Barks, the Good Duck Artist." *Comics Journal*. July 1982, pp. 54-57, 60-63.

4167. Decker, Dwight R. "Duck Kapital by Karl Barx." *Comics Journal*. August 1981, pp. 6-7.

4168. Gabbard, Frank. *Reprint Guide to Carl Barks*. Selah, Washington: 1980. 20 pp.

4169. Hamilton, Bruce. "Interview des Jahres: Bruce Hamilton im Gespräch mit Carl Barks und Floyd Gottfredson." In *Comic-Jahrbuch 1986*, edited by Martin Compart and Andreas C. Knigge, pp. 120-128. Frankfurt: Ullstein GmbH, 1985.

4170. Luciano, Dale. "Appreciating Carl Barks." *Comics Journal*. August 1983, pp. 47-56.

4171. Luciano, Dale. "Classic Barks." *Comics Journal*. September 1981, pp. 33-35.

4172. Nichols, John. "Barks for Beginners." *The Barks Collector*. April 1981.

4173. Nichols, John. "Gladstone Gander in the Magic Land, OR: Winning IS a Form of Work!" *The Barks Collector*. March 1985, pp. 2-15.

4174. Odemark, Tor. "The Seven Cities of Cibola." *Duckburg Times*. December 15, 1981, pp. 8-9.

4175. "Sketchbook: Carl Barks." *Comics Journal*. July 1992, pp. 105-109.

4176. Spillmann, Klaus. "Der Unveröffenlichte Carl Barks." *Comixene* (Hanover). 8:38 (1981), pp. 46-51.

Baron, Mike

4177. Dutter, Barry. "30 Questions—Mike Baron." *Four Color Magazine*. March 1987, pp. 44-49.

4178. "Mike Baron." *Comics Interview*. No. 63, 1988, pp. 4-19.

4179. "Mike Baron and Steve Grant." *Comics Interview*. February 1984, pp. 15-27.

4180. "OK, Then, Is Mike Baron Overworked?" *Comics Scene*. No. 3 (Vol. 3, Series 13), pp. 45-47.

4181. Smay, Dave. "The Story Rules: An Interview with Mike Baron." *Comics Journal*. August 1986, pp. 78-104.

Barry, Dan

4182. Arbesú, Faustino R. "Tanto Monta... Dan Barry Como Alex Raymond." *El Wendigo*. No. 54, 1991, p. 7.

4183. Barry, Dan. "Interview." *Amazing Heroes*. March 1988.

4184. "Dan Berry." *Comics Interview*. No. 82, 1990.

4185. Pérez, Ramón Fermín. "Dan Barry." *El Wendigo*. No. 54, 1991, p. 7.

4186. Pérez, Ramón Fermín. "Dos Exposiciones de 'Restallu.'" *El Wendigo*. No. 54, 1991, p. 6.

4187. Rodríguez, Sofía Carlota. "Dan Barry: Un Mito del Cómic." *El Wendigo*. No. 54, 1991, pp. 4-5.

Bates, Cary

4188. "An Interview with Cary Bates." *Comics Feature*. January 1981, pp. 24-33.

4189. Greenberger, Robert. "Cary Bates 17 Years with the Man of Steel." *Comics Scene*. September 1983, pp. 32-36.

4190. Lillian, Guy H., III. "Cary Bates and Elliot Maggin: The Men Behind the Super Typewriter." *The Amazing World of DC Comics*. September-October 1974, pp. 2-7.

Beck, C.C.

4191. "About 'Captain Marvel' and C.C. Beck." *FCA/S.O.B.* June/July 1982, pp. 8-9.

4192. Beck, C.C. "Les Super-Héros dans la Grèce Antique." *Le Nouveau Bédésup* (Marseilles). 34, 1985, pp. 29-30.

4193. "C.C. Beck Dies." *CAPS Newsletter*. December 1989, p. 4.

4194. "C.C. Beck Død, 79 År." *Serieskaberen*. March 1990, p. 14.

4195. "C.C. Beck, June 9, 1910-November 22, 1989." *Comics Journal*. December 1989, p. 23.

4196. *A Complete Collection of Captain Marvel Adventures from Whiz Comics 7-28*. East Moline, Illinois: Special Edition Publishers, 1974. 320 pp.

4197. DeFuccio, Jerry. "C.C. Beck: Fine Artist." *Comics Journal*. July 1989, pp. 58-59.

4198. DeFuccio, Jerry. "Charles Clarence Beck: The World's Second Mightiest Mortal." In *The Comic Book Price Guide 1985-86*, edited by R.M. Overstreet, pp. A-78-A-88. Cleveland, Tennessee: 1985.

4199. Groth, Gary. "'With One Magic Word...'—An Interview with C.C. Beck." *Comics Journal*. February 1985, pp. 57-77.

Binder, Otto

4200. Beck, C.C. "Otto Binder 1911-1974." *FCA/S.O.B.* February/March 1982, p. 6; *Rocket's Blast Comic Collector*. No. 115, 1973.

4201. Binder, Otto. "Letter to Roy Thomas." *Amazing World of DC Comics*. April 1978.

Biro, Charles

4202. Spicer, Bill. "Charles Biro's Tops." *Fanfare*. Summer 1981, p. 35.

4203. Scott, Art. "The Illustories of Charles Biro." *Fanfare*. Summer 1981, pp. 25-34.

Bisley, Simon

4204. Hawton, Zoe. "Nobody Beats the Biz—Simon Bisley Interview." *Comics Values Monthly*. November 1992, pp. 16-18.

4205. Sanderson, Peter. "Simon Bisley." *Comics Interview*. No. 99, 1991, pp. 18-25.

4206. "Simon Bisley and Alan Grant Interview." *Comics Scene*. No. 26, 1992.

Bissette, Steve

4207. Bissette, Stephen. "Evolution of a Comic Book Artist—Part I." *Cartoonist PROfiles*. September 1985, pp. 30-35; Part II, December 1985, pp. 78-81.

4208. Bissette, Stephen. "Interview." *Comics Journal*. September 1984.

4209. Bissette, Steve. "Spotlight: Cerebus." *Comics Interview*. No. 107, 1992, pp. 8-41.

4210. Cannon, Martin. *Swamp Thing, Green Mansions*. Critics Choice Files Magazine. Canoga Park, California: Psi Fi Movie Press, 1987. 53 pp.

4211. "Sketchbook. Steve Bissette." *Comics Journal*. September 1990, pp. 107-111.

Blackbeard, Bill

4212. Schwartz, Ron. "A Visit With... Bill Blackbeard." *The Funnie's Paper*. March 1984, pp. 11-12.

4213. Strzyz, Klaus. "Interview mit Bill Blackbeard." *Comic Forum* (Vienna). 25/26, 1984, pp. 46-49.

Bolland, Brian

4214. Monks, Joe. "Brian Bolland." *Comics Buyer's Guide*. January 22, 1993, pp. 44, 48.

4215. Pirani, Adam. "Panel Boarder." *Comics Scene Spectacular*. September 1990, pp. 10-14.

4216. Plowright, Frank. "Brian Bolland." *Comics Interview*. January 1985, pp. 20-38.

Boltinoff, Murray

4217. Snyder, Robin. "Murray Boltinoff." *Comics Journal*. July 1985, pp. 79+.

4218. Snyder, Robin. "Murray Boltinoff Interview." *Comics Journal*. Winter 1980, pp. 132-138.

Brown, Chester

4219. Grammel, Scott. "Chester Brown im Gespräch. Ein Interview mit dem Yummy Fur-Magier." *Comic Info*. May-June 1993, pp. 28-29.

4220. Grammel, Scott. "Chester Brown: from the Sacred to the Scatological." *Comics Journal*. April 1990, pp. 66-90.

Burden, Bob

4221. "Bob Burden." *Comics Interview*. No. 40, 1986, pp. 22-41.

4222. "Bob Burden Interview." *Comics Scene*. No. 21, 1991.

4223. "Bob Burden, the Carrot Man." *Speakeasy*. March 1990, pp. 43-45, 47.

4224. Mallette, Jack. "Bob Burden." *Comics Interview*. No. 41, 1986, pp. 18-37.

Burns, Charles

4225. "Charles Burns: Sketchbook." *Comics Journal*. December 1987, pp. 119-125.

4226. Gladstone, Jim. "Doc Boy's Big Daddy." *Philadelphia City Paper*. November 17-24, 1989, pp. 1, 10-11.

4227. Jerome, Fiona. "Charles Burns: Crown Prince of the New Pulp." *Speakeasy*. April 1990, pp. 48-49, 51.

4228. Sullivan, Darcy. "Charles Burns." *Comics Journal*. February 1992, pp. 52-65, 67-68, 70-85, 87-88.

Burroughs, Edgar R.

4229. Cantey, Bill. "The Legacy of Edgar Rice Burroughs." *The Collector*. Winter 1973, pp. 6-11.

4230. Cochran, Russ. *The Edgar Rice Burroughs Library of Illustration*. 3 Vols. West Plains, Missouri: 1976-1984.

4231. "Edgar Rice Burroughs, the Artists Behind Him." *Fantastic* (Flushing, New York). November 1966.

4232. *Library Review* (Louisville, Kentucky). May 1980. Issue on Edgar Rice Burroughs and collection of his work at University of Kentucky. Prepared by George T. McWhorter. 38 pp.

4233. McGreal, Dorothy. "The Burroughs No One Knows." *The World of Comic Art*. Fall 1966, p. 204 +.

4234. "Me Tarzan, Me Rich: Edgar Rice Burroughs." *Forbes*. February 15, 1975, pp. 22-23.

4235. Porges, Irwin. *Edgar Rice Burroughs: The Man Who Created Tarzan.* Provo, Utah: Brigham Young University Press, 1975. 820 pp.

4236. *Remember When* (Carrollton, Texas). February 1972 issue dedicated to works of Edgar Rice Burroughs.

4237. *Tarzan of the Apes.* London: Williams, 1971. 144 pp.

4238. Vohland, Duffy. "A Look at the DC Burroughs Book Adaptions." *The Collector.* Winter 1973, pp. 4-5.

Buscema, John

4239. Buscema, John. *The Art of John Buscema.* Brooklyn, New York: S. Quartuccio, 1978. 32 pp.

4240. "John Buscema." *Comics Feature.* July 1986.

4241. "John Buscema." *Comics Interview.* No. 62, 1988, pp. 16-26.

4242. Peel, John. "John Buscema." *Comics Feature.* September-October 1984, pp. 11-18, 63-66.

Byrne, John

4243. *The Art of John Byrne.* Foreword by Roger Stern. Brooklyn, New York: SQ Productions, 1980. 72 pp.

4244. Byrne, John. *The Art of John Byrne.* Brooklyn, New York: S.Q. Productions, 1980. 64 pp.

4245. Byrne, John. "Byrne Takes the Bat." *Speakeasy.* February 1989, p. 34.

4246. Byrne, John. "On Creator's Rights." *Comics Scene.* March 1982, pp. 56-57.

4247. "Byrne, Baby, Byrne." *Speakeasy.* December 1988, pp. 24-25, 46.

4248. Carlota, Sofia. "John Byrne: Ahora Es la Edad de Oro del Comic." *El Wendigo.* Winter 1988-1989, pp. 30-32.

4249. Catron, Michael. "John Byrne Get Back to the Basics." *Best of Amazing Heroes.* No. 1, 1982, pp. 60-67.

4250. Cuervo, Javier. "John Byrne: Esto Es un Espectaculo." *El Wendigo.* March-April 1987, pp. 26-30.

4251. Gammill, Kerry. "John Byrne Agrees and Disagrees with Jan Strnad, Gary Groth, and Kerry Gammill." *Comics Journal.* September 1982, pp. 62-74.

4252. Hansen, Neil A. "Byrne's Next Frontier." *Comics Values Monthly.* September 1992, pp. 12-14.

4253. "John Byrne." *Comics Interview.* No. 43, 1987, pp. 25-29.

4254. "John Byrne." *Comics Interview.* No. 71, 1989, pp. 4-57.

4255. "John Byrne." *Comics Scene.* No. 5; April 1990; No. 19, 1991.

4256. "John Byrne: The Interview." *Comics Feature.* January-February 1984, pp. 19-39.

4257. Juanmartí, Jordi and Javier Riva. "Omac: No Future." *El Wendigo.* No. 59, 1993, pp. 40-42.

4258. McConnell, Kevin C. "Byrned Out." *Comics Journal.* October 1983, pp. 6-7.

4259. McConnell, Kevin C. "Byrne Unleashed." *Comics Journal.* December 1981,p.48.

4260. Sodaro, Robert J. "John Byrne: A Brief Chat." *Comics Buyer's Guide.* May 8, 1987, pp. 40, 42.

4261. Wilcox, John A. and Robert J. Sodaro. "From the Fantastic 4 to Superman! John Byrne." *Cartoonist PROfiles.* September 1986, pp. 66-73.

Carter, John

4262. Wolfman, Marv. "John Carter of Marvel." *Baycon III Program Book.* 1977, pp. 42-43.

4263. "John Carter of Mars." *Comics Club.* No. 1, 1967, p. 23.

Chadwick, Paul

4264. Baisden, Greg and Dale Crain. "Man of Stone: Paul Chadwick." *Comics Journal.* November 1989, pp. 76-102.

4265. "The Chadwick Collection." *Comics Interview.* No. 61, 1988, pp. 22-27.

4266. "Paul Chadwick." *Comics Interview*. No. 61, 1988, pp. 4-21.

Chaykin, Howard

4267. Arbesú, Faustino Rodríguez. "El Crepúsculo de los Dioses." *El Wendigo*. No. 59, 1993, pp. 4-5.

4268. Bethke, Marilyn. "An Interview with Howard Chaykin." *Comics Journal*. November 1979, pp. 55-69.

4269. Chaykin, Howard. *The Shadow, Blood and Judgement*. New York: DC Comics, 1987. 128 pp.

4270. Cohn, Mitch. "Howard Chaykin." *Comics Interview*. May 1983, pp. 37-41.

4271. Green, Stuart. "Chaykin: The Black Kiss Off." *Speakeasy*. December-January 1989-1990, p. 53.

4272. Groth, Gary. "'I Have a Hard Time with Vigilantes'—An Interview with Howard Chaykin." *Comics Journal*. July 1986, pp. 70-104.

4273. "Howard Chaykin: An Interview with the Creator of 'American Flagg.'" *Comics Buyer's Guide*. January 25, 1985, pp. 20, 22, 24, 26, 28, 38.

4274. Mitchell, Steve. "Who Is Howard Chaykin and Why Is He on This Planet?" *Baycom III Program Book*. 1977, pp. 26-27.

4275. Rehm, Dirk. "Blackhawk und Andere Comics—Zeichen und Syntax bei Howard Chaykin." *Comic Info*. May-June 1993, pp. 31-36.

4276. Rodi, Rob. "Whole Lotta Chaykin Goin' On." *Comics Journal*. August 1988, pp. 29-33.

4277. Rodríguez, Sofía Carlota and Faustino R. Arbesú." Lo Otra Cara de Howard Chaykin." *El Wendigo*. Verano, 1990, pp. 6-8.

4278. Shapiro, Marc. "Flash of TV Worlds." *Comics Scene*. December 1990, pp. 9-12, 32.

4279. "Writer/Artist: Howard Chaykin." *Comics Interview*. No. 75, 1989, pp. 44-77.

Claremont, Chris

4280. "Chris Claremont." *Society of Strip Illustration Newsletter*. May 1989, pp. 3-4.

4281. "Chris Claremont Interview." *Comics Scene*. No. 17, 1991.

4282. Green, Stuart. "Claremont—The Mutant Master." *Speakeasy*. February 1990, pp. 27, 29, 31.

4283. Groth, Gary. "Chris Claremont." *Comics Journal*. October 1979, pp. 48-69.

4284. MacDonald, Heidi D. "Alas, Poor Claremont, I Knew Him Well." *Comics Journal*. June 1985, pp. 53-56.

4285. MacDonald, Heidi D. "Chris Claremont." *Comics Journal*. July 1985, pp. 80-82.

4286. O'Neill, Patrick D. "Chris Claremont." *Comics Interview*. No. 56, 1988, pp. 5-15.

4287. Sanderson, Peter. "The Third Generation of X-Men." *Comics Journal*. August 1982, pp. 56-69.

4288. Schutz, Diana. "Chris Claremont—Superstar." *Comics Scene*. September 1983, pp. 20-25.

4289. Schutz, Diana. "X-Men: Chris Claremont Interview Part II." *Comics Collector*. Winter 1984, pp. 25-30, 32.

4290. Thompson, Kim H. "Chris Claremont." *Comics Journal*. August 1992, pp. 71-88.

4291. Truck, Walter. "Hiebe and Triebe." *ICOM*. January 1993, pp. 36-37.

Clowes, Dan

4292. Groth, Gary. "Daniel Clowes Revealed." *Comics Journal*. November 1992, pp. 46-92.

4293. "Sketchbook: Dan Clowes." *Comics Journal*. September 1991, pp. 101-106.

Colan, Gene

4294. McGregor, Don. "The Gene Colan Interview: Hopalong Cassidy to Batman." *Comics Scene*. September 1982, pp. 60-64.

4295. McGregor, Don. "The Gene Colan Interview: Part One: Creating His Own Destiny." *Comics Scene*. July 1982, pp. 41-45.

4296. Mougin, Lou. "Gene Colan." *Comics Interview*. No. 59, 1988, pp. 21-31.

Cole, Jack

4297. Goulart, Ron. *Focus on Jack Cole*. Agoura, California: Fantagraphics Books, 1986. 78 pp.

4298. Toth, Alex. "About Jack Cole." *Robin Snyder's History of the Comics*. July 1991, p. 71.

Cole, L.B.

4299. Boatner, E.B. "L.B. Cole: The Man Behind the Mask." In *The Comic Book Price Guide 1981-82*, edited by R.M. Overstreet, pp. A-55-A-72. Cleveland, Tennessee: 1981.

4300. Irons, Christopher. "The Man Behind the Cover: L.B. Cole." *The Comic Book Price Guide*. No. 18, 1988, p. A-77.

Collins, Max A.

4301. Gold, Mike. "Max Allan Collins." *Comics Journal*. November 1982, pp. 68-89.

4302. Gorman, Ed. "Ms. Tree's Creators: Interview with Max Collins and Terry Beatty." *Comics Collector*. Winter 1984, pp. 14, 16-20.

4303. McDonnell, David and Kim H. Johnson. "Max Allan Collins—The Mystery Novelist Who Writes Comics." *Comics Scene*. November 1982, pp. 29-32.

4304. "Max Allan Collins." *Comics Scene*. August 1990, pp. 29-39.

4305. "Max Collins and Terry Beatty." *Comics Interview*. June 1985, pp. 7-23.

Conway, Gerry

4306. Gustaveson, Rob. "Gerry Conway Talks Back to the Comics Journal." *Comics Journal*. December 1981, pp. 70-83.

4307. Kraft, David A. "Gerry Conway." *Comics Interview*. July 1984, pp. 9-27.

4308. "Writer: Gerry Conway." *Comics Interview*. No. 75, 1989, pp. 6-14.

Corben, Richard V.

4309. Bharucha, Fershid. *Richard Corben, Flights into Fantasy*. Brooklyn, New York: Thumb Tack Books, 1981. 200 pp.

4310. Bharucha, Fershid. *Richard Corben, Vols Fantastiques*. Paris: Ed. Neptune, 1982.

4311. Corben, Richard. *Complete Works*. 3 Vols. New York: Catalan Communications, 1985-1987.

4312. Legaristi, Francisco. "Monocomics—Richard Vance Corben." *Trix*. No. 2, n.d., p. 35.

4313. Schnurrer, Achim. "Wer Hat Angst vor Richard Corben?" *Comixene* (Hanover). 6:25 (1979), pp. 14-16.

Costanza, Pete

4314. Beck, C.C. "A Conversation with Pete Costanza." *FCA/S.O.B.* June/July 1982, p. 10.

4315. Pierce, John. "Pete Costanza." *FCA/S.O.B.* June 1980, p. 3.

Crumb, Robert

4316. Alessandrini, Marjorie. *Robert Crumb*. Paris: Albin Michel Coll. "Graffiti," 1974. 120 pp.

4317. Barrier, Mike. "On Comix." *Comics Journal*. November 1985, pp. 93-99.

4318. Bjørklid, Finn. "TEGN Presenterer Robert Crumb." *TEGN*. No. 3 (13), 1989, pp. 30-35.

4319. Bloodstone, Maggie. "All I Needed To Know I Learned in the Comics: How R. Crumb Taught Me the Facts of Life." *Comics Journal*. July 1991, pp. 71-75.

4320. Crumb, Robert. *The Complete Crumb Comics*. Agoura, California: Fantagraphics Books, 1987-.

4321. Crumb, Robert. *The Complete Fritz the Cat*. New York: Belier Press, 1978. 128 pp.

4322. Crumb, Robert. "Down Home Crumb." *Co-Evolution Quarterly*. Summer 1982, pp. 52-53.

4323. Crumb, Robert. *Fritz the Cat*. New York: Ballantine Books, 1969.

4324. Crumb, Robert. *Head Comix*. New York: Ballantine Books, 1970.

4325. Crumb, Robert. *R. Crumb's Yum Yum Book*. Scrimshaw Press, 1975. 150 pp.

4326. Crumb, Robert. *Robert Crumb's Carload o' Comics: An Anthology of Choice Strips and Stories—1968 to 1976*. New York: Belier Press, 1976. 176 pp.

4327. Crumb, Robert. *Sketchbook July, 1978 to November, '83*. 3 Vols. Frankfurt: Zweitausendeins, 1984. 382 pp.

4328. Crumb, Robert. *Sketchbook Late 1967 to Mid 1974*. Frankfurt: Zweitausendeins, 1986. 388 pp.

4329. Crumb, Robert. *Sketchbook 1966-67*. Frankfurt: Zweitausendeins, 1981. 361 pp.

4330. Crumb, Robert. *Sketchbook November 1974 to January 1978*. Frankfurt: Zweitausendeins, 1978. 310 pp.

4331. Crumb, Robert, *et al. The Complete Foo!* Chicago, Illinois: Bijou Publishing Empire, 1980.

4332. Crumb, Robert, *et al. The Snatch Sampler*. San Francisco, California: K. Green, 1977. 160 pp.

4333. de Gaudemar, Antoine. "Crumb, le Grand Robert." *Libération*. Supplement Special Angoulême 1992, p. v.

4334. Delio, Michelle. "In Search of Crumb." *Art? Alternatives*. October 1992, pp. 41-55.

4335. Dreyfus, Antoine. "Crumb: Le Dessin ou le Néant." *Le Quotidien de Paris*. January 22, 1992, p. xiii.

4336. Duncan, B.W. "Let's Hear It For Crumb!" *Comics Journal*. December 1989, pp. 52-54.

4337. Fiene, Donald. "Crumb Chronology." *Comics Journal*. April 1988, pp. 121-123.

4338. Green, Keith. "What's a Nice Counter-Culture Visionary Like Robert Crumb Doing on a Secluded Farm in California." *Inside Comics*. Spring 1974, pp. 18-23, 25.

4339. Groth, Gary. "A Couple of White Guys Sitting Around Talking: An Interview with R. Crumb." *Comics Journal*. July 1991, pp. 77-92.

4340. Groth, Gary. "Robert Crumb." *Comics Journal*. April 1993, pp. 67-76.

4341. Groth, Gary. "Robert Crumb—Tegneserier på Live og Død." *TEGN*. No. 3 (13), 1989, pp. 22-29.

4342. Groth, Gary. "The Straight Dope from R. Crumb." *Comics Journal*. April 1988, pp. 48-120.

4343. Hackett, G. "R. Crumb Keeps on Drawing." *Newsweek*. July 25, 1983, p. 9.

4344. Maremma, T. "Who Is This Crumb? Underground Cartoons of the Late Sixties." *New York Times Magazine*. October 1, 1972, pp. 12-13+. "Discussion," October 29, 1972, p. 12+.

4345. Pekar, Harvey. "Rapping about Cartoonists; Particularly Robert Crumb." *Journal of Popular Culture*. Spring 1970, pp. 677-688.

4346. "R. Crumb. Sketchbook." *Comics Journal*. July 1987, pp. 106-109.

4347. Ringgenberg, Steve. "Gary Groth on *The Complete Crumb*." *Gauntlet*. No. 5, 1993, pp. 163-166.

4348. "Robert Crumb—Comics." *New York Times*. October 1, 1972, VI, p. 12.

4349. Schechter, Harold. "Deep Meaning Comix: The Archetypal World of R. Crumb." *San Jose Studies*. November 1977, pp. 6-21.

4350. Scholz, Carter. "Expansive Early Crumb." *Comics Journal*. May 1981, pp. 120-121.

4351. Sherman, Bill. "Hup with Crumb." *Comics Journal*. December 1987, pp. 55-57.

Cruse, Howard

4352. Cruse, Howard. "At the Reunion." *Comics Scene*. May 1983, pp. 38-40.

4353. Cruse, Howard. *Dancin' Nekkid with the Angels*. New York: St. Martin's Press, 1987.

4354. Cruse, Howard. *Early Barefootz*. Seattle, Washington: Fantagraphics, 1990. 104 pp.

4355. Cruse, Howard. "Me, Barefoontz, and Underground Comix." *Cartoonist PROfiles*. June 1980, pp. 56-61.

4356. Cruse, Howard. *Wendel*. New York: Gay Presses of New York, 1985.

4357. Ringgenberg, Steve. "Sexual Politics and Comic Art: An Interview with Howard Cruse." *Comics Journal*. September 1986, pp. 64-94, 96.

Davis, Alan

4358. Nazzaro, Joe. "Punchlines." *Comics Scene*. December 1992, pp. 45-48, 50.

4359. Rodríguez, Sofía Carlota and Faustino R. Arbesú. "Alan Davis: Imaginación sin Salir de Casa." *El Wendigo*. Verano 1990, pp. 39-40.

DeCarlo, Dan

4360. Lee, Stan. "A Salute to Dan DeCarlo." *Robin Snyder's History of the Comics*. July 1991, p. 75.

4361. Metzger, Kim. "Dan DeCarlo, An Interview with Archie's Chief Artist." *Comics Buyer's Guide*. July 26, 1985, pp. 37-38.

Deitch, Kim

4362. Beauchamp, Monte. "Kim Deitch." *Comics Journal*. July 1988, pp. 56-79.

4363. Cohen, Aaron. "The Nine Lives of Kim Deitch." *Comics Journal*. January 1993, pp. 88-89.

4364. "Sketchbook Kim Deitch." *Comics Journal*. November 1991, pp. 99-103; December 1991, pp. 77-83.

De Matteis, J. Marc

4365. Hansom, Dick. "J.M. De Matteis, Just Desserts." *Speakeasy*. March 1990, pp. 32-33, 35, 37.

4366. Higgins, Mike. "J. Marc De Matteis." *Comics Interview*. No. 38, 1986, pp. 20-35; No. 39, 1986, pp. 7-19; No. 40, 1986, pp. 6-21.

Dent, Lester

4367. "Lester (*Doc Savage*) Dent." *Comics Scene*. No. 28, 1992.

4368. Murray, Will. "Who Was (or Were) Kenneth Robeson?" *Comics Buyer's Guide*. February 12, 1993, pp. 36, 40, 44.

Ditko, Steve

4369. Catron, Mike. "Shade: Ditko's New Book Shows Potential." *Comics Journal*. April 1977, pp. 8-11.

4370. Ditko, Steve. *The Ditko Collection*. Thousand Oaks, California: Fantagraphics Books, 1984. 112 pp.

4371. Ditko, Steve. *The Ditko Collection*. Edited and Intro. by Robin Snyder. 2 Vols. Agoura, California: Fantagraphics Books, 1985-1986.

4372. "First Look: A Steve Ditko Strip." *Amazing Heroes*. No. 99, 1987, pp. 42-47.

4373. Groth, Gary. "Dada Ditko." *Comics Journal*. October 1991, pp. 53-55.

4374. Murray, Will. "Ditko Before the Code." *The Comics Buyer's Guide*. November 23, 1984, pp. 58-59, 63.

4375. Sodaro, Bob. "The Amazing Spider-Man: Ditko Days." *Best of Amazing Heroes*. No. 1, 1982, pp. 41-47.

4376. Wileman, Michael L. *A 50's Ditko Cover Gallery*. Kansas City, Kansas: 1982. 27 pp.

Douglas, Steve

4377. Dunn, Robert. "Steve Douglas." *The Cartoonist*. August 1967, p. 26.

4378. Smith, Al. "Steve Douglas." *The Cartoonist*. August 1967, p. 27.

DuBois, Gaylord

4379. Mougin, Lou. "Gaylord DuBois." *Comics Interview*. November 1984, pp. 9-13.

4380. Ziemann, Irvin H. "Gaylord DuBois: Chapter One, Concluded." *Comics Buyer's Guide*. October 13, 1989, pp. 62-64.

4381. Ziemann, Irvin H. "Gaylord DuBois: King of the Comics Writers." *Comics Buyer's Guide*. October 6, 1989, pp. 60, 62-65; November 3, 1989, pp. 46-50.

4382. Ziemann, Irvin H. "Gaylord DuBois: King of the Comics Writers. Chapter 5: From Rag-Dolls to Spaceships." *Comics Buyer's Guide*. May 4, 1990, pp. 50-51, 54, 56, 58, 60, 63-64.

4383. Ziemann, Irvin H. "Gaylord DuBois. Writer of 3000 Comics Scripts Is 90." *Comics Buyer's Guide*. September 8, 1989, pp. 1, 3.

Eisner, Will

4384. Barrier, Michael. "Comics Master: The Art and Spirit of Will Eisner." *Print*. November-December 1988, pp. 88-97.

4385. Benson, John. "An Interview with Will Eisner." *Witzend*. No. 6, 1970, p. 7-9+.

4386. Bouyer, Sylvain. "Du Visuel au Sonore." *Les Cahiers de la Bande Dessinée* (Grenoble). 61, 1985, pp. 95-96.

4387. Castelli, Alfredo. "The Spirit." *Comics*. No. 4, 1966, pp. 18-23.

4388. Chante, Alain. "L'Appel de l'Espace ou le Monde Selon Eisner." *Les Cahiers de la Bande Dessinée* (Grenoble). 61, 1985, pp. 90-91.

4389. de Cortanze, Gérard. "Etre Juif à New York." *Les Cahiers de la Bande Dessinée* (Grenoble). 61, 1985, p. 85.

4390. de Moya, Álvaro. "Will Eisner." *Abigraf*. November-December 1991, pp. 18-22.

4391. Eisner, Will. "Art and Commerce: An Oral Reminiscence." *Panels*. Summer 1979, pp. 4-21.

4392. Eisner, Will. "Catch the Spirit: An Interview with Will Eisner." *Four-Color Magazine*. January 1987, pp. 28-34, 66.

4393. Eisner, Will. "The Comics." *New York Herald Tribune Magazine*. January 9, 1966, p. 8.

4394. Eisner, Will. "'Future Schlock.' Will Eisner on the State—and Future—of Comics." *Comics Journal*. November 1991, pp. 86-89.

4395. Eisner, Will. *How To Avoid Death and Taxes... And Live Forever.* New York: Poorhouse Press, 1975.

4396. Eisner, Will. "Interview." In *Comic Book Price Guide*, edited by R.M. Overstreet. Cleveland, Tennessee: Overstreet Publications, 1976.

4397. Eisner, Will. "Interview." *Comics Journal.* March 1984.

4398. Eisner, Will. "A Life Force." *Cartoonist PROfiles.* September 1990, pp. 22-26.

4399. Eisner, Will. *Will Eisner's Gallery of New Comics, 1974.* New York: School of Visual Arts, 1974. 32 pp.

4400. Eisner, Will. *Will Eisner's Gleeful Guide to Communicating with Plants To Help Them Grow.* New York: Harmony Books, 1974. 64 pp.

4401. Eisner, Will. *Will Eisner's Gleeful Guide to Living with Astrology.* New York: Harmony Books, 1974. 64 pp.

4402. Eisner, Will. *Will Eisner's Gleeful Guide to Occult Cookery.* New York: Harmony Books, 1974. 64 pp.

4403. Eisner, Will. *Will Eisner's Incredible Facts, Amazing Statistics, Monumental Trivia.* New York: Harmony Books, 1974. 64 pp.

4404. Feiffer, Jules. "Jules Feiffer Talks About The Spirit." *Panels.* Summer 1979, pp. 22-27.

4405. Fermín Pérez, Ramón. "Will Eisner: La Vuelta del Viejo Maestro." *El Wendigo.* No. 22, pp. 3-5.

4406. Flórez, Florentino. "Will Eisner: Dibujante de Historietas." *El Wendigo.* Autumn/Winter 1989-1990, pp. 4-6.

4407. Groensteen, Thierry and Thierry Smolderen. "Entretien avec Will Eisner." *Les Cahiers de la Bande Dessinée* (Grenoble). 61, 1985, pp. 86-89.

4408. Groth, Gary. "Will Eisner: A Second Opinion." *Comics Journal.* January 1988, pp. 3-7.

4409. Horn, Maurice. "An Introduction...." *The Spirit.* No. 1. Milwaukee, Wisconsin: Krupp Comics Works, 1973.

4410. Hurd, Jud. "Will Eisner." *Cartoonist PROfiles.* September 1990, pp. 18-21.

4411. "Kitchen Sink News: More Eisner." *Comics Journal.* September 1986, p. 27.

4412. Lecigne, Bruno and Jean-Pierre Tamine. "L'Oeil Était dans la Tombe." *Les Cahiers de la Bande Dessinée* (Grenoble). 61, 1985, pp. 92-94.

4413. Luciano, Dale. "Three from Eisner." *Comics Journal*. May 1984, pp. 41-46.

4414. Luciano, Dale. "Will Eisner." *Comics Journal*. July 1985, pp. 83-89+.

4415. Mercer, Marilyn. "The Only Real Middle-Class Crimefighter." *New York* (*Herald Tribune*). January 9, 1966, pp. 8-9, 55.

4416. O'Neill, Patrick D. "Winners and Losers: Harsh Memories from Will Eisner." *Comics Journal*. May 1979, pp. 52-53.

4417. Pohl, Peter. "A Contract with God?—Will Eisner und Sein Werk." *Comic Forum* (Vienna). 4:14 (1982), pp. 45-51.

4418. Pohl, Peter. "Interview mit Will Eisner." *Comic Forum* (Vienna). 4:14 (1982), pp. 52-53.

4419. Pomerleau, Luc. "The Spirit of Will Eisner." *La Nouvelle Barre du Jour*. February 1982, pp. 61-67.

4420. Potter, Gregory. "Eisner the Master Stylist." *Comics Journal*. July 1979, pp. 49-57.

4421. Rodríguez Arbesú, Faustino. "Una Obra Diferente: 'Question.'" *El Wendigo*. Autumn/Winter 1989-1990, pp. 10-11.

4422. Sanderson, Peter. "End Notes." *Comics Feature*. November 1980, pp. 80+.

4423. "Spirit by Will Eisner." *Cartoonist PROfiles*. September 1991, pp. 36-51.

4424. "Will Eisner Interview." *Graphixus*. June-July 1978, pp. 30-34.

4425. "Will Eisner Plans More New Material." *Comics Journal*. September 1981, p. 29.

4426. Yronwode, Catherine. *The Art of Will Eisner*. Princeton, Wisconsin: Kitchen Sink Press, 1982. 136 pp.

4427. Yronwode, Cat. "Spirit: Will Eisner Interview." *Comics Journal*. May 1979, pp. 34-41, 43-46, 48-49; July 1979, pp. 41-48.

4428. Yronwode, Cat. "Will Eisner: Reminiscences and Hortations." *Comics Journal*. May 1984, pp. 73-97.

4429. Yronwode, Catherine and Denis Kitchen. *La Bande Dessinée Selon Will Eisner*. Paris: Futuropolis, 1983.

Ellison, Harlan

4430. Askegren, Pierce. "A Mixed Bag Of Ellison." *Comics Journal*. August 1979, p. 29.

4431. Groth, Gary. "The Harlan Ellison Interview." *Comics Journal*. Winter [January?] 1980, pp. 68-107.

4432. Groth, Gary. "Harlan Ellison's Flamboyant Philistinism for the '80s." *Comics Journal*. January 1989, pp. 5-15.

4433. "Harlan Ellison Vs Mr. X." *Comics Journal*. August 1981, pp. 54-63.

4434. Scholz, Carter. "Exploring Ellison." *Comics Journal*. September 1976, pp. 28-29.

4435. Smith, Ken. "Opening Shots." *Comics Journal*. January 1989, pp. 3-4.

Englehart, Steve

4436. Joplin, Marlakan. "Behind the Point Man: An Interview with Steve Englehart." *Comics Feature*. December 1981, pp. 51-57.

4437. Kraft, David A. "Englehart." *Comics Interview*. August 1984, pp. 23-39.

4438. Lanyi, Ronald L. "Comic Books and Authority: An Interview with 'Stainless Steve' Englehart." *Journal of Popular Culture*. Fall 1984, pp. 139-148.

4439. Macchio, Ralph. "Steve Englehart in Transition." *Comics Journal*. Spring 1981, pp. 264-283.

4440. Sanderson, Peter. "An Interview with Steve Englehart." *Comics Feature*. September 1980, pp. 12-31, 34.

4441. Sanderson, Peter. "Steve Englehart." *Comics Journal*. July 1985, pp. 90-92.

4442. Via, Ed. "Steve Englehart: Triple-Threat Writer." *Comics Journal*. July 1979, pp. 25-27.

4443. "Writer: Steve Englehart." *Comics Interview*. No. 70, 1989, pp. 31-45.

Evanier, Mark

4444. Evanier, Mark. "Foreward." *Comics Feature*. November 1982, p. 29.

4445. Evanier, Mark. "Mighty Magnor." *Comics Buyer's Guide*. April 23, 1993, p. 30. (Mark Evanier, Sergio Aragones).

4446. Jones, Ken. "This Business of Comics: An Interview with Mark Evanier." *Comics Journal*. November 1986, pp. 60-72, 75-90, 93-98; Part 2, December 1986, pp. 72-92.

4447. O'Neill, Patrick D. "Hooray for Hollywood." *Comics Scene*. December 1990, pp. 50-52, 68.

4448. Schwartz, David. "Interview Me: Mark Evanier." *Amazing Heroes*. October 1986, pp. 24-34.

Evans, George

4449. Dellinges, Al, ed. *A Display of Art Work by George Evans*. San Francisco, California: Cartoonews, 1979. 27 pp.

4450. "George Evans: The Flying Swifts." *Squa Tront*. No. 3, 1969, pp. 60-72.

Everett, Bill

4451. Everett, Bill. "Auto-biography: A Letter to Jerry De Fuccio from Bill Everett Dated May 19, 1961." *Robin Snyder's History of the Comics*. July 1991, pp. 72-73.

4452. Everett, Bill. "Everett on Everett." *Alter Ego*. No. 11, 1978.

4453. Korkis, Jim. "Wild Bill Everett: That Man From Atlantis." *Amazing Heroes*. October 1986, pp. 37-41.

4454. Korkis, Jim. "Wild Bill: That Man from Atlantis." *Golden Age of Comics*. February 1984.

4455. Thomas, Roy. "Everett on Everett." *Alter Ego*. No. 11, 1978, pp. 10-32.

Fine, Lou

4456. Dellinges, Al, ed. *The Art of Lou Fine*. San Francisco, California: Cartoonews, 1979. 32 pp.

4457. Fine, Lou, *et al. The Ray and Black Condor*. Special Edition Series, No. 2. East Moline, Illinois: Special Edition Reprints, 1974. 316 pp.

Fleisher, Michael

4458. Catron, Michael. "The Blessed Life of Michael Fleisher: An Interview with the Man Who Stuffed Jonah Hex." *Comics Journal*. June 1980, pp. 42-71.

4459. Decker, Dwight R. "Chasing Fleisher." *Comics Journal*. December 1980, pp. 126-133.

Fox, Gardner

4460. Fox, Gardner. "Interview." *Amazing Heroes*. March 15, 1987.

4461. Mougin, Lou. "Gardner Fox." *Comics Interview*. March 1984, pp. 15-21.

4462. Phillips, Gene. "The Thinking Man's Hero: The Works of Gardner Fox." *Comics Feature*. November 1982, pp. 85-87.

4463. Thomas, Roy. "Gardner F. Fox (1911-1986): A Personal Remembrance." *Comics Journal*. February 1987, p. 34.

Fox, Gill

4464. Dellinges, Al, ed. *The Art of Gill Fox*. San Francisco, California: Cartoonews, 1979. 32 pp.

4465. "Gill Fox." *Comics: The Golden Age*. May 1984.

4466. "Gill Fox Tells About a Different Style Approach to Cartoon Success." *Cartoonist PROfiles*. No. 6, 1970, pp. 74-80.

Frazetta, Frank

4467. Barrett, Bob. "The Frazetta Collector." *Squa Tront*. No. 3, 1969, pp. 25-37.

4468. Frazetta, Frank. *The Comic Strip Frazetta*. New York: Pure Imagination, 1980. 56 pp.

4469. Frazetta, Frank. *The Fantastic Art of Frank Frazetta*. New York: Scribner's, 1975. Unpaginated.

4470. Frazetta, Frank. *The Frazetta Treasury*. 1975. 48 pp.

4471. Frazetta, Frank. *Thunda, King of the Congo*. Adel, Iowa: R. Cochran, 1973. 32 pp.

4472. Frazetta, Frank. *Untamed Love*. Adel, Iowa: R. Cochran, 1973. 32 pp.

4473. Frazetta, Frank. *White Indian*. New York: Pure Imagination, 1981. 52 pp.

4474. Frazetta, Frank and Peter De Paolo. *Johnny Comet*. New York: Pure Imagination, 1975. 56 pp.

4475. "Frank Frazetta." *Comics Interview*. No. 42, 1987, pp. 24-64.

4476. Murray, Doug. "Interview! Frank Frazetta." *Infinity Two*. No. 2 (n.d.), pp. 24-30.

4477. Pohl, Peter. "Frank Frazetta." *Comic Forum* (Vienna). 5:18 (1983), pp. 45-48.

4478. Pohl, Peter. "Interview mit Frank und Ellie Frazetta. Aufgenommen am 11. September 1975 in Pennsylvania." *Comic Forum*. Vienna, 5:18 (1983), pp. 50-51.

4479. Van Hise, James. "Frank Frazetti." *Comics Scene*. May 1983, pp. 25-28.

Friedrich, Mike

4480. Borax, Mark. "Agents: Mike Friedrich and Sharon Cho." *Comics Interview*. No. 117, 1993, pp. 40-43, 45-46, 48-49, 51.

4481. Borax, Mark. "Mike Friedrich." *Comics Interview*. No. 116, 1992, pp. 44-49, 51, 53-56.

4482. Thompson, Kim. "Reaching for the Stars with Mike Friedrich." *Comics Journal*. April 1982, pp. 79-92.

4483. Wochner, Lee. "Mike Friedrich." *Comics Journal*. July 1985, pp. 93-96.

Gaiman, Neil

4484. Biggers, Cliff. "The Neil Gaiman-Jill Thompson Interview." *Comic Shop News*. September 2, 1992, pp. 4-7.

4485. Evans, Liz. "Dream On." *Speakeasy*. October 1990, pp. 37-39, 41.

4486. Herding, Kemberly. "Neil Gaiman." *Comics Interview*. No. 116, 1992, pp. 4-16, 19, 21-23.

4487. Herding, Ken. "Neil Gaiman on Chicago." *Comics Buyer's Guide*. June 11, 1993, p. 59.

4488. "Interview: Neil Gaiman." *Fantazia*. No. 4, 1990, pp. 15-18.

4489. Muñoz, Pedro Augosto. "Los Libros de la Magia: Neil Gaiman, el Último Mago." *El Wendigo*. No. 59, 1993, pp. 8-9.

4490. Nicholls, Stan. "Visual Cases." *Comics Scene*. May 1992, pp. 18-22, 52.

4491. Thompson, Kim. "Neil Gaiman." *Comics Journal*. January 1993, pp. 64-69, 71-80, 83.

Gaines, William M.

4492. Decker, Dwight R. and Gary Groth. "William Gaines: An Interview with the Man Behind EC." *Comics Journal*. May 1983, pp. 53-85.

4493. "Gaines Interview." *Qua Bront*. No. 1, 1985, pp. 4-8.

4494. Groth, Gary. "Will Gaines." *Comics Journal*. July 1985, pp. 103+.

4495. Jacobs, Frank. *The Mad World of William M. Gaines*. Secaucus, New Jersey: Lyle Stuart, 1972. 271 pp.

4496. Weber, John. "SAD." *WittyWorld*. Summer/Autumn 1992, p. 7.

4497. "William Gaines Interview." *Comics Scene*. No. 21, 1991.

Gerber, Steve

4498. Bethke, Marilyn. "An Introduction to Steve Gerber." *Comics Journal*. August 1978, pp. 26-27.

4499. Bethke, Marilyn. "The Prodigal Iconoclast Returns to Comics: Gerber Speaks Again." *Comics Journal*. June 1980, pp. 85-93.

4500. Cover, Arthur B. "Steve Gerber." *Comics Journal*. July 1985, pp. 97-102+.

4501. Dawson, Jim. "Caught in the Steve Gerber Trap." *Comics Journal*. August 1978, pp. 19-20.

4502. Gerber, Steve and Gene Colan. "Howard the Duck." *Comics Journal*. December 1977, pp. 68-74.

4503. Groth, Gary. "An Interview with Steve Gerber." *Comics Journal*. August 1978, pp. 28-44.

4504. Kraft, David A. "The Foom Interview: Steve Gerber." *Foom*. No. 15, 1976, pp. 7-16.

4505. Luciano, Dale. "An Unapologetic and Eulogistic Critical Survey of Steve Gerber's Howard the Duck." *Comics Journal*. September 1981, pp. 152-162.

4506. Oberkrieser, Stacy. "Stever Gerber Discusses His Ultraverse Title: Exiles." *Comics Buyer's Guide*. July 30, 1993, pp. 26-27, 30, 36.

4507. Sanderson, Peter. "Steve Gerber." *Comics Feature*. September-October 1981, pp. 114-127.

4508. "Steve Gerber." *Amazing Heroes*. July 1989.

4509. "Steve Gerber." *Comics Interview*. February 1983, pp. 16-30.

4510. "Steve Gerber." *Comics Interview*. No. 38, 1986, pp. 6-19.

4511. "Steve Gerber Interview." *Comics Scene*. No. 15, 1990.

4512. Yronwode, Cat. "The Gerber Story." *Comics Journal*. October 1978, pp. 38-39.

4513. Zimmerman, Dwight J. "Steve Gerber." *Comics Interview*. No. 37, 1986, pp. 6-17.

Gibbons, Dave

4514. "Dave Gibbons." *Comics Interview*. October 1984, pp. 50-66.

4515. "Dave Gibbons Interview." *Comics Scene*. No. 15, 1990.

4516. Flórez, Florentino and Faustino Rodríguez Arbesú. "Dave Gibbons: El Dibujo al Servicio de Una Gran Obra." *El Wendigo.* No. 42, 1988, pp. 10-11.

4517. Rodríguez, Sofía C. "Dave Gibbons: A la Popularidad por Una Obra." *El Wendigo.* Autumn/Winter 1989-1990, pp. 32-33.

4518. Stewart, Bhob. "Dave Gibbons: Pebbles in a Landscape." *Comics Journal.* July 1987, pp. 97-103.

Giffen, Keith

4519. Burbey, Mark. "The Trouble with Keith Giffen." *Comics Journal.* February 1986, pp. 9-14.

4520. "Keith Giffen." *Comics Interview.* February 1985, pp. 29-35.

4521. "Keith Giffen and Andy Helfer." *Comics Interview.* No. 66, 1989, pp. 51-60.

4522. "The Omega Men: Roger Slifer and Keith Giffen." *Comics Interview.* February 1983, pp. 6-15.

4523. Pérez, Ramón F. "Keith Giffen: 'El Efecto Foto-matón.'" *El Wendigo.* Verano 1990, pp. 11-13.

4524. Sodaro, Bob. "Keith Giffen." *Comics Interview.* No. 99, 1991, pp. 26-33.

Gilbert, Michael T.

4525. Gilbert, Michael T. *Strange Brew.* Kitchener, Ontario: Aardvark-Vanaheim, 1982. 64 pp.

4526. "Michael Gilbert." *Comics Interview.* No. 29, 1985, pp. 16-35.

4527. Stewart, Bhob. "An Interview with Michael T. Gilbert." *Comics Journal.* September 1983, pp. 56-78.

Giordano, Dick

4528. "Creating the Comics: Dick Giordano on Pencilling." *Comics Scene.* March 1982, pp. 52-54.

4529. "Dick Giordano." *Comics Interview.* June 1983, 37-44.

4530. "Dick Giordano, Comic Book Editor." *Cartoonist PROfiles*. No. 6, 1970, pp. 43-50.

4531. Durrwachter, Jerry. "For Fun or Fortune: A Discussion with Dick Giordano." *Whizzard*. February 1981, pp. 12-16.

4532. "Guest Spot: A Few Words from Dick Giordano." *Comics Scene*. September 1983, pp. 30-31.

4533. Groth, Gary. "Dick Giordano." *Comics Journal*. January 1988, pp. 70-75, 78-86.

4534. Groth, Gary. "An Interview with Dick Giordano." *Comics Journal*. March 1981, pp. 44-79.

4535. MacDonald, Heidi D. "Giordano." *Comics Journal*. July 1985, pp. 104-107.

4536. Peel, John. "DC's 50th Anniversary: Dick Giordano." *Comics Feature*. November-December 1984, pp. 19-26, 53-55.

Gold, Mike

4537. Landau, Nick. "Interview: Mike Gold." *Comic Reader*. December 1977, pp. 8-13; January 1978, pp. 8-13.

4538. "Mike Gold." *Comics Interview*. No. 67, 1989, pp. 31-43; No. 68, 1989, pp. 50-61.

Goodwin, Archie

4539. "Archie Goodwin." *Comics Interview*. No. 36, 1986, pp. 24-39.

4540. "EPIC: One Year Later. An Interview with Archie Goodwin." *Comics Feature*. February 1981, pp. 61-65.

4541. MacDonald, Heidi D. "Goodwin." *Comics Journal*. July 1985, pp. 108-110.

4542. Ringgenberg, Steve. "Archie Goodwin." *Comics Journal*. December 1982, pp. 61-80.

4543. Skidmore, Martin. "Archie Goodwin." *FA*. October 1989, pp. 46-52.

4544. Stern, Roger. "Infoomation Interviews Archie Goodwin." *Foom*. June 1976, pp. 28-29.

Gould, Chester

4545. Gould, Chester. *Dick Tracy*. Long Beach, California: T. Raiola, 1982. 72 pp.; 1982. 96 pp.; 1983. 48 pp. (*Feature Book*, No. 6, No. 4, No. 3, 1937).

4546. Gould, Chester. *Dick Tracy and Scottie of Scotland Yard*. Long Beach, California: T. Raiola, 1983. 48 pp.

4547. Gould, Chester. *Dick Tracy and the Famon Boys*. Long Beach, California: T. Raiola, 1982. 72 pp.

4548. Gould, Chester. *Dick Tracy and the Kidnapped Princess*. Long Beach, California: T. Raiola, 1983. 48 pp.

4549. Gould, Chester. *Dick Tracy Fools the Mad Doc Hump*. Long Beach, California: T. Raiola, 1982. 48 pp.

4550. Gould, Chester. *Dick Tracy Meets the Blank*. Long Beach, California: T. Raiola, 1983. 72 pp.

4551. Gould, Chester. *Dick Tracy, the Racket Buster*. Long Beach, California: T. Raiola, 1982. 72 pp.

Grant, Alan

4552. "Alan Grant Interview 2." *Comics Scene*. No. 17, 1991.

4553. Collins, Andrew. "Heroes and Villains: Talking to Alan Grant." *Speakeasy*. May 1990, pp. 36-37, 39.

4554. Nutman, Philip. "One Man's Psychosis." *Comics Scene*. December 1990, pp. 20-24.

4555. Sanderson, Peter. "Alan Grant." *Comics Interview*. No. 99, 1991, pp. 10-17.

Green, Justin

4556. Burbey, Mark. "My Dinner with Justin Green." *Comics Journal*. January 1986, p. 48.

4557. Burbey, Mark. "On Comics and Catholics: The Justin Green Interview." *Comics Journal*. January 1986, pp. 37-49.

4558. "Sketchbook: Justin Green." *Comics Journal*. August 1992, pp. 121-125.

Grell, Mike

4559. Greenberger, Robert. "From Skataris to Sable: A Chat with Storyteller Mike Grell." *Comics Scene*. May 1983, pp. 49-50, 52-53, 65.

4560. "The Name's Grell... Mike Grell." *Penstuff*. June 1989, pp. 4-5.

4561. "Writer/Artist: Mike Grell." *Comics Interview*. No. 69, 1989, pp. 22-44.

Griffith, Bill

4562. "Bill Griffith." *Comics Interview*. February 1984, pp. 29-37.

4563. Griffith, Bill and Jay Kinney, eds. *The Young Lust Reader*. San Francisco, California: And/Or Press, 1974. 127 pp.

4564. Groth, Gary. "Politics, Pinheads and Post-Modernism: Bill Griffith." *Comics Journal*. March 1993, pp. 50-61, 63-74, 76-84, 86-92, 94-98.

4565. Strzyz, Klaus. "Ein Interview mit Bill Griffith." *Comixene* (Hanover). 8:42 (1981), pp. 46-50.

4566. Walker, Brad. "A Talk with Bill Griffith, the Man Behind Zippy." *Comics Feature*. November 1980, pp. 54-61.

Hernandez Brothers

4567. Fiore, R. "Pleased To Meet You. Love and Rockets. The Hernandez Bros. Interview." *Comics Journal*. January 1989, pp. 60-113.

4568. Green, Stuart. "To Live and Die in L.A." *Speakeasy*. December-January 1990-1991, pp. 45-47.

4569. Hernandez, Gilbert. *Heartbreak Soup*. London: Titan Books, 1987. 127 pp.

4570. Hernandez, Jaime. *Love and Rockets*. London: Titan Books, 1987. 127 pp.

4571. Hernandez, Jaime, Gilbert Hernandez, and Mario Hernandez. *Love and Rockets*. Agoura, California: Fantagraphics Books, 1985. 145 pp.

4572. "'I'm Drawing What I Want To Draw.'" *Comics Journal*. May 1992, pp. 60-65. (Jaime Hernandez).

Hoberg, Rick

4573. "Rick Hoberg." *Comics Interview*. March 1985, pp. 37-53.

4574. "Rick Hoberg—Comic Book Artist." *Penstuff*. May 1990, pp. 3, 7.

Howard, Robert E.

4575. Killian, Peter. "Robert E. Howard." *Comic Forum* (Vienna). 4:15 (1982), pp. 17-18.

4576. Kirkland, Skip. "Robert E. Howard: The Man Who Created Conan!" *Foom*. June 1976, pp. 15-17.

Howarth, Matt

4577. McEnroe, Richard S. "Bad Boys, Bright Girls, and Bug-Eyes Monsters." *Amazing Heroes*. July 1988, pp. 20-21.

4578. Vick, Edd. "Post Apocalypse: The Matt Howarth Interview." *Amazing Heroes*. July 1988, pp. 23-34.

Infantino, Carmine

4579. Dionnet, J.P. "Carmine Infantino." *Phénix*. No. 15, 1970.

4580. Hanerfeld, Mark. "Carmine Infantino: A Short Biography." In *The Confident Collector*, edited by Jerry Weist, pp. 54-63. New York: Avon, 1992.

4581. Rozarkis, Bob and Jack C. Harris. "The Incredible Infantino." *Amazing World of DC Comics*. September 1975.

Ingels, Graham

4582. "Graham Ingels, 1915-1991." *Comics Journal*. June 1991, p. 12.

4583. Hill, Roger. "EC Horror Artist Graham Ingels Dies." *Comics Buyer's Guide*. May 24, 1991, pp. 1, 3, 42, 44.

4584. Hill, Roger. "The Last Ingels Folio." *Qua Brot*. No. 1, 1985, pp. 11-14.

4585. "The 'Pulpy' Roots of Graham Ingels." *Comics Journal*. July 1991, pp. 18-19.

Jackson, Jack (Jaxon)

4586. Förster, Gerhard. "Jack Jaxon und der Wahre Wilde Westen" *Comic Forum* (Vienna). 2:5 (1980), pp. 35-40.

4587. Groth, Gary. "Jack Jackson on His Work in the Underground and His New Book, *Los Tejanos*." *Comics Journal*. September 1982, pp. 75-84.

4588. Groth, Gary. "Jaxon." *Comics Journal*. July 1985, pp. 111-114.

4589. Jackson, Jack. *Comanche Moon*. San Francisco, California: Rip Off Press and Last Gasp Eco-Funnies, 1979. 128 pp.

4590. Jackson, Jack. "Learning Texas History: The Painless Way." *Comics Journal*. January 1987, pp. 97-100.

4591. Phillips, Gene. "Tejanos Revisited." *Comics Journal*. June 1985, p. 51.

4592. Sherman, Bill. "Tejano Cartoonist: An Interview with Jack Jackson." *Comics Interview*. Winter [November?] 1981, pp. 100-111.

4593. Sweeney, Bruce. "Jaxon." *Comics Interview*. March 1984, pp. 40-49.

Johnson, Russ

4594. Luciano, Dale. "Fifty Years with Russ Johnson." *Comics Journal*. August 1983, pp. 83-94.

4595. von Cannon, K. "Meet Cartoonist Russ Johnson." *The Funnie's Paper*. July 1985, pp. 4-5.

Jones, Gerard

4596. "Is Gerard Jones Overworked?" *Comics Scene*. August 1990, pp. 13-18.

4597. Stanley, Kelli. "Gerard Jones." *Comics Buyer's Guide*. May 24, 1991, pp. 66, 68, 70, 72, 74, 76.

Jones, Jeff

4598. Denkena, Kurt S. "The Studio. 4:Jeff Jones." *Comixene* (Hanover). 7:31 (1980), pp. 52-54.

4599. Groensteen, Thierry. "Entretien avec Jeff Jones." *Les Cahiers de la Bande Dessinée* (Grenoble). 66, 1985, pp. 51-54.

4600. Groensteen, Thierry. "Une Simplicité Énigmatique." *Les Cahiers de la Bande Dessinée* (Grenoble). 66, 1985, pp. 54-56.

Jones, Kelley

4601. "Kelley Jones." *Comics Interview*. March 1985, pp. 27-35.

4602. Lucas, Mike. "Kelley Jones." *Comics Interview*. No. 117, 1993, pp. 4-15.

Jurgens, Dan

4603. Bittner, Drew. "Playing in a New League." *Comics Scene*. May 1992, pp. 25-28, 52. (Also Gerard Jones).

4604. "Dan Jurgens." *Comics Interview*. October 1984, pp. 31-49.

Kaluta, Michael

4605. "Mike Kaluta Interviewed." *Comics Feature*. No. 25, 1983, pp. 55-61.

4606. Strzyz, Klaus. "The Studio. 1:Michael Kaluta." *Comixene* (Hanover). 7:28 (1980), pp. 22-25.

4607. Trumbo, Phil. "Lurking in the Hearts of Men: The Michael Kaluta Interview." *Comics Journal*. November 1985, pp. 50-79.

Kane, Bob

4608. "Artist: Bob Kane." *Comics Interview*. No. 70, 1989, pp. 46-59.

4609. "Bob Kane Interview." *Comics Scene*. No. 27, 1992.

4610. Kane, Bob with Tom Andrae. *Batman and Me: An Autobiography*. Forestville, California: Eclipse Books, 1989. 156 pp.

4611. Kane, Bob. *Famous First Edition, C-28*. New York: National Periodical Publications Inc., 1974.

4612. Kane, Bob. *Famous First Edition, F-5*. New York: National Periodical Publications Inc., 1975.

Kane, Gil

4613. "Gil Kane." *Cartoonist PROfiles*. March 1978, pp. 32-35.

4614. "Gil Kane." *Comics Journal*. July 1981; July 1984. (Interviews).

4615. "Gil Kane on the Evolution of Comics Artists and the State of the Art." *Comics Journal*. September 1982, pp. 52-61.

4616. Groth, Gary. "An Interview with Gil Kane." *Comics Journal*. February 1977, pp. 34-46.

4617. Harvey, R.C. "Gil Kane, Past and Present." *Comics Journal*. December 1982, pp. 98-109.

4618. Kane, Gil. *Blackmark*. New York: Bantam Books, 1971.

4619. Kane, Gil. "Eyes Fixed on Comics." *Comics Journal*. January 1988, p. 115.

Kanigher, Robert

4620. Kanigher, Robert. "Detour!... Danger Trail." *Robin Snyder's History of Comics*. April 1990.

4621. Morrissey, Richard. "The Golden Age Gladiator: Robert Kanigher." *Comics Journal*. October 1983, pp. 51-85.

4622. Snyder, Robin. "The Golden Gladiator: The Conclusion of Our Interview with Robert Kanigher." *Comics Journal*. November 1983, pp. 71-100.

Katz, Jack

4623. Evanier, Mark. "About Jack Katz." *Baycon III Program Book*. 1977, pp. 19-20.

4624. Katz, Jack. "Solar Sailing: Poetry with Art." *Comics Scene*. January 1981, p. 45.

4625. Sherman, Bill. "The Kingdom and the Power of Jack Katz." *Comics Journal*. February 1977, pp. 51-52, 54-55.

4626. Zimmerman, Howard. "Jack Katz and the First Kingdom." *Comics Scene*. July 1982, pp. 37-40, 64.

Kieth, Sam

4627. Lucas, Mark. "Sam Kieth." *Comics Interview*. No. 117, 1993, pp. 32-38.

4628. "Sam Kieth Interview." *Comics Scene*. No. 23, 1991 or 1992.

Kirby, Jack

4629. Borax, Mark. "Jack Kirby." *Comics Interview*. No. 41, 1986, pp. 38-55.

4630. Boyd, Alex. "The Once and Future 'King!'" *Foom*. No. 11, 1975, pp. 10-13.

4631. Buckler, Rich and Joe Sinnott. "Kirby Speaks." *Foom*. No. 11, 1975, pp. 4-7.

4632. Comtois, Pierre. "The Deification of Jack Kirby." *Comics Journal*. May 1981, pp. 33-34.

4633. Decker, Dwight R. "Kirby and the Kids." *Baycon III Program Book*. 1977, pp. 3-5.

4634. Groth, Gary. "Jack Kirby." *Comics Journal*. February 1990, pp. 57-99.

4635. Hanke, Brock J. "Jack Kirby's Fourth World: A Retrospective." *Comics Journal*. February 1990, pp. 109-112.

4636. Heintjes, Tom. "The Negotiators." *Comics Journal*. February 1986, pp. 53-59.

4637. Isabella, Tony. "Tony's Tips!" *Comics Buyer's Guide*. December 4, 1992, p. 40.

4638. "Jack Kirby." *Comics Feature*. May 1986.

4639. Jacobs, Will and Gerard Jones. "Pure Kirby." *Comics Journal*. August 1986, pp. 27-30.

4640. Katschke, Edward and George Leedom. "Jack's a Hack." *Comics Journal*. February 1991, pp. 31-33.

4641. Kirby, Jack. *Kirby Unleashed.* Newbury Park, California: Communicators Unlimited, 1971. 40 pp.

4642. Kirby, Jack. Interview. *Golden Age of Comics.* November 1983.

4643. Kirby, Jack. "Shop Talk: Jack Kirby." *Will Eisner's Spirit Magazine No. 39.* February 1982.

4644. "Kirby—An Historical Perspective." *Comics Scene.* March 1982, p. 29.

4645. "Kirby Awards End in Controversy." *Comics Journal.* June 1988, pp. 19-20.

4646. Lanyi, Ronald L. "Idea and Motive in Jack 'King' Kirby's Comic Books: A Conversation." *Journal of Popular Culture.* Fall 1983, pp. 22-30.

4647. Mougin, Lou. "New Gods for Old: A Hero History of Jack Kirby's Fourth World Part I." *Amazing Heroes.* August 1986, pp. 36-49.

4648. Potter, Greg. "The Gods and Heroes of Jack Kirby." *Comics Journal.* October 1980, pp. 84-93.

4649. Theakston, Greg. "That Old Jack Magic." *Amazing Heroes.* August 1, 1986, pp. 70-77.

4650. Thompson, Kim H. "From Dinosaurs to Robots: Kirby Strikes Out Again." *Comics Journal.* April 1977, pp. 52-53.

4651. Zimmerman, Howard. "Kirby Takes on the Comics." *Comics Scene.* March 1982, pp. 25-28.

Krenkel, Roy

4652. Barish, K.G. "RGK—Portfolio." *Heroic Fantasy.* February 1984, pp. 18-25.

4653. Benson, John. "Krenkel and Creepy." *Squa Tront.* No. 7, 1977, pp. 3-14.

4654. "Memorial: Roy G. Krenkel, 1918-1983." *Heroic Fantasy.* February 1984, p. 17.

4655. "Roy G. Krenkel." *Comics Interview.* June 1983, pp. 22-31.

4656. "Roy Krenkel, A Portfolio." *Infinity Two.* No. 2 (n.d.), pp. 31-33.

4657. "Roy Krenkel, EC Artist/Illustrator, Dead at 64." *Comics Journal.* March 1983, pp. 15-16.

4658. Stewart, Bhob. "RGK—A Few Less People at the Table." *Qua Brot.* No. 1, 1985, pp. 18-26.

Krigstein, Bernard

4659. "Bernard Krigstein Død, 71 År." *Serieskaberen.* June 1990, p. 12.

4660. Potter, Greg. "The EC Progressives: Part Two: Bernard Krigstein." *Comics Journal.* April 1982, pp. 107-112.

4661. Spiegelman, Art. "Krigstein: An Eulogy." *Comics Journal.* February 1990, p. 13.

4662. Stewart, Bhob. "B. Krigstein, an Evaluation." *Squa Tront.* No. 6, 1975, pp. 53-55.

4663. Stewart, Bhob. "Krigstein Revisited." *Comics Journal.* August 1982, pp. 24-25.

4664. Stewart, Bhob and John Benson. "An Interview with Bernard Krigstein." *Squa Tront.* No. 6, 1975, pp. 3-40.

Kubert, Joe

4665. Hambrecht, Robert. "Kubert's Command." *Comics Scene.* February 1990, pp. 13-16, 24.

4666. "Joe Kubert." *Cartoonist PROfiles.* March 1986, pp. 48-50.

4667. Kubert, Joe. *A Display of Art Work by Joe Kubert.* The Golden Age Art of Joe Kubert, Book 2. San Francisco, California: A. Dellinges and B. Sheridan, 1979. 42 pp.

4668. Kubert, Joe. *Kubert Goes to War.* San Francisco, California: A. Dellinges, 1979. 32 pp.

4669. Kubert, Joe. "Shop Talk: Joe Kubert." *Will Eisner's Spirit Magazine No. 40.* April 1983.

4670. Pérez, Ramón F. "Joe Kubert: Un Maestro Desconocido." *El Wendigo.* September-October 1984, pp. 19-21.

4671. Salicrup, Jim. "Kubert." *Comics Interview.* March 1984, pp. 51-57, 60-69.

Kurtzman, Harvey

4672. Benson, John. "A Conversation with Harvey Kurtzman and Bill Elder," *Squa Tront*. No. 9, 1983, pp. 66-79.

4673. Benson, John. "A Conversation with Harvey Kurtzman and Bill Gaines." *Squa Tront*. No. 9, 1983, pp. 82-92.

4674. Dutrey, Jacques. "Leapin' Lizards! Playboy's Comics Strip Tease." *Comics Journal*. October 1992, pp. 77-80.

4675. *Frontline Combat*. The Complete EC Library. 3 Vols. West Plains, Missouri: R. Cochran, 1982.

4676. Groth, Gary. "Goodbye, Harvey." *Comics Journal*. March 1993, p. 3.

4677. "Harvey Kurtzman." *Comics Journal*. October 1992, pp. 92-95.

4678. "Harvey Kurtzman, Genius." In *San Diego Comic Convention 1993*, pp. 120-125. San Diego, California: 1993.

4679. "Harvey Kurtzman: Rubble!" *Comics Journal*. October 1992, pp. 96-102.

4680. Hefner, Hugh M. "Little Annie Fanny." (Preface). *Playboy Press*. Chicago, Illinois: AMH Publication Company, 1966.

4681. Hewetson, Alan. "An Interview with Harvey Kurtzman." *Fandom Annual*. 1967, p. 53.

4682. "Hey Look! Kurtzman Tributes." *Comics Journal*. October 1992, pp. 70-74.

4683. James, J.P.C. "H. Kurtzman." *Comics Journal*. October 1992, pp. 47-55.

4684. Johnson, Kim H. and Randy and Jean-Marc Lofficier. "Harvey Kurtzman." *Comics Scene*. December 1990, pp. 45-48, 68.

4685. Kitchen, Denis. "Harvey Kurtzman, Inspiration and Mentor." *Comics Buyer's Guide*. April 2, 1993, p. 36.

4686. Kurtzman, Harvey. *Fast-Acting Help!* Greenwich, Connecticut: Gold Medal, 1961.

4687. Kurtzman, Harvey. *Hey Look! Cartoons by MAD Creator, Harvey Kurtzman*. Princeton, Wisconsin: Kitchen Sink Press, 1992. 192 pp.

4688. Kurtzman, Harvey. "H. Kurtzman." *Cartoonist PROfiles*. June 1975, pp. 46-49.

4689. Kurtzman, Harvey, ed. *The Humbug Digest*. New York: Ballantine Books, 1957. 157 pp.

4690. Kurtzman, Harvey. *Kurtzman Komix*. Princeton, Wisconsin: Kitchen Sink Enterprises, 1976.

4691. Kurtzman, Harvey, with Howard Zimmerman. *My Life As a Cartoonist*. New York: Minstrel Books, 1988. 108 pp.

4692. Kurtzman, Harvey. "Takin' the Lid Off the Id." *Esquire*. June 1971, pp. 128-136.

4693. Kurtzman, Harvey and Will Elder. *Goodman Beaver*. Princeton, Wisconsin: Kitchen Sink Press, 1984. 159 pp.

4694. Kurtzman, Harvey and Will Elder. *Playboy's Little Annie Fanny*. 2 Vols. Chicago, Illinois: Playboy Press, 1966, 1972. 159 pp.

4695. "Kurtzman." *Comics Journal*. July 1984, pp. 103-108.

4696. "Kurtzman Ade!" *Comic Info*. May-June 1993, pp. 14, 16.

4697. "Kurtzman, Kane, and a Career in Comics." *Comics Journal*. March 1993, pp. 13-17.

4698. Latona, Robert. "Interview with Harvey Kurtzman." *Vanguard*. No. 1, 1966, pp. 25-30.

4699. Neal, Jim and Don Thompson. "Harvey Kurtzman Dies, Creator of 'Mad.'" *Comics Buyer's Guide*. March 19, 1993, p. 6.

4700. O'Brien, Geoffrey. "Stark Raving 'Mad'—Harvey Kurtzman's Last Laugh." *Voice*. Literary Supplement, October 1989, pp. 10-12.

4701. Ogg, Doug. "Harvey Kurtzman." *Comics Journal*. March 1993, pp. 4-17.

4702. Pascale, Michael. "Good Lord! (Choke)." *Comics Journal*. April 1993, pp. 3-4.

4703. Pinkwater, Daniel. "On First Looking into Kurtzman's Mad." *First Whistle*. Reading, Massachusetts: Addison-Wesley, 1989.

4704. Potter, Greg. "The EC Progressives, Part One: Harvey Kurtzman." *Comics Journal*. October 1981, pp. 101-107.

4705. Preiss, Byron. "Harvey Kurtzman Today." *Comics Journal*. October 1992, pp. 57-61.

4706. Preiss, Byron, *et al.* "Harvey Kurtzman: the Modest Genius." *Comics Buyer's Guide*. April 2, 1993, pp. 30-31, 36.

4707. Schröder, Ulrich. "Interview mit Harvey Kurtzman." *Comic Forum* (Vienna). 24, 1984, pp. 27-33.

4708. Thompson, Don and Maggie. "Editorial: Harvey Kurtzman." *Comics Buyer's Guide*. March 19, 1993, p. 4.

4709. Thompson, Kim and Gary Groth. "An Interview with the Man Who Brought Truth to the Comics, Harvey Kurtzman." *Comics Journal*. October 1981, pp. 68-107.

4710. Witek, Joseph. "H. Kurtzman. More Thrilling Than Fiction: Kurtzman, Kirby, and History." *Comics Journal*. October 1992, pp. 83-90.

4711. Wochner, Lee. "Harvey Kurtzman." *Comics Journal*. July 1985, pp. 115-117.

Lee, Jim

4712. Kanalz, Hank. "Mutant Artist." *Comics Scene*. October 1991, pp. 9-12.

4713. "Jim Lee." *Comics Interview*. No. 63, 1988, pp. 30-43.

Lee, Stan

4714. Ayers, Dick. "Inker's View." *Comics Journal*. December 1987, pp. 38-39.

4715. Bierbaum, Tom. "Stan Lee's Imperfect Heroes Lifted Marvel to Top of Heap." *Variety*. September 17, 1986, pp. 81, 88.

4716. Clark, John. "Lunch with Stan Lee." *Fantazia*. No. 4, 1992, pp. 30-31.

4717. Dawson, Jim. "Hello, Culture Lovers! Stan the Man Raps with Marvel Maniacs at James Madison University." *Comics Journal*. October 1978, pp. 45-55.

4718. Edelman, Scott. "Stan Lee Was My Co-Pilot." *Comics Journal*. June 1985, pp. 93-94.

4719. Green, Robin. "Face Front: Clap Your Hands! You're on the Winning Team." *Rolling Stone*. September 16, 1971, p. 34+.

4720. "Interview with Stan Lee." *IT*. September 24, 1970.

4721. Khoo, Eric. "Here's Stan the Man... 'Nuff Said." *Big O*. January 1991, pp. 39-42.

4722. Kraft, David A. "Stan Lee." *Foom*. March 1977, pp. 7-17.

4723. Lee, Stan. *The Amazing Spider-Man*. New York: Simon and Schuster, 1979.

4724. Lee, Stan. *Bring on the Bad Guys*. New York: Simon and Schuster, 1976. 253 pp.

4725. Lee, Stan. *Captain America*. New York: Simon and Schuster, 1979. 127 pp.

4726. Lee, Stan. *Dr. Strange*. New York: Simon and Schuster, 1979. 127 pp.

4727. Lee, Stan. *The Fantastic Four*. New York: Simon and Schuster, 1979, 127 pp.

4728. Lee, Stan. *The Incredible Hulk*. New York: Simon and Schuster, 1978.

4729. Lee, Stan. *The Invincible Iron Man*. New York: Marvel Comics, 1984.

4730. Lee, Stan. *Marvel's Greatest Superhero Battles*. New York: Simon and Schuster, 1978. 253 pp.

4731. Lee, Stan. "Stan Lee Sounds Off: How Do I Get My Ideas." *Comics Feature*. January 1986, pp. 8-10.

4732. Lee, Stan. "Twenty-Five Years? I Don't Believe It!" *The Comic Book Price Guide*. No. 16, 1986, pp. A-82-A-84.

4733. Lee, Stan, ed. *The Best of Spidey Super Stories*. New York: Simon and Schuster, 1978. 126 pp.

4734. Lee, Stan, ed. *Mighty Marvel Team-Up Thrillers*. New York: Marvel Comics Group, 1983. 159 pp.

4735. Lee, Stan, ed. *The Power of Iron Man*. New York: Marvel Comics Group, 1984. 162 pp.

4736. Lee, Stan, ed. *The Uncanny X-Men*. New York: Marvel Comics Group, 1984. 185 pp.

4737. Menéndez, Germán and Norman Fernández. "Bienvenido Mr. Lee." *El Wendigo*. No. 51, 1991, pp. 8-9.

4738. Roth, A. "Stan Lee Comic-Book Hero." *American Film*. October 1989, p. 12.

4739. "Stan Lee." *Comics Feature*. May 1986.

4740. "Stan Lee." *Comics Interview*. July 1983.

4741. "Stan Lee." *Comics Interview*. No. 64, 1988, pp. 5-23.

4742. "Stan Lee and 'Marvel Comics.'" *Cartoonist PROfiles*. Fall 1969, pp. 48-52.

4743. White, Ted. "A Conversation with the Man Behind Marvel Comics: Stan Lee." *Castle of Frankenstein*. No. 12, 1968, pp. 8-10, 60.

Leialoha, Steve

4744. Gafford, Carl. "Steve Leialoha: Warlocks to Warriors." *Baycon III Program Book*. 1977, pp. 29-30.

4745. Péréz, Ramón F. "Steve Leialoha: Uno de la Bounty." Program of Centro Cultural Campoamor, Oviedo, Spain. December 1988, pp. 9-10.

4746. "Steve Leialoha." *Comics Interview*. April 1984, pp. 28-41.

Levitz, Paul

4747. "Eleven Critics Respond to Paul Levitz's Call for Higher Criticism." *Comics Journal*. November 1979, pp. 32-37.

4748. "Paul Levitz." *Comics Interview*. October 1984, pp. 19-29.

4749. Zilber, Jay and Gary Groth. "An Interview with DC's Boy Wonder, Paul Levitz." *Comics Journal*. April 1978, pp. 26-29, 31-34, 35-38.

McCloud, Scott

4750. Bissette, Steve. "Understanding Comics." *Comics Buyer's Guide*. March 12, 1993, pp. 26-28, 32, 36, 40, 44.

4751. McCloud, Scott. "Sketches." *New Yorker*. June 11, 1984, pp. 32-33.

4752. Salicrup, Jim and Kurt Busiek. "Scott McCloud." *Comics Interview*. December 1984, pp. 18-35; January 1985, pp. 47-59.

McFarlane, Todd

4753. Butler, Don. "Todd McFarlane." *Comics Buyer's Guide.* October 1, 1993, pp. 28, 34, 38.

4754. Groth, Gary. "Todd McFarlane." *Comics Journal.* August 1992, pp. 45-70.

4755. "Todd McFarlane." *Canadian Cartoonist.* April 1989, pp. 17-20.

4756. "Todd McFarlane Interview." *Comics Scene.* No. 27, 1992.

McGregor, Don

4757. Burton, Richard. "Interview." *Comic Reader.* No. 147 (Super Summer 1977), pp. 11-14, 19.

4758. Phillips, Gene. "Heroes and Antiheroes in a Vulgar Valhalla: Cultural Patterns in the Comics Writing of Don McGregor and Steve Gerber." *Comics Journal.* April 1980, pp. 63-64.

4759. Phillips, Gene. "McGregor and Myths." *Comics Journal.* September 1986, pp. 110-112.

Mayer, Sheldon

4760. Catron, J. Michael. "Sheldon Mayer." *Comics Journal.* February 1992, pp. 90-96.

4761. "Sheldon Mayer." *Amazing World of DC Comics.* March 1975.

4762. "Sheldon Mayer Dies." *CAPS.* February 1992, p. 17.

4763. "Sheldon Mayer, Wizard of the Golden Age." *Comics Journal.* February 1992, pp. 18-19.

4764. Wasserman, Jeffrey H. "Sheldon Mayer, 'Superfolks' and Garry Trudeau." *Comics Journal.* June 1978, pp. 53-54.

Mazzucchelli, David

4765. Arbesú, Faustino R. "Mazzucchelli: el Maestro." *El Wendigo.* No. 57, 1992, pp. 4-5.

4766. "David Mazzucchelli en Gijón." *El Wendigo*. No. 58, 1993, pp. 6-7.

4767. Kieffer, Bill. "David Mazzucchelli." *Comics Interview*. No. 117, 1993, pp. 17-22, 24, 26-28.

4768. Lim, C.T. "Whatever Happened to David Mazzucchelli?" *Big O Magazine*. October 1992, p. 92.

4769. "Sketchbook: David Mazzucchelli." *Comics Journal*. May 1992, pp. 145-149.

4770. Young, Frank. "David Mazzucchelli." *Comics Journal*. August 1992, p. 114-120.

Messner-Loebs, William

4771. Messner-Loebs, William. *Tall Tales*. Journey, Book 1. Agoura, California: Fantagraphics Books, 1987. 94 pp.

4772. Thompson, Kim. "Interview: William Messner Loebs." *Amazing Heroes*. September 1986, pp. 26-35.

4773. Waldroop, Bill. "A Few Minutes with William Messner-Loebs." *Comics Buyer's Guide*. May 26, 1989, pp. 20, 24.

4774. "Writer-Artist: William Messner-Loebs." *Comics Interview*. No. 73, 1989, pp. 24-43.

Miller, Frank

4775. Barr, Mike. "Frank Miller Said." *The Elektra Saga* (New York). March 1984.

4776. Borchert, Karlheinz and Walter Truck. "Frank Miller: Comics aus dem Bauch!" *Comic Info*. May-June 1993, pp. 41-44.

4777. Catron, Michael. "Devil's Advocate." *Amazing Heroes*. September 1981, pp. 49-55.

4778. Decker, Dwight R. "Frank Miller." *Comics Journal*. January 1982, pp. 68-93.

4779. Erickson, Steve. "The World of Frank Miller." *LA Weekly*. May 3-May 9, 1991, pp. 18-22.

4780. Fermín Pérez, Ramón. "Ronin: El Resbalon de los Dioses." *El Wendigo*. 14:43 (1988), pp. 21-23.

4781. "Frank Miller." *Comics Interview*. No. 52, 1987, pp. 4-15.

4782. "Frank Miller—The Friend I Hardly Know." *Comics Feature*. No. 25, 1983, pp. 87-93.

4783. "Frank Miller Interview." *Comics Scene*. No. 17, 1991.

4784. "Frank Miller Says...." *Comics Interview*. No. 43, 1987, pp. 22-24.

4785. "Frank Miller's Back." *Big O Magazine*. July 1990, pp. 45-46.

4786. "Frank Miller Speaks Out Against MPS Paperback." *Comics Journal*. August 1986, p. 15.

4787. Groth, Gary. "Frank Miller Interview." *Comics Journal*. December 1987, pp. 74-83.

4788. Hansom, Dick. "Dark Knight: Inside the Asylum." *Speakeasy*. November 1989, pp. 31-33, 35.

4789. Harvey, R.C. "McKenzie and Miller's Daredevil: Skillful Use of the Medium." *Comics Journal*. September 1980, pp. 92-94.

4790. Howell, Richard and Carol Kalish. "An Interview with Frank Miller." *Comics Feature*. December 1981, pp. 17-26.

4791. Miller, Frank. *Batman: The Dark Knight Returns*. New York: DC Comics, 1986. 200 pp.

4792. Miller, Frank. *Frank Miller, a Work in Progress*. Edited by Hal Schuster. Great Comic Artist File, Vol. 1. Canoga Park, California: Heroes Publishing, 1986. 58 pp.

4793. Miller, Frank. "God Save the King." *Comics Journal*. February 1986, pp. 63-68.

4794. Miller, Frank. *Ronin*. New York: DC Comics, 1987. 298 pp.

4795. "Miller Joins Samurai Comic." *Comics Feature*. May 1987, p. 7.

4796. Olsson, Kurt. "Frank Miller Makes Daredevil Come Alive." *Comics Journal*. December 1981, pp. 28-31.

4797. Schuster, Hal. "Frank Miller." *Comics Feature*. No. 25, 1983, pp. 31-45.

4798. Thompson, Kim. "Frank Miller: Return of the Dark Knight." *Comics Journal*. August 1985, pp. 58-79.

4799. Via, Ed. "Miller's Daredevil." *Comics Journal*. January 1982, pp. 94-99.

Moench, Doug

4800. Greenberger, Bob. "Aztec Ace." *Comics Interview.* April 1984, pp. 7-19.

4801. Greenberger, Bob. "Doug Moench." *Comics Interview.* May 1984, pp. 7-25.

4802. Moench, Doug. "Buckler and Me and Deathlok Makes Three." *Foom.* April 1974.

4803. Via, Ed. "Originality and Transcendency in the Work of Doug Moench." *Comics Journal.* September 1981, pp. 112-116.

Moore, Alan

4804. "Alan Moore." *Amazing Heroes.* May 15, 1985.

4805. "Alan Moore." *Comics Interview.* June 1984, pp. 9-27.

4806. "Alan Moore." *Comics Interview.* No. 65, 1988, pp. 5-23.

4807. "Alan Moore: Last Big Words." *Comics Journal.* February 1991, pp. 72-85.

4808. "Alan Moore on (Just About) Everything." *Comics Journal.* March 1986, pp. 38-46.

4809. Boatz, Darrel. "Alan Moore." *Comics Interview.* No. 48, 1987, pp. 7-20.

4810. Cannon, Martin. *Swamp Thing.* Canoga Park, California: Psi Fi Movie Press, 1987. 49 pp.

4811. Fernández, Norman. "Su Majestad Alan Moore!" *El Wendigo.* Año 15, No. 46, 1989, pp. 8-9.

4812. Flórez, Florentino and Faustino Rodríguez Arbesú. "Alan Moore: Un Watchmen del Buen Comic." *El Wendigo.* No. 42, 1988, pp. 12-13.

4813. Groth, Gary. "Alan Moore." *Comics Journal.* August 1992, pp. 89-100.

4814. Groth, Gary. "Alan Moore. Big Words." *Comics Journal.* December 1990, pp. 78-109.

4815. Groth, Gary. "Alan Moore Interview." *Comics Journal.* December 1987, pp. 60-72.

4816. Groth, Gary. "Pornographer Laureate: An Interview with Alan Moore." *Comics Journal.* July 1991, pp. 116-123.

4817. Moore, Alan. "Alan Moore on Writing for Comics: Part One." *Comics Journal*. January 1988, pp. 90-95; Part 2, March 1988, pp. 99-102; Part 3, April 1988, pp. 133-138.

4818. Moore, Alan and Dave Gibbons. "A Portal to Another Dimension." *Comics Journal*. July 1987, pp. 80-87.

4819. Nutman, Philip. "From Hell and Beyond: Alan Moore and Jack the Ripper." *Comics Buyer's Guide*. May 3, 1991, pp. 64, 66, 68, 70.

4820. Stewart, Bhob. "Alan Moore: Synchronicity and Symmetry." *Comics Journal*. July 1987, pp. 89-95.

Morrison, Grant

4821. "Grant Morrison." *Comics Scene*. April 1990.

4822. "Grant Morrison Interview." *Comics Scene*. No. 28, 1992.

Motter, Dean

4823. Herzog, Marty. "Dean Motter." *Comics Interview*. No. 39, 1986, pp. 60-77.

4824. Herzog, Marty. "Dean Motter and Mark Askwith." *Comics Interview*. No. 77, 1989, pp. 4-20.

Murray, Doug

4825. Murray, Doug and Michael Golden. *The 'Nam*. New York: Marvel Comics, 1987-.

4826. "Writer: Doug Murray." *Comics Interview*. No. 53, 1987, pp. 6-19.

Nasser, Michael

4827. "Mike Nasser." *The Fans of Central Jersey*. July 1977, pp. 2-6.

4828. Thomas, Kenn and Ed Mantels-Seeker. "A Revealing Conversation with Nasser." *Whizzard*. February 1981, pp. 24-29.

Nostrand, Howard

4829. Nostrand, Howard. "Nostrand by Nostrand." *Comics Journal*. February 1985, pp. 79-86.

4830. Stewart, Bhob. "The Mystery Artist: Howard Nostrand." *Comics Journal*. March 1985, pp. 93-111.

4831. Stewart, Bhob. "The Nostrand Zone." *Comics Journal*. March 1985, pp. 79-92.

O'Neil, Denny

4832. Cavalieri, Joey and Mitch Cohn. "The Denny O'Neil Interview." *Daredevil Chronicles*. February 1982, pp. 37-40.

4833. "Denny O'Neil." *Comics Feature*. July-August 1980, pp. 18-28.

4834. Groth, Gary. "War and Peace with Denny O'Neil." *Comics Journal*. September 1981, pp. 56-.

4835. Wochner, Lee. "Denny O'Neil." *Comics Journal*. July 1985, pp. 123-125.

4836. Zimmerman, Dwight J. "Writer/Editor: Denny O'Neil." *Comics Interview*. No. 35, 1986, pp. 22-37.

O'Neill, Kevin

4837. Mills, Pat and Kevin O'Neill. "I Am the Law!" *Speakeasy*. December-January 1990-1991, pp. 39-41, 43.

4838. Plowright, Frank. "Kevin O'Neill Interview." *Comics Journal*. June 1988, pp. 87-105.

Ordway, Jerry

4839. "Jerry Ordway: Super-Artist." *Comics Scene*. No. 3 (Vol. 3, Series 13), pp. 36-41.

4840. Martínez, Rodolfo. "Jerry Ordway: La Evolucion de un Artesano." *El Wendigo*. No. 50, 1990, pp. 34-35.

Panter, Gary

4841. Luciano, Dale. "Living for the Day: Gary Panter Interviewed." *Comics Journal*. July 1985, pp. 215-225.

4842. Panter, Gary. *Road Kill*. Somerville, Massachusetts: Carnage Press, 1986. 32 pp.

4843. "Sketchbook: Gary Panter." *Comics Journal*. April 1991, pp. 107-112; June 1991, pp. 103-108.

Parker, Ken

4844. Arbesú, Faustino Rodríguez and Florentino Flórez. "Ken Parker, la Saga de las Últimas Décadas." *El Wendigo*. No. 59, 1993, pp. 10-13.

4845. Condero, Moncho. "Ken Parker: Un Doble Homenaje." *El Wendigo*. December 1984-January 1985, pp. 60-62.

4846. Rodríguez Arbesú, Faustino. "Algo Mas Que 'Bellos' Dibujos." *El Wendigo*. May 1984, pp. 4-9.

Pekar, Harvey

4847. Fiene, Donald M. "From Off the Streets of Cleveland: The Life and Work of Harvey Pekar." *Comics Journal*. April 1985, pp. 65-88.

4848. Groth, Gary. "Harvey Pekar: Stories About Honesty, Money, and Misogyny." *Comics Journal*. April 1985, pp. 44-64.

4849. Hunt, Leon. "Pekar and Realism." *Comics Journal*. January 1989, pp. 47-51.

4850. Pearl, Jonathan. "Harvey Pekar's America." *Fanfare*. Summer 1983, pp. 33-37.

4851. Pekar, Harvey. "Blood and Thunder." *Comics Journal*. April 1990, pp. 27-34.

4852. Pekar, Harvey. *From Off the Streets of Cleveland Comes... American Splendor: The Life and Times of Harvey Pekar*. Garden City, New York: Doubleday, 1986. 160 pp.

4853. Pekar, Harvey. *From Off the Streets of Cleveland Comes... More American Splendor: The Life and Times of Harvey Pekar*. New York: Doubleday, 1987. 160 pp.

4854. Pekar, Harvey. "Getting Dave's Goat." *Cleveland Edition*. September 22, 1988, p. 1+.

4855. Pekar, Harvey. "Late Night of the Soul with David Letterman." *Village Voice*. August 25, 1987, pp. 45-46.

4856. Pekar, Harvey. "*Maus* and Other Topics." *Comics Journal*. December 1986, pp. 54-57.

4857. Pekar, Harvey. "Me 'n' Dave Letterman." *Cleveland Plain Dealer*. February 1, 1987, p. H-1.

4858. Pekar, Harvey. "The Potential of Comics." *Comics Journal*. July 1988, pp. 81-88.

4859. Pekar, Harvey. "Working-Class Cavemen." *Comics Journal*. December 1991, pp. 38-39.

Pérez, George

4860. Cuervo, Javier. "George Pérez: La Minuciosidad No Es una Minucia." *El Wendigo*. Winter 1988-1989, pp. 11-12.

4861. "George Pérez Interview, Pt. 2." *Fans-Zine*. Spring-Summer 1979, pp. 21-23, 38.

4862. Greenberger, Robert. "The Ultimate Team Player: A Look at the Career and Art of George Pérez." *Comics Scene*. January 1982, pp. 30-38.

4863. Groth, Gary, *et al*. "'I Was Born To Be a Comic Book Artist': An Interview with the Most Popular Artist in Comics: George Pérez." *Comics Journal*. January 1983, pp. 72-85.

4864. Heintjes, Tom, ed. *Focus on George Pérez*. Agoura, California: Fantagraphics Books, 1985. 119 pp.

4865. Heintjes, Tom. "Pérez." *Comics Journal*. July 1985, pp. 127-128.

4866. O'Neill, Patrick D. "Able To Leap Panel Borders in a Single Bound." *Comics Scene*. February 1990, pp. 48-52.

4867. Pérez, George and Ralph Macchio. *Pérez, Accent on the First "E."* Detroit, Michigan: Omnibus, 1977. 52 pp.

4868. Ringgenberg, Steve and Gary Groth. "'I Love This Job': An Interview with George Pérez." *Comics Journal*. March 1983, pp. 54-69.

Pini, Richard and Wendy

4869. Decker, Dwight R. "From Elfland to Smallville." *Comics Journal.* March 1982, pp. 53-56.

4870. Decker, Dwight R. "From Poughkeepsie to Elfland: An Interview with Wendy and Richard Pini." *Comics Journal.* Spring [May?] 1981, pp. 127-151.

4871. Dorf, Shel. "Shel Dorf Interviews Richard and Wendy Pini." *Comics Buyer's Guide.* March 18, 1983, pp. 1, 31-32, 34, 36, 38, 40-46.

4872. "Elfquest Preview: A Look at Wendy Pini's Coloring for *Book II.*" *Comics Scene.* January 1982, pp. 25-29.

4873. O'Neill, Patrick D. "Writers/Artist: Wendy and Richard Pini." *Comics Interview.* No. 87, 1990, pp. 21-23, 25-41.

4874. Pini, Wendy and Richard Pini. *ElfQuest.* 4 Vols. Virginia Beach, Virginia: Donning, 1981-84.

4875. Sanderson, Peter. "Wendy and Richard Pini." *Comics Journal.* July 1985, pp. 129-134.

4876. Thomas, Ron. "Saga of the Wolfriders." *Four Color Magazine.* March 1987, pp. 28-35.

4877. "Wendy and Richard Pini." *Comics Interview.* No. 60, 1988, pp. 16-37.

4878. Yeh, Phil. "Wendy and Richard Pini." *Uncle Jam International.* September-October 1984, pp. 5-6.

Reed, Rod

4879. Beck, C.C. "Rod Reed." *FCA/S.O.B.* October-November 1980, p. 7.

4880. "Rod Reed." *Comics Interview.* December 1984, pp. 9-17.

Robinson, Jerry

4881. "The Last Laugh." *Provincetown Arts.* 1988.

4882. Ringgenberg, Steve. "Jerry Robinson." *Comics Interview.* No. 56, 1988, pp. 28-31, 33, 36-37, 39, 41, 43, 45, 47; No. 57, 1988, pp. 17-19, 21, 23-25, 27, 29, 33; No. 58, 1988, pp. 38-43, 45, 47-49, 51-53, 55.

4883. Robinson, Jerry. "Pleasantry and Mirth." *The Cartoonist*. April 20, 1965.

Rogers, Boody G.

4884. Rogers, Boody G. *Homeless Bound*. Seagraves, Texas: Pioneer Book Publishers, 1984. 199 pp.

4885. Yoe, Craig. "Boody Rogers." *Comics Buyer's Guide*. March 8, 1985, pp. 20, 22, 26, 28, 30, 32, 34, 36, 45.

Rogers, Marshall

4886. Groth, Gary. "From Detective to Detectives Inc. An Interview with Marshall Rogers." *Comics Journal*. March 1980, pp. 56-70.

4887. Harvey, R.C. "A Lingering Look at the Comics Art of Marshall Rogers." *Comics Journal*. March 1980, pp. 71-74.

4888. Wochner, Lee. "Marshall Rogers." *Comics Journal*. July 1985, pp. 140-143.

Romita, John, sr. and jr.

4889. Commer, Dick. "John Romita—Spider-Man." *Cartoonist PROfiles*. September 1978, pp. 30-33.

4890. Guzzo, Gary. "John Romita, Jr. on 'Daredevil: Man Without Fear.'" *Comics Buyer's Guide*. August 6, 1993, pp. 27-28.

4891. "John Romita." *Cartoonist PROfiles*. December 1978, pp. 77-79.

4892. Khoo, Eric. "Leapin' Spiders." *Big O Magazine*. October 1991, pp. 94-97.

4893. Kraft, David A. "John Romita." *Foom*. June 1977, pp. 8-14.

4894. Talley, Brian. "John Romita, jr." *Comics Interview*. May 1984, pp. 28-45.

Rosa, Don

4895. Campiti, David. "The Keno Don Rosa Interview Part One!" *Comics Buyer's Guide*. December 28, 1984, p. 58.

4896. Clark, John and Bruce Hamilton. "An Interview with Don Rosa and William Van Horn." *Comics Buyer's Guide*. February 26, 1993, pp. 26-27.

4897. Harvey, R.C. "Adventures of Don Rosa in Scandinavia and Elsewhere." *Comics Buyer's Guide*. August 13, 1993, pp. 26-28.

4898. Harvey, R.C. "Don Rosa—One Happy Fella." *Cartoonist PROfiles*. September 1993, pp. 54-61.

4899. Mougin, Lou. "Don Rosa." *Comics Interview*. July 1984, pp. 28-45.

Rude, Steve

4900. "Sketchbook: Steve Rude." *Comics Journal*. September 1987, pp. 114-119.

4901. Strnad, Jan. "A Chat with Steve Rude." *Amazing Heroes*. No. 99, 1987, pp. 12-14.

Russell, P. Craig

4902. Lobdell, Scott. "Operatic Evenings." *Comics Scene*. December 1990, pp. 16-19.

4903. Paeth, Craig. "P. Craig Russell." *Comics Journal*. December 1991, pp. 44-64, 66-73.

4904. Ringgenberg, Steve. "P. Craig Russell." *Comics Interview*. May 1983, pp. 8-17.

Saba, Arn

4905. Shainblum, Mark. "Arn Saba." *Comics Interview*. January 1985, pp. 7-19; February 1985, pp. 13-23.

4906. Thompson, Kim. "Tripping the Light Fantastic: An Interview with Arn Saba." *Comics Journal*. June 1985, pp. 57-67.

Sable, Jon

4907. Grell, Mike. *Jon Sable, Freelance*. New York: Ballantine, 1987. 192 pp.

4908. Groth, Gary. "Jon Sable's 'Real People.'" *Comics Journal*. September 1985, pp. 7-8.

Sakai, Stan

4909. Dobashi, Mas. "Stan Sakai: A CAPS Look at the Creator of Usagi Yojimbo." *CAPS*. June 1993, pp. 20-24.

4910. Sakai, Stan. *Usagi Yojimbo*. Agoura, California: Fantagraphics Books, 1987. 144 pp.

4911. "Stan Sakai." *Comics Interview*. No. 44, 1987, pp. 24-37.

4912. Yeh, Phil. "Samurai Rabbit: WittyWorld Interview with Stan Sakai." *WittyWorld*. Summer 1987, pp. 18-19.

Schultz, Mark

4913. Beauchamp, Monte. "Mark Schultz." *Comics Journal*. May 1992, pp. 108-143.

4914. "Mark Schultz Interview." *Comics Scene*. No. 27, 1992.

Schwartz, Julius

4915. "Julius Schwartz." *Amazing World of DC Comics*. March 1977.

4916. "Julius Schwartz." *Comics Feature*. July 1984.

4917. "Julius Schwartz." *Comics Interview*. No. 88, 1990.

4918. "Julius Schwartz and the Comics of the Fantastic." *Comics Feature*. November 1982, pp. 64-67.

4919. Lillian, Guy A. "Strange Schwartz Stories." *Amazing World of DC Comics*. November 1974.

Scroggy, David

4920. Dorf, Shel. "David Scroggy." *Comics Buyer's Guide*. November 4, 1983, pp. 30, 32, 36.

4921. Gelb, Jeff. "David Scroggy." *Comics Interview*. May 1984, pp. 53-71.

Shaffenberger, Kurt

4922. Asherman, Allan. "Remembering." *The Amazing World of DC Comics*. September-October 1974, pp. 26-27.

4923. Howell, Richard. "A Talk with Kurt Schaffenberger." *Comics Feature*. September 1982, pp. 68+.

4924. Lage, Matt. "Kurt Schaffenberger." *FCA/S.O.B.* April 1980, pp. 2-3.

Shelton, Gilbert

4925. Shelton, Gilbert. *The Adventures of Fat Freddy's Cat*. Rev. Ed. San Francisco, California: Rip Off Press, 1982.

4926. Shelton, Gilbert. *The Best of Fat Freddy's Cat*. London: Knockabout Comics, 1983.

4927. Shelton, Gilbert. *The Fabulous Furry Freak Brothers* (The Best of the Rip Off Press, Vol. 2). New York: Rip Off Press, 1974.

4928. Walker, Brad. "Gilbert Shelton and Hunt Emerson." *Comics Feature*. June 1980, pp. 39-46.

Shooter, Jim

4929. Broertjes, Harry C. "Shooter's Dismissal: Retailers Unconcerned." *Retail Express*. August 7, 1987, p. 6.

4930. "Comic Fan from Childhood, Shooter Is Man Behind Those Superheroes." *Variety*. September 17, 1986, p. 82.

4931. "Defiant and the Defiant Universe." *Comics Buyer's Guide*. May 7, 1993, pp. 26-27.

4932. Dutter, Barry. "Jim Shooter." *Comics Buyer's Guide*. September 27, 1985, pp. 20, 22, 24, 26.

4933. Groth, Gary. "Pushing Marvel into the Eighties: An Interview with Jim Shooter." *Comics Journal*. November 1980, pp. 56-83.

4934. Groth, Gary. "What Made Jimmy Run?" *Comics Journal*. September 1987, pp. 5-6.

4935. Harvey, R.C. "Shooter, Colan, and the Marvel Way." *Comics Journal*. November 1981, pp. 89-95.

4936. "Jim Shooter Announces Details of Defiant Launch." *Comics Buyer's Guide*. March 26, 1993, p. 22.

4937. "Jim Shooter Fired." *Comics Journal*. July 1987, pp. 13-14.

4938. "Jim Shooter Interview." *Comics Scene*. No. 20, 1991.

4939. "Jim Shooter: Story of a Defiant Dreamer." *Comics Buyer's Guide*. April 9, 1993, pp. 27-28.

4940. Jones, R.A. "Straight Shooter." *Comics Buyer's Guide*. July 31, 1987, p. 30.

4941. "The Return of Jim Shooter." *Speakeasy*. April 1990, p. 17.

4942. Shooter, Jim. "Marvel and Me." *Comics Buyer's Guide*. No. 16, 1986, pp. A-85-A-96.

4943. "Shooter Speaks Out on Kirby Art." *Comics Journal*. January 1986, p. 9-11.

4944. Thompson, Kim. "An Interview with Marvel's Head Honcho: Jim Shooter." *Comics Journal*. June 1978, pp. 38-47.

4945. Thompson, Maggie. "Jim Shooter's Back." *Comics Buyer's Guide*. December 25, 1992, p. 22.

Shuster, Joe and Jerry Siegel

4946. Andrae, Thomas. "Of Supermen and Kids with Dreams: An Interview with Jerry Siegel and Joe Shuster." *The Comic Book Price Guide*. No. 18, 1988, pp. A-78-A-98.

4947. "Cartoonist Short-Changed by Superman: Joe Shuster." *The Jester*. September 1992, p. 13. Reprinted from *Daily Mail* (London). August 10, 1992.

4948. Fuchs, Wolfgang J. "Superman-Comics." *Comic Forum* (Vienna). 6:23 (1984), pp. 24-25. (Joe Shuster).

4949. "Joe Shuster... Forever Up, Up and Away." *Comics Journal*. October 1992, pp. 20-24.

4950. Siegel, Jerry. "The Facts About 'Superman.'" *Comics Buyer's Guide*. September 6, 1985, p. 32.

4951. Siegel, Jerome and Joe Shuster. *Famous First Edition, C-26*. New York: National Periodical Publications, 1974.

4952. Siegel, Jerome and Joe Shuster. *Famous First Edition, C-61*. New York: National Periodical Publications, 1979.

4953. Siegel, Jerry and Joe Shuster. *Superman Archives 1*. New York: DC Archive Editions, 1989.

4954. Siegel, Jerry and Joe Shuster. Interview. *Nemo*. August 1983.

4955. Siegel, Jerry and Joanne Siegel. "A Tribute to Joe Shuster." In *San Diego Comic Convention 1993*, p. 136. San Diego, California: 1993.

4956. "Siegel and Shuster: Date Line 1930s." *Eclipse Comics*. November 1984.

4957. "Siegel, Shuster and Superman." *Amazing World of DC Comics*. February 1976, pp. 28-29.

4958. "Superman Artist Joe Shuster Dead at 78." *CAPS*. August 1992, p. 4.

4959. Urbanek, Hermann. "Superman in Deutschland." *Comic Forum* (Vienna). 6:23 (1984), pp. 26-27. (Joe Shuster).

Sienkiewicz, Bill

4960. "Artist: Bill Sienkiewicz." *Comics Interview*. No. 53, 1987, pp. 32-33.

4961. Bernard, Jami. "The Substance of Style: Part I." *Comics Scene*. February 1990, pp. 25-28; Part II, April 1990.

4962. "Bill Sienkiewicz: El Arte por El Arte." *El Wendigo*. 14:43 (1988), pp. 6-7.

4963. "Comic Book Artist Bill Sienkiewicz." *Cartoonist PROfiles*. December 1984, pp. 22-29.

4964. Curson, Nigel. "Big Numbers: The Mathematics of Mankind." *Speakeasy*. April 1990, pp. 28-29, 31, 33.

4965. Noble, Steve. "Forked Tale—Bill Sienkiewicz's Stray Toasters." *FA*. October 1988, pp. 13-15.

4966. Sanderson, Peter. "Slow Dancing on the Cutting Edge: An Interview with Bill Sienkiewicz." *Comics Journal*. April 1986, pp. 58-77.

4967. "Visual Jazz: Bill Sienkiewicz." *Best of Amazing Heroes*. No. 1, 1982, pp. 55-57.

Sim, Dave

4968. Bissette, Steve. "Cerebus by Dave Sim." *Comics Interview*. No. 107, 1992, pp. 8-39.

4969. Denn, Matt. "Dave Sim and Deni Loubert: Portrait of the Artist As a Young Aardvark." *Comics Buyer's Guide*. March 29, 1985, pp. 38, 40, 42.

4970. Groensteen, Thierry. "Tout le Monde ne Peut Pas Être Oryctérope." *Les Cahiers de la Bande Dessinée* (Grenoble). 68, 1986, pp. 75-77.

4971. Groth, Gary. "Opening Shots: A Reply to Dave Sim." *Comics Journal*. February 1991, pp. 3-4.

4972. Groth, Gary. "Repentant Publisher (Dave Sim)." *Comics Journal*. July 1989, pp. 80-124.

4973. Groth, Gary. "The Two Daves, Or The Babbitization of Dave Sim." *Comics Journal*. January 1993, pp. 3-8.

4974. Hansom, Dick. "Sim and Self-Published Aardvark." *Speakeasy*. December-January 1989-1990, pp. 32-33, 35.

4975. MacDonald, Heidi D. "Dave Sim." *Comics Journal*. July 1985, pp. 144-148.

4976. McDonnell, David. "Dave and Deni Sim: Part One." *Comics Scene*. March 1983, pp. 20-24; Part 2, May 1983, pp. 56-60, 62.

4977. Pomerleau, Luc. "Entretien Avec Dave Sim." *Les Cahiers de la Bande Dessinée* (Grenoble). 68, 1986, pp. 70-74.

4978. Sim, Dave. "A Declaration of Independence." *Comics Journal*. February 1986, pp. 87-90.

4979. Sim, Dave. *Church and State*. Kitchener, Ontario: Aardvark-Vanaheim, 1987. 592 pp.

4980. Sim, Dave. "Dave Sim's Vision of Comic Shop's Future." *Comics Journal*. February 1989, pp. 3-4.

4981. Sim, Dave. *High Society*. Kitchener, Ontario: Aardvark-Vanaheim, 1986. 512 pp.

4982. Sim, Dave. *Swords of Cerebus*. 6 Vols. Kitchener, Ontario: Aardvark-Vanaheim, 1981-1984.

4983. Thompson, Kim. "Dave and Deni Sim, Part I." *Comics Journal*. July 1983, pp. 66-85; Part II, August 1983, pp. 59-82.

Simon, Joe

4984. Groth, Gary. "Joe Simon." *Comics Journal*. February 1990, pp. 101-108.

4985. Simon, Joe. "Memoirs of a Comic Book Maker." *Comics Scene*. October 1990.

4986. Simon, Joe. "Shop Talk: Joe Simon." *Will Eisner's Spirit Magazine No. 37*. October 1982.

Simonson, Walt

4987. Cuervo, Javier. "Walt Simonson: 'Los Superheroes son Descendientes de la Mitologia Europea.'" *El Wendigo*. 14:43 (1988), pp. 11-12.

4988. Harris, Jack C. "Walt Simonson." *Comics Interview*. March 1984, pp. 22-39.

4989. Sanderson, Peter. "Walt and Louise Simonson." *Comics Interview*. No. 39, 1986, pp. 42-57.

4990. Simonson, Walt and Louise. "At Work in Comics: How Walt and Louise Simonson Approach the Job." *Comics Collector*. Summer 1984, pp. 22-23.

4991. "Upstart Associates: Walt Simonson on Working with Other Creators." *Comics Collector*. Summer 1984, pp. 26-28.

4992. "Walt Simonson Speaks!" *Comics Scene*. No. 3 (Vol. 3, Series 14), p. 17.

Smith, Ken

4993. Groth, Gary. "An Interview with Kenneth Smith." *Comics Journal*. Summer 1979, pp. 104-119.

4994. Groth, Gary. "Kenneth Smith." *Comics Journal*. July 1985, pp. 149-155.

4995. "Sketchbook: Kenneth Smith." *Comics Journal*. December 1989, pp. 97-101.

Spiegelman, Art and Francoise Mouly

4996. Bolhafner, J. Stephen. "Art for Art's Sake: Spiegelman Speaks on *Raw's* Past, Present and Future." *Comics Journal*. October 1991, pp. 97-99.

4997. Cavalieri, Joey. "An Interview with Art Spiegelman and Francoise Mouly." *Comics Journal*. August 1981, pp. 98-125.

4998. Dreifus, C. "Art Spiegelman." *The Progressive*. November 1989, pp. 34-37.

4999. Green, Stuart. "Art Spiegelman, Raw and Read." *Speakeasy*. April 1990, pp. 42-43, 45, 47.

5000. Groensteen, Thierry. "Entretien Avec Art Spiegelman." *Les Cahiers de la Bande Dessinée* (Grenoble). 66, 1985, pp. 62-66.

5001. Lindon, Mathieu. "Art Spiegelman: des BD, des Souris et des Hommes." *Libération*. Supplement Special Angoulême 1992, pp. ii-iii.

5002. Martin, Doug. "RAW: An Interview with Art Spiegelman." *Gauntlet*. No. 2, 1991, pp. 208-212.

5003. Pachter, Richard. "Maus/Art Spiegelman." *Comics Interview*. No. 108, 1992, pp. 4-13.

5004. "Raw Magazine: An Interview with Art Spiegelman and Francoise Mouly." *Comics Feature*. July-August 1980, pp. 49-56.

5005. Roland, Niels. "Livet Som en Koncentrationslejr." *Seriejournalen*. June 1992, pp. 18-19.

5006. "Slaughter on Greene Street: Art Spiegelman and Francoise Mouly Talk about *RAW*." *Comics Journal*. August 1982, pp. 70-82.

5007. Smith, Graham. "From Micky to Maus: Recalling the Genocide Through Cartoon." *Oral History*. 15:1 (1987), pp. 32+.

5008. Spiegelman, Art. *Breakdowns*. New York: Belier Press, 1977. 42 pp.

5009. Spiegelman, Art and Francoise Mouly, eds. *Read Yourself Raw*. New York: Pantheon Books, 1987. 90 pp.

5010. Tucker, Ken. "The Holocaust As a (Serious) Comic." *Philadelphia Inquirer*. October 20, 1986, pp. E-1, E-8.

5011. Van Biema, D. "Art Spiegelman Battles the Holocaust's Demons—and His Own—in an Epic Cat-and-Mouse Comic Book." *People Weekly*. October 27, 1986, pp. 98-100+.

Starlin, Jim

5012. Fernández, Norman. "La Metamorfosis de Jim Starlin." *El Wendigo*. No. 52, 1991, pp. 36-37.

5013. "Jim Starlin." *Comics Interview*. June 1983, pp. 6-21.

5014. "Jim Starlin Interview." *Comics Scene*. No. 19, 1991; No. 27, 1992.

5015. "Jim Starlin Interviewed." *Comics Feature*. June 1983, pp. 22-40.

5016. White, Ted. "Botched 'Novel,' Dishonest Politics from Starlin." *Comics Journal*. December 1982, pp. 52-57.

Staton, Joe

5017. Bethke, Marilyn. "From E-Man to Batman: The Joe Staton Interview." *Comics Journal*. March 1979, pp. 37-45.

5018. Dorf, Shel. "Joe Staton." *Comics Buyer's Guide*. July 1, 1983, pp. 40, 42-43.

5019. Greenberg, Fred. "An Interview with Joe Staton." *Omnibus*. March 1978, pp. 30-39.

5020. Greenberger, Robert. "Joe Staton." *Comics Journal*. July 1985, pp. 157-161.

5021. "Interview with Joe Staton." *Dreamline*. March 1982, pp. 68-75.

5022. Schuster, Hal. "Joe Staton Interviewed." *Comics Feature*. No. 25, 1983, pp. 65-76.

Steranko, Jim

5023. Blackwith, Ed. "The Men Behind the Comics: Steranko." *Castle of Frankenstein*. 1967, pp. 30-31.

5024. Groth, Gary. "Visual Vivisectors." *Comics Journal*. August 1979, pp. 25-29.

5025. Paniceres, Ruben. "Jim Steranko: Sombras Recobradas." *El Wendigo*. No. 45, 1989, pp. 35-36.

5026. Winnipeg Art Gallery. *Steranko: Graphic Narrative*. Winnipeg, Manitoba: 1978. 108 pp.

Stevens, Dave

5027. "Dave Stevens Interview." *Comics Scene*. No. 18, 1991.

5028. Groth, Gary. "Unmasking the Rocketeer: The Dave Stevens Interview." *Comics Journal*. September 1987, pp. 68-85.

St. John, J. Allen

5029. Brueckel, Frank. "On St. John and Dinosaurs." *ERB-DOM*. June 1969.

5030. Cazedessus, Camille, jr. "Burroughs Artist—J. Allen St. John." *ERB-DOM*. October 1968.

5031. Coriell, Vernell. *J. Allen St. John Portfolio*. Kansas City, Missouri: Greystoke, 1964.

5032. Estes, Arthur B. "J. Allen St. John." *Metropolitan Magazine*. November 1898, pp. 503-506+.

5033. Ivie, Larry. "Burroughs and St. John—An Analysis." *ERB-DOM*. July 1963, pp. 8, 104+.

5034. "J. Allen St. John Portfolio." *Fantastic*. April 1972.

5035. Richardson, Darrell C. *J. Allen St. John*. West Plains, Missouri: Russ Cochran, 1976.

5036. Richardson, Darrell C. "J. Allen St. John: America's Most Famous Fantasy Illustrator." *Other World's Science Stories*. July 1951.

5037. Richardson, Darrell C. "J. Allen St. John, Dean of Fantasy Illustrators." *The Fanscient*. Spring 1950.

5038. Richardson, Darrell C. "The Magic Paint Brush of J. Allen St. John." *Near Mint*. 1980 (no monthly date), 9 pp.

5039. "Special St. John Issue." *The Burroughs Bulletin*. Spring 1972.

5040. "A Special St. John Issue." *ERB-DOM*. November 1972. Includes: Camille Cazedessus, jr., "J. Allen St. John" and "Henry Hardy Heins on St. John."

5041. Turner, George E. "St. John: Artist, Teacher, Friend." *The Burroughs Bulletin* (N.S.). January 1991. 9 pp.

5042. Vinson, Stanleigh B. "J. Allen St. John." *The World of Comic Art*. Fall 1966, p. 272+.

Strnad, Jan

5043. "Jan Strnad." *Comics Interview*. No. 30, 1986, pp. 7-15.

5044. Strnad, Jan. "My Brilliant Career at Marvel." *Comics Journal*. September 1982, pp. 41-49.

Sutton, Tom

5045. Petrucha, Stefan. "Tom Sutton." *Comics Interview*. No. 80, 1990, pp. 32-59.

5046. Reece, Warren. "About the Artist: Tom Sutton." *Foom*. December 1976, pp. 20-21.

5047. Thompson, Kim H. "Tom Sutton, the Unknown Artist." *Comics Journal*. June 1978, p. 29.

5048. "Tom Sutton." *Cartoonist PROfiles*. December 1974, pp. 68-72.

Swan, Curt

5049. Morrissey, Richard, *et al*. "35 Years at DC Comics—Curt Swan: An Interview with Superman's Main Artist." *Comics Journal*. July 1982, pp. 64-66, 68-71, 73-75, 77-81.

5050. "Superman by Curt Swan." *Cartoonist PROfiles*. 1:2 (1969), pp. 24-30.

Thomas, Roy

5051. Gustaveson, Rob. "Fifteen Years at Marvel: An Interview with Roy Thomas." *Comics Journal*. December 1980, pp. 74-99.

5052. Macchio, Ralph. "Thomas Speaks!" *Foom*. June 1976, pp. 3-14.

5053. Malin, Adam. "Roy Thomas." *Comics Journal*. April 1982, pp. 94-96.

5054. "Roy Thomas." *Cartoonist PROfiles*. Fall 1969, pp. 53-54.

5055. "Roy Thomas." *Comics Feature*. May 1986.

5056. "Roy Thomas." *Comics Interview*. No. 66, 1989, pp. 5-32; No. 67, 1989, pp. 5-24; No. 68, 1989, pp. 5-28.

5057. "Roy Thomas and Gerry Conway." *Comics Scene*. May 1983, pp. 30-31.

5058. Sanderson, Peter. "From Here to Infinity." *Amazing Heroes*. December 1, 1983, pp. 28-48.

5059. Thomas, Roy. "'Star Wars' and Me." *Comics Buyer's Guide*. April 16, 1993, pp. 26-27.

5060. Thompson, Kim and J. Collier. "Creatures Great and Small...and Super Heroes All!" *Amazing Heroes*. March 1982, pp. 32-39. (Also Scott Shaw!).

Toth, Alex

5061. "Alex Toth Art." *Near Mint*. No. 1, 1980, pp. 4-7.

5062. Davis, Vincent. "Still the Artist's Artist: An Interview with Alex Toth." *Comics Journal*. May 1985, pp. 59-77.

5063. "The Monument by Alex Toth." *Cartoonist PROfiles*. No. 13, 1972, pp. 54-59.

5064. Phillips, Gene. "Bravo for Toth." *Comics Journal*. November 1980, pp. 40-41.

5065. Strzyz, Klaus. "Ein Interview mit Alex Toth." *Comixene*. 7:33 (1980), pp. 9-12, 18.

5066. Toth, Alex. *Bravo for Adventure*. Bravo for Adventure, No. 1. Toronto, Ontario: Dragon Lady Press, 1987. 70 pp.

5067. Toth, Alex. *A Display of Art Work by Alex Toth*. San Francisco, California: Feature Associates, 1977. 59 pp.

Truman, Tim

5068. Downs, Steve. "An Interview with Timothy Truman." *Comics Buyer's Guide*. July 23, 1993, pp. 26-28, 30.

5069. Groth, Gary. "Down Home with Tim Truman." *Comics Journal*. September 1991, pp. 66-86.

5070. Juanmartí, Jordi. "El Apocalipsis de Tim Truman." *El Wendigo*. No. 58, 1993, pp. 8-9.

5071. "Timothy Truman: Cómic Shaman." *El Wendigo*. No. 59, 1993, pp. 32-33.

5072. "Tim Truman." *Comic Scene*. April 1990.

Turner, Ron

5073. "Ron Turner." *Comics Interview*. No. 43, 1987, pp. 30-41.

5074. Shaw, Jonathan. "Mind Candy for the Masses." *Art? Alternatives*. October 1992, pp. 16-19.

Van Horn, William

5075. Lustig, John. "Wm. Van Horn." *Comics Interview*. No. 77, 1989, pp. 21-29.

5076. Oakley, Peter. "Donald Duck Cartoonist Bill Van Horn Addresses Standing-Room-Only Crowd." *CAPS*. September 1991, pp. 13-14.

Vansant, Wayne

5077. "Artist: Wayne Vansant." *Comics Interview*. No. 53, 1987, pp. 20-31.

5078. Biggers, Cliff. "Wayne Vansant." *Comic Shop News*. August 21, 1991, pp. 4-7.

Veitch, Rick

5079. Kreiner, Rich. "Hail and Farewell: An Irish Wake for Rick Veitch's *Swamp Thing*." *Comics Journal*. May 1989, pp. 3-4.

5080. "Rick Veitch." *Comics Scene*. August 1990.

5081. "Rick Veitch Quits *Swamp Thing*." *Comics Journal*. May 1989, pp. 7-10.

5082. Veitch, Rick. "Comic Book Artist/Writer." *Cartoonist PROfiles*. September 1984, pp. 10-17.

Verheiden, Mark

5083. Green, Stuart. "All American Aliens Boy." *Speakeasy*. February 1991, pp. 21-23.

5084. "Mark Nelson and Mark Verheiden." *Comics Interview*. No. 68, 1989, pp. 29-49.

5085. O'Neill, Patrick D. "Writer: Mark Verheiden." *Comics Interview*. No. 87, 1990, pp. 12-19.

Vogel, Henry

5086. Woodcock, Julie. "Henry Vogel." *Comics Interview*. No. 55, 1988, pp. 6-27.

5087. "X-Thieves and Southern Knights: Henry Vogel and Mark Propst." *Comics Interview*. No. 35, 1986, pp. 6-21.

Wagner, Matt

5088. Chadwick, Bill. "Matt Wagner." *Comics Interview*. August 1984, pp. 40-47.

5089. "Like a Bat Out of Hell." *Before I Get Old*. January 1987, pp. 29-30.

5090. Wagner, Matt. *Magebook*. 2 Vols. Norristown, Pennsylvania: Comico the Comic Company, 1985.

5091. Walker, Leigh A. "Matt Wagner: Not Just for Kids." *Philadelphia People*. Winter/Spring 1987, p. 27.

Waller, Reed

5092. Fletcher, Ken. "Reed Waller and Kate Worley." *Comics Interview*. No. 59, 1988, pp. 4-19.

5093. "Reed Waller." *Comics Journal*. May 1989, pp. 86-88.

Wein, Len

5094. Greenberger, Robert. "Len Wein." *Comics Journal*. July 1985, pp. 162-168.

5095. Jankiewicz, Pat. "Len Wein." *Comics Interview*. No. 92, 1991, pp. 58-65.

5096. Slifer, Roger. "Len Wein." *Comics Journal*. Summer 1979, pp. 73-99.

Williams, J.R.

5097. Campbell, Gordon. "J.R. Williams." *Cartoonist PROfiles*. December 1982, pp. 68-73.

5098. "Cowboy Cartoonist: J.R. Williams." *Time*. May 13, 1940, pp. 57-59.

5099. Phelps, Donald. "The Panel Art of J.R. Williams—Reveries of a Rumpled Age." *Nemo*. October 1983, pp. 41-45.

5100. "Sketchbook: J.R. Williams." *Comics Journal*. May 1992, pp. 55-59.

5101. West, Gordon. "J.R. Williams, Cowboy Cartoonist." *Frontier Times* (Austin, Texas). December-January 1971.

5102. Williams, J.R. *Born Thirty Years Too Soon*. New York: Scribner's, 1945.

5103. Williams, J.R. *The Bull of the Woods*. New York: Charles Scribner's Sons, 1944.

5104. Williams, J.R. *Why Mothers Get Gray*. New York: Charles Scribner's Sons, 1945.

Williamson, Al

5105. "Al Williamson." *Comics Interview*. No. 62, 1988, pp. 43-59.

5106. "The Al Williamson Story." *Cartoonist PROfiles*. Summer 1969, pp. 30-39.

5107. Arbesú, Faustino R. "Al Williamson: Elegancia, Asimilación y Modernidad." *El Wendigo*. No. 57, 1992, pp. 14-15.

5108. Heintjes, Tom. "Al Williamson." *Comics Journal*. July 1985, pp. 127-128.

5109. Ringgenberg, S.C. "Al Williamson: A Talk with the Celebrated EC Science Fiction Artist." *Comics Journal*. June 1984, pp. 63-94.

5110. "A 3/4 Score (Al Williamson)." *Squa Tront*. No. 8, 1978, pp. 14-20.

5111. Van Hise, James. *The Art of Al Williamson*. San Diego, California: Blue Dolphin Enterprises, 1983. 144 pp.

5112. Van Hise, James and Andrew Mayfair. "Flashing Across the Empire with Al Williamson." *Comics Scene*. July 1983, pp. 32-36.

Williamson, Skip

5113. Green, Grass. "The Strange World of Snappy Sammy Snoot." *Comics Journal*. January 1986, pp. 50-74.

5114. "Meet Cartoonist Skip Williamson." *The World of Comic Art*. June 1966, p. 17.

5115. "Skip Williamson Sketchbook." *Comics Journal*. May 1993, pp. 114-118.

5116. Williamson, Skip. "Skip to 1985." *Comics Journal*. January 1985, p. 74.

Wilson, S. Clay

5117. Pfouts, Chris. "S. Clay Wilson: Putting the 'Ugh' in Underground." *Art? Alternatives*. April 1992, pp. 73-81.

5118. "S. Clay Wilson: a Profile." In *The Official Underground and Newave Comix Price Guide*, edited by Jay Kennedy, p. 27. Cambridge, Massachusetts: Boatner Norton Press, 1982.

Wolfman, Marv

5119. "The Comics Scene: Marv Wolfman and Peter David Discuss Heroic Fare." *Comics Scene*. No. 3 (Vol. 3, Series 14), pp. 8-10.

5120. Decker, Dwight R. "Marv Wolfman: On the New Teen Titans. Part I." *Comics Journal*. January 1983, pp. 86-98.

5121. "An Interview with Marv Wolfman." *Orion*. 1:2 (1982), pp. 10-17.

5122. Johnson, Kim H. "Of Titans and Terminators." *Comics Scene*. February 1991, pp. 10-16.

5123. Kraft, David A. "Marv Wolfman." *Comics Interview*. May 1983, pp. 18-30.

5124. MacDonald, Heidi D. "Marv Wolfman." *Comics Journal*. July 1985, pp. 171-173+.

5125. MacDonald, Heidi. "Marv Wolfman on the *New* Teen Titans: Part Two." *Comics Journal*. March 1983, pp. 70-85.

5126. "Marv Wolfman." *Comics Interview*. No. 74, 1989, pp. 9-11.

5127. "Marv Wolfman Discovers the DC Universe." *Comics Feature*. February 1987, pp. 8-10.

5128. "Marv Wolfman Fired by DC As Editor." *Comics Journal*. April 1987, pp. 9-10.

5129. Sanderson, Peter. "Marv Wolfman." *Comics Feature*. September-October 1981, pp. 34-64.

5130. Thompson, Kim. "An Interview with Marv Wolfman." *Comics Journal*. January 1979, pp. 34-51.

5131. Wolfman, Marv. "The Creators Reply...." *Comics Journal*. January 1988, pp. 87-88.

Wolverton, Basil

5132. Cameron, Oregon Eddy. "A Visit with Basil Wolverton." *Baycon III Program Book*. 1977, pp. 38-39.

5133. Voll, Dick. "Basically Basil." *Qua Brot*. No. 1, 1985, pp. 44-46.

5134. Voll, Dick. "The Spaghetti and Meatball School of Design." *Comics Journal*. September 1985, pp. 85-89.

5135. Wolverton, Basil. *Spacehawk*. Cambridge, Massachusetts: Archival Press, 1978. 63 pp.

5136. Zone, Ray. "Boltbeak The Art of Basil Wolverton." *Journal of Popular Culture*. Winter 1987, pp. 145-163.

Wood, Wally

5137. Benson, John. "Wood Has Done It!" *The Cartoonist*. October 1966, p. 31.

5138. "Cover Ideas from the Wood File." *Squa Tront*. No. 9, 1983, pp. 45-50.

5139. Decker, Dwight R. "X-Rated Wally Wood." *Comics Journal*. October 1981, pp. 55-56.

5140. Decker, Dwight R. and Kim Thompson. "Newswatch: Wally Wood Dead at 54." *Comics Journal*. December 1981, pp. 8-12.

5141. "Early Wood." *Squa Tront*. No. 9, 1983, pp. 26-33.

5142. Stewart, Bhob. "Memories of Wally Wood: There Are Good Guys and Bad Guys." *Comics Journal*. January 1982, pp. 50-67.

5143. Webb, Steve. "The Devil and Wally Wood." *The Daredevil Chronicles*. February 1982, pp. 4-6.

5144. Wood, Wallace. *The Marvel Comics Art of Wally Wood*. Brooklyn, New York: Thumbtack Books, 1982. 62 pp.

5145. Wood, Wallace. "My Strange Move, or How I Learned To Stop Working and Joined the Fans." *The Cartoonist*. October 1966, pp. 32-34.

5146. Wood, Wallace. *The Wallace Wood Sketchbook*. Bridgeport, Connecticut: B. Crouch, 1980, 48 pp.

5147. Wood, Wallace. *The Wallace Wood Treasury*. New York: Pure Imagination, 1980. 52 pp.

5148. "Wood. Galaxy Folio." *Qua Brot*. No. 1, 1985, pp. 39-43.

Workman, John

5149. Groth, Gary. "Das Heavy Metal Interview." *Comic Forum* (Vienna). 4:13 (1982), pp. 28-30. (Julie Simmons and John Workman).

5150. Simmons, Julie and John Workman. "'We're All Lunatics': The Heavy Metal Interview." *Comics Journal*. September 1979, pp. 42-50.

5151. Wochner, Lee. "John Workman." *Comics Journal*. July 1985, pp. 174-178.

Wrightson, Berni

5152. Christie, Andrew. "Wrightson." *Comics Journal*. July 1985, pp. 179-181.

5153. Groensteen, Thierry. "Entretien Avec Berni Wrightson." *Les Cahiers de la Bande Dessinée* (Grenoble). 66, 1985, pp. 57-59.

5154. Groth, Gary. "Zombies, Homunculi, and (Swamp) Things That Go Bump in the Night: An Interview with Berni Wrightson." *Comics Journal*. October 1982, pp. 80-134.

5155. Lecigne, Bruno. "Wrightson et les EC Comics." *Les Cahiers de la Bande Dessinée* (Grenoble). 66, 1985, pp. 60-61.

5156. Maier, Jürgen. "The Studio. 3:Bernie Wrightson." *Comixene* (Hanover). 7:30 (1980), pp. 54-57.

5157. Malin, Adam. "Berni Wrightson Interview." *Infinity Two*. No. 2 (n.d.), pp. 10-23.

5158. Wrightson, Berni. *Back for More*. Cambridge, Massachusetts: Archival Press, 1978. 62 pp.

5159. Wrightson, Berni. *The Berni Wrightson Treasury*. Detroit, Michigan: Omnibus Publishing, 1975. 48 pp.

5160. Zavisa, Christopher. *Berni Wrightson, a Look Back*. Detroit, Michigan: Land of Enchantment, 1979. 358 pp.

Zeck, Mike

5161. "Artist Mike Zeck." *Comics Interview*. No. 72, 1989, pp. 14-34.

5162. "Mike Zeck: Another Fandom Talent Emerges." *Rocket's Blast Comic Collector*. No. 119, 1975, pp. 14-15.

ANTHOLOGIES, REPRINTS, REVIEWS

5163. "Aztec Ace." *Comics Interview*. April 1984, pp. 7-19.

5164. Baron, Mike and Steve Rude. *The Original Nexus*. First Graphic Novel, No. 4. Chicago, Illinois: First Comics, 1985. 104 pp.

5165. Bethke, Marilyn. "Fandom Review." *Comics Journal*. May 1979, pp. 59-62.

5166. Bittner, Drew. "Feeling Paranoia." *Comics Scene*. February 1991, pp. 53-56, 60.

5167. Bittner, Drew. "Wetworks." *Comic Scene*. December 1992, pp. 25-28, 52.

5168. Bittner, Drew. "Wild Cards." *Comics Scene Spectacular*. September 1990, pp. 50-53.

5169. Boxell, Tim. *Commies from Mars—The Red Planet, The Collected Works*. San Francisco, California: Last Gasp, 1985.

5170. Boyd, Robert. "Mini-malism." *Comics Journal*. March 1992, pp. 45-47.

5171. Chrissinger, Craig W. "Corporate Wars." *Comics Scene*. December 1992, pp. 21-24.

5172. "Christmas Guide." *Before I Get Old*. December 1986, pp. 40-42.

5173. "Classical Comics: Excerpts from Great Comic-Books." *Horizon*. 8 (1966), pp. 116-120.

5174. "Collectors Highlights: What's New in Comics." *Comic Book Collector*. January 1993, pp. 28-29, 31, 33.

5175. Cutler, David W., *et al*. *Two Decades of Comics, a Review*. Bexleyheath, Kent, England: Slings and Arrows, 1981. 112 pp.

5176. Delich, Craig, ed. *All Star Comics Revue*. Kansas City, Kansas: Delich, 1977. 83 pp.

5177. Dellinges, Al, ed. *The Book of Jumbo Comics Covers*. San Francisco, California: 1979. 52 pp.

5178. Dellinges, Al, ed. *Five Stories from Planet Comics*. San Francisco, California: n.d. 38 pp.

5179. Dickholtz, Daniel. "Bombs Away! The Boston Bombers." *Comics Scene*. December 1990, pp. 13-15, 32.

5180. Eagan, Tim. "Subconscious Comics." Reviewed by Liz Sizensky. *Fine Print*. January 1986, pp. 39-40.

5181. Findley, John. *Tex Arcana*. New York: Catalan Communications, 1987. 72 pp.

5182. Fiore, R. "Funnybook Roulette." *Comics Journal*. Continuing column of reviews.

5183. Fox. *The Book of Redfox*. Northwood, Middlesex, England: Harrier Publishing, 1986. 112 pp.

5184. "Futures." *Before I Get Old*. December 1986, p. 39.

5185. Gafford, Carl. "The Reviewing Stand." *The Amazing World of DC Comics*. September-October 1974, pp. 28-29.

5186. Griffith, Bill, *et al. Four Sketchbooks and a Tale of Useful Information*. San Francisco, California: Apex Novelites, 1973. 48 pp. (Bill Griffith, Justin Green, Spain Rodríguez, Art Spiegelman).

5187. Griffith, Ralph, Stu Kerr, and Guy Davis. *The Realm*. Ypsilanti, Michigan: Arrow Comics, 1987-.

5188. Harvey, R.C. "Bringing Back the Reprints." *Comics Journal*. September 1986, pp. 56-58, 60-61.

5189. Harvey, R.C. "Reprint Revolution." *Comics Journal*. October 1992, pp. 121-125.

5190. Hunt, Leon. "Sketches from the Lowbrow Media Bath." *FA*. October 1989, pp. 16-20.

5191. *Jerry Iger's Classic Wings Comics*. El Cajon, California: Blackthorne, 1985. 71 pp.

5192. Johns, T.L. "Another Game Afoot!" *Comics Scene*. No. 13, 1990, pp. 28-31, 52.

5193. Johnson, Kim H. "Heart Surgeon." *Comics Scene*. December 1992, p. 41-44, 50.

5194. Johnson, Kim H. "Light Years." *Comics Scene*. February 1991, pp. 61-64, 66.

5195. Johnson, Kim H. "Reliving History." *Comics Scene*. May 1992, pp. 49-51.

5196. "Kewpies." *Near Mint*. October 1982, pp. 1-13.

5197. Kreiner, Rich. "A Half-Filled Glass from a Tapped-Out Barrel." *Comics Journal*. August 1992, pp. 39-44.

5198. Kyle, Richard. "Graphic Story Review." *Fantasy Illustrated*. No. 7, 1967, pp. 24-27; *Graphic Story Magazine*. October 1967, pp. 30-32.

5199. Lang, Jeffrey. "Vertigo Aims To Put You on the Lip of the Abyss." *Comics Buyer's Guide*. January 22, 1993, pp. 26-28.

5200. Lim Cheng Tju. "Ain't It Distracting." *Big O Magazine*. March 1988, pp. 18-20.

5201. Lim, C.T. "Killing and Firing." *Big O Magazine*. October 1992, pp. 90-91.

5202. Lynch, Jay, ed. *The Best of Bijou Funnies*. New York: Links Books, 1975.

5203. McDonald, Heidi. "Comics in Review." *Amazing Heroes*. June 15, 1987, pp. 66-70.

5204. Marschall, Richard, ed. *Nemo: The Classics Comics Library #9*. Thousand Oaks, California: Fantagraphics, 1984.

5205. Mason, Tom. "Introducing: Dinosaurs for Hire." *Comics Buyer's Guide*. January 1, 1993, p. 27.

5206. Mathews, Kevin. "The Best in the Mainstream." *Big O Magazine*. December 1992, pp. 92-93.

5207. Niderost, Eric. "Zone Continuum." *Comics Scene*. February 1991, pp. 21-24, 60.

5208. "1980 Year in Review." *Comics Feature*. February 1981, pp. 34-60.

5209. "'Nuff Is 'Nuff." *Before I Get Old*. September 1986, pp. 50-51.

5210. Pack, Jim. "The Critical Eye." *The Comicist*. April 1990, pp. 13-18; June 1990, pp. 12-14; July 1990, pp. 20-25; August 1990, pp. 18-21; September 1990, pp. 15-18. (Small press comics reviews).

5211. Pennsylvania. University. Institute of Contemporary Art. *The Spirit of the Comics*. [Catalogue of an exhibition held] October 1-November 9, 1969. [Philadelphia] 1969. 32 pp.

5212. Phillips, Gene. "The Great Originals." *Comics Feature*. November 1982, pp. 88-92.

5213. "Richard Sala Sketchbook." *Comics Journal*. August 1993, pp. 107-111.

5214. Roche, Ruth and Matt Baker. *Flamingo*. Jerry Iger's Golden Features, No. 1. El Cajon, California: Blackthorne, 1986. 32 pp.

5215. Rodi, Rob. "What Price Role Models?" *Comics Journal*. August 1992, pp. 23-25.

5216. Rodi, Rob, *et al*. "Saints and Sinners." *Comics Journal*. December 1987, pp. 47-52.

5217. "A Rogue's Gallery." *Squa Tront*. No. 9, 1983, pp. 80-81.

5218. Schanes, Steve and Bill Schanes, eds. *Planet Comics*. San Diego, California: Blue Dolphin, 1984. 70 pp.

5219. Shelton, Gilbert. *Thoroughly Ripped with the Fabulous Furry Freak Brothers*. San Francisco, California: Rip Off Press, 1978. 63 pp.

5220. "Short Changed." *Squa Tront*. No. 9, 1983, pp. 42-44.

5221. Soron, Bob. "Twinkle Twinkle. Little Star...." *Comics Feature*. November 1982, pp. 56-59.

5222. Tan, Mike. "Hard Times." *Before I Get Old*. January 1991, p. 81.

5223. Tan, Stephen. "Ain't It Distracting." *Before I Get Old.* December 1986, pp. 46-47.

5224. Tan, Stephen. "Comics Stop 'Growing.'" *Before I Get Old.* July 1987, pp. 22-24.

5225. Tan, Stephen. "Heartbreak Hotel." *Before I Get Old.* August 1986, pp. 42-44.

5226. Tan, Stephen. "Promising First Half." *Before I Get Old.* July 1987, pp. 27-28.

5227. Tan, Stephen. "The Story Counts Too." *Before I Get Old.* May 1987, pp. 27-30.

5228. Tan, Stephen. "Turnout a Letdown." *Before I Get Old.* February 1987, pp. 24-25.

5229. Teo, Billy. "Ain't It Distractin.'" *Before I Get Old.* July 1987, pp. 25-26.

5230. Wochner, Lee. "Comics 1983: The Year in Review." *Comics Journal.* May 1984, pp. 62-71.

LEGAL ASPECTS

5231. "Dispute Ends Kirby Awards." *Comics Buyer's Guide.* April 15, 1988, p. 64.

5232. "ECA Denies Granting Credits for Comics in Germany." *Publisher's Weekly.* December 11, 1948, p. 2346.

5233. Edelman, M. "American Style Comics and the Law." *Publishers Circular and Booksellers Report* (London). 166:4493 (1952), pp. 1150-1151.

5234. Edelman, Scott. "Opportunity Knocked." *Comics Journal.* November 1985, pp. 100-102.

5235. "Establishment Uproar." *Speakeasy.* April 1990, p. 21.

5236. "Fantagraphics Sues Ex-*Comics Journal* Editor." *Comics Journal.* August 1993, pp. 11-15.

5237. "FBI Investigates Letters Sent to Kay Reynolds." *Comics Journal.* July 1987, p. 22.

5238. Gaines, William M. "Fighting Mad." *CAPS Newsletter.* October 1990, pp. 21-22.

5239. Groth, Gary. "Is This Any Way To Run a Protest?" *Comics Journal.* December 1987, pp. 5-7.

5240. Groth, Gary. "Things Change." *Comics Journal.* August 1993, pp. 7-8.

5241. "Hasbro Forces Marvel to Recall G.I. Joe Issue, Print Retraction." *Comics Journal*. December 1986, p. 23.

5242. Ingersoll, Robert M. "The Law Is a Ass." *Comics Buyer's Guide*. Continuing column from August 26, 1983.

5243. "Lawsuits Filed." *Comics Feature*. January 1981, pp. 9-10.

5244. Lynch, Jay. "Destroying Idols: The Role of Satire and the Free Press in Comics." *Comics Journal*. February 1987, pp. 76-94.

5245. Lynch, Jay. "The First Amendment Was Easier Then." In *The Official Underground and Newave Comix Price Guide*, edited by Jay Kennedy, pp. 16-18. Cambridge, Massachusetts: Boatner Norton Press, 1982.

5246. McGreal, Dorothy. "The Curious Case of the Ink-Stained Attorney." *The World of Comic Art*. 2:1 (1967), pp. 17-21.

5247. Metz, C. "Jack Chick's Anti-Catholic *Alberto* Comic Book Is Exposed As a Fraud." *Christianity Today*. March 13, 1981, p. 50+.

5248. "Right To Spoof—How Far Does It Go?" *Comics Journal*. January 1986, p. 13.

5249. Snyder, Robin. "Freedom of the Press: Opening Shots." *Comics Journal*. September 1987, p. 9.

5250. "State Flip-Flops, Tells Mavrides To Pay Up." *Comics Journal*. May 1993, p. 9.

5251. "Stuff v. EC Publications, Inc., *et al*." *U.S. Patent Quarterly*. Fed. Ct. of Appeals for the 2d Cir.: 1965, 560.

5252. Tan, Stephen. "Means to an End: Pt. II." *Before I Get Old*. September 1986, pp. 55-57.

5253. "Thomas, Kupperberg Respond to *Hour 25* Allegations." *Comics Journal*. April 1987, pp. 18-20.

5254. "WaRP files $4 Million Lawsuit." *Comics Journal*. April 1987, pp. 11-12.

Censorship, Control

5255. "Adult Comics Seized in Florida." *Comics Journal*. December 1990, pp. 9-10.

5256. Allport, T.A. "Comic Book Control Can Be a Success." *American City*. January 1949, p. 100.

5257. Ang, Benjamin. "A Case for Censorship." *Before I Get Old*. September 1986, pp. 57-60.

5258. "As the Dust Settles." *Comics Journal*. December 1987, pp. 58-72, 74-83. (Alan Moore and Frank Miller on censorship).

5259. Beck, C.C. "Those Hysterical Cries Against Censorship... Are They To Be Heeded?" *Comics Journal*. December 1989, pp. 115-116.

5260. "Better Than Censorship." *Christian Century*. July 28, 1948, p. 750.

5261. "Bindery Refuses *Yummy Fur* and *Omaha* Collections." *Comics Journal*. November 1989, p. 13.

5262. Bissette, Stephen R. "'Fulce-ifying' Evidence." *Gauntlet*. No. 2, 1991, pp. 227-236.

5263. "Booksellers' Group May Expel Chick (anti-Catholic comic book, *Alberto*)." *Christianity Today*. October 31, 1981, p. 62.

5264. Cafasso, Ed. "The Chilling Effect of Corporate Extortion on the Arts." *Gauntlet*. No. 5, 1993, pp. 146-163.

5265. "Catalogs Restrict Adult Comics Listings." *Comics Journal*. June 1991, pp. 13-14.

5266. "Comic Legends Quits Obscenity Appeal." *Comics Journal*. November 1989, p. 14.

5267. "Comic Shop Busted." *Comics Journal*. February 1987, pp. 13-15.

5268. "Comic Shop Claims Police Harassment." *Comics Journal*. July 1990, pp. 11-12.

5269. "Comics Store Manager Arrested in Florida." *Comics Journal*. July 1992, pp. 9-10.

5270. "Controversy Raised over Explicit *Miracleman* Birth Scenes." *Comics Journal*. November 1986, p. 11.

5271. "Enter the PC Superheroes." *The Jester*. March 1993, p. 2.

5272. Flagg, Michael. "Comic Books Not Just Kid Stuff." *Los Angeles Times*. March 1, 1991, pp. E-1, E-3.

5273. "Florida Retailer Is Acquitted." *Comics Journal*. June 1991, pp. 10-11.

5274. "Friendly Frank's Closes." *Comics Journal*. January 1989, p. 25.

5275. "Friendly Frank's Manager Found Guilty." *Comics Journal*. March 1988, p. 5.

5276. "Friendly Frank's; New Evidence." *Comics Journal*. July 1987, p. 20.

5277. "Friendly Frank's Wins on Appeal." *Comics Journal*. December 1989, pp. 13-15.

5278. Gaines, William M., *et al*. "Censorship in Comics." *Comics Journal*. November 1982, pp. 91-101.

5279. "*Gauntlet*: Exploring the Limits of Free Expression." *Magazine Week*. November 9, 1992, p. 17.

5280. "Gerber Pulls Howard Script." *Comics Journal*. August 1985, pp. 14-19.

5281. Gordon, George. "Popeye Artist Fired for Pouring Oyl on Troubled Waters." *The Jester*. September 1992, p. 12. Reprinted from *Daily Mail* (London). July 23, 1992.

5282. Groth, Gary. "Censored for Real." *Comics Journal*. March 1988, p. 3.

5283. Groth, Gary. "Courage Before Freelancers, Cowardice Before Censorship." *Comics Journal*. April 1989, pp. 3-4.

5284. Groth, Gary. "Protection Vs. Censorship: Buddy Saunders." *Comics Journal*. July 1987, pp. 29-34.

5285. Groth, Gary. "Thomas Radecki Interview." *Comics Journal*. December 1989, pp. 66-75.

5286. "Happy Hal's Howlings." *Comics Feature*. May 1987, p. 12.

5287. "*Homo Patrol* Causes Uproar in the Midwest." *Comics Journal*. January 1993, p. 22.

5288. "Isabella Withdraws *Everett True* from the *Buyer's Guide* Due to Censorship." *Comics Journal*. February 1987, pp. 25-26.

5289. Johnson, Larry. "Self-Censorship." *The Comicist*. August/September 1991, pp. 12-13.

5290. Legman, Gershon. *Love and Death: A Study in Censorship*. New York: Breaking Point, 1949; New York: Hacker Art Books, 1963.

5291. Levin, Bob. "Attack on the Salmonheads." *Comics Journal*. April 1991, pp. 3-5.

5292. "Lone Star Comics Restricts Sales of 'Inappropriate' Material to Children." *Comics Journal*. December 1986, pp. 14-15.

5293. "*Lone Wolf* and *Club* Branded 'Harmful.'" *Comics Journal*. June 1991, p. 15.

5294. MacDonald, Heidi. "In the Beginning Was the Word: Interview with Frank Miller on Censorship." *WittyWorld*. Summer 1987, pp. 5-7.

5295. "Marvel To Be Sued Twice for Same Comic Book." *Comics Journal*. December 1992, p. 11.

5296. Mescallado, Ray. "Exploring the Limits of Free Expression. *Gauntlet* 1992 Edition." *Comics Journal*. January 1993, pp. 90-93.

5297. "Mike Barr Fired from DC over Letter He Wrote to *The Comics Journal*." *Comics Journal*. February 1987, pp. 24-25.

5298. "Miller, Evanier, Wolfman Discuss Comics 'Censorship' with Ellison on *Hour 25*." *Comics Journal*. April 1987, pp. 16-18.

5299. Miller, John J. "Comics on Trial." *Comics Journal*. December 1989, pp. 85-86.

5300. Mitchell, Steve. "The Best Is The Worst: Love, 'Classics,' and the ACMP." *Comics Buyer's Guide*. July 19, 1985, pp. 25, 28, 30, 32, 38.

5301. Moore, Alan. "The Politics and Morality of Ratings and Self-Censorship." *Comics Journal*. September 1987, pp. 35-36.

5302. O'Neill, Patrick D. "Censor Censure." *Comics Journal*. July 1986, pp. 39-41.

5303. "Police Crack Down on California Comics Stores." *Comics Journal*. July 1992, pp. 10-11.

5304. "*Popeye* Artist Fired." *Comics Journal*. August 1992, p. 12.

5305. Rodi, Rob. "Repeat Until Spanked." *Comics Journal*. February 1987, pp. 57-61.

5306. Schultz, Henry E. "Censorship or Self Regulation?" *Journal of Educational Sociology*. December 1949, pp. 215-224.

5307. Shetterly, Will. "Graphic Comics Stir Controversy." *Utne Reader*. May-June 1991, pp. 32, 34.

5308. "Some Milestone Comics Drop Comics Code." *Comics Journal*. July 1993, p. 12.

5309. Strnad, Jan. "Bitter Harvest." *Comics Journal*. October 1983, pp. 87-96.

5310. Sweeney, Bruce. "Publisher: Bernd Metz." *Comics Interview*. No. 35, 1986, pp. 38-45.

5311. Tan, Stephen. "Censorship Is No Solution." *Before I Get Old*. June 1987, pp. 18-20.

5312. "Testimony Given; Friendly Frank's Case Goes on Trial May 13." *Comics Journal*. April 1987, p. 24.

5313. Thompson, Don. "Comics Guide." *Comics Buyer's Guide*. February 10, 1993, pp. 28, 32.

5314. Williams, J.P. "Why Superheroes Never Bleed: The Effects of Self-Censorship on the Comic Book Industry." *Free Speech Yearbook*, Volume 26, 1987, edited by S.A. Smith, pp. 60-69. Carbondale, Illinois: Southern Illinois University Press, 1988.

5315. Worley, Kate. "Finding the Cost of Freedom." *Gauntlet*. No. 3, 1992, pp. 156-162.

5316. "Zealous Feds." *Comics Journal*. December 1989, pp. 17-21.

Copyright, Licensing, Plagiarism

5317. "Cå May Regulate Collectables [sic]." *Comics Journal*. April 1993, p. 22.

5318. "A Case of Plagiarism." *Comics Journal*. September 1990, p. 25.

5319. "Copyright Troubles for Revolutionary Comics." *Comics Journal*. February 1990, p. 9.

5320. "Copyright Udløbet for Mickey Mouse." *Serieskaberen*. December 1989, pp. 10-11.

5321. Desris, Joe. "Licensing Comics Characters." *Comics Buyer's Guide*. December 18, 1987, pp. 28-30.

5322. "Piracy in the Public Domain?" *Comics Journal*. April 1991, pp. 16-17.

5323. "Swipe File." *Squa Tront*. No. 7, 1977, p. 15-17; No. 8, 1978, pp. 10-13.

5324. "Tom DeFalco on Licensing." *Comics Business*. July 1987, pp. 1, 3.

Creator's Rights

5325. "Amy Grant Sues Marvel." *Comics Journal*. July 1990, p. 13.

5326. Bissette, Steve, Scott McCloud, and Gary Groth. "What Are Creator's Rights?" *Comics Journal*. September 1990, pp. 66-92.

5327. Bode, Janet. "A Comic Book Artist KO'd: Jack Kirby's Six-Year Slugfest with Marvel." *Village Voice*. December 8, 1987, pp. 30-32, 34, 36, 38.

5328. "Comics Contracts: What the Various Companies Offer." *Comics Journal*. December 1986, pp. 19-22.

5329. "Comics Creators Mobilize in Response to Guidelines and Rumors of Guidelines." *Comics Journal*. February 1987, pp. 17-22.

5330. "Controversy over Warren Art." *Comics Journal*. October 1984, pp. 8-11.

5331. "Creators Discuss the Pros and Cons of Contracts." *Comics Journal*. December 1986, pp. 22-23.

5332. Dorschner, John. "Fighting Mad." *CAPS*. August 1990, pp. 9-12, 15-16; *Miami Herald, Tropic*. May 20, 1990.

5333. "Eight Top Creators Petition Innovation." *Comics Journal*. July 1989, pp. 16-19.

5334. Friedrich, Mike. "Creator's Rights in the Real World." *Comics Journal*. December 1990, pp. 110-114.

5335. Groth, Gary. "Creator's Rights: The Latest Panacea." *Comics Journal*. December 1983, pp. 6-8.

5336. "Jack Kirby Vs. Marvel Comics: The Public's Outrage." *Comics Journal*. August 1986, pp. 31-44.

5337. Kirby, Jack. "Jack Kirby Replies to Marvel Statement." *Comics Buyer's Guide*. October 3, 1986, pp. 1, 3.

5338. "The Kirby Art Work." *Comics Journal*. September 1986, pp. 9-14.

5339. "Marvel Returns Art to Kirby, Adams." *Comics Journal*. July 1987, p. 15.

5340. "Marvel's Art Return on Hold." *Comics Journal*. April 1986, pp. 9-10.

5341. "Marvel Takes Legal Action." *Comics Journal*. July 1987, pp. 16-17.

5342. "Marvel To Return Original Art." *Comics Journal*. February 1985, pp. 8-10.

5343. "Marvel Vice President Michael Z. Hobson Releases Statement on Kirby Art Dispute: Jack and Roz Kirby Respond." *Comics Journal*. September 1986, p. 10.

5344. "Mavrides Makes a Stand for Cartoonists' Rights." *Comics Journal*. October 1992, pp. 28-29.

5345. "'Sad Sack' Artist Wins $2.58 Million in Suit." *Comics Journal*. July 1983, p. 12.

5346. "Senate Considering Work-Made-for-Hire Bill That Favors Artists." *Comics Journal*. September 1986, pp. 16-18.

5347. Siegel, Jerry and James Steranko. "The Case Against Superman." *Mediascene*. January-February 1976, pp. 25-28.

5348. "Supersuit; Rights to Superman." *Newsweek*. April 14, 1947, p. 65.

5349. Thompson, Don. "Don Martin Leaves 'Mad' for 'Cracked.'" *Comics Buyer's Guide*. November 13, 1987, pp. 1, 3.

5350. "Twelve Creators Sue Donning Company." *Comics Journal*. November 1991, pp. 21-22.

5351. "U.S. Supreme Favors Artist 9-0." *Comics Journal*. July 1989, pp. 10-13.

5352. "Where Did All the Art Go?" *Comics Journal*. February 1986, pp. 16-22.

5353. "Work-for-Hire Bill in Legislative Limbo." *Comics Journal*. February 1990, p. 8.

Guidelines, Ratings

5354. "Aircel's 'New' Nudity Policy 18 Months Old." *Comics Journal*. August 1988, p. 15.

5355. "DC Guidelines Spawn Reaction." *Comics Journal*. February 1987, pp. 16-17.

5356. "DC Responds to Miller, Moore, Chaykin and Wolfman's Letter." *Comics Journal*. April 1987, pp. 21-22.

5357. "DC Senior Editor Schwartz Avoids Questions on DC Guidelines on *Hour 25*." *Comics Journal*. April 1987, p. 21.

5358. "Diamond Policies Questioned." *Comics Journal*. July 1987, pp. 18-20.

5359. Giordano, Dick. "What Ratings? By Whom?" *Comic Scene*. September 1983, pp. 30-31.

5360. "Measures by the Giants: DC's Guidelines; Marvel's Return to the Code." *Comics Journal*. December 1986, p. 18.

5361. National Institute of Municipal Law Officers, Washington, D.C. *NIMLO Model Comic Book Ordinance*. Washington, D.C.: 1954? 4 pp.

5362. "Ratings and Standards in Comics?" *Comics Journal*. December 1987, pp. 15-17.

5363. "The Ratings Debate." *Comics Journal*. January 1984, pp. 71-84; Part 2, pp. 86-94.

5364. Rhyne, Charles S. "Comic Books—Municipal Control of Sale and Distribution. A Preliminary Study." Washington, D.C.: National Institute of Municipal Law Officers, 1949.

Libel

5365. "Closing Arguments." *Comics Journal*. April 1987, pp. 129-142.

5366. "*Comics Journal* Wins Fleisher Libel Suit." *Comics Journal*. December 1986, p. 11.

5367. "The Deposition of Dean Mullaney." *Comics Journal*. April 1987, pp. 65-73.

5368. Ellison, Harlan. "Preliminary Thoughts on the 'Big Lawsuit.'" *Comics Journal*. April 1987, pp. 61-62.

5369. Groth, Gary. "How Much Does Freedom of the Press Cost? A Couple Hundred Thousand Dollars, Thank You Very Much." *Comics Journal*. February 1987, pp. 8-9.

5370. Groth, Gary. "Notes on the Testimony." *Comics Journal*. April 1987, p. 63.

5371. Groth, Gary. "Reflections of an Expert Witness." *Comics Journal*. October 1988, pp. 3-4.

5372. Sacco, Joe. "The Fight for 1st Amendment Rights." *Comics Journal*. April 1987, pp. 51-55.

5373. Sacco, Joe. "Personal Comments: Jurors' Recollections." *Comics Journal*. April 1987, pp. 57-58.

5374. "The Testimony of Gary Groth." *Comics Journal*. April 1987, pp. 119-128.

5375. "The Testimony of Harlan Ellison." *Comics Journal*. April 1987, pp. 109-117.

5376. "The Testimony of Jim Shooter." *Comics Journal.* April 1987, pp. 75-107.

Obscenity, Pornography, Violence

5377. "Adult Content: Whose Responsibility?" *Comics Interview.* No. 43, 1987, pp. 8-21.

5378. "Cartoonist Charged in Florida Obscenity Case." *Comics Journal.* July 1993, pp. 10-11.

5379. "Concern over Comics' Contents Escalates Inside Industry and Out." *Comics Journal.* December 1986, pp. 12-14.

5380. Edelman, Scott. "Death, Be Not Bland." *Comics Journal.* January 1986, pp. 92-94.

5381. "Filth on Trial." *Comics Journal.* July 1988, pp. 91-100, 102-107.

5382. "Frank Miller Reacts to the Controversy." *Comics Journal.* December 1986, p. 18.

5383. Gattuso, Steve. "Golden Shower of Porn." *Comics Journal.* June 1991, pp. 27-28.

5384. Groth, Gary. "Everybody's a Critic." *Comics Journal.* June 1991, pp. 5-7.

5385. Groth, Gary. "Obscenity and the Rights of the Individual—John Weston." *Comics Journal.* June 1988, pp. 127-132.

5386. Groth, Gary. "Todd Loren: First Amendment Advocate or Lying Sack of Shit?" *Comics Journal.* October 1990, pp. 5-6.

5387. Groth, Gary. "Violence and the Evil of Banality." *Comics Journal.* December 1989, pp. 7-8.

5388. Harvey, R.C. "Sex and Violence Galore." *Comics Journal.* December 1989, pp. 103-109.

5389. Kreiner, Rick. "The Quality of Violence." *Comics Journal.* December 1989, pp. 91, 95-96.

5390. McGuire, Dave, City Director of Public Relations to Mayor Morrison and the Commission Council of the City of New Orleans. *Report on Comic Books.* October 18, 1948.

5391. "'Mature' Comics Fall into an Unfavorable Media Spotlight." *Comics Journal.* January 1988, pp. 9-16.

5392. Rodman, Larry. "Reality Check: Violence in the Media." *Comics Journal.* December 1989, pp. 9-11.

5393. "The Sad Truth Behind a Media Circus." *Comics Journal.* December 1990, p. 17.

5394. Scholz, Carl. "Seduction of the Ignorant." *Comics Journal.* March 1983, pp. 48-53.

5395. Smith, Kenneth. "Violence: Decivilization and Dissonance." *Comics Journal.* December 1989, pp. 111-114.

5396. Stallman, David. "An Inquiry into Violence." *Comics Journal.* September 1981, pp. 85-91.

5397. "Violent Comics Draw Unfavorable Media Spotlight." *Comics Journal.* July 1989, pp. 5-10.

5398. "Washington, D.C. Television Station Reports on 'Sick Comics.'" *Comics Journal.* December 1986, pp. 16-18.

5399. "'X-Rated Adult Comics' Discussed on TV Show." *Comics Journal.* October 1990, p. 11.

TECHNICAL ASPECTS

5400. "Blue Line Presents How to... Chapter 1, Page Layout." *Comics Arena.* July 1992, p. 28.

5401. "Eclipse." *Cartoonist PROfiles.* March 1992, pp. 22-27.

5402. Johnson, Kim H. "Classic Style." *Comics Scene.* February 1990, pp. 17-20, 24.

5403. Kuhn, W.B. "Don't Laugh at the Comics, Opportunity for the Freelancer." *Writer.* February 1951, pp. 46-48.

5404. Levitz, Paul. "How a Comic Is Created." *The Amazing World of DC Comics.* September-October 1974, pp. 30-32.

5405. "The Mighty Marvel Comics Submissions Guide." *Cartoonist PROfiles.* June 1992, pp. 38-41.

5406. Morrissey, Rich. "Covers, Backups, and Mysteries. The Path to Success in Comic Books." *LOC*. January 1980, pp. 41-47.

5407. "Once Trained, How Can a Newcomer in Your Field Get Work?" *Comics Collector*. Winter 1986, pp. 38-39.

5408. Pack, Jim. "Advertising Your Comic Book: An Economical Approach." *The Comicist*. August 1990, pp. 11-13.

5409. Pini, Richard and Wendy. "Breaking In: Tips and Advice." *Comics Scene*. July 1982, pp. 54-56.

5410. Prahl, Jack. "What Will Editors Buy?" *Cartoonist PROfiles*. September 1986, pp. 26-29.

5411. Pratt, Douglas R. "The Comics Forum: A Convention in Your Computer." *CAPS*. September 1991, pp. 17-18.

5412. Previtali, Kenneth. "Frank McLaughlin: Cartooning and Judo Instructor." *Cartoonist PROfiles*. September 1977, pp. 78-83.

5413. Soron, Bob. "Writing and Art in Comics—Friends or Foes?" *LOC*. January 1980, pp. 67-70.

5414. Stoutsenberger, Leo. "Ask Leo." *Cartoonist PROfiles*. March 1990, pp. 52-53; March 1991, pp. 44-49; continuing column.

5415. "WAP! The Freelancers' Newsletter Debuts." *Comics Journal*. June 1988, pp. 15-17.

5416. "What Training or Background Should a Beginner Get Before Becoming a Professional in Your Field?" *Comics Collector*. Winter 1986, pp. 36-37.

5417. Wolfman, Marv. "Writer + Artist + Editor = Comic Book." *Comics Scene*. March 1983, pp. 30-31.

Drawing

5418. Buckler, Rich. *How To Become a Comic Book Artist*. Brooklyn, New York: Solson Publications, 1986. 79 pp.

5419. Buckler, Rich. *How To Draw Super-Heroes*. Brooklyn, New York: Solson Publications, 1986. 94 pp.

5420. Eisner, Will. "Comics and Sequential Art." *Cartoonist PROfiles*. March 1991, pp. 10-16.

5421. Giordano, Dick. "DC Guidelines for Would-Be Comic Book Artists and Writers." *Cartoonist PROfiles*. December 1991, pp. 54-57.

5422. Greenberger, Robert. "Creating the Comics Part Four A: Inking." *Comics Scene*. September 1982, pp. 56-59, 65.

5423. Greenberger, Robert. "Creating the Comics Part Four B: Inking." *Comics Scene*. November 1982, pp. 58-63.

5424. Greenberger, Robert. "Creating the Comics. Part Two: Pencilling." *Comics Scene*. March 1982, pp. 52-55.

5425. Greenberger, Robert. "Creating the Comics: Part Three: Lettering." *Comics Scene*. July 1982, pp. 58, 60-61.

5426. Henderson, Rik. "Pixelized Panels: Comics and Computers." *Speakeasy*. December-January 1989-1990, pp. 50-51.

5427. Hogarth, Burne. *Dynamic Wrinkles Drapery*. New York: Watson-Guptill, 1992.

5428. "How To Print and Publish Your Own Comic Book. Part Five. Drawing the Comic Strip." *Comic Book Newsletter*. March 1988, pp. 12-14.

5429. "How To Print and Publish Your Own Comic Book. Part Six. Creating the Final Art." *Comic Book Newsletter*. April 1988, pp. 18-19.

5430. Janson, Klaus, *et al*. "Creating the Comics. Part Four C: Inking." *Comics Scene*. January 1982, pp. 59-60.

5431. Johnson, Larry. "Classic Comics Characters." *The Comicist*. February 1992, pp. 10-11.

5432. Lee, Stan and John Buscema. *How To Draw Comics the Marvel Way*. New York: Simon and Schuster, 1978. 160 pp.

5433. McKenzie, Alan. *How To Draw and Sell Comic Strips for Newspapers and Comic Books*. Cincinnati, Ohio: North Light Books, 1987. 143 pp.

5434. "Narrative Illustration: The Story of the Comics." *Print*. Summer 1943, pp. 1-14.

5435. Sanderson, Peter. "Comics As an Artistic Form." *Comics Feature*. June 1983, p. 47.

5436. Schmitt, Ronald. "Deconstructive Comics." *Journal of Popular Culture*. Spring 1992, pp. 153-161.

5437. Smith, Frank C. *I Can Draw Comics and Cartoons*. New York: Wanderer Books, 1982.

5438. Steranko, Jim. "Breaking into Comics: Part Two—The Laws of Action." *Mediascene*. July-August 1978, p. 18+.

5439. Tallarico, Anthony. *Let's Draw Comics*. New York: Grosset and Dunlap, 1976.

5440. "3-D: Many Levels." *Squa Tront*. No. 5, 1974, p. 25-27.

5441. Willette, Allen. *Top Cartoonists Tell How They Create America's Favorite Comics*. Fort Lauderdale, Florida: 1964.

5442. Windham, Ryder. "Hogarth 101." *Comics Journal*. November 1992, pp. 40-43.

5443. Young, Eddie. "Illustration and Design." *Cartoonist PROfiles*. March 1988, pp. 76-81.

Publishing

5444. Arthur, Robert. "How the Comics Are Made." *FCA/S.O.B.* April/May 1982, pp. 3-6.

5445. Brodsky, Gary. *How To Publish Comics*. Brooklyn, New York: Solson, 1987. 32 pp.

5446. Cummings, Richard. *Make Your Own Comics for Fun and Profit*. New York: H.Z. Walck, 1976. 118 pp.

5447. Eaton, Edward R. "Color Plates for Comics." In *Eighth Graphic Arts Production Yearbook*. New York: Colton Press, 1948.

5448. Feazell, Matt. "Anyone Can Make Their Own Comics! It's Fun and Easy!" *Small Press Comics Explosion*. July 1986, pp. 9-11.

5449. Fox, Janet. "So You Want To Publish a Small Press Zine." *Citizens Publishing*. December 1988, pp. 19-22.

5450. Gold, Mike. "Technocomics." *Comics Journal*. August 1985, pp. 94-96.

5451. MacLeod, John. "Speaking of Which." *Citizens Publishing*. October-November 1988, p. 3.

5452. Oakley, Peter. "Publishing Comics for Fun and Money." *Penstuff*. May 1992, p. 7.

5453. Pack, Jim. "Creating Comic Books: 'Color Separation.'" *The Comicist*. November 1990, p. 18.

5454. Pack, Jim. "Economics of Publishing." *The Comicist*. July 1990, pp. 16-18.

5455. Pack, Jim. "How To Print and Publish Your Own Comic Book." *Comic Book Newsletter*. January 1988, pp. 9-11; July 1988, p. 13-14.

5456. Pack, Jim. "How To Print and Publish Your Own Comic Book." *The Comicist*. December 1989, pp. 12-14; September 1990, pp. 13-14; February 1990, pp. 18-20.

5457. Pack, Jim. "How To Print and Publish Your Own Comic Book: Preparing the Final Art." *Comicist*. April 1990, pp. 10-12.

5458. Pack, Jim. "How To Print and Publish Your Own Comic Book: Selecting a Printer." *The Comicist*. June 1990, pp. 9-10.

5459. Pack, Jim. "Mass Distribution of Your Comic." *Citizen Publishing*. October-November 1988, pp. 19-20.

5460. Pack, Jim. "Small Press Menu." *Citizens Publishing*. December 1988, pp. 23-30.

5461. Pack, Jim. "The World of the Small Press." *Comic Book Newsletter*. January 1988, pp. 13-15.

5462. Yeh, Phil. "Making and Selling Your Own Book: Just Do It." *Uncle Jam Quarterly*. Summer 1990, pp. 2, 7.

Writing

5463. David, Peter. "Writing for Comic Books: A Non-Absolute 'How To' Essay." *Comics Buyer's Guide 1993 Annual*, pp. 11-12, 14. Iola, Wisconsin: Krause, 1992.

5464. Gheno, D. "Adventures of the Comic Book Writer." *Writer's Digest*. March 1974, pp. 28-30.

5465. "Gil Kane and Denny O'Neil on Comics Writing." *Comics Journal*. July 1981, pp. 61-79.

5466. Greenberger, Robert. "Creating the Comics Part Five: Editing." *Comics Scene*. May 1983, pp. 46-48.

5467. Greenberger, Robert. "Creating the Comics. Part One—Writing Comic Books." *Comics Scene*. January 1981, pp. 36-38.

5468. Howell, Richard. "The School of Comics Over-Writing." *LOC*. January 1980, pp. 13-16.

5469. Jennings, Bob. "'How To Make $20,000 a Year Writing Sword-and-Sorcery Clap-Trap.'" *Comics Feature*. November 1980, pp. 25-28.

5470. Lee, Stan. "There's Money in the Comics!" *Writer's Digest*. November 1947.

3

Comic Strips

GENERAL STUDIES

5471. Astor, David. "G-Rated Comics in an X-Rated World?" *Editor and Publisher*. November 7, 1992, pp. 32-33.

5472. Bagdikian, Ben H. "Stop Laughing: It's the Funnies." *New Republic*. January 8, 1962, pp. 13-15.

5473. Beiswinger, George L. "They Talk about Creative 'Block Busters.'" *Editor and Publisher*. October 14, 1989, pp. 56-58.

5474. Bertieri, Claudio. "'Trent' Anni Dopo: *Il Bertoldo*." *Il Lavoro*. August 25, 1967.

5475. Bindig, Bob. "Boos and Bouquets." *The Funnie's Paper*. May 1985, pp. 11-12.

5476. Bingham, Barry. "Advice from the Comics for Unquiet Americans." *Louisville Courier-Journal*. May 25, 1958.

5477. Blank, Dennis M. "Comics Aren't Funny Telling Off the World." *Editor and Publisher*. 99:26 (1966), pp. 7, 52.

5478. Bogart, Leo. "Adult Talk About Newspaper Comics." *American Journal of Sociology*. January 1956, pp. 26-30.

5479. Bond, C. "The Far Side of NMNH." *Smithsonian*. April 1987, p. 168.

5480. Brednich, R.W. "Comic Strips As a Subject of Folk Narrative Approach." In *Folklore Today. A Festschrift for Richard M. Dorson*, edited by L. Degn, H. Glassie and F.J. Oinas, pp. 45-55. Bloomington, Indiana: Indiana University Research Center for Language and Semiotic Studies, 1976.

5481. Buckner, Jennie. "You Think You Have It Tough? Try Picking the Comics!" *The Funnie's Paper*. February 1984, p. 13.

5482. Caniff, Milton and Jules Feiffer. "Strip Time: The Comics Observed." In *The Festival of Cartoon Art*, pp. 7-30. Columbus, Ohio: Ohio State University Libraries, 1986.

5483. Carlinsky, D. "They're Serious About the Funnies." *Senior Scholastic*. December 11, 1972, pp. 26-27.

5484. Carter, Del. *Good News for Grimey Gulch*. Valley Forge, Pennsylvania: Judson Press, 1977.

5485. Chamberlain, D. "Lizard Power in Aspen." *Rolling Stone*. February 5, 1981, p. 14.

5486. Collings, James L. "Comics." *Editor and Publisher*. May 29, 1954.

5487. "Comic Realities." *Newsweek*. November 23, 1970, pp. 98-99B.

5488. "Comic Strip and Popular Culture." *Intellect*. September 1975, pp. 84-85.

5489. "The Comic Strip in American Life: A British View." *Times Literary Supplement*. September 17, 1954.

5490. "Comic Strip Struggle." *New York Times*. September 13, 1954.

5491. Condor, Bob. "A Ray of Hope." *New York Daily News*. October 9, 1988.

5492. "'Create the Comics of the 90's.'" *Cartoonist PROfiles*. March 1991, pp. 32-37.

5493. Culhane, J. "Funnies Are Us." *Reader's Digest*. August 1979, pp. 163-164.

5494. "Daily News Comic Strip Wins Freedom Foundation Award." *Chicago Daily News*. March 19, 1954, p. 3.

5495. de Haven, Tom. "Strip Mining." *Entertainment Weekly*. October 5, 1990, pp. 44-47.

5496. Denney, Reuel. *The Revolt Against Naturalism in the Funnies. The Astonished Muse*. Chicago, Illinois: University of Chicago Press, 1957.

5497. Dickenson, F. "Fascinating Funnies." *Reader's Digest*. November 1971, pp. 201-204+.

5498. "Drawing the Line." *Newsweek*. July 14, 1969, p. 38.

5499. Dubois, Claude. "Le Titi. Retombe en Enfance." *Figaroscope*. January 22, 1992, p. 8.

5500. Dunn, Bob. "Said and Dunn." *Cartoonist PROfiles*. June 1975, pp. 44-45; September 1977, pp. 76-77.

5501. Dunn, Bob. "Who Will Draw the Next Blockbuster Comic Strip?" *Cartoonist PROfiles*. 1:1 (1969), pp. 32-37.

5502. Eco, Umberto. *Apocalittici e Integrati*. Milan: Bompiani, 1965.

5503. "Editorial: Keeping Apprised." *Nemo*. September 1987, pp. 5-6.

5504. Engli, Frank. "2,000,000 Comic Strip Words." *Cartoonist PROfiles*. No. 9, 1971, pp. 54-61.

5505. "Erst Comic-Strips dann Verbrechen und Massengrab. 'Amerikanische Lebensweise' auf Deutschem Boden." *Neues Deutschland* (East Berlin). June 26, 1954.

5506. "Fabulous Funnies—Das Spiegelkabinett Amerikas. 1." Deutsches Fernsehen (ARD) (Hamburg). 3. Programm, December 31, 1969.

5507. Federman, Michael. "Arbiters of the Comic Page." Boston, Massachusetts: Boston University Report, 1960.

5508. Fermín Pérez, Ramón. "Un Viaje al Pais de las Maravillas." Program of Centro Cultural Campoamor, Oviedo, Spain. November 1988, pp. 35-41.

5509. Fiore, R. "Newspaper Strips." *Comics Journal*. April 1991, pp. 59-64.

5510. Frapat, J. "Tac au Tac in America." *Phénix* (Paris). No. 21, 1971.

5511. "The Funnies As an American Phenomenon and Her Influence." *Graphic Arts*. January 1964.

5512. "Für und Gegen Amerikanische Comic-Strips." *Die Deutsche Zeitung* (Düsseldorf). 4:11 (1950), p. 26.

5513. "Getting Close to 100." *Penstuff*. July 1990, p. 3.

5514. Gibbs, Maureen. "Of 'Maus' and Men." *Penstuff*. June 1992, p. 3.

5515. Glubok, Shirley. *The Art of the Comic Strip*. New York: Macmillan; London: Collier Macmillan, 1979. 52 pp.

5516. Goldberg, Reuben L. "Present: the 60s." *The Cartoonist*. Special Number, 1966, pp. 26-28.

5517. "Government Seeks Artist for Strips." *Editor and Publisher*. October 27, 1956, p. 50.

5518. Gray, H. "Why Two Newspaper Editors Like the Comics." *Media Decisions*. 1977, pp. 12, 69, 133.

5519. Gray, Kevin. "Chasing Purloined Panels." *Gannett Westchester Newspapers*. March 11, 1990, p. A-8.

5520. "Great Comic Cats." *Cartoonist PROfiles*. June 1982, pp. 30-31.

5521. Harvey, R.C. "Chiaroscuro Kipling and a Bit of Lace." *Comics Journal*. January 1988, pp. 111-113.

5522. Harvey, R.C. "Half a Loaf Is Better Than Two in the Bush." *Comics Journal*. November 1981, pp. 32-36.

5523. Harvey, R.C. "Three Classic Adventure Strips." *Comics Journal*. May 1989, pp. 89-92.

5524. Harvey, R.C. "Three Vintage Strips in Print Again." *Comics Journal*. February 1987, pp. 61-70.

5525. "Has This Opus Drawn to an End?" *Newsweek*. May 15, 1989, p. 65.

5526. "Heaven Can Wait." *U.S. News and World Report*. April 17, 1989, p. 14.

5527. Horak, Carl. "Double Take." *The Funnie's Paper*. September 1984, pp. 8-10.

5528. Horak, Carl. "You Should Be Seein' Stars." *The Funnie's Paper*. May 1986, pp. 7-10.

5529. Inge, M. Thomas. "The Comics." In *Humor in America: A Research Guide to Genres and Topics*, edited by Lawrence E. Mintz, pp. 35-48. Westport, Connecticut: Greenwood Press, 1988.

5530. Inge, M. Thomas. "Comics Strips." In *Handbook of American Popular Culture*, edited by M. Thomas Inge, pp. 205-228. Westport, Connecticut: Greenwood Press, 1989.

5531. Inge, M. Thomas. "What's So Funny About the Comics?" In *American Humor*, edited by Arthur P. Dudden, pp. 76-84. New York: Oxford University Press, 1987.

5532. "'Inside' Humor." *Cartoonist PROfiles*. Summer 1969, pp. 66-67.

5533. "Jach Spake: Funny Papers on Strike!" *Comics Journal*. February 1979, pp. 64-66.

5534. Janensch, Paul. "It's Official: Madam Adam Will Return." *Louisville Courier Journal*. October 8, 1965.

5535. Kinnaird, Clark. "Cavalcade of the Funnies." *The Funnies Annual*. No. 1, 1959.

5536. Laas, William. "The Comic Strip." *USA*. 1:10.

5537. Larsen, Tom. "International Page." *The Funnie's Paper*. July 1985, p. 6.

5538. Lasky, Mark. "The Education of an Assistant." *Cartoonist PROfiles*. September 1975, pp. 66-69.

5539. Levine, George and Stewart Slocum. "The 'Wednesday Rounds.'" *Cartoonist PROfiles*. September 1985, pp. 24-29.

5540. "Life in Comic Strip World." *Science News Letter*. August 1, 1953, p. 71.

5541. Love, Phil. "Love to All" *Cartoonist PROfiles*. September 1975, p. 74. Continuing column.

5542. McCabe, Michael. "Carping in America." *The Funnie's Paper*. February 1984, pp. 4-5.

5543. McCarty, Al. "Mindless Musings of a Misbegotten Maniac!" *The Funnie's Paper*. September 1985, pp. 7-8; July 1985, pp. 21-22.

5544. Mad Magazine. "The Comics." *Mad Super Special Number 36*. Fall 1981.

5545. Maeder, Jay. "*The Miami Herald*." *Cartoonist PROfiles*. June 1980, pp. 36-37.

5546. Mano, D.K. "Funnies." *National Review*. June 22, 1973, pp. 688-689.

5547. Marion, Philippe. "Graphic Tracings, Narrative Figuration and Communication. Notes on the Comic Strip and Its Reader." *Recherches Sociologiques*. 21:3 (1990), pp. 353-371.

5548. Marschall, Richard. "Commentary Strips of the '80s: The Emperor's Latest New Clothes." *Comics Journal*. September 1983, pp. 104-112.

5549. Marschall, Richard. "Old World, New Names; Old Strips, New Looks." *Nemo*. May 1985, p. 4.

5550. Marschall, Richard. "Overture." *Comics Journal*. April 1980, pp. 65-67.

5551. Marschall, Richard, *et al*. "Weirdworld." *Comics Journal*. Summer 1979, pp. 45-65.

5552. Martin, D. "Favorites from the Funnies." *Hobbies*. February 1966, pp. 118-119.

5553. Martin, Man. "Sibling Revelry." *Cartoonist PROfiles*. June 1990, pp. 24-29.

5554. "Mary Worm and Mr. Rapp." *New Republic*. September 23, 1957, p. 8.

5555. Mendelsohn, Lee. "The Fabulous Funnies!" *The Cartoonist*. January 1968, pp. 12-13.

5556. Miller, K. "A Feel for the Funnies." *Esquire*. May 1985, pp. 25-26.

5557. Moliterni, Claude. "Bloc-Notes USA/Septembre 1969." *Phénix*. No. 12, 1969.

5558. "Motley: News Puts Prizes in the Kitty for Lookalike." *Cartoonist PROfiles*. March 1979, pp. 84-88.

5559. Neal, Jim. "Cartoonists Campaign for Stamps Honoring Comic Strip." *Comics Buyer's Guide*. May 7, 1993, p. 122.

5560. "New Look on the Funny Pages." *Newsweek*. March 5, 1973, pp. 76-77.

5561. "New Publication Offers Hope to Aspiring Comic Strip Creators." *WittyWorld*. Summer/Autumn 1991, p. 55.

5562. "Newspaper Comics Can Breathe in Riverside!" *Cartoonist PROfiles*. December 1977, pp. 92-93.

5563. Newspaper Comics Council. *Calvacade of American Comics. Report*. October 13-19, 1963. New York, 16 pp.

5564. Newspaper Comics Council. *Parade of the Comics, A Coloring Book*. New York: 1967.

5565. "No Laughing Matter." *Newsweek*. March 8, 1965, p. 39.

5566. Norwood, Rick. "Strip Tease: Year in Review." *Comics Feature*. No. 25, 1983, pp. 77-83.

5567. "O. Bleak." *Saturday Review*. November/December 1985, pp. 49-51.

5568. O'Hara, Frank. "The City: 'Neon in Daylight Is a Great Pleasure.'" *Newsletter* of Society of Strip Illustration. December 1988, p. 6.

5569. "Old Folks Take It Harder Than Junior." *Collier's*. July 9, 1949, p. 74.

5570. Pascal, David. "Comics: Ein Amerikanischer Expressionismus." *Graphis-Sonderband* (Zurich). 1972, pp. 80-87.

5571. Paulssen, Ernst. "Heroen aus der Retorte. Comic Strips von Babylon bis New York." *Deutsche Zeitung* (Cologne). August 19-20, 1961.

5572. "Phil Love." *Cartoonist PROfiles*. December 1977, p. 46.

5573. "Politics Is Funny." *Time*. May 25, 1962, p. 54.

5574. Pollock, Dennis. "US Media Fall for Comics Hoax." *Media Information Australia*. May 1988, pp. 47-48.

5575. Powell, Kathleen. "Breathing Life into a Comic Strip." *The Funnie's Paper*. November 1983, pp. 4-6.

5576. "Readers Catch Up on Comics, Ads, News As Three Cleveland Papers Publish Again." *Wall Street Journal*. November 28, 1956, p. 1.

5577. Reiner, John. "The Laughter Lives On." *Cartoonist PROfiles*. September 1989, pp. 12-17.

5578. Rhodes, Elizabeth. "Baby Boom Is Big Boon." *The Funnie's Paper*. January 1984, pp. 10-11.

5579. Rogow, Lee. "New Comic Strip." *Saturday Review*. February 7, 1953, pp. 18-20.

5580. Seidman, David. "The Comics Editor's Desk." *Cartoonist PROfiles*. December 1989, pp. 24-31.

5581. Sheridan, Martin. "Comics and Their Creators." *The Funnie's Paper*. January 1986, p. 6.

5582. Silk, Mark. "Comic Wars." *Boston Review*. June 1986, p. 15.

5583. Smith, S.D. "Book of Comic Strips." *New York Times*. September 3, 1972, p. VII-15.

5584. Snowden, George. "Panels in My Life." *Qua Brot*. 1, 1985, pp. 47-51.

5585. Stevens, M. "Comics and Not-So-Comics." *Newsweek*. August 22, 1983, p. 71.

5586. "Stolen Strips Still Missing." *Comics Journal*. December 1990, pp. 17-18.

5587. Stredicke, Victor. "P-I. Comics Change Is No Laughing Matter." *Penstuff*. August 1990, p. 5.

5588. Szathmary, Richard. "The 21st Century Comics Project." *Editor and Publisher*. February 16, 1985, pp. 1C-2C.

5589. Teng, Justina. "Where Innocence Is Bliss." *Comment* (Singapore). March 16-23, 1991, p. 22.

5590. Tucker, Ken. "Black and White." *Entertainment Weekly*. October 5, 1990, pp. 34-37, 40-42.

5591. Tucker, Ken. "Cats, Mice, and History—The Avant-Garde of the Comic Strip." *New York Times Book Review*. May 26, 1985, p. 3.

5592. Tucker, Ken. "On the Making of a Standout Comic." *Philadelphia Inquirer Daily Magazine*. April 28, 1987. pp. 1-D, 3-D.

5593. Turner, Kathleen J. "Comic Strips: A Rhetorical Perspective." *Central States Speech Journal*. Spring 1977, pp. 24-35.

5594. Viertel, G. "Dirigible: Comic Strip." *Harper's Bazaar*. January 5, 1971, pp. 62-65; February 1971, pp. 124-125; March 1971, pp. 156-157; April 1971, pp. 140-141; May 1971, pp. 144-145.

5595. Vinogradoy, S. and E. Goldberg. "Adventures of Rhoda Gravure: Comic Strip." *Seventeen*. January 1974, pp. 102-104.

5596. Walker, Mort. "Cartooning Is Alive and Well." *Comics Journal*. September 1990, pp. 99-100.

5597. Walker, Mort. *Comics*. Florida: Harold Publications, 1964.

5598. Walker, Mort. *The Lexicon of Comicana*. Port Chester, New York: Museum of Cartoon Art, 1980; Bedford, New York: Comicana, 1986. 96 pp.

5599. Wasserman, Jeffrey H. "Funny Papers on Strike!" *Comics Journal*. January 1979, pp. 64-65.

5600. Weaver, Tom. "Crimestopper's Heritage." *Comics Scene*. August 1990, pp. 29-32, 52.

5601. West, Richard S. "Comic Page Cynics." *Target*. Spring 1985, p. 16.

5602. White, David M. "Funnies: An American Idiom." *Newsweek*. January 17, 1963, pp. 92-93; *Saturday Review of Literature*. October 19, 1963, p. 35.

5603. White, David M. and R.H. Abel, eds. *The Funnies: An American Idiom*. New York: Macmillan, 1963.

5604. Wills, Franz H. "Ablenkung vom Alltag. Comic-Strips Made in USA." *Gebrauchsgraphik* (Munich). 42:1 (1970), pp. 38-45.

5605. Wolff, Louie. "Carving Comic Strip Characters." *The Funnie's Paper*. May 1985, p. 16.

5606. "The World's Greatest Newspaper." *Time*. May 11, 1942, p. 55.

Business Aspects

5607. Astor, David. "Once Not Enough for Two Newspapers." *Editor and Publisher*. November 2, 1985, pp. 40-41.

5608. Astor, David. "A Rise in Features for Young Adults." *Editor and Publisher*. October 17, 1992, pp. 38-40.

5609. Beiswinger, George L. "Cartoonists Hoping for Tax Law Changes." *Editor and Publisher*. July 22, 1989, pp. 50-52.

5610. Beiswinger, George L. "The Early Licensing of Comic Characters." *Editor and Publisher*. March 26, 1988, pp. 38-39.

5611. Cohen, Mark J. and Morrie Turner. "Selling with Humor." *Cartoonist PROfiles*. September 1986, pp. 48-53.

5612. Erwin, Ray. "Comics Need Better Position, Promotion." *Editor and Publisher*. March 17, 1962.

5613. Fitzgerald, Mark. "Breathed and Peters Criticize Trends in Comic World." *Editor and Publisher*. November 2, 1985, pp. 41-42.

5614. "Funnies Business." *Vogue*. May 1987, p. 256.

5615. McCoy, F. and A. Edmond, jr. "Serious Business." *Black Enterprise*. September 1989, pp. 86-88.

5616. McManus, K. "Funny Business." *Forbes*. June 4, 1984, p. 212.

5617. Markow, Jack. "Current Market Information." *Cartoonist PROfiles*. No. 24, 1974, pp. 58-62.

5618. Neal, Jim. "Newspaper Offers Comic Strips on Wheels." *Comics Buyer's Guide*. May 21, 1993, p. 112.

5619. Peoples, Tom. "This Funny Business." *Cartoonist PROfiles*. No. 22, 1974, pp. 66-69.

5620. Philips, Adam and Benjamin Svetkey. "Funny Business." *Entertainment Weekly*. October 5, 1990, p. 43.

5621. "Pigeons-Eye View of the Market, Blue Chips Comic Strips." *Business Weekly*. May 26, 1962, p. 143.

5622. "REMCO Still Struggling." *Comics Journal*. May 1992, pp. 18-19.

5623. "Remco Transferring Assets to Printer." *Comics Journal*. March 1992, p. 20.

5624. Robinson, Keith. "Making It. A Survival Guide for Today." *Cartoonist PROfiles*. March 1989, pp. 48-53.

5625. Rykken, Rolf. "Comics Reach Target Groups." *presstime*. September 1991, pp. 22-23.

5626. Stredicke, Victor. "All the Comics That Fit, They Print." *Penstuff*. March 1992, p. 3.

5627. Watterson, Bill. "The Cheapening of the Comics." *WittyWorld*. Summer/Autumn 1989, pp. 21-27; *Comics Journal*. September 1990, pp. 93-98.

5628. Weiner, S.B. "Funny Money." *Forbes*. December 12, 1988, pp. 272+.

Contents

5629. "Batton Lash." *The Funnie's Paper*. November 1985, pp. 4-5.

5630. Becker, Stephen. "The Changing Face of the Funnies." New York: Comics Council, March 13, 1960.

5631. Brewster, P.G. "Folklore Invades the Comic Strips." *Southern Folklore Quarterly*. 14 (1950), pp. 97-102.

5632. "Chili in the Comics." *The Funnie's Paper*. May 1986, p. 20.

5633. "Cigars in the Comics." *The Funnie's Paper*. January 1986, pp. 12-13.

5634. "Comic Strips in Drift to Soap Opera." *The Iowa Quest*. August 1959, p. 5.

5635. Considine, Robert. "The Comic-Strip Story." *New York Journal American*. May 5, 1953, p. 23.

5636. Culhane, J. "Leapin' Lizards! What's Happening to the Comics?" *New York Times Magazine*. May 5, 1974, pp. 16-17+. "Discussion." May 26, 1974, pp. 49-51.

5637. Cunningham, Richard P. "The Funnies Get Political." *The Quill*. January 1989, pp. 10-11.

5638. Cunningham, Richard P. "A Little Powder on the Comic Pages." *The Quill*. September 1985, pp. 8-9.

5639. Curtis, Richard H. "Masonry in the Strips." *The Funnie's Paper*. December 1983, pp. 5-9.

5640. "Decision-Making in the Comics." *The Funnie's Paper*. January 1985, pp. 4-5.

5641. Fearing, Franklin, Carl Terwillinger and Marvin Spiegelmann. "The Content of Comic Strips: A Study of a Mass Medium of Communication." *Journal of Psychology*. 35 (1952), pp. 37-57.

5642. Fearing, Franklin, Carl Terwillinger, and Marvin Spiegelmann. "The Content of Comics: Goals and Means to Goals of Comic-Strip Characters." *Journal of Psychology*. May 1953, pp. 189-203.

5643. Fern, A. *Comics As Serial Fiction*. Chicago, Illinois: University of Chicago, 1968. 60 pp.

5644. "Flyswatters in the Comics." *The Funnie's Paper*. November 1985, p. 10.

5645. "French Fries in the Comics." *The Funnie's Paper*. September 1985, p. 14.

5646. Gallacher, S.A. "The Ideal Hero of Antiquity and His Counterpart in the Comic Strips of Today." *Southern Folklore Quarterly*. 11, 1947, pp. 141-148.

5647. "Hair in the Comics." *The Funnie's Paper*. May 1984, pp. 18-19.

5648. "Honesty in the Comics." *The Funnie's Paper*. September 1984, pp. 22-23.

5649. Horn, Maurice. "American Dreaming: An Analysis of the Adventure Strip." *Inside Comics*. No. 3, 1974.

5650. "Leapin' Lizards! Look What's Happened to the Comics!" *U.S. News and World Report*. June 9, 1975, pp. 44-46.

5651. LeVasseur, Tom. "Bicycles in the Comics." *The Funnie's Paper*. July 1985, p. 11.

5652. McLellan, Dennis. "Artists Bank on Surfing's Draw." *Los Angeles Times*. March 1, 1991, pp. E-1, E-3.

5653. Panetta, G. "Comic Strip, Dramatization of Jimmy Potts Gets a Haircut." *America*. June 21, 1958, p. 359; *Catholic World*. August 1958, pp. 386-387.

5654. Randolph, Nancy. "Chic-Chat. What's Going on Here? Annie, Dick, Abner." *New York Sunday News*. May 16, 1956.

5655. Sargeant, Winthrop. "The High Spots in Lowly Comics. Animals Supply Satire and Fantasy in America's Most Popular Art Form." *Life*. 17:2 (1954), p. 26.

5656. Schwartz, Ron. "The Mouse and the Comic Strip." *Cartoon Art Museum Newsletter*. Winter 1986, p. 2.

5657. Schwartz, Ronald L. "Sleuths in the Strips." *The Funnie's Paper*. April 1984, pp. 11-12; May 1984, pp. 15-16; January 1985, pp. 9-10; March 1985, pp. 4-6; May 1985, pp. 17-20; September 1985, pp. 17-20.

5658. Schwartz, Ronald L. "Storm Warning." *The Funnie's Paper*. September 1984, pp. 24-25.

5659. Scott, Randy. "Mosquitoes in the Comics." *The Funnie's Paper*. May 1985, p. 13.

5660. "Soap Operas Take to Print." *Time*. August 8, 1977, pp. 42-43.

5661. "Spiders in the Comics." *The Funnie's Paper*. March 1987, p. 4.

5662. Stewart, H. Alan. "King Arthur in the Comics." *Avalon to Camelot*. 2:1 (1986), pp. 12-14.

5663. Stredicke, Vic. "Spiders." *Penstuff*. October 1990, pp. 6-7.

5664. Thompson, Don. "Dramatic Newspaper Comic Strips Fare Poorly in Study." *Comics Buyer's Guide*. June 10. 1983, p. 1.

Legal Aspects

5665. Andriola, Alfred. "Comic-Strip Taboos." *Newsletter*. December 1965, pp. 9-14.

5666. Astor, David. "Arnold Schwartzman Admits Guilt Again." *Editor and Publisher*. February 24, 1990, pp. 40-41.

5667. Astor, David. "Class-Action Lawsuit, Apology in Schwartzman Case." *Editor and Publisher*. May 12, 1990, pp. 36-37.

5668. Benenson, Lisa. "Advice and Contempt." *News Inc*. October 1990, pp. 12-13, 15-17.

5669. Cunningham, Richard P. "'... Freedom of Expression Belongs to the Owners.'" *The Quill*. March 1989, pp. 12-13.

5670. Jaquith, James R. "Tabooed Words in Comic Strips. A Transparent Mask." *Anthropological Linguistics*. 14:3 (1972), pp. 71-77.

5671. "Lawyer Admits He Cheated Cartoonists." *Comics Journal*. October 1990, pp. 12-13.

5672. Lederer, Richard. "Sometimes, Language in the Comics Ain't Funny." *ASNE Bulletin*. October 1992, p. 13.

5673. "No Comment." *WittyWorld*. Summer/Autumn 1991, pp. 26-27.

5674. Phifer, G. and T.R. King. "Censoring ('Editing') the Comics." *Journalism Quarterly*. Spring 1986, pp. 174-177.

5675. Pond, Pamela. "How Free Is the Cartoonist's Pen?" *Iowa Journalist*. Fall 1987, p. 8.

Readership

5676. "Another View on Comics—All Categories of Them Have Lost Readership Says Philadelphia Editor." *Inland Bulletin*. March 16, 1955.

5677. Astor, David. "Do Comics Get Respect in U.S.?" *Editor and Publisher*. April 13, 1991, pp. 36-40.

5678. Baize, N.C. "A Factor Analysis of Comic Strip Readership." Master's thesis, Southern Illinois University, Carbondale, Illinois, 1971.

5679. Bogart, Leo. "Comic Strips and Their Adult Readers." Ph.D. dissertation, University of Chicago, 1950.

5680. Bogart, Leo. "Comic Strips and Their Adult Readers." In *Mass Culture: The Popular Arts in America*, edited by Bernard Rosenberg and David M. White, pp. 189-198. Glencoe, Illinois: The Free Press, 1957.

5681. "Cartoon Strips Rule As Readers Call the Shots." *Media Asia*. 15:3 (1988), p. 173.

5682. "The Funnies Paper Survey Results." *The Funnie's Paper*. May 1984, pp. 4-6.

5683. Haskins, Jack B. and Leonard Kubas. "Validation of a Method for Pre-Testing Reader Interest in Newspaper Content." *Journalism Quarterly*. Summer 1979, pp. 269-276.

5684. Lawing, J.V., jr. "Refiner's Fire: Popularity of the Funnies." *Christianity Today*. February 15, 1974, pp. 18-22+.

5685. Robinson, Edward J. and David M. White. "Comic Strip Reading in the United States." Boston, Massachusetts: Report No. 5, Communications Research Center, Boston University, 1962.

5686. Stempel, Guido H. "Comic Strip Reading: Effect of Continuity." *Journalism Quarterly*, Summer 1956, p. 366.

5687. Wells, John. "Newspaper Poll Threatens Strips." *Comics Buyer's Guide*. April 23, 1993, p. 52.

Sunday Funnies

5688. Barcus, Francis E. "Advertising in the Sunday Comics." *Journalism Quarterly*. Spring 1962, pp. 196-202.

5689. Barcus, Francis E. "A Content Analysis of Trends in Sunday Comics, 1900-1959." *Journalism Quarterly*. Spring 1961, pp. 171-180.

5690. Berenstain, S. and J. Berenstain. "Bedlam on Sunday." *Collier's*. October 2, 1948, p. 30.

5691. Kraws, James R. and Tim Rosenthal. "The Sunday Funnies Are Serious Business!" *Cartoonist PROfiles*. March 1989, pp. 64-67.

5692. Lehman, H.C. "The Compensatory Function of the Sunday Funny Paper." *Journal of Applied Psychology*. June 11, 1927, pp. 202-211.

5693. Marschall, Richard, ed. *The Sunday Funnies, 1896-1950*. New York: Chelsea House, 1978. 48 pp.

5694. Snider, Arthur J. "Like Weekend Comics? Here Are Reasons Why." *Chicago Daily News*, May 25, 1956, p. 16.

5695. Social Research Inc. "The Sunday Comics, a Socio-Psychological Study of Their Function and Character." Chicago, Illinois: Prepared by Social Research Inc., for Metropolitan Sunday Newspaper, 1954, pp. 1-11.

Technical Aspects

5696. Anderson, Carl. *How To Draw Cartoons Successfully*. New York: World Book, 1935.

5697. Arnold, Henry. "What Makes a Great Strip." *The Cartoonist*. March 1968, pp. 25-28.

5698. "Button Briefs by Ford Button." *Cartoonist PROfiles*. September 1984, pp. 72-73.

5699. Crane, Roy. "Roy Crane Scrapbook." *Cartoonist PROfiles*. No. 30, 1976, pp. 58-59; No. 32, 1976, pp. 72-76.

5700. Dumas, Jerry, "Saving Time." *Cartoonist PROfiles*. March 1979, pp. 62-69.

5701. Gillespie, Sarah. "On Developing Comic Strips." *Cartoonist PROfiles*. March 1986, pp. 40-43.

5702. Goodrich, Sherman. "A Cartoonist's Guide to What They're *Not* Buying." *Cartoonist PROfiles*. December 1992, pp. 64-69.

5703. Horak, Carl. "Just for Fun: Be a Stripper." *Comic Cellar*. Summer 1982, pp. 39-43, 50-56.

5704. Howe, Andrew. "Comic Strip Technique." *Printer's Ink*. September 12, 1935, p. 12.

5705. Little, Lewis A. "If Your Comic Reaches First Base...." *Cartoonist PROfiles*. June 1981, pp. 26-27.

5706. Lynn, Richard. "The Sons of Liberty." *Cartoonist PROfiles*. December 1977, pp. 78-81.

5707. Muse, Ken. *The Secrets of Professional Cartooning*. Englewood Cliffs, New Jersey: Prentice-Hall, 1981. 330 pp.

5708. North, Harry. "MAD Kong." *Cartoonist PROfiles*. June 1977, pp. 68-72.

5709. Rio, Michel. "Frame, Plan, Reading; Cadre, Plan, Lecture." *Communications*. 24 (1976), pp. 94-107.

5710. Scott, Jerry. "A 55-Foot 'Nancy.'" *Cartoonist PROfiles*. March 1990, pp. 12-17.

5711. Sherry, Richard. "Newspaper Comics and the Economy." *Cartoonist PROfiles*. June 1982, p. 11.

5712. Smith, Ha. "Preparation for Strip Submission." *WittyWorld*. Spring 1988, p. 42.

5713. Steele, Philip. "Fundamentals for Creating Your Own Character for Your Comic Strip." *Cartoonist PROfiles*. September 1980, pp. 58-61.

5714. Stoutsenberger, Leo. "Ask Leo." *Cartoonist PROfiles*. December 1989, pp. 58-61; September 1992, pp. 72-75.

5715. "Submitting Strips." *Cartoonist PROfiles*. September 1977, pp. 74-75.

5716. "Tools of the Trade." *Breaking In*. Premiere Issue, 1992, pp. 30-31.

5717. Toth, Alex. "Felt-Tip Pens." *Cartoonist PROfiles*. June 1982, pp. 78-82.

5718. United States. Copyright Office. *Cartoon and Comic Strips*. Circular R44. Washington, D.C.: Library of Congress, Copyright Office, 1981. 2 pp.

5719. Walker, Mort. "Comicana—the Absolutely Fascinating Science of COMICANA." *Cartoonist PROfiles*. December 1978, pp. 74-76.

5720. Winterbotham, Russell R. *How Comic Strips Are Made*. Girard, Kansas: Haldermann Julius, 1946.

HISTORICAL ASPECTS

5721. "Again... Curses, Foiled Again!" *Nemo*. October 1985, pp. 35-48.

5722. Alloway, L. "Art: Exhibition of 75 Years of the Comics." *The Nation*. August 30, 1971, pp. 157-158.

5723. Andrae, Tom. "Of Supermen and Kids with Dreams." *Nemo*. August 1983, pp. 6-12, 14-19.

5724. Angelo, Ernidio (Mike). "Nostalgic Portraits." *Cartoonist PROfiles*. No. 9, 1971, pp. 24-26.

5725. Barnette, Mark. "Wot's Dis?" *Comics Journal*. October 1992, pp. 44-45.

5726. Barrier, Mike. "Writing a History of American Cartoons." *Funnyworld*. Fall 1977, pp. 4-7.

5727. Beaumont, Charles. "Who's Got the Funnies?" In *Remember, Remember?* New York: Macmillan Co., 1963.

5728. Berger, Arthur A. *The Comic-Stripped American*. Baltimore, Maryland: Penguin Books, 1974. 225 pp.; New York: Walker, 1973.

5729. Blackbeard, Bill. "Q's and A's about Comic Strips!" *Cartoonist PROfiles*. September 1978, pp. 34-36; December 1978, pp. 66-72; March 1979, pp. 54-55.

5730. Blackbeard, Bill. "Reprint Follies II." *Funnyworld*. Spring 1983, pp. 56, 58, 60.

5731. Blackbeard, Bill and Martin Williams, eds. *The Smithsonian Collection of Newspaper Comics*. Washington, D.C.: Smithsonian, 1978. 336 pp.

5732. Blosser, Merrill. "Nostalgia." *Cartoonist PROfiles*. No. 32, 1976, p. 92.

5733. Blum, Geoffrey. "The Joyous Season." *Nemo*. June 1984, pp. 16-17.

5734. Cerdeirinha, Agnaldo. "Mundo—Porco." *Boletim de HQ*. May-June 1992, p. 5.

5735. "Comics and Joseph Patterson." *Time*. January 13, 1947, pp. 59-62.

5736. "Comics: Exhibition To Celebrate Diamond Jubilee of Comic Strips." *New Yorker*. May 1, 1971, pp. 32-33.

5737. Crane, Roy. "Rise and Fall of the Comic Strip." *Cartoonist PROfiles*. No. 20, 1973, pp. 30-31.

5738. Cruse, Howard. "The Other Side of the Coin." *Comics Scene*. March 1983, pp. 59-62.

5739. "The Diary of a Deluded Dandy." *Nemo*. December 1985, pp. 7-14.

5740. Disbrow, Jay. "The Original Comics Heroes." *Comics Buyer's Guide*. July 19, 1985, pp. 66-70.

5741. Dogiakos, James. "Ye Olde Comic Strips." *The Funnie's Paper*. November 1985, pp. 11-14.

5742. Dunn, Bob. "Said and Dunn." *Cartoonist PROfiles*. No. 17, 1973, p. 30; No. 18, 1973, pp. 56-59; No. 19, 1973, pp. 46-47; No. 20, 1973, pp. 32-33; No. 21, 1974, pp. 44-45; No. 22, 1974, pp. 60-61; No. 24, p. 57; No. 29, 1976, pp. 10-11; No. 30, 1976, pp. 40-45; No. 31, 1976, pp. 54-57; No. 32, 1976, pp. 55-57; March 1977, pp. 46-49; June 1977, pp. 21-23; March 1978, pp. 48-54; June 1978, pp. 66-69; December 1978, pp. 32-35; September 1979, pp. 62-65; March 1980, pp. 20-21; June 1980, pp. 76-79; September 1980, pp. 72-73; March 1982, pp. 63-64; March 1983, pp. 78-80.

5743. Fermín Pérez, Ramón. "'Que No Te den Liebre por Gata." *El Wendigo*. No. 51, 1991, p. 39.

5744. Fine, Herbert S. "The Reign of the Super-Man." *Nemo*. August 1983, pp. 20-28.

5745. Glasser, Jean-Claude. "De Sherlock Holmes à Fearless Fosdick. La Parodie dans le Comic Strip Américain." *Les Cahiers de la Bande Dessinée* (Grenoble). 61, 1985, pp. 68-70.

5746. Goulart, Ron. "Leaping Tall Buildings, Falling on Faces." *Nemo*. August 1983, pp. 30-34.

5747. "The Great Time Machine by Jay Maeder." *Cartoonist PROfiles*. June 1982, pp. 60-61.

5748. Hogben, Lancelot. *From Cave Painting to Comic Strip*. New York: Chanticleer Press, 1949. 288 pp.

5749. Hohman, Edward J. "Those Early Cartoon Contests... Humble Beginnings for Today's Greats." *Nemo*. September 1987, pp. 8-11.

5750. Inge, M. Thomas. "Faulkner Reads the Funny Papers." In *Faulkner and Humor*, edited by Doreen Fowler and Ann J. Abadie, pp. 153-190. Jackson, Mississippi: University Press of Mississippi, 1986.

5751. Inge, M. Thomas. "William Faulkner Reads the Comics." *Nemo*. November 1987, pp. 36-44.

5752. Ivey, Jim. "When Comics Wore Toppers." *Nemo*. April 1986, pp. 44-55.

5753. Ivey, Jim. "When Newspapers Respected Their Features." *Nemo*. July 1986, p. 21-42.

5754. "Jack Markow." *Cartoonist PROfiles*. June 1978, pp. 52-56; June 1979, pp. 66-71.

5755. Johnson, Mark. "Squirrel Food." *Nemo*. April 1987, pp. 61-66.

5756. Johnson, Mark. "The Two Worlds of Danny Dreamer." *Nemo*. June 1984, pp. 40-45.

5757. Kasen, Jill H. "Exploring Collective Symbols: America As a Middle-Class Society." *Pacific Sociological Review*. July 1979, pp. 348-381.

5758. Kasen, Jill H. "Portraits from the Dream. The Myth of Success in the Comic Strip, 1925-1975." Doctoral dissertation, Rutgers University, 1978.

5759. Kasen, Jill H. "Whither the Self-Made Man? Comic Culture and the Crisis of Legitimation in the United States." *Social Problems*. December 1980, pp. 131-148.

5760. Kennedy, Malcolm. "Andrew Shelduck: Profile of a Troubleshooter." *The Barks Collector*. May 1985, pp. 21-22.

5761. Kidson, Mike. "Modest Proposals." *FA*. October 1989, pp. 34-37.

5762. Kutlowski, Edward. *Cavalcade of Old Time Comic Strips*. Danvers, Massachusetts: Tower Press, 1967.

5763. Lahue, Kalton C. *Continued Next Week*. Norman, Oklahoma: University of Oklahoma Press, 1964.

5764. Love, Phil. "Cartoonists' Goofs Get Quick Reaction." *Cartoonist PROfiles*. June 1978, p. 57.

5765. Love, Phil. "Newspaperman Reminisces." *Cartoonist PROfiles*. No. 21, 1974, p. 27; No. 22, 1974, p. 42; No. 23, 1974, p. 29.

5766. Markow, Jack. "Balloons." *Cartoonist PROfiles*. September 1982, pp. 60-65.

5767. Marschall, Richard. "Comic Masters." *Horizon*. July 1980, pp. 42-51.

5768. Marschall, Richard. "Death at the Drawing Board." *Comics Journal*. July 1982, pp. 91-96.

5769. Marschall, Richard. "God Save the King." *Nemo*. August 1986, pp. 5+.

5770. Marschall, Richard. "The Stage Is Set." *Comics Journal*. September 1980, pp. 84-87.

5771. Moliterni, Jeannine. "U.S.A. Comics." In *Histoire Mondiale de la Bande Dessinée*, edited by Pierre Horay, pp. 210-232. Paris: Pierre Horay Éditeur, 1989.

5772. "N.E.A. Nostalgia." *Cartoonist PROfiles*. December 1979, pp. 64-68.

5773. Newspaper Comics Council. *Milestones of the Comics. Report*, March 10, 1957. New York.

5774. Norwood, Rick. "Strip Tease." *Comics Feature*. November 1982, pp. 81-84.

5775. "Nostalgia in the Comics." *Cartoonist PROfiles*. September 1975, pp. 51-58.

5776. "One Bachelor Bites the Dust; Another Has a Close Shave." *Editor and Publisher*. March 29, 1952, p. 57.

5777. O'Sullivan, Judith. *The Art of the Comic Strip*. College Park, Maryland: University of Maryland, Department of Art/Art Gallery, 1971. 95 pp.

5778. O'Sullivan, Judith. *The Great American Comic Strip*. Boston, Massachusetts: Little, Brown and Co., 1990. 200 pp.

5779. Phelps, Donald. "The Tenants of Moonshine." *Nemo*. August 1985, pp. 5-18.

5780. "Phil Love." *Cartoonist PROfiles*. September 1977, pp. 32-33.

5781. Robinson, Jerry. *The Comics, an Illustrated History of Comic Strip Art*. New York: G.P. Putnam's Sons, 1974. 256 pp.

5782. Robinson, Jerry. "The Comic Strip: An American Art Form." In *San Diego Comic Convention 1989* program book, pp. 24-27. San Diego, California: San Diego Comic-Con Committee, 1989.

5783. Rothweiler, Kyle. "'Ideelism' in Comics and Law." *Comics Journal*. April 1991, pp. 71-72.

5784. Schwartz, Ron. "Debut. It All Began This Month." *The Funnie's Paper*. January 1986, pp. 4-5; May 1986, p. 4.

5785. "Simplicity Itself." *Nemo*. February 1987, pp. 20-21.

5786. Snowden, George. "Panels in My Life." *Qua Brot*. No. 1, 1985, pp. 47-51.

5787. *What's So Funny? The Humor Comic Strip in America*. Exhibit and Catalog Sponsored by: The Salina Art Center, Salina, Kansas, February 18-March 31, 1988. Salina, Kansas: The Salina Art Center, 1988. 48 pp.

5788. "When Knights Were Bold, But More So the Damsels." *Nemo*. July 1986, p. 5.

5789. Zlotnick, Joan. "The Medium Is the Message, or Is It?: A Study of Nathaniel West's Comic Strip Novel." *Journal of Popular Culture*. 5:1 (1971), pp. 236-240.

5790. Zschiesche, Bob. "Roy and Les." *Cartoonist PROfiles*. March 1979, pp. 56-59.

Comic Periodicals

5791. Dennis, Everette E. and Christopher Allen. "Puck, the Comic Weekly." *Journalism History*. Spring 1979, pp. 2-7, 13.

5792. Gabriel, Gilbert W. "The Comic Supplement: An Irregular Glimpse of the Rich Young Revue Which Foreswore New York." *New York Telegram*. February 2, 1925.

5793. Marschall, Richard. "The Age of Funny Pictures: The History of the Comic Strip Part 3: Judge Magazine." *Comics Journal*. November 1980, pp. 87-91.

5794. Marschall, Richard. "The Stage Is Set: The History of the Comic Strip, Part 2: Decline and Death of Puck Magazine." *Comics Journal*. September 1980, pp. 84-87.

5795. Marschall, Richard. "What Fools These Mortals Be: The History of the Comic Strip. Part 1: Puck Magazine." *Comics Journal*. June 1980, pp. 134-139.

5796. Marschall, Richard. "Where There's Life There's Hope. The History of the Comic Strip, Part Four: 'Life' Magazine." *Comics Journal*. March 1981, pp. 86-89.

5797. Marvin, Keith. "The Gulf Funny Weekly." *Comics Buyer's Guide*. January 20, 1989, p. 48.

5798. West, Richard S. "A Yankee Doodle Dirge: Being an Examination into the Failure of Mid-Nineteenth Century American Comic Weeklies." *The Puck Papers*. Spring 1981, pp. 1-7.

Periods

Pre-1920

5799. Bergengren, Ralph. "Humor of the Colored Supplement." *Atlantic*. August 1906, pp. 269-273.

5800. Caine, Matthew T. "Hunting for Sketches." *Cartoons*. January 1913, p. 16.

5801. "Comic-ers." *Everybody's*. July 1915, pp. 71-77.

5802. "The Comic Nuisance." *Outlook*. March 6, 1909, p. 527.

5803. Hershfield, Harry. "Very Past: The Pre-20s." *The Cartoonist*. Special Number, 1966, pp. 16-18.

5804. "The Hoosier Cat of the Indianapolis Star." *Cartoons*. January 1913, p. 46.

5805. Irwin, Wallace. "The Comics." *New York Times*. October 22, 1911.

5806. Jenkins, W. "Illustration of the Daily Press in America." *International Studio*. October 1902, pp. 281-291.

5807. Marschall, Richard. "'Life' Under Gibson—and Beyond. The History of the Comic Strip, Part Five." *Comics Journal*. September 1981, pp. 312-319.

5808. Marschall, Richard. "Shibboleths: Exploding Myths, Looking for New Origins, Redefining Our Terms: The Advent of the Comic Strip." *Comics Journal*. November 1981, pp. 79-87.

5809. Newspaper Comics Council. *Cavalcade of American Funnies A History of Comic Strips from 1896*. New York: 1970.

5810. Reynolds, Edward S. "Tige the Mascot of the Portland Oregonian." *Cartoons*. January 1913, p. 24.

5811. Robinson, Jerry. "From Cave Drawing to Comic Strip." *Children's Digest*. Spring 1972, pp. 22-32.

5812. Shelton, William H. "Comic Papers in America." *Critic*. September 1901.

5813. Swartz, John. "The Anatomy of the Comic Strip and the Value World of Kids." Ph.D. dissertation, Ohio State University, 1978. 533 pp.

5814. "True Love Will Out; Cartoon Strip Dating to c. 1875." *American Heritage*. February 1976, pp. 42-43.

5815. Winkler, John K. *William Randolph Hearst: A New Appraisal*. New York: Hastings House, 1955. (Appendix, pp. 300-315, on comics).

1920-1940

5816. "American Funnies at Home Throughout the World." *Newsweek*. May 26, 1934. pp. 3-28.

5817. Aronson, J. "What's Funny About Funnies?" *Ill. Scholastic*. March 26, 1938, p. 18E.

5818. Berkman, A. "Sociology of the Comic Strip." In *American Spectator*. June 1936.

5819. Brennecke, Ernest. "The Real Mission of the Funny Paper." *Century*. March 1924, pp. 665-675.

5820. Brisbane, Arthur. "The Comics." *Literary Digest*. December 12, 1936, p. 19.

5821. Broun, Heywood. "Fifty Million Readers." *Vanity Fair*. August 1935.

5822. Broun, Heywood. "The Newspapers Comic Strip." *The Nation*. July 23, 1930, p. 87.

5823. Broun, Heywood. "Wham! and Pow! The Comic Strip." *New Republic*. May 17, 1939, p. 44.

5824. "Comic History." *Saturday Review of Literature*. September 16, 1933, p. 108.

5825. "Comic Strips Are America's Favorite Fiction." *Life*. June 5, 1939, pp. 8-11.

5826. Dangerfield, George. "I'll See You in the Funnies." *Harper's Bazaar*. October 1939, pp. 87, 112-114.

5827. Field, Eugene. "Excerpts from *The Complete Tribune Primer*." *The World of Comic Art*. June 1966, pp. 30-33.

5828. "Fortune Survey: What Is Your Favorite Comic Strip." *Fortune*. April 1937, pp. 190+.

5829. "Funnies: Colored Comic Strips in the Best of Health at 40." *Newsweek*. December 1934, pp. 26-27.

5830. "Funnies; Photographs." *Collier's*. February 12, 1927, pp. 12-13.

5831. "The Funny Papers." *Fortune*. April 1933, pp. 45-49, 92, 95, 98, 101.

5832. "Ghost Cartoonists Assure Immortality to Strips." *Newsweek*. December 23, 1936, p. 34.

5833. Goldberg, Reuben L. "Comics: New Style and Old." *Saturday Evening Post*. December 15, 1928, pp. 12-13.

5834. Goulart, Ron. "'The Adventurous Decade.'" *Cartoonist PROfiles*. June 1975, pp. 50-51.

5835. Goulart, Ron. *The Adventurous Decade: Comic Strips of the Thirties*. New York: Arlington House, 1973.

5836. Goulart, Ron. "Funnies in the Thirties, Part I: Mock Heroics." *Comics Buyer's Guide*. January 1, 1988, pp. 20, 22, 26, 28, 32, 34.

5837. Goulart, Ron. "Funnies in the Thirties: Part V: Out West." *Comics Buyer's Guide*. January 13, 1989, pp. 32, 34, 36, 38-39.

5838. Goulart, Ron. "Funnies in the Thirties: Part 8: In Uniform." *Comics Buyer's Guide*. November 3, 1989, pp. 42, 44, 46.

5839. "Grandpa's Pa." *Time*. November 14, 1938, p. 47.

5840. Harvey, R.C. *Cartoons of the Roaring Twenties. Volume One: 1921-1923*. Seattle, Washington: Fantagrahics, 1991. 72 pp.

5841. "Hoosegaw Herman." *Time*. October 17, 1938, pp. 36-37.

5842. Lowrie, S.D. "Comic Strips." *Forum*. April 1928, pp. 527-536.

5843. McCord, David F. "The Social Rise of the Comics." *American Mercury*. July 1935, pp. 360-364.

5844. Markow, Jack. "Remembering the Thirties." *Cartoonist PROfiles*. December 1978, pp. 80-83.

5845. "Nostalgia Dept. — How They Looked in 1925." *Cartoonist PROfiles*. November 1970, p. 17.

5846. Patterson, Russel. "The Past: The Roaring Twenties." *The Cartoonist*. Special Number, 1966, pp. 6-13.

5847. Pennell, Elisabeth R. "Our Tragic Comics." *North American Review*. February 1920, pp. 248-258.

5848. Politzer, Heinz. "From Little Nemo to Li'l Abner." *Commentary*. October 8, 1949, pp. 346-355.

5849. Price, B. "Comics Go Big Business." *World's Work*. August 1931, pp. 35-37.

5850. Roberts, Elzey. "What Is a Comic Page?" *St. Louis Star Times*. March 17, 1938.

5851. Seldes, Gilbert. "The 'Vulgar' Comic Strip." In *The Seven Lively Arts*, by Gilbert Seldes, pp. 193-205. New York: Harper and Bros., 1924.

5852. Sheridan, Martin. "A Ghost Remembers: Life in the King Features Bullpen in the 1930s." *Nemo*. October 1984, pp. 52-55.

5853. Sheridan, Martin. "This Serious Business of Being Funny." *St. Nicholas*. December 1937, pp. 21-23.

5854. Smith, S.M. "Friends of the Family; the Comics." *Pictorial Review*. January 1935, pp. 24-25.

5855. Stone, Sylvia S. "Let's Look at the Funnies." *People*. May 1937, pp. 5-9.

5856. Tarcher, J.D. "The Serious of the Comic Strip." *Printers Ink*. April 28, 1932.

5857. Thompson, Lovell. "America's Day Dream: The Funnies." *Saturday Review of Literature*. November 13, 1937, pp. 3-4, 16.

5858. "Time and the Funnies." *Atlantic Monthly*. October 1936, pp. 510-511.

5859. Tricoche, Georges N. "Remarques sur les Typus Populaires Créés par la Litérature Comique Américaine." *Révue de Litérature Comparée* (Paris). 11 (1931), pp. 250-261.

5860. Weitenkampf, Frank. "The Inwardness of the Comic Strip." *The Bookman*. July 1925, pp. 574-577.

5861. "Winnie on a Bus." *Time*. February 20, 1939, p. 48.

5862. Wolf, S.C.J. "Tribute to Comic Strip Artists." *Literary Digest*. April 7, 1934, p. 51.

5863. Young, William H., jr. "Images of Order: American Comic Strips During the Depression, 1929-1938." Ph.D. dissertation, Emory University, 1972.

5864. Young, William H., jr. "The Serious Funnies: Adventure Comics During the Depression, 1929-1938." *Journal of Popular Culture*. Winter 1969, pp. 404-427.

5865. Zahniser. "The Comics." *Christian Century*. May 8, 1936, p. 607.

1941-1960

5866. Arden, Stuart. "The Good Soldier Schweik and His American Cartoon Counterparts." *Journal of Popular Culture*. Summer 1975, pp. 26-30.

5867. "Chicago's Col. M' Cosmic Makes Hit." *Life*. May 11, 1942, pp. 28-29.

5868. "Comics Stripped." *Newsweek*. March 13, 1950, p. 32.

5869. "Comic Strip Cookies." *New York Times*. August 3, 1948.

5870. "Editors, Specialists Discuss the Comics." *Editor and Publisher*. November 22, 1947, p. 14.

5871. "Escape Artist." *Time*. January 13, 1947, pp. 59-62.

5872. "50 Years of Comics." *Minneapolis Sunday Tribune*. June 3, 1948.

5873. "The Funnies." *Newsweek*. January 7, 1946, p. 64.

5874. "The Funnies." *Parents' Magazine*. March 1951.

5875. Goulart, Ron. "Funnies in the 40's. Part 3: Paper Bullets." *Comics Collector*. Fall 1985, pp. 50-55.

5876. Goulart, Ron. "Funnies in the 40's, Part IV: The Adventurers." *Comics Collector*. Winter 1986, pp. 72-77.

5877. Goulart, Ron. "Funnies of the Forties VII: Our Fighting Men." *Comics Buyer's Guide*. July 4, 1986, pp. 20, 22.

5878. "Grim Comic Strip Pamphlet Depicts U.S. Seized by Telegram." *New York Telegram*. December 5, 1947, p. 12.

5879. Hadsel, Fred L. "Propaganda in the Funnies." *Current History*. December 1941, pp. 365-368.

5880. Haskins, Jack B. and Robert L. Jones. "Trends in Newspaper Reading: Comic Strips, 1949-1954." *Journalism Quarterly*. 32 (1955).

5881. Henne, Frances. "Whence the Comic Strip: Its Development and Content." *Supplementary Educational Monographs*. December 1942, pp. 153-158.

5882. Klonsky, M. "Comic-Strip-Tease of Time." *American Mercury*. December 1952, pp. 93-99.

5883. "Paper Personalities." *Popular Mechanics*. January 1949, p. 141.

5884. "Pok! Ack! Pitooooon!" *New Republic*. March 11, 1957, p. 7.

5885. "Primitive in the Papers." *Newsweek*. April 11, 1960, p. 110.

5886. "Stirrup Strips." *Newsweek*. December 12, 1949, p. 55.

5887. "Stuff of Dreams." *Time*. December 1, 1947, p. 71.

5888. Sugrue, Thomas. "From Comic Strip to Comic Art." *Saturday Review of Literature*. February 16, 1946, pp. 15-16.

5889. "Superseding Superman, P-D Color Comics." *Newsweek*. July 19, 1948, pp. 51-53.

5890. "This Little Gag Went." *Time*. August 12, 1946, p. 65.

5891. "Trib Comics: Slipping?" *Newsweek*. October 11, 1948, p. 62.

5892. Vlamos, J.F. "Sad Case of the Funnies; Comic Strips Have Gone He-Man, Haywire and Hitlerite." *American Mercury*. April 1941, pp. 411-416.

CHARACTERS and TITLES

5893. Amend, Bill. "Fox Trot." *Cartoonist PROfiles*. December 1989, pp. 18-23.

5894. "The Badge Guys—Brand New Police Comic." *Cartoonist PROfiles*. September 1971, pp. 76-78.

5895. Barson, Michael. "The Haunting Beauty of White Boy." *Nemo*. November 1987, pp. 45-66.

5896. Bates, Bill. *Cartoons by Bates*. Approximately 80 cartoons by the Cartoonist of "Ping." New York: Bobbs Merrill Co., 1964.

5897. "Battle for Belinda." Catalogue of Exhibition, "Battle for Belinda." Philadelphia, Pennsylvania, June 2-29, 1988. Radnor, Pennsylvania: The Tosubi Group, 1988. 16 pp.

5898. "'Benchley' by Jerry Dumas and Mort Drucker." *Cartoonist PROfiles*. March 1985, pp. 44-51.

5899. "Bench Warmers by Richard Torrey." *Cartoonist PROfiles*. March 1992, pp. 44-49.

5900. Berrill, Jack. *Gil Thorp Silver Anniversary Yearbook*. Arlington, Illinois: Take 5 Productions, 1984. 143 pp.

5901. Berry, Romeyn. *Sport Stuff*. Reprinted from "Sport Stuff" in the *Cornell Alumni News*. Ithaca, New York: Cornell University, 1927. 94 pp.

5902. Biamonte, S.G. "Moby Dick." *Sgt. Kirk*. No. 3, 1967, pp. 63-64.

5903. "Big Chief Wahoo Hits Hollywood." *Nemo*. June 1986, pp. 55-66.

5904. "Big for Her Age: Honeybelle." *Newsweek*. January 24, 1949, p. 48.

5905. Bittle, Jerry. *Let's Burn That Bridge When We Come to It*. Kansas City, Missouri: Andrews, McMeel and Parker, 1985. 127 pp. ("Geech").

5906. Blackbeard, Bill. "Max, Maurice, and Willie: The Saga of a Little Yellow Book." *Nemo*. August 1983, pp. 48-52.

5907. Blackbeard, Bill, ed. *Classic American Comic Strips*. 22 Vols. Westport, Connecticut: Hyperion Press, 1977. (Percy Crosby, "Skippy"; Billy De Beck, "Barney Google"; Clare Dwiggins, "School Days"; Harry Fisher, "A. Mutt"; Frank Godwin, "Connie"; Rube Goldberg, "Bobo Baxter"; George Herriman, "Baron Bean"; George Herriman, "The Family Upstairs"; Harry Hershfield, "Abie the Agent"; Harry Hershfield, "Dauntless Durham of the U.S.A."; Clifford McBride, "Napoleon"; Winsor McCay, "Winsor McCay's Dream Days"; George McManus, "Bringing Up Father"; Gus Mager, "Sherlocko the Monk"; Dick Moores, "Jim Hardy"; Frederick Opper, "Happy Hooligan"; Richard Outcault, "Buster Brown"; Elzie C. Segar, "Thimble Theater, Introducing Popeye"; Cliff Sterrett, "Polly and Her Pals"; George Storm, "Bobby Thatcher"; Harry Tuthill, "The Bungle Family"; and Edgar S. Wheelan, "Minute Movies.")

5908. Blankfort, Henry and Sergio Aragones. *Henry, the Smiling Dog*. New York: 1967.

5909. "The Blue Tracer by Fred Gardineer." *Cartoonist PROfiles*. No. 31, 1976, pp. 46-53.

5910. Boardman, John. "Li'l Who?" *The Pointing Vector*. September 1964; *Comic Art*. October 1964, p. 3.

5911. "Born Loser by A. Sansom." *Cartoonist PROfiles*. No. 9, 1971, pp. 72-77.

5912. Brady, Pat. "Rose Is Rose." *Cartoonist PROfiles*. September 1984, pp. 40-45.

5913. "Breaking In '10.'" *Breaking In*. January 1993, pp. 18-28.

5914. "Buck Brady Rides in Paris." *Newsweek.* March 24, 1947, p. 66.

5915. "The Buckets by Scott Stantis." *Cartoonist PROfiles.* June 1992, pp. 12-17.

5916. Burnett, Jim. "Winston." *Cartoonist PROfiles.* December 1985, pp. 50-53.

5917. Campbell, Sandy. "Pop's Place." *Cartoonist PROfiles.* June 1986, pp. 16-21.

5918. "Campus Clatter from Doolittle College, by Larry Lewis." *Cartoonist PROfiles.* December 1974, pp. 20-24.

5919. "The Car Pool by John H. 'Jake' Schuffert." *Cartoonist PROfiles.* No. 19, 1973, pp. 59-60.

5920. Chalkley, Tom. "Comic Tonic." *Balitmore City Paper.* October 1992.

5921. Chesney, Earle D. *Eggburt and Other Navy Cartoons.* Washington, D.C.: Anderson House, 1945.

5922. Childress, James. *Conchy #2.* New York: Grosset and Dunlap, 1976.

5923. Childress, James. *Conchy on the Half-Shell.* New York: Grosset and Dunlap, 1973.

5924. "A Christmas Strip." *Cartoonist PROfiles.* December 1971, pp. 54-58.

5925. Coll, Charles and Ray Thompson. *The Strange Adventures of Myra North, Special Nurse.* Greenfield, Wisconsin: Arcadia Publications, 1987. 80 pp.

5926. Colley, Ed and Janet Alfieri. "Suburban Cowgirls." *Cartoonist PROfiles.* December 1991, pp. 14-21.

5927. Collins, Max A. "Strip Search: Fearless Fosdick, the 'Ideel' Comic Strip Detective." *Comics Feature.* January-February 1985, pp. 14-15, 38.

5928. Collins, Max A. "Strip Search: The Mr. Oswald Story." *Comics Feature.* November-December 1984, pp. 10-11, 36-38.

5929. Coma, Javier. "L'Origine de 'Ming Foo' au Coeur de 'Little Annie Rooney.'" *Le Nouveau Bédésup.* 35, 1985, pp. 40-47.

5930. "A Comic Panel Set in Outer Space." *Editor and Publisher.* June 27, 1987, p. 37.

5931. "Comics, Gal Tennis Hypo." *New York World Telegram and Sun.* February 16, 1956, p. 34.

5932. Compart, Martin. "Krieg im Abenteuer-Comic." In *Comic-Jahrbuch 1986*, edited by Martin Compart and Andreas C. Knigge, pp. 22-37. Frankfurt: Ullstein GmbH, 1985.

5933. Couperie, Pierre. "Don Winslow a Presque Existé." *Phénix* (Paris). No. 13, 1969.

5934. Craven, T. *Cartoon Cavalcade*. New York: Simon and Schuster, 1943.

5935. Cronel, Hervé. "Rip Kirby, Batman, Barbarella u.a. Zwischen Epos und Zauberwelt—Erster Aufriß Einer Geschichte der Comic Strips." *Die Welt* (Hamburg). October 30, 1971, pp. III-IV.

5936. "Dallas." *Cartoonist PROfiles*. March 1981, pp. 8-14.

5937. DeFuccio, Jerry and Alex Toth. "'Skool' Yardley... Our Man on the Corner." *Cartoonist PROfiles*. No. 15, 1972, p. 23.

5938. Della Corte, Carlos. "Ernie Pike." *Sgt. Kirk*. No. 4, 1967, pp. 26-27.

5939. Della Corte, Carlos. "Gordon e Mandrake Preannunciarono la Fantascienza." *Italia Domani* (Milan). November 8, 1959.

5940. Dickenson, Steve. "Tar Pit by Steve Dickenson." *Cartoonist PROfiles*. June 1993, pp. 54-59.

5941. "Doctor Smock by George Lemont." *Cartoonist PROfiles*. December 1974, pp. 52-56.

5942. Dodson, Reynolds. "Splitsville by Baginski and Dodson: The True Story Behind That New 'Divorce' Cartoon Strip." *Cartoonist PROfiles*. June 1979, pp. 24-27.

5943. "Don Q by David Gantz." *Cartoonist PROfiles*. September 1975, pp. 10-17.

5944. Dozier, R.J. "Odets and Little Lefty." *American Literature*. January 1977, pp. 597-598.

5945. "The Dropouts by H. Post." *Cartoonist PROfiles*. No. 9, 1971, pp. 32-38.

5946. Dunn, Bill. "High School Dropouts." *Cartoonist PROfiles*. No. 10, 1971, pp. 68-73.

5947. "Dusty Chaps Dude Ranch." *Cartoonist PROfiles*. September 1981, pp. 16-20.

5948. Dwiggins, Clare V. *School Days*. The Hyperion Library of Classic American Comic Strips. Westport, Connecticut: Hyperion, 1977. 152 pp.

5949. "Ed Reed." *Cartoonist PROfiles*. March 1978, pp. 46-47.

5950. Edwina. *Sinbad. A Dog's Life*. New York: Coward McCann. 1930. Unpaginated.

5951. Eisner, Will. *Hawks of the Seas*. Papeete, Tahiti: Transtar Pacific C.C. Publishers, 1985. 52 pp.

5952. "Ella Cinders by Charlie Plumb." *Cartoonist PROfiles*. No. 14, 1972, p. 37.

5953. "Elwood by Tom Forman." *Cartoonist PROfiles*. September 1984, pp. 74-77.

5954. English, James W. *The Rin Tin Tin Story*. New York: Dodd, Mead and Co., 1955. 248 pp.

5955. Erichsen, Kurt. *Savoir-Fairy*. Murphy's Manor, Vol. 1. Toledo, Ohio: 1986, 28 pp.

5956. Erwin, Ray. "'Beauregard!' Laughs Through Civil Wars." *Editor and Publisher*. February 25, 1961.

5957. Erwin, Ray. "Husband-Wife Team Draws Funny Oldsters." *Newsletter*. May 1965, p. 20.

5958. Evans, Greg. "Luann." *Cartoonist PROfiles*. March 1985, pp. 36-41.

5959. "Fantasy in the Comics—A Punk Mother Goose. Wells and Kaber's *Lovely Lilly*." *Nemo*. November 1987, pp. 22-27.

5960. "Fenton by Wiley Miller." *Cartoonist PROfiles*. June 1984, pp. 52-57.

5961. François, Edouard. "Clifton." *Phénix*. No. 20, 1971.

5962. Frank, Phil. *Travels with Farley*. San Francisco, California: Troubador Press, 1980. 96 pp.

5963. "Freddy by Rupe." *Cartoonist PROfiles*. No. 21, 1974, pp. 14-19.

5964. Freyse, Bill. "Major Hoople and Co." *Cartoonist PROfiles*. 1:1 (1969), pp. 53-58.

5965. Galewitz, Herb, ed. *Great Comics Syndicated by the Daily News-Chicago Tribune*. New York: Crown Publishers, 1972. 319 pp.

5966. Gary, Jim. *King of Royal Mounted*. Dragon Lady Productions, No. 1. Toronto, Ontario: Dragon Lady Comic Shop, 1985. 67 pp.

5967. Gehman, R.B. "Deadwood Dick to Superman." *Science Digest*. June 1949, pp. 52-57.

5968. Gerber, Steve and Gene Colan. *It's Adventure Time with Howard the Duck*. Buffalo, New York: J. Zawadzki, 1978. 24 pp.

5969. Gerberg, Mort. "Koky: A Contemporary Strip about Today's Family." *Cartoonist PROfiles*. September 1980, pp. 62-67.

5970. Glasberg, Ronald. "Sam and His Laugh: A Comic Strip Reflection of Turn-of-the-Century America." *Journal of American Culture*. Spring 1985, pp. 87-93.

5971. Godwin, Frank. *Connie*. Intro. by Maurice Horn. The Hyperion Library of Classic American Comic Strips. Westport, Connecticut: Hyperion, 1977. 161 pp.

5972. Goldberg, Rube. *Bobo Baxter*. The Hyperion Library of Classic American Comic Strips. Westport, Connecticut: Hyperion, 1977. 151 pp.

5973. Gooch, Larry. "A Wind of the Spirit: Cultural Paths in Search of Transcendental Truths: As Evidenced by the Ducks and the Tralla Lallians." *The Barks Collector*. 31/32, 1985, pp. 11-20.

5974. "Good News. Bad News—Henry Martin." *Cartoonist PROfiles*. December 1982, pp. 62-67.

5975. Goulart, Ron. "Beyond Mars: A Forgotten SF Strip Classic." *Nemo*. June 1985, pp. 34-52.

5976. Goulart, Ron. "The Life and Hard Times of Bunker Hill, Jr." *Nemo*. October 1983, pp. 46-58.

5977. "Griff and the Unicorn by Dave Sokoloff." *Cartoonist PROfiles*. No. 17, 1973, p. 2.

5978. Guren, Peter. "Ask Shagg." *Cartoonist PROfiles*. September 1988, pp. 48-53.

5979. Gustafson, Bob. "Gamin and Patches." *Cartoonist PROfiles*. June 1987, pp. 24-30.

5980. Haessle, Jacques. "Etude de Trois Bandes Dessinée Axées sur le Merveilleux." *Le Nouveau Bédésup*. 29/30, 1984, pp. 91-97. ("Little Nemo," "Krazy Kat," "Mandrake").

5981. Hammond, Chris. "Speed Walker, Private Eye." *Cartoonist PROfiles*. December 1983, pp. 18-23.

5982. Harvey, R.C. "Mickey, Mutt and Jeff, and Myra North." *Comics Journal*. June 1988, pp. 140-143.

5983. Hatlo, Jimmy. *They'll Do It Every Time*. Philadelphia, Pennsylvania: David McKay, 1945; New York: Avon, 1951. 192 pp.

5984. Hegerfors, Sture. "Deckaren Peter Falk, Elegant Bildad Ungkarl." *GT Söndags Extra* (Göteborg). November 19, 1967.

5985. Henley, Marian. *Maxine*. New York: American Library, 1987. 128 pp.

5986. Herriman, George. *Baron Bean 1916-1917*. The Hyperion Library of Classic American Comic Strips. Westport, Connecticut: Hyperion, 1977. 101 pp.

5987. Hess, Erwin L. *Golden Yesterdays*. 2 Vols. Westlake, Ohio: Hess Press Reproductions, 1981.

5988. Hodgins, Dick and Dick Ericson. "The Bank Dicks." *Cartoonist PROfiles*. 1:2 (1969), pp. 40-42.

5989. Hoest, Bill. *Howard Huge*. New York: Lyle Stuart Inc. 1981. Unpaginated.

5990. Hogarth, Burne. *Drago*. Long Beach, California: Pacific Comics Club, 1985. 54 pp.

5991. "Hoppy's Re-Deal." *Newsweek*. January 8, 1951, p. 36.

5992. Horak, Carl. "Reprint Reviews." *The Funnie's Paper*. March 1987, pp. 21-22.

5993. Hudson, Gunboat. "Mixing with the Best of Them." *Nemo*. August 1986, pp. 56-57.

5994. Huisking, Charlie. "Captain Vincible." *Cartoonist PROfiles*. March 1983, pp. 24-31.

5995. Hurd, Jud. "Brainstormers by Mike Smith." *Cartoonist PROfiles*. March 1991, pp. 74-77.

5996. Hurd, Jud. "Cobwebs by Gorrell and Brookins." *Cartoonist PROfiles*. March 1987, pp. 30-35.

5997. Hurd, Jud. "Moose Miller." *Cartoonist PROfiles*. December 1992, pp. 46-53.

5998. Irwin, Walter. "America's Typical Teen-ager." *Comics Collector*. Fall 1985, pp. 56-57, 59-67.

5999. "It's a Crock by Bill Rechin and Don Wilder." *Cartoonist PROfiles*. December 1981, pp. 38-45.

6000. Ittork, Nek. "S2C Boondocker and His Author Face Life's Problems Together." *The Navy News*. January 13, 1946.

6001. "James Bond und die Comic Strips." *Neue Zürcher Zeiting* (Zürich). June 26, 1965.

6002. Jesuele, Kim. "Big Nate by Lincoln Peirce." *Cartoonist PROfiles*. June 1991, pp. 10-17.

6003. Jesuele, Kim. "The Grizzwells by Bill Schorr." *Cartoonist PROfiles*. June 1993, pp. 66-71.

6004. "Jetz Bin Ich da: Conny." *Constanze* (Hamburg). No. 42, 1968.

6005. "Jim Henson's Muppets by Guy and Brad Gilchrist." *Cartoonist PROfiles*. September 1981, pp. 8-13.

6006. "Just a Kid in a Big White House: Miss Caroline." *Time*. July 26, 1963, p. 56.

6007. Keaton, Russel. *Flyin' Jenny*. Greenfield, Wisconsin: Arcadia Publications, 1987. 72 pp.

6008. Kirby, Jack and Wallace Woody. *Sky Masters of the Space Force*. Comic Art Showcase, No. 1. Buffalo, New York: Quality Comic Art Productions, 1980. 61 pp.

6009. "Lala Palooza." *Time*. November 9, 1936, p. 51.

6010. Lang, Jeffrey. "The Incredibly Intelligent, Eminently Readable, Incisive, and Fun-Filled Article About Gregory and Herman Vermin." *Comics Buyer's Guide*. December 11, 1992, pp. 26, 28.

6011. Lee, Stan. *The Best of Spider-Man*. New York: Ballantine, 1986. 201 pp.

6012. Le Gallo, Claude. "Blake, Mortimer et la Science-Fiction." *Phénix*. No. 4, 3 Trimestre, 1967, pp. 23-26.

6013. Leiffer, Paul. "The Space Patrol Returns." *Vangaurd*. No. 2, 1968.

6014. Leonard, Lank. "Mickey Finn." *Cartoonist PROfiles*. No. 5, 1970, pp. 40-49.

6015. Le Pelley, Guernsey. "Six Children and a Dog; Tubby and Buddy and Co." *Christian Science Monitor Magazine*. March 31, 1937, p. 15.

6016. Lichty, George. *Grin and Bear It*. New York: McGraw-Hill, 1954.

6017. "Li'l Sports by Cliff Wirth." *Cartoonist PROfiles*. December 1975, pp. 64-65.

6018. Love, Philip. "Kerry Drake Is on Stage Artist Model." *The Cartoonist*. January 1968, p. 59.

6019. Lynn, Ernest. "Boots and Her Buddies by Edgar E. Martin." *Cartoonist PROfiles*. No. 13, 1972, pp. 63-69.

6020. McDonnell, Patrick. "Bad Baby." *Cartoonist PROfiles*. September 1993, pp. 36-43.

6021. McEldowney, Brooke. "9 Chickweed Lane." *Cartoonist PROfiles*. September 1993, pp. 44-51.

6022. McGeean, Ed. "New Comic Strip Prevue." *CAPS*. February 1992, p. 13.

6023. McGraw, Tug and Mike White. "Scroogie." *Cartoonist PROfiles*. September 1975, pp. 62-65.

6024. McPherson, John. "Close to Home." *Cartoonist PROfiles*. June 1993, pp. 14-19.

6025. Mack, Stan. *Stan Mack's Out-Takes*. Woodstock, New York: Overlook Press, 1984. 128 pp.

6026. Marschall, Richard. "An American Classic and a Classic Comic Strip." *Nemo*. December 1985, pp. 19-33.

6027. Marschall, Richard. "A Complete Fantasy Classic: The Explorigator." *Nemo*. February 1984, pp. 7-21.

6028. Marschall, Richard. "Crock by Bill Rechin and Brant Parker." *Cartoonist PROfiles*. December 1975, pp. 12-14.

6029. Marschall, Richard. "The Force Was With Him—The Escapades and Escapes of Slim Jim." *Nemo*. May 1985, pp. 48-66.

6030. Marschall, Richard. "Oh, You Kid. A Strip of Leviathan Quality." *Comics Journal*. March 1989, pp. 73-77.

6031. Marschall, Richard. "Threats and Thrills, Fantasy and Fortune Cookies: Ming Foo." *Nemo*. February 1989, pp. 45-63.

6032. Martin, Joe. *Warning, Willy 'n Ethel*. Chicago, Illinois: Turnbull and Willoughby, 1984. 100 pp.

6033. Martin, Ted. "Pavlov." *Cartoonist PROfiles*. September 1985, pp. 36-41.

6034. Maxson, Randy. *The Geek Book*. Malden, Massachusetts: Zeke Publishing, 1986. 112 pp.

6035. May, Carl. "Suzann Says by Ollie." *Cartoonist PROfiles*. September 1992, pp. 84-87.

6036. "Meet Curtis: New Kid on Post Comics Page." *Cincinnati Post*. May 22, 1989.

6037. "The Middletons by Ralph Dunagin and Dana Summers." *Cartoonist PROfiles*. December 1987, pp. 56-61.

6038. "Mixed Singles by William F. Brown and Mel Casson." *Cartoonist PROfiles*. No. 17, 1973, pp. 4-13.

6039. "Moe Has a Moral." *New York Times Magazine*. November 17, 1963, pp. 96+.

6040. Moore, Alan. *Maxwell the Magic Cat*. London: Acme Press, 1986-87.

6041. Moore, Robin and Joe Kubert. *Tales of the Green Beret*. 3 Vols. Comic-Strip Preserves. El Cajon, California: Blackthorne, 1985-1986.

6042. Moores, Dick. *Jim Hardy*. The Hyperion Library of Classic American Comic Strips. Westport, Connecticut: Hyperion, 1977. 100 pp.

6043. Mösch, Inge. "Mickymaus, Snoopy, Superman; Ausstellung 'Comics' im Kunsthaus in Hamburg." *Hamburger Abendblatt*. June 24, 1971.

6044. Munce, Howard. "Randall Enos... He Doesn't Come in Pairs." *Cartoonist PROfiles*. June 1993, pp. 20-25.

6045. Murray, Will. "Nick Carter Turns 100." *Comics Buyer's Guide*. September 26, 1986, pp. 22, 24.

6046. Neal, Jim. "Editors Flushed Over Cathy's 'Swirley.'" *Comics Buyer's Guide*. May 28, 1993, p. 36.

6047. "New Cartoon Features Half-Pint Infant." *Newsweek*. March 31, 1934, p. 28.

6048. "New Panel Dolly Shows Modern Miss." *Newsletter*. May 1965, p. 20.

6049. Nintzel, Jim. "Tune in Tomorrow." *Metro Times*. November 4-10, 1992, pp. 10-11.

6050. Nordling, Klaus, *et al*. *Lady Luck*. 2 Vols. Park Forest, Illinois: K. Pierce, 1980.

6051. *Nostalgia Comics*. 6 Vols. Franklin Square, New York: Nostalgia Press, 1971-1974.

6052. Nugent, Arthur. "Uncle Nugent's Funland, World's Leading Puzzlemaker." *Cartoonist PROfiles*. No. 6, 1970, pp. 11-15.

6053. Nutzle, Futzie. *Futzie Nutzle's Modern Loafer*. New York: Thames and Hudson, 1981.

6054. Ohff, Heinz. "Pluto und Superman am Hanseatenweg. Zur 'Comic-Strip'—Austellung in der Akademie der Künste." *Der Tagesspiegel* (Berlin). December 14, 1969.

6055. Oliphant, Tim. *Suzann Says*. Bell Buckle Press, 1992.

6056. Oroyan, Susanna. "John Lucas Loves Katy Keene." *Doll Reader*. May 1988, pp. 177-180.

6057. "Out for the Count." *Nemo*. October 1986, pp. 15-24.

6058. Overgard, William. *Rudy in Hollywood*. New York: Holt, Rinehart and Winston, 1984. 128 pp.

6059. Partch, V.F. *Big George*. New York: Duell, Sloan, 1962.

6060. "Pogo, Dennis Star at Lunch Club Meeting." *Publisher's Weekly*. December 20, 1952, pp. 2377-2378.

6061. "Prime Time." *Cartoonist PROfiles*. September 1979, pp. 22-25.

6062. "Professor Doodle's Just for Kids Corner." *Cartoonist PROfiles*. December 1987, pp. 24-31.

6063. "A Real Corporate Soap Opera in Dallas." *Comics Journal*. October 1990, pp. 14-15.

6064. "Redeye (Gordon Bess)." *Cartoonist PROfiles*. No. 19, 1973, pp. 28-35.

6065. Reed, Rod and Jose Luis Salinas. *The Cisco Kid*. Park Forest, Illinois: K. Pierce, 1983. 81 pp.

6066. "Report on the Comic Strip 'Visit to America.'" *Time*. March 16, 1962, p. 15.

6067. Roberts, Cliff. "Sesame Street." *Cartoonist PROfiles*. December 1971, pp. 60-64.

6068. "Roy Howard's Bird, Arpad." *Newsweek*. June 7, 1943, p. 80.

6069. Sadoux, Jean-Jacques. "Bande Dessinée et Publicité: La Fin du Purgatoire?" *Les Langues Modernes* (Paris). 5/6, 1980, pp. 579-586. ("B.C.," "Blondie," "Peanuts," "The Ryatts").

6070. Saunders, Allen and Elmer Woggon. *Steve Roger and Wahoo*. 2 Vols. Comic-Strip Preserves. El Cajon, California: Blackthorne, 1986-.

6071. Scmidmaier, Werner. "Werbung Ist Sündhaft Teuer (Dagobert Duck)." *Werben und Verkaufen* (Munich). November 20, 1970.

6072. Schmuckler, Eric. "Free Peanuts! Free Beetle Bailey!" *Forbes*. October 30, 1989, pp. 159-160.

6073. Schorr, Bill. *Conrad*. New York: Pocket Books, 1985. 95 pp.

6074. Shapiro, Marc. "The Big Chill—Archie." *Comics Scene*. August 1990, pp. 61-64.

6075. Shapiro, Marc. "'The People Next Door' Move In." *Comics Scene*. No. 10, 1989, pp. 58-59.

6076. "Snake Tales." *Cartoonist PROfiles*. June 1984, pp. 24-29.

6077. "Snoopy and Fred Basset." *Cartoonist PROfiles*. September 1977, pp. 10-11.

6078. "Sonny Pew by James Estes." *Cartoonist PROfiles*. June 1982, pp. 22-27.

6079. Spillane, Mickey and Ed Robbins. *Mike Hammer, the Comic Strip*. Park Forest, Illinois: Pierce, 1982. 64 pp.

6080. Stamaty, Mark. *MacDoodle St.* New York: Congdon and Lattes, 1980. 94 pp.

6081. Starr, Leonard. *Annie*. Book 1. Reuben Award Winner Series. El Cajon, California: Blackthorne, 1985. 72 pp.

6082. Storm, George. *Bobby Thatcher, Including Phil Hardy*. The Hyperion Library of Classic American Comic Strips. Westport, Connecticut: Hyperion, 1977. 168 pp.

6083. "The Strange World of Mr. Mum, by Phillips." *Cartoonist PROfiles*. Fall 1969, pp. 61-68.

6084. Streter, Sabin C. *Hollenhead*. New York: NAL Penguin, 1987. 123 pp.

6085. "Strip Collections Top Bestseller List." *Comics Journal*. July 1987, p. 26.

6086. Sullivan, Ed. "Life with Priscilla." *Cartoonist PROfiles*. December 1981, pp. 74-.

6087. Tallarico, Tony. "Trivia Treat." *Cartoonist PROfiles*. June 1987, pp. 64-65.

6088. Tercinet, Alain. "Bronc Peeler." *Giff-Wiff*. No. 20, 1966, p. 21.

6089. "Three Men on a Cartoon; Ching Chow." *Newsweek*. February 10, 1947, p. 58.

6090. Thruelsen, R. "Saddest Man in the Funnies." *Saturday Evening Post*. May 24, 1953, pp. 22-23.

6091. Torrey, Rich. *American Hartland*. New York: New American Library, 1986. 96 pp.

6092. Trinchero, Sergio. "Bat Star." *Super Albo Spada*. No. 51, 1963.

6093. Trinchero, Sergio. "Cassius Clay." *Sgt. Kirk*. No. 2, 1967.

6094. Trinchero, Sergio. "Twiggy." *Sgt. Kirk*. No. 6, 1967, pp. 108-109.

6095. Tufts, Warren. *Casey Ruggles*. 3 Vols. Long Beach, California: Western Wind Production, 1979.

6096. "25 Years of the Nebbs." *Newsweek*. May 31, 1948. p. 53.

6097. Van Amerongen, Jerry. "Ballard Street." *Cartoonist PROfiles*. September 1991, pp. 52-57.

6098. Van Amerongen, Jerry. *The Neighborhood*. New York: Simon and Schuster, 1984. 96 pp.

6099. Van Buren, Raeburn. *Abbie an' Slats*. 2 Vols. Park Forest, Illinois: K. Pierce, 1983-1984.

6100. "The Virtue of Vera Valiant by Stan Lee and Frank Springer." *Cartoonist PROfiles*. March 1977, pp. 62-71.

6101. Walker, Mort. *Backstage at the Strips*. New York: A and W Visual Library, 1975. 311 pp.

6102. Walt Disney Productions. *Walt Disney Animated Features and Silly Symphonies*. New York: Abbeville Press, 1980. 152 pp.

6103. Watzke, Oswald. "Umgang Mit Comics im 4. Schuljahr. Wir Lesen Einen Funny Strip 'Rotfuchs,' Einen Anderen Strip 'Tarzan' und Einen Fantastic Strip 'Little Nemo.'" In *Kinder und Jugendlektüre im Unterricht*, edited by Theodor Karst, pp. 168-185. Heilbrunn/Obb.: Klinkhardt, 1978.

6104. Weaver, Charlotte and Gray Morrow. *Barbara Cartland Romances*. New York: Quick Fox, 1981. 126 pp.

6105. "We Need Your Opinion!" *Cartoonist PROfiles*. September 1991, pp. 62-70.

6106. Wheelan, Ed. *Minute Movies*. The Hyperion Library of Classic American Comic Strips. Westport, Connecticut: Hyperion, 1977. 163 pp.

6107. Wilder, Don. "Out of Bounds by Rechin and Wilder." *Cartoonist PROfiles*. December 1986, pp. 53-58.

6108. Williamson, Al. *Secret Agent Corrigan*. 2 Vols. Comic Art Showcase, No. 2-3. Buffalo, New York: Quality Comic Art Productions, 1980.

6109. Williamson, Jack and Lee Elias. *Beyond Mars*. Comic-Strip Preserves. El Cajon, California: Balckthorne, 1987. 72 pp.

6110. Woggon, Bill. *Count Your Blessings with Little Ben*. Cincinnati, Ohio: Standard, 1973.

6111. "Wright Angles by Larry Wright." *Cartoonist PROfiles*. March 1978, pp. 54-57.

6112. "Zeus by Corky Trinidad." *Cartoonist PROfiles*. September 1979, pp. 8-13.

6113. Zschiensche, Bob. "Our Folks." *Cartoonist PROfiles*. June 1980, pp. 12-20.

6114. Zuñiga, Angel. "Lo Que Va de Tillie a Millie." *Destino* (Barcelona). No. 1551, 1967, pp. 30-31.

"Alley Oop"

6115. "Alley Oop by Dave Graue." *Cartoonist PROfiles*. September 1980, pp. 50-57.

6116. Bertieri, Claudio. "Alley Oop Candido Cavernicolo." *Il Lavoro* (Genoa). August 4, 1966.

6117. Bertieri, Claudio. "A Temple for Alley Oop." *Comics* (Lucca). 1968.

6118. François, Edouard. "Alley Oop." *Phénix* (Paris). No. 2, 1967, p. 35.

6119. Vance, Michael. "Alley Oop." *Dreamline*. March 1982, pp. 86-91.

"Baby Blues"

6120. "Baby Blues." *Cartoonist PROfiles*. March 1990, pp. 40-45.

6121. Beiswinger, George L. "'Baby Blues' Has a Successful Formula." *Editor and Publisher*. December 1, 1990, pp. 40-41.

"Barnaby"

6122. "Barnaby Has His I.Q. for Cartoon-Strip Humor." *Life*. October 4, 1943, pp. 10-13.

6123. "End of a Fairy Tale: Barnaby." *Time*. January 28, 1952, p. 77.

6124. "Escape Artist; Barnaby Strip." *Time*. September 2, 1946, pp. 49-50.

6125. Johnson, Crockett. *Barnaby*. Garden City, New York: Blue Ribbon Books, 1943. 361 pp.

6126. Johnson, Crockett. *Barnaby*. 6 Vols. New York: Ballantine, 1985-1986.

6127. Johnson, Crockett. *Barnaby and Mr. O'Malley*. New York: Henry Holt and Co., 1944. 328 pp.; New York: Dover, 1975. 134 pp.

6128. Kalish, Carol B. "When Worlds Collide." *Comics Feature*. September 1980, pp. 62-63.

"Barney Google"

6129. "Barney Google Man." *Newsweek*. November 23, 1942, pp. 62-63.

6130. "Barney Google's Birthday." *Newsweek*. October 4, 1943, pp. 10-13.

6131. "Barney Google's Birthday, But He Is Eclipsed by the Toughie, Snuffy Smith." *Newsweek*. October 14, 1940, pp. 59-60.

6132. DeBeck, Billy. *Barney Google*. The Hyperion Library of Classic American Comic Strips. Westport, Connecticut: Hyperion, 1977. 102 pp.

6133. DeBeck, Billy. *Barney Google and His Faithful Nag Spark Plug*. New York: Cupples and Leon, 1923.

6134. Goulart, Ron. "Barney Google." *Comics Scene*. July 1982, pp. 20-23.

6135. Sagarin, Edward. "The Deviant in the Comic Strip: The Case History of Barney Google." *Journal of Popular Culture*. Summer 1971, pp. 179-193.

"Batman"

6136. "Batman." *Cartoonist PROfiles*. 1:1 (1969), pp. 74-75.

6137. Horn, Maurice. "Starts Today: Batman, The Original 1940s Newspaper Strip." *New York Daily News Magazine*. July 16, 1989, pp. 20-21.

6138. Richler, M. "Batman at Midlife: Or, the Funnies Grow Up." *New York Times Book Review*. May 3, 1987, p. 35.

"B.C."

6139. Astor, David. "'B.C.' Comic Joining Ann Landers at CS." *Editor and Publisher*. March 21, 1987, pp. 58-59.

6140. "B.C. by Johnny Hart." *Cartoonist PROfiles*. June 1975, pp. 63-67; June 1988, pp. 44-47.

6141. Bertieri, Claudio. "L'Antichissimo Mondo di B.C." *Il Lavoro Nuovo* (Genoa). January 23, 1966.

6142. Fossati, Franco. "B.C." *Fantapolitica* (Rome). February 1966.

6143. Hart, Johnny. *Ala Ka Zot!* New York: Fawcett, 1979.

6144. Hart, Johnny. *B.C. Color Me Sunday*. Greenwich, Connecticut: Fawcett, 1977. 144 pp.

6145. Hart, Johnny. *Big Wheel!* Greenwich, Connecticut: Fawcett, 1969.

6146. Hart, Johnny. *Hey! B.C.* Greenwich, Connecticut: Fawcett, 1959.

6147. Sherry, Richard. "Zot! The King Is a Fink." *The World of Comic Art*. Summer 1967, pp. 24-33.

6148. Wells, Michael. "The B.C. Open." *Cartoonist PROfiles*. September 1987, pp. 62-63.

"Beetle Bailey"

6149. "Beetle at the Pentagon." *Cartoonist PROfiles*. December 1990, pp. 56-57.

6150. "Beetle Bailey." *Cartoonist PROfiles*. No. 15, 1972, pp. 34-39.

6151. "Beetle Bailey's Miss Buxley Proves Controversial; To Be Toned Down in Future." *Comics Journal*. October 1984, pp. 12-13.

6152. "Beetle Busted." *Newsweek*. January 18, 1954, p. 29.

6153. "Beetle's 30th." *Cartoonist PROfiles*. December 1980, pp. 58-59.

6154. Bertieri, Claudio. "Beetle Bailey." *Photographia Italiana*. No. 152, 1970.

6155. "Drummer Bailey." *Editor and Publisher*. February 18, 1958, p. 74.

6156. "The Evolution of a Beetle." *Cartoonist PROfiles*. December 1980, pp. 56-57.

6157. "General Halftrack Mooned." *Comics Journal*. April 1990, p. 17.

6158. Walker, Mort. *Beetle Bailey and Sarge*. New York: Dell Publishing, 1958. Unpaginated.

6159. Walker, Mort. *The Best of Beetle Bailey*. New York: Holt, Rinehart and Winston, 1984. 240 pp.; Bedford, New York: Comicana, 1986. 240 pp.

"Believe It or Not!"

6160. Campbell, Gordon and Mary. "'Believe It or Not.'" *Cartoonist PROfiles*. December 1983, pp. 12-17.

6161. Leamy, H. "Strange Things under the Sun; R.L. Ripley's Believe It or Not Cartoons." *American Mercury*. October 1929, pp. 42-43.

6162. Ripley, Robert L. *Ripley's Giant Believe It or Not!* New York: Warren Books, 1976.

"The Better Half"

6163. "The Better Half Team Cruises Round World." *The Cartoonist*. January 1968, p. 38.

6164. Saxon, C. "Better Half Fare." *New York Times Magazine*. December 5, 1948, p. 20.

"Betty Boop"

6165. Fleischer, Max. *Betty Boop*. New York: Avon Books, 1975. 104 pp.

6166. Fleischer, Max and Bud Counihan. *Betty Boop*. 3 Vols. Comic-Strip Preserves. El Cajon, California: Blackthorne, 1986-1987.

6167. Kreinz, Glória. "Betty Boop—Mulher em HQ." *Boletim de HQ*. January-February 1992, p. 2.

"Big Ben Bolt"

6168. Hegerfors, Sture. "Benjamin Bolt Har Lagt Upp." *Göteborgs-Tidningen* (Göteborg). Söndags-Extra, December 3, 1967.

6169. Murphy, John Cullen. *Big Ben Bolt*. 2 Vols. Vienna, Austria: Pollischansky; New York: King Features Syndicate, 1978-1981.

"Blondie"

6170. Alexander, J. "Dagwood and Blondie Man." *Saturday Evening Post*. April 10, 1948, pp. 15-17.

6171. "Blondie and Dagwood Are America's Favorites." *Life*. August 17, 1942, pp. 8-11.

6172. "Blondie by Young and Drake." *Cartoonist PROfiles*. December 1986, pp. 32-39.

6173. "Blondie Is World's Top Blonde." *Trinidad Guardian*. April 27-May 6, 1990, p. 3.

6174. "Blondie Macht das Rennen." *Allgemeine Zeitung*. April 7, 1951.

6175. Bono, Giani. "Blondie." *Sgt. Kirk* (Genoa). No. 15, 1968. p. 66.

6176. Bryan, Joseph. "His Girl Blondie." *Collier's*. March 15, 1941, p. 14.

6177. "Dagwood Splits the Atom." *Popular Science*. September 1948, pp. 146-149.

6178. Guisto-Davis, J. "Harper To Celebrate 50 Years of Blondie." *Publisher's Weekly*. July 10, 1981, pp. 39-40+.

6179. "Happy 50th Birthday, Blondie!" *Good Housekeeping*. September 1980, p. 70.

6180. Harvey, R.C. "The Old and the Youngs: Blondie at 50." *Comics Journal*. May 1982, pp. 36-42.

6181. Hegerfors, Sture. "Dagobert Forlorade Billioner pa Att Gifta Sig Med Blondie." *GT Söndags Extra* (Göteborg). October 29, 1967.

6182. Hubert-Rodier, Lucienne. "Le Père de Blondie Est Venue à Paris pour Apprendre à Flaner." *Samedi-Soir* (Paris). August 16, 1952.

6183. Krauss, Bob. "Blondie by Young and Raymond." *Cartoonist PROfiles*. September 1980, pp. 24-25.

6184. "Moderner Herd für Blondie." *Westdeutsche Allgemeine Zeitung* (Essen). December 28, 1965.

6185. Nuhn, M. "Blondie and Dagwood—Fifty Years Young." *Hobbies*. September 1980, pp. 68-69.

6186. "$100,000-a-Year Family; Comic Strip Blondie." *Newsweek*. June 23, 1941, p. 64.

6187. Péus, Gunter. "70 Millionen Lieben Familie Bumstead." *Die Welt* (Hamburg). January 31, 1959.

6188. Teisseire, Guy. "Illico, Blondie, Le Fantôme, les Héros des Bandes Dessinées Ont Désormais une Histoire... et des Historiens." *L'Aurore* (Paris). March 15, 1966.

6189. Young, Chic. *Adventures of Blondie and Dagwood*. London: Associated Newspapers, (ca. 1955).

6190. Young, Chic. *Blondie and Dagwood's Adventure in Magic*. Racine, Wisconsin: Whitman Publishing Co., 1944. 248 pp.

6191. Young, Dean and Stan Drake. *Blondie*. Intro. by Shel Dorf. Comic-Strip Preserves. El Cajon, California: Blackthorne, 1986-.

6192. Young, Dean and Rick Marschall. *Blondie and Dagwood's America*. New York: Harper and Row, 1981, 144 pp.

"Bloom County"

6193. Breathed, Berke. *Billy and the Boingers Bootleg*. Boston, Massachusetts: Little, Brown, 1987. 121 pp.

6194. Breathed, Berke. *Bloom County Babylon*. Boston, Massachusetts: Little, Brown, 1986. 224 pp.

6195. Breathed, Berke. *Bloom County: Loose Tails*. Boston, Massachusetts: Little, Brown, 1983. 148 pp.

6196. Breathed, Berke. *Penguin Dreams and Stranger Things*. Boston, Massachusetts: Little, Brown, 1985. 120 pp.

6197. Breathed, Berke. *Tales Too Ticklish To Tell*. Boston, Massachusetts: Little, Brown, 1988.

6198. Breathed, Berke. *'Toons for Our Times*. Boston, Massachusetts: Little, Brown, 1984. 96 pp.

6199. Grauer, N.A. "The Great Bloom County Feud." *Columbia Journalism Review*. September/October 1987, pp. 52-53.

6200. Hurd, Jud. "Bloom County by Berke Breathed." *Cartoonist PROfiles*. December 1987, pp. 12-18.

6201. Stredicke, Victor. "'Bloom County' Dies a Natural Death." *Penstuff*. August 1989, p. 4-5.

"Boner's Ark"

6202. "Boner's Ark." *Cartoonist PROfiles*. No. 15, 1972, pp. 35, 38.

6203. "Boner's Ark, by Addison." *Cartoonist PROfiles*. 1:1 (1969), pp. 44-49.

"Brick Bradford"

6204. Bertieri, Claudio. "Brick Bradford: An Half Hero." *Sgt. Kirk* (Genoa). No. 26, 1969.

6205. Fossati, Franco. "Brick Bradford." *Special SF*. August-October 1966.

6206. François, Edouard. "Brick Bradford ou Cl. Gray le Mal-Aimé. *Phénix* (Paris). No. 12, 1969.

6207. Gray, Clarence. *Brick Bradford, Voyage in a Coin*. The Golden Age of the Comics. Papeete, Tahiti: Comics Stars in the World and Pacific Comics Club, 1976. 96 pp.

6208. Ritt, William and Clarence Gray. *Brick Bradford in the City Beneath the Sea*. The Golden Age of the Comics. Papeete, Tahiti: Comics Stars in the World and Pacific Comics Club, 1976. 92 pp.

6209. Ritt, William and Clarence Gray. *Brick Bradford in the Land of the Lost*. Papeete, Tahiti: Pacific Comics Club, 1981. 52 pp.

6210. Ritt, William and Clarence Gray. *Brick Bradford in the Middle of the Earth*. Papeete, Tahiti: J. Taoc/Pacific Comics Club, 1976. 42 pp.

6211. Trinchero, Sergio. "Brick Bradford." *"Brick Bradford"—L'Olimpo dei Fumetti (Sugar)*. June 1970.

6212. Trinchero, Sergio. "Brick Bradford—l'Autore e il Personaggio." *L'Enciclopedia dei Fumetti*. No. 14, 1970.

"Bringing Up Father"

6213. Braun, Wilbur. *Bringing Up Father, An Original Based on George McManus's Famous Cartoon*. New York: S. French, 1936.

6214. "Bringing up Father by Geo. McManus." *Cartoonist PROfiles*. December 1979, pp. 14-23.

6215. *Bringing Up Father in Politics*. Chicago, Illinois: H. Rossiter Music Co., 1916.

6216. *Bringing Up Father on Broadway*. Chicago, Illinois: H. Rossiter Music Co., 1920.

6217. Galewitz, Herb. *Bringing Up Father. Starring Maggie and Jiggs*. New York: Charles Scribner's Sons. 1973. 179 pp.

6218. "Jiggs: the 25th Anniversary of a Corned Beef and Cabbage Craze." *Newsweek*. November 16, 1935, p. 29.

6219. "Jiggs: The 29th Anniversary of a Corned Beef and Cabbage Craze." *Newsweek*. August 25, 1941, p. 46.

6220. "Jiggs 30 Years." *Newsweek*. November 23, 1942. pp. 64-65.

6221. La Cossitt, H. "Jiggs and I." *Collier's*. January 19, 1952, pp. 9-11; January 26, 1952, pp. 24-25+; February 2, 1952, pp. 30-31+.

6222. McManus, George. *Bringing Up Father*. London: A.V.N. Jones and Co., 1919.

6223. McManus, George. *Bringing Up Father*. Third Series. New York: Cupples and Leon, 1919. 4th Series, 1921.

6224. McManus, George. *Bringing Up Father*. Series Number 22. New York: Cupples and Leon Co., 1932; 1918-.

6225. McManus, George. *Bringing Up Father*. The Hyperion Library of Classic American Comic Strips. Westport, Connecticut: Hyperion, 1977. 166 pp.

6226. McManus, George. *Bringing Up Father, Starring Maggie and Jiggs*. New York: Bonanza, 1973. 179 pp.

6227. McManus, George. *Jiggs Is Back*. Library of Irish American Literature and Culture, Vol. 1. Berkeley, California: Celtic Book Company, 1986. 64 pp.

6228. Murtfeldt, E.W. "Making of a Funny; Bringing Up Father, from the Drawing Board of George McManus, to Its Appearance in the Newspapers." *Popular Science*. June 1940, pp. 84-88.

"Broom Hilda"

6229. "Broom-Hilda." *Cartoonist PROfiles*. September 1983, pp. 30-35.

6230. "Broom Helda by Russell Myers." *Cartoonist PROfiles*. June 1972, pp. 14-23.

6231. Myers, Russell. *Broom-Hilda, Sore Loser*. New York: Fawcett, 1987.

"Brother Juniper"

6232. Irwin, T. "Wistful World of Brother Juniper." *Coronet*. September 1960, pp. 162-167.

6233. McCarthy, Justin. *Brother Juniper at Work and Play*. New York: Hanover House, 1960. 127 pp.

6234. McCarthy, Justin. *Brother Juniper Strikes Again*. New York: Pocket Books, 1961. 127 pp.

"Brother Sebastian"

6235. Day, Chon. *Brother Sebastian at Large*. New York: Doubleday and Co. 1961. 95 pp.

6236. Day, Chon. *Brother Sebastian Carries On*. New York: Doubleday and Co. 1959. 95 pp.

"Buck Rogers"

6237. Bertieri, Claudio. "Buck Rogers." *Il Lavoro* (Genoa). May 17, 1968.

6238. Bertieri, Claudio. "Rogers: The First Viking of the Space." *Photographia Italiana*. No. 132, 1968.

6239. Bradbury, Ray. "Buck Rogers in Apollo, Year One." In *The Collected Works of Buck Rogers in 25th Century*, pp. xi-xiv. New York: Bonanza Books, 1969.

6240. "Buck's Luck." *Time*. February 24, 1958, p. 57.

6241. Dille, Robert C. *The Collected Works of Buck Rogers in the 25th Century*. New York: 1970.

6242. Kane, George. "Buck Rogers: Harbinger of Decade." *Rocky Mountain News* (Denver). December 28, 1969, pp. 5, 8.

6243. Lawrence, Jim and Gray Morrow. *Buck Rogers*. New York: Quick Fox, 1981. 179 pp.

6244. Nowlan, Phil and Dick Calkins. "Buck Rogers: An Autobiography." In *The Collected Works of Buck Rogers in the 25th century*, pp. xv-xxiii. New York: Bonanza Books, 1969.

6245. Nowlan, Phil and Dick Calkins. *Buck Rogers 25th Century A.D.* Ann Arbor, Michigan: E.M. Aprill, 1971. 180 pp.

6246. Nowlan, Phil and Dick Calkins. *The Collected Works of Buck Rogers in the 25th Century*. Edited by Robert C. Dille. New York: Chelsea House, 1969. 376 pp.

6247. Nowlan, Phil and Dick Calkins. *The Collected Works of Buck Rogers in the 25th Century*. Edited by Robert C. Dille. Rev. Ed. New York: A & W Publishers, 1977. 288 pp.

6248. Sherman, Sam. "Buck Rogers, Part 1-2." *Spacemen*. No. 5, 1962, pp. 34-42; No. 6, 1963, pp. 16-21.

"The Bungle Family"

6249. "The Bungle Family." *Cartoonist PROfiles*. June 1977, pp. 52-61.

6250. Phelps, Donald. "The Bungle Family's Little Glories of Inanity." *Nemo*. February 1984, pp. 39-50.

6251. Tuthill, Harry J. *The Bungle Family*. The Hyperion Library of Classic American Comic Strips. Westport, Connecticut: Hyperion, 1977. 134 pp.

"Buster Brown"

6252. "Buster Brown. Merchandising's Oldest Comic Trademark." *The World of Comic Art*. June 1966, p. 41.

6253. Caldiron, Orio. "Buster Brown." *Sgt. Kirk* (Genoa). No. 15, 1968, pp. 44-46.

6254. Fabrizzi, Paolo, Sergio Trinchero, and Rinaldo Traini. "Buster Brown." *Mondo Domani*. Supplemento Mondo Ragazzi. July 28, 1968.

6255. Nuhn, R. "The Valentines of Buster Brown and Friends." *Hobbies*. February 1984, pp. 102-105.

6256. Outcault, Richard F. *Buster Brown*. The Hyperion Library of Classic American Comic Strips. Westport, Connecticut: Hyperion, 1977. 110 pp.

6257. Outcault, Richard F. *Buster Brown, Early Strips in Full Color*. Edited by August Derleth. New York: Dover, 1974. 30 pp.

"Buz Sawyer"

6258. "Buz Sawyer by Roy Crane." *Cartoonist PROfiles*. No. 5, 1970, pp. 51-56; No. 6, 1970, pp. 71-73; No. 15, 1972, p. 48.

6259. Crane, Roy. *Buz Sawyer*. 2 Vols. Comic Art Showcase, No. 5-6. Buffalo, New York: Quality Comic Art Productions, 1980.

6260. Crane, Roy. "Roy Crane and Buzz Sawyer." *Cartoonist PROfiles*. Summer 1969, pp. 4-13.

"Calvin and Hobbes"

6261. "Calvin and Hobbesian Dilemma." *News Inc.* February 1992, p. 7.

6262. Marschall, Rick. "Oh, You Kid." *Comics Journal*. February 1989, pp. 73-77.

6263. Watterson, Bill. *Calvin and Hobbes*. Kansas City, Missouri: Andrews, McMeel and Parker, 1987. 127 pp.

6264. Watterson, Bill. "Calvin and Hobbes." *Cartoonist PROfiles*. December 1985, pp. 36-41.

6265. Watterson, Bill. *Something Under the Bed Is Drooling*. Kansas City, Missouri: Andrews and McMeel, 1988.

"Captain Easy"

6266. Goulart, Ron. "Captain Easy." *Comics Scene*. November 1982, pp. 41-44.

6267. Traini, Rinaldo. "Captain Easy." *Sgt. Kirk*. No. 11/12, 1968, pp. 1-4.

"Caspar Milquetoast"

6268. Basso, H. "Profiles: The World of Caspar Milquetoast." *The New Yorker*. November 5, 1949, pp. 44-50, 53-55, 119.

6269. "Caspar Rides Again." *Newsweek*. April 13, 1953, p. 31.

"Charlie Chan"

6270. Andriola, Alfred. *Charlie Chan, A Mystery Strip*. New York: McNaugh Syndicate, Inc., 1950.

6271. Andriola, Alfred. "You Can't Do That!" Manuscript presented at Comic-Kongress, Bordighera, Italy, February 1965.

6272. "Charlie Chan by Alfred Andriola." *Cartoonist PROfiles*. No. 14, 1972, p. 40; No. 15, 1972, p. 49.

6273. Horn, Maurice "Charlie Chan." *Phénix* (Paris). No. 2, 1967, pp. 1-4.

6274. Lacassin, Francis. "Charlie Chan, ou le Sage aux Sept Fleurs." *Club du Livre Policier, Editions Opta* (Paris). February 1966.

"Dennis the Menace"

6275. "Dennis the Menace and His Family Go on the Great American Weekend." *Look*. June 2, 1953, p. 88.

6276. "Dennis Turns 39." *Trinidad Guardian*. April 27-May 6, 1990, p. 3.

6277. "From Cartoon to Big Business with Dennis the Menace." *Publisher's Weekly*. January 9, 1961, pp. 34-35.

6278. Hanscom, Leslie. "Dennis the Menace Is 37, Going on 5." *Newsday* story in *Philadelphia Inquirer*. November 29, 1987, p. 5-J.

6279. Karrer, Wolfgang. "The Analysis of Comics: The Example of 'Dennis the Menace.' Zur Analyse von Comics: Am Beispiel 'Dennis the Menace.'" *Anglistik und Englischunterricht*. October 1977, pp. 93-108.

6280. Ketcham, Hank. "An All-American Classic—Dennis the Menace." *Cartoonist PROfiles*. June 1986, pp. 11-15.

6281. Ketcham, Hank. *Dennis the Menace... Here Comes Trouble*. Greenwich, Connecticut: Fawcett, 1966. Unpaginated.

6282. Ketcham, Hank. *Dennis the Menace Household Hurricane*. New York: Pocket Books, 1958. Unpaginated.

6283. Ketcham, Hank. *Dennis the Menace Vs Everybody*. New York: Crest Books, 1962. Unpaginated.

6284. Ketcham, Hank. *Dennis the Menace, Who Me?* New York: Random, 1962. Unpaginated.

6285. Ketcham, Hank. *Happy Half-Pint*. New York: Random, 1961. Unpaginated.

6286. Johansen, Arno. "Dennis the Menace." *Parade*. January 24, 1960, p. 8.

6287. "Menace Gets Dressed." *Look*. October 6, 1953, p. 87.

6288. "Speaking of Pictures: Boys Resembling Dennis the Menace." *Life*. March 30, 1953, pp. 14-15.

6289. Wilson, B. "Menace Pays Off." *Américas*. June 1953, pp. 7-9.

"Dick Tracy"

6290. Bernazzali, Nino and Giani Bono. "Dick Tracy in Italia." *Comics World* (Genoa). September 1967.

6291. "Bonny Braids." *New Yorker*. July 7, 1951, pp. 14-15.

6292. "B.O.'s Wedding Night." *Newsweek*. August 26, 1946.

6293. Broes, Arthur T. "*Dick Tracy*: The Early Years." *Journal of Popular Culture*. Spring 1992, pp. 97-122.

6294. "Candles for Tracy." *Newsweek*. October 22, 1956, p. 30.

6295. Collins, Max A. and Rick Fletcher. *Dick Tracy*. The Complete Max Collins/Rick Fletcher Dick Tracy, No. 1. Toronto, Ontario: Dragon Lady Press, 1986. 61 pp.

6296. Collins, Max A. and Dick Locher. *The Dick Tracy Casebook: Favorite Adventures, 1931-1990*. New York: St. Martin's Press, 1990(?).

6297. Collins, Max A. and Dick Locher. *Dick Tracy: Tracy's Wartime Memories*. U.S. Classic Series, Park Forest, Illinois: K. Pierce, 1986. 64 pp.

6298. "The Comics." *MAD Super Special*. Fall 1981. (Dick Tracy parodies).

6299. Counts, Kyle. "Dick Tracy." *Comics Scene*. August 1990, pp. 33-39.

6300. Crouch, Bill, jr. *Dick Tracy: America's Most Famous Detective*. Secaucus, New Jersey: Citadel, 1987. 256 pp.

6301. Culhane, John. "Dick Tracy, the First Law and Order Man." *Argosy*. June 1974.

6302. Del Buono, Oreste. "Dick Tracy Comics Al Cappone." *Linus*. No. 3, 1965.

6303. "Detective Tracy's Mansion." *Time*. December 25, 1950, p. 35.

6304. "Dick Tracy." *Cartoonist PROfiles*. No. 15, 1972, p. 45.

6305. "Dick Tracy in Orbit; Diet Smith's Space Coupe." *Newsweek*. January 14, 1963, p. 47.

6306. "Dick Tracy Strip Accused of Libel." *Comics Journal*. January 1988, p. 16.

6307. "Dick Tracy Wrist Radio Developed by Signal Corps." *Tampa Morning Tribune*. December 23, 1954, p. 3.

6308. Edwards, William. "How Dick Tracy Gets His Man." *Guns Magazine*. August 1955.

6309. Gould, Chester. *The Celebrated Cases of Dick Tracy, 1931-1951*. Edited by Herb Galewitz. New York: Chelsea House, 1970. 291 pp.

6310. Gould, Chester. *Dick Tracy*. 2 Vols. Long Beach, California: T. Raiola, 1982.

6311. Gould, Chester. *Dick Tracy*. 13 Vols. Reuben Award Winner Series. El Cajon, California: Blackthorne, 1984-1987.

6312. Gould, Chester. "Dick Tracy Looks at Television." *TV Guide*. May 1-7, 1953.

6313. Gould, Chester. "Dick Tracy No. 1." *Cartoonist PROfiles*. No. 6, 1970, pp. 16-27.

6314. Gould, Chester. *Dick Tracy, the Early Years*. El Cajon, California: Blackthorne, 1987-.

6315. Gould, Chester. *Dick Tracy, the Unprinted Stories*. El Cajon, California: Blackthorne, 1987-.

6316. Gould, Chester. *Dick Tracy, the Thirties: Tommy Guns and Hard Times*. Edited by Herb Galewitz. New York: Chelsea House, 1978. 285 pp.

6317. Hencey, Robert. "Dick Tracy, King of the Detectives." *Antique Trader Weekly*. May 7, 1986.

6318. Johnson, Kim H. "Crimestopper's Casebooks." *Comics Scene*. August 1990, pp. 40-44, 52.

6319. Lacassin, Francis. "Dick Tracy Meets Muriel." *Sight and Sound* (London). Spring 1967, pp. 101-103.

6320. McSpadden, "DC." "The History of Dick Tracy." *Collector's Club Newsletter*. September 1980, pp. 5-6.

6321. Maeder, Jay. *Dick Tracy. The Life and Times of America's No. 1 Crimestopper*. New York: Penguin, 1990. 218 pp.

6322. Margolick, David. "In Dick Tracy's Latest Caper, 'The Case of the Purloined Panels,' a Law Firm Is Embarrassed." *New York Times*. October 20, 1989, p. 8.

6323. "Million Dollar Baby." *Time*. August 18, 1947, p. 42.

6324. "Miniature Wrist Radio." *Life*. October 3, 1947.

6325. Mooney, L.A. and C.M. Fewell. "Crime in One Long-Lived Comic Strip: An Evaluation of Chester Gould's 'Dick Tracy.'" *American Journal of Economics and Sociology*. January 1989, pp. 89-100.

6326. Museum of Cartoon Art. *Dick Tracy, the Art of Chester Gould*. Port Chester, New York: 1978. 48 pp. Catalog of an exhibition held October-November 1978.

6327. Orphan, Dennis. "Dick Tracy: For 30 Years, Flint-Jawed Crime Fighter." *The Quill*. April 1962, 14-15.

6328. Price, Bob. "The Dick Tracy Story." *Screen Thrills Illustrated*. No. 1, 1962, pp. 52-59.

6329. Resnais, Alain. "Dick Tracy ou L'Amérique en 143 Visages." *Giff-Wiff* (Paris). No. 21, 1966.

6330. Roberts, Garyn Glyn. "Black Days, Grotesque Rogues and Square-Jawed Justice: The World of Dick Tracy." *Dissertation Abstracts International*. March 1987.

6331. Romer, Jean-Claude. "Dick Tracy à l'Écran." *Giff-Wiff* (Paris). No. 21, 1966.

6332. Rosemont, Franklin. "Surrealism in the Comics II: Dick Tracy (Chester Gould)." In *Popular Culture in America*, edited by Paul Buhle, pp. 128-131. Minneapolis, Minnesota: University of Minnesota Press, 1987.

6333. Serbell, John. "50 Golden Years." *Media History Digest*. Spring 1981, pp. 41-55.

6334. "Sparkle Plenty: From Comic-Strip Dick Tracy." *Life*. August 25, 1947, p. 42.

6335. Stuckey, William. "Dick Tracy: The Inner Man." *Northwestern Review*. Winter 1967.

6336. "Syndicate Rubs Out Max Collins as 'Tracy' Writer." *Comics Buyer's Guide*. February 26, 1993, p. 6.

6337. "Too Harsh in Putting Down Evil." *Time*. June 28, 1968, p. 53.

6338. "Top Cop." *Newsweek*. October 16, 1961.

6339. Van Hise, James. *Calling Tracy! Six Decades of Dick Tracy*. Las Vegas, Nevada: Pioneer, 1990. 148 pp.

"Dickie Dare"

6340. Caniff, Milton. *The Complete Dickie Dare*. Intro. by Rick Marschall. Agoura, California: Fantagraphics Books, 1986. 147 pp.

6341. Marschall, Rick. "Of Stout Fellahs and Real Thrills: Milton Caniff's Early Adventure Strip, *Dickie Dare*." *Nemo*. October 1985, pp. 5-26.

"Dilbert"

6342. Adams, Scott. "The Making of Dilbert." *Cartoonist PROfiles*. December 1989, pp. 38-45.

6343. Goodman, J.B. "Dilbert, USN; Lieut. Comdr. R.C. Osborn Creates Dilbert Posters for the Navy." *Flying*. August 1944, pp. 55+.

6344. "Navy Airmen Learn from Dilbert; Cartoons by R. Osborn." *Life*. May 17, 1943, pp. 8-10.

6345. Osborn, R.C. "Story of Dilbert; or, How Not To Fly." *New York Times Magazine*. November 1, 1942, p. 15.

"Dondi"

6346. "Dondi by Gus Edson and Irwin Hasen." *Cartoonist PROfiles*. No. 15, 1972, p. 53.

6347. "Dondi by Irwin Hasen." *Cartoonist PROfiles*. 1:2 (1969), pp. 19-23.

"Doonesbury"

6348. Alter, Jonathan. "Doonesbury Contra Sinatra." *Newsweek*. June 24, 1985, p. 82.

6349. Alter, Jonathan, *et al*. "Comics in Yuppiedom: The 'Doonesbury' Strip Returns to Funny Pages Far Different from the Sedate, Safe Days of 'Blondie.'" *Newsweek*. October 1984, pp. 76-79.

6350. "Dan, Drugs, and Doonesbury." *Comics Journal*. December 1991, pp. 16-17.

6351. "Doonesburying Reagan." *Newsweek*. November 10, 1980, p. 121.

6352. "'Doonesbury' Series Brouhaha." *Editor and Publisher*. September 12, 1987, p. 61.

6353. "'Doonesbury' Will Hit Its 20th Anniversary This Week." *Editor and Publisher*. October 20, 1990, p. 43.

6354. Henry, W.A. "Attacking a 'National Amnesia.'" *Time*. December 8, 1986, p. 107.

6355. Kelly, J. "Ol' Black Eyes." *Time*. June 24, 1985, p. 66.

6356. Lamb, Christopher. "Changing with the Times: The World According to 'Doonesbury.'" *Journal of Popular Culture*. Spring 1990, pp. 113-129.

6357. Lamb, Chris. "Doonesbury and the Limits of Satire." Paper presented at Association for Education in Journalism and Mass Communication, Portland, Oregon, July 1988.

6358. Leonard, Tom. "Brought to Light in the Cartoon Strip." *The Guardian*. February 20, 1989.

6359. McConnell, F. "Zonker's Sunset Strip." *Commonweal*. November 19, 1982, pp. 624-625.

6360. Maeder, Jay. "Doonesbury." *Cartoonist PROfiles*. June 1980, pp. 36-37.

6361. "Newspaper Editor Edits *Doonesbury*." *Comics Journal*. November 1989, pp. 17-18.

6362. Palomo, Juan. "The Great Doonesbury Uproar." *The Quill*. August 1979, p. 26.

6363. Ricci, James. "The Doonesbury Shuffle." *Menomonee Falls Guardian*. September 24, 1973, pp. 3-6, 11-15. Reprinted from *Akron Beacon Journal*. November 5, 1972.

6364. "Savage Pen." *Time*. November 12, 1984, p. 89.

6365. Trudeau, Garry B. *Ask for May, Settle for June*. New York: Holt, Rinehart and Winston, 1982.

6366. Trudeau, Garry B. *Bull Tales*. New Haven, Connecticut: *Yale Daily News*, 1969.

6367. Trudeau, Garry B. "Doonesbury." *Life*. October 1984, pp. 55-62.

6368. Trudeau, Garry B. *The Doonesbury Chronicles*. New York: Holt, Rinehart and Winston, 1975. 224 pp.

6369. Trudeau, Garry B. *Doonesbury Classics*. 4 Vols. New York: Holt, Rinehart and Winston, 1980. (*Dare To Be Great Ms Caucus; Any Grooming Hints for Your Young Fans, Rollie?, As the Kid Goes for Broke, Stalking the Perfect Tan*).

6370. Trudeau, Garry B. *Doonesbury Deluxe: Selected Glances Askance*. New York: Henry Holt, 1987. 224 pp.

6371. Trudeau, Garry B. *Doonesbury Dossier: The Reagan Years*. New York: Holt, Rinehart and Winston, 1980, 1981, 1982, 1983, 1984. 222 pp.

6372. Trudeau, Garry B. *Doonesbury's Greatest Hits*. New York: Holt, Rinehart and Winston, 1978. 224 pp.

6373. Trudeau, Garry B. *Doonesbury Special. A Director's Notebook*. Kansas City, Missouri: Sheed, Andrews, McMeel, Inc., 1977. 128 pp.

6374. Trudeau, Garry B. "The 'Doonesbury' You Probably Didn't See." *Ms*. November 1985, pp. 101-102.

6375. Trudeau, Garry B. *Guilty, Guilty, Guilty!* New York: Holt, Rinehart and Winston, 1973.

6376. Trudeau, Garry B. *In Search of Reagan's Brain*. New York: Holt, Rinehart and Winston, 1981. Unpaginated.

6377. Trudeau, Garry B. *The Original Yale Cartoons*. Kansas City, Missouri: Sheed, Andrews and McMeel, 1976.

6378. Trudeau, Garry B. *The People's Doonesbury*. New York: Holt, Rinehart and Winston, 1981. 204 pp.

6379. Trudeau, Garry B. *A Tad Overweight, But Violet Eyes To Die For*. New York: Holt, Rinehart and Winston, 1980. Unpaginated.

6380. Trudeau, Garry B. *The Week of the "Rusty Nail."* New York: Holt, Rinehart, and Winston, 1983.

6381. Trudeau, Garry B. *You're Never Too Old for Nuts and Berries*. New York: Holt, Rinehart and Winston, 1976.

6382. Trudeau, Garry B. and Nicholas Von Hoffman. *Tales from the Margaret Mead Taproom*. Kansas City, Missouri: Sheedy and Ward, 1976.

6383. "Washington Post's Suspension of Doonesbury." *Time*. June 18, 1979, p. 68.

6384. Wasserman, Jeffrey H. "Doonesbury: Too O' the Charts." *Comics Journal*. March 1979, p. 36.

"Drabble"

6385. "Drabble by Kevin Fagan." *Cartoonist PROfiles*. March 1980, pp. 30-33.

6386. Fagan, Kevin. *Drabble in the Fast Lane*. New York: Fawcett, 1985. 128 pp.

6387. Fagan, Kevin. *The First Book of Drabble*. New York: Fawcett, 1981. 127 pp.

6388. Fagan, Kevin. "Seventeen-Second Interview; Drabble Cartoonist." *Seventeen*, October 1979, p. 58.

"Emmy Lou"

6389. Links, Marty. *Bobby Sox. The Life and Times of Emmy Lou*. New York: Hawthorn Books, 1954.

6390. Mitchell, Ed. "Emmy Lou by Marty Links." *Cartoonist PROfiles*. March 1977, pp. 50-55.

6391. Neuhaus, Cynthia. "Emmy Lou." *Newsletter*. June 1966, p. 8.

"Eyebeam"

6392. Hurt, Sam. *Eyebeam, Therefore I Am*. Austin, Texas: Distributed by AAR/Tantalus, 1984. 128 pp.

6393. Hurt, Sam. *Eenie Meenie Minie Tweed*. Austin, Texas. Blunt Books, 1985. 122 pp.

6394. Hurt, Sam. *I'm Pretty Sure I've Got My Death-Ray in Here Somewhere*. Austin, Texas: Distributed by AAR/Tantalus, 1982. 128 pp.

6395. Hurt, Sam. *The Mind's Eyebeam*. Kansas City, Missouri: Andrews, McMeel and Parker, 1986. 123 pp.

6396. Hurt, Sam. *Our Eyebeam's Twisted*. Austin, Texas: Blunt Books, 1985. 122 pp.

6397. Nybakken, Scott. "15 Years of Beamophilia. An Appreciation of Sam Hurt's *Eyebeam*." *Comics Journal*. May 1993, pp. 40-43, 45.

"Family Circus"

6398. Keane, Bil. "The Family Circus Album." *Cartoonist PROfiles*. March 1985, pp. 62-65.

6399. Keane, Bil. *The Family Circus Parade*. Kansas City, Missouri: Andrews, McMeel and Parker, 1984. 104 pp.

"The Far Side"

6400. Kelly, J. "All Creatures Weird and Funny." *Time*. December 1, 1986, p. 86.

6401. Kinoshita, L. "A View from 'The Far Side.'" *Saturday Review*. November/December 1984, pp. 36-37+.

6402. Lanzafama, E. "Life on 'The Far Side.'" *National Wildlife*. October/November 1984.

6403. Larson, Gary. *The Far Side Gallery*. Kansas City, Missouri: Andrews, McMeel and Parker, 1984. 206 pp.

6404. Larson, Gary. *The Far Side Gallery 2*. Kansas City, Missouri: Andrews, McMeel and Parker, 1986. 192 pp.

6405. Larson, Gary. *In Search of the Far Side*. Kansas City, Missouri: Andrews, McMeel and Parker, 1984.

6406. Larson, Gary. *The PreHistory of the Far Side: A 10th Anniversary Exhibit*. Kansas City, Missouri: Andrews and McMeel, 1989. 288 pp.

6407. Larson, Gary. "The Real Story from 'The Far Side.'" *The Oregonian*. January 5, 1990, p. B-1.

6408. Larson, Gary. *Wildlife Preserves: A Far Side Collection*. Kansas City, Missouri: Andrews and McMeel, 1989.

6409. "Near the Far Side." *Comics Scene*. No. 10 (Vol. 4, Series 21), pp. 58-60.

6410. Richmond, Peter. "Creatures from the Black Cartoon: In Gary Larson's Wildly Funny Comic Strip, 'The Far Side,' Animals Act Like Humans and Humans Act Like Animals." *Rolling Stone*. September 1987, p. 79.

"Ferd'nand"

6411. Hegerfors, Sture. "Ferd'nand 30, 40 Miljoner Läser Hopnan Varje Dag!" *GT Söndags Extra* (Göteborg). September 10, 1967.

6412. Mikkelson, H.D. *Ferd'nand by Mik*. New York: Greenberg, 1953.

"Flash Gordon"

6413. "The Ace of Space: Flash Gordon." *Spacemen, Annual 1965 (Philadelphia)*. pp. 16-21.

6414. Amadieu, G. "Scénario de Flash Gordon." *Phénix*. No. 3, 1967, p. 12-16.

6415. Arbesu, Faustino R. "Crónicas Gijonesas de 'Flash Gordon.'" *El Wendigo*. No. 53, 1991, p. 4.

6416. Behlmer, Rudy. "The Sage of Flash Gordon." *Screen Facts*. No. 10, 1967, pp. 53-63.

6417. Briggs, Austin. *Flash Gordon*. 4 Vols. Long Beach, California: Pacific Comics Club, 1981.

6418. Castelli, Alfredo. "Bibliografia di Flash Gordon Negli Stati Uniti. *Comics*. No. 4, 1966, pp. 13-14.

6419. Couperie, Pierre and Edouard François. "Flash Gordon." *Phénix* (Paris). No. 3, 1967, pp. 2-7.

6420. Cwiklik, Gregory. "When Adventure Was an Art." *Comics Journal*. February 1993, pp. 90-94.

6421. Del Buono, Oreste. "Caro Vecchio Flash Gordon." *Corriere d'Informazione*. 1964.

6422. Del Buono, Oreste. "Flash Gordon." *Linus*. No. 4, 1965.

6423. Del Buono, Oreste. "Ma Chi Era Gordon?" *Linus*. No. 44, 1968, p. 30.

6424. Gasca, Luis. "El Buen Amigo 'Flash Gordon.'" *La Voz de España* (Madrid). August 6, 1963.

6425. Hegerfors, Sture. "Blixt Gordon-Superh-Jälten." *Dagens Nyheter* (Stockholm). February 5, 1967.

6426. Horn, Maurice. "The Adventure Strip." Introduction to *Flash Gordon in the Ice Kingdom of Mongo*. Franklin Square, New York: Nostalgia Press, 1967.

6427. Horn, Maurice. "Flash Gordon." *Nostalgia Comics*. No. 1, 1969.

6428. Jodorowsky, Alexandro." The Flash Contra Gurdjieff." *Nueva Dimensión* (Barcelona). No. 4, 1968, pp. 145-146.

6429. Leborgne, André. "Monstres et Antropomorphes de Notre Enfance. Flash Gordon le Tournoi de Mongo." *Rantanplan* (Brussels). No. 5, 1967, pp. 6-7.

6430. Leborgne, André. "Monstres et Antropomorphes de Notre Enfance. Flash Gordon por Alex Raymond." *Rantanplan* (Brussels). No. 4, 1966/1967, pp. 14-15.

6431. Leydi, Roberto. "Il Ritorno di Gordon Flash." *L'Europeo*. August 10, 1964.

6432. Littlejohn, Tom. "The Return of Flash Gordon!" *The Collectors' Club Newsletter*. September 1980, pp. 7-9.

6433. Mariani, Enzo. "Gordon." *Fantascienza Minore*. Sondernummer 1967, pp. 61-62.

6434. Nicoletti, Manfredi. "Flash Gordon und die Utopie des 20. Jahrhunderts." *Bauen und Wohnen*. 22 (1967), Chronik, pp. V. 4, 6, 8.

6435. Norwood, Rick. "A Surprising Collaboration: Kurtzman and Frazetta's Contributions to Dan Barry's Flash Gordon." *Nemo*. December 1983, pp. 7-26.

6436. Pohl, Peter. "Flash Gordon. Der Comic. Eine Bestandsaufnahme." *Comic Forum* (Vienna). 3:9 (1981), pp. 40-47.

6437. Ponce de Leon, A. "Flash Gordon, Tinha Razao." *Manchete* (Lisbon). 1968.

6438. Raymond, Alex. *Flash Gordon*. Franklin Square, New York: Nostalgia Press, 1967.

6439. Raymond, Alex. *Flash Gordon*. 5 Vols. Franklin Square, New York: Nostalgia Press, 1974-1978.

6440. Raymond, Alex. *Flash Gordon*. Papeete, Tahiti: Pacific Comics Club, 1977. 55 pp.

6441. Raymond, Alex. *Flash Gordon in the Planet Mongo*. Franklin Square, New York: Nostalgia Press, 1974.

6442. Raymond, Alex. *Flash Gordon in the Underwater World of Mongo*. Franklin Square, New York: Nostalgia Press, 1974.

6443. Raymond, Alex. *Flash Gordon into the Water World of Mongo*. Intro. by Maurice Horn. Franklin Square, New York: Nostalgia Press, 1971.

6444. Rodari, Gianni. "Gordon Ritorna." *Paese Sera* August 17, 1964.

6445. Scott, Kenneth W. "A Propos de Flash Gordon." *Midi-Minuit Fantastique* (Paris). No. 9, 1964, pp. 53-55.

6446. Trinchero, Sergio. "Flash Gordon." *Super Albo*. No. 86, 1964.

6447. Trinchero, Sergio. "Minculpop Contro Flash Gordon." *Hobby* (Milan). No. 1, 1966.

6448. Trinchero, Sergio. "Il Trionfo di Gordon." *Gordon*. No. 2, 1964.

6449. Trinchero, Sergio and Alfredo Castelli. "Bibliographia Italiana di Gordon." *Comics*. No. 4, 1966, pp. 15-16.

6450. Zanotto, Piero. "Ritorna in America il Gordon Che Entusiasmò Negli Anni Trenta." *Il Gazzettino* (Venice). May 15, 1967.

"For Better or for Worse"

6451. "Caught in Controversy; *For Better or for Worse*." *Comics Journal*. May 1993, pp. 10-11.

6452. Johnston, Lynn. *Is This One of Those Days, Daddy?* Kansas City, Missouri: Andrews and McMeel, 1982. 127 pp.

6453. Johnston, Lynn. *It Must Be Nice To Be Little*. Kansas City, Missouri: Andrews and McMeel, 1983. 128 pp.

6454. Johnston, Lynn. *It's All Downhill from Here*. Kansas City, Missouri: Andrews, McMeel and Parker, 1987. 126 pp.

6455. Johnston, Lynn. *I've Got the One-More-Washload Blues*. Kansas City, Missouri: Andrews and McMeel, 1981. 127 pp.

6456. Johnston, Lynn. *Just One More Hug*. Kansas City, Missouri: Andrews, McMeel and Parker, 1984. 128 pp.

6457. Johnston, Lynn. *Keep the Home Fries Burning*. Kansas City, Missouri: Andrews, McMeel and Parker, 1986. 127 pp.

6458. Johnston, Lynn. *The Last Straw*. Kansas City, Missouri: Andrews, McMeel and Parker, 1985. 128 pp.

6459. Neal, Jim. "Family-Oriented Comic Strip Character Says He's Gay." *Comics Buyer's Guide*. April 23, 1993, p. 6.

"Foxy Grandpa"

6460. Bunny. *Foxy Grandpa Plays Ball*. Chicago, Illinois: M.A. Donahue, 1908(?).

6461. Bunny. *Foxy Grandpa Plays Santa Claus*. Chicago, Illinois: M.A. Donahue, 1908(?).

6462. Bunny. *Foxy Grandpa Rides the Goat*. Chicago, Illinois: M.A. Donahue, 1908(?).

6463. Bunny. *Foxy Grandpa's Fancy Shooting*. Chicago, Illinois: M.A. Donahue, 1908(?).

6464. Bunny. *Foxy Grandpa Shows the Boys Up-to-Date Sports*. Chicago, Illinois: M.A. Donahue, 1908(?).

"Frank and Ernest"

6465. "Frank and Ernest." *Cartoonist PROfiles*. September 1975, pp. 44-47.

6466. Thaves, Bob. "Frank and Ernest." *Cartoonist PROfiles*. June 1988, pp. 18-24.

"Funky Winkerbean"

6467. Batiuk, Tom. *Closed Out!* New York: Grosset and Dunlap, 1977.

6468. Batiuk, Tom. *Funky Winkerbean.* New York: Fawcett, 1984. 96 pp.

6469. Batiuk, Tom. *Funky Winkerbean Yearbook #3.* New York: Tempo, 1980.

6470. Batiuk, Tom. *Play It Again, Funky!* New York: Grosset and Dunlap, 1975.

6471. "Funky Winkerbean." *Cartoonist PROfiles.* September 1992, pp. 30-38.

6472. "Funky Winkerbean by Tom Batiuk." *Cartoonist PROfiles.* No. 22, 1974, pp. 12-17.

"Garfield"

6473. Conça, Paulo. "Garfield: O Cinismo Crítico." *Boletim de HQ.* January-February 1992, p. 6.

6474. Davis, Jim. *Garfield at Large.* New York: Ballantine, 1980. 128 pp.

6475. Davis, Jim. *Garfield Treasury.* New York: Ballantine, 1982. 117 pp.

6476. Davis, Jim. *Here Comes Garfield.* New York: Ballantine, 1982.

6477. Davis, Jim. *The Second Garfield Treasury.* New York: Ballantine, 1983.

6478. Davis, Jim. *U.S. Acres Goes Half Hog.* New York: Topper Books, 1987. 125 pp.

6479. Hurd, Jud. "Garfield—Jim Davis." *Cartoonist PROfiles.* September 1986, pp. 12-19.

6480. Japinga, Jeff. "Garfield by Jim Davis." *Cartoonist PROfiles.* December 1978, pp. 62-65.

6481. McDowell, E. "Behind the Best Sellers." *New York Times Book Review.* July 27, 1980, p. 25.

"Gasoline Alley"

6482. Banks, Michael A. "Sixty-Three and Counting. Gasoline Alley Marches On." *Comics Collector.* Spring 1984, pp. 72-73, 90.

6483. Black, Ed. "Gasoline Alley." *Cartoonist PROfiles*. September 1987, pp. 64-69.

6484. "Gasoline Alley: Fifty Years from Today." *Comics Buyer's Guide*. May 23, 1986, p. 36.

6485. "Gasoline Alley's Flights of Fancy." *Nemo*. February 1989, pp. 5-17.

6486. King, Frank. *Skeezix and Pal*. [New York]: Reilly and Lee, 1925. 105 pp.

6487. King, Frank. *Skeezix and Uncle Walt*. [New York]: Reilly and Lee, 1924. 122 pp.

6488. King, Frank. *Skeezix at the Circus*. [New York]: Reilly and Lee, 1926. 106 pp.

6489. Marschall, Rick. "Graphic Delights Along Gasoline Alley." *Nemo*. June 1983, pp. 44-48.

6490. Moores, Dick. *Gasoline Alley*. New York: Avon Books, 1976. 137 pp.

6491. Moores, Dick. *Rover from Gasoline Alley*. Reuben Award Winner Series. El Cajon, California: Blackthorne, 1984. 72 pp.

6492. Oliphant, H.N. "Skeezix: King of the Comics." *Coronet*. February 1949, pp. 77-80.

6493. "Skeezix Is 21." *Time*. February 23, 1942, p. 65.

6494. "Skeezix Scoops." *Newsweek*. May 24, 1943, pp. 93-94.

6495. "Speaking of Pictures Little-Businessman Skeezix Hires His Ex-Sergeant." *Life*. April 15, 1946, pp. 14-15.

6496. "Twenty Years of Skeezix." *Newsweek*. February 17, 1941, p. 71.

"Gordo"

6497. Arriola, Gus. *Gordo*. Garden City, New York: Doubleday, 1950. Unpaginated.

6498. Arriola, Gus. *Gordo's Critters*. San Diego, California: Oak Tree Publications, 1983; Concord, California: Nitty Gritty Productions, 1972.

6499. Arriola, Gus. *Gordo the Lover*. Concord, California: Nitty Gritty Productions, 1972.

6500. "Arriola's Gordo." *Cartoonist PROfiles*. December 1972, pp. 34-41.

"The Heart of Juliet Jones"

6531. Drake, Stan. "The Heart of Juliet Jones." *Cartoonist PROfiles*. November 1969, pp. 4-13.

6532. Drake, Stan and Elliot Caplin. *Juliet Jones*. Greenfield, Wisconsin: Arcadia Publications, 1986. 96 pp.

6533. Drake, Stan and Elliot Caplin. *Juliet Jones in Big Business*. Greenfield, Wisconsin: Arcadia Publications, 1987. 64 pp.

6534. "Heart of Juliet Jones by Stan Drake." *Cartoonist PROfiles*. No. 15, 1972, p. 53.

"Heathcliff"

6535. Gately, George. "Heathcliff: 1973-1993. 20th Anniversary of 'Heathcliff.'" *Cartoonist PROfiles*. September 1993, pp. 10-15.

6536. Gately, George. *Heathcliff, Rockin' and Rollin'*. New York: Charter Books, 1986. 128 pp.

6537. "Heathcliff by George Gately." *Cartoonist PROfiles*. March 1975, pp. 30-33.

"Hello Carol"

6538. "Hello Carol." *Cartoonist PROfiles*. June 1981, pp. 34-41.

6539. Johnson, B. *Hello Carol*. New York: Ace Books, 1982. 160 pp.

"Henry"

6540. Anderson, Carl. *Henry*. New York: Greenberg, 1935.

6541. Anderson, Carl. *Henry*. Philadelphia, Pennsylvania: D. Mackay, 1945.

6542. Bono, Giani. "Henry." *Sgt. Kirk* (Genoa). No. 15, 1968, p. 68.

6543. DeLeon, Clark. "The Funnies: Henry Sells Out." *Philadelphia Inquirer*. October 11, 1987, p. 2B.

6544. "Henry by Jack Tippit." *Cartoonist PROfiles*. December 1984, pp. 54-57.

6545. Trachte, Don. "Henry." *Cartoonist PROfiles*. June 1989, pp. 22-28.

"Herman"

6546. Rumley, Larry. "Gloomy 'Herman' Makes People Chuckle." *The Funnie's Paper*. March 1984, pp. 18-19.

6547. Unger, Jim. *The 1st Treasury of Herman*. Kansas City, Missouri: Andrews and McMeel, 1979. 223 pp.

6548. Unger, Jim. *Herman, the Fourth Treasury*. Kansas City, Missouri: Andrews, McMeel and Parker, 1984. 204 pp.

6549. Unger, Jim. *Herman, the Third Treasury*. Kansas City, Missouri: Andrews and McMeel, 1982. 207 pp.

6550. Unger, Jim. *Herman Treasury 5*. Kansas City, Missouri: McMeel and Parker, 1986. 203 pp.

6551. Unger, Jim. *The Second Herman Treasury*. Kansas City, Missouri: Andrews and McMeel, 1980. 207 pp.

"Hi and Lois"

6552. Browne, Dik. "Hi and Lois." *Cartoonist PROfiles*. No. 15, 1972, pp. 35-36.

6553. Walker, Brian. "A Family Album of Hi and Lois." *Nemo*. December 1986, pp. 33-45.

6554. Walker, Mort and Dik Browne. *The Best of Hi and Lois*. Edited by Brian Walker. Bedford, New York: Comicana Books, 1986. 240 pp.

"Hubert"

6555. "Dick Wingert—'Hubert.'" *Cartoonist PROfiles*. June 1982, pp. 66-69.

6556. "'Hubert.'" *Cartoonist PROfiles*. December 1987, pp. 74-77.

"Inspector Wade"

6557. Bono, Giani. "Due Parole su...l'Ispettore Wade." *Comics World* (Genoa). No. 2, 1968, p. 1.

6558. "l'Ispettore Wade, Vorwort Zu 'La Chiave d'Argento.'" *Comics Club*. Supplement, No. 1, 1967.

6559. "Publicazione Italiana de L'Ispettore Wade." *Comics World*. March 1968, p. 2.

"Joe Palooka"

6560. Boyle, R.H. "Champ for All Time! Joe Palooka." *Sports Illustrated*. April 19, 1965, pp. 120-124.

6561. Crouch, Bill, jr. "Tony Di Preta, Joe Palooka Cartoonist." *Cartoonist PROfiles*. No. 23, 1974, pp. 8-13.

6562. "Joe and Joe." *Time*. November 30, 1942, pp. 68, 70.

6563. "Joe Palooka." *Newsweek*. June 4, 1951, p. 33.

6564. "Joe Palooka, Public Hero." *Newsweek*. December 8, 1939, pp. 42-43.

6565. "Joe Palooka...Then and Now!" *The Cartoonist*. February 1967, pp. 19-23.

6566. Marschall, Rick. "Joe Palooka Retains the Title!" *Nemo*. October 1986, pp. 15-24.

6567. "Mr. and Mrs. Palooka." *Time*. June 27, 1949, pp. 45-46.

6568. "Palooka and Ann? Yes." *Newsweek*. June 7, 1948, p. 56.

6569. "Presenting Ann." *New York Times Magazine*. January 16, 1944, p. 18.

6570. "Reconverting Palooka." *Newsweek*. September 3, 1945, p. 68.

6571. "Reprieve." *Time*. July 18, 1938, p. 27.

6572. Updegraff, Marie. "Don't Be Surprised. You Must Be Next. Name-Borrowing Solves Many a Problem in Creation of Joe Palooka Cartoons." *The Cartoonist*. February 1967, pp. 17-18.

"Johnny Hazard"

6573. Della Corte, Carlos. "Jonny Hazzard: Divertire, Non Convertire." *Smack.* No. 2, 1968, pp. 1-2.

6574. "Johnny Hazard by Frank Robbins." *Cartoonist PROfiles.* November 1970, pp. 26-37; No. 15, 1972, p. 51.

6575. Robbins, Frank. *Johnny Hazard.* 9 Vols+. Papeete, Tahiti: Pacific Comics Club, 1979-1980.

6576. Robbins, Frank. *Johnny Hazard.* Long Beach, California: Pacific Comics Club, 1981.

6577. Robbins, Frank. *Johnny Hazard.* Long Beach, California: Raiola; Park Forest, Illinois: K. Pierce, 1984?-.

6578. Robbins, Frank. *Johnny Hazard.* Comic Art Showcase, No. 7. Buffalo, New York: Magnum Entertainment Productions, 1981. 59 pp.

"Judge Parker"

6579. "ABA Honors Judge Parker." *Editor and Publisher.* August 21, 1954.

6580. "Judge Parker by Harold Le Doux." *Cartoonist PROfiles.* 1:2 (1969), pp. 15-18.

6581. "Judge Parker Has Too Many Friends." *San Francisco News.* January 23, 1957, p. 14.

6582. "Judge Parker of Mirror Honored." *New York Daily Mirror.* March 18, 1954, p. 16.

6583. "Legal Aid Lawyers Cite 'Judge Parker.'" *Chicago Daily News.* August 18, 1954, p. 39.

"Jungle Jim"

6584. Amadieu, G. "Jim la Jungle." *Phénix* (Paris). No. 3, 1967, pp. 21-24.

6585. Groensteen, Thierry. "Une Jungle Sans Mystère." *Les Cahiers de la Bande Dessinée* (Grenoble). 72, 1986, pp. 13-15.

6586. Raymond, Alex. *Jungle Jim.* Menomonee Falls, Wisconsin: Street Enterprises, 1972. 31 pp.

6587. Raymond, Alex. *Jungle Jim*. 4 Vols. Papeete, Tahiti: Pacific Comics Club, 1972.

6588. Raymond, Alex. *Jungle Jim*. 6 Vols. Papeete, Tahiti: Pacific Comics Club, ca. 1977.

6589. Trinchero, Sergio. "Jim della Giungla." *Super Albo* (Fratelli Spada). No. 93, 1964.

"Katzenjammer Kids" and "Captain and the Kids"

6590. Black, Ed. "The Katzenjammer Kids by Joe Musial." *Cartoonist PROfiles*. June 1981, pp. 50-55.

6591. "The Captain and the Kids by Rudolph and John Dirks." *Cartoonist PROfiles*. No. 18, 1973, pp. 4-17.

6592. Dirks, Rudolph. *The Cruise of the Katzenjammer Kids*. New York: F.A. Stokes, 1907.

6593. Dirks, Rudolph. *The Katzenjammer Kids: A Series of Comic Pictures*. New York: New York American and Journal, 1902 or 1903.

6594. Dirks, Rudolph. *The Katzenjammer Kids, Early Strips in Full Color*. New York: Dover Publications, 1974. 29 pp. First published as *The Komical Katzenjammers*. New York: F.A. Stokes, 1908.

6595. "Dirk's Bad Boys, Katzenjammer Kids." *Time*. March 4, 1957, p. 48.

6596. Lent, John A. "Katzies Take (and Give) Abuses for 90 Years." *WittyWorld*. Spring 1988, pp. 33-35.

6597. Lowe, Jim. "The 'Dittenhofer' File." *Vot der Dumboozle?* Spring 1988, pp. 20-23.

6598. Lowe, Jim. "The Katzaddendum and Knerratum Page." *Vot der Dumboozle?* Spring 1988, p. 19.

6599. Lowe, Jim. "What's in a Name?" *Vot der Dumboozle?* Spring 1988, pp. 14-18.

6600. Lowe, Jim. "Who Were 'The Shenanigan Kids'?" *Vot der Dumboozle?* Spring 1988, pp. 6-13.

6601. Musial, Joe. *Katzenjammer Kids*. New York: Pocket Books, 1970.

6602. Russell, F. "Farewell to the Katzenjammer Kids." *National Review*. July 16, 1968, pp. 703-705.

6603. Schwartz, J. "Katzenjammer Kids Still Mischievous after 58 Years." *Arizona Republic*. December 13, 1982, p. B-12.

6604. Simeth, Franz. "Die Katzenjammer Kids." *Deutsche Tagespost*. 1956.

6605. Strzyz, Klaus. "Die Katzenjammer Kids." *Comic Forum* (Vienna). 7:30 (1985), pp. 56-58.

6606. Walsh, J. "Classics of the Comics: the Katzenjammers." *Hobbies*. April 1953, pp. 146-149.

"Krazy Kat"

6607. "Among the Unlimitless Ethos (Krazy Kat and His Creator)." *Time*. May 8, 1944, pp. 94-96.

6608. Cavallone, Bruno. "Krazy Kat." *Linus*. No. 6, 1965.

6609. Engle, Gary. "Krazy Kat and the Spirit of Surrealism." *Gamut*. Fall 1984, pp. 28-39.

6610. François, Edouard. "Krazy Kat." *Phénix* (Paris). No. 18, 1971.

6611. Gasca, Luis. "Krazy Kat." *Boletin de Cine Club San Sebastian*. November 1963.

6612. Gelman, Barbara. "Introduction" to *Krazy Kat*. New York: Madison Square Press, 1969. 168 pp.

6613. *Geo. Herriman's Krazy and Ignatz: The Komplete Kat Komics: Vol. 1—1916*. Intro. by Bill Blackbeard. Forestville, California: Eclipse Books/Turtle Island Foundation, 1988. 59 pp.

6614. Harvey, R.C. "Krazy Kat in Prose Not Pix." *Comics Journal*. July 1989, pp. 139-141.

6615. Herriman, George. *The Family Upstairs: Introducing Krazy Kat 1910-1912*. Intro. by Bill Blackbeard. Westport, Connecticut: Hyperion Press, 1977. 212 pp.

6616. Herriman, George. *Krazy Kat*. Intro. by e.e. cummings. New York: Henry Holt and Co., 1946.

6617. Herriman, George. *Krazy Kat*. Intro. by e.e. cummings. New York: Grosset and Dunlap, 1969.

6618. Herriman, George. *Krazy Kat*. Intro. by e.e. cummings. New York: Madison Square Press, September 1969. 168 pp.

6619. Inge, M. Thomas. "*Krazy Kat* As Pure American Dada Humor." In *Social Change and New Modes of Expression: The United States, 1910-1930*, edited by Rob Kroes and Allessandro Portelli, pp. 173-177. Amsterdam: Free University Press, 1986.

6620. "Krazy Kat, George Herriman." Catalogue of exhibition at University of Arizona Museum of Art, November 5-December 3, 1972.

6621. Rosemont, Franklin. "Surrealism in the Comics I: Krazy Kat (George Herriman)." In *Popular Culture in America*, edited by Paul Buhle, pp. 119-127. Minneapolis, Minnesota: University of Minnesota Press, 1987.

6622. Sorel, Edward. "Krazy Kat: A Love Story." *American Heritage*. August/September 1982, pp. 72-77.

6623. Sorel, Edward. "'Krazy Kat,' A Love Story." *Nemo*. Winter 1992, pp. 22-25.

6624. Tamine, Jean-Pierre. "Relecture: Krazy Kat." *Les Cahiers de la Bande Dessinée* (Grenoble). 59, 1984, pp. 86-87.

6625. Warshow, Robert. "Krazy Kat." *Partisan Review*. November-December 1956.

6626. Weales, G. "Krazy Kat, by G. Herriman. Review." *Life*. December 12, 1969, p. 12.

6627. Weaver, William. "On Krazy Kat and Peanuts." *New York Review of Books*. June 13, 1985, pp. 16-17.

6628. Young, Stark. "Krazy Kat." *New Republic*. October 11, 1922, pp. 175-176.

"Kudzu"

6629. Astor, David. "Paper Pulls 'Kudzu' Comics Satirizing Jesse Helms." *Editor and Publisher*. October 20, 1990, p. 44.

6630. Marlette, Doug. *A Doublewide with a View: The Kudzu Chronicles*. Atlanta, Georgia: Longstreet Press, 1989.

6631. Marlette, Doug. *Just a Simple Country Preacher*. Nashville, Tennessee: T. Nelson, 1985. 112 pp.

6632. Marlette, Doug. *Kudzu*. New York: Ballantine Books, 1982.

6633. Marlette, Doug. *There's No Business Like Soul Business*. Atlanta, Georgia: Peachtree Publishers, 1987. 109 pp.

6634. Wepman, Dennis. "Did Kudzu Help Marlette Win the Pulitzer Prize?" *WittyWorld*. Winter/Spring 1990, pp. 50-55.

"Lance"

6635. Toth, Alex. "A Forgotten Western Classic: Lance." *Nemo*. December 1983, pp. 43-55.

6636. Tufts, Warren. *Lance*. The Books of Comics Land, No. 1. Genoa, Italy: N. Bernazzali, 1979. 28 pp.

"Life in Hell"

6637. Groening, Matt. *Love Is Hell*. New York: Pantheon Books, 1985. 48 pp.

6638. Groening, Matt. *School Is Hell*. New York: Pantheon Books, 1987. 48 pp.

6639. Groening, Matt. *Work Is Hell*. New York: Pantheon Books, 1986. 48 pp.

6640. Rodi, Rob. "Repeat Until Spanked." *Comics Journal*. February 1987, pp. 57-61.

"Li'l Abner"

6641. Berger, Arthur A. "Li'l Abner: An American Satire." Ph.D. dissertation, University of Minnesota, 1965.

6642. Berger, Arthur A. *Li'l Abner, a Study in American Satire*. New York: Twayne, 1970. 191 pp.

6643. Bertieri, Claudio. "Il Bravo Cittadino Yokum." *Il Lavoro* (Genoa). September 12, 1966.

6644. Capp, Al. *Bald Iggle. The Life It Ruins May Be Your Own*. New York: Simon and Schuster, 1956. Unpaginated.

6645. Capp, Al. *The Best of Li'l Abner*. New York: Holt, Rinehart and Winston, 1978. 190 pp.

6646. Capp, Al. *The Hardhat's Bedtime Story Book*. New York: Harper and Row, 1971. 120 pp.

6647. Capp, Al. "It's Hideously True; Li'l Abner." *Life*. March 31, 1952, pp. 100-102+; "Discussion." April 21, 1952, pp. 11+.

6648. Capp, Al. *The Life and Times of the Shmoo*. New York: Simon and Schuster, 1948. 90 pp.

6649. Capp, Al. *Li'l Abner*. Princeton, Wisconsin: Kitchen Sink Press, 1988-.

6650. Capp, Al. *Li'l Abner*. Reuben Award Winner Series. El Cajon, California: Blackthorne, 1985-.

6651. Capp, Al. "Miracle of Dogpatch, Review of Life and Times of the Shmoo." *Time*. December 27, 1948, p. 48.

6652. Capp, Al. "There Is a Real Shmoo." *New Republic*. March 21, 1949, pp. 14-15.

6653. Capp, Al. "Unforgettable Li'l Abner." *Reader's Digest*. June 1978, pp. 109-113.

6654. Capp, Al. *The World of Li'l Abner*. New York: Farrow, Straus and Young, 1953; New York: Ballantine Books, 1965.

6655. "Capp-italist Revolution; Al Capp's Shmoo Offers a Parable of Plenty." *Life*. December 20, 1948, p. 22.

6656. "Capp's New Girl!" *Newsweek*. June 24, 1954, p. 49.

6657. "Capp's New Girl: Long Sam." *Newsweek*. June 14, 1954, p. 92.

6658. Carano, Ranieri. "Prologo" to *Il Cittadino Yokum*. Milano: Libri Edizioni, 1967, pp. 5-9.

6659. "Daisy Mae's Friends." *Time*. May 27, 1946, p. 92.

6660. Goodman, M. "Train Doesn't Stop at (Choke!) Dogpatch Anymore." *New Times*. January 9, 1978, p. 100.

6661. "Harvest Shmoon." *Time*. September 13, 1948, p. 29.

6662. "Kigmy Sweet." *Newsweek*. October 3, 1949, p. 58.

6663. "Lena the Unseena: Li'l Abner Strip." *Newsweek*. July 1, 1946, p. 58.

6664. "Leviticus Vs. Yokum." *Newsweek*. November 29, 1948, p. 58.

6665. Lewin, Willy. "Steinbeck and Li'l Abner." *O Estado de São Paulo*. December 15, 1962.

6666. "Li'l Abner." *Newsweek*. August 7, 1950, p. 40.

6667. *Li'l Abner. Dailies. Volume One: 1934-1935. By Al Capp*. Princeton, Wisconsin: Kitchen Sink Press, 1988. 232 pp.

6668. *Li'l Abner. Dailies. Volume Two: 1936. By Al Capp*. Princeton, Wisconsin: Kitchen Sink Press, 1988. 160 pp. (R.C. Harvey, Milton Caniff and Al Capp, "Nightowls in the Bullpen," and Dave Schreiner, "1936: The Innocents Abroad and at Home").

6669. "Li'l Abner Helps Navy Recruiter." *Berkshire Eagle*. August 10, 1959, p. 3.

6670. "Li'l Abner Meets the Bald Iggle: The Who's Zoo of Al Capp." *Nemo*. April 1986, pp. 18-32.

6671. "Li'l Abner's Chillum." *Newsweek*. July 17, 1950, pp. 38-39.

6672. "Miracle of Dogpatch; Review of Life and Times of the Shmoo." *Time*. December 27, 1948, p. 48.

6673. "On Sadie Hawkins Day Girls Chase Boys in 201 Colleges." *Life*. December 11, 1939, pp. 32-33.

6674. Romer, Jean-Claude. "Li'l Abner à l'Écran." *Giff-Wiff*. No. 23, 1967, p. 15.

6675. "Sacking of the Shmoo, London Sunday Pictorial." *Time*. May 23, 1949, p. 63.

6676. "Sadie Hawkins at Yale." *Time*. November 11, 1940, p. 51.

6677. "Shmoos." *New Yorker*. January 1, 1949, pp. 14-15.

6678. "Shmoos Make Noos." *Newsweek*. October 11, 1948, p. 62.

6679. "Shmoo's Return; Li'l Abner Comic Strip." *New Yorker*. October 26, 1963, pp. 39-40.

6680. "Speaking of Pictures; 500,000 People Draw Lena the Hyena." *Life*. October 28, 1946, pp. 14-16.

6681. "Tain't Funny; Li'l Abner Walks a Dangerous Rope." *Time*. September 29, 1947, p. 79.

6682. "Taming of the Shmoo." *Newsweek*. September 5, 1949, p. 49.

6683. "Trials of Little Abner." *Newsweek*. February 26, 1940, p. 40.

6684. Trinchero, Sergio. "Li'l Abner, Trent' Anni di Suspense." *Hobby*. No. 5, 1967.

6685. "Unthinkable: Li'l Abner's Marriage." *Time*. March 31, 1952, p. 53.

6686. "U.S. Becomes Shmoo—Struck." *Life*. September 20, 1948, p. 46.

6687. White, David M. *From Dogpatch to Slobbovia: The World of Li'l Abner*. Boston, Massachusetts: Beacon Press, 1964.

6688. White, David M. "How To Lead Li'l Abner Intelligently." In *Mass Culture*, edited by Bernard Rosenberg and David M. White. Boston: The Free Press of Glencoe, 1957.

6689. Williams, Martin. "The Hidden World of 'Li'l Abner.'" *Comics Journal*. December 1991, pp. 74-75.

6690. "Writ by Hand: Li'l Abner." *Newsweek*. June 3, 1946, p. 58.

6691. "Yokum Gold." *Newsweek*. July 21, 1947.

"The Little King"

6692. Dunn, Bob. "The Little King by O. Soglow." *Cartoonist PROfiles*. June 1975, pp. 60-62.

6693. Soglow, Otto. *The Little King*. London: Duckworth, 1933.

"Little Lulu"

6694. "About Melvin Monster." *The Hollywood Eclectern*. No. 1, 1992, p. 9.

6695. Caen, Michel. "La Villaine Lulu." *Plexus* (Paris). No. 9, 1967, pp. 154-157.

6696. Cuesta Fernández, Fernando. "La Pequeña Lulu: El Trasfondo de una Historieta 'Intrascendente.'" *El Wendigo*. December 1984-January 1985, pp. 4-8.

6697. Cushman, Howard. "Little Lulu Is Really a Lulu." *The Hollywood Eclectern*. August 1993, pp. 10-12.

6698. "Little Lulu in King Comics?" *The Hollywood Eclectern*. No. 1, 1992, pp. 5-6.

6699. Marge. (Marjorie H. Buell). *Laughs with Little Lulu*. New York: David McKay, 1942. 60 pp.

6700. Marge. (Marjorie H. Buell). *Little Lulu at Grandma's Farm*. Springfield, Massachusetts: McLoughlin Bros., 1946(?).

6701. Marge. (Marjorie H. Buell). *Little Lulu at the Seashore*. Springfield, Massachusetts: McLoughlin Bros., 1946(?).

6702. Marge. (Marjorie H. Buell). *Little Lulu on Parade*. Philadelphia, Pennsylvania: David McKay, 1941. Unpaginated.

6703. Marge. (Marjorie H. Buell). *Little Lulu Plays Pirate*. Springfield, Massachusetts: McLoughlin Bros., 1946. 40 pp.

6704. "Redrawn Stories in the Little Lulu Library." *The Hollywood Eclectern*. No. 1, 1992, pp. 3-4.

6705. Saint-Laurent, Ives. *La Villaine Lulu*. Paris: Edition Tchou, 1966.

6706. Tenan, Bradley. "A Little Lulu Chronology." *The Hollywood Eclectern*. August 1993, pp. 4-5.

6707. Tenan, Bradley. "Peekskill Revisited: A Retrospective." *The Hollywood Eclectern*. No. 2, 1992, pp. 3-5.

6708. Thompson, Maggie. "Little Ms. Moppet." *Comics Collector*. Winter 1984, pp. 67-72.

6709. Thompson, Maggie. "Little Ms. Moppet, Part II." *Comics Collector*. Spring 1984, pp. 67-71.

6710. Weiner, Gina. *Marge's Little Lulu*. New York: Golden Press, 1962.

"Little Nemo"

6711. Ciment, Gilles. "Traces de Little Nemo dans la BD Contemporaine." *Les Cahiers de la Bande Dessinée* (Grenoble). 63, 1985, pp. 84-86.

6712. Derleth, August. "Preface" to *Little Nemo in Slumberland*. New York: McCay Features Syndicate, 1957.

6713. Fresnault, Pierre. "Little Nemo in Slumberland." *Phénix* (Paris). No. 21, 1971.

6714. Inge, M. Thomas. "Little Nemo." *Crimmer's The Journal of Narrative Arts*. Spring 1976, pp. 44-51.

6715. "A Landmark Publishing Event: Waking Up in Slumberland." *Nemo*. April 1989, pp. 5-27.

6716. Levine, Edna S. *Little Nemo in Slumberland*. New York: Rand McNally and Co., 1941. 63 pp.

6717. McCay, Winsor. *Dreams of a Rarebit Fiend*. New York: Dover Publications, 1973. 62 pp.

6718. McCay, Winsor. *Little Nemo*. Franklin Square, New York: Nostalgia Press, 1972. 263 pp.

6719. McCay, Winsor. *Little Nemo*. 2nd. Ed. Intro. by Woody Gelman. Franklin Square, New York: Nostalgia Press, 1974. 263 pp.

6720. McCay, Winsor. *Little Nemo—1905-1906*. Intro. by Woody Gelman. New York: Nostalgia Press, 1976. 59 pp.

6721. McCay, Winsor. *Little Nemo in the Palace of Ice*. New York: Dover, 1976. 32 pp.

6722. McCay, Winsor. *Little Nemo in Slumberland*. 2 Vols. Comic-Strip Preserves. El Cajon, California: Blackthorne, 1986.

6723. McCay, Winsor. *Winsor McCay's Dream Days*. Intros. by Bill Blackbeard and Woody Gelman. The Hyperion Library of Classic American Comic Strips. Westport, Connecticut: Hyperion, 1977. 178 pp.

6724. Marschall, Rick. "Of Daydreams and Nightmares." *Nemo*. July 1986, pp. 43-64.

6725. Metken, Günter. "Klein-Nemo im Traumland. Zur Neuausgabe des Comicstrips von Winsor McCay." *Der Tagesspiegel* (Berlin). December 30, 1969.

6726. Moliterni, Claude. "Little Nemo." *Graphis* (Zürich). 28:159 (1972-1973), pp. 44-51.

6727. Remesar, A. "La Particular Odisea de Little Nemo." *Neuróptica. Estudios Sobre el Cómic* (Zaragoza). 2, 1984, pp. 76-93.

6728. Trinchero, Sergio. "E'tornato 'Little Nemo.'" *Momento Sera*. No. 277, 1969.

6729. Trinchero, Sergio. "Il Fumetto Liberty: Little Nemo." *Hobby*. No. 6, 1967.

6730. Trinchero, Sergio. "Nemo 11." *Linus*. No. 57, 1969.

6731. Weales, G. "Little Nemo, by W. McCay. Review." *Commonweal*. April 19, 1974, pp. 171-173.

6732. Zanotto, Piero. "Da Little Nemo a Tenebrax: Favolinus 1968." *Il Gazzettino*. December 31, 1967.

"Little Orphan Annie"

6733. "Annie Doesn't Live There." *Newsweek*. August 30, 1943, p. 78-79.

6734. "Annie Orphaned." *Newsweek*. July 7, 1967, p. 49.

6735. Auster, Donald. "A Content Analysis of 'Little Orphan Annie.'" *Social Problems*. July 1954, pp. 26-33.

6736. Auster, Donald. "A Content Analysis of 'Little Orphan Annie.'" In *Sociology: The Progress of a Decade*, edited by S. Lipset and N. Smelser. Englewood Cliffs, New Jersey: Prentice-Hall, 1961.

6737. "Back from the Grave; Orphan Annie." *Newsweek*. August 6, 1945, p. 67.

6738. Barker, Kenneth. "The Life and Love, Friends and Foes, Trials and Triumphs of Little Orphan Annie." *Nemo*. August 1984, pp. 8-31.

6739. Barker, K.S. "Annie—Yesterday and Today." *Theology Today*. October 1982, pp. 303-313.

6740. "Censoring Orphan Annie." *Time*. February 26, 1965, p. 52.

6741. Daviss, B. "World of Funnies Is 'Warped with Fancy, Woofed with Dreams.'" *Smithsonian*. November 1987. pp. 180-183+.

6742. "Fascism in the Funnies: Little Orphan Annie, H. Gray Continues His Attacks upon the New Deal." *New Republic*. September 18, 1935, p. 147.

6743. Gehman, R. "But What Goes After the Third Line? Little Orphan Annie." *Saturday Review*. July 12, 1969, p. 4.

6744. Gray, Harold. *Arf! The Life and Hard Times of Little Orphan Annie 1935-1945*. Intro. by Al Capp. New Rochelle, New York: Arlington House, 1970. 714 pp.

6745. Gray, Harold. *Little Orphan Annie*. New York: Cupples and Leon Co., 1926.

6746. Gray, Harold. *Little Orphan Annie*. Intro. by Rick Marschall. The Nemo Bookshelf. Agoura, California: Fantagraphics Books, 1987-.

6747. Gray, Harold. *Little Orphan Annie and Little Orphan Annie in Cosmic City*. New York: Dover, 1974. 178 pp. Reprint of *Little Orphan Annie*. New York: Cupples and Leon, 1926 and *Little Orphan Annie in Cosmic City*. New York: Cupples and Leon, 1933.

6748. Gray, Harold. *Little Orphan Annie Bucking the World*. New York: Cupples and Leon, 1929. 86 pp.

6749. Gray, Harold. *Little Orphan Annie in the Great Depression*. New York: Dover, 1979. 58 pp.

6750. Gray, Harold. *Little Orphan Annie, Never Say Die!* New York: Cupples and Leon, 1930. 86 pp.

6751. Hamaker, Gene E. "Alla-Ca-Zaba! Gazah! Presto! Some Observations on the Role of the Orient in 'Little Orphan Annie' (1924-1968)." *Journal of Popular Culture*. Fall 1975, pp. 331-342.

6752. Kehl, J.A. "Defender of the Faith: Orphan Annie and the Conservative Tradition." *South Atlantic Quarterly*. Autumn, 1977, pp. 454-465.

6753. "Little Orphan Annie." *Cartoonist PROfiles*. November 1970, pp. 70-75.

6754. "Little Orphan Annie." *The Nation*. October 23, 1935, p. 454.

6755. "Little Orphan Annie." *New Republic*. February 25, 1957, p. 6.

6756. "Little Orphan Annie. Das Mädchen von Gestern, Heute und Morgen." *Comic Forum* (Vienna). 4:16 (1982), pp. 19-21.

6757. "Little Orphan Delinquent: Little Orphan Annie." *Time*. March 19, 1956, pp. 70-71.

6758. Marschall, Rick. "The Ageless Golden Age of Little Orphan Annie." *Nemo*. December 1986, pp. 5-32.

6759. Marschall, Richard. "Little Orphan Annie Bucking the World." *Nemo*. August 1984, pp. 49-66.

6760. "Moppet in Politics." *Time*. August 30, 1943, pp. 47-48.

6761. Neuberger, Richard L. "Hooverism in the Funnies; Little Orphan Annie, Creation of H. Gray." *New Republic*. July 11, 1934, pp. 234-235.

6762. "Orphan in a Storm." *Newsweek*. March 19, 1956, p. 80.

6763. Phelps, Donald. "Little Icon Annie: 'Who's That Little Chatterbox?'" *Nemo*. August 1984, pp. 33-38.

6764. Reston, James. "Daddy Warbucks Finds the Answer." *New York Times*. May 11, 1958, p. 8E.

6765. Rhoads, E. "Little Orphan Annie and Lévi-Strauss: The Myth and the Method." *Journal of American Folklore*. October 1973, pp. 345-357.

6766. Romer, Jean-Claude. "La Petite Annie." *Giff-Wiff* (Paris). No. 5, 1965, p. 2.

6767. Ryan, S.P. "Orphan Annie Must Go!" *America.* December 8, 1956, pp. 293-295; "Discussion." January 19, 1957, p. 437.

6768. Serbell, John. "'Tomorrow, Tomorrow,' She's the Same Annie." *Media History Digest.* Fall 1980, pp. 18-24.

6769. Shannon, Lyle W. "The Opinions of Little Orphan Annie and Her Friends." *Public Opinion Quarterly.* Summer 1954, pp. 169-179.

6770. Shannon, Lyle W. "The Opinions of Little Orphan Annie and Her Friends." In *Mass Culture: The Popular Arts in America,* edited by Bernard Rosenberg and David M. White, pp. 212-217. Glencoe, Illinois: The Free Press, 1957.

6771. Smith, Bruce. *The History of Little Orphan Annie.* New York: Ballantine, 1982. 149 pp.

6772. Smith, Bruce. *The World According to Daddy Warbucks.* Piscataway, New Jersey: New Century Publishers, 1982.

6773. "Tougher Than Hell with a Heart of Gold." *Time.* September 4, 1964, pp. 71-72.

6774. Warshow, Robert. "Woofed with Dreams." *Partisan Review.* 13:5 (1946).

6775. Young, William H. "That Indomitable Redhead: Little Orphan Annie." *Journal of Popular Culture.* Fall 1974, pp. 309-316.

"Lone Ranger"

6776. Horak, Carl. "The Lonely Ranger." *The Funnie's Paper.* January 1985, pp. 17-19.

6777. "The Lone Ranger by Russ Heath and Cary Bates." *Cartoonist PROfiles.* September 1981, pp. 30-34.

6778. Scapperotti, Dan. "Lone Ranger: 50 Years of Action." *Comics Collector.* Winter 1984, pp. 33-38.

6779. Striker, Fran. *The Lone Ranger and Tonto.* New York: 1940.

"Lunchbucket"

6780. "Lunchbucket by Rex May." *Cartoonist PROfiles.* March 1993, pp. 60-67.

6781. McGeean, Ed. "New Comic Strip Introduction." *CAPS.* April 1993, pp. 11-12.

"McGonigle"

6782. Huscha, N. "A Comic Strip Artist and His Computer." *Personal Computer*. July 1985, pp. 33+.

6783. "McGonigle of *The Chronicle* by Jeff Danziger." *Cartoonist PROfiles*. March 1984, pp. 58-63.

"Male Call"

6784. Caniff, Milton. *Male Call*. New York: Simon and Schuster, 1945. 56 pp.

6785. Caniff, Milton. *Male Call*. New York: Grosset and Dunlap, 1959.

6786. Caniff, Milton. *Male Call*. Paris: Futuropolis, 1983.

6787. Caniff, Milton. *Male Call*. Princeton, Wisconsin: Kitchen Sink Press, 1987. 120 pp.

6788. Poplaski, Peter, ed. *Male Call by Milton Caniff 1942-1946 Featuring Miss Lace*. Princeton, Wisconsin: Kitchen Sink Press, 1988.

"Mandrake the Magician"

6789. Arbesú, Faustino R. "Mandrake: Un Mito un el Olimpo del Comic." Program of Caja de Ahorras de Asturias, Oviedo, Spain, November 1989, pp. 50-60.

6790. Augusto, Sergio. "Os Dois Fantasmas Rondam a Carlota de Mandrake." *Jornal do Brasil* (Rio de Janeiro). August 18, 1967.

6791. Del Buono, Oreste. "All 'Università: Mandrake e Paperino." *Settimana Incom* (Milan). 1964.

6792. Detowarnicki, Frederic. "Mandrake Psychoanalyste." *L'Express* (Paris). April 1-7, 1968.

6793. Falk, Lee and Phil Davis. *Mandrake in Hollywood*. Intro. by Maurice Horn. The Golden Age of the Comics, No. 7. Franklin Square, New York: Nostalgia Press, 1970. 96 pp.

6794. Falk, Lee and Phil Davis. *Mandrake the Magician*. Franklin Square, New York: Nostalgia Press, 1970. 96 pp.

6795. Falk, Lee and Phil Davis. *Three Thrillings for Mandrake*. The Golden Age of the Comics. Papeete, Tahiti: Comics Stars in the World and Pacific Comics Club, 1976. 144 pp.

6796. Fini, Luciano and A. Massarelli. "Un Personaggio della Fantasia: Mandrake, l'Uomo del Misterio." *Sagittarius*. June 1965, p. 3.

6797. Fossati, Franco. "Mandrake." *Vega SF*. March 1966.

6798. Hegerfors, Sture. "Ett Försummat Kapitel. Stalmannen, Mandrake och Dragos." *Folkbladet Ostgöten*. October 28, 1967.

6799. Hegerfors, Sture. "Mandrake Larde Nup Resnais." *Expressen* (Stockholm). January 10, 1966.

6800. Hegerfors, Sture. "Mandrake-mon Amour." *Expressen* (Stockholm). May 27, 1967.

6801. Hegerfors, Sture. "Mandrake Utan Pappa." *Expressen* (Stockholm). January 18, 1965.

6802. Hegerfors, Sture. "Mandrake Var en Gang Hitlers Favorit-Serie." *GT Söndags Extra* (Göteborg). November 5, 1967.

6803. Hronik, Tom. "A Magician Named Mandrake." *Voice of Comicdom*. No. 5, August 1965.

6804. Lacassin, Francis. "A la Poursuite de Mandrake." *Midi-Minuit Fantastique* (Paris). No. 6, 1963. p. 88.

6805. Lacassin, Francis. "Du Temps Que Mandrake N'Avait Pas Peur de la Magie." Prefrace to *Mandrake, Roi de la Magie*. Paris: CELEG, 1964.

6806. Lacassin, Francis. "Mandrake en Liberté Provisoire." *Midi-Minuit Fantastique* (Paris). No. 3, 1962, p. 49.

6807. "Mandrake Sale in Cattedra." *L'Espresso*. July 17, 1964.

6808. Rodríguez Arbesú, Faustino. "Mandrake: Un Heroe Atipico." *El Wendigo*. May 1983, pp. 27-31.

6809. Rodríguez Arbesú, Faustino. "Un Añadido en la Vida Sentimental de Merlin Narda." *El Wendigo*. January 1984, pp. 41-45.

6810. Trinchero, Sergio. "Mandrake l'Imprevedibile." *Super Albo "Mandrake"* (Fratelli Spada, Milan). No. 28, 1963.

6811. Vosburg, Mike. "Mandrake the Magician." *Masquerader*. No. 2, 1962, pp. 11-13.

6812. Zanotto, Piero. "Concluso con le Premazioni il Festival di Mandrake." *Il Gazzettino* (Venice). September 26, 1966.

6813. Zanotto, Piero. "Mandrake e Barbarella Sullo Schermo." *Corriere del Giorno*. March 13, 1965.

"Mark Trail"

6814. "Mark Trail by Ed Dodd." *Cartoonist PROfiles*. No. 20, 1973, pp. 42-48.

6815. Elrod, Jack. "Mark Trail." *Cartoonist PROfiles*. December 1983, pp. 50-53; March 1991, pp. 66-69.

"Mary Worth"

6816. Cleghorn, R. "Upwardly Mobile Apple Mary." *Christian Century*. November 5, 1975, p. 990.

6817. "Mary Worth—Allen and John Saunders." *Cartoonist PROfiles*. September 1978, pp. 62-65.

6818. "Mary Worth Faces Life." *Newsweek*. March 10, 1947, p. 64.

6819. "Mary Worth: The Saunders Duo." *Cartoonist PROfiles*. June 1978, pp. 10-15.

6820. McGeean, Ed. "Bill Ziegler Dies; Drew 'Mary Worth' Strip." *Comics Buyer's Guide*. September 17, 1993, pp. 40, 46.

6821. Saunders, Allen and Ken Ernst. *Mary Worth*. Comic-Strip Preserves. El Cajon, California: Blackthorne, 1986-.

6822. Welsh, Nick. "Changing of the Pens at Mary Worth." *Cartoonist PROfiles*. September 1993, pp. 62-65.

"Mickey Mouse"

6823. Ackermann, Lutz. "Die Linke und die Micky Maus." *Spontan* (Frankfurt). 3:2 (1970), pp. 32-33.

6824. Cramon, Corinna and F. Müller-Scherz. "Micky Maus Wählt CSU." *AZ-Feuilleton* (Abendzeitung) (Munich). 1970, p. 8.

6825. Fouilhé, P. "Benjamin, le Journal de Mickey." *Educateurs* (Paris). No. 51, 1954.

6826. Friedrich, Heinz. "Die Micky-Mäuse der Kulturrevolution. Inhumane Comic-Strips." *Neue Zürcher Zeitung* (Zurich). February 23, 1969.

6827. Gottfredson, Floyd. *Goofy Explores Cave Man Island*. Best Comics. New York: Abbeville Press, 1980. 34 pp.

6828. Gottfredson, Floyd. *Mickey Mouse and the Bat Bandit of Inferno Gulch*. The Best of Walt Disney Comics. Racine, Wisconsin: Western, 1974. 48 pp.

6829. Gottfredson, Floyd. *Mickey Mouse Joins the Foreign Legion*. Best Comics. New York: Abbeville Press, 1980. 42 pp.

6830. Gottfredson, Floyd. *Mickey Mouse 1932*. Collana Grandi Adventure. Genoa, Italy: Club Anni Trenta, 1971. 137 pp.

6831. Gottfredson, Floyd. *Walt Disney Mickey Mouse*. Best Comics. New York: Abbeville Press, 1978. 104 pp.

6832. "Mickey Mouse Newspaper Strip Ceases After 60 Years." *CAPS Newsletter*. November 1989, p. 12.

6833. Willits, Malcom. "Mickey Mouse, the First Golden Decade." *Vanguard*. No. 2, 1968, pp. 19-28.

6834. Pittoni, Hans. "Micky Maus und die Comics." *Die Furche* (Vienna). No. 2, 1957, p. 10.

6835. West, Dick. "What Happened to Disney's Comics?" *Masquerader*. Spring 1964, pp. 26-28.

6836. Zboron, Hagen. "Aspekte der Beschwichtigung in 'Micky Maus.'" *Anabis*. 18 (1966/1967), pp. 83-88.

"Miss Peach"

6837. Horn, Maurice. "Miss Peach, ou le Chemin des Écoliers." *Phénix* (Paris). No. 5, 4 Trimester 1967, pp. 2-4.

6838. Lazarus, Mell. *Miss Peach*. Englewood Cliffs, New Jersey: Prentice-Hall, 1958.

6839. Lazarus, Mell. *Miss Peach*. New York: Ace Books, 1962.

6840. Lazarus, Mell. *Miss Peach*. New York: Tempo Books, 1973.

6841. Lazarus, Mell. *Miss Peach, Are These Your Children?* New York: Dial, 1982.

"Modesty Blaise"

6842. Billard, Pierre. "Modesty Blaise—la Super Femme." *L'Express* (Paris). May 2-8, 1966, pp. 66-68, 75.

6843. Drew, Bernard A. "He Nails 'Em with Modesty: Peter O'Donnell's *Femme Fatale* Uses Everything To Fight Evil Forces." *Armchair Detective*. Winter 1987, pp. 26-30.

6844. Drew, Bernard A. "Modesty Blaise—Two Decades of Adventure." *Comics Collector*. Fall 1984, pp. 48-53.

6845. Florez, Florentino. "Modestia Aparte." *El Wendigo*. No. 45, 1989, pp. 10-11.

6846. "James Bond Ist Tot—Es Lebe Modesty Blaise." *Der Stern* (Hamburg). No. 44, 1966.

6847. Lundin, Bo. "Fire Gode Grunner til å Lese Modesty Blaise." *TEGN*. No. 3, 1989, pp. 10-11.

6848. Mauriac, Claude. "De Modesty Blaise à Polly Maggoo." *Le Figaro Littéraire* (Paris). October 27, 1966.

6849. "Modesty Blaise." *Il Fumetto*. September 1973, pp. 19-23.

6850. "Modesty Blaise—Optischer Zirkus." *Film* (Hanover). No. 11, 1966, p. 38.

6851. "Nach James Bond Nun das Superweib (Modesty Blaise)." *Constanze* (Hamburg). No. 8, February 15, 1966.

6852. Parinaud, André. "Modesty Blaise: Une Monte Religieuse Snob." *Arts* (Paris). October 19, 1966.

6853. Rizzo, Renato. "Modesty Blaise." *Il Fumetto*. September 1973, pp. 24-56.

6854. Sanderson, Peter. "A Blaise of Glory." *Comics Feature*. June 1980, pp. 49-51.

6855. Schaffer, Bernhard. "Modesty Blaise. Die Tödliche Lady." *Comic Forum* (Vienna). 3:11 (1981), pp. 33-35.

"Momma"

6856. Lazarus, Mell. *Momma*. New York: Dell, 1972.

6857. Lazarus, Mell. *The Momma Treasury*. Kansas City, Missouri: Sheed Andrews and McMeel, 1978. 224 pp.

6858. Lazarus, Mell. *Momma, We're Grownups Now!* New York: Grosset and Dunlop, 1979.

6859. Lazarus, Mell. *The Phantom Momma Strikes Again!* New York: Bantam, 1981.

"Moon Mullins"

6860. Fisher, Raymond. "Moon Mullins Today." *The World of Comic Art*. June 1966, pp. 6-9.

6861. Howard, C. "Magnificent Roughneck; Moon Mullins." *Saturday Evening Post*. August 9, 1947, pp. 20-21 +.

6862. Johnson, Ferd. "Moon Mullins." *Cartoonist PROfiles*. Fall 1969, pp. 33-39.

6863. Lardner, J. "King of the Lowdowns, Moon Mullins." *Newsweek*. January 27, 1958, p. 67.

6864. Willard, Frank H. "Moon Mullins and Me." *Colliers*. May 7, 1949, p. 68.

6865. Willard, Frank H. *Moon Mullins, Two Adventures*. New York: Dover, 1976. 96 pp. Reprints of *Moon Mullins, Series 3*. New York: Cupples and Leon, 1929; *Moon Mullins, Series 5*. New York: Cupples and Leon, 1931.

"Mother Goose and Grimm"

6866. Peters, Mike. *Four-Wheel Grimmy*. New York: Pharos Books/Topper, 1989. 128 pp.

6867. Peters, Mike. *Mother Goose and Grimm*. New York: Dell, 1986. 128 pp.

6868. Peters, Mike. "Mother Goose and Grimm." *Cartoonist PROfiles*. March 1988, pp. 12-17.

6869. Peters, Mike. *The Portable Mother Goose and Grimm*. New York: Dell, 1987. 128 pp.

6870. Peters, Mike. *Steel-Belted Grimm*. New York: Topper, 1988. 128 pp.

"Motley's Crew"

6871. "Motley's Crew." *Cartoonist PROfiles*. December 1978, pp. 88-93.

6872. "Motley's Crew by Ben Templeton and Tom Forman." *Cartoonist PROfiles*. September 1992, pp. 25-29.

"Mr. Boffo"

6873. Martin, Joe. *Boffo*. Chicago, Illinois: Turnbull and Willoughby, 1986. 128 pp.

6874. Martin, Joe. "Great Uncanny Humor, Mr. Boffo." *Cartoonist PROfiles*. March 1989, pp. 12-17.

"Mutt and Jeff"

6875. Black, Ed. "Officially Banned from Newark." *Cartoonist PROfiles*. June 1993, pp. 76-81.

6876. Blackbeard, Bill. "Bill of Fare: Mutton Jeff. Mutt and Jeff's Family Album." *Nemo*. December 1984, pp. 46-52.

6877. Blackbeard, Bill. "Introduction." In *A. Mutt. An Original Compilation: First Collection of the Complete First Years of the Daily Strip, 1907-1908*, edited by Harry C. Fisher, pp. v-xiv. Westport, Connecticut: Hyperion, 1977.

6878. "Fans Are Loyal to Mutt and Jeff." *Newsletter*. March 1965, p. 6.

6879. Fisher, Bud. *A. Mutt*. The Hyperion Library of Classic American Comic Strips. Westport, Connecticut: Hyperion, 1977. 162 pp.

6880. Fisher, Bud. *Mutt and Jeff*. Boston, Massachusetts: Ball Publishing, 1910-.

6881. Fisher, Bud. *Mutt and Jeff*. New York: Cupples and Leon, 1926. Unpaginated.

6882. Fisher, Bud. *The Mutt and Jeff Cartoons*. Greenfield, Wisconsin: Arcadia Publications, 1987. 64 pp.

6883. "Mutt and Jeff." *Newsweek*. April 23, 1951, p. 40.

6884. "Mutt and Jeff Celebrate 82nd Anniversary." *Trinidad Guardian*. April 27-May 6, 1990, p. 2.

6885. "Mutt and Jeff 75 Years!" *Cartoonist PROfiles*. December 1982, pp. 54-57.

6886. "Plastica: Los Nietos de Mutt y Jeff." *Primera Plana* (Buenos Aires). No. 287, 1968, p. 70.

"Nancy"

6887. Bushmiller, Nancy. *Nancy*. New York: Pocket Books, 1961.

6888. Hegerfors, Sture. "Hur Fritzi Ritz, en Rik Skön Amazon, Blev Ungarna Lisa och Sluggo." *GT Söndags Extra* (Göteborg). January 7, 1968.

6889. "Nancy!" *Cartoonist PROfiles*. March 1986, pp. 61-65.

6890. "Nancy, Sluggo and Ernie." *Newsweek*. June 28, 1948, p. 60.

6891. Walker, Brian, ed. *The Best of Ernie Bushmiller's Nancy*. New York: Comicana/Henry Holt, 1988.

6892. Wildman, George. *Nancy and Sluggo*. New York: Random House, 1981.

"Napoleon"

6893. Herbert, Jack. "'Napoleon' and 'Uncle Elby.'" *Cartoonist PROfiles*. September 1977, pp. 58-62.

6894. McBride, Clifford. *Napoleon*. Intro. by Jack Herbert. The Hyperion Library of Classic American Comic Strips. Westport, Connecticut: Hyperion, 1977. 101 pp.

6895. McBride, Clifford. *Napoleon and Uncle Elby*. Intro. by Don Herold. McBride and Co., 1945.

6896. "Napoleon and Uncle Elby." *The Nation*. May 10, 1947, p. 531.

"Odd Bodkins"

6897. O'Neill, Dan. *The Collective Unconscience of Odd Bodkins*. San Francisco, California: Glide Publications, 1973. 112 pp.

6898. O'Neill, Dan. *Hear the Sound of My Feet Walking Drown the Sound of My Voice Talking*. Rev. Ed. San Francisco, California: Glide Publications, 1975. 62 pp.

"On Stage"

6899. "'On Stage' Returns to the Free Press." *Detroit Free Press*. June 8, 1958, p. A-11.

6900. Starr, Leonard. "Mary Perkins on Stage." *Cartoonist PROfiles*. No. 10, 1971, pp. 74-83.

6901. Starr, Leonard. *On Stage*. Reuben Award Winner Series. El Cajon, California: Blackthorne, 1985. 72 pp.

"On the Fastrack"

6902. Holbrook, Bill. *On the Fastrack*. New York: Putnam, 1985.

6903. "On the Fastrack by Bill Holbrook." *Cartoonist PROfiles*. March 1984, pp. 8-13.

"Our Boarding House"

6904. McCormick, Tom. "Our Boarding House (with Major Hoople)." *Cartoonist PROfiles*. March 1985, pp. 66-69.

6905. Phelps, Donald. "Boarding House Days and Arabian Nights." *Nemo*. July 1985, pp. 60-66.

"Outbursts of Everett True"

6906. Blackbeard, Bill. "Black 'Everett True.'" *Comics Buyer's Guide*. October 10, 1986, p. 38.

6907. Condo, A.D. and J.W. Raper. *The Outbursts of Everett True*. Vestal, New York: Vestal Press, 1983. 94 pp.

6908. Johnson, Mark. "Grilling the Prime Beefs: The Outbursts of Everett True." *Nemo*. September 1987, pp. 54-66.

"Out Our Way"

6909. Black, Ed. "Ed Sullivan, Out Our Way Cartoonist." *Cartoonist PROfiles*. No. 23, 1974, pp. 30-34.

6910. Williams, J.R. *The Bull of the Woods and Out Our Way*. New York: Scribner's, 1952.

6911. Williams, J.R. *Cowboys Out Our Way*. New York: Scribner's, 1951.

6912. Williams, J.R. *Kids Out Our Way*. New York: Charles Scribner's Sons, 1946.

6913. Williams, J.R. *Out Our Way*. New York: Scribner's Sons, 1943.

6914. Williams, J.R. *Twenty Years of Out Our Way*. New York: NEA Service, 1942(?).

"Ozark Ike"

6915. Collins, Max A. "Strip Search: A Talk with Ray Gotto." *Comics Feature*. January 1986, pp. 14-15, 42-43.

6916. "El Asombroso Exito de Ozark Ike." *Dibujantes* (Buenos Aires). No. 13, 1955, pp. 4-5.

6917. Garnett, Bill. "Ozark, Ray and Me: 'My Search for Ray Gotto.'" The *Funnie's Paper*. September 1984, pp. 4-6.

6918. Pollak, R. Robert. "Ozark Ike: Ray Gotto's Baseball Strip." *Comics Buyer's Guide*. September 1, 1989, pp. 42, 44.

"Peanuts"

6919. "Alles über die Peanuts." *RTV* (Nürnberg). No. 47, 1972, p. 23.

6920. Anton, Uwe. "Ich Liebe die Welt—Aber Liebt Sie Mich? Das Mikrouniversum der Peanuts." *Comixene* (Hanover). 8:35 (1981), pp. 18-20.

6921. Augusto, Sergio. "Peanuts No Sofá." *Jornal do Brasil* (Rio de Janeiro). March 31, 1967.

6922. Augusto, Sergio. "A Solidao de Charlie Brown." *Jornal do Brasil* (Rio de Janeiro). April 7, 1967.

6923. Augusto, Sergio. "Tres Autores à Procura de Charlie Brown." *Jornal de Brasil* (Rio de Janeiro). September 1, 1967.

6924. Berger, Arthur A. "Peanuts: An American Pastoral." *Journal of Popular Culture*. Summer 1969, pp. 1-8.

6925. Berger, Arthur A. "Peanuts: The Americanization of Augustine." In *Humor in America*, edited by Enid Veron, pp. 298-305. New York: Harcourt, Brace, Jovanovich, 1976.

6926. Borgzinner, J. "Inept Heroes, Winners at Last. C.M. Schulz's Peanuts Characters." *Life*. March 17, 1967, pp. 74-78+.

6927. Butzkamm, Wolfgang. "Peanuts. Ein Amerikanischer Comic für den Englischen Anfangsunterricht." *Englisch-Amerikanische Studien* (Cologne). 2, 1984, pp. 288-295.

6928. Cavallone, Bruno. "Alla Scoperta dei Peanuts." *Linus*. No. 1, 1965.

6929. Cecchi, Ottavio. "Si, Lucy è una Fascista." *L'Unità* (Milan). January 24, 1965.

6930. Chaboud, Jack. "*Le Chien dans la B.D.* Snoopy Super Star." *Le Nouveau Bédésup*. 34:2 (1985).

6931. "Charlie Brown at Forty." *Media Development*. 4, 1990, p. 1.

6932. "Charlie Brown's New Pal." *Newsweek*. July 29, 1968, pp. 66-67.

6933. "Charlie Brown und Seine Freunde." *Der Spiegel* (Hamburg). No. 52, 1970, p. 126.

6934. "Charlie Ist zu Albern." *Hamburger Morgenpost*. No. 270, 1969, p. 31.

6935. "Charlie und Sein Hund Snoopy." *Neue Ruhr-Zeitung* (Essen). April 2, 1969.

6936. Demski, Eva. "Peanuts—Ein Comic Strip als Lebenshilfe." *Titel, Thesen, Temperamente, 1. Deutsches Fernsehen (ARD)*, (Baden-Baden). January 25, 1971.

6937. Demski, Eva and S. Ehrentreich. "Die Peanuts—Lebenshilfe durch Comics." *Radius* (Stuttgart). 2, 1971, pp. 44-47.

6938. "Doing Business with Charlie Brown Is No Peanuts for 68 Publishers and Licensees." *Publisher's Weekly*. July 7, 1975, pp. 72-73.

6939. Eco, Umberto. "Charlie Brown e i Fumetti." *Linus*. No. 1, 1965.

6940. Eco, Umberto. "Die Welt von Charlie Brown." In *Apokalyptiker und Intergrierte. Zur Kritischen Kritik der Massenkultur. Aus dem Italienischen übersetzt von Max Looser*, edited by Ders, pp. 223-232. Frankfurt: S. Fischer Verlag, 1984.

6941. Eco, Umberto. "Il Mondo di Charlie Brown." *Milano Libri*. 1963.

6942. Eco, Umberto and Max Looser. "Die Welt von Charlie Brown." *Neue Rundschau*. 95:4 (1984), pp. 5-14.

6943. "Ein Junge Namens Charlie Brown Erobert die Filmleinwand." *Hamburger Abendblatt*, January 10-11, 1970, p. 27.

6944. Eppert, Franz. "Erzählen und Diskurs. Grundsätzliches zum Einsatz von Kommunikationsgeschichten im Zielsprachenunterricht Deutsch als Fremdsprache." *Jahrbuch Deutsch als Fremdsprache* (Munich). 4, 1978, pp. 22-40.

6945. Erwin, Ray. "Good News Charlie Brown: Peanuts Wins." *Editor and Publisher*. 99:28 (1966), p. 57.

6946. "Für und Wider Charlie Brown." *Hamburger Morgenpost*. No. 276, 1969, p. 30.

6947. Gauthier, Guy. "La Mirada Discreta de Linus." Translated by Jaime B. Andrew. *Cuadernos de Semiótica* (México). September 1982, pp. 1-16.

6948. Gauthier, Guy. "Peanuts: An Idiomatic Way of Writing (Les Peanuts: Un Graphisme Idiomatique)." *Communications* (Paris). 24 (1976), pp. 108-139.

6949. Gerteis, Klaus. "Charlie Brown und die Seinen." *Die Welt* (Hamburg). December 7, 1968, p. II.

6950. "Good Grief." *Time*. April 9, 1965, pp. 80-84.

6951. "Good Grief: Curly Hair: Peanuts." *Newsweek*. March 6, 1961, pp. 42-43, 68.

6952. "Good Grief, $150 Million." *Newsweek*. December 27, 1971, pp. 32-36.

6953. "Good Grief: The World According to Peanuts." *Time*. April 9, 1965, pp. 42-46.

6954. "Gospel According to Peanuts." *Time*. January 1, 1965, p. 28.

6955. Green, Robin. "Face Front—Clap Your Hands! You're on the Winning Team." *Rolling Stone*. September 1971, pp. 28-34.

6956. Hartlaub, Geno. "Snoopy, Asterix und Charley Brown." *Deutsches Allgemeines Sonntagsblatt* (Cologne). July 11, 1971, p. 24.

6957. Hornung, Werner. "Charlie Brown, Valentina & Co." *Schweizer National-Zeitung* (Basel). December 12, 1971.

6958. Inge, M. Thomas. "*Peanuts* and American Culture." In *The Graphic Art of Charles Schulz*, pp. 48-61. Oakland, California: Oakland Museum, 1985. Presented at Popular Culture Association, Montreal, March 1987.

6959. Inge, M. Thomas. "We Can Compare Peanuts and Ibsen." *The Buyer's Guide for Comic Fandom*. January 30, 1976, p. 31.

6960. "Introducing Peanuts." *The Observer Review* (London). December 31, 1967, p. 17.

6961. Kael, Pauline. "A Boy Named Charlie Brown." *New Yorker*. January 17, 1970.

6962. Kanner, B. "You're a Good Salesman, Charlie Brown." *New York*. February 4, 1985, pp. 19-20.

6963. "Kartes Licenses Peanuts from Sister Company." *Publisher's Weekly*. April 24, 1987, pp. 50 +.

6964. Kempkes, Wolfgang. "'Charlie Brown'—Buch von Ravensburg." *Bulletin: Jugend & Literatur*. No. 6, 1970, p. 6.

6965. Kempkes, Wolfgang. "Peanuts on Board!" *Bulletin: Jugend + Literatur*. No. 7, 1970, p. 12.

6966. Kerr, Walter. "You're a Good Man, Charlie Brown." *New York Times*. March 9, 1967.

6967. Knight, Arthur. "A Boy Named Charlie Brown." *Saturday Review*. January 17, 1970.

6968. Le Carpentier, P. "Peanuts." *Phénix* (Paris). No. 13, 1969.

6969. Limmer, Wolfgang. "Zeichentrickfilm-Snoopy." *Fernsehen und Film* (Hanover). No. 2, 1971, p. 25.

6970. Linnenkohl, Ute. "Comics." *Lehrer Journal* (Munich). 53: 7/8 (1985), pp. 311-314.

6971. "Linus in Love." *Senior Scholastic*. November 4, 1959, p. 1.

6972. "Look Who's Turned 35!" *Good Housekeeping*. December 1985, p. 156.

6973. Loria, Jeffrey H. *What's It All About, Charlie Brown? Peanuts Kids Look at America Today*. New York: Holt, Rinehart and Winston, 1968.

6974. Mendelson, Lee and Charles M. Schulz. *Happy Birthday, Charlie Brown*. New York: Random House, 1979. 160 pp.

6975. Miner, M.E. "Charley Brown Goes to School." *English Journal*. November 3, 1969, pp. 1183-1185.

6976. Morrow, H. "Success of an Utter Failure." *Saturday Evening Post*. January 12, 1957, pp. 34-35.

6977. Naumann, Michael. "You're an Old Man, Charlie Brown Older: Die Misere Eines Gezeichneten Lebens." *Zeit-magazin* (Hamburg). December 4, 1970, p. 31.

6978. Neal, Jim. "Charlie Brown Ends 42-Year Losing Streak." *Comics Buyer's Guide*. May 7, 1993, p. 64.

6979. Oomen, Ursula. "Wort-Bild-Nachricht: Semiotische Aspekte des Comic Strip 'Peanuts.'" *Linguistik und Didaktik* (Munich). 6:24 (1975), pp. 247-259.

6980. Oliver, Tom. "Snoopy als Star." *Der Abend* (Berlin). August 17, 1972.

6981. Orlando, R. "Dove Corrie, Charlie Brown?" *L'Europeo*. January 24, 1965.

6982. "Peanuts." *Cartoonist PROfiles*. December 1980, pp. 60-61.

6983. "Peanuts, the Thinking Man's Diet." *The World of Comic Art*. 1:1 (1966), pp. 42-48.

6984. "Peanuts To Enjoy a Colorful Life." *Cartoon Art Museum Newsletter*. 2:1 (1987), p. 4.

6985. Pei, Mario. "We Love You Carlos, Caroline, Charlot Brown!" *Quinto Lingo*. August/September 1970, pp. 40D-40G.

6986. "Portrait of the Artist As a Christian Beagle." *Education 2000* (Paris). 21, 1982, pp. 2-13.

6987. Schmidt, Hans J. "Comics im Mathematikunterricht der Sekundarstufe 1." *Neue Unterrichtspraxis* (Hanover). 13:4 (1980), pp. 216-220.

6988. Schulz, Charles M. *A Boy Named Charlie Brown*. New York: Holt, Rinehart and Winston, 1969.

6989. Schulz, Charles M. *A Charlie Brown Christmas*. New York: United Features, 1965. Unpaginated.

6990. Schulz, Charles M. *Charlie Brown's All-Stars*. New York: United Features, 1966. Unpaginated.

6991. Schulz, Charles M. *Fun with Peanuts*. Greenwich, Connecticut: Fawcett, 1957. Unpaginated.

6992. Schulz, Charles M. *Happiness Is a Warm Puppy*. San Francisco, California: Determined Productions, 1962. Unpaginated.

6993. Schulz, Charles M. *Hey Peanuts!* Greenwich, Connecticut: Fawcett, 1954. Unpaginated.

6994. Schulz, Charles M. *Home Is on Top of a Doghouse*. San Francisco, California: Determined Productions, ca. 1966. Unpaginated.

6995. Schulz, Charles M. "Linus Gets a Library Card." *Wilson Library Bulletin*. December 1960, pp. 312-313.

6996. Schulz, Charles M. *More Peanuts*. New York: Rinehart, 1954. Unpaginated.

6997. Schulz, Charles M. "New Peanuts Happiness Book; Excerpts." *McCall's*. October 1967, pp. 90-91.

6998. Schulz, Charles M. *Peanuts Classics*. New York: Holt, Rinehart and Winston, 1970. 224 pp.

6999. Schulz, Charles M. "Peanuts Festival, Excerpts from Peanuts Books." *McCall's*. September 1966, pp. 106-111.

7000. Schulz, Charles M. *Peanuts Treasury*. New York: Holt, Rinehart and Winston, 1968. 256 pp.

7001. Schulz, Charles M. *Race for Your Life, Charlie Brown*. New York: Holt, Rinehart and Winston, 1978.

7002. Schulz, Charles M. *Security Is a Thumb and a Blanket*. London: Paul Hamlyn, 1963. Unpaginated.

7003. Schulz, Charles M. *Snaps, Scraps and Souvenirs*. New York: United Features, 1967. Unpaginated.

7004. Schulz, Charles M. *Snoopy and the Red Baron*. New York: Holt, Rinehart and Winston, 1967. 63 pp.

7005. Schulz, Charles M. *Snoopy Come Home*. New York: 1962.

7006. Schulz, Charles M. *The "Snoopy Come Home" Movie Book*. New York: Holt, Rinehart and Winston, 1972.

7007. Schulz, Charles M. *The Snoopy Festival*. New York: Holt, Rinehart and Winston, 1974.

7008. Schulz, Charles M. *Sunday's Fun Day, Charlie Brown*. New York: Holt, 1965. Unpaginated.

7009. Schulz, Charles M. *Thanks for Nothing, Snoopy*. New York: Holt, Rinehart and Winston, 1975.

7010. Schulz, Charles M. *What Next, Charlie Brown?* Greenwich, Connecticut: Fawcett, 1956. Unpaginated.

7011. Schulz, Charles M. *The Wonderful World of Peanuts*. Greenwich, Connecticut: Fawcett, 1954. Unpaginated.

7012. Schulz, Charles M. *You Don't Look 35, Charlie Brown!* New York: Holt, Rinehart and Winston, 1985. 224 pp.

7013. Schulz, Charles M. *You're Barking Up the Wrong Tree, Snoopy*. [New York]: Scholastic Book Service, 1980.

7014. Schulz, Charles M. *You've Had It, Charlie Brown*. New York: Holt, Rinehart and Winston, 1969.

7015. Schulz, Monte and Jody Millward. *The Peanuts Trivia and Reference Book*. New York: Henry Holt, 1986. 138 pp.

7016. Schulze, Hartmut. "Zokroarr Wumm. Unserem Charlie Brown zum 20. Geburtstag." *Hamburger Morgenpost*. November 12, 1970, p. 4.

7017. Short, Robert L. *Ein Kleines Volk Gottes. Die Peanuts*. Basel: F. Reinhardt Verlag, 1966.

7018. Short, Robert L. *The Gospel According to Peanuts*. Atlanta, Georgia: John Knox, 1965.

7019. Short, Robert L. "The Gospel According to Peanuts." *Coronet*. May 1968, pp. 126-161.

7020. Short, Robert L. *The Parables of Peanuts*. New York: Harper and Row, 1968. 328 pp.

7021. Short, Robert L. "Peanuts and the Bible." *Americas*. April 1964, pp. 16-20.

7022. Short, Robert L. "Peanuts at 35; Distilled Love." *Christian Century*. November 13, 1985, p. 1022.

7023. Short, Robert L. and Roy P. Nelson. "Gospel According to Peanuts." *Christian Century*. March 3, 1965, p. 276.

7024. Siegmann. "Volk Gottes in den Comic Strips (Peanuts)." *Die Schülerbücherei, Beilage zur "Schulwarte"* (Stuttgart). July 1967, p. 2.

7025. *Snoopy Around the World. Dressed by Top Fashion Designers*. New York: Harry N. Abrams, 1990. 128 pp.

7026. Spraker, Nancy. "He's Your Dog, Charlie Brown." *Woman's Day*. February 1968, pp. 58-60.

7027. Taylor, Robert. "With Nancy, Shopping Is More Fun." *Boston Herald*. December 17, 1959, p. 23.

7028. Thompson, A. "Baseball's Most Winning Losers." *McCall's*. July 1984, pp. 94-95.

7029. Trenquel, Rogé. "Une Combinatoire Confictuelle (sic!) les Peanuts. A Guy Gauthier, Peanutsophile." *Le Nouveau Bédésup*. 34, 1985, pp. 3-11.

7030. Vittorini, Elio and Oreste Del Buono. "Charlie Brown e i Fumetti." *Linus*. No. 1, April 1965.

7031. Von Berg, Robert. "Verdammt, der Rote Baron! Zur Musikalischen Inszenierung von 'Peanuts' in New York." *Süddeutsche Zeitung* (Munich). March 31, 1967.

7032. Wakin, Edward. "The Gospel According to Peanuts...." *The Funnie's Paper*. April 1984, pp. 4-9.

7033. Warzecha, Marion. "Comic: Schülerlotse Charlie Braun." *Pädagogische Welt*. 35:7 (1981), pp. 431-432.

7034. Weales, G. "Good Grief, More Peanuts!" *Reporter*. April 30, 1959, pp. 45-46.

7035. "Weitermalen (Snoopy)." *Bild* (Hamburg). July 1, 1970, p. 15.

7036. "Woes of a Peanuts Manager." *Sports Illustrated*. June 20, 1966, pp. 46-50.

7037. Zanotto, Piero. "Charlie Brown a Rapallo." *Linus* (Milan). 5:47 (1969), p. 71.

7038. Zanotto, Piero. "Una Candelina per i Peanuts." *Nazione Sera*. May 17, 1966.

7039. Zanotto, Piero. "Il Provocatorio Candare di Charlie Brown." *Corriere del Giorno*. March 8, 1967.

"Penny"

7040. Haenigsen, H. "Penny and Me." *Collier's* February 5, 1949, p. 22.

7041. "Penny Fashions Planned for Fall." *New York Herald Tribune*. May 9, 1950, p. 25.

7042. "Penny's Fall Hats Set a Teen Trend." *New York Herald Tribune*. July 25, 1949, p. 17.

7043. Sheppard, Eugenia. "Penny Says Yes to Hats." *New York Herald Tribune*. August 12, 1948, p. 20.

"Peter Rabbit"

7044. Dowhan, Michael W., jr. "Peter Rabbit: Harrison Cady's Masterwork. An Overview." *Cartoonist PROfiles*. September 1983, pp. 36-39.

7045. "Peter Rabbit's New Creator." *Newsweek*. September 20, 1948, p. 67.

"The Phantom"

7046. Barry, Sy. "Me and My Phantom." *Comics Scene*. January 1981, pp. 58-61.

7047. Bouyxou, Jean-Pierre. "Le Fantôme du Bengale." *Mercury* (Paris). No. 6, 1967.

7048. Caen, Michel. "Le Fantôme du Bengale." *Plexus* (Paris). No. 12, 1967, pp. 150-152.

7049. "Comic-Strips—Phantom Unter Palmen." *Der Spiegel* (Hamburg). No. 10, 1965, p. 112.

7050. Falk, Lee and Ray Moore. *The Phantom*. Intro. by Maurice Horn. Franklin Square, New York: Nostalgia Press, 1969.

7051. Falk, Lee and Ray Moore. *The Phantom*. n.p.: ca. 1973. 46 pp.

7052. Falk, Lee and Ray Moore. *The Phantom, Diana Aviatrix Lost*. The Golden Age of the Comics. Papeete, Tahiti: Comics Stars in the World, 1981(?) 64 pp.

7053. Falk, Lee and Ray Moore. *The Phantom, the Game of Alvar*. The Golden Age of the Comics. Papeete, Tahiti: Coimics Stars in the World, 1980(?) 44 pp.

7054. Falk, Lee and Ray Moore. *The Phantom, the Sea-Horse*. The Golden Age of the Comics. Papeete, Tahiti: Comics Stars in the World, 1981(?). 56 pp.

7055. Falk, Lee and Ray Moore. *The Phantom Versus the Singh Brotherhood*. Concord, California: Comic Art Publishing Co., 1979. 78 pp.

7056. Falk, Lee and Ray Moore. *The Phantom Vs. the Sky Maidens*. Park Forest, Illinois: K. Pierce, 1982. 80 pp.

7057. Falk, Lee and Ray Moore. *The Phantom's Treasure*. The Golden Age of the Comics. Papeete, Tahiti: Comics Stars in the World, 1981(?). 60 pp.

7058. Falk, Lee and Ray Moore. *The Sky Band*. Collana Grandi Adventure. Genova, Italy: Club Anni Trenta, 1972. 52 pp.

7059. Fini, Luciano and A. Massarelli. "Il Giustiziere della Jungla: The Phantom." *Sagittarius*. July 1965, p. 3.

7060. Lacassin, Francis. "La Résurrection du Fantôme." *Midi-Minuit Fantastique* (Paris). No. 6, 1963, p. 88.

7061. Lacassin, Francis. "Rider Haggard ou le Juste en Proie aux Fantômes." Préface à "Elle." Paris: J.J. Pauvert, 1965.

7062. Laura, Ernesto G. "L'Uomo Bianco e il 'Terzo Mondo' Attraverso il Personaggio di 'The Phantom.'" *Quaderni di Communicazioni di Massa*. No. 1, 1965, pp. 93-102.

7063. "Les Fils de Fantomas." *Stop* (Paris). No. 70, 1967.

7064. "The Life and Times of *The Phantom*." *Comic Hotline*. 1:1 (1986), pp. 20-22.

7065. Vene, Gianfranco. "Fantomas e Figlik." *L'Europeo*. April 11, 1965.

7066. Von Zitzewitz, Monika. "Das Phantom, das Rache Schwört." *Die Weltwoche* (Basel). October 21, 1966, p. 37.

"Pogo"

7067. "Advance Look at New Pogo Book." *Pogo Is Back*. 3:3 (1992), p. 1.

7068. Bertieri, Claudio. "Le Aventure di Pogo et di Albert." *Il Lavoro Nuovo* (Genoa). March 10, 1966.

7069. Breit, Harvey. "Go Pogo." *New York Times Book Review*. October 10, 1954.

7070. Bruckner, Carl. "Walt Kelly's *Pogo*: The Eye of the Whole Man." *Studies in American Humor*. NS 2.3 (1983-1984), pp. 161-170.

7071. "Carefree Camp Siberia: The Saga of the Cheerful Charlies." *Fort Mudge Most*. May 1990, pp. 5-13.

7072. Cassel, Andrew. "'Pogo' Reborn." *Philadelphia Inquirer*. January 3, 1989, pp. 1-D, 8-D.

7073. Cavallone, Bruno. "Pogo and Okefenokee County." *Linus*. July 1965.

7074. Cavallone, Bruno. "Pogo e la Contea di Okefenokee." *Linus*. No. 4, 1965.

7075. "The Christmas Song." *Fort Mudge Most*. November 1989, pp. 14-15.

7076. Clifford, G. "Fed Up with the Presidential Candidates? No Need To Play Possum When You Can Go Pogo." *People*. May 26, 1980, pp. 34-35.

7077. Crouch, Bill, jr. "More Pre-Syndicated Pogo Comic Strips from the New York Star." *Okefenokee Star*. Summer 1977, pp. 22-30.

7078. Crouch, Bill, jr. "Pogo as Fine Art: The One Man Shows at Springfield and Greenwich." *Okefenokee Star*. Spring 1977, pp. 29-32.

7079. Dominguez, Joe. "Pogonomics." *In Context: A Quarterly of Humane Sustainable Culture*. Summer 1990.

7080. "Extinction of the Longhorn." *Time*. March 29, 1968.

7081. Gantt, Barry and Sandra Pungor. "In Pogo We Remember." *Comics Scene*. February 1990, pp. 29-32, 60.

7082. Hale, Norman. *All Natural Pogo*. New York: Thinker's Books, 1991. 96 pp.

7083. Hale, Norman. "Natural Foods." *Comics Journal*. February 1991, pp. 59-60.

7084. "Hark! The Herald Tribune Sings." *Fort Mudge Most*. July 1991, pp. 4-10.

7085. Harvey, R.C. "More on Pogo (And Not a Minute Too Soon)." *Comics Journal*. October 1982, pp. 52-56.

7086. Harvey, R.C. "Pogo Runs Only in Reruns." *Comics Journal*. February 1993, pp. 89-90.

7087. Horn, Maurice. "Admirable Pogo." *Giff-Wiff*. September 1964.

7088. "I Go Pogo: The Movie." *Fort Mudge Most*. May 1989, pp. 18-19.

7089. Inge, M. Thomas. "Pogo's Victory Celebration." *The Okefenokee Star*. Summer 1982, pp. 12-13.

7090. Kelly, Selby and Bill Crouch, jr., eds. *The Best of Pogo*. New York: Simon and Schuster, 1982. 224 pp.

7091. Kelly, Selby and Bill Crouch, jr., eds. *Outrageously Pogo*. New York: Simon and Schuster, 1985. 223 pp.

7092. Kelly, Selby and Bill Crouch, jr., eds. *Pogo Even Better*. New York: Simon and Schuster, 1984. 224 pp.

7093. Kelly, Selby and Bill Crouch, jr., eds. *Walt Kelly's Pluperfect Pogo*. New York: Simon and Schuster, 1987. 223 pp.

7094. Kelly, Selby D. and Steve A. Thompson. *Pogo Files for Pogophiles: A Retrospective on 50 Years of Walt Kelly's Classic Comic Strip*. Richmond, Minnesota: Spring Hollow Books, 1992. 256 pp.

7095. Kelly, Walt. *Beau Pogo*. New York: Simon and Schuster, 1960. 191 pp.

7096. Kelly, Walt. *The Complete Pogo Comics*. Forestville, California: Eclipse Books. *Pogo and Albert*. Vol. 1, 1989. 63 pp.; *At the Mercy of the Elephants*. Vol. 2, 1990. 63 pp.

7097. Kelly, Walt. *Deck Us All with Boston Charlie*. New York: Simon and Schuster, 1963. 128 pp.

7098. Kelly, Walt. *G.O. Fizzicle Pogo*. New York: Simon and Schuster, 1958. 191 pp.

7099. Kelly, Walt. *Gone Pogo*. New York: Gregg Press, 1977, ca. 1961. 127 pp.

7100. Kelly Walt. *I Go Pogo*. New York: Simon and Schuster, 1952. 190 pp.

7101. Kelly, Walt. *The Incompleat Pogo*. New York: Simon and Schuster, 1954. 191 pp.; New York: Gregg Press, 1977. 191 pp.

7102. Kelly, Walt. *The Jack Acid Society Black Book*. New York: Simon and Schuster, 1957, 1961, 1962. 96 pp.

7103. Kelly, Walt. *Phi Beta Pogo*. New York: Simon and Schuster, 1989. 256 pp.

7104. Kelly, Walt. *Pogo*. New York: Simon and Schuster, 1951. 182 pp.

7105. Kelly, Walt. *Pogo à la Sundae*. New York: Gregg Press, 1977. 127 pp.

7106. Kelly, Walt. *Pogo Extra*. New York: Simon and Schuster, 1960. 144 pp.

7107. Kelly, Walt. "Pogo Looks at the Abominable Snowman." *Saturday Review*. August 30, 1958.

7108. Kelly, Walt. *A Pogo Panorama*. New York: Simon and Schuster, 1977.

7109. Kelly, Walt. *The Pogo Papers*. New York: Simon and Schuster, 1953. 192 pp.

7110. Kelly, Walt. *The Pogo Peek-a-Book*. New York: Simon and Schuster, 1955. Unpaginated.

7111. Kelly, Walt. *The Pogo Poop Book*. New York: Simon and Schuster, 1966. 132 pp.

7112. Kelly, Walt. *Pogo Primer for Parents (TV division)*. Washington, D.C.: U.S. Government Printing Office, 1961. 24 pp.

7113. Kelly, Walt. *The Pogo Stepmother Goose*. New York: Simon and Schuster, 1954. 89 pp.

7114. Kelly, Walt. *The Pogo Sunday Book*. New York: Simon and Schuster, 1956. 192 pp.

7115. Kelly, Walt. *The Pogo Sunday Brunch*. New York: Simon and Schuster, 1959.

7116. Kelly, Walt. *The Pogo Sunday Parade*. New York: Simon and Schuster, 1958. 127 pp.

7117. Kelly, Walt. *Positively Pogo*. New York: Simon and Schuster, 1957. 189 pp.

7118. Kelly, Walt. *Potluck Pogo*. New York: Simon and Schuster, 1955. 179 pp.

7119. Kelly, Walt. *The Return of Pogo*. New York: Simon and Schuster, 1965.

7120. Kelly, Walt. *Uncle Pogo So-So Stories*. New York: Gregg Press, 1977. 92 pp.

7121. Kidder, Rushworth M. "All Over Gulpy." *Fort Mudge Moan*. 1984, p. 9. Reprinted from *Christian Science Monitor*.

7122. Lamb, Chris. "Cartooning Duo Talk About New 'Pogo.'" *Editor and Publisher*. August 19, 1989, pp. 52-55.

7123. Lennon, Dan. "Growing Up with Pogo." *Fort Mudge Most*. 2:3 (1988), p. 13.

7124. Lennon, Dan. "Growing Up with Pogo III." *Fort Mudge Most*. March 1989, p. 19.

7125. Maresca, Peter. "Making Pogo Tick." *Comedy*. Winter 1981, pp. 20-23.

7126. Mendelson, E. "Possum Pastoral." *Yale Review*. Spring 1978, pp. 470-480.

7127. Monath, Norman. *Songs of the Pogo*. New York: Simon and Schuster, 1956. 152 pp.

7128. "No Go Pogo." *America*. June 2, 1962, p. 337.

7129. Norwood, Rick. "In the Beginning." *Fort Mudge Most*. March 1989, pp. 14-16.

7130. "Our Archives of Culture: Enter the Comics and Pogo." *Newsweek*. June 21, 1954, pp. 60 +. "Discussion." July 12, 1954, p. 6.

7131. "Out Goes Pogo." *Time*. December 1, 1958, p. 40.

7132. "The Overseas Okefenokee: Pogo in Translation." *Fort Mudge Most*. May 1992, pp. 9-45.

7133. "Pan-Am Mania." *Fort Mudge Most*. September 1990, pp. 10-13.

7134. "P and G Giveaways: 21 Years Old in May." *Fort Mudge Most*. July 1990, pp. 9-11.

7135. "Pogo." *Collier's*. March 8, 1952.

7136. "Pogo Again." *Collier's*. April 29, 1955.

7137. "Pogo Against McCarthy." *Newsweek*. September 6, 1954, p. 42.

7138. "Pogo for President." *Newsweek*. July 2, 1956, pp. 48-49.

7139. "Pogo Gets Animated: A Brief Guide." *Fort Mudge Most*. July 1990, pp. 5-7.

7140. "Pogo Problem; Khrushchev-Castro Satire." *Commonweal*. June 8, 1962, pp. 267-268.

7141. "Pogo's Progress." *Newsweek*. May 30, 1949, p. 56.

7142. "Possum Time: Pogo." *Time*. December 18, 1950, pp. 81-82.

7143. "Presenting the Complete and 'Official' Six Verses to 'Deck Us All with Boston Charlie!'" *Pogo Is Back*. 3:3 (1992), p. 8.

7144. Refior, Donna. "We Have Met the Enemy and He Is Us II." *Fort Mudge Most*. March 1990, pp. 8-11.

7145. Rosen, I. "FBI Couldn't Nail Pogo Possum; Investigation of Cartoonist W. Kelly." *New Times*. June 12, 1978, p. 18.

7146. Smith, Kenneth. "Pogophilia: Pogo and Albert." *Comics Journal*. February 1991, pp. 41-42.

7147. "Speaking of Pictures: Pogofenokee Land." *Life*. May 12, 1952, pp. 12-14; May 11, 1953.

7148. "Strangers in a Strange Land: Pogo, Albert and Churchy on Mars." *Fort Mudge Most*. January 1991, pp. 8-10.

7149. Thompson, Michelle. "On the Distaff Side." *Fort Mudge Most*. April 1988, p. 20.

7150. Thompson, Steve and Phil Knotts. "Buttons, Buttons, Who's Got the Buttons?" *Fort Mudge Most*. July 1991, pp. 12-21.

7151. "Un Poco Pogo." *Fort Mudge Most*. April 1988, pp. 9-13.

7152. "Un Poco Pogo." *Fort Mudge Most*. 2:3 (1988), pp. 5-7.

7153. "Wade, Down Upon the Suwanee River." *Fort Mudge Most*. November 1990, pp. 12-14.

7154. "A Walt Kelly Sketchbook." *Comics Journal*. February 1991, pp. 70-71.

7155. Watterson, Bill. "Some Thoughts on Pogo." *Comics Journal*. February 1991, pp. 63-66.

7156. Yronwode, Cat. "Pogo the Pup Dog." *Fort Mudge Most*. September 1989, pp. 12-13.

"Polly and Her Pals"

7157. Lecigne, Bruno and Jean-Pierre Tamine. "Relecture: Polly and Her Pals." *Les Cahiers de la Bande Dessinée* (Grenoble). 66, 1985, pp. 76-79.

7158. Sterrett, Cliff. *Polly and Her Pals*. The Hyperion Library of Classic American Comic Strips. Intro. by Bill Blackbeard. Westport, Connecticut: Hyperion, 1977. 124 pp.

"Popeye"

7159. Blackbeard, Bill. "You Are Cordially Invited to the Reopening of Thimble Theater." An Introduction to *Popeye the Sailor*. Franklin Square, New York: Nostalgia Press, 1970.

7160. Bretieri, Claudio. "A Mad Sailor (Popeye)." *Il Lavoro* (Genoa). October 11, 1968.

7161. Caen, Michel. "Popeye." *Plexus* (Paris). No. 10, 1967, pp. 148-151.

7162. "Did Popeye Marry Ms Oyl?" *The Jester*. September 1992, p. 15. Reprinted from *Sunday Times* (London). July 19, 1992.

7163. Forest, Jean-Claude. "Plus d'Épinards pour Popeye." *Giff-Wiff* (Paris). No. 3, 1965, p. 21.

7164. Forest, Jean-Claude. *Popeye et les Harpies*. Paris: CELEG, 1964.

7165. Gowans, Alan. "Popeye and the American Dream." *Perspectives IV*. 1979, pp. 549-557.

7166. Gowans, Alan. *Prophetic Allegory: Popeye and the American Dream*. Watkins Glen, New York: American Life Books, 1983. 311 pp.

7167. Gowans, Alan. "Remarks on Arts and Utopias in the 1930s, à Propos of Some Excerpts from 'Popeye's Ark.'" *Racar* (Québec). 1:1 (1974), pp. 5-22.

7168. Kempkes, Wolfgang. "Popeye-Comic-Heftserie." *Bulletin: Jugend + Literatur*. No. 4, 1970, p. 12.

7169. Lacassin, Francis. "Popeye ou le Matelot Venu par Hasard." *Giff-Wiff* (Paris). No. 17, 1966, pp. 3-8.

7170. Lecigne, Bruno. "Relecture Popeye." *Les Cahiers de la Bande Dessinée* (Grenoble). 56, 1984, pp. 70-75.

7171. Lob, Jacques. "Popeye Parodies ou Popeye, Poopeye, Poopik et Cie." *Giff-Wiff*. No. 17, 1966, p. 23.

7172. "Olive Oyl's Right To Choose." *Philadelphia City Paper*. November 27, 1992, p. 6.

7173. "Passing of Olive Oyl." *Newsweek*. December 27, 1954, p. 38.

7174. "Popeye." *Cartoonist PROfiles*. September 1977, pp. 84-85.

7175. "Popeye by E.C. Segar." *Cartoonist PROfiles*. No. 13, 1972, pp. 14-23.

7176. "Popeye on His 50th Birthday." *Cartoonist PROfiles*. June 1979, pp. 22-23.

7177. "Popeye Reaches His 60th Birthday." *Editor and Publisher*. February 25, 1989, p. 40.

7178. Ranke, Richard. "Popeye and the Depression." *Nemo*. October 1983, pp. 14-15.

7179. Ringgenberg, Steve. "Abortion Wars: The Canning of Popeye Comic Strip Writer Bobby London." *Gauntlet*. No. 2, 1992, pp. 119-123.

7180. Romer, Jean-Claude. "Popeye à l'Écran." *Giff-Wiff*. No. 17, 1966, pp. 13-14.

7181. Sagendorf, Bud. *Popeye—Die Ersten Fünfzig Jahre*. Stuttgart: Ehapa Verlag, 1979.

7182. Sagendorf, Bud. *Popeye, the First Fifty Years*. New York: Workman, 1979. 142 pp.

7183. Schröder, Horst. "Popeye. Der Sensible Raufbold." *Comic Forum* (Vienna). 3:12, pp. 24-28.

7184. Segar, E.C. *The Complete E.C. Segar Popeye*. 10 Vols. The Nemo Bookshelf. Agoura, California: Fantagraphics Books, 1984-.

7185. Segar, E.C. *Popeye and the Jeep*. Long Beach, California: T. Raiola, 1982. 84 pp.

7186. Segar, E.C. *Thimble Theatre, Introducing Popeye*. The Hyperion Library of Classic American Comic Strips. Westport, Connecticut: Hyperion 1977. 173 pp.

7187. Segar, E.C. *Thimble Theatre, Starring Popeye the Sailor*. The Golden Age of the Comics No. 8. Franklin Square, New York: Nostalgia Press, 1971. 125 pp.

7188. Shepperd, Jean. "The Return of the Smiling Wimpy Doll." *Playboy*. December 1967, pp. 180-232.

7189. Siclier, Jacques. "Bonne-Année, Popeye." *Giff-Wiff* (Paris). No. 17, 1966, p. 11.

7190. "Successful Sailor." *Time*. October 12, 1940, p. 48.

7191. Sullerot, Eveline. "Popeye Cause." *Giff-Wiff* (Paris). No. 17, 1966, pp. 9-10.

7192. Terry, Bridget. *The Popeye Story*. New York: Tom Doherty Associates, 1980.

7193. Watson, Frank. "The Delightful Antics of Popeye, Olive Oyl, and Brutus." *Comics Journal*. December 1978, p. 33.

"Prince Valiant"

7194. Bertieri, Claudio. "Valiant i un Principe Coraggioso con ré Artu." *Il Lavoro* (Genoa). July 24, 1965.

7195. Delafuente, Francisco. "Neuvième Art: Prince Valiant." *U.N. Special*. No. 220, 1968, pp. 4-5, 23.

7196. Foster, Harold. *Prince Valiant*. New York: Nostalgia Press, 1974-.

7197. Foster, Harold. *Prince Valiant*. 2 Vols. Wayne, New Jersey: Manuscript Press, 1982-1984.

7198. Foster, Harold. *Prince Valiant*. Vols. 26-31. Agoura, California: Fantagraphics Books, 1984-1987.

7199. Foster, Harold. *Prince Valiant and the Golden Princess*. Book 5. Text by Max Trell. New York: Hastings House, 1955. 128 pp.; New York: Nostalgia Press, 1976. 127 pp.

7200. Foster, Harold. *Prince Valiant Companions in Adventure*. Franklin Square, New York: Nostalgia Press, 1974.

7201. Foster, Harold. *Prince Valiant in the Days of King Arthur*. New York: Hastings House, 1951. 128 pp.

7202. Foster, Harold. *Prince Valiant in the Days of King Arthur*. 3 Vols. Franklin Square, New York: Nostalgia Press, 1974-1978.

7203. Foster, Harold. *Prince Valiant in the Days of King Arthur*. Long Beach, California: Pacific Comics Club, 1979-1982.

7204. Foster, Harold. *Prince Valiant in the New World*. New York: Hastings House, 1956. 95 pp.

7205. Foster, Harold. *The Prince Valiant Scrapbook*. Bridgeport, Connecticut: B. Crouch, jr., 1981. 49 pp.

7206. Foster, Harold. *Prince Valiant's Perilous Voyage*. New York: Nostalgia Press, 1976. 128 pp.

7207. Greenberger, Robert. "Doing *Prince Valiant* Right." *Comics Scene*. July 1982, pp. 48-49.

7208. Krause, Horst-Burkhardt. "Mittelalter in Sprechblasen. Zur Rezeption des Mittelalters im Comic." In *Mittelalter—Rezeption II. Gesammelte Vorträge des 2. Salzburger Symposions "Die Rezeption des Mittelalters in Literatur, Bildender Kunst und Musik des 19. und 20. Jahrhunderts*, edited by Jürgen Kühnel, *et al.*, pp. 281-299. Göppingen: Kümmerle Verlag, 1982.

7209. Murphy, John C. *Prince Valiant in the Days of King Arthur*. 2 Vols. Reuben Award Winner Series. El Cajon, California: Blackthorne, 1986.

7210. Pérez, Ramón Fermín. "La Obra de Una Vida." *El Wendigo*. June-August 1987, pp. 4-10.

7211. "Prince Valiant." *Cartoonist PROfiles*. June 1983, pp. 45-49.

7212. "Prince Valiant." *Cartoonist PROfiles*. March 1987, pp. 49-51.

7213. *Prince Valiant: Lithway's Law*. Thousand Oaks, California: Fantagraphics, 1984(?).

"Private Breger"

7214. Breger, David. "Day in the Life of a Private." *New York Times Magazine*. April 12, 1942, p. 16.

7215. Breger, Dave. *G.I. Joe. From the Pages of "Yank" and "Stars and Stripes."* Garden City, New York: Doubleday, 1945.

7216. Breger, Dave. *Private Breger. His Adventures in an Army Camp*. New York: Rand McNally, 1942.

7217. Breger, Dave. *Private Breger in Britain*. London: Pilot Press, 1945.

7218. Breger, David. *Private Breger's War. His Adventures in Britain and at the Front*. New York: Random House, 1943. Unpaginated.

7219. Nuhn, R. "G.I. Joe's Dad Dave Breger." *Hobbies*. January 1985, pp. 60-65.

"Red Barry"

7220. Ferraro, Ezio and Giani Bono. "Pubblicazione Italiana di Red Barry." *Comics World*. No. 1, 1968.

7221. François, Edouard. "Red Barry." *Phénix* (Paris). No. 22, 1972.

7222. Marschall, Rick. "The 1930s Comics Noir World of Red Barry, Undercover Man." *Nemo*. July 1985, pp. 7-36.

"Red Ryder"

7223. Harman, Fred. *Red Ryder*. Long Beach, California: Western Wind Production, 1979. 18 pp.

7224. Harman, Fred. *Red Ryder*. Dragon Lady Productions, No. 2. Toronto, Ontario: Dragon Lady Press, 1985. 66 pp.

7225. Poling, J. "Ryder of the Comic Page." *Collier's*. August 14, 1948, pp. 16-17.

7226. Tercinet, Alain. "Red Ryder, ou l'Quest Bien Défini." *Giff-Wiff*. September 1964.

7227. Thomas, H.C. *Red Ryder and the Adventure at Chimney Rock*. Racine, Wisconsin: Whitman, 1946.

7228. Trout, Bernard. "Red Ryder." *Informations et Documents*. August 1974.

7229. Winterbotham, R.R. *Red Ryder and the Mystery of Whispering Walls*. Racine, Wisconsin: Whitman, 1941.

"Rev. David Crane"

7230. "Clergyman as Hero." *Newsweek*. March 12, 1956, p. 92.

7231. "Comic Cleric: Rev. David Crane." *Time*. March 12, 1956, pp. 90, 92.

7232. "David Crane." *Cartoonist PROfiles*. Summer 1969, pp. 20-29.

7233. Rowland, Gil. "Creator of David Crane Strip Sees Ethics in Everyday Living." *Newsletter*. June 1966, p. 9.

"Rex Morgan"

7234. Dorlaque, Joseph. "Doctors Endorse This Comic Strip." *Popular Science*. September 1956, pp. 172-174.

7235. "Operation on the Doctor; Rex Morgan, M.D." *Time*. December 25, 1950, pp. 34-35.

7236. "Rex Morgan, M.D." *Cartoonist PROfiles*. No. 15, 1972, p. 52.

7237. "Rex Morgan Revealed." *Time*. January 25, 1954, pp. 39-40.

"Rip Kirby"

7238. Cartier, E. "Rip Kirby." *Phénix* (Paris). No. 3, 1967, p. 28.

7239. Marquez, Miguel R. "Rip Kirby, el Defensor de la Ley." *Cuto* (San Sebastian). May 1967, pp. 3-5.

7240. Martín, Antonio. "Rip Kirby en España." *Cuto* (San Sebastian). May 1967, pp. 6-7.

7241. Prentice, John. "Rip Kirby and John Prentice." *Cartoonist PROfiles.* 1:2 (1969), pp. 34-39.

7242. Raymond, Alex. *Rip Kirby.* 16 Vols. Long Beach, California: Pacific Comics Club, 1980.

7243. Raymond, Alex. *Rip Kirby.* Comic Art Showcase, No. 4. Buffalo, New York: Quality Comic Art Productions, 1980. 56 pp.

7244. Smolderen, Thierry. "Un Détective Tranquille Qui en Jette Plein la Vue." *Les Cahiers de la Bande Dessinée* (Grenoble). 72, pp. 32-34.

7245. Trinchero, Sergio. "Cino e Franco." *Super Albo "Rip Kirby,"* No. 98, Supplemento, *Fratelli Spada*, August 1964.

7246. Trinchero, Sergio. "Si Parla di....Rip Kirby." *Super Albo* (Fratelli Spada). No. 54, 1963.

"Robotman"

7247. Meddick, Jim. *Robotman Takes Off.* New York: World Almanac Publications, 1986. 136 pp.

7248. Meddick, Jim. *Robotman, the Untold Story.* New York: Topper Books, 1986. 126 pp.

7249. "Robotman." *Cartoonist PROfiles.* March 1985, pp. 8-13.

"Rubes"

7250. Rubin, Leigh. *Rubes.* New York: Perigee Books, 1988. 195 pp.

7251. Rubin, Leigh. "Rubes." *Cartoonist PROfiles.* September 1990, pp. 68-73.

"Sad Sack"

7252. Baker, George. *The Sad Sack.* New York: Simon and Schuster, 1944. 237 pp.

7253. Campbell, Gordon and Mary. "Sad Sack." *Cartoonist PROfiles.* March 1986, pp. 70-73.

7254. Fields, A.C. "Still the Sad Sack." *Saturday Review of Literature*. July 6, 1946, p. 7.

7255. "Sack in the War." *Newsweek*. November 8, 1943, pp. 81-82.

7256. "Sad Sack Booklet Destroyed by Army." *New York Herald Tribune*. September 21, 1951.

7257. "Yank, Army's Famous Magazine, Stars 'Sad Sack.'" *Life*. November 15, 1943, pp. 118-124.

"Sally Forth"

7258. Howard, Greg. *Sally Forth*. New York: Fawcett Columbine-Ballantine Books, 1987. 127 pp.; New York: St. Martin's Press, 1982.

7259. Howard, Greg. "Sally Forth." *Cartoonist PROfiles*. June 1992, pp. 42-49.

"Sam's Strip"

7260. Marschall, Rick. "Sam's Strip Returns!" *Nemo*. May 1985, pp. 5-9.

7261. "*Sam's Strip* Returns." *Nemo*. August 1985, pp. 49-50.

7262. Walker, Mort and Jerry Dumas. *Sam's Strip Lives*. Greenwich, Connecticut: Carriage House, n.d. 52 pp.

"Scorchy Smith"

7263. Gebers, Keith. "Strip Search: Scorchy Smith." *Comics Feature*. January-February 1984, pp. 10-12.

7264. Goulart, Ron. "Scorchy Smith." *Comics Scene*. January 1981, pp. 30-33.

7265. Sickles, Noel. *Scorchy Smith*. 2 Vols. Franklin Square, New York: Nostalgia Press, ca. 1977.

"Secret Agent X-9"

7266. Bouyer, Sylvain. "X-9 Est Fou." *Les Cahiers de la Bande Dessinée* (Grenoble). 72, 1986, p. 19.

7267. Charteris, Leslie and Charles Flanders. *Secret Agent X-9*. Long Beach, California: Pacific Comics Club, 1980. 16 pp.

7268. Charteris, Leslie and Alex Raymond. *Secret Agent X-9*. Long Beach, California: Pacific Comics Club, 1980. 16 pp.

7269. De La Croix, Arnaud. "Agent Secret X-9: Rencontre au Sommet." *Les Cahiers de la Bande Dessinée* (Grenoble). 72, 1986, pp. 16-18.

7270. Della Corte, Carlos. "Agent Secret X-9, d'Hier à Aujourd'hui." *Les Héros du Mystère* (Lyon). No. 2, 1967, pp. 25-32.

7271. Ferraro, Ezio. "7 Volti per X-9." *Sgt. Kirk*. No. 10, 1968.

7272. Hammett, Dashiell and Alex Raymond. *Dashiell Hammett's Secret Agent X-9*. IPL Library of Crime Classics. New York: International Polygonics, 1983. 225 pp.

7273. Horn, Maurice. "Agent X-9." *Phénix* (Paris). No. 3, 1967, pp. 25-27.

7274. Schwartz, Ron. "Sleuths in the Strips. Secret Agent X-9." *The Funnie's Paper*. July 1985, pp. 15-20.

7275. Trinchero, Sergio. "Agente Secreto X-9." *Albo dell'Avventuroso*. No. 16, 1963.

7276. Trinchero, Sergio. "Agente Secreto X-9: Autore e Personaggio." *L'Enciclopedia dei Fumetti*. No. 22, 1970.

7277. Trinchero, Sergio. "X-9, Primo Amore di Raymond." *Super Albo* (Fratelli Spada). No. 129, 1965.

7278. Williamson, Al. *Secret Agent X-9*. Dragon Lady Press, No. 6. Toronto, Ontario: Dragon Lady Press, 1987. 70 pp.

"Sherlock Holmes"

7279. Barry, William H. *Sherlock Holmes, a Graphic Novel*. Glendale, California: CB Publications, 1987. 74 pp.

7280. Blackbeard, Bill. *Sherlock Holmes in America*. New York: Harry N. Abrams, 1981. 240 pp.

7281. Wilder, G. "Adventure of Sherlock Holmes' Smarter Brother; Comic Strip Version." *Esquire*. July 1975, pp. 84-87.

"Sherlocko the Monk"

7282. Mager, Gus. *Sherlocko the Monk*. The Hyperion Library of Classic American Comic Strips. Intro. by Bill Blackbeard. Westport, Connecticut: Hyperion, 1977. 272 pp.

7283. "Sherlocko the Monk, Gus Mager." *Cartoonist PROfiles*. June 1978, pp. 80-85.

"Shoe"

7284. "Jeff MacNelly—An Interview with the Creator of 'Shoe.'" *Clockwatch Review*. Spring 1985, pp. 47-57.

7285. MacNelly, Jeff. *The Greatest Shoe on Earth*. New York: Holt, Rinehart and Winston, 1985.

7286. MacNelly, Jeff. *The New Shoe*. New York: Avon, 1981. 123 pp.

7287. MacNelly, Jeff. *One Shoe Fits All*. New York: H. Holt, 1987. 128 pp.

7288. MacNelly, Jeff. *The Other Shoe*. New York: Avon, 1980. 121 pp.

7289. MacNelly, Jeff. *A Shoe for All Seasons*. New York: Holt, Rinehart and Winston, 1983.

7290. MacNelly, Jeff. *The Shoe Must Go On*. New York: Holt, Rinehart and Winston, 1984. 128 pp.

7291. MacNelly, Jeff. *Too Old for Summer Camp and Too Young To Retire*. New York: St. Martin's Press, 1988.

7292. MacNelly, Jeff. *The Very First Shoe Book*. New York: Avon, 1978. 121 pp.

7293. Muro, Mark. "The Man Behind 'Shoe.'" *Boston Globe*. October 11, 1983.

"Short Ribs"

7294. McCoy, Bill. "Satirical 'Short Ribs' Stands Alone." *Cartoonist PROfiles*. June 1977, p. 102.

7295. O'Neal, Frank. *Short Ribs*. Greenwich, Connecticut: Fawcett, 1961.

"Skippy"

7296. Crosby, Percy L. *Skippy*. Intro. by Oliver Herford. New York: Greenberg, 1925. 64 pp.

7297. Crosby, Percy L. *Skippy, from Life*. New York: Henry Holt, 1924.

7298. Crosby, Percy L. *Skippy*. Intro. by Bill Blackbeard. The Hyperion Library of Classic American Comic Strips. Westport, Connecticut: Hyperion, 1977. 147 pp.

7299. Crosby, Percy L. *Skippy Rambles*. New York: G.P. Putnam's Sons., 1932. 179 pp.

7300. Crosby, Percy L. *That Bookie from the 13th Squad*. New York: Harper and Bros., 1918.

7301. "Skippy on a Hobby Horse." *Newsweek*. June 30, 1945, p. 63.

"Smilin' Jack"

7302. Hayes, Ed. "'Smilin' Jack' Still Adventurous." *Near Mint*. April 1981, p. 18.

7303. Mosley, Zack. *De-Icers Galore*. Stuart, Florida: 1980. 53 pp.

7304. Mosley, Zack. *The Hot Rock Glide*. Stuart, Florida: 1979. 104 pp.

7305. Phelps, Donald. "Wild Blue Yonder: Smilin' Jack?" *Nemo*. June 1984, pp. 5-10.

7306. Von Cannon, K. "Smilin' Jack." *Near Mint*. April 1981, p. 19.

"Smitty"

7307. Berndt, Walter. "48 Fun-Filled Years with Smitty." *Cartoonist PROfiles*. Summer 1969, pp. 50-57.

7308. Berndt, Walter. *Smitty*. New York: Cupples and Leon, 1928.

"The Spirit"

7309. Calzavara, Elisa. "The Spirit." *Comics Almanacco*, Salone Internationale dei Comics (Rome). June 1967, p. 90.

7310. Castelli, Alfredo. "Bibliografia di The Spirit." Comics. No. 4, 1966, p. 24.

7311. Castelli, Alfredo. "The Spirit." *Comics*. No. 4, 1966, pp. 18-23.

7312. Eisner, Will. *The Spirit*. Collectors Edition. 1972-1973. 41 fascicles.

7313. Eisner, Will. *The Spirit*. 4 Vols. Richton Park, Illinois: Funny Paper Book Store, 1977-1980.

7314. Eisner, Will. *Spirit Color Album*. 3 Vols. Princeton, Wisconsin: Kitchen Sink Press, 1982?-1983.

7315. Eisner, Will. *Will Eisner Color Treasury*. Text by Cat Yronwode. Princeton, Wisconsin: Kitchen Sink Press, 1981. 109 pp.

7316. Eisner, Will, Jules Feiffer, and Wallace Wood. *Outer Space Spirit, 1952*. Princeton, Wisconsin: Kitchen Sink Press, 1983. 87 pp.

7317. Hegerfors, Sture. "The Spirit." *Expressen* (Stockholm). August 25, 1966.

7318. "The Spirit." *Linus*. No. 43, 1968, p. 60.

7319. Thompson, Maggie. "The Spirit: Blue Suit, Blue Mask, Blue Gloves—and No Socks." *Comics Collector*. Winter 1986, pp. 59-69.

"Star Hawks"

7320. Goulart, Ron. "Star Hawks." *Cartoonist PROfiles*. September 1977, pp. 26-31.

7321. Goulart, "Star Hawks." *Menomonee Falls Gazette*. March 3, 1978, pp. 4-5, 7.

7322. Kane, Gil and Ron Goulart. *Star Hawks*. 4 Vols. Comic-Strip Preserves. El Cajon, California: Blackthorne, 1986-1987.

"Steve Canyon"

7323. Caniff, Milton. *Milton Caniff's Steve Canyon*. New York: Golden Press, 1959.

7324. Caniff, Milton. *Milton Caniff's Steve Canyon*. Princeton, Wisconsin: Kitchen Sink Press, 1983.

7325. Caniff, Milton. *Steve Canyon*. 4 Vols. Concord, California: Comic Art Publishing Co., 1977.

7326. Caniff, Milton. "Steve Canyon." *Cartoonist PROfiles*. December 1985, pp. 23-25.

7327. Caniff, Milton. *Steve Canyon: Operation Convoy*. New York: Grosset and Dunlap, 1959.

7328. Caniff, Milton. *Steve Canyon: Operation Eel Island*. New York: Grosset and Dunlap, 1959.

7329. Caniff, Milton. *Steve Canyon: Operation Foo Ling*. New York: Grosset and Dunlap, 1959.

7330. Caniff, Milton. *Steve Canyon: Operation Snowflower*. New York: Grosset and Dunlap, 1959.

7331. Couperie, P. "Le Mariage de Stève Canyon." *Phénix* (Paris). No. 17, 1970.

7332. De Gaetani, Giovanni. "Steve Canyon." *Comics Club*. No. 1, 1967, pp. 67-69.

7333. Dorf, Shel. "Handling Reality: Steve Canyon Tells His Life Story." *Comics Buyer's Guide*. May 16, 1986, p. 28.

7334. Eco, Umberto. "Le Hura di Steve Canyon." In *Communicazioni di mmassa e Teoria della Cultura di Massa*, edited by Umberto Eco, 2nd Ed., pp. 134-187. Milan: Bompiani, 1965.

7335. Eco, Umberto. "Lektüre von 'Steve Canyon.'" In *Apokalyptiker und Integrierte. Zur Kritischen Kritik der Massenkultur. Aus dem Italienischen übersetzt von Max Looser*, edited by Ders, pp. 116-159. Frankfurt: S. Fischer Verlag GmbH, 1984.

7336. Eco, Umberto. "Lettura di Steve Canyon." *Quaderni di Communicazioni di Massa*. No. 4-5, 1967.

7337. Eco, Umberto. "A Reading of Steve Canyon." *Twentieth Century Studies*. December 1976. Reprinted in Catalogue. *Comic Iconoclasm*. London, 1987.

7338. Franchini, Rolando and Alfredo Castelli. "Bibliografia di Steve Canyon." *Comics Club*. No. 1, 1967, p. 70.

7339. "Not for Kids, Milton Caniff's New Comic: Steve Canyon." *Time*. December 2, 1946, p. 61.

7340. Scotto, U. "Steve Canyon, Un IBM et les Viet-Congs." *Phénix* (Paris). No. 12, 1969.

7341. "Steve Canyon." *Cartoonist PROfiles*. September 1979, pp. 48-51.

7342. "Steve Canyon." *Cartoonist PROfiles*. March 1982, pp.6-9.

7343. "Steve Canyon in Italia." *Comics World*. No. 0, 1966.

7344. "Such Language: London Daily Express Trial Run of Steve Canyon." *Time*. August 25, 1947, p. 54.

7345. Tyson, Patrick. "The Canyon Wave: Steve Started It." *New York Sunday Mirror*. April 6, 1947, p. 12.

"Tank McNamara"

7346. Millar, Jeff and Bill Hinds. *And I'm Tank McNamara with the Norts Spews*. Kansas City, Missouri: Sheed and Ward, 1976. 95 pp.

7347. Millar, Jeff and Bill Hinds. *Another Day, Another $11,247.63*. Kansas City, Missouri: Andrews and McMeel, 1983. 127 pp.

7348. Millar, Jeff and Bill Hinds. *God Intended Blond Boys To Be Quarterbacks*. Kansas City, Missouri: Sheed, Andrews and McMeel, 1977. 78 pp.

7349. Millar, Jeff and Bill Hinds. "Tank McNamara." *Cartoonist PROfiles*. June 1975, pp. 34-38.

"Tarzan"

7350. Bertieri, Claudio. "Tarzan, The First Hero." *Il Lavoro* (Genoa), April 19, 1968.

7351. "Bibliografia di Tarzan." *Comics Club*. No. 1, 1967, p. 22.

7352. "'Blondie,' der Weibliche Tarzan." *Die Welt* (Hamburg). April 24, 1950.

7353. Boujut, Michel. "Tarzan ou Johnny-d'une Jungle à l'Autre." *Construire* (Geneva). February 21, 1968.

7354. Bowman, David. "The Motive Behind Tarzan." *Oparian*. 1: (1965), pp. 14-15.

7355. Bretagne, Christian. "Il y a du Michel-Ange dans Tarzan." *Le Nouveau Candide* (Paris). No. 348, 1967, p. 25.

7356. Burroughs, Edgar R. and Burne Hogarth. *Tarzan, Seigneur de la Jungle*. Paris: 1967.

7357. Castelli, Alfredo. "Cronologia di Tarzan." *Comics Club*. No. 1, 1967, pp. 35-38.

7358. Castelli, Alfredo. "Tarzan Nei Comic Books." *Comics Club*. No. 1, 1967, pp. 33-34.

7359. Cowart, David. "The Tarzan Myth and Jung's Genesis of the Self." *Journal of American Culture*. Summer 1979, pp. 220-230.

7360. Foster, Hal. *Tarzan in Color: Volume 1 (1931-1932)*. New York: NBM Publishing, 1992. 64 pp.

7361. Franchini, Rolando and Alfredo Castelli. "Bibliografia di Tarzan." *Comics Club*. No. 1, 1967, pp. 39-40.

7362. François, Edouard. "Les Humanités de Mongo." *Phénix* (Paris). No. 14, 1970.

7363. Free, Ken. "Tarzan and the Barton Werper." *Oparian*. 1:1 (1965), pp. 40-42.

7364. Fuchs, Wolfgang J. "Zum Beispiel Tarzan." *Jugend-Film-Fernsehen* (Munich). 16:4 (1972), pp. 29-36.

7365. Goldberg, Todd H. "The Tarzan Newspaper Strip." *Comics Buyer's Guide*. August 8, 1986, p. 39.

7366. Göpfert, Peter H. "Tarzan in der Akademie. Berliner Ausstellung Zeigt Comic-Strips." *Westdeutsche Allgemeine Zeitung* (Essen). December 27, 1969, 4.

7367. Gutter, Agnes. "Die Naiven und der Tarzan." Vortrag. Seraphisches Liebeswerk für Jugendliteratur, 1955. (Solothurn).

7368. Harwood, J. and H.W. Starr. "Korak, Son of Tarzan." *The Burroughs Bulletin*. No. 16, 1965, pp. 8-27.

7369. Hegerfors, Sture. "Tarzans Historia." *Kvällsposten* (Malmö). November 10, 1967.

7370. Hogarth, Burne. *The Golden Age of Tarzan, 1939-1942*. New York: Chelsea House; Schonau, Germany: N. Hethke, 1979. 117 pp.

7371. Hogarth, Burne. *Jungle Tales of Tarzan*. Intro. by Walter J. Miller. New York: Watson-Guptill, 1976. 157 pp.

7372. Hogarth, Burne. *Tarzan*. Intro. by Maurice Horn. New York: Watson-Guptill, 1972. 110 pp.

7373. Hogarth, Burne. *Tarzan*. Intro. by Maurice Horn. 2 Vols. Comic-Strip Preserves. El Cajon, California: Blackthorne, 1986.

7374. Holtsmark, Erling. *Tarzan and Tradition: Classical Continuity in a Popular Type*. Iowa City, Iowa: Com IV, Ltd., 1979.

7375. Holtsmark, Erling. *Tarzan and Tradition: Classical Myth in Popular Literature*. Westport, Connecticut: Greenwood Press, 1981.

7376. Horn, Maurice. "Introduction." In Burne Hogarth. *Tarzan: Seigneur de la Jungle*. Paris: Editions Azur, 1967.

7377. Horn, Maurice. "The Many Faces of Tarzan." Introduction to *The Golden Age of Tarzan*. New York: Chelsea House, 1977.

7378. Hornung, Werner. "Tarzan Oder Zokroarrwumm." *Kölner Stadt-Anzeiger* (Cologne). December 5/6, 1970.

7379. Kane, Gil, Archie Goodwin and Mike Grell. *Tarzan*. Comic-Strip Preserves. El Cajon, California: Blackthorne, 1986. 72 pp.

7380. Lacassin, Francis. "Tarzan à Cinquante Ans." *Cinéma 62* (Paris). No. 65, 1962.

7381. Lacassin, Francis. "Tarzan, Mythe Triomphant, Mythe Humilié." *Bizarre* (Paris). No. 29-30, 1963.

7382. Lacassin, Francis. "Tarzan, le Seigneur de la Jungle Bien Que Septuagénaire, Reste Toujours Tres Vert." *V-magazine* (Paris). 1967.

7383. "La Visita del Padre de Tarzan." *Primera Plana* (Buenos Aires). No. 303, 1968.

7384. Laclos, Michel. "Tarzan au Musée." *Paris-Jour*. April 8, 1967.

7385. Manning, Russ. *Tarzan*. Comic-Strip Preserves. El Cajon, California: Blackthorne, 1986. 72 pp.

7386. Maxon, Rex. *Tarzan the Ape Man*. Wytheville, Virginia: House of Greystoke, ca. 1985. 62 pp.

7387. Pendleton, Thomas A. "Tarzan of the Papers." *Journal of Popular Culture*. Spring 1979, pp. 691-701.

7388. Soumille, Gabriel. "Tarzan, l'Homme-Singe." *Educateurs* (Paris). No. 48, 1953, pp. 299-301.

7389. Sueiro, Victor. "El Papá de Tarzan." *Gente* (Buenos Aires). October 17, 1968, pp. 50-52.

7390. "Tarzan en el Di Tella." *Analisis* (Buenos Aires). No. 382,1968, pp. 62-63.

7391. "Tarzan, 75 Years Old and Still Swinging." *Cartoon Art Museum Newsletter*. Fall 1987, p. 3.

7392. "Tarzan, Special Couleur." *Phénix* (Paris). No. 1, 1970.

7393. "Tarzan Verschwindet." *Die Zeit* (Hamburg). No. 3, 1967.

7394. Theroux, Paul. "Tarzan: un Affreux au Pays des Merveilles." *Jeune Afrique* (Paris). January 14, 1968.

7395. Traini, Rinaldo. "Tarzan, il Mito della Libertà." *Sgt. Kirk*. No. 5, 1967, pp. 19-21.

7396. Traini, Rinaldo and Sergio Trinchero. "Tarzan Contro Bond." *Comics Club*. No. 1, 1967; *Hobby* (Rome). No. 2, 1967.

7397. Traini, Rinaldo and Sergio Trinchero. "Tarzan, 1967 Balla lo Shake." *Hobby*. No. 2, 1967.

7398. Trinchero, Sergio. "Tarzan of the Apes." *Comics Club*. No. 1, 1967, pp. 18-19.

7399. Vielle, Henri. "Un Cousin de Tarzan, Drago." *Giff-Wiff* (Paris). No. 18, 1966.

7400. Vigilax. "Le Mythe de Tarzan." *Educateurs* (Paris). No. 28, 1950.

7401. Zanotto, Piero. "Ariva Tarzan." *Nazione Sera* (Florence). July 11, 1967.

7402. Zanotto, Piero. "Il Tout-Paris Legge Tarzan: Lussuoso Album per i Fumetti di Hogarth." *Nazione Sera* (Florence). January 22, 1968.

"The Teenie Weenies"

7403. Cahn, Joseph M. *The Teenie Weenies Book: The Life and Art of William Donahey*. La Jolla, California: The Green Tiger Press, 1986. 128 pp.

7404. Donahey, William. "Fantasy in the Comics: The Teenie Weenies." *Nemo*. April 1984, pp. 31-38.

"Terry and the Pirates"

7405. Bainbridge, J. "Flip Corkin." *Life*. August 9, 1943, pp. 42-44+.

7406. Biamonte, S.G. "Terry and the Pirates, un Fumetto per Faldi." *Sgt Kirk* (Genoa). No. 15, 1968, pp. 72-73.

7407. Caniff, Milton. *Terry and the Pirates*. Chicago, Illinois: Whitman, 1935. 424 pp.

7408. Caniff, Milton. *Terry and the Pirates*. New York: Random House,1946. 115 pp.

7409. Caniff, Milton. *Terry and the Pirates*. New York: Chicago Tribune/New York News Syndicate and Museum of Cartoon Art, 1979. 56 pp.

7410. Caniff, Milton. *Terry and the Pirates*. Long Beach, California: T. Raiola, 1982. 48 pp.

7411. Caniff, Milton. *Terry and the Pirates*. Long Beach, California: T. Raiola, 1983. 48 pp.

7412. Caniff, Milton. *Terry and the Pirates*. Long Beach, California: T. Raiola, 1983. 64 pp.

7413. Caniff, Milton. *Terry and the Pirates*. Long Beach, California: T. Raiola, 1983. 52 pp.

7414. Caniff, Milton. *Terry and the Pirates*. 12 Vols. Flying Buttress Classics Library. New York: Nantier-Beall-Minoustchine, 1984-1987.

7415. Caniff, Milton. *Terry and the Pirates*. Intros. by Milton Caniff and Maurice Horn. The Golden Age of the Comics. New York: Nostalgia Press, 1970. 208 pp.

7416. Caniff, Milton. *Terry and the Pirates, China Journey*. The Golden Age of the Comics. New York: Nostalgia Press, 1977. 108 pp.

7417. Caniff, Milton. *Terry and the Pirates, Enter the Dragon Lady*. New York: Nostalgia Press, 1975. 90 pp.

7418. Caniff, Milton. *Terry and the Pirates Meet Burma*. New York: Nostalgia Press, 1975. 97 pp.

7419. Caniff, Milton. *Terry and the Pirates. The Normandie Affair*. New York: Nostalgia Press, 1977.

7420. Coma, Javier. *Caniff's Terry--The Strips of Our Lives*. Rome: Comic Art, 1987.

7421. Crouch, Bill, jr. "Terry and the Pirates." *Cartoonist PROfiles*. No. 20,1973, pp. 49-53.

7422. De Gaetani, Giovanni and Alfredo. Castelli. "Terry and the Pirates." *Comics Club*. No. 1, 1967, pp. 61-64.

7423. Della Corte, Carlos. "Terry e i Pirati." *Sgt. Kirk*. No. 1, 1967, p. 70.

7424. Franchini, Rolando and Alfredo Castelli. "Bibliografia di Terry." *Comics Club*. No. 1, 1967, p. 65.

7425. Fuchs, Wolfgang J. "Serie: Die Abenteurer: Terry and the Pirates (2)." *Comixene* (Hanover). 7:31 (1980), pp. 56-58.

7426. Goulart, Ron. "Terry and the Pirates." *Comics Scene*. May 1983, pp. 41-45.

7427. Irvine, David J. "I Remember Terry." *Comics Journal*. September 1980, pp. 6-7.

7428. Pérez, Ramón F. "Piratas de Tinta China." *El Wendigo*. No. 45, 1989, pp. 7-9.

7429. Small, Collie. "Strip Teaser in Black and White: M. Caniff's Terry and the Pirates." *Saturday Evening Post*. August 10, 1946, pp. 22-23.

7430. Smolderen, Thierry. "Résurrections d'une Femme-Dragon sur les Rives du Fleuve Jaune." *Les Cahiers de la Bande Dessinée* (Grenoble). 66, 1985, pp. 18-21.

7431. "Terry and the Pirates Invade New York Gallery." *Life*. January 6, 1941, pp. 34+.

7432. "Terry and the Pirates Storm Art Gallery in New Adventure." *Newsweek*. December 16, 1940, p. 48.

7433. Wiley, George T. "*Terry and the Pirates* in 1942: War, the Ultimate Adventure." Paper presented at Popular Culture Association, New Orleans, Louisiana, April 8, 1993.

"Texas History Movies"

7434. Patton, Jack and John Rosenfeld, jr. *Texas History Movies*. Dallas, Texas: P.L. Turner Co., 1943. 217 pp.

7435. Patton, Jack and John Rosenfeld, jr. *Texas History Movies*. Collector's Limited Edition. Dallas, Texas: Pepper Jones Martinez, 1970.

7436. Patton, Jack and John Rosenfeld, jr. *Texas History Movies*. Abridged and Revised. Dallas, Texas: Pepper Jones Martinez, 1985.

7437. Patton, Jack and John Rosenfeld, jr. *Texas History Movies*. Abridged and Revised. Austin, Texas: Texas Historical Association,1986.

"Tim Tyler's Luck"

7438. Coma, Javier. "The Costumes of Tim Tyler, the Disguises of Lyman Young--A Ghost-Hunting Expedition." *Nemo*. October 1985,pp. 27-31.

7439. Horn, Maurice. "Tim Tyler's Luck." *Nostalgia Comics*. No. 1, 1969.

7440. Horn, Maurice. "Tim Tyler's Luck." Introduction to *Cino e Franco*. Milan: Garzanti, 1973.

7441. Young, Lyman. *Tim Tyler's Luck*. Papeete, Tahiti: Pacific Comics Club, 1972. 44 pp.

"Toonerville Trolley"

7442. Clark, Arthur "Ted." "The World's Longest Trolley Ride." *Nemo*. December 1986, pp. 46-65.

7443. Couperie, P. "Toonerville Folks." *Phénix* (Paris). No. 15, 1970.

7444. Fox, Fontaine. *Toonerville Trolley*. New York: Charles Scribner's Sons, 1972. 184 pp.

"Tumbleweeds"

7445. Pinella, P. "Rolling Along with Tumbleweeds; T.K. Ryan." *Saturday Evening Post*. November 1979, pp. 70-72.

7446. "Tumbleweeds by T.K. Ryan." *Cartoonist PROfiles*. March 1978, pp. 36-39.

"Wash Tubbs"

7447. Crane, Roy. *Wash Tubbs*. New York: Luna Press, 1974. 304 pp.

7448. Crane, Roy. *Wash Tubbs*. Dragon Lady Press, No. 3. Toronto, Ontario: Dragon Lady Press, 1986. 62 pp.

7449. Crane, Roy. *Wash Tubbs and Captain Easy*. Intro. by Bill Blackbeard. Flying Buttress Classics Library. New York: Nantier-Beall-Minoustchine, 1987-.

7450. Crane, Roy. *Wash Tubbs Featuring Captain Easy*. Dragon Lady Press, No. 7. Toronto, Ontario: Dragon Lady Press, 1987, 55 pp.

7451. Stack, Frank. "Easy Reader." *Comics Journal*. April 1990, pp. 47-52.

"The Yellow Kid"

7452. Campbell, Gordon. "The Yellow Kid." *Cartoonist PROfiles*. September 1981, pp. 44-49.

7453. Del Buono, Oreste. "Il Monstruoso Yellow Kid." *Linus*. 5:51 (1969), pp. 1-10.

7454. Harvey, R.C. "The Yellow Kid and Commercial Success." *Comics Journal*. December 1982, p. 21.

7455. Harvey, Steve. "Kid Granddaddy of Comics and Yellow Journalism. *Los Angeles Times*. March 18, 1973, pt. VI, p. 5.

"Ziggy"

7456. Hurd, Jud. "Ziggy." *Cartoonist PROfiles*. June 1988, pp. 10-14.

7457. Wilson, Tom. *Encore! Encore!* Intro. by Cathy Guisewite. Kansas City, Missouri: Andrews and McMeel, 1979. 224 pp.

7458. Wilson, Tom. *Ziggy's Ins and Outs*. New York: New American Library, 1985.

7459. Wilson, Tom. *Ziggy's Sunday Funnies*. Kansas City, Missouri: Andrews and McMeel, 1981. 56 pp.

7460. Wilson, Tom. *The Ziggy Treasury*. Kansas City, Missouri: Andrews and McMeel, 1977. 224 pp.

"Zippy the Pinhead"

7461. Griffith, Bill. *King Pin*. New York: E.P. Dutton, 1987. 144 pp.

7462. Griffith, Bill. *Zippy, Nation of Pinheads*. Berkeley, California: And/Or Press, 1982. 96 pp.

7463. Griffith, Bill. *Zippy, Pindemonium*. San Francisco, California: Last Gasp, 1986. 96 pp.

7464. Griffith, Bill. *Zippy, Pointed Behavior*. San Francisco, California: Last Gasp, 1984. 96 pp.

7465. Griffith, Bill. *Zippy Stories*. Berkeley, California: And/Or Press, 1981. 158 pp.

CARTOONISTS

7466. Ahern, Jodie and Martin Keller. "See You in the Funnies." *Minnesota Monthly*. June 1992, pp. 42-44, 70-71, 73.

7467. "Alberto Dorne 1904-1965." *Newsletter*. January 1966, pp. 9-12.

7468. "Artemus Cole." *Cartoonist PROfiles*. September 1986, pp. 23-25.

7469. Barsotti, Charles. "P.J. McFey." *Cartoonist PROfiles*. December 1985, pp.12-15.

7470. Beiswinger, George L. "Mal Has Wide Range of Cartoon Features." *Editor and Publisher*. April 21, 1990. pp. 132+.

7471. Beiswinger, George L. "What Ex-Creators Are Doing These Days." *Editor and Publisher*. December 17, 1988, pp. 34-36.

7472. Berchtold, William E. "Men of Comics." *New Outlook*. April 1935, pp. 34-40; May 1935, pp. 43-47.

7473. Bernard, Jami. "Short Stories." *Comics Scene*. December 1990, pp. 41-44, 66.

7474. Bertieri, Claudio. "Rudolph Dirks and Harold Gray." *Il Lavoro* (Genoa). June 1, 1968.

7475. Bester, Alfred. "King of the Comics." *Holiday*. June 1958.

7476. "Best Seller Showcase, Elliott Caplin." *Cartoonist PROfiles*. March 1978, pp. 60-63.

7477. "Betty Boop and Felix Meet the Walker Brothers." *Cartoonist PROfiles*. December 1984, pp. 8-13.

7478. "Bill Overgard." *Cartoonist PROfiles*. March 1983, pp. 53-59.

7479. "Bill Schorr Has Created a New Comic Strip for LATS." *Notebook*. Spring 1990. p. 11.

7480. "Bill Yates." *Cartoonist PROfiles*. December 1990, pp. 44-47.

7481. "Biography by John Roman." *Cartoonist PROfiles*. September 1987, pp. 22-27.

7482. Black, Ed. "Roger Bollen." *Cartoonist PROfiles*. No. 32, 1976, pp. 58-65.

7483. Blackbeard, Bill. "The Career of a Pioneer." *Nemo*. October 1986, pp. 59-64.

7484. Blosser, Merrill. "Blosser." *Cartoonist PROfiles*. December 1975, pp. 57-63.

7485. Bowman, David. "Whatever Happened to Droodles? Whatever Happened to Roger Price?" *Journal of Popular Culture*. 9:1 (1975), pp. 20-25.

7486. Bradfield, Roger. "Dooley's World." *Cartoonist PROfiles*. June 1975, pp. 10-15.

7487. Brandel, Max. "Namelies." *Cartoonist PROfiles*. No. 10, 1971, pp. 48-51.

7488. "Brandon Walsh." *Dibujantes* (Buenos Aires). No. 17, 1955, p. 29.

7489. Brown, Lloyd W. "Comic-Strip Heroes: Leroi Jones and the Myth of American Innocence." *Journal of Popular Culture*. Fall 1969, pp. 191-204.

7490. Browne, Dik. "The Night We Took in Shing-Dang-Dong-Sung-Dong-Ku." *The Cartoonist*. April 24, 1967.

7491. "Bud Sagendorf." *The Funnie's Paper*. May 1983, p. 4.

7492. Busino, Orlando. "Roughing It." *Cartoonist PROfiles*. 1:1 (1969), pp. 59-61.

7493. "Capsules (Guy Vasilovich)." *CAPS Newsletter*. March 1991, pp. 17-20.

7494. "Cartoonist Former H.H.S. Student." *The Funnie's Paper*. September 1983, p. 1.

7495. "Cartoonists Honor Boyd Lewis As Ace." *Newsletter*. May 1965, p. 15.

7496. "Cartoons by Kaz." *Cartoonist PROfiles*. June 1979, pp. 56-59.

7497. Cohen, Mark J. "Jim Toomey and Sherman's Lagoon." *Cartoonist PROfiles*. June 1992, pp. 86-91.

7498. "Comic Strips: Brant Parker Begins New Strip." *Comics Journal*. March 1980, p. 23.

7499. "Congressional Record (Jack Rosen)." *Cartoonist PROfiles*. No. 16, 1972, pp. 22-27.

7500. Couperie, P. "Clayton Knight." *Phénix* (Paris). No. 12, 1969.

7501. Couperie, Pierre. "Martin Branner, Jay Irving, H. Gray." *Phénix*. No. 16, 1970.

7502. Crane, Brian. "How I Got Pickled." *Cartoonist PROfiles*. September 1992, pp. 66-71.

7503. "Dave Miller." *Cartoonist PROfiles.* March 1993, pp. 38-43.

7504. De Fuccio, Jerry. "The Art of Bob Clarke--From Robert L. Ripley to Alfred E. Neuman." *Cartoonist PROfiles.* December 1986, pp. 70-77.

7505. De Fuccio, Jerry. "Guy Stuff's Jim Ryan." *Cartoonist PROfiles.* June 1992, pp. 74-79.

7506. De Fuccio, Jerry. "Ralph Fuller." *Cartoonist PROfiles.* September 1990. pp.30-39.

7507. De Fuccio, Jerry. "Tiger by Bud Blake." *Cartoonist PROfiles.* March 1976, pp. 13-23.

7508. "Dick Dugan's Talented Brush Reflects His Own Glory Days." *The Cartoonist.* August 1967, p. 39.

7509. Dikas, Mike. "Strictly Classified." *Cartoonist PROfiles.* September 1988, pp. 54-59.

7510. Doty, Roy. "Doty Has Done It Again." *Cartoonist PROfiles.* 1:1 (1969), pp. 26-31.

7511. Douglas, George H. "Howard R. Garis and the World of Uncle Wiggily." *Journal of Popular Culture.* Winter 1974, pp. 503-512.

7512. Drake, Bob. "Kit 'N' Carlyle." *Cartoonist PROfiles.* March 1981, pp. 50-53.

7513. Dunn, Bob. "Said and Dunn." *Cartoonist PROfiles.* December 1974, p. 57; March 1975, pp. 64-65; June 1979, pp. 52-55; March 1981, pp. 54-55.

7514. Dunn, Robert. "Vernon Creene." *The Cartoonist.* September 1965, p. 9.

7515. "Eric Gurney." *Cartoonist PROfiles.* March 1976, pp. 57-66.

7516. Erwin, Ray. "Syndicates. Phyllis Diller Begins Her Own Comic Strip." *Editor and Publisher.* 101:1 (1968), p. 37.

7517. Fastner, Steve. "Bill Fugate." *Minnesota Cartoonist.* April 15, 1991, p. 3.

7518. Fett, George. "Engineer, Crow Hunter, Cartoonist." *Cartoonist PROfiles.* 1:2 (1969), pp. 50-53.

7519. Fox, Fontaine. *Cartoons.* New York: Harper and Bros., n.d.

7520. "Four Kings of Comics." *Cartoonist PROfiles.* September 1990, pp. 80-82.

7521. "Frank Bellamy." *Society of Strip Illustration Newsletter.* January 1988, pp. 6-7.

7522. "Frank Johnson." *Cartoonist PROfiles*. June 1984, pp. 18-23.

7523. "Fran Matera: Cartoonist, Illustrator." *Cartoonist PROfiles*. December 1982, pp. 32-39.

7524. Fries, Sandy. "'Super' Duper Cartoonist Bil Kresse." *Cartoonist PROfiles*. No. 13, 1972, pp. 34-41.

7525. Goldstein, Kalman. "Al Capp and Walt Kelly: Pioneers of Political and Social Satire in the Comics." *Journal of Popular Culture*. Spring 1992, pp. 81-95.

7526. Goulart, Ron. "George Storm: Pioneer of the Adventure Strip." *Nemo*. December 1983, pp. 57-62.

7527. Goulart, Ron. "The Many Careers of Tom McNamara." *Comic Art*. October 1964, pp. 12-14.

7528. Goulart, Ron. "Strip Search." *Comics Feature*. October 1986, pp. 40-43.

7529. Greene, Daniel. "The Titans of the Funnies. How the Artists View Their Work." *National Observer*. September 12, 1966, p. 24.

7530. Habblitz, Harry. "Jesse Marsh: Post Impressionist of the Comic Page." *Fantasy Illustrated*. No. 7, 1967, p. 47.

7531. "Hall of Fame--Milton Caniff and Chester Gould." *Cartoonist PROfiles*. June 1982, pp. 28-29.

7532. Hampton, Ed. "Cartooning's Child Prodigy—Randy Glasbergen." *Breaking In*. January 1993, pp. 7-16.

7533. Hampton, Ed. "Interview with...Johnny Sajem." *Breaking In*. January 1993, pp. 31-39.

7534. Hanscom, Sally. "Color Them Suburban." *The World of Comic Art*. Winter 1966/1967, pp. 42-47. (Dik Browne, Mort Walker).

7535. Harvey, R.C. "Crane and Caniff: Homages and Tributes." *Comics Journal*. March 1988, pp. 117-122.

7536. "Henry Boltinoff." *Cartoonist PROfiles*. December 1980, pp. 95-98.

7537. Hoffman, Pete. "Life After Jeff Cobb." *Cartoonist PROfiles*. September 1983, pp. 58-63.

7538. "Howard Munce: A Contented Newspaper Artist." *Cartoonist PROfiles*. June 1992, pp. 30-35.

7539. Hurd, Jud. "Harry Devlin: A Retrospective." *Cartoonist PROfiles*. September 1991, pp. 10-17.

7540. Hurd, Jud. "Henny Youngman." *Cartoonist PROfiles*. No. 32, 1976, pp. 90-91.

7541. Hurd, Jud. "Robert Mankoff." *Cartoonist PROfiles*. June 1987, pp. 48-53.

7542. "The Incomparable Dorgan—Tad." *Nemo*. July 1985, pp. 37-55.

7543. Inge, M. Thomas. "Studying the Geniuses of Comic Strips." *Chronicle of Higher Education*. September 13, 1976, p. 16.

7544. "Inside Woody Allen (Stu Hample)." *Cartoonist PROfiles*. June 1978, pp. 22-26.

7545. "An Interview with Leonard Starr." *Comics Feature*. February 1981, pp. 19-34.

7546. "Jerry Marcus, Heart Specialist, Criminal Lawyer, Cartoonist." *Cartoonist PROfiles*. 1:1 (1969), pp. 62-64.

7547. Jesuele, Kim. "Meet Betty." *Cartoonist PROfiles*. June 1992, pp. 24-29. (Gerry Rasmussen).

7548. "John Gallagher." *Cartoonist PROfiles*. December 1971, pp. 8-17.

7549. "John Lane and 'Ben Swift.'" *Cartoonist PROfiles*. June 1981, pp. 28-31.

7550. "John Locher." *Cartoonist PROfiles*. September 1986, p. 37.

7551. Johnson, Mark. "Frank King's Make-Believe World. The Pre-Gasoline Era." *Nemo*. June 1985, pp. 25-33.

7552. Kelly, John. "Mark Newgarden." *Comics Journal*. August 1993, pp. 74-80, 82-83, 85, 87-89, 91.

7553. Kinoshita, L. "Matt Groening (Life in Hell Strip)." *Saturday Review*. March/April 1985, pp.50-53.

7554. Klein, I. "Memories of Milt Gross." *Cartoonist PROfiles*. June 1972, pp. 54-62.

7555. Klein, I. "Vacationing for Fun and Gags." *Cartoonist PROfiles*. December 1980, pp. 62-67.

7556. Kreffel and Steadham. "The Care and Treatment of Caniff-cappschulzwalkerbrowneparkerhartomania." *Near Mint*. No. 1, 1980, pp. 1-3.

7557. Lansky, Bernie. "Lansky's Look: Bernie Lansky, Creator of Lansky's Look." *Cartoonist PROfiles*. December 1974, pp. 63-67.

7558. Levy, D.S. "A Hooligan Who Wields a Pen." *Time*. December 25, 1989, pp. 10+.

7559. Lewis, Jerry D. "The Man Who's Serious about the Funnies." *The Funnie's Paper*. April 1984, pp. 14-16; *Ford Times*. January 1984.

7560. "Life of James J. Walker." *Cartoonist PROfiles*. No. 6, 1970, p. 10.

7561. "Locher." *Cartoonist PROfiles*. December 1984, pp. 69-74.

7562. Louthan, John. "Briefcase." *Cartoonist PROfiles*. March 1991, pp. 28-32.

7563. Lowe, Channing. "Get the Lowe Down." *Cartoonist PROfiles*. June 1986, pp. 74-78.

7564. Lynde, Sidne. "The Creator of J.P. Doodles, Barry McWilliams." *Cartoonist PROfiles*. December 1986, pp. 84-89.

7565. Lynde, Stan. "On the Range: The Western Art of Fred Harman (1934-1938)." *Nemo*. August 1983, pp. 53-59.

7566. "McCall of the Wild. *Cartoonist PROfiles*. December 1987, pp. 40-45.

7567. McGreal, Dorothy. "More Irons in the Fire Than a Blacksmith." *The World of Comic Art*. 2:4 (1967), pp. 44-55.

7568. Marschall, Richard. *America's Great Comic-Strip Artists*. New York: Abbeville, 1989. 295 pp.

7569. Marschall, Richard. "Comic Masters." *Horizon*. July 1980, pp. 42-51.

7570. Marschall, Richard. "The Man Who Loved Comics." *Nemo*. October 1986, p. 5.

7571. Marschall, Richard. "The Master." *Nemo*. August 1984, pp. 5-6.

7572. Marschall, Richard. "Snappy Art, Sappy Copy. The Comic Strip Ads of Milton Caniff and Noel Sickles." *Nemo*. April 1987, pp. 36-46.

7573. "Meet Conrad and Bill Schorr." *The Funnie's Paper*. April 1983, pp. 1-2.

7574. "Men of Comics." *New Outlook*. April 1935, pp. 34-40; May 1935, pp. 43-47, 64.

7575. "Mice to Men." *Cartoonist PROfiles*. March 1982, pp. 58-61.

7576. Miller, Bob. "Bob Curtis and 'Mother Goose and Grimm': The Life of a Line Producer." *Comic Buyer's Guide*. November 27, 1992, pp. 94, 98, 100.

7577. "Most Neglected Genius, Charles William Kahles." *Cartoonist PROfiles*. No. 31, 1976, pp. 22-29.

7578. Munce, Howard. "Bert Dodson." *Cartoonist PROfiles*. March 1993, pp. 68-73.

7579. Nash, P. "America's Comic Draughtsmen." *Living Age*. November 1931, pp. 227-278.

7580. Nelson, Roy P. "The Day a Cartoonist Fought Kid McCoy." *The World of Comic Art*. 1:2 (1966), pp. 18-19.

7581. Oakley, Peter. "Frank Shiers Jr., Self-Syndicated, Self-Taught." *Penstuff*. February 1991, pp. 1, 3.

7582. Oakley, Peter. "Steve Willis Anticipates the Demise of Paper." *Penstuff*. March 1991, pp. 1, 6.

7583. O'Neill, Pat. "John Celardo." *Comics Interview*. No. 80, 1990, pp. 26-31.

7584. Perrin, Steve. "He Who Walked the Night." *Comic Art*. No. 5, 1964, pp. 28-30.

7585. "Phil Love." *Cartoonist PROfiles*. March 1978, pp. 64-66.

7586. "Prize Winning Cartoon (Morrie Brickman)." *Cartoonist PROfiles*. No. 18, 1973, p. 55.

7587. Quentmeyer, Dick. "Aerospace Engineer...Cartoonist." *Cartoonist PROfiles*. March 1992, pp. 31-33.

7588. "Questionnaire for a Comic-Strip Artist." *New York Evening Post*. December 4, 1922.

7589. Reinert, Rick. "No Lessons, Just the Right Father." *Newsletter*. June 1966, p. 41.

7590. "The 'Reuben.'" *Cartoonist PROfiles*. June 1982, p. 10.

7591. Roberts, Johnnie L. "Nicholas Launches New Cartoon Career After Time Warner." *Wall Street Journal*. June 15, 1992, p. B-6.

7592. Roche, Art. "The Big Break." *Breaking In*. December 1992, pp. 29-38.

7593. Roskin, R. Terrance. "Cavelli Makes Distractions Pay." *Cartoonist PROfiles*. June 1977, p. 85.

7594. Rouson, John. "He Does Four Daily Strips!" *Cartoonist PROfiles*. No. 6, 1970, pp. 28-34.

7595. Ruth, Gerry and Jim. "Pineapple Euphoria: Hawaiian Cartoonists." *Cartoonist PROfiles*. December 1977, pp. 53-55.

7596. Ruth, Jim and Gerry. "Her Son the Cartoonist!" *Cartoonist PROfiles*. June 1972, pp. 44-53.

7597. "Serie: Die Pioniere der Comic-Strips: (6) Clarence Gray." *Comixene* (Hanover). 7:30, pp. 58-59.

7598. Sherburne, E.C. "Serious Business, the Funnies; Well-Known Cartoonists." *Christian Science Monitor Magazine*. May 2, 1942, pp. 4+.

7599. Sheridan, Martin. *Comics and Their Creators*. New York: Hale, 1944 and 1971.

7600. Sherry, Richard. "The Electric Cartoonist." *Cartoonist PROfiles*. June 1981, pp. 32-33.

7601. "A Sketch in Time Is Gold Mine for Freelance Cartoonist, 21." *Cartoonist PROfiles*. December 1978, pp. 36-40. (Randy Glasbergen).

7602. Smith, George and Virginia. "The Smith Family." *Cartoonist PROfiles*. June 1987, pp. 44-47.

7603. "The Stainless Texan." *Time*. January 3, 1955, pp. 32-33.

7604. "Stan Stamaty." *Cartoonist PROfiles*. September 1978, pp. 46-53.

7605. "Steve Greenberg." *Cartoonist PROfiles*. September 1986, pp. 30-36.

7606. Stoutsenberger, Leo. "Bud Blake and Tiger." *Cartoonist PROfiles*. September 1991, pp. 26-31.

7607. Stoutsenberger, Leo. "Memoirs of a Journeyman Cartoonist." *Cartoonist PROfiles*. March 1984, pp. 32-37.

7608. Strzyz, Klaus. "Interview mit Steven Jehorek." *Comic Forum* (Vienna). 25/26, 1984, pp. 40-46.

7609. Szorady, Mark. "Riding the Bench and Drawing Comics." *Cartoonist PROfiles*. March 1992, pp. 34-35.

7610. "A Talk with Greg Howard." *Minnesota Monthly*. June 1992, pp. 45, 73-75.

7611. Thompson, Steve. "An Interview with Peter Kelly." *Fort Mudge Most*. September 1992, pp. 7-12.

7612. Thompson, Thomas. "A Place in the Sun All Her Own." *Life*. April 1968, pp. 66-70.

7613. "Three Men on a Cartoon, Ching Chow." *Newsweek*. February 10, 1947, p. 58.

7614. "Tom McCormick." *Cartoonist PROfiles*. June 1985, pp. 68-69; September 1985, pp. 66-69.

7615. "Tony Auth and Daniel Pinkwater Launch Daily Comic Strip." *Comics Journal*. November 1989, p. 21.

7616. Toole, Fred. "... One of the World's Best Selling Authors..." *The Cartoonist*. February 1967, pp. 11-13.

7617. Trinchero, Sergio. "Hanno Detto de... l'Uomo Mascherato: 'Coulton Waugh.'" *L'Uomo Mascherato* (Milan). No. 65, 1964.

7618. "Verbena—What Becomes a Legend?" *Cartoonist PROfiles*. June 1981, pp. 10-16.

7619. Vest, Jake. "That's Jake." *Cartoonist PROfiles*. March 1990, pp. 60-65.

7620. Vojtko, Bob. "Working Class Cartoonist." *Cartoonist PROfiles*. March 1992, pp. 28-30.

7621. Wagner, Charles A. "Dave Gerard: Crawfordsville's Citizen Smith." *Cartoonist PROfiles*. June 1980, pp. 72-75.

7622. Walker, Mort. "Let's Get Down to Grawlixes." *The Cartoonist*. January 1968, pp. 23-25.

7623. "Walter Gibson." *Orlandocon '77*. 1977, p. 5.

7624. "War Correspondent, Syndicate President, Oil Painter, Cartoonist!" *Cartoonist PROfiles*. September 1981, pp. 24-29.

7625. Warren, Julianne. "Result of a Cartoonist Becoming Immersed in His Work!" *Cartoonist PROfiles*. No. 10, 1971, pp. 14-21.

7626. "Where Are They Now?" *Newsweek*. April 25, 1966.

7627. "Where Are They Now? Creators of Buck Rogers and Flash Gordon." *Newsweek*. August 4, 1969, p. 8.

7628. White, Leo. "Mr. Versatility." *Cartoonist PROfiles*. June 1975, pp. 53-55.

7629. "Whitney Darrow, jr." *Cartoonist PROfiles*. No. 7, 1970, pp. 52-61.

7630. Wolf, S.C.J. "Tribute to Comic Strip Artists." *Literary Digest*. April 7, 1934, p. 51.

7631. Yeo, Henry. *Warren Tufts Retrospective*. Long Beach, California: Western Wind, 1980. 158 pp.

Anderson, Brad

7632. "His Work Is Dog-Gone Funny! Marmaduke." *National Geographic World*. May 1979, pp. 28-31.

7633. "Marmaduke by Brad Anderson." *Cartoonist PROfiles*. December 1982, pp. 18-25.

Anderson Carl

7634. McGreal, Dorothy. "Silence Is Golden: Carl Anderson 1865-1948." *The World of Comic Art*. Winter 1966/1967, pp. 10-12.

7635. McGreal, Dorothy. "Silence Is Golden—Part II: The Family at 'Henry's House.'" *The World of Comic Art*. Winter 1966/1967, pp. 12-17.

7636. Rath, Jay. "Silents, Please! The Unspeakable Greatness of Carl Anderson's Henry." *Nemo*. September 1987, pp. 42-52.

Andriola, Alfred

7637. Andriola, Alfred. "Don't Sit on Your Big Fat Complacency!" New York: Newspaper Comics Council, March 15, 1967.

7638. Andriola, Alfred. "The Most for Your Money." *The Cartoonist*. Autumn 1957, pp. 11-12, 36, 38.

7639. Andriola, Alfred. "Pas Question de Faire Ça." *Giff-Wiff*. No. 20, 1966, p. 29.

7640. Andriola, Alfred. "A Project Chairman Makes a Report." *Newsletter*. 1965.

7641. Andriola, Alfred. "Story Strip History." *Cartoonist PROfiles*. No. 14, 1972, pp. 32-42; No. 15, 1972, pp. 45-54.

7642. François, Edouard. "Alfred Andriola." *Mongo*. No. 0, 1966; *Phénix*. No. 21, 1971.

7643. Goulart, Ron. "Andriola and the Commandos." *Nemo*. June 1983, pp. 62-69.

Armstrong, Roger

7644. Fisher, Raymond and John Barnard. "Roger Armstrong: Triple Threat Artist." *The World of Comic Art*. Winter 1966/1967, pp. 22-27.

7645. Harvey, R.C. "Comics by Roger Armstrong." *Cartoonist PROfiles*. June 1991, pp. 50-59.

7646. "Roger Armstrong." *Comics Interview*. No. 45, 1987, pp. 34-47.

Armstrong, Tom

7647. Craft, Jerry. "Marvin: Famous 'Toon Is Actually a High School Student." *Cartoonist PROfiles*. September 1992, pp. 10-11.

7648. McAllister, Deborah. "Marvin's Father." *Express*. February 1985, pp. 27-35.

7649. "Marvin by Tom Armstrong." *Cartoonist PROfiles*. September 1987, pp. 48-55.

Arriola, Gus

7650. Coker, Paul, jr. "Horrifying Cliches Cartoonist Interviews Gus Arriola." *Cartoonist PROfiles*. No. 16, 1972, pp. 32-41.

7651. Patterson, Russell. "A Tribute to Gus...." *The Cartoonist*. February 1967, pp. 25-28.

Barks, Carl

7652. Blum, Geoffrey. "A Letter from the Duck Man." *Nemo*. June 1984, pp. 20-21.

7653. Kirby, Paul. "Flights of Fancy: Escapism and the Stories of Carl Barks." *The Barks Collector*. October 1984, pp. 2-10.

7654. Lendacky, Andrew. "The Barks 'Hookey' Stories." *The Barks Collector*. July 1981, pp. 5-10.

7655. Wagner, Dave. "Donald Duck: An Interview." *Radical America*. 7:1 (1973), pp. 1-19.

Basset, Brian

7656. "Brian Basset." *Cartoonist PROfiles*. March 1985, pp. 18-25.

7657. Harvey, R.C. "Brian Basset's Juggling Act." *Cartoonist PROfiles*. March 1992, pp. 14-21.

Batiuk, Tom

7658. Batiuk, Tom. "How I Get My Ideas... and Why It Probably Won't Work for You." *Cartoonist PROfiles*. June 1989, pp. 50-53.

7659. "Batiuk Creates New Strip; Raps Ownership Practices." *Editor and Publisher*. June 27, 1987, p. 37.

7660. "Crankshaft." *Cartoonist PROfiles*. September 1987, pp. 40-45.

7661. "John Darling by Tom Batiuk and Tom Armstrong." *Cartoonist PROfiles*. March 1980, pp. 8-13.

7662. Myers, Greg W. "'I Was Drawing All the Time'—An Interview with Funky Winkerbean Creator Tom Batiuk." *Comics Collector*. Summer 1985, pp. 52-61.

Berry, Jim

7663. "Benjy by Jim Berry and Bill Yates." *Cartoonist PROfiles*. No. 20, 1973, pp. 14-20.

7664. Berry, Jim. "Berry's Day with a Relaxed LBJ." *Newsletter*. October 1965, pp. 10-11.

7665. Berry, Jim. *Berry's World*. New York: Four Winds, 1967.

7666. Berry, Jim. "Berry's World." *Cartoonist PROfiles*. No. 7, 1970, pp. 42-51.

7667. Fouse, Marnie. "Berry's World." *The World of Comic Art*. Summer 1967, pp. 40-47.

7668. Gilles, D.B. "Berry's World." *Cartoonist PROfiles*. September 1978, pp. 72-75.

7669. "Jim Berry in Russia." *Cartoonist PROfiles*. March 1989, pp. 24-29.

7670. Wood, Tim. "Jim Berry—Cartoonist with a Conscience." *Cartoonist PROfiles*. December 1984, pp. 36-41.

Blaisdell, Philip

7671. Blaisdell, Philip T. "Background 'on' and 'by' Blaisdell." *Newsletter*. June 1966, pp. 10-14.

7672. "Little Orphan Annie by Philip Blaisdell." *Cartoonist PROfiles*. No. 7, 1970, pp. 26-34.

Boughner, Howard

7673. "Howard Boughner." *Cartoonist PROfiles*. June 1977, pp. 87-91.

7674. "Howard Boughner." *Cartoonist PROfiles*. March 1981, pp. 33-35.

7675. Simons, Jeannie. "Mrs. Bee and Mrs. Boughner, Cartoon Has Real Life Counter Part." *The Cartoonist*. August 1967, p. 30.

Boynansky, Bill

7676. Boynansky, Bill. "From 'Roughs' to Riches." *The World of Comic Art*. June 1966, pp. 26-29.

7677. "Meet Artist-Author Bill Boynansky." *The World of Comic Art*. 1:1 (1966), p. 16.

Breathed, Berke

7678. "Berke Breathed Ends *Bloom County*." *Comics Journal*. July 1989, pp. 24-25.

7679. Breathed, Berke. "The Pariah Speaks." *Comics Journal*. August 1988, pp. 104-107.

7680. Buchalter, G. "Cartoonist Berke Breathed Feathers His Nest by Populating Bloom County with Rare Birds." *People's Weekly*. August 6, 1984, pp. 93-94+.

7681. Cashwell, Peter. "Every Breathed You Take: A Waste of Trees." *Comics Journal*. December 1987, p. 129.

7682. Jannot, Mark. "Can Breathed Be Taken Seriously?" *Comics Journal*. October 1988, pp. 74-106.

7683. "Outlandish Breathed Interview." *Penstuff*. February 1990, p. 7.

7684. Sayers, John. "An Interview with Bloom County's Berke Breathed." *Comics Collector*. Winter 1984, pp. 48-49, 52-53, 55-56.

7685. Wepman, Dennis. "Berke Breathed Moves On." *WittyWorld*. Summer/Autumn 1989, p. 29.

Browne, Chris

7686. Browne, Chris. "Son of Hägar." *Canadian Cartoonist*. 6/7, 1990, pp. 3-4.

7687. Crouch, Bill, jr. "Chris Browne." *Cartoonist PROfiles*. December 1977, pp. 87-91.

7688. Lent, John A. "God Willing, I Will Avoid the Venus Flytrap of Hackdom—Chris Browne." *WittyWorld*. Winter 1993, pp. 30-31, 33-35.

Browne, Dik

7689. "Dik Browne." *Cartoonist PROfiles*. September 1989, pp. 43-45.

7690. "Dik Browne Død, 71 År." *Serieskaberen*. December 1989, p. 10.

7691. "Dik Browne: 1917-1989." *National Cartoonists Society Newsletter*. July 1989, p. 6.

7692. Huisking, Charlie. "The Joan Browne Cartoon Classic." *Cartoonist PROfiles*. June 1988, pp. 72-74.

7693. Lent, John A. "Creator of 'Hägar the Horrible' Dik Browne Succumbs to Cancer." *WittyWorld*. Summer/Autumn 1989, p. 11.

7694. Marschall, Rick. "Browne the Magnificent: On Comics, Commentary, and Contentment." *Nemo*. June 1983, pp. 28-42.

7695. Meyer, Brian. "An Overview of Hägar the Horrible: 'We Have Met the Barbarians and They Are Us.'" *Comics Feature*. September-October 1981, pp. 91-93.

Burroughs, Edgar R.

7696. Lefevre, Gaston. "Edgar Rice Burroughs et Son Oeuvre." *Rantanplan* (Brussels). No. 3, 1966, pp. 2-3; No. 4, 1966/1967, pp. 11-13.

7697. Lupoff, Richard A. *Edgar Rice Burroughs: Master of Adventure*. 2nd Ed. New York: Ace Books, 1968; Canaveral Press, 1965. 294 pp.

7698. McGreal, Dorothy. "The Burroughs No One Knows." *The World of Comic Art*. Fall 1966, pp. 12-15.

7699. McGreal, Dorothy. "Il Burroughs Sconosciuto." *Comics Club*. No. 1, 1967, pp. 19-20.

7700. Proges, Irwin. *Edgar Rice Burroughs: The Man Who Created Tarzan*. Provo, Utah: Brigham Young University Press, 1975.

Bushmiller, Ernie

7701. Barnette, Mark. "'What Bushmiller Seems To Be Saying Here....'" *Comics Journal*. June 1991, pp. 52-54.

7702. Bushmiller, Ernie. "Nancy and Me." *Collier's*. September 18, 1948, p. 23.

7703. Harvey, R.C. "Bushmiller's Awe-full Awful and Other Vintage Mixes." *Comics Journal*. November 1989, pp. 111-115.

7704. Marschall, Rick. "*Nancy* Creator Ernie Bushmiller Dead at 76." *Comics Journal*. October 1982, p. 22.

7705. Walker, Brian. "'Dumb It Down': The Comic-Strip Craftsmanship and Common Denominators of Ernie Bushmiller." *Nemo*. April 1989, pp. 30-43.

Caniff, Milton

7706. Adams, John P. *Milton Caniff, Rembrandt of the Comic Strip*. New York: David McKay, 1946.

7707. Adams, John Paul and Richard Marschall. *Milton Caniff, Rembrandt of the Comic Strip*. Endicott, New York: Flying Buttress, 1981. 62 pp.

7708. Andriola, Alfred. "How Milton Caniff Became a Character in 'Kerry Drake.'" *Cartoonist PROfiles*. March 1983, pp. 72-77.

7709. "The Art of Milton Caniff." *Pageant*. May 1953.

7710. Bainbridge, John. "Significant Sig and the Funnies; Milton Caniff." *New Yorker*. January 8, 1944, pp. 25-30.

7711. Balthazar, Edward J. "Air Force Awards Multiple Honors to Milton Caniff." *Magazine of Sigma Chi*. February 1957, p. 14.

7712. "Banshees Give Silver Lady to Milton Caniff." *Editor and Publisher*. December 3, 1960.

7713. Bertieri, Claudio. *Il Cittadino Caniff*. Genoa: Ed. "Kirk," 1969.

7714. Bertieri, Claudio. "The Knight of the Roaring Cross." In *Citizen Caniff*. Genoa: Ed. "Kirk," 1969.

7715. Caniff, Milton. "As í Nació Steve Canyon." *Dibujantes* (Buenos Aires). No. 30, 1959, pp. 30-31.

7716. Caniff, Milton. "Cartoon Feature." *Design*. May 1958, pp. 200-201.

7717. Caniff, Milton. "Day in Life of...." *Cartoonist PROfiles*. 1:1 (1969), pp. 19-25.

7718. Caniff, Milton. "Detour Guide for an Armchair Marco Polo." *Report of the King Features Syndicate* (New York). 1955.

7719. Caniff, Milton. "Don't Laugh at the Comics." *Cosmopolitan*. November 1958, pp. 43-47.

7720. Caniff, Milton. "Don't Shoot the Flannelmouth." *The Cartoonist*. Autumn 1957, pp. 3, 5, 26-27.

7721. Caniff, Milton. "En-qui-rer!" 41st Anniversary Cartoonist Reuben Awards Dinner *Program*. New York, May 24, 1987.

7722. Caniff, Milton. "Guia Detallada para un Marco Polo Sedentario." *Trix*. 1:6 (1988), pp. 66-68.

7723. Caniff, Milton. *Male Call*. New York: Grosset and Dunlop, 1959.

7724. Caniff, Milton. "Male Call." *Sgt. Kirk* (Genoa). No. 9, 1968, p. 93.

7725. Caniff, Milton. "Steve Canyon and Me." *Collier's*. November 20, 1948, p. 36.

7726. Caniff, Milton. "Syndicated Cartoon Feature." *Design*. June 1953, pp. 212-213.

7727. "Caniff, Canyon and Calhoon." *Newsweek*. January 20, 1947, p. 64.

7728. "Caniff Inducted into Air Police." *Philadelphia Inquirer*. November 11, 1959, p. 49.

7729. "Caniff's Private War To Save Steve Canyon." *Nemo*. Winter 1992, pp. 4-21.

7730. Couperie, Pierre. "Milton Caniff, Portfolio." *Phénix*. No. 17, 1970.

7731. De Gaetani, Giovanni. "Milton Caniff." *Comics Club*. No. 1, 1967, p. 60.

7732. Delafuente, Francisco. "Le Grand Milton Caniff." *U.N. Special*. No. 225, 1968, pp. 4-7, 15.

7733. De La Croix, Arnaud and Luc Dellisse. "Lames de Fond à Bruxelles." *Les Cahiers de la Bande Dessinée* (Grenoble). 66, 1985, pp. 39-41.

7734. Dorf, Shel. "Milton Caniff and Real People." *Cartoonist PROfiles*. June 1984, pp. 36-42.

7735. Dorf, Shel. "Milton Caniff: Reminiscence by Shel Dorf." *Cartoonist PROfiles*. March 1989, pp. 72-75.

7736. "Dumas from Ohio." *Newsweek*. April 24, 1950, pp. 58-61.

7737. "Field Day for Caniff." *Newsweek*. January 15, 1945, p. 80.

7738. Gallo, Bill. "Remembering Milton Caniff." *National Cartoonists Society Newsletter*. Reuben Ed., 1988, pp. 1, 4.

7739. "General Caniff Does It Again!" *Newsletter*. June 1966, pp. 32-35.

7740. Glasser, Jean-Claude. "Naissance d'un Style." *Les Cahiers de la Bande Dessinée* (Grenoble). 66, 1985, pp. 16-17.

7741. Goulart, Ron. "The Caniff School." *Comic Art*. No. 6, 1966, pp. 12-16.

7742. Goulart, Ron. "Milton Caniff: His Career." *Comics Buyer's Guide*. April 29, 1988, pp. 20, 22, 24, 26, 28.

7743. Groensteen, Thierry and Thierry Smolderen. "Entretien Avec Milton Caniff." *Les Cahiers de la Bande Dessinée* (Grenoble). 66, 1985, pp. 6-15.

7744. Guitar, Mary Anne. "Interview." *Famous Artists Magazine*. 8:3 (1960), n.p.

7745. Harvey, R.C. "Contradictions." *Caniffites*. December 1989, pp. 5-8.

7746. Harvey, R.C. "Milton Caniff, A Tribute." *Comics Buyer's Guide*. April 29, 1988, pp. 12, 14, 16, 20.

7747. Harvey, R.C. "Of Miscellany and Milt." *Comics Journal*. April 1989, pp. 33-38.

7748. Heimer, Mel. "Milton Caniff." *Comics World*. No. 0, 1966.

7749. Hidalgo, F. "Milton Caniff." *Phénix*. No. 12, 1969.

7750. Horn, Maurice. "Milton Caniff, In Memoriam." *Bédésup*. 2 Trim. 1988, p. 1.

7751. Lecigne, Bruno. "Eye Call." *Les Cahiers de la Bande Dessinée* (Grenoble). 66, 1985, pp. 27-28.

7752. Leguebe, Eric. "Le Coup de 'Caniff.'" *Bédésup*. 3rd-4th Trim., 1989, pp. 21-23.

7753. Lent, John A. "Milton Caniff 1907-1988." *WittyWorld*. Summer 1988, pp. 4-5.

7754. McQuiston, John T. "Milton Caniff, 81, Creator of 'Steve Canyon,' Dies." *New York Times*. April 5, 1988, p. D-25.

7755. Marschall, Rick. "Milton Caniff Dead at 81." *Comics Journal*. June 1988, pp. 23-24.

7756. Marschall, Rick. "Milton Caniff: The Man Who Made Comics Serious Art." *Philadelphia Inquirer*: April 10, 1988, p. 7-D.

7757. "Milt Caniff Dies at the Age of 81." *Editor and Publisher*. April 9, 1988, p. 58.

7758. "Milton Caniff." *Cartoonist PROfiles*. March 1975, pp. 60-63.

7759. "Milton Caniff." *Cartoonist PROfiles*. December 1977, pp. 32-39.

7760. "Milton Caniff." *Cartoonist PROfiles*. June 1989, pp. 76-81.

7761. "Milton Caniff." *Dibujantes* (Buenos Aires). No. 15, 1955, p. 31.

7762. "Milton Caniff." *Near Mint*. July 1982, pp. 40-44.

7763. "Milton Caniff." *Trix*. 1:6 (1988), p. 65.

7764. "Milton Caniff and Jimmy Swinnerton." *Cartoonist PROfiles*. December 1971, pp. 18-27.

7765. "Milton Caniff, Cartoonist of 'Terry and the Pirates.'" *Philadelphia Inquirer*. April 4, 1988, p. 13-D.

7766. "Milton Caniff, Master Craftsman." *Ohio Schools*. October 1957, pp. 8-44.

7767. "Milton Caniff, 'Rembrandt of Comics.'" *Philadelphia Daily News*. April 4, 1988, p. 25.

7768. "Milton Caniff Remembered." *Comics Revue*. No. 30, 1988, pp. 26-29, 64.

7769. Mintz, Lawrence E. "Fantasy, Formula, Realism, and Propaganda in Milton Caniff's Comic Strips." *Journal of Popular Culture*. Spring 1979, pp. 653-680.

7770. Pohl, Peter. "Terry und die Caniffianer." *Comic Forum* (Vienna). 25/26, 1984, pp. 85-97.

7771. Raiola, Antonio. "I Grandi Cartoonists Americani: Milton Caniff." *Il Fumetto*. September 1973, pp. 2-3.

7772. Raiola, Antonio. "Intervista con Mr. Caniff." *Il Fumetto*. September 1973, pp. 4-16.

7773. Rockwell, Richard W. "Remembering Caniff." *Cartoonist PROfiles*. September 1989, pp. 32-37.

7774. Saba, Arn. "'I'm Just a Troubadour Singing for My Supper'—Milton Caniff." *Comics Journal*. May 1986, pp. 60-102.

7775. "A Salute to Milton Caniff on His 75th Year." *The Cartoonist*. April 1982. 60 pp.

7776. Serie: Die Pioniere der Comic-Strips: (1) Milton Caniff." *Comixene* (Hanover). 6:25, pp. 58-61.

7777. Smolderen, Thierry, ed. *Images de Chine: Milton Caniff*. Chaville: Gilou, 1986.

7778. Staunton Helen M. "Milton Caniff Unveils His New Strip with Hero Who Has Been Around." *Editor and Publisher*. November 23, 1946.

7779. Sterckx, Pierre. "Le Rembrandt de la BD." *Les Cahiers de la Bande Dessinée* (Grenoble). 66, 1985, pp. 24-26.

7780. Trinchero, Sergio. "Un Italiano in Cartoonland (1-3; 4: "Il Grande Milton"; 5; 6: Russell e Remington pre Fumetto Yankee; 7: Jerry Robinson e Dick Ericson; 8: Addio a Chinatown)." *Sgt. Kirk*. No. 15-22, 1968-1969.

7781. Trinchero, Sergio. "Milton Caniff—George Wunder." *"Terry"—L'Olimpio dei Fumetti (Sugar)*. June 1970.

7782. "Waiting for a Boat to Civilization: Caniff's Great Pirate Episode." *Nemo*. June 1983, pp. 7-20; August 1983, pp. 36-46.

7783. Winchester, James H. "Milt Caniff's Air Force." *Air Force Magazine*. July 1957, pp. 41-47.

7784. Yronwode, Catherine. "The Greatest Comic Strip Studio of All Time." *Comics Collector*. Spring 1983, pp. 28-34.

Capp, Al

7785. Abel, Robert H. "Al Capp Vs. Just About Everybody." *Cavalier*. 17:9 (1967), pp. 25-101.

7786. Benayoun, Roberto. "La Tragédie Américaine de (Gulp!) Al Capp." *Giff-Wiff* (Paris). No. 23, 1967, pp. 2-7.

7787. Berger, Arthur A. "La Castration dans la Comédie Cappienne." *Giff-Wiff*. No. 23, 1967, pp. 16-18.

7788. Bittorf, W. "Al Capps Menschliche Komödie." *Süddeutsche Zeitung* (Munich). September 5, 6, 1953.

7789. Buckley, William F. "Al Capp at Bay." *National Review*. October 20, 1970, p. 1124.

7790. Caplin, Elliott. "We Called Him Alfred." *Cartoonist PROfiles*. December 1980, pp. 79-83.

7791. Capp, Al. "Capp's Column." *Time and Tide* (London). November 1-8, 1962.

7792. Capp, Al. "The Care and Feeding of Sacred Cows." *Saturday Evening Post*. 245 (1973), pp. 46-49.

7793. Capp, Al. "'The Comic Page Is the Last Refuge of Classic Art.'" *Nemo*. April 1986, pp. 16-17.

7794. Capp, Al. "From Dogpatch to Slobbovia." *Saturday Review*. February 29, 1964, p. 29.

7795. Capp, Al. "Mort Sahl or Joe Phillips." *Time and Tide* (London). October 11-18, 1962. p. 14.

7796. Capp, Al. "My Life As an Immortal Myth." *Life*. June 14, 1965, pp. 56-62.

7797. Capp, Al. "My Life As an Immortal Myth; Experiences at the First International Exhibition of the Comics." *Life*. April 30, 1965, pp. 97-100+.

7798. Capp, Al. *My Well-Balanced Life on a Wooden Leg: Memoirs*. Santa Barbara, California: John Daniel and Company, 1991. 126 pp.

7799. Capp, Al. "New Comic Strip; Reply with Rejoinder." *Saturday Review*. April 11, 1953, p. 27.

7800. Capp, Al. "1994." *Time and Tide* (London). October 25-November 1, 1962. p. 12.

7801. Capp, Al. "The Raw Recruit." *Time and Tide* (London). September 20-27, 1962.

7802. Carano, Ranieri. "Un Nobel per Al Capp." *Linus*. No. 2, 1965.

7803. Chaplin, Charles. "Foreword" to *The World of Li'l Abner*. New York: Ballantine, 1966.

7804. "Comical Protest Is Strummed Up by Joanie Phoanie." UPI dispatch in *Minneapolis Tribune*. January 11, 1967.

7805. De Moya, Alvaro and Syllas Roserg. "O Satirico Al Capp, um Genio Americano." *O Tempo* (São Paulo). December 10, 1950.

7806. "Dogpatch Is Ready for Freddie; Retirement of A. Capp." *Time*. October 17, 1977, p. 78.

7807. Furlong, W. "Recap on Al Capp." *Saturday Evening Post*. Winter 1971, pp. 40-45+.

7808. Hegerfors, Sture. "Joan Baez vs. Al Capp. Fejd Som Skakar Serie-USA." *Göteborgs Tidningen*. July 12, 1967.

7809. "Li'l Abner's Mad Capp." *Newsweek*. November 24, 1947, p. 60.

7810. "Li'l Al." *Newsweek*. July 17, 1961, p. 54.

7811. Maloney, R. "Li'l Abner's Capp." *Life*. June 24, 1946, pp. 58-62.

7812. Marschall, Rick. "Al Capp: A Last Interview with Comics' Master Satirist." *Comics Journal*. March 1980, pp. 45-55.

7813. Marschall, Rick. "'Saying Something About the Status Quo': Al Capp, Master Satirist of the Comics." *Nemo*. April 1986, pp. 7-12, 15.

7814. Marschall, Richard. "The Truth about Al Capp!! by Li'l Abner." *Cartoonist PROfiles*. March 1978, pp. 10-20.

7815. "Playboy Interview: Al Capp." *Playboy*. December 1966, pp. 89-100.

7816. Politzer, Heinz. "From Little Nemo to Li'l Abner." *Commentary*. 8 (1949), pp. 346-355.

7817. Rafferty, Max. "Al Capp—An Authentic Homegrown Genius Type." *The World of Comic Art*. Fall 1966, p. 2.

7818. "Rap for Capp." *Time*. September 9, 1957, pp. 89-90.

7819. Resnais, Alain. "Entretien Avec Al Capp." *Giff-Wiff* (Paris). March 1967, pp. 23-28.

7820. Richards, E. "Rap for Capp." *Saturday Review of Literature*. May 1, 1948, p. 21.

7821. Sanderson, Peter. "A Cappital Farce." *Comics Feature*. July-August 1980, pp. 69-71.

7822. "Speaking of Pictures... Al Capp Puts the Likenesses of Famous People in His 'Li'l Abner.'" *Life*. June 12, 1944, pp. 12-13.

7823. "Special Al Capp." *Giff-Wiff*. March 1967.

7824. Steinbeck, John. "Introduction" to *The World of Li'l Abner*. New York: Ballantine Books, 1966.

7825. "Which One Is the Phoanie?" *Time*. January 20, 1967, p. 47.

7826. White, David M. "The Art of Al Capp." In *From Dogpatch to Slovovia*. Boston: Beacon Press, 1964.

7827. White, David M. *The Art of Al Capp. A Bibliography*. Boston: Boston University, Communications Research Center, Report, No. 2, 1961.

7828. Zanotto, Piero. "Al Capp Riduce Gli Uomini Alle Dimensioni di Una Verme." *Il Gazzettino* (Venice). July 17, 1967.

7829. Zanotto, Piero. "Ammira Chaplin il Padre de Li'l Abner." *Carlino Sera* (Bologna). July 26, 1966; *Nazione Sera*. July 26 1966.

Crane, Roy

7830. Bindig, Bob. "How I Was Hooked by a Crane." *The Funnie's Paper*. April 1984, pp. 22-24.

7831. Bindig, Bob. "Royston Campbell Crane—1901-1977." *The Funnie's Paper*. April 1984, p. 21.

7832. Bono, Giani. "Dopo Roy Crane...." *Comics World* (Genoa). No. 3, 1968, pp. 11-12.

7833. Couperie, Pierre. "Roy Crane." *Phénix* (Paris). No. 2, 1967, pp. 5-14.

7834. Couperie, Pierre. "Roy Crane, Un Artista, due Eroi." *Comics World* (Genoa). No. 3, 1968, pp. 4-10.

7835. Crane, Roy. "Roy Crane Sketchbook." *Cartoonist PROfiles*. No. 13, 1972, pp. 48-50.

7836. Harvey, R.C. "A Flourish of Trumpets: Roy Crane and the Adventure Strip." *Comics Journal*. March 1993, pp. 101-106.

7837. "Roy Crane." *Cartoonist PROfiles*. September 1977, pp. 42-43.

7838. "Roy Crane—1901-1977—In Memoriam." *Orlandocon '77*. 1977, pp. 24-27.

7839. "Roy Crane Scrapbook." *Cartoonist PROfiles*. No. 9, 1971, pp. 78-79; December 1975, pp. 15-19; March 1976, pp. 35-37; December 1977, pp. 47-49; June 1978, pp. 94-97.

7840. Strzyz, Klaus. "Serie: Die Pioniere der Comic-Strips: (10) Roy Crane." *Comixene* (Hanover). 8:41 (1981), pp. 56-58.

Crosby, Percy

7841. Crosby, Percy L. *Always Belittlin.'* New York: Unicorn Press, 1927.

7842. Crosby, Percy. *A Cartoonist's Philosophy*. MacLean, Virginia: Percy Crosby, 1931. 252 pp.

7843. Crosby, Percy L. *Dear Sooky*. New York: G.P. Putnam's Sons, 1929. 124 pp.

7844. Crosby, Percy L. *Sport Drawings*. McLean, Virginia: Percy Crosby, 1933.

7845. Kaler, Dave. "Percy Leo Crosby." *Cartoonist PROfiles*. June 1977, pp. 28-33.

7846. Marschall, Rick. "The Slum Kids of Percy Crosby." *Nemo*. August 1986, p. 58.

7847. Robinson, Jerry. *Skippy and Percy Crosby*. New York: Holt, Rinehart, and Winston, 1978. 155 pp.

Dallis, Nick

7848. "AMA Cites Dr. Dallis, 'Rex Morgan' Author." *Chicago Daily News*. June 22, 1954, p. 4.

7849. Astor, David. "Creator of Three Enduring Serial Strips." *Editor and Publisher*. June 29, 1985, pp. 30-32.

7850. "Dr. Morgan's Creator Wins Freedom Award." *San Francisco News*. May 26, 1954, p. 23.

7851. Papke, D.R. "Cartoon Doctor; Rex Morgan, M.D." *Saturday Evening Post*. November 1975, pp. 22+.

7852. Porter, Philip W. "Rex Morgan, M.D., Judge Parker, Apartment 3-G." *Cartoonist PROfiles*. September 1975, pp. 38-41.

7853. "*Rex Morgan* Creator Dallis Dies." *Comics Journal*. September 1991, p. 14.

7854. Wagner, M. "Psychiatrist at the Drawing Board: Nick Dallis." *Today's Health*. August 1963, pp. 14-17.

Davis, Jim

7855. Astor, David. "Jim Davis Is the Reuben Award Winner." *Editor and Publisher*. May 12, 1990, pp. 34-35.

7856. Baker, J.F. "PW Interviews J. Davis (of "Garfield")." *Publisher's Weekly*. March 13, 1981, pp. 6-7.

7857. Friedwald, Will. "An Interview with Jim Davis," *Comics Buyer's Guide*. November 2, 1984, pp. 40+.

7858. Pauer, Frank. "From 'Gnorm Gnat' to 'Garfield': The Astounding Success of Jim Davis." *WittyWorld*. Autumn 1988, pp. 20-33.

7859. Pauer, Frank. "The Nine Lives of Jim Davis." *The Magazine (Dayton Daily News)*. June 19, 1988, pp. 6-7, 10-11, 15, 17.

7860. Shapiro, Walter. "The Jim Davis Interview." *Comics Review*. 1:3 (1984), pp. 22-26.

7861. "U.S. Acres by Jim Davis." *Cartoonist PROfiles*. December 1986, pp. 48-52.

Dean, Abner

7862. Dean, Abner. *And on the Eighth Day*. New York: Simon and Schuster, 1949. 111 pp.

7863. Dean, Abner. *Come As You Are*. New York: Simon and Schuster, 1952.

7864. Dean, Abner. *Wake Me When It's Over*. New York: Simon and Schuster, 1955.

7865. Dean, Abner. *What Am I Doing Here?* New York: Simon and Schuster, 1947.

7866. "Punch-Drunk Prophet; Abner Dean." *Life*. November 23, 1942, pp. 150-153.

De Beck, Bill

7867. "De Beck Dies." *Time*. November 23, 1942, pp. 51-52.

7868. Inge, M. Thomas. "The Appalachian Backgrounds of Bill De Beck's Snuffy Smith." *Appalachian Journal*. Winter 1977, pp. 120-132. Also in *Cartonaggio*, January 1978, pp. 7-19.

Dodd, Ed

7869. "Ed Dodd Earns SDX Cartooning Award." *The Rainbow*. February 1950, p. 57.

7870. "Ed Dodd y Mark Trail." *Dibujantes* (Buenos Aires). No. 30, 1959, pp. 4-6.

7871. Shalett, S. "Nature Lore: Ed Dodd's Mark Trail." *Américas*. July 1958, pp. 14-18.

Drake, Stan

7872. Cuesta Fernandez, Fernando. "Kelly Green: Stan Drake se Viste de Negro." *El Wendigo*. May-June 1985, pp. 37-38.

7873. Dorf, Shel. "Stan Drake." *Comics Interview*. No. 26, 1985, pp. 27-41; No. 27, 1985, pp. 36-41.

7874. Drake, Stan. "Juliet Jones Cartoonist Describes Trip to Spain." *Cartoonist PROfiles*. No. 17, 1973, pp. 44-46.

7875. Drake, Stan. "Juliet Jones Cartoonist Writes from Spain." *Cartoonist PROfiles*. No. 21, 1974, pp. 37-39.

7876. "Stan Drake." *Cartoonist PROfiles*. June 1979, pp. 14-19.

Elrod, Jack

7877. "Interview with Jack Elrod." *Breaking In*. December 1992, pp. 8-16.

7878. Salmon, Ray. "Jack Elrod, The Ryatts Cartoonist." *Cartoonist PROfiles*. No. 30, 1976, pp. 46-51.

Falk, Lee

7879. Astor, David. "Fifty Years of Magic and a Masked Man." *Editor and Publisher*. December 20, 1986, pp. 26-28.

7880. "Lee Falk." New York: King Features Syndicate, Biographical Series. No. 2-R 1969.

7881. "Lee Falk." *Cartoonist PROfiles*. September 1975, pp. 20-24.

7882. Meana. "El Salon de Oviedo y Lee Falk." *El Wendigo*. Año 15, No. 46 (1989), pp. 40-42.

7883. Resnais, Alain. "Entretien Avec Lee Falk." *Les Lettres Françaises* (Paris). No. 1138, 1966.

7884. Traini, Rinaldo and Sergio Trinchero. "Incontro con Lee Falk." *Comic Art in Paperback* (Milan). No. 3, 1966.

7885. Trinchero, Sergio. "Lee Falk in Italia." *L'Uomo Mascherato* (Milan). No. 120, 1965.

7886. Rodríguez Arbesú, Faustino. "Lee Falk y Phil Davis. Mandrake." *El Wendigo*. January 1982, pp. 28-31.

Feininger, Lyonel

7887. Feininger, Lyonel. *The Kin-der-Kids*. Intros. by Bill Blackbeard, Maurice Horn. New York: Dover, 1980. 32 pp.

7888. Feininger, T. Lux. *Lyonel Feininger—City at the Edge of the World*. New York: Frederick A. Praeger, 1965.

7889. Flemming, Hanns. "Lyonel Feininger: Karikaturen, Comic Strips, Illustration—Andreas Feininger: Fotografien." *Die Weltkunst* (Munich). 51:3 (1981), pp. 172-173.

7890. Gallick, Rosemary. "The Comic Art of Lyonel Feininger, 1906." *Journal of Popular Culture*. Winter 1976, pp. 664-676.

7891. Hess, Hans. *Lyonel Feininger*. New York: Harry N. Abrams, 1955.

7892. Horn, Maurice. "Lyonel Feininger, Cartoonist." *Eureka*. No. 114, 1973.

7893. Luckhardt, Ulrich. *Lyonel Feininger: Die Karikaturen und das Zeichnerische Frühwerk: Der Weg der Selbstfindung zum Unabhängigen Künstler, mit Einem Exkurs zu den Karikaturen von Emil Nolde und George Grosz*. Munich: Scaneg, 1987. 222 pp.

7894. Marschall, Richard. "The Concentrated Visions of Lyonel Feininger." *Comics Journal*. September 1981, pp. 98-102.

7895. Scheyer, Ernst. *Lyonel Feininger, Caricature and Fantasy*. Detroit, Michigan: Wayne State University Press, 1964.

Fisher, Bud

7896. "Bud Fisher Scrapbooks." *Cartoonist PROfiles*. Fall 1969, pp. 58-60.

7897. Fisher, Bud. "Confessions of a Cartoonist." *Saturday Evening Post*. July 28, August 4, August 11, August 18, 1928, pp. 10-11; 26-28; 28-30; 31.

7898. Milne, Peter. "Bud Fisher's Mutt and Jeff Pictures." *Motion Picture News*. April 15, 1916.

7899. "Recent Discovery! Bud Fisher Scrapbooks." *Cartoonist PROfiles*. Summer 1969, pp. 40-49.

Fisher, Ham

7900. Fisher, Ham. "Joe Palooka and Me." *Collier's*. October 16, 1948, p. 28.

7901. "Ham Fisher Defends Comic Strips." *Philadelphia Bulletin*. March 27, 1949, p. 3.

Flanders, Charles

7902. Horn, Maurice. "Charles Flanders, or the Eternal Second." *Nostalgia Comics*. No. 1, 1969.

7903. Horton, Andrew S. "Ken Kesey, John Updike and the Lone Ranger." *Journal of Popular Culture*. Winter 1974, pp. 570-581.

Foster, Hal

7904. "Advice from Hal Foster!" *Cartoonist PROfiles*. June 1985, pp. 74-75.

7905. Couperie, Pierre. "Harold Foster se Retire." *Phénix*. No. 17, 1970.

7906. Craggs, R.S. "Father of the Adventure Strip." *The World of Comic Art*. Fall 1966, pp. 4-11.

7907. Crouch, Bill, jr. "Harold R. Foster, Creator of Prince Valiant." *Cartoonist PROfiles*. No. 22, 1974, pp. 44-53.

7908. Fini, Luciano and A. Massarelli. "Harold Foster." *Sagittarius*. August 1965, p. 3.

7909. Grünewald, Dietrich. "Behinderte im Comic. Unterrichtsanregung für die Orientierungsstufe am Beispel 'Prinz Eisenherz' von H. Foster." *Kunst + Unterricht* (Hanover). 69, 1981, pp. 62-63.

7910. "Hal Foster." *Cartoonist PROfiles*. No. 5, 1970, pp. 36-39.

7911. "Hal Foster Dead at 89." *Comics Journal*. October 1982, pp. 15-16.

7912. "Hal Foster, Special Couleur." *Phénix* (Paris). No. 9, 1969.

7913. Heimer, Mel. "Hal Foster." New York: King Features Syndicate, Biographical Series, No. 9, 1970.

7914. Howard, Clive. "Prince Valiant's Hal Foster." *Pageant*. 5:6 (1949), pp. 104-109.

7915. Lacassin, Francis. "Foster, o la Serenità. Hogarth, o l'Inquietudine." *Comics Club*. No. 1, 1967, pp. 27-28.

7916. Marschall, Richard. "A Candid, Unpublished Interview: The Master, Hal Foster." *Nemo*. October 1984, pp. 7-19.

7917. Potter, Greg. "Hal Foster the Classicist." *Comics Journal*. September 1981, pp. 285-287.

7918. Saba, Arn. "Drawing Upon History." *Comics Journal*. September 1985, pp. 61-84.

7919. "Serie: Die Pioniere der Comic-Strips: (4) Harold Foster." *Comixene* (Hanover). 7:28, pp. 52-55.

Fox, Fontaine

7920. Campbell, Gordon. "Fontaine Fox." *Cartoonist PROfiles*. March 1982, pp. 26-31.

7921. Fox, Fontaine. *Fontaine Fox's Toonerville Trolley*. Compiled by Herb Galewitz and Don Winslow. New York: Weathervane Books, 1972. 184 pp.

7922. Simonelli, Y.M. "Fontaine Fox and His Toonerville Trolley." *Antiques Journal*. August 1978, pp. 20-26+.

Goldberg, Rube

7923. Berry, Michael. "Long Day's Journey with Mac and Mike." *The Cartoonist*. January 1968, pp. 15-19.

7924. Blackbeard, Bill. "Rube Goldberg's First Comic Strip." *Cartoonist PROfiles*. No. 24, 1974, pp. 73-75.

7925. Campbell, Gordon. "Rube Goldberg." *Cartoonist PROfiles*. March 1983, pp. 60-65.

7926. "Cartooning: To Make Them Laugh." *Time*. May 1, 1964, p. 66.

7927. Couperie, Pierre. "Rube Goldberg." *Phénix*. No. 16, 1970.

7928. "Exhibit at Smithsonian." *Cartoonist PROfiles*. No. 9, 1971, pp. 39-43.

7929. George, George. "Young Rube." *Cartoonist PROfiles*. March 1989, pp. 60-63.

7930. Goldberg, Reuben L. *Chasing the Blues*. New York: Doubleday, Page and Co., 1912, 94 pp.

7931. Goldberg, Reuben L. "Comics, New Style and Old." *Saturday Evening Post*. December 15, 1928, pp. 12-13.

7932. Goldberg, Reuben L. "From Reuben...." *The Cartoonist*. April 20, 1965.

7933. Goldberg, Reuben L. "Gripe of an Inventor." *The Cartoonist*. Summer 1957, pp. 26-27.

7934. Goldberg, Reuben. *Guide to Europe*. New York: Vanguard, 1954.

7935. Goldberg, Rube. *How To Remove the Cotton from a Bottle of Aspirin*. New York: Doubleday, 1959.

7936. Goldberg, Rube. "It Happened to a Rube." *Saturday Evening Post*. November 10, 1928, pp. 20-21.

7937. Goldberg, Rube. "My Answer to the Question: How Did You Put It Over?" *American Magazine*. March 1922, pp. 36-39.

7938. Goldberg, Rube. *Rube Goldberg, a Retrospective*. Intro. by Philip Garner. New York: Delilah Communications, distributed by Putnam, 1983. 95 pp.

7939. Goldberg, Rube. "This Cartoon Business." *Nemo*. February 1987, pp. 28-44.

7940. Ivey, Jim. "The Many Comic Inventions of Rube Goldberg." *Nemo*. February 1987, pp. 5-18.

7941. Keller, Charles. *The Best of Rube Goldberg*. Englewood Cliffs, New Jersey: Prentice-Hall, 1979.

7942. Kinnaird, Clark, ed. *Rube Goldberg Vs. the Machine Age*. New York: Hastings House, 1968. 214 pp.

7943. Marzio, Peter C. "Art, Technology and Satire: The Legacy of Rube Goldberg." *Leonardo* (London). 5:4 (1972), pp. 315-324.

7944. Marzio, Peter C. *Do It the Hard Way, Rube Goldberg and Modern Times*. Washington, D.C.: The Smithsonian Institution, 1970.

7945. Marzio, Peter C. *Rube Goldberg: His Life and Work*. New York: Harper and Row, 1973. 322 pp.

7946. "New Bunch of Books by Rube." *Life International*. October 18, 1965.

7947. "Rube Goldberg Drawings for Newspaper Cartoons, c. 1930-1936." *Apropos*. No. 1, 1983, pp. 136-137.

7948. "Rube Goldberg: Inventions and Comics." *Cartoonist PROfiles*. March 1977, pp. 42-43.

7949. "Rube Goldberg: Prisoner of War." *Nemo*. February 1987, pp. 22-27.

7950. "Rube Goldberg's New Leaf; Contract with New York Sun." *Newsweek*. December 5, 1938, p. 27.

7951. "The Works of Rube Goldberg." *Nemo*. February 1987, p. 19.

Gould, Chester

7952. Bainbridge, John. "Chester Gould: The Harrowing Adventures of His Cartoon Hero Dick Tracy Give Vicarious Thrills to Millions." *Life*. August 14, 1944, pp. 43-53.

7953. Bono, Giani. "Chester Gould." *Comics World* (Genoa). September 1967.

7954. Brandenburg, John. "Gould and Tracy, Partners in Crime for 25 Years." *Editor and Publisher*. October 6, 1956.

7955. "Chester Gould." *Cartoonist PROfiles*. No. 17, 1973, pp. 24-29.

7956. "Chester Gould." *Cartoonist PROfiles*. June 1985, pp. 14-15.

7957. "Chester Gould's Golden Moldies." *Esquire*. December 1973, pp. 166-167.

7958. Crump, Stuart, jr. "Chester Gould—the Creator of Dick Tracy." *Personal Communications*. January/February 1985.

7959. "Dick Tracy (Chester Gould) Cops." *New York Daily News*. October 10, 1949, p. 17.

7960. Gould, Chester. "A Christmas Fillum Fable." *Cartoonist PROfiles*. No. 16, 1972, p. 64.

7961. Gould, Chester. "Dick Tracy and Me." *Collier's*. December 11, 1948, p. 54.

7962. Gould, Chester. "Dick Tracy: The Detective Who Wouldn't Let Me Give Up." *Guideposts*. April 1976.

7963. Gould, Chester. "Interview." *Orange County (California) Register*. January 17, 1971.

7964. King, Robert. "Chester Gould's Dick Tracy." *Fanfare*. Summer 1983, pp. 18-24.

7965. Marschall, Richard, ed. "Chester Gould and Dick Tracy, A Comprehensive Look at a Comic Strip Master." *Nemo*. February 1986.

7966. Packard, Oakes. "The Sanguinary Squire from Pawnee." *The World of Comic Art*. Winter 1966/1967, pp. 28-31.

7967. "Serie: Die Pioniere der Comic-Strips: (5) Chester Gould." *Comixene* (Hanover). 7:29, pp. 58-59.

7968. Yoder, Robert M. "Dick Tracy's Boss." *Saturday Evening Post*. December 17, 1949, pp. 22-23.

Grace, Bud

7969. Drevets, Tricia. "Bud Grace: Physicist Turned Cartoonist." *Editor and Publisher*. April 9, 1988, pp. 58-59.

7970. Mills, David. "Drawing Trouble." *Philadelphia Inquirer*. March 7, 1992, pp. D-1, D-8.

Gray, Harold

7971. Barker, K.S. "Annie, Warbucks, and Harold Gray's Gospel." *Theology Today*. July 1978, pp. 178-190.

7972. McCracken, Harry. "Harold Gray, Cartoonist and Mythologist: Annie's Real 'Daddy.'" *Nemo*. August 1984, pp. 40-47.

7973. Marschall, Rick. "Harold Gray's Other Orphan: Little Joe." *Nemo*. August 1986, pp. 35-54.

Hamlin, V.T.

7974. Hamlin, V.T. "Alley Oop and Me." *Collier's*. March 19, 1949, p. 28.

7975. Hamlin, V.T. "Nostalgia Department." *Cartoonist PROfiles*. No. 5, 1970, pp. 60-68.

7976. Neal, Jim. "'Alley Oop' Creator V.T. Hamlin Dies at 93." *Comics Buyer's Guide*. July 16, 1993, p. 6.

7977. Norwood, Rick. "King of the Jungle Jive." *Nemo*. April 1984, pp. 39-49.

7978. "V.T. Hamlin, Creator of *Alley Oop*, Dead at 93." *Comics Journal*. July 1993, pp. 13-14.

7979. "V.T. Hamlin Retires As Comic-Artist." *New York Times*. December 2, 1971, p. 59.

7980. "Vincent Trout Hamlin." *The Jester*. August 1993, p. 18.

Hart, Johnny

7981. Hart, Johnny. "One Man's Family." *The World of Comic Art*. Summer 1967, pp. 22-24.

7982. Hart, Johnny. *Well, This Is Another Fine How Do You Do*. New York: Fawcett, 1982.

7983. "Johnny Hart." *Cartoonist PROfiles*. December 1980, pp. 10-16; March 1981, pp. 46-49.

7984. Neubauer, Martin. "'American Way of Life' und Mittelalter: Der Comic Strip 'The Wizard of Id.'" In *Mittelalter—Rezeption II. Gesammelte Vorträge des 2. Salzburgers Symposions "Die Rezeption des Mittelalters in Literatur, Bildender Kunst und Musik des 19. und 20. Jahrhunderts."* edited by Jürgen Kühunel, *et al.*, pp. 301-315. Göppingen: Kümmerle Verlag, 1982.

7985. Siepe, Klaus. "Johnny Hart." *Comic Forum* (Vienna)l 2:6 (1980), pp. 30-33.

Held, John, jr.

7986. Held, John, jr. "23 Skiddoo!" *Nemo*. October 1986, pp. 6-14.

7987. Lynes, Russell. "John Held's Mad World." *Harper's Magazine*. November 1967, pp. 24-36.

7988. Marschall, Rick. "The Bee's Knees; The Cat's Pajamas: John Held's Flapper Strips." *Nemo*. October 1986, pp. 6-13.

7989. Tarrant, Dorothy and John. "It Was the Jazz Age and John Held, jr. Drew It and Lived It." *Smithsonian*. September 1986, pp. 94-104.

Herriman, George

7990. Blackbeard, Bill. "The Forgotten Years of George Herriman." *Nemo*. June 1983, pp. 50-60.

7991. Bonner, Anthony J. "George Herriman, His Life and Work." Thesis, Syracuse University, n.d.

7992. Caskey, Marie. "George Herriman." In *Dictionary of American Biography*. Supplement 3, 1941-1945, pp. 356-357. New York: Charles Scribner and Sons.

7993. "Death of Herriman." *Art News*. May 1-14, 1944, p. 7.

7994. "A Genius of the Comic Page." *Cartoons*. ca. 1916.

7995. "George Herriman, Noted Cartoonist." *New York Times*. April 27, 1944, Late City ed., sec. 1, p. 23.

7996. Gopnik, A. "The Genius of George Herriman." *New York Review of Books*. December 18, 1986, pp. 19-20+.

7997. Inge, M. Thomas. "George Herriman, Creator of Krazy Kat." *Cartoonist PROfiles*. June 1974, p. 43.

7998. Inge, M. Thomas, ed. "George Herriman's Early Years: A Biographical Portrait by a Friend." *Cartoonist PROfiles*. December 1992, pp. 54-59.

7999. "Krazy Kat's Kreator." *Newsweek*. May 8, 1944, p. 96.

8000. Landenberger, Mary. "Herriman Stumbles on Krazy Kat and Has Been Embarrassed Ever Since." *Nashville Tennessean*. May 1930.

8001. McArdell, Roy, ed. *George Herriman's "Krazy Kat."* New York: Grosset and Dunlap, 1977.

8002. McDonnell, Patrick, Karen O'Connell, and George Riley de Havenon. *Krazy Kat: The Comic Art of George Herriman*. New York: Harry Abrams, 1986. 224 pp.

8003. Rosemont, Franklin. "George Herriman (Krazy Kat)." *Cultural Correspondence*. Fall 1974.

8004. Strzyz, Klaus. "Serie: Die Pioniere der Comic-Strips: (11) George Herriman." *Comixene* (Hanover). 8:42 (1981), pp. 56-60.

Hershfield, Harry

8005. "Harry Hershfield." *The Cartoonist*. October 1966, pp. 6-11.

8006. "Harry Hershfield." *Cartoonist PROfiles*. March 1975, pp. 41-42.

8007. Hershfield, Harry. *Abie the Agent*. The Hyperion Library of Classic American Comic Strips. Westport, Connecticut: Hyperion, 1977. 98 pp.

8008. Hershfield, Harry. *Dauntless Durham of the U.S.A.* The Hyperion Library of Classic American Comic Strips. Intro by Bill Blackbeard. Westport, Connecticut: Hyperion, 1977. 108 pp.

8009. Nizer, Louis. "Goodbye, Harry. A Famed Trial Lawyer's Tribute to Harry Hershfield, Including Many of the Cartoonist's Favorite Stories." *Cartoonist PROfiles*. June 1975, pp. 22-25.

Hoest, Bill

8010. "Agatha Crumm by Bill Hoest." *Cartoonist PROfiles*. September 1977, pp. 66-69.

8011. Hoest, Bill. *Bumper Snickers*. New York: New American Library, 1976.

8012. Hoest, Bill. *A Taste of Carrot*. New York: Atheneum, 1967.

8013. Hurd, Jud. "What a Guy! A New Comic Strip by Bill Hoest." *Cartoonist PROfiles*. June 1987, pp. 34-40.

Hogarth, Burne

8014. "Burne Hogarth." *Cartoonist PROfiles*. June 1977, pp. 8-12; September 1977, pp. 40-41.

8015. "Burne Hogarth." *Mongo* (Paris). No. 0, 1967.

8016. *Catalogue Burne Hogarth*. Paris: Socerlid, 1966.

8017. Da Silva Nunes, Luis. "Introducao ao 'Diabrete,' o Tarzan de Hogarth." *Républica* (Lisbon). April 24-May 5, 1968, p. 3.

8018. Horn, Maurice. "La Carrière et l'Oeuvre d'Hogarth." Introduction to *Tarzan, Seigneur de la Jungle*. Paris: Editions Azur, 1967.

8019. Horn, Maurice. "The Magic of Burne Hogarth." An introduction to *Tarzan of the Apes*. New York: Watson-Guptill, 1972.

8020. Lacassin, Francis. "Hogarth Between Wonder and Madness." *Giff-Wiff*. No. 13, 1965.

8021. Lacassin, Francis. "Introducing Hogarth: Hogarth Entre le Merveilleux et la Démence." *Giff-Wiff* (Paris). No. 18, 1966.

8022. Le Gallo, Claude. "Burne Hogarth." *Phénix*. No. 19, 1971.

8023. Leguebe, Eric. "Burne Hogarth." *Phénix* (Paris). No. 7, 3 Trim. 1968, pp. 6-8.

8024. Leguebe, Eric. "Interview Hogarth." *Le Nouveau Bédésup*. 34, 1985, p. 27.

8025. Oppetit, Danielle, Elisabeth Hardy and Jean-Claude Faur. *Hogarth, 1935-1985*. Marseilles: Ville de Marseilles, 1985.

8026. Pascal, David. "Burne Hogarth il Michelangelo dei Fumetti." *Comics, Archivio Italiano della Stampa a Fumetti*. No. 1, 1966, pp. 8-13.

8027. Pascal, David. "Hogarth Répond." *Giff-Wiff* (Paris). No. 18, 1966.

8028. "Serie: Die Pioniere der Comic-Strips: (2) Burne Hogarth—Michelangelo der Comics." *Comixene* (Hanover). 6:26, pp. 55-58.

8029. "Sketchbook: Burne Hogarth." *Comics Journal*. March 1992, pp. 81-85.

8030. Zanotto, Piero. "Il Tout-Paris Legge Tarzan: Lussuoso Album per i Fumetti di Hogarth." *Il Piccolo*. November 24, 1967; *Nuova Sardegna*. December 21, 1967.

8031. Zanotto, Piero. "Nei Fumetti di Hogarth, il Ritorno di Tarzan." *Il Gazzettino* (Venice). January 15, 1968.

8032. Zimmerman, Howard. "An Informal Chat with Burne Hogarth, the World's Greatest Living Comics Artist." *Comics Scene*. September 1982, pp. 32-39.

Holbrook, Bill

8033. "Interview with Bill Holbrook." *Breaking In*. Premiere Issue, 1992, pp. 6-13.

8034. "Safe Haven." *Cartoonist PROfiles*. June 1989, pp. 70-75.

Holman, Bill

8035. "Bill Holman and Smokey Stover." *Cartoonist PROfiles*. March 1978, pp. 26-31; June 1980, pp. 25-27.

8036. Holman, Bill. *Smokey Stover*. Comic-Strip Preserves. El Cajon, California: Blackthorne, 1985. 72 pp.

8037. Robinson, Jerry. "Holman Revisited." *The Cartoonist*. February 1957, pp. 7-8, 33.

Johnson, Ferd

8038. Johnson, Tom. "Working on the Moon: Moon Mullins." *Cartoonist PROfiles*. June 1983, pp. 8-15.

8039. Marschall, Rick. "Good Moon Rising: An Interview with Ferd Johnson." *Nemo*. February 1989, pp. 18-43.

Keane, Bil

8040. Astor, David. "Keane Gets Ownership of 'Family Circus.'" *Editor and Publisher*. February 4, 1989, pp. 36-37.

8041. "Bil Keane." *Cartoonist PROfiles*. December 1975, pp. 80-85; December 1980, pp. 84-87; September 1986, pp. 44-47.

8042. "Bil Keane and Family Circus." *Cartoonist PROfiles*. December 1977, pp. 12-17; March 1979, pp. 60-61.

8043. Brophy, Blake. "The Wonderful World of Bil Keane." *The Cartoonist*. October 1966, pp. 12-17.

8044. Greenberger, Robert. "Of Circuses and Mickey Mouse." *Comics Scene*. March 1983, pp. 42-43.

8045. Keane, Bil. *The Family Circus Is Very Keane*. New York: Fawcett, Columbine, 1988.

8046. Keane, Bil. "Report from Paradise Valley." *Cartoonist PROfiles*. No. 5, 1970, pp. 31-35.

8047. Lund, William R. "The Three-Ring Circus of Bil Keane." *Comics Scene*. March 1983, pp. 41-42, 44-45.

Kelly, Walt (also Selby)

8048. "Anybody Here Seen Kelly?" *Fort Mudge Most*. January 1988, pp. 8-9.

8049. Beiman, Nancy. "Walt and Selby Kelly." *Cartoonist PROfiles*. December 1983, pp. 26-31.

8050. "Cartoonist's Wife Continues Sunday Pogo Strip." *Cartoonist PROfiles*. No. 23, 1974, pp. 24-28.

8051. "Cartoons by Walt Kelly." *Fort Mudge Most.* May 1991, pp. 16-12.

8052. "The Charitable Walt Kelly." *Fort Mudge Most.* September 1989, pp. 5-9.

8053. "Christmas Cards." *Fort Mudge Most.* November 1989, pp. 18-22.

8054. "The Complete Text of an Unpublished Strip Kitty Malone." *Fort Mudge Most.* July 1990, pp. 14-22.

8055. "Creator of Pogo Composes a Gay Carol." *Newsweek.* June 26, 1955, pp. 38-39.

8056. Crouch, Bill, jr. "George Ward Talks About Kelly, Pogo and Times Past." *Okefenokee Star.* Spring 1977, pp. 21-28; Summer 1977, pp. 38-42.

8057. Crouch, Bill, jr. "Ray Dirgo Remembers Walt Kelly." *Okefenokee Star.* Summer 1977, pp. 7-21.

8058. "Early Kelly." *Okefenokee Star.* Spring 1977, pp. 36-37.

8059. Fisher, Harrison. "Pogo's Pal Kelly." *Maclean's Magazine.* April 15, 1950, pp. 20-21, 52.

8060. "Gremlins by Walt Kelly." *Fort Mudge Most.* March 1991, pp. 16-23.

8061. Inge, M. Thomas. "Walt Kelly and Me." *Okefenokee Star.* Summer 1977, pp. 36-37.

8062. "In the Beginning...." *Pogo Is Back!* 4:1 (1993), p. 1.

8063. Kane, Gil. "Walt Kelly." *Comics Journal.* February 1991, pp. 50-58.

8064. Kelly, Walt. "A Crying Need for the Cleansing Lash of Laughter." *Fort Mudge Most.* July 1989, pp. 12-14.

8065. Kelly, Walt. "Our Comic Heritage." *The Cartoonist.* April 20, 1965; *Okefenokee Star.* Summer 1977, pp. 31-35.

8066. Kelly, Walt. "Remember the Two Frogs." *Fort Mudge Most.* 1984, p. 6.

8067. Kelly, Walt. *Ten Ever-Lovin' Blue Eyed Years with Pogo* (1949-1959). New York: Simon and Schuster, 1971.

8068. Kelly, Walt. "Walt Kelly's Views on Conservation." *Fort Mudge Most.* March 1990, pp. 14-15.

8069. "Kelly's Politics." *Okefenokee Star.* Spring 1977, pp. 38-45.

8070. "Kelly's Wisdom." *Okefenokee Star.* Spring 1977, pp. 34-35.

8071. Lockwood, Georg J. "Walt Kelly." *Cartoonist PROfiles*. September 1985, pp. 48-49.

8072. Mayerson, Mark. "Walt and Walt: Kelly at Disney." *Fort Mudge Most*. May 1989, pp. 4-6.

8073. Mishkin, Daniel. "Pogo = Walt Kelly's American Dream." *Journal of Popular Culture*. Spring 1979, pp. 681-690.

8074. "Reilly, Starling and Kelly: Two Irishmen and a Scot." *Fort Mudge Most*. July 1989, pp. 16-18.

8075. Robinson, M. "Pogo's Papa." *Collier's*. March 8, 1952, pp. 20-21+.

8076. Thompson, Don and Maggie. "Walt Kelly." *Okefenokee Star*. Summer 1977, pp. 43-50.

8077. Thompson, Maggie. "Walt Kelly, Creator of 'Pogo' Comic Strip, Dies at 60." *Menomonee Falls Guardian*. November 5, 1973, pp. 3-6.

8078. Thompson, Steve. "A Walt Kelly Biography." *Comics Journal*. February 1991, pp. 67-70.

8079. Thompson, Steve. "Post-Historical Kelly: Upward Ho!" *Fort Mudge Most*. March 1991, pp. 8-13.

8080. "The Very Early Walt Kelly." *Fort Mudge Most*. March 1989, pp. 5-8.

8081. [Walt Kelly]. *Linus*. June 1965.

8082. "Walt Kelly." *New York Times*. October 19, 1973, p. 42.

8083. "Walt Kelly: A Retrospective Exhibition To Celebrate the Seventy-Fifth Anniversary of His Birth." *Fort Mudge Most*. September 1988, pp. 14-15.

8084. "Walt Kelly Canines with a Little Extra Bite." *Fort Mudge Most*. May 1991, pp. 12-14.

8085. "Walt Kelly Comes to Life." *Fort Mudge Most*. May 1991, pp. 6-11.

8086. "Walt Kelly in High School." *Okefenokee Star*. Spring 1977, pp. 5-10.

8087. "What Do You Know About the New York Star?" *Okefenokee Star*. Spring 1977, pp. 11-20.

8088. "The World of Pogo. Walt Kelly's Menagerie of Characters from the Okefenokee Swamp." *Cartoonist PROfiles*. December 1974, pp. 43-45.

8089. Zanotto, Piero. "Walt Kelly Presenta Pogo." *Tribuna del Mezzogiorno* (Messina). December 31, 1955.

Ketcham, Hank

8090. Ager, Susan. "Ketcham's Family Affair." *The Funnie's Paper*. December 1983, pp. 12-15.

8091. Easthope, Anthony. *What a Man's Gotta Do*. London: Paladin, 1986.

8092. Edson, L. "Man Behind the Menace." *Coronet*. October 1959, pp. 68-73.

8093. Greenberger, Robert. "Making Mischief and Mayhem with the Man Behind Dennis the Menace." *Comics Scene*. July 1983, pp. 19-22.

8094. "Hank Ketcham." *Cartoonist PROfiles*. March 1981, pp. 56-61.

8095. Ketcham, Hank. "Half Hitch." *Cartoonist PROfiles*. September 1971, pp. 50-57.

8096. Ketcham, Hank. *Hank Ketcham: The Merchant of Dennis (the Menace)*. New York: Abbeville Press, 1990. 256 pp.

8097. Ketcham, Hank. "Hank Ketcham Writes from Switzerland." *Newsletter*. September 1965, pp. 15-17.

8098. "Ketcham's Menace, Billy de Beck Award." *Newsweek*. May 4, 1953, p. 57.

8099. "The Merchant of Dennis the Menace." *Cartoonist PROfiles*. September 1990, pp. 10-17.

Key, Ted

8100. Beiswinger, George L. "Hazel by Ted Key." *Cartoonist PROfiles*. June 1988, pp. 56-62.

8101. Beiswinger, George L. "Hazel's Here—and Everywhere." *Media History Digest*. Fall 1985, pp. 8-13.

8102. Beiswinger, George L. "Ted Key, Creator of 'Hazel.'" *Courier, Syracuse University Library Associates*. Fall 1988, pp. 45-56.

8103. Hohman, Edward J. "What Maids Are Dreamed Of." *Comics Scene*. May 1992, pp. 57-60.

8104. Key, Ted. *The Biggest Dog in the World*. New York: Dutton, 1960. 44 pp.

8105. Key, Ted. *Fasten Your Seat Belts!* New York: E.P. Dutton and Co., 1956.

8106. Key, Ted. *Many Happy Returns*. New York: E.P. Dutton and Co., n.d.

8107. Key, Ted. "People's Choice." *Saturday Evening Post*. September 11, 1948, pp. 34-35.

8108. Key, Ted. *Ted Key's Phyllis*. New York: Dutton and Co., 1957.

8109. Key, Theodore. "Wrong Number." *Saturday Evening Post*. May 1, 1948, pp. 36-37.

Knerr, Harold

8110. Lowe, Jim. "Behind the Scenes with Harold Knerr." *Vot Der Dumboozle?* Summer 1988, pp. 9-13.

8111. "The Katzaddendum and Knerratum Page." *Vot Der Dumboozle?* Summer 1988, pp. 21-22.

8112. Lowe, Jim. "Knerr: The Art of the Swimsuit." *Vot Der Dumboozle?* Summer 1988, pp. 14-16.

8113. Lowe, Jim. "The Supporting Cast." *Vot Der Dumboozle?* Summer 1988, pp. 17-20.

Kubert, Joe

8114. Dionnet, J.P. "Joe Kubert." *Phénix*. No. 16, 1970.

8115. "The Enemy Ace by Joe Kubert." *Cartoonist PROfiles*. No. 17, 1973, pp. 58-60.

8116. "Joe Kubert." *Cartoonist PROfiles*. September 1981, pp. 42-43.

8117. "Our Army at War by Joe Kubert." *Cartoonist PROfiles*. No. 17, 1973, p. 55.

8118. Russell, Scott. "Dynamic Kubert, Master Artist." *Masquerader*. No. 6, 1964, pp. 22-25.

8119. "Tarzan by Joe Kubert." *Cartoonist PROfiles*. No. 17, 1973, pp. 52, 56-57, 63.

Larson, Gary

8120. Bernstein, F. "Loony 'toonist Gary Larson Takes Millions for a Daily Walk on the Far Side." *People's Weekly*. February 4, 1985, pp. 103-105.

8121. "The Far Side of Gary Larson." *Reader's Digest*. July 1985, pp. 98-99.

8122. Feeney, Sheila Anne. "Gary Larson." *The Funnie's Paper*. May 1984, pp. 8-10.

8123. Richmond, P. "Creatures from the Black Cartoon." *Rolling Stone*. September 24, 1987, pp. 79-80+.

8124. Shute, Nancy. "On the Far Side: Gary Larson." *Vis à Vis*. March 1988, pp. 74-75.

8125. "Taking a Break from 'The Far Side.'" *Newsweek*. October 10, 1988, p. 81.

8126. Weiner, S.B. "Funny Money." *Forbes*. December 12, 1988, pp. 272+.

8127. Wilstein, Steve. "Larson Lives on 'the far side.'" *The Reporter* (Lansdale, Pa). Associated Press dispatch. December 14, 1985, pp. B-3, B-5.

Lasswell, Fred

8128. "Fred Lasswell." *Cartoonist PROfiles*. December 1979, pp. 76-77.

8129. Young, D. "Snuffy Smith's Pappy." *Southern Living*. July 1987, p. 106.

Lazarus, Mell

8130. Dorf, Shel. "The Mell Lazarus Interview." *Nemo*. December 1984, pp. 13-20.

8131. Lazarus, Mell. *Arthur, Isn't the Atmosphere Polluted Enough?* New York: Bantam, 1981.

8132. Lazarus, Mell. *I Guess He'll Do Until the Right Man Comes Along*. Toronto: Bantam, 1982.

8133. "Mell Lazarus." *Cartoonist PROfiles*. December 1971, pp. 38-49.

Lynde, Stan

8134. "Latigo by Stan Lynde." *Cartoonist PROfiles*. June 1979, pp. 36-45.

8135. Lynde, Stan. "Conniption." *Cartoonist PROfiles*. No. 7, 1970, pp. 18-23.

8136. Lynde, Stan. "Rick O'Shay." *Cartoonist PROfiles*. 1:1 (1969), pp. 3-8.

8137. "Stan Lynde." *Cartoonist PROfiles*. June 1981, pp. 77-80.

McCay, Winsor

8138. Bertieri, Claudio. "The McCay's Perspective." *Photographia Italiana* (Milan). No. 149, 1970.

8139. Campbell, Gordon. "Winsor McCay." *Cartoonist PROfiles*. June 1980, pp. 38-45.

8140. Canemaker, John. *Winsor McCay, His Life and Art*. New York: Abbeville Press, 1987. 223 pp.

8141. Dinges, Richard. "John Canemaker on the Art of Winsor McCay." *Uncle Jam Quarterly*. Summer 1988, pp. 11-12.

8142. Fitzsimmons, John A. "Winsor McCay." *Cartoonist PROfiles*. March 1984, pp. 20-25.

8143. Harvey, R.C. "Winsor McCay: A Pioneer in Dreamland." *Comics Journal*. October 1991, pp. 107-112.

8144. Inge, M. Thomas. "Fantasy and Reality in Winsor McCay's Little Nemo." *Proceedings of the Fifth National Popular Culture Association*, pp. 167-179. Bowling Green, Ohio: Bowling Green University Popular Press, 1975.

8145. "John Canemaker Writes Winsor McCay Biography." *Cartoonist PROfiles*. September 1985, p. 15.

8146. Könemann, Ludwig. "Serie: Die Pioniere der Comic-Strips: (8) Winsor McCay." *Comixene* (Hanover). 8:35, pp. 56-58.

8147. Marschall, Richard, ed. *Daydreams and Nightmares: The Fantastic Visions of Winsor McCay*. Westlake Village, California: Fantagraphics Books, 1988. 170 pp.

8148. O'Sullivan, Judith. "The Art of Winsor Z. McCay. 1871-1934." Ph.D. dissertation, University of Maryland, 1976. 860 pp. Available through University Microfilms International.

8149. "Penmen of the Past: Winsor McCay." *Nemo*. April 1986, pp. 34-43.

8150. "Winsor McCay." *Cartoonist PROfiles*. September 1987, pp. 10-13.

McManus, George

8151. "George McManus." *Cartoonist PROfiles*. March 1975, pp. 66-70.

8152. "George McManus." *The Funnie's Paper*. October 1983, p. 4.

8153. La Cossit, H. "Jiggs and I, G. McManus." *Collier's*. January 19, 1952, pp. 9-11; January 26, 1952, pp. 24-25; February 2, 1952, pp. 30-31.

8154. McGreal, Dorothy. "The Inimitable George." *The World of Comic Art*. 1:1 (1966), pp. 34-40.

8155. Marschall, Rick. "The Decorative Art of George McManus." *Nemo*. August 1985, pp. 19-32.

8156. Marschall, Rick. "George M. McManus's Pioneer Work of Fantasy." *Nemo*. October 1984, pp. 21-37.

8157. Zanotto, Piero. "McManus." *Il Lavoro* (Genoa). June 12, 1959.

8158. Zanotto, Piero. "Ricordo di George McManus." *Enciclopedia Motta*. No. 150, September 5, 1959.

Manning, Russ

8159. Barrett, Robert R. *Russ Manning: A Bibliography*. Wichita, Kansas: Bob Barrett, 1992. 30 pp.

8160. Barrett, Robert R. "Tarzan's Third Great Comic Strip Artist: Russell G. Manning (1929-1981)." *Burroughs Bulletin*. January 1993, pp. 11-21.

8161. "Bill Stout, Dave Stevens and Bill Rotsler Discuss the Russ Manning Years." *Comics Feature*. November-December 1983, pp. 41-66.

8162. Dorf, Shel. "An Interview with Russ Manning." *Comics Feature*. November-December 1983, pp. 4-9, 11-31.

8163. Royer, Mike. "On Russ Manning." *Comics Feature*. November-December 1983, pp. 32-40.

Martin, Don

8164. "Don Martin Starts Daily Strip." *Comics Journal*. May 1992, p. 24.

8165. Hurd, Jud. "Don Martin and the Nutheads." *Cartoonist PROfiles*. December 1990, pp. 20-25.

Montana, Bob

8166. "Archie by Bob Montana." *Cartoonist PROfiles*. No. 6, 1970, pp. 4-9.

8167. "Bob Montana." *Cartoonist PROfiles*. March 1975, p. 29.

8168. Sanville, Cathy. "Montana: The Man That Started It All!" *The Funnie's Paper*. September 1983, pp. 2-6.

Moores, Dick

8169. Black, Ed. "Gasoline Alley Cartoonist Dick Moores." *Cartoonist PROfiles*. No. 30, 1976, pp. 70-77.

8170. "Dick Moores." *Orlandocon '77*. 1977, p. 4.

8171. Howard, D.W. "Dick Moores of 'Gasoline Alley.'" *Comics Buyer's Guide*. May 16, 1986, p. 30.

8172. Wells, John. "Dick Moores: Some Memories of 'Gasoline Alley.'" *Comics Buyer's Guide*. May 23, 1986, pp. 36, 38, 40, 42.

Mosley, Zack

8173. Deutsch, B. "Smilin' Zack." *Flying*. October 1949, pp. 24-25.

8174. Mosley, Zack. *Brave Coward Zack*. Rev. Ed. St. Petersburg, Florida: Valkyrie Press, 1976. 102 pp.

8175. Mosley, Zack. "Smilin' Jack and Zack." *Near Mint*. April 1981, pp. 14-17.

8176. von Cannon, K. "Meet Cartoonist Zack Mosley." *The Funnie's Paper*. September 1985, pp. 4-5.

Murphy, John Cullen

8177. Crouch, Bill, jr. "John Cullen Murphy and Big Ben Bolt." *Cartoonist PROfiles*. No. 24, 1974, pp. 36-42.

8178. Fuchs, Wolfgang J. "John Cullen Murphy." *Comics Forum* (Vienna). 2:7/8 (1980), pp. 65-68.

8179. "Murphy: Drew Toots-Casper Cartoon Strip." *Newsletter*. March 1965, p. 16.

8180. Pohl, Peter. "Interview mit John Cullen Murphy." *Comixene* (Hanover). 8:34 (1981), pp. 12-13.

Myers, Russell

8181. Gorner, Peter. "He Lives Off the Earnings of a Drunken Witch." *Menomonee Falls Guardian*. September 1, 1973, pp. 4, 6, 12-13. Reprinted from *Chicago Tribune*. March 13, 1973.

8182. Myers, Russell. *Doing What I Do Best*. New York: Ballantine, 1984.

8183. Myers, Russell. *X Rated X-Rays*. New York: Grosset and Dunlap, 1978.

Opper, Frederick B.

8184. Campbell, Gordon. "On Frederick Opper." *Cartoonist PROfiles*. March 1980, pp. 22-28.

8185. Flower, B.O. "Frederick Opper: A Cartoonist of Democracy." *The Arena*. June 1905, pp. 583-593.

8186. Milum, Richard A. "Faulkner and the Comic Perspective of Frederick Burr Opper." *Journal of Popular Culture*. Winter 1982, pp. 139-150.

8187. Opper, Frederick B. *The Folks in Funnyville*. New York: R.H. Russell, 1900.

8188. Opper, Frederick B. *John, Jonathan, and Mr. Opper*. London: Grant Richards, 1903.

8189. Opper, Frederick B. *Just for Fun*. New York: Keppler and Schwarzmann, 1895.

8190. Opper, Frederick B. *Puck's Opper Book*. New York: Keppler and Schwarzmann, 1888.

8191. Opper, Frederick. *This Funny World As Puck Sees It*. New York: Keppler and Schwarzmann, 1890.

8192. Opper, Frederick B. *Willie and His Papa*. New York: Grosset and Dunlap, 1901.

Outcault, Richard F.

8193. Tank, Kurt Lothar. "Es Begann Mit Dem Mehlsack des Mr. Outcault." *Die Welt* (Hamburg). June 12, 1954.

8194. Westerman, Harry J. "Outlines Career of R.F. Outcault, Ohio-Born Artist." *The Ohio Newspaper*. December 1933.

Partch, Virgil

8195. Stewart, Bhob. "Virgil's Aeneid: R.I.P. Vip." *Nemo*. August 1985, pp. 39-48.

8196. "Virgil Partch." *Cartoonist PROfiles*. No. 31, 1976, pp. 30-37.

Prince, Bernard

8197. "Bernard Prince." *Cartoonist PROfiles*. No. 16, 1972, pp. 56-63.

8198. François, Edouard. "Bernard Prince." *Phénix*. No. 16, 1970.

Raymond, Alex

8199. Couperie, Pierre. "Le Style d'Alex Raymond." *Phénix*. No. 3, 1967, pp. 8-11.

8200. Delafuente, Francisco. "Alex Raymond." *U.N. Special* (Genoa). No. 221, 1968.

8201. "El Bultre y Julio de Diego: Alex Raymond Extrajo de la Vida Real Uno de Sus Más Conocidos Personajes." *Dibujantes* (Buenos Aires). No. 29, 1959, p. 18.

8202. Fini, Luciano and A. Massarelli. "Alex Raymond." *Sagittarius*. May 1965, p. 3.

8203. Glasser, Jean-Claude. "Alex Raymond Illustrateur." *Les Cahiers de la Bande Dessinée* (Grenoble). 72, 1986, pp. 27-29.

8204. Glasser, Jean-Claude. "Alex Avant Raymond." *Les Cahiers de la Bande Dessinée* (Grenoble). 72, 1986, pp. 10-12.

8205. Glasser, Jean-Claude. "D'Austin Briggs à Daniel Torres: Quel(s) Héritage(s)?" *Les Cahiers de la Bande Dessinée* (Grenoble). 72, 1986, 35-38.

8206. Groensteen, Thierry. "Dossier: Alex Raymond." *Les Cahiers de la Bande Dessinée* (Grenoble). 72, 1986, pp. 7-9.

8207. Muscio, L. "Omaggio a Raymond." *Comic Art*. No. 4, 1967.

8208. Potter, Greg. "Alex Raymond the Romantic." *Comics Journal*. September 1981, pp. 289-293.

8209. "Serie: Die Pioniere der Comic-Strips: (3) Alex Raymond." *Comixene* (Hanover). 6:27 (1979), pp. 56-59.

8210. Trinchero, Sergio. "Alex Raymond." *Super Albo Spada*. No. 61, 1963.

Robbins, Frank

8211. Commer, Dick. "Frank Robbins of Johnny Hazard." *Cartoonist PROfiles*. June 1979, pp. 76-83.

8212. Hidalgo, F. "Frank Robbins." Phénix. No. 23, 1972.

Robinson, Jerry

8213. Bertieri, Claudio. "Still Life of Jerry Robinson." *Sgt. Kirk*. No. 4, 1967, pp. 1-5.

8214. "Jerry Robinson. Still Life." *Cartoonist PROfiles*. No. 13, 1972, pp. 24-29.

8215. Le Carpentier, P. "Jerry Robinson." *Phénix*. No. 14, 1970.

8216. "True Classroom Flubs and Fluffs by Jerry Robinson." *Cartoonist PROfiles*. No. 13, 1972, pp. 30-33.

Saunders, Allen and John

8217. "Dateline: Danger! by John Saunders and Alden McWilliams." *Cartoonist PROfiles*. No. 15, 1972, pp. 40-44, 54.

8218. Ernst, Ken and Allen Saunders. "Mary Worth and Us." *Collier's*. January 8, 1949, p. 45.

8219. Marschall, Rick. "From the Secret Saunders File: Kerry Drake and the Mystery of the Disappearing Inker." *Nemo*. June 1986, pp. 5-24.

8220. Ridgeway, Ann N. "Allen Saunders." *Journal of Popular Culture*. 5:2 (1971), pp. 385-420.

8221. Saunders, Allen. *A Career for Your Child in the Comics?* New York: The Newspaper Comics Council, 1959, 12 pp.

8222. Saunders, Allen. "It's A Sin To Be Serious?" *The Cartoonist*. Summer 1957, pp. 11-12.

8223. Saunders, Allen. "Mornings at the Blackboard, Afternoons and Evenings at the Drawing Board." *Nemo*. February 1984, pp. 54-56.

8224. Saunders, Allen. "Playwright for Paper Actors: The Allen Saunders Autobiography." *Nemo*. December 1983, pp. 27-32, 64-66; June 1984, pp. 47-50; August 1985, pp. 31-37; April 1986, pp. 57-63.

8225. Saunders, Allen. "Playwright for Paper Actors: The Allen Saunders Autobiography. The Craft of Strip Writing." *Nemo*. December 1984, pp. 54-57.

8226. Saunders, Allen. "Playwright for Paper Actors: The Allen Saunders Autobiography: Hilarity in the Newsroom." *Nemo*. October 1984, pp. 46-50.

8227. Saunders, Allen. "The Playwright for Paper Actors: The Allen Saunders Autobiography. The Social Impact of Comics." *Nemo*. June 1986, pp. 51-54.

8228. "Saunders Considers the Comic Strip 'One of the Best' Narrative Art Forms." *Toledo Blade*. July 21, 1957, p. 1.

8229. "A Story Mill Starts To Grind: The Allen Saunders Biography, Chapter Four." *Nemo*. April 1984, pp. 52-57.

Schneider, Howie

8230. "Howie by Howie Schneider." *Cartoonist PROfiles*. June 1985, pp. 47-51.

8231. Lippman, Petder. "Howie Schneider." *Cartoonist PROfiles*. No. 31, 1976, pp. 58-63.

8232. Schneider, Howie. "Of Mice and Howie Schnieder." *Cartoonist PROfiles*. 1:2 (1969), pp. 63-68.

Schulz, Charles

8233. Adams, Paul. "Snoopy, Schroeder und ihr Schöpfer. Der Dollarmillionar mit dem Zeichenstift: Charles M. Schulz." *Frankfurter Rundschau*. April 12, 1969.

8234. Astor, David. "'Peanuts' Creator Discusses His Comic." *Editor and Publisher*. October 12, 1985, pp. 38-39.

8235. Bianchi, P. "L'Umanità in Erba del Disegnatore Schulz." *Il Giorno* (Genoa). July 31, 1963.

8236. Bindig, Bob. "Charles Schulz Was Right." *The Funnie's Paper*. January 1985, pp. 20-21.

8237. Carlinsky, D. "Pleasant Chat with the Creator of Peanuts; Interview with C.M. Schulz." *Seventeen*. December 1977, pp. 106-107.

8238. "The Charles M. Schulz Award." *Cartoonist PROfiles*. December 1986, pp. 78-79.

8239. "Charles M. Schulz, Reuben Winner 1965." *Newsletter*. May 1965, p. 10.

8240. "Charles Schulz." *Cartoonist PROfiles*. December 1979, pp. 46-55.

8241. "Charles Schulz." *Comics Interview*. No. 47, 1987, pp. 6-25.

8242. "Charles M. Schulz." *New York Times*. October 7, 1971, p. 63.

8243. Conrad, B. "You're a Good Man, Charlie Schulz." *New York Times Magazine*. April 16, 1967, pp. 32-35+; *Reader's Digest*. July 1967, pp. 168-172.

8244. Groensteen, Thierry. "The Schulz System: Why Peanuts Works." *Nemo*. January 1992, pp. 26-41.

8245. Jennings, C.R. "Good Grief, Charlie Schulz!" *Saturday Evening Post*. April 25, 1964, pp. 26-27.

8246. Johnson, Rheta. *Good Grief: The Story of Charles M. Schulz*. New York: Pharos, 1989. 256 pp.

8247. Koeppel, Dan. "The Legacy of Charles Schulz." *News Inc.* July/August 1990, pp. 20-23.

8248. Lidz, F. "Good Ol' Charles Schulz." *Sports Illustrated.* December 23-30, 1985, p. 111-123.

8249. McIntosh, Barbara. "Life, As Seen by the Creator of 'Peanuts.'" Knight-Ridder News Service dispatch in *Philadelphia Inquirer.* January 26, 1986, pp. I-1, I-6.

8250. Marschall, Rick and Gary Groth. "Charles Schulz Interview." *Nemo.* January 1992, pp. 5-24.

8251. Mendelson, Lee. *Charlie Brown and Charlie Schulz.* New York: World, 1970. 160 pp.

8252. Obertello, Nicoletta. "L'Apologia dell' Esingenza di Sicurezza nel Mondo Fanciullesco di Schulz." *Quaderni di Communicazioni de Massa.* 1965.

8253. "'Peanuts' by Schulz. The Thinking Man's Diet." *The World of Comic Art.* June 1966, pp. 43-48.

8254. Roebuck, Joan, ed. *The Graphic Art of Charles Schulz.* Oakland, California: Oakland Museum, 1985. 128 pp. Exhibition Catalogue.

8255. Schulz, Charles M. "But a Comic Strip Has To Grow." *Saturday Review.* April 12, 1969, pp. 73-74.

8256. Schulz, Charles M. "Charles Schulz and 'Peanuts.'" *Cartoonist PROfiles.* December 1971, pp. 4-7.

8257. Schulz, Charles M. *The International Pavilion of Humor of Montreal Presents Charles M. Schulz. 1978 Cartoonist of the Year.* Montreal: 1978. 75 pp.

8258. Schulz, Charles M. *Peanuts Jubilee: My Life and Art with Charlie Brown and Others.* New York: Holt, Rinehart and Winston, 1975. 221 pp.

8259. Schulz, Charles M., with R. Smith Kiliper. *Charlie Brown, Snoopy and Me.* New York: Fawcett Columbine, 1980. 128 pp.

8260. Szabo, Joe. "'I Just Know How To Do It... Yet, I Am Not Picasso or Andrew Wyeth'—A Candid Interview with Charles M. Schulz." *WittyWorld.* Winter/Spring 1992, pp. 16-20, 22-23.

8261. Tebbel, John. "Not-So Peanuts World of Charles M. Schulz." *Saturday Review.* April 12, 1969, pp. 72-74.

8262. Trimboli, Giovanni. *Charles M. Schulz: 40 Years, Life and Art.* New York: Pharos Books, 1990. 173 pp.

8263. Vidal, Marion. *Monsieur Schulz et Ses Peanuts*. Paris: Albin Michel, 1976.

Segar, E.C.

8264. Black, Ed. "Elzie Crisler Segar: The Forgotten Creator of Popeye." *Comics Collector*. Summer 1984, pp. 58-65.

8265. Blackbeard, Bill. "E.C. Segar's Knockouts of 1925 (And Low Blows Before and After): The Unknown Thimble Theatre Period." *Nemo*. October 1983, pp. 6-25.

8266. Könemann, Ludwig. "Serie: Die Pioniere der Comic-Strips: (7) Segar." *Comixene* (Hanover). 7:32 (1980), pp. 54-56.

8267. Segar, E.C. *Charlie Chaplin in the Army*. Chicago: M.A. Donohue, 1917.

8268. "Segar, Student and Teacher." *Nemo*. October 1983, p. 17.

8269. "Through an Ink-Bottle Darkly... Oof! Zam! Plop! Segar Pokes Fun at His Own Profession of Cartooning." *Nemo*. October 1983, pp. 20-25.

Sickles, Noel

8270. Caniff, Milton. "Caniff on Sickles." *Near Mint*. January 1983, pp. 2-3.

8271. Crouch, Bill, jr. "Scorchy Smith and Noel Sickles." *Cartoonist PROfiles*. March 1976, pp. 48-56.

8272. Dorf, Shel. "I Wish I'd Known Him Better." *Near Mint*. January 1983, pp. 6-7.

8273. Dorf, Shel. "Toth on Sickles." *Near Mint*. January 1983, pp. 10-13.

8274. "Noel Sickles. *Near Mint*. January 1983, pp. 14-50.

8275. "Noel Sickles, Friend of Milton Caniff, Draws 'Scorchy Smith' for 200 Papers." *Dayton (Ohio) Journal*. July 21, 1935.

8276. Toth, Alex. "Noel Sickles." *Near Mint*. January 1983, pp. 8-9.

Smith, Sidney

8277. Clark, N.M. "Sidney Smith and His Gumps." *American Mercury*. March 1923, pp. 18-20.

8278. "Gumps: Andy, Min and Chester Carry on Without Sidney Smith." *Newsweek*. November 2, 1935, pp. 21-22.

Soglow, Otto

8279. "Otto Soglow." *Dibujantes* (Buenos Aires). No. 13, 1955, p. 23.

8280. Soglow, Otto. *Everything's Rosy*. New York: Farrar and Rinehart, 1932.

8281. Soglow, Otto. "Most Overrated People in America." *Scribner's*. September 1938, pp. 22-23.

8282. Soglow, Otto. *Soglow's Confidential History of Modern England*. New York: Frederick A. Stokes To. 1939. Unpaginated.

Sternecky, Neal

8283. "Doyle and Sternecky." *Fort Mudge Most*. January 1989, pp. 12-23. (also Larry Doyle).

8284. Harvey, R.C. "Neal Sternecky and Walt Kelly's Pogo." *Cartoonist PROfiles*. December 1992, pp. 31-37.

8285. Thompson, Steve. "Sternecky." *Fort Mudge Most*. July 1992, pp. 6-11.

Sterrett, Cliff

8286. Groth, Gary. "The Comic Genius of Cliff Sterrett." *Nemo*. June 1983, pp. 21-26.

8287. Harvey, R.C. "A Pretty Girl Is Like a Malady." *Comics Journal*. December 1991, pp. 84-90.

8288. Mruz, Dave. "Cliff Sterrett." *Minnesota Cartoonist*. March 19, 1991, p. 3.

Swinnerton, Jimmy

8289. Campbell, Gordon. "Swinnerton." *Cartoonist PROfiles*. September 1983, pp. 51-56.

8290. Davidson, Harold G. *Jimmy Swinnerton: The Artist and His Work*. New York: Hearst Books, 1985. 160 pp.

8291. Lyons, Jim. "First Comic Strip: 'Swin' and His Magical Bears." *Newspaper Collector's Gazette*. August-September 1972, pp. 1-4.

8292. Phelps, Donald. "Jimmy and Company." *Nemo*. October 1986, pp. 36-37, 40-57.

8293. Phelps, Donald. "Swin." *Nemo*. October 1986, pp. 38-58.

Trudeau, Garry

8294. Alter, Jonathan. "Real Life with Garry Trudeau." *Newsweek*. October 15, 1990, pp. 60-66.

8295. Buckley, W.F., jr. "Humane Letters; G. Trudeau's Doonsebury." *National Review*. September 15, 1978, pp 1158-1161.

8296. "Doonesbury: Drawing and Quartering for Fun and Profit." *Time*. February 9, 1976, pp 57-60, 65-66.

8297. "Doonesbury on Leave." *Newsweek*. September 20, 1982, p. 102.

8298. "Doonesbury Scoops U.S. Journalists." *Extra!* January-February 1992, pp. 14-15.

8299. "Garry Trudeau." *Cartoonist PROfiles*. September 1988, pp. 12-15.

8300. Grove, Lloyd. "Trudeau." *Target*. Spring 1987, pp. 13-22.

8301. Hendley, W.C. "Horatian Satire of Trudeau's Doonesbury." *Journal of Popular Culture*. Spring 1983, pp. 103-115.

8302. Kelly, Kevin. "The Trudeau Touch." *Boston Globe*. December 22, 1985.

8303. Marschall, Rick. "Who's Got the Arrogance?" *Comics Journal*. September 1987, pp. 63-66.

8304. O'Neil, Dennis. "Profile: Garry Trudeau."*Comics Journal*. September 1981, pp. 252-255.

8305. Pike, Rayner. "'Doonesbury' Cartoonist Takes Aim at Bush." *Philadelphia Inquirer*. October 24, 1992, p. A-5.

8306. Salisbury, Stephen. "The Scathing Wit of 'Doonesbury's' Creator." *Philadelphia Inquirer*. July 19, 1987, pp. 1-K, 8-K.

8307. Trudeau, Garry B. "*Doonesbury* Vs. President Reagan." In *Maincurrents in Mass Communications*, edited by Warren K. Agee, Phillip H. Ault and Edwin Emery, pp. 375-379. New York: Harper and Row, 1986.

8308. Trudeau, Garry B. "Maggie and Jiggs and Blondie and Dagwood and Lucy and Charlie." *Couples*. (New York: *New York Magazine*, 1973), pp. 29-33.

8309. Trudeau, Garry B. "Speech to the ANPA." *Cartoonist PROfiles*. September 1988, pp. 12-15.

8310. "Trudeau, by a Jury of His Peers." *Esquire*. December 1985, pp. 137-139.

8311. "Trudeaumania: G. Trudeau's Comic Strip, Doonesbury." *Newsweek*. January 13, 1975, p. 49.

8312. Wartofsky, Alona. "Garry Trudeau: Q and A." *City Paper* (Washington, D.C.). November 24, 1986.

8313. Wasserman, Jeffrey H. "Sheldon Mayer, 'Superfolks,' and Garry Trudeau." *Comics Journal*. June 1978, pp. 53-55.

Unger, Jim

8314. "Herman by Jim Unger." *Cartoonist PROfiles*. December 1975, pp. 76-79.

8315. Weber, John. "A Little Bit Removed from Reality—Unger." *WittyWorld*. Winter/Spring 1989, pp. 46-53.

Van Buren, Raeburn

8316. Harris, Stephen L. "Raeburn Van Buren." *Cartoonist PROfiles*. June 1988, pp. 76-80.

8317. "Raeburn Van Buren." *Cartoonist PROfiles*. December 1980, pp. 46-51.

8318. Van Buren, Raeburn. "And Without Getting Wet." *The World of Comic Art*. 1:4 (1967), pp. 23-32.

Walker, Mort

8319. Marschall, Rick. "Man Bites Dog: Mort Walker." *Comics Journal*. July 1987, pp. 134-138, 141-144.

8320. Marschall, Rick. "Mort Walker Talks Candidly About His Career, Comics' Future, History and Funny Stuff." *Nemo*. February 1984, pp. 23-37.

8321. "Mort Walker." *Cartoonist PROfiles*. March 1990, pp. 66-69.

8322. "Mort Walker Biography." New York: King Features Syndicate, No. 139, 1967.

8323. "Mort Walker Converses with Dik Browne." *Cartoonist PROfiles*. March 1979, pp. 12-27.

8324. "Sam and Silo by Jerry Dumas and Mort Walker." *Cartoonist PROfiles*. March 1977, pp. 24-29.

8325. Walker, Hermanos. "My Father Draws Beetle Bailey." *The Cartoonist*. October 1966, pp. 24-28.

8326. Walker, Mort. *Backstage at the Strips*. New York: Mason/Charter, 1975. 311 pp.

8327. Walker, Mort. "Comicana: The Absolutely Fascinating Science of Comicana." *Cartoonist PROfiles*. December 1978, pp. 69-75; Part II, September 1979, pp. 36-39.

8328. Walker, Mort. "The Evermores by Johnny Sajem." *Cartoonist PROfiles*. December 1982, pp. 48-53.

8329. Walker, Mort. "Look, Ma! I'm an Artist!" *Cartoonist PROfiles*. Summer 1969, pp. 46-47.

8330. Walker, Mort. "Love!" *Cartoonist PROfiles*. No. 7, 1970, pp. 40-41.

Watterson, Bill

8331. McGeean, Ed. "Ink Blots." *CAPS Newsletter*. December 1989, pp. 7-8, 13.

8332. "Watterson Returns, Demands His Space." *Comics Journal*. February 1992, pp. 14-15.

8333. West, Richard Samuel. "Interview: Bill Watterson." *Comics Journal*. March 1989, pp. 56-71.

Wilson, Tom, jr.

8334. Robinson, R. "Drawing on His Inheritance, Tom Wilson Jr. Unveils a Ziggyfied, Hard-luck Hero Named UG." *People Weekly*. January 7, 1985, pp. 81-83.

8335. "Tom Wilson, Ziggy." *Cartoonist PROfiles*. No. 19, 1973, pp. 4-13.

8336. "UG! by Tom Wilson Jr." *Cartoonist PROfiles*. September 1984, pp. 18-23.

Young, Chic and Dean

8337. Alexander, J. "Dagwood and Blondie Man." *Saturday Evening Post*. April 10, 1948, pp. 15-17.

8338. "Blondie's Pop." *Newsweek*. November 1, 1948, p. 54.

8339. "Chic Young." New York: King Features Syndicate, Biographical Series, No. 8-A, 1970.

8340. "Dean Young and Blondie." *Cartoonist PROfiles*. June 1980, pp. 21-24.

8341. "Quien Es Quien en el Dibujo: Chic Young." *Dibujantes* (Buenos Aires). No. 16, 1955, p. 25.

Author Index

Subject Index

CARTOONING PERSONNEL

CHARACTERS, TITLES

COMPANIES, FANZINES, and PERIODICALS

GENERAL SUBJECTS

About the Compiler

JOHN A. LENT began studying comics in 1963–1964 when he conducted a readership/causal relationship analysis of fourth graders in Syracuse, New York. Over the years, he has pursued cartooning, studying comic books as part of a larger mass communications project in the Philippines in 1964–1965, and presenting the featured address at the first comic art exhibition in Malaysia in 1973. In 1984, he founded the comic art working group within the International Association for Mass Communication Research, and in 1986, compiled the first international comic art bibliography published in the United States. He also founded the quarterly newsletter, *Berita*, of which he is editor, and the Malaysia/Singapore/Brunei Studies Group in the mid-1970s.

Dr. Lent has been managing editor of *WittyWorld International Cartoon Magazine* since its inauguration in 1987. The author or editor of 46 books and monographs and hundreds of articles, he also serves on the editorial boards of *Comics Journal, Big O Magazine, Studies of Latin American Popular Culture*, and other periodicals. Some of his works have concentrated on comic art, beginning with a 1966 monograph, *3 Research Studies*; followed by *Comic Art: An International Bibliography* (1966), a special issue of *Philippine Communication Journal* (1993); *Cartoonometer: Taking the Pulse of the World's Cartoonists*; *Asian Popular Culture*; and the four-volume bibliography of comic art worldwide (Greenwood, 1994). In preparation for a book on Asian comic and cartoons, Dr. Lent has interviewed about 190 cartoonists in 15 Asian countries; he has also interviewed cartoonists from Europe, North and South America, and the Caribbean.

A professor since 1960, Dr. Lent has taught at universities in the Philippines, where he was a Fulbright Scholar; in Malaysia, where he started the first mass communications program in that country; and has taught at universities and colleges in West Virginia, Wyoming, Wisconsin, and Pennsylvania.

ISBN 0-313-28211-0
90000>
EAN
9 780313 282119
HARDCOVER BAR CODE